Windows on Arabic and Its Culture

(For College Students and Adults)

Level 1 for Beginning Arabic

Second Expanded and Improved Edition

By

Fadel Abdallah & Khalil Tahrawi

DEDICATION

This book is dedicated in loving memory of Fadel Abdalla, the co-author of " Windows on Arabic and its Culture". Fadel dedicated years of his life to education and many of his final days to the completion of the improved edition of this book. Fadel's hard work and dedication will be relived and revisited each time this book is opened and closed. You are dearly missed.

Photos / images in Part 1 are by Shutterstock, Inc.

Illustrations in Parts 2 & 3 are by Andrea Guerrero.

www.kendallhunt.com
Send all inquiries to:
4050 Westmark Drive
Dubuque, IA 52004-1840

ISBN 978-1-4652-8684-0

Printed in the United States of America

Table of Contents

* * *

* * *

* * *

* * *

*   *   *

*   *   *

* * *

* * *

* * *

* * *

* * *

THE AUTHORS' INTRODUCTION TO

WINDOWS ON ARABIC LANGUAGE & ITS CULTURE

Arabic, in its present form, is a language that has been spoken, written and articulated for some 1,500 years. It is estimated that over 400 million people speak Arabic as their native national language. Over 1.5 billion Muslims, in every corner of the world, venerate Arabic as their religious language, and use it for prayers and other religious rituals. Arabic is also one of the major official languages of the United Nations, and has been designated by the State Department and other U.S. Government organs as one of the most critical languages of our times. In a recent book by Barry Farber, a foreign language-learning advocate, he commented on the merits of learning Arabic as being "**very rewarding**."

It is ironic that the tragic events of 9/11, followed by the unfortunate recent war in Iraq, have raised the value of Arabic linguists to unprecedented levels. Government organs and private corporations are seeking personnel who are proficient in Arabic. We hope that after war peace will prevail, and even then, the value of Arabic linguists will naturally go higher. Whether in time of war or peace, knowledge of Arabic and its related culture are destined to remain at the center of world affairs for many years to come.

The authors of this book, and other subsequent ones, naturally agree with the assertion of many language-learning advocates who believe that language knowledge will eventually breed world peace. Since it is impossible to learn a language and not learn a great deal about the countries and people who are natives of that language, it is then natural that those who learn about a country and its people are bound to develop a better understanding of that nation.

An Arabic proverb puts it, "**A man is an enemy of what he is ignorant about**." Moreover, there is nothing like learning a language and its related culture and value system that has the potential of eliminating ignorance and opening the doors of enlightenment.

Before you embark on the challenging and rewarding task of learning Arabic, you need to know that linguists call the language you are about to learn through this book as "**Modern Standard Literary Arabic (MSLA)**." MSLA is essentially the same language that has been articulated and used for over 1500 years; the main difference being the large new vocabulary, consisting of classical words with new meanings, and loan words from other languages. As the fundamental grammar of written Arabic has hardly changed over the last 1,500 years, Modern Standard Literary Arabic may well serve as an introduction to the rich classical, as well as to the written and spoken language of the modern Arab World; i.e. newspapers, magazines, books, radio, television and public speeches.

This book is a **second, revised and expanded edition** of a previously published work by **Kendall Hunt Publishing Co**. It is the first in a series of an ambitious project, which focuses on developing three graded textbooks, to teach Arabic to college students and adult learners, over a period of three years or six semesters. The Second Volume within this series was published two year ago by the same publishing house. Since the publication of the first volume, and using it as a textbook in several institutions, the authors developed insight into producing the improved and expanded second edition you have in your hands now. Those who are familiar with the first edition of this work will notice some new features of this second edition. Among these are more concise and systematic linguistic material. Moreover, this new edition has a coloring scheme lacking in the first edition. An expanded Glossary is another noticeable feature of this new edition, containing linguistic idioms, which were used in the conversational and the reading texts of the book. The concise explanations of the fine linguistic and grammatical points were further made more concise and pointed through contextual examples from the texts and vocabulary introduced.

This book,, along with the subsequent volumes within this series, are the outcome of many years of teaching Arabic to college and adult English-speaking students by two experienced instructors of Arabic, in different settings, at the University of Minnesota, Northwestern University, the American Islamic College in Illinois, Bowling Green State University and the University of Toledo, both in Ohio, and more recently at the American University, Lake Forest College in Illinois, Johns Hopkins University, in Maryland, and North Virginia Community Colleges in Virginia.

This work is also, in some way, a parallel effort to an earlier endeavor by the authors, which resulted in the development and publication of a series of graded textbooks and workbooks, designed to teach Arabic, as a second language, at six graded levels, for children and youth in elementary, junior and high school. These were published by the Chicago based IQRA' International Educational Foundation, under the generic title of "**IQRA' Arabic Reader Series.**"

As to the format of the present book, it consists of **four parts**. The **First Part**, entitled "**Preliminary Essentials,**" consists of sixteen short and concise lessons on the phonetics of Arabic, to teach the pronunciation and articulation of the sounds of individual words and a variety of basic linguistic structure, as well as learning the basics of the writing system, along with the shapes and forms of Arabic letters. A writing workbook will accompany this part for practice.

Part Two consists of fifteen short conversational texts, with English meanings of the vocabulary and linguistic idioms. These texts concentrate on teaching the most common language used in greetings, getting acquainted situations and courtesy expressions, and other basic themes relevant to common everyday themes. The learning process in this section will focus in pairing students to enact these short conversations to build up their confidence in communicating in Arabic.

Part Three consists of another **ten unit-lessons**. Each unit contains a **conversational text for oral enactment in the class**. Another section focuses on five to seven **grammatical themes**, related to issues raised in the conversation text, as well as the reading aloud text, which would follow later in the unit. Linguistic and grammatical rules are explained through examples mostly taken from the text of the lesson. The focal points are duly highlighted through different devices, which make them easy to recognize. Then there is a **section on exercises** intended to reinforce the grammatical concepts learned in the previous section. In a following lesson, there is **reading aloud text**, followed by a **vocabulary list**, arranged according to the order of their introduction in the text. Then follows a section on **comprehension questions**, to be done orally in class as an interactive drilling.. Furthermore, each unit contains a section on Arabic adages, proverbs or wise-sayings; through which the learners will gain insight into the culture and value system of Arabic-speaking peoples. This is an important dimension, noted and appreciated by numerous non-Arab scholars, who had the opportunity to study the Arabic culture at depth. Moreover, these selections represent the idiomatic Arabic language at its best, and have been proven very useful to train students in moving from word-by-word translations to idiomatic ones.

As noted above, each unit within part three contains a text in a conversational format and another in narrative style for reading and comprehension. The purpose of these conversational texts is to provide conversational formulas and patterns for the students to emulate and role-play. These are very close imitations of real life situations. Then, using the vocabulary list, provided in conjunction with these conversational texts, the students would get an extra opportunity to receive training in translation. The last feature with which the lesson-unit concludes is intended to provide learning through diversion in the form of crossword puzzles focusing on word-search. Occasionally, recordings of Arabic TV programs, Arabic songs and music, as well as Arabic talk shows will be played in class as a cultural dimension to the course.

The ultimate goal of this course, however, is to train the learners to read Modern Standard Literary Arabic with comprehension, and to use the language verbally in connection with basic conversational settings related to getting acquainted situations and exchanging basic courtesies, as well tackling basic questions and answers related to all natural settings of human socialization.

Writing in Arabic is also drilled, both as a language skill in its own right, as well as to aid the learners in the mastery of reading, speaking and building up their vocabulary repertoires. Because this course is the first step in a 3-year-long term of structured learning, towards a well-rounded general knowledge of Arabic and its related culture, a total approach to learning all the related skills has been adopted. Therefore, the course covers, besides reading, writing, speaking and listening, aspects of phonology, morphology and syntactic structures of the language.

An Audio CD, in the sounds of native speakers, accompanies this textbook, to help the students master the sounds of Arabic with extra listening activity at home.

Finally, the authors would like to inform those instructors, who adopt this this textbook for teaching, that they are available for consultation and providing syllabus formats, along with extra useful handouts, lessons / units vocabulary and grammar tests, as well as Power-Points presentations for grammar teaching, all free of charge. The authors can be contacted at the following:
fadel.abdallah@ymail.com; fabdallah@luc.edu; ktahrawi@gmail.com; kaltahrawi@nvcc.edu

ACKNOWLEDGEMENT:

Last but not least, the authors would like to express their deep gratitude and sincere acknowledgment to the students of Arabic at Bowling Green State University, the University of Toledo, Lake Forest College, the American University, the Johns Hopkins University, the American Islamic College, North Virginia Community Colleges and Loyola University Chicago, for being the first to learn from earlier initial drafts of material covered in this book, which was offered to them as loose paper handouts on an installment basis. They have in many ways helped in improving the quality of this book. It is to those young men and women that we dedicate this book, with love and appreciation. Special thanks go to Professor **Peter Chomwicz** of Maryland Institute College of Arts in Baltimore, who proofread the English of the final version in the course of studying Arabic under Khalil Tahrawi, one of the co-authors of this work, and provided invaluable editorial corrections.

Special thanks go to **Lara Sanders** and **Bev Kraus**, of **Kendall Hunt Publishing**, for their diligent work as Manager of the Authors' Contracts and Coordinator of this publication. Other special thanks go to Professor **Shaghaf Ibrahim Hazimeh** of the American University, for her kind participation in the recorded material on the accompanying audio CD. Other special thanks go to **Conrad Osipowicz** engineer at Blue Room Productions, for his diligent work on supervising and producing the final Audio CD. Last, but not least, special thanks go **Andrea Guerrero** for her work on producing a good part of the illustrations, used in **Par Two** and **Part Three** of this book.

The Authors:

Fadel Abdallah & Khalil Tahrawi

July 1, 2016

PART ONE .... القِسمُ الأَوَّل

PRELIMINARY ESSENTIALS .... مَبادِئ تَـمهيدِيَّة

نَتمَنّى لَكُم التَّوْفِيق وَالنَّجاحَ!

Lesson One

The Arabic Alphabet

Names of the Letters, Writing Symbols and Transliteration

The Arabic Alphabet consists of **twenty-eight** characters, written from right to left. All twenty-eight characters represent **consonants**. **Three** of them are also symbols for **long vowels**. The letters, as they appear in isolation or when they are standing alone, are as follows:

Transliteration Symbols	Name of the Letter	Arabic Symbol
’	*Hamzah / Hamzated Alif*	ء / أ
B	*Baa (Bā)*	ب
T	*Taa (Tā)*	ت
Th	*Thaa (Thā)*	ث
J	*Jeem (Jīm)*	ج
Ḥ	*Ḥaa (Ḥā)*	ح
Kh	*Khaa (Khā)*	خ
D	*Daal (Dāl)*	د
Dh	*Dhaal (Dhāl)*	ذ
R	*Raa (Rā)*	ر
Z	*Zaa / Zayn (Zā)*	ز
S	*Seen (Sīn)*	س
Sh	*Sheen (Shīn)*	ش
Ṣ	*Ṣaad (Ṣād)*	ص
Ḍ	*Ḍaad (Ḍād)*	ض
Ṭ	*Ṭaa (Ṭā)*	ط

Ẓ	*Ẓaa* (*Ẓā*)	ظ
‘	*‘Ayn*	ع
<u>Gh</u>	*<u>Gh</u>ayn*	غ
F	*Faa* (*Fā*)	ف
Q	*Qaaf* (*Qāf*)	ق
K	*Kaaf* (*Kāf*)	ك
L	*Laam* (*Lām*)	ل
M	*Meem* (*Mīm*)	م
N	*Noon* (*Nūn*)	ن
H	*Haa* (*Hā*)	هـ
W	*Waaw* (*Wāw*)	و
Y	*Yaa* (*Yā*)	ي

* * *

Important Notes:

1. Many language books give *Alif* (ا) as the first letter of the Arabic Alphabet. In reality, they should give a *Hamzated Alif*, whereas the *Alif* is only a **chair** on top of which the *Hamzah* sits at the beginning of a word. Thus, the *Alif* itself has no independent phonetic value.
2. The symbols (ي / و / ا) are also to be seen as long vowels, and will be introduced later. You will also see these symbols as ‘**chairs**’ for the *Hamzah*.
3. The following consonants have no exact sound equivalent in English. As such, they constitute difficult sounds to articulate and master. Students must exert special effort and spend extra time working on mastering these sounds, especially by imitating a native speaker. These are:

ء / ح / خ / ذ / ص / ض / ط / ظ / ع / غ / ق

Lesson Two	Greetings, Courtesy Expressions & Class Management Prompts

Peace be upon you! = Greetings of Peace!	*As-Salāmu 'alaykum!*	السَّلامُ عَلَيْكُمْ !
And unto you may Peace be! (*response*)	*Wa-'alaykum-us-Salām!*	وَعَلَيْكُمْ ٱلسَّلام !
Good morning!	*Ṣabāḥ al-khayr!*	صَباحَ ٱلخَيْر !
Good morning (light)! (*response*)	*Ṣabāḥ an-noor!*	صَباحَ ٱلنُّور !
Good evening!	*Masaa' al-khayr!*	مَساءَ ٱلخَيْر !
Good evening (light)! (*response*)	*Masaa' an-noor!*	مَساءَ ٱلنُّور !
How are you? (*generic*)	*Kayfa-al-Ḥāl?*	كَيْفَ الحال ؟
Well (fine), praise be to God! (*response*)	*Bi-khayr, al-ḥamdu li-(A)llāh!*	بِخَيْر ، الحَمْدُ لِلَّه !
Hello! Hi! Welcome!	*Marḥaban / Marḥaba!*	مَرْحَباً / مَرْحَبا !
Hello and welcome!	*Ahlan wa-marḥaba!*	أَهْلاً وَمَرْحَبا !
Welcome! (*upon receiving someone at your place*)	*Ahlan wa-sahlan!*	أَهْلاً وَسَهْلاً !
Welcome to you! (*male / female*)	*Ahlan bi-ka / Ahlan bi-ki!*	أَهْلاً بِكَ / أَهْلاً بِكِ !
Thanks! / Thanks a lot!	*Shukran / Shukran jazeelan!*	شُكْراً / شُكْراً جزيلاً !
(You're) welcome! (*response*)	*'Afwan! / Al-'Afw*	عَفْواً ! / العَفْو
Excuse me! Pardon me!	*'Afwan! / Ma'dhirah!*	مَعْذِرَة !
Don't worry! Take it easy! (*male / female*)	*Laa ba'sa 'alayka / 'alaiki!*	لا بَأْسَ عَلَيْكَ / عَلَيْكِ !
With your permission! If you please! (*male / female*)	*'An 'idhnika / 'An 'idhniki!*	عَنْ إِذْنِكَ / عَنْ إِذْنِكِ!
Yes, kindly proceed! (*male / female*)	*Tafaḍḍal / Tafaḍḍali*	تَفَضَّلْ ! / تَفَضَّلِي!
Nice (happy) opportunity (for meeting you)!	*Furṣah Ṭayyiba (Sa'eedah)!*	فُرْصَة طَيِّبَة (سَعيدَة)!
Nice opportunity! / And I am happier!	*Furṣah Ṭayyiba! / Wa-'Ana 'as'ad!*	فُرْصَة طَيِّبَة! / وأنا أَسْعَد!
Please! If you please! (*male / female*)	*Min faḍlika / Min faḍliki!*	مِنْ فَضْلِكَ / مِنْ فَضْلِكِ!

Yes, please! Yes, kindly! (*male / female*)	*Na'am, tafaḍḍal / tafaḍḍali!*	نَعَمْ ، تَفَضَّلْ / تَفَضَّلِي!
Kindly (Please) come in! (*male / female*)	*Tafaḍḍal 'udkhul!* *Tafaḍḍali 'udkhuli!*	تَفَضَّلْ أُدْخُلْ! / تَفَضَّلِي أُدْخُلِي!
Thanks! I thank you! (to male) I thank you! (to female)	*Shukran!* *'Ashkuruka! / 'Ashkuruki!*	شُكْراً ! أَشْكُرُكَ / أَشْكُرُكِ!
Kindly (Please) sit down! (*male / female*)	*Tafaḍḍal 'ijlis!* *Tafaḍḍali 'ijlisi!*	تَفَضَّلْ اِجْلِسْ! تَفَضَّلِي اِجْلِسِي!
Thanks! I thank you! (to male) I thank you! (to female)	*Shukran!* *'Ashkuruka! / 'Ashkuruki!*	شُكْراً ! أَشْكُرُكَ / أَشْكُرُكِ!
Kindly (Please) have coffee! (*male / female*)	*Tafaḍḍal Al-Qahwa!* *Tafaḍḍali Al-Qahwa!*	تَفَضَّلْ ٱلْقَهْوَة! تَفَضَّلِي ٱلْقَهْوَة!
Thanks! I thank you! (to male) I thank you! (to female)	*Shukran!* *'Ashkuruka! / 'Ashkuruki!*	شُكْراً ! أَشْكُرُكَ / أَشْكُرُكِ!
Kindly (Please) have tea! (*male / female*)	*Tafaḍḍal Ash-Shaay!* *Tafaḍḍali Ash-Shaay!*	تَفَضَّلْ ٱلشَّاي! تَفَضَّلِي ٱلشَّاي!
Thanks! I thank you! (to male) I thank you! (to female)	*Shukran!* *'Ashkuruka! / 'Ashkuruki!*	شُكْراً ! أَشْكُرُكَ / أَشْكُرُكِ!
Congratulations! / May it be blessed!	*Mabruuk! / Mubaarak!*	مَبْرُوك! / مُبارَك!
May God bless you (too)! (to male/ female)	*Baaraka Allahu feeka / feeki!*	بارَكَ ٱللَّهُ فِيكَ / فِيكِ!
Until we meet again! Bye!	*'Ilal-liqaa'!*	إِلى ٱللِّقاء!
Until we meet again! Goodbye! Go safely!	*'Ilal-liqaa' / ma'a-salaamah!*	إِلى ٱللِّقاء / مَعَ ٱلسَّلامَة!

Class Management: Complements and Prompts!

Well done! (*masculine / feminine / plural*)	*'Ahsanta / 'Ahsanti / 'Ahsantum!*	أَحْسَنْتَ/ أَحْسَنْتِ / أَحْسَنْتُمْ !
Excellent! (*masculine / feminine / plural*)	*Mumtaaz / Mumtaazah / Mumtaazuun*	مُمْتاز / مُمْتازَة / مُمْتازُون !
Good! (*masculine / feminine / plural*)	*Jayyid / Jayyidah / Jayyiduun!*	جَيِّد / جَيِّدَة / جَيِّدُون !
Very Good! (*masculine / feminine / plural*)	*Jayyid Jiddan / Jayyidah Jiddan / Jayyiduun Jiddan!*	جَيِّد جِدّاً/ جَيِّدَة جِدّاً / جَيِّدُون جِدًّا !
Open! (*command verb for masculine, feminine, & plural*)	*'Iftah / 'Iftahi / 'Iftahuu*	اِفْتَحْ / اِفْتَحِي / اِفْتَحُوا!
Listen! (*command verb for masculine, feminine, & plural*)	*'Istami' / 'Istami'i / 'Istami'uu*	اِسْتَمِعْ / اِسْتَمِعِي / اِسْتَمِعُوا!
Read! (*command verb for masculine, feminine, & plural*)	*'Iqra' / 'Iqra'i / 'Iqra'uu*	اِقْرَأْ / اِقْرَئِي / اِقْرَؤُوا !
Write! (*command verb for masculine, feminine, & plural*)	*'Uktub / 'Uktubi / 'Uktubuu*	أُكْتُبْ / أُكْتُبِي / أُكْتُبُوا !
Repeat! (*command verb for masculine, feminine, & plural*)	*Raddid / Raddidi / Raddiduu*	رَدِّدْ / رَدِّدي / رَدِّدُوا !
Study! (*command verb for masculine, feminine, & plural*)	*'Udrus / 'Udrusi / 'Udrusuu*	أُدْرُسْ / أُدْرُسِي / أُدْرُسُوا !
Hush! (*command verb for masculine, feminine, & plural*)	*'Uskut / 'Uskuti / 'Uskutuu*	أُسْكُتْ / أُسْكُتِي / أُسْكُتُوا !
Sit down! (*command verb for masculine, feminine, & plural*)	*'Ijlis / 'Ijlisi / 'Ijlisuu*	اِجْلِسْ / اِجْلِسِي / اِجْلِسُوا !
Come out! Go out! (*command verb for masculine, feminine, & plural*)	*'Ukhruj / 'Ukhruji / 'Ukhrujuu*	أُخْرُجْ / أُخْرُجِي / أُخْرُجُوا !
Come here! (*command verb for masculine, feminine, & plural*)	*Ta'aala / Ta'aalay / Ta'aalaw*	تَعالَ / تَعالَيْ / تَعالَوْا !

Take! (*command verb for masculine, feminine, & plural*)	***Khudh / Khudhii, Khudhuu***	خُـذْ/ خُـذِي/ خُـذُوا !
Bring! Give! (*command verb for masculine, feminine, & plural*)	***Haati / Haatii / Haatuu***	هـاتِ / هـاتِـي / هاتُـوا !

* * *

Lesson Three

Arabic Short & Long Vowels

- In literary Arabic, there are three short vowels and three corresponding long vowels.
- The short vowels signs are represented by diacritical marks placed on top of or underneath the consonant letters.
- The long vowels, however, are represented by letter forms.

- **The short vowels are respectively:**
  1. *Fatḥah* (فَتْحَة), a small diagonal stroke above a consonant, as in

     (بَ/ *ba*), (تَ/ *ta*).
  2. *Dammah* (ضَمَّة), a small (*Wāw* /و) above a consonant, as in

     (جُ/ *ju*), (فُ/ *fu*) .
  3. ***Kasrah*** (كَسْرَة), a small diagonal stroke under a consonant , as in

     (كِ/ *ki*), (نِ/ *ni*) .
- **The long vowels are respectively:**
  1. *Alif al-Madd* (أَلِف الـمَدّ), the letter named *Alif* (ـا / *aa* or *ā*); such as:

     (ثـا), (جـا).
  2. *Wāw al-Madd* (واو الـمَدّ), the letter named *Wāw* (ـُـو / *uu* or *ū*), as in

     (سُو), (يُـو) .
  3. *Yā al-Madd* (ياء الـمَدّ), the letter named *Yā* (ـِـي / *ii* or *ī*), as in

     (شِـي), (مِـي) .
- **Two Important Notes:**
- When the ***Hamzah*** bears a ***Kasrah***, both *Hamzah* and *Kasrah* are written under an *Alif*, such as: (إِ).
- The sounds represented by the vowel signs are, of course, all influenced by the surrounding consonants. It is to be especially noted that when the *Fathah* is above

one of the <u>velarized consonants</u> (ص / ض / ط / ظ / ق) and above the

(ر), its sound tends to be that of the "**a**" in "**sofa**" or "**abound**." In other cases, it tends to be like the "**e**" in "**end**." The question of vowel variations, however, settles itself automatically because of the mechanics of proper consonant articulation.

- The following table represents the vowel system paradigm in Arabic:

(*aa*) or (*ā*) ـا	(*a*) ـَ
(*uu*) or (*ū*) ـو	(*u*) ـُ
(*ii, ee*) or (*ī*) ـِي	(*i*) ـِ

* * *

Important Note:

- The combination of a consonant with a short or long vowel in Arabic does not only serve to form syllabic parts in larger words, but many of such combinations form actual words and particles with their own meanings. The following list is intended to introduce you to the most common of such one syllabic words:

أَهـذا أَبـوكَ؟	Is… / Are…? *(as interrogative particle)*	أَ
أَنا طـالـب بـالـجامِعَة . سـافَرْتُ بـالسَّيَّارَة .	at, by *(as preposition)*	بِ
تـاَللَّهِ!	by *(as an oath particle)*	تا
لِـي أُخْت واحِدَة . لَـهُ أخ واحِد . نُـسافِرُ لِـنَـزُورَ الأَهْلَ .	1. **have, belong to** *(as possessive particle)* 2. **in order to** *(as a subjunctive particle before verbs)*	لِـ / لَـ
لا أَشْرَب قَهْوَة .	**no,** do not *(as a negating particle)*	لا / لا
أَنا وَأَنْتَ صَـديقان . وَاَللَّه!	1. **and** *(as conjunction particle)* 2. **by** *(as an oath particle)*	وَ
هَذا أَخـي وَهَـذِهِ أُخْـتِـي .	**my** *(as a possessive pronoun when attached to the end of nouns)*	ـِي

Lesson Four	**Notes on** *Sukūn* (السُّكُون) **and** *Shaddah* (الشَّدَّة), **Aspects of** Accent, Diphthongs **and the** Dagger *Alif*

- Besides the three diacritical signs used for the short vowels, as introduced in Lesson 3, there are three other signs which will be seen over the Arabic consonants:

1. One sign is called *Sukūn*; it is formed like a small circle written above the consonant. Its sign is (ْ). This sign indicates the absence of any particular vowel from the consonant bearing it. In other words, the *Sukūn* indicates a vowelless consonant. Examples:

مِنْ / مَنْ / هَلْ / أَنْتَ / نَعَمْ / مِصْرُ / بَغْدَادُ / لُبْنَانُ / مَرْيَمُ

2. The other sign is called **Shaddah**. Its sign is (ّ) written above the consonant.

<u>This sign results from two identical consonants following each other without another consonant in between.</u> The first of these identical consonants is *Sākin*, which means bearing a *Sukūn*, and the second is *Mutaḥarrik*, which means bearing one of the short vowels. The doubled consonant is written only once, and the sign of the *Shaddah* is written above it. Thus, letters which have **Shaddah** over them are commonly said to be doubled. Examples:

شَدَّ (شَدْ+دَ) / عَلَّمَ (عَلْ+لَ+مَ) / سَلَّمْ (سَ+لْ+لِ+مْ) /

قُدُّوسٌ (قُ+دْ+دُ+و+سٌ) / مُدَرِّسٌ (مُ+دَ+رْ+رِ+سٌ)

3. <u>**Accent or Stress:**</u> In Arabic, words of <u>two syllables</u> are accented on the first syllable; this rule applies when a word consists of two consonants with their own vowels, or when a word consists of three consonants, but the second consonant bears a *Sukūn*. Examples:

أَبٌ / أَخٌ / فَمٌ / يَدٌ / عِلْمٌ / زَهْرٌ / بَعْدَ / وَعْدُ / سَهْلٌ / بَحْرٌ

4. Words of <u>three syllables</u> are also <u>accented on the</u> <u>first syllable</u>, unless the <u>middle syllable is closed</u>, in which case it receives the accent. A closed syllable may be defined as one which consists of a consonant, a short vowel, and a vowelless consonant. An open syllable, on the other hand is one which consists of consonants always followed by their own vowels. Examples respectively are:

(ّ)	أَكَلَ / شَرِبَ / دَرَسَ .
(ْ)	نَكْتُبُ / رَغْبَةُ / دَرَسْنَ .

9

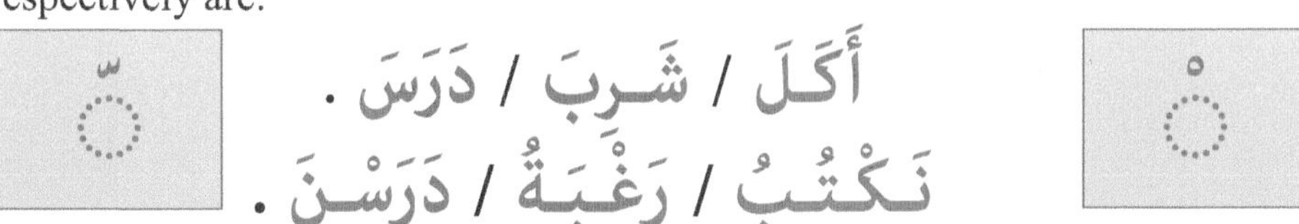

5. **Diphthongs:** There are two diphthongs in Arabic, represented by the combinations:

ـَوْ / ـَيْ and transliterated respectively as: (*aw*) and (*ay*).

The sound represented by the former is similar to that of the "*ow* " in "**fowl.**" The sound represented by the latter is similar to that of the word "**eye** ". However, in literary Arabic diphthongs, the glide is carried all the way to the consonant positions of the " *w* " and " *y* " respectively. Diphthongs are closed syllables. Examples:

أَوْ / كَيْ / كَيْفَ / لَوْنُ / بَيْتُ

6. **The Dagger *Alif*** : In few words, the long vowel (ـَا) is expressed, in writing, by a short vertical stroke (in reality **a miniature *Alif*,** known also as a **Dagger *Alif***) written raised above the consonant and following the *Fathah.* The pronunciation, however, is the same as the regular long vowel (ـَا). In modern written Arabic, this **Dagger *Alif*,** of the old writing system, is not written, but assumed, or written as a regular long vowel. Examples:

هٰذا / هٰذِهِ / ذٰلِكَ / لٰكِنَّ / الرَّحْمٰنُ

* * *

Exercise 1: Listen and repeat first, then read on your own, with due concentration on the aspects of *Sukūn* and accents:

نَفْسٌ / تَحْتَ / بَعْدَ / لَحْمُ / بَدْرٌ / قُدْسٌ / ذَهَبَ / سَمِعَ / قَلَمُ / طُهْرٌ / رَكَضَ /

طَبْلُ / كَتَبْتُ / سَمِعْتُ / يَكْتُبْنَ / لُبْنانُ / مِصْرُ / بَغْدادُ

* * *

Exercise 2: Listen and repeat first, then read on your own, with due concentration on the aspect of *Shaddah*:

سَلَّمَ / عَلَّمَ / كَلَّمَ / جَمَّعَ / وَدَّعَ / وَدَّ / عَدَّ / مُدَرِّسٌ / مُعَلِّمُ / سُلَّمُ / حُبٌّ

وُدٌّ / مَدَّ / تَكَلَّمَ / تَعَلَّمَ / جَلَّ / قُدُّوسُ / جَبَّارُ / حَرَّمَ / صَفَّقَ

* * *

Exercise 3: Listen and repeat first, then read on your own, with due concentration on the aspect of diphthongs :

لَوْلا / لَيْثُ / عَيْنُ / بَيْروتُ / رَوْض / قَوْلُ / بَيْع / صَوْمُ / أَوْلادُ / يَوْمُ /
أَيْدِي / بَيْض / ثَوْبُ / جَيْش / حَوْض / وَيْلُ / لَيْمُونُ

* * *

Vocabulary Repertoire Building: The words highlighted in green in the sections above are recommend to be learned as vocabulry at this early stage of learning Arabic. Thus, they are listed again in the following table, along with their English meanings. The green color in Arabic culture stands for fertility!

I wrote	كَتَبْتُ	pen	قَلَم	after	بَعْدَ
he went	ذَهَبَ	soul, self	نَفْس	Lebanon	لُبْنان
he heard	سَمِعَ	I heard	سَمِعْتُ	I wrote	كَتَبْتُ
Egypt	مِصْر	happy	سَعيد	Baghdad	بَغْداد
he spoke to someone	كَلَّمَ	he taught	عَلَّمَ	he saluted	سَلَّمَ
he spoke up	تَكَلَّمَ	love	حُبّ	teacher	مُعَلِّم
eye, spring of water	عَيْن	instructor, teacher	مُدَرِّس	he learned	تَعَلَّمَ
eggs	بَيْض	boys, children	أَوْلاد	Beirut	بَيْروت
lemon	لَيْمون	garment	ثَوْب	day	يَوْم

* * *

Lesson Five

حَرْف الهَمْزَة والأَلِف: (ء) (ا) نُطقاً وكِتابَةً

The letters *Hamzah* (ء) and *Alif* (ا): Aspects of Articulation, Pronunciation and Writing

(ء) The ***Hamzah*** represents a glottal stop, produced by completely stopping the breath momentarily in the glottis and then releasing it explosively as if you lift something heavy; thus it is called glottal stop sound. It is part of the English sound system though it is not represented by a letter. The sound is frequently made in English at the beginning of a word with an initial vowel, particularly if emphasized; e.g. "***absolutely essential***." It is similar to the first sound of the English "***ouch***".

At the beginning of words, the *Hamzah* takes the *Alif* as a seat, and the sound of the *Hamzah* is absorbed into the short vowel that follows. Thus, for the untrained ear, one can hardly distinguish where the sound of the *Hamzah* stops and the sound of the short vowel begins.

As a consonant in Arabic, the *Hamzah* can appear in writing at the beginning, middle and final positions of words. At the beginning of words, the *Hamzah* takes the *Alif* as a seat, and hence the overlapping of these two letters in the minds of some educators and learners.

Now listen to your instructor pronouncing the following isolated *Hamzah* seated on an *Alif* in combination with the three short vowels: *Fathah*, *Dammah* and *Kasrah*; then pronouncing them in context of actual words:

إِ	أُ	أَ
إِذا	أُمّ	أَب

Important Note: The rules of writing the *Hamzah* in the middle and final positions of words are rather complicated, and will be treated separately in one lesson at the end of this section of the textbook!

(ا) The *Alif* has two main functions: (1) It is either a seat for the *Hamzah*, as in (أَ) and (أُ), or the *Hamzah* is a seat for it, as in (إِ), at the beginning of words as illustrated above. In a text without the vowel signs, the *Alif* substitutes for the *Hamzah*, which is left out in writing, thus in unvowelled text, the words in the section above will appear as: (اب), (ام) and (اذا).

(2) The other function of the *Alif*, without any diacritical mark affiliated with it, is the sign for the long vowel (ـا / ا = *aa* or *ā*) after any other consonant, as in the following examples:

سَمـاء	تـاب	بـاب

Lesson Six

حَرْف الباء والتَّاء والثَّاء: (ب) (ت) (ث) نُطقاً وكِتابَةً

The letters *Baa* (ب), *Taa* (ت) & *Thaa* (ث): Aspects of Articulation, Pronunciation and Writing

ب (*Baa*): The sound of this letter is identical to the letter (b) in English words, such as **bat**, **boy** or **beam**.

In terms of writing, the letter (*Baa*) assumes the following three forms in initial, middle and final positions of words:

Now observe visually, then listen and repeat!

Final Position	Middle Position	Initial Position
ـب / ب	ـبـ / بـ	بـ
أب / حَبِيب	جَبَل / أَبَتِ	باب / بَيْت

* * *

ت (*Taa*): The sound of this letter is identical to the letter (t) in English words, such as **tan**, **tea** or **tool**.

In terms of writing, the letter (*Taa*) assumes the following three forms in initial, middle and final positions of words:

Now observe visually, then listen and repeat!

Final Position	Middle Position	Initial Position
ـت / ت	ـتـ / تـ	تـ
تَحْتَ / باتَ	بَتَرَ / أَتَتْ	تابَ / تُوت

* * *

ث (*Thaa*) represents almost the same sound as does the unvoiced "*th*" of English "**mouth**" or "**thing**".

In terms of writing, the letter (*Thaa*) assumes the following three forms in initial, middle and final positions of words. Now observe the written shapes, then listen and repeat!

Final Position	Middle Position	Initial Position
ـث / ث	ـثـ / ثـ	ثـ
ثُلُث / ثَلاث	عَثَرَ / أَثَر	ثَوْب / ثُوم

Important Note About Writing the Two or Three Dots That Are Part of Certain Letters:

In handwriting and in one established script in Arabic, the two or three separate dots which accompany certain letters can be represented by one thick dash for two dots (▬), and by one miniture symbol of a two-sided triangle (^), such as:

Exercise: Now, listen to your instructor pronouncing the letters ث / ت / ب in combination with the three short vowels and the corresponding three long vowels:

Long Vowel	Short Vowel	Long Vowel	Short Vowel	Long Vowel	Short Vowel
بي	بِ	بو	بُ	با	بَ
تي	تِ	تو	تُ	تا	تَ
ثي	ثِ	ثو	ثُ	ثا	ثَ

* * *

Exercise: Now, listen to your instructor pronouncing the following words which contain the letters ث / ت / ب in combination with short and long vowels:

بابا	ثابَ	تابَ	بابُ	باتَ
ثُبوتُ	ثَوابُ	ثَوْبُ	توتُ	ثابِتُ
ثَوْبي	بُيوتُ	بَيْتُ	بابي	أبي

* * *

Vocabulary Repertoire Building: Continue building your vocabulary repertoire by learning the words in the following table:

father	أب	house	بَيْت	door	باب
three	ثَلاث	beloved	حَبيب	mother	أُمّ
mountain	جَبَل	sky, heaven	سَماء	One-third	ثُلُث

Lesson Seven

حَرْف الجيم والحاء والخاء:
(ج) (ح) (خ) نُطقاً وكِتابَةً

The letters *Jeem* (ج), *Ĥaa* (ح) & *Khaa* (خ): Aspects of Articulation, Pronunciation and Writing

ج **(*Jeem*):** The sound of this letter is identical to the letter (j) in English words, such as **jam**, **judge** or **jeep**. In some Arabic regions, such as Lebanon and Syria, it is pronounced like the letter (s) in a word like "**pleasure**." In parts of Egypt and Yemen, it is pronounced like the letter (g) in a word like "**gap**."

In terms of writing, the letter (***Jeem***) assumes the following three forms in initial, middle and final positions of words:

Now observe visually, then listen and repeat!

Final Position	Middle Position	Initial Position
ـج / ج	ـجـ / ـجـ	جـ
حَـجَّ / حـاجّ	حِـجاب / أَجـاب	جـابَ / جُـثَـثٌ

* * *

ح **(*Ĥaa*):** It can be said that the letter (*Ĥaa*) is a (hard *h*), in the sense that it's articulated like the (*h*) but with an accompanying friction in the throat. In articulating this sound, the epiglottis is broght soo close to the pharyngeal wall that the air escapes with a friction. This consonant is voiceless; that is, no vibrations of the vocal cords occur.

In terms of writing, the letter (***Ĥaa***) assumes the following three forms in initial, middle and final positions of words:

Now observe visually, then listen and repeat!

Final Position	Middle Position	Initial Position
ـح / ح	ـحـ / ـحـ	حـ
بَـلَـحُ / بـاحَ	بَـحَـثَ / بـاحِـث	حَـبيبُ / حَـجَـبَ

* * *

خ (***Khaa***): It can be said that the sound of this consonant is similar to the final consonant of the German "***Bach***" and the Scotiish "***loch***". In the articulation of this consonant, the back of the tongue lightly touches the soft palate (velum) and the air escapes with friction. Like the previous consonant, this one is also voiceless.

In terms of writing, the letter (***Khaa***) assumes the following three forms in initial, middle and final positions of words:

Now observe visually, then listen and repeat!

Final Position	Middle Position	Initial Position
خ / ـخ	ـخـ / ـخـ	خـ
تـاريـخ / أرَّخَ	بُـخـارُ / أخـيـر	خَـبـيـثُ / خُـبْـزُ

* * *

Exercise: Now, listen to your instructer pronouncing the the letters خ / ح / ج in combination with the three short vowels and the corresponding three long vowels:

Long Vowel	Short Vowel	Long Vowel	Short Vowel	Long Vowel	Short Vowel
جـي	جِ	جـو	جُ	جـا	جَ
حـي	حِ	حـو	حُ	حـا	حَ
خـي	خِ	خـو	خُ	خـا	خَ

* * *

Exercise: Now, listen to your instructor pronouncing the following words which containn the letters خ / ح / ج in combination with short and long vowels:

تاجُ	أجابَ	جَوابُ	جابَ	جاءَ
باحَ	أحَبَّ	حاجِبُ	حَبيبي	حُوتُ
خَوْخُ	أخْبارُ	أخْتي	أخي	خابَ

* * *

Drills.. تَمْرينات

1. Connect the isolated letters to form words you encountered in Lessons 4, 5 & 6, as in the given example. *It is preferable to do this exercise on a note book:*

ح+ج+ا+ب = حِجاب

١- أ + ب = ____________

٢- ث+ب+ا+ت = ____________

٣- ح+ب+ي+ب = ____________

٤- ب+ا+ب = ____________

٥- ت+ح+ت = ____________

٦- ب+ي+ت = ____________

٧- أ+ب+ي = ____________

٨- خ+و+خ = ____________

٩- أ+خ+ت+ي = ____________

١٠- ح+و+ت = ____________

١١- ب+ح+ث = ____________

١٢- أ+ج+ا+ب = ____________

١٣- ح+ج+ج = ____________

١٤- ب+ي+و+ت = ____________

١٥- خ+ب+ز = ____________

١٦- ت+ا+ر+ي+خ = ____________

* * *

2. Listen to your instructor pronouncing the following items and fill in, in writing, the missing letters:

١- تا.......... ٢- بـ..........ـت ٣- ....حِث ٤- ....تي

٥- أَ.......... ٦- ثا..........ت ٧- ....اب ٨- بُـ..........ر

* * *

3. Listen to your instructor pronouncing one word from each group of two, and circle the one you hear:

١- حابَ خابَ ٢- حَدُّ خَدُّ

٣- حُبُّ خُبُّ ٤- حارَ خارَ

* * *

Vocabulary Repertoire Building: Continue to build up your vocabulary repertoire by learning the words in the following table:

Meaning	Arabic	Meaning	Arabic	Meaning	Arabic
brother	أَخ	mother	أُمّ	father	أَب
I love, I like	أُحِبّ	beloved	حَبيب	sister	أُخْت

Lesson Eight

حَرْف الدَّال والذَّال والرَّاء والزَّاء: (د) (ذ) (ر) (ز) نُطقاً وكِتابَةً

The letters *Daal* (د), *Dhaal* (ذ), *Raa* (ر) & *Zaa* (ز): Aspects of Articulation, Pronunciation and Writing

د (*Daal*): The sound of this letter is identical to the letter (d) in English words, such as **Dan**, **doom** or **dear**.

In terms of writing, the letter (*Daal*) assumes the following three forms in initial, middle and final positions of words:

Now observe visually, then listen and repeat!

Final Position	Middle Position	Initial Position
ـد / د	ـد / د	د
أحَـد / وَدود	حَـديـد / جَـديـد	دار / دُبّ

* * *

ذ (*Dhaal*): The sound of this letter is identical to the English combination (th) in English words, such as **that**, **those** or **then**.

In terms of writing, the letter (*Dhaal*) assumes the following three forms in initial, middle and final positions of words:

Now observe visually, then listen and repeat!

Final Position	Middle Position	Initial Position
ـذ / ذ	ـذ / ذ	ذ
خُـذْ / إِذْ	حِـذاء / أذوب	ذابَ / ذُباب

* * *

ر (*Raa*): Though this consonant is similar to the English (r), it is different from it. It is rather closer to the Spanish (r) in a word such as (perro), where the tip of the tongue flaps against the alveolar ridge behind the upper front teeth.

In terms of writing, the letter (*Raa*) assumes the following three forms in initial, middle and final positions of words:

Now observe visually, then listen and repeat!

Final Position	Middle Position	Initial Position
ـر / ر	ـر / ر	ر
أخِيـر / دار	بَـريـد / خـارِج	رَبـاح / رَذاذ

* * *

ز (*Zaa*): The sound of this consonant is identical to the English (**z**) in words such as **zone**, **zebra** or **zipper**, where the front of the tongue touches against the alveolar ridge behind the upper front teeth.

In terms of writing, the letter (*Zaa*) assumes the following three forms in initial, middle and final positions of words:

Now observe visually, then listen and repeat!

Final Position	Middle Position	Initial Position
ـز / ز	ـز / ز	ز
بَـزّ / باز	تَـزْداد / أزيـز	زَبـيـب / زاد

* * *

Exercise: Now, listen to your instructor pronouncing the letters د / ذ / ر / ز in combination with the three short vowels and the corresponding three long vowels:

Long Vowel	Short Vowel	Long Vowel	Short Vowel	Long Vowel	Short Vowel
دي	دِ	دو	دُ	دا	دَ
ذي	ذِ	ذو	ذُ	ذا	ذَ
ري	رِ	رو	رُ	را	رَ
زي	زِ	زو	زُ	زا	زَ

* * *

Exercise 1: Now, listen to your instructor pronouncing the following words which contain the letters د / ذ / ر / ز in combination with short and long vowels:

جَديد	أَسَد	دَرَس	دُور	دار
حِذاء	بُـذور	أَخَذَ	ذُباب	ذابَ

حَرير	حارّ	أَحْرَزَ	دَرْب	رَ بِح
بـاز	بَـزَّ	وَزيـر	زَبيب	زيـر

* * *

<u>Exercise 2</u>: In this exercise we will compare and contrast the sounds of the letters (ث) and (ذ) in actual words, so listen and repeat:

١- ثـابَ	ذابَ
٢- بُـثـور	بُـذور
٣- بَـثَّ	بَـذَّ
٤- آثـار	آذار
٥- ثَواب	ذَواب

* * *

<u>Important Note</u>: You might have observed that <u>in writing</u>, <u>most of the Arabic letters are two way connecters; they can be connected to preceding and following letters</u>. However, <u>the *Alif* (ا), the *Hamzated Alif* (أ), and the *Waaw* (و) are one-way connecters</u>; <u>they connect only to preceding letters, but not to following letters</u>. Now we can add to this list of one-way connecters the other letters to complete the group, as they appear inside the following box:

أ ، ا ، و ، د ، ذ ، ر ، ز

Lesson Nine

حَرْف السِّين والشِّين والصَّاد والضَّاد: (س) (ش) (ص) (ض) نُطقًا وكِتابَةً

The letters *Seen* (س), *Sheen* (ش), *Šaad* (ص) & *Ďaad* (ض): Aspects of Articulation, Pronunciation and Writing

س (*Seen*): The sound of this letter is identical to the letter (s) in English words, such as **Sam**, **soon** or **seen**.

In terms of writing, the letter (*Daal*) assumes the following three forms in initial, middle and final positions of words:

Now observe visually, then listen and repeat!

Final Position	Middle Position	Initial Position
ـس / س	ـسـ / سـ	س
أَحَسَّ / أساس	حِساب / أسير	سَراب/ سَحَر

* * *

ش (*Sheen*): The sound of this letter is identical to the English combination (*sh*) in English words, such as **sharp**, **hush** or **sheep**.

In terms of writing, the letter (*Sheen*) assumes the following three forms in initial, middle and final positions of words:

Now observe visually, then listen and repeat!

Final Position	Middle Position	Initial Position
ـش / ش	ـشـ / شـ	ش
حَشيش / بَشوش	بَشير / أَشرَبُ	شَراب / شَجَر

* * *

ص (*Šaad*): This **consonant** represents an "**emphatic**" **velarized** correlative of س. It is formed by placing the tip of the tongue in approximately the same position as the *Seen*, and raising the back of the tongue toward the velum.

In terms of writing, the letter (*Šaad*) assumes the following three forms in initial, middle and final positions of words. Now observe visually, then listen and repeat!

Final Position	Middle Position	Initial Position
ـص / ص	ـصـ / صـ	ص
حِصَص / أَبْرَص	بَصير / أَصْبَح	صَباح / صابِر

* * *

ض (*Ďaaḍ*): This consonant represents an "emphatic" velarized correlative of د. It is formed in the same way as in *Šaad* / ص :

In terms of writing, the letter (*Ďaaḍ*) assumes the following three forms in initial, middle and final positions of words. Now observe visually, then listen and repeat!

Final Position	Middle Position	Initial Position
ـض / ض	ـضـ / ضـ	ض
أَبْيَض / خاضَ	أَخْضَر / أَضْرِبُ	ضَرَبَ / ضابِط

* * *

Exercise: Now, listen to your instructor pronouncing the letters س / ش / ص / ض in combination with the three short vowels and the corresponding three long vowels:

Long Vowel	Short Vowel	Long Vowel	Short Vowel	Long Vowel	Short Vowel
سي	سِ	سو	سُ	سا	سَ
شي	شِ	شو	شُ	شا	شَ
صي	صِ	صو	صُ	صا	صَ
ضي	ضِ	ضو	ضُ	ضا	ضَ

* * *

Exercise: Now, listen to your instructor pronouncing the following words which contain the letters س / ش / ص / ض in combination with short and long vowels:

جَحْش	رَأْس	سور	حِساب	سارَ
حَشيش	بَشَّر	شَباب	أَشْرَبُ	شَراب
صَبَر	سَبَر	أَصْبَحَ	صادَ	صابِر
بَصير	بَشير	حَضَر	أَضْرِبُ	ضَرَبَ

Oral Exercise 1: In this exercise we will compare and contrast the sounds of the letters (س) and (ص) in actual words, so listen and repeat:

١- سَبَرَ	صَبَرَ
٢- سَيْف	صَيْف
٣- سارَ	صارَ
٤- أَسْبَح	أَصْبَح
٥- سُوَر	صُوَر

* * *

Oral Exercise 2: In this exercise we will compare and contrast the sounds of the letters (د) and (ض) in actual words, so listen and repeat:

١- دَرْب	ضَرْب
٢- بَيْداء	بَيْضاء
٣- دَرَّ	ضَرَّ
٤- فَرْد	فَرْض
٥- رُدود	رُضُوض

* * *

Listening Exercise 3: Listen to your instructor pronounce one of two words in each group, and then circle the one you hear:

١- بَيْضاء / بَيْداء ٢- ضَرْب / دَرْب ٣- سادَ / صادَ

٤- بادَتْ / باضَتْ ٥- حَسَدَ / حَصَدَ ٦- سُور / صُور

٧- دار / ضار ٨- دَرَّ / ضَرَّ ٩- عَدَّ / عَضَّ ١٠- سَريرُ / صَريرُ

* * *

Listening & Writing Exercise 4: Listen to your instructor pronounce the following five words in each group, and then write in each blank the missing letter you hear:

١- ...... يْف ٢- ...... باب ٣- بَيْ ...... ٤- حَـ ...... د ٥- بَـ ...... ير

* * *

Dictation: Listening & Writing Exercise 5: Listen to your instructor selectively pronouncing five words introduced in the lesson; your task is to write down the word you hear with the right spelling:

١- .... ٢- .... ٣- ....

٤- .... ٥- ....

* * *

Writing Exercise 5: Connect the isolated letters in each group to form a full-fledged word:

١- ش+ا+د+ي = ______________ ٢- ص+ب+ا+ح = ______________

٣- س+ح+ر = ______________ ٤- ب+ص+ي+ص = ______________

٥- خ+ض+ا+ر = ______________ ٦- ح+س+و+د = ______________

٧- ص+ب+و+ر= ______________ ٨- ح+ش+ي+ش = ______________

٩- ص+ر+ي+ح= ______________ ١٠- ب+ي+ض = ______________

١١- أ+خ+ض+ر = ______________ ١٢- ب+ش+و+ش= ______________

Important Note: **A hand-written variation of writing the (س) and (ش) letters can be seen underlined in the following chart; this is called the (رِقْعَة / *Riq'ah*) script. Also notice the variations in other letters!**

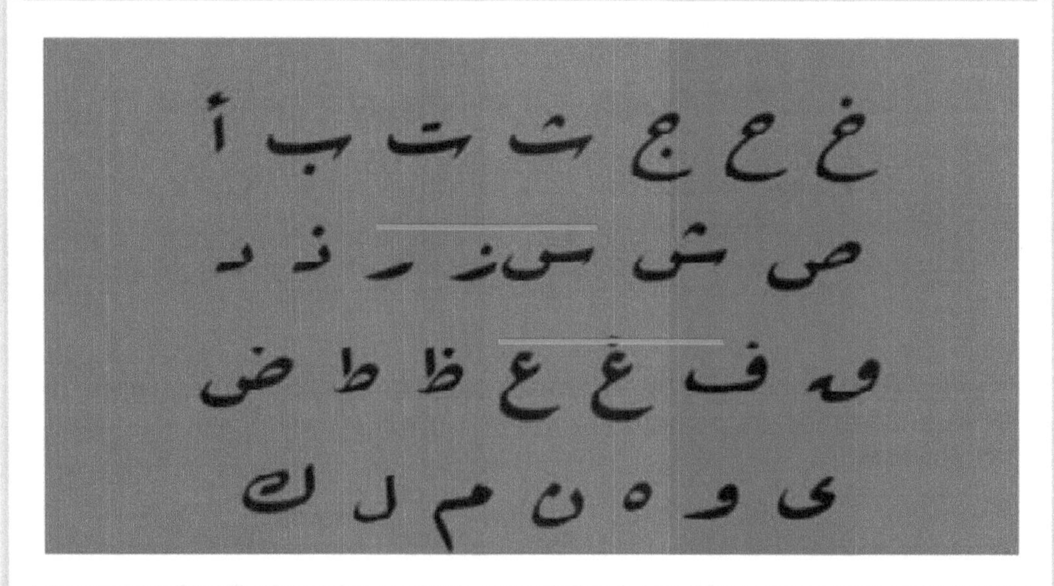

Vocabulary Repertoire Building: Continue to build up your vocabulary repertoire by learning the words in the following table:

professor	أُسْتاذ	class	صَفّ	lesson	دَرْس
I study	أَدْرُس	bread	خُبْز	morning	صَباح
I drink	أَشْرَب	tea	شاي	head	رَأْس
patience	صَبْر	one	أَحَد	home, house	دار
shoes	حِذاء	new	جَديد	drink	شَباب
counting	حِساب	lion	أَسَد	hot	حارّ
white	أَبْيَض	body	جَسَد	drink	شَراب
true, correct	صَواب	he came, he attended	حَضَرَ	green	أَخْضَر

* * *

Lesson Ten

حَرْف الطَّاء والظَّاء والعَيْن والغَيْن:

(ط)(ظ)(ع)(غ) نُطقاً وكِتابَةً

The letters *Ťaa* (ط), *Žaa* (ظ), *'Ayn* (ع) & *Ghayn* (غ):

Aspects of Articulation, Pronunciation and Writing

ط (*Ťaa*): The sound of this letter might sound identical to the (ت) sound to the untrained ear.This consoant represents an "emphatic" velarized correlative of ت. It is produced with the back of the tongue raised toward the soft palate. It is close in sound to the English (t) in a word like Todd.

In terms of writing, the letter (*Ťaa*) assumes the following three forms in initial, middle and final positions of words. Now observe visually, then listen and repeat!

Final Position	Middle Position	Initial Position
ـط / ط	ـطـ / طـ	طـ
رَبَـط / رِباط	حَطب / أَطْيَب	طَبيب/ طيِّب

ظ (*Žaa*): The sound of this letter might sound to the untrained ear like (ذ). However, the (ظ) is the pharyngealized counterpart of the (ذ), and it is produced with the back of the tongue raised toward the soft palate. But in colloquial Egyptian and Syrian dialects, this sound is often pronounced as that of ***Zaa*** / ز .

In terms of writing, the letter (*Žaa*) assumes the following three forms in initial, middle and final positions of words:

Now observe visually, then listen and repeat!

Final Position	Middle Position	Initial Position
ـظ / ظ	ـظـ / ظـ	ظـ
حَظّ / حُظوظ	حُظوظ / وَظّف	ظَبْيِ / ظِباء

* * *

ع (*'Ayn*): This consonant might sound like the letter (ء) to the untrained ear. It is a very difficult sound for the average Westerner to articulate, and it is best mastered in connection with a native speaker. It is generally regarded that *'Ayn* is a voiced correlative of *Ĥaa* / ح. This supposition is only partially true; for if *'Ayn* is unvoiced, something close to *Ĥaa* results. However, if the process is reversed, and the *Ĥaa* is voiced, it will be found that the general tenseness in the pharynx is greatly increased; there may be other physical modifications as well:

In terms of writing, the letter (*'Ayn*) assumes the following three forms in initial, middle and final positions of words. Now observe visually, then listen and repeat!

Final Position	**Middle Position**	**Initial Position**
ـع / ع	ـعـ / عـ	عـ
إصْبَع / بَيّاع	بَعيد / أعزب	عرَب / عجيب

* * *

غ (*Ghayn*): It is a voiced velar fricative. It is almost the voiced correlative of خ , but the correlation is not exact; for in *Ghayn* there is no velar scrape. This sound is similar to the Parisian " r " in a word like Paris.

In terms of writing, the letter (*Ghayn*) assumes the following three forms in initial, middle and final positions of words. Now observe visually, then listen and repeat!

Final Position	Middle Position	Initial Position
ـغ / غ	ـغـ / غـ	غـ
صَبَغَ / صاغَ	بَغداد / راغِب	غُراب / غرب

* * *

<u>Exercise</u>: Now, listen to your instructor pronouncing the letters ط / ظ / ع / غ in combination with the three short vowels and the corresponding three long vowels:

Long Vowel	Short Vowel	Long Vowel	Short Vowel	Long Vowel	Short Vowel
طي	طِ	طو	طُ	طا	طَ
ظي	ظِ	ظو	ظُ	ظا	ظَ
عي	عِ	عو	عُ	عا	عَ
غي	غِ	غو	غُ	غا	غَ

* * *

<u>Exercise</u>: Now, listen to your instructor pronouncing the following words which contain the letters ط / ظ / ع / غ in combination with short and long vowels:

بَطّ	عُطْر	بَطَرَ	طِبّ	طالِب
حُظوظ	حَظّ	حَظْر	ظَرْف	ظَريف
بَديع	بارِع	تَعْبير	عيد	عَبَّرَ
بَعيد	بَغيض	غَرْب	غُبار	غُرَف

* * *

<u>Oral Exercise</u> 1: In this exercise we will compare and contrast the sounds of the letters (ت) and (ط) in actual words, so listen and repeat:

١- تابَ طابَ ٢- تَرَكَ طَرَقَ ٣- فَتَرَ فَطَرَ

٤- تابِع طابِع ٥- بَتَر بَطَر

* * *

<u>Oral Exercise</u> 2: In this exercise we will compare and contrast the sounds of the letters (ذ) and (ظ) in actual words, so listen and repeat:

١- نَذَرَ　　نَظَرَ　　　٢- نَذير　　نَظير

٣- بُذور　　بُظور　　　٤- شَذا　　شَظا

٥- حَذَر　　حَظَر

* * *

<u>Oral Exercise</u> 3: In this exercise we will compare and contrast the sounds of the letters (خ) and (غ) in actual words, so listen and repeat:

١- خَيْر　غَيْر　　　٢- خابَ غابَ

٣- خَرير　غَرير　　٤- خَرَّ　غَرَّ　٥- خابَتْ　غابَتْ

* * *

<u>Oral Exercise 4</u>: In this exercise we will compare and contrast the sounds of the letters (أ) and (ع) in actual words, so listen and repeat:

١- باءَ　باعَ　　٢- أَبَدَ　عَبَدَ　　٣- أَثَر　عَثَر

٤- سائِد　ساعِد　　٥- أَرْض　عَرْض

* * *

<u>Listening Exercise</u> 5: Listen to your instructor pronounce one of two words in each group, and then circle the one you hear:

١- إِبَر / عِبَر　٢- عَلَتْ / غَلَتْ　٣- طابِع / تابِع

٤- خَبَّر / غَبَّر　٥- خابَ / غابَ　٦- بَتَّ / بَطَّ

٧- تَبَعَ / طَبَعَ　٨- أَجيب / عَجيب

* * *

<u>Listening & Writing Exercise 6</u>: Listen to your instructor pronounce the following five words, and then write in each blank the missing letter you hear:

١- ......يْب　٢- بَـ......داد　٣- ......بيب　٤- حافِ......　٥- بَـ......يد

<u>Dictation: Listening & Writing Exercise</u> 7: Listen to your instructor selectively pronouncing five words introduced in the lesson; your task is to write down the word you hear with the right spelling:

١- .... ٢- .... ٣- ....

٤- .... ٥- ....

* * *

<u>Writing Exercise</u> 8: Connect the isolated letters in each group to form a full-fledged word:

١- س+ع+ي+د = ____________ ٢- ب+غ+د+ا+د = ____________

٣- ظ+ر+ف = ____________ ٤- ب+ط+ا+ط+ا = ____________

٥- ب+د+ي+ع = ____________ ٦- ع+ي+د = ____________

٧- ط+ب+ع = ____________ ٨- ط+ب+ي+ب = ____________

٩- ب+ع+ي+د = ____________ ١٠- ر+غ+د = ____________

١١- ظ+ب+ي = ____________ ١٢- س+ع+ي+د = ____________

١٣- ط+ب+خ = ____________ ١٤- ط+ب+ب+ا+خ = ____________

١٥- غ+ر+ا+ب = ____________ ١٦- ع+ر+ب+ي+ي = ____________

* * *

Vocabulary Repertoire Building: Continue to build up your vocabulary repertiore by learning the words in the following table:

deer	ظَبْي	doctor, M.D.	طَبيب	fine, delicious	طَيِّب
an Arab, Arabic	عَرَبِيّ	Arabs	عَرَب	envelope	ظَرْف
finger	إِصْبَع	happy	سَعيد	distant, far away	بَعيد
stamp	طابِع	raven	غُراب	west	غَرْب
holiday	عيد	strange, alien	غَريب	watermelon	بَطِّيخ
onion	بَصَل	he sold	باعَ	potatoes	بَطاطا

Lesson Eleven

حَرْف الفاء والقاف والكاف والـلّام: (ف) (ق) (ك) (ل) نُطقاً وكِتابَةً

The letters *Faa* (ف), *Qaaf* (ق), *Kaaf* (ك) & *Laam* (ل): Aspects of Articulation, Pronunciation and Writing

ف (*Faa*): The sound represented by this letter is identical to the sound of the English (**f**) in words such as fat, fool or feel.

In terms of writing, the letter (***Faa***) assumes the following three forms in initial, middle and final positions of words:

Now observe visually, then listen and repeat!

Final Position	Middle Position	Initial Position
ـف / ف	ـفـ / ف	فـ
عَفيف / حَرف	حَفِيد / رَفَعَ	فَجْر / فَتَحَ

* * *

ق (*Qaaf*): This is a voiceless uvular stop, which can be reproduced by taking the point of contact in the "*ik, ak, uk*" series (see above under *Khaa* / خ) one stage further back, so that contact may be made at the extremity of the velum. In various areas, especially the Arabian Gulf, *Qaaf* is pronounced like the hard "g " in " gas " :
In terms of writing, the letter (***Qaaf***) assumes the following three forms in initial, middle and final positions of words. Now observe visually, then listen and repeat!

Final Position	Middle Position	Initial Position
ـق / ق	ـقـ / ق	قـ
حَقّ / سُوق	عَقْرَب / دَقيق	قَعَدَ / قُعود

* * *

ك (***Kaaf***): The sound represented by this letter is identical to sound of the English (**k**) in words such as **Kansas**, **Kafka**, or **keep**, or to the sound of the (**c**) in words such as **cat**, **course**, or **cute**.

In terms of writing, the letter (***Kaaf***) assumes the following three forms in initial, middle and final positions of words:

Now observe visually, then listen and repeat!

Final Position	Middle Position	Initial Position
ـك / ك	ـكـ / كـ	كـ
ديـك / شُـبَّاك	تَـكْـتُـب / أكْـبَـر	كِـتاب / كَـيْـف...؟

* * *

ل (*Laam*): The sound represented by this letter is very close to the sound of the English (l) in words such as **lab**, **loop** or **sleep**. However, the Arabic (ل) is generally lighter. It is pronounced with the back of the tongue lowered and the tip touching the alveolar ridge, just behind the upper teeth. By contrast, the American English (l) is usually dark, with the back of the tongue raised toward the soft palate. The word 'little", for example, has two occurrences of (l); the first one is light and the secomd one is heavy.

There are, however, instances of heavy (ل) in Arabic. The best example occures in the word (الله) for "God." Also heavy (ل) occurs when it is adjacent to one of the pharyngealized sounds of (ص / ض / ط / ظ).

In terms of writing, the letter (*Laam*) assumes the following three forms in initial, middle and final positions of words. Now observe visually, then listen and repeat!

Final Position	Middle Position	Initial Position
ـل / ل	ـلـ / لـ	لـ
أَصْـل / أصـول	جَـلَـسَ / جالِـس	لَـعِـبَ / لِـبـاس

* * *

Exercise: Now, listen to your instructor pronouncing the letters ف / ق / ك / ل in combination with the three short vowels and the corresponding three long vowels:

Long Vowel	Short Vowel	Long Vowel	Short Vowel	Long Vowel	Short Vowel
فـي	فِ	فـو	فُ	فـا	فَ
قـي	قِ	قـو	قُ	قـا	قَ
كـي	كِ	كـو	كُ	كـا	كَ
لـي	لِ	لـو	لُ	لا / لا	لَ

تـركيـب (لام أَلِف) (لا) (لا)

The Construct of the (*Laam*) with (*Alif*) as a Long Vowel to Form (لا) (لا)

The combination of the letter (***Laam***) followed by the long vowel (***Alif***) is a highly frequent occurance in Arabic, to form syllables and one actual word for the English "**no** / **not**." Due to this fact, there is even one key on the Arabic keyboard that automatically combine these two characters together. The form (لا) is the shape this combination appears as when you hit the keyboard designated for it. The form (لـا) is the shape resulting when you hit two keys separately. This last is the form mostly used in handwriting.

Now listen to your instructor pronounce actual words containing the (ـا+ل) combination:

لاحَ	لاذَ	لا
جَـلال	أَوْلاد	بِـلاد
خَـلا	بِـلا	سَـلا

* * *

Exercise: Now, listen to your instructor pronouncing the following words which contain the letters ف / ق / ك / ل in combination with short and long vowels:

لِـحاف	فَـضْل	حَـرْف	طِـفْـل	فَـرَس
حَـلّاق	إِبْـريـق	عِـقْـد	قَـلْـب	قَـلَـيـل
بِـلاد	خَـلـيـل	كـاتِـب	كُـتُـب	كِـتـاب
سُـؤال	بَـصَل	قَـلْـب	لاعِـب	لَـيْـث

* * *

<u>Oral Exercise</u>: In this exercise we will compare and contrast the sounds of the letters (ك) and (ق) in actual words, so listen and repeat:

١- كَـلْـب قَـلْـب ٢- كـادَ قـادَ ٣- سَـبَـكَ سَـبَـقَ

٤- سَـلَـكَ سَـلَـقَ ٥- كـالَ قـالَ

Listening Exercise 1: Listen to your instructor pronounce one of two words in each group, and then circle the one you hear:

١- سَبَكَ / سَبَقَ ٢- دَكَّ / دَقَّ ٣- كَلَّ / قَلَّ

٤- رَكِيك / رَقِيق ٥- كَرَّ / قَرَّ ٦- كَلْب / قَلْب

* * *

Listening & Writing Exercise 2: Listen to your instructor pronounce the following five words, and then write in each blank the missing letter you hear:

١- ......ريب ٢- ......فاح ٣- ......ولا ٤- بِ......د ٥- مِ......تاح

* * *

Dictation: Listening & Writing Exercise 3: Listen to your instructor selectively pronouncing five words introduced in the lesson; your task is to write down the word you hear with the right spelling:

١- .... ٢- .... ٣- ....

٤- .... ٥- ....

* * *

Writing Exercise: Connect the isolated letters in each group to form a full-fledged word:

١- ط+ف+ل = ____________ ٢- أ+و+ل+ا+د = ____________

٣- ك+ت+ب = ____________ ٤- ك+ت+ا+ب = ____________

٥- ك+ل+ب = ____________ ٦- ق+ل+ب = ____________

٧- ق+ا+ل = ____________ ٨- ف+ت+ح = ____________

٩- أ+ك+ت+ب = ____________ ١٠- أ+ف+ل+ح = ____________

١١- ج+ل+س = ____________ ١٢- ل+ا+ع+ب = ____________

١٣- س+و+ق = ____________ ١٤- ب+ل+ا+د = ____________

١٥- ح+ر+ف = ____________ ١٦- ق+ل+و+ب = ____________

Vocabulary Repertoire Building: Continue to build up your vocabulary repertiore by learning the words in the following table:

he sat	جَلَسَ	he did	فَعَلَ	he said	قالَ
heart	قَلْب	child, baby	طِفْل	shades	ظِلال
chair	كُرْسِي	player	لاعِب	market	سُوق
a book	كِتاب	a writer	كاتِب	he wrote	كَتَبَ
an alphabet letter	حَرْف	bigger, greater	أَكْبَر	dog	كَلْب
countries	بِلاد	children	أَوْلاد	no, not	لا

* * *

Visual Activity: Use your visual power to recognize some of the letters that you see in the following Arabesque piece and attempt to pronouce them!

Lesson Twelve

حَرْف الـميم والنُّون والهاء والواو والياء: (م) (ن) (هـ) (و) (ي) نُطقاً وكِتابَةً

The letters *Meem* (م), *Noon* (ن), *Haa* (هـ) *Wāw* (و) & *Yaa* (ي): Aspects of Articulation, Pronunciation and Writing

م (*Meem*): The sound represented by this letter is identical to the sound of the English (m) in words such as mother, moon or meat.

In terms of writing, the letter (*Meem*) assumes the following three forms in initial, middle and final positions of words:

Now observe, then listen and repeat!

Final Position	Middle Position	Initial Position
ـم / م	ـمـ / مـ	مـ
عَالِم / إمام	أَحْمَد / أمين	مُحَمَّد / مُمْتاز

* * *

ن (*Noon*): The sound represented by this letter is identical to the sound of the English (n) in words such as, moon, mother or meat.

Now observe visually, then listen and repeat!

Final Position	Middle Position	Initial Position
ـن / ن	ـنـ / نـ	نـ
حَسَن / حِصان	عِنَب / أنيق	نَامَ / نَبيل

* * *

هـ (*Haa*): The sound represented by this letter is identical to a great extent to sound of the English (h) in words such as **house**, **hose**, or **heat**. However, the difference between the Arabic and the English sounds is that in English, it is found mainly at the beginning of a syllable, whereas in Arabic it can be seen at the beginning, in the middle or at the end.

In terms of writing, the letter (*Haa*) assumes the following three forms in initial, middle and final positions of words. Now observe visually, then listen and repeat!

Final Position	Middle Position	Initial Position
ـه / ه	ـهـ / ـهـ / هـ	هـ
وَجْه / وُجوه	بَهيج/ جُهْد / زَهْر	هَرَم / هُم

* * *

و (***Waaw***): The (و) has two functions:

(1) It is the written symbol of the long vowel (ـو) transliterated as (*OO/ū*) and corresponding to the short vowel (*Dammah* ـُ), and free from any diacritical mark associated with consonants. As a long vowel its sound is equivalent to an (*OO*) in words such as boot, food.

(2) Its other function is that of full-fleged consonant, identical in sound to the (**W**) of English, in words such as wool, water, or wet. As a consonant, the vowel diacritial marks learned before can be seen over it. However, it is easy to distinguish between the two functions of the (و) because in Arabic a syllable does not start with a vowel, nor does it allow two different vowels consecutively.

- The (و) as a consonant is one of the two **diphthongs** in Arabic when the preceeding letter bears a (*Fathah*) vowel and the (*Waaw*) itself bears a "*Sukoon*," such as (لَوْ), (أَوْلاد).
- In terms of writing, the letter (و) as consonant assumes the usual three forms in initial, middle and final positions of words. However, it is one of the six letters which are one way connecters. Now observe visually, then listen and repeat!

Final Position	Middle Position	Initial Position
ـو / و	ـو / و	و
دَلْوْ / أوْ	يَوْم / أوَّل	وَلَد / وِداد

* * *

ي (***Yaa***): As was explained with the (و) above, the letter (ي) has two functions:

(1) It is the written symbol of the long vowel ـي) transliterated as (*ii/ī*) and corresponding to the short vowel (*Kasrah* ـِ), and free from any diacritical mark associated with consonants. As a long vowel its sound is equivalent to an (*ee /ea*) in words such as seed, meat or beat.

(2) Its other function is that of full-fleged consonant, identical in sound to the (y) of English, in words such as youth, yard, or yet. As a consonant, the vowel diacritial marks learned before can be seen over it. However, it is easy to distinguish between the two functions of the (ي) because in Arabic a syllable does not start with a vowel, nor does it allow two different vowels consecutively.

- The (ي) as a consonant is one of the two **diphthongs** in Arabic when the preceeding letter bears a (*Fathah*) vowel and the (*Yaa*) itself bears a "*Sukoon*," such as (كَـيْ), (كَـيْـفَ).
- In terms of writing, the letter (ي) as consonant assumes the usual three forms in initial, middle and final positions of words. Furthermore, it is a two-way connecter. Now observe visually, then listen and repeat!

Final Position	Middle Position	Initial Position
ـي / ي	ـيـ / يـ	يـ
ظَـبْـيُ / والِـدَيَّ	لَـيْـث / أيّـام	يَـوْم / يَـمـيـن

* * *

Exercise: Now, listen to your instructor pronouncing the letters ي / و / ه / ن / م in combination with the three short vowels and the corresponding three long vowels:

Long Vowel	Short Vowel	Long Vowel	Short Vowel	Long Vowel	Short Vowel
مي	مِ	مو	مُ	ما **	مَ
ني	نِ	نو	نُ	نا	نَ
هي	هِ	هو	هُ	ها	هَ
وي	وِ	وو*	وُ	وا	وَ
* يي	يِ	يو	يُ	يا *	يَ

تركيب (ما) (يا)

The Construct of the (*Meem*) with (*Alif*) and (*Yaa*) with (*Alif*) to form Two Actual Particles

(يا) (ما)

The combination of the letter (*Meem*) followed by the long vowel (*Alif*) results in two actual particles with different semantic meanings, with highly frequent usage:

1. In a sentence like (ما هَذا؟), which means, (<u>What</u> is this?), (ما) is functioning as an <u>interrogative particle</u>.
2. However, in a sentence like (ما شَرِبْتُ قَهْوَةً .), which means, (**I did not drink coffee.**), (ما) is functioning as a <u>negating particle, negating the past tense verb following it</u>.
3. The combination of the letter (*Yaa*) followed by the long vowel (*Alif*) results in an actual particle, called "vocative" or "calling" particle, in a sentence such as, (يا اللّه!), which means, (O God!). The particle (يا) is used to invoke the name of God. Moreover, in every day speech, people use the particle (يا) before the name of the person they are addressing, as a **<u>term of endearment</u>**, such as:
يا مُحَمَّد ، أَيْنَ كُنْتَ أَمْس؟, which means, "**O Muhammad, where were you yesterday?!**

* * *

<u>Exercise 1</u>: Now, listen to your instructor pronouncing the following words which contain the letters م / ن / هـ / و / ي in combination with short and long vowels:

سَلام	قَلَم	عَمَل	مَرْيَم	مَحْمود
كان	مِنْ / مَنْ	مَصْنَع	نَلْعَبُ	نَحْنُ
وُجوه	وَجيه	نَهْر	هَذا	هُوَ
وَ	دَلْو	مَوْعِد	وَعَدَ	وَدود
شاي	بَيْت	بَيْنَ	يَعْقوبُ	يَسْكُنُ

* * *

<u>Oral Exercise</u> 2: In this exercise we will compare and contrast the sounds of the letters (ح) and (هـ) in actual words, so listen and repeat:

١- حَرَم   هَرَم
٢- حَلَّ   هَلَّ
٣- حَزَم   هَزَم
٤- سَحَر   سَهَر
٥- شُحوب   شُهوب

* * *

Listening Exercise 3: Listen to your instructor pronounce one of two words in each group, and then circle the one you hear:

١- حُروب / هُروب ٢- حادي / هادي ٣- حَجَر / هَجَر

٤- أَفْحَمَ / أَفْهَمَ / ٥- حَرَمُ / هَرَمُ ٦- حُبوب / هُبوب

* * *

Listening & Writing Exercise 4: Listen to your instructor pronounce the following five words, and then write in each blank the missing letter you hear:

١- ......لِك ٢- ......واء ٣- ......ور ٤- نَـ......ار ٥- ......الِد......

* * *

Dictation: Listening & Writing Exercise 5: Listen to your instructor selectively pronouncing five words introduced in the lesson; your task is to write down the word you hear with the right spelling:

١- .... ٢- .... ٣- ....

٤- .... ٥- ....

* * *

Writing Exercise 6: Connect the isolated letters in each group to form a full-fledged word:

١- أ+ن+ا = ____________ ٢- ع+ط+ش+ا+ن = ____________

٣- ن+و+ر = ____________ ٤- ت+ع+ب+ا+ن = ____________

٥- ن+ا+ر = ____________ ٦- م+ج+ن+و+ن = ____________

٧- م+ه+ا = ____________ ٨- م+ص+ر+ي+ي = ____________

٩- ن+ا+س = ____________ ١٠- م+ك+ت+ب = ____________

١١- م+ط+ر = ____________ ١٢- ج+م+ي+ل = ____________

١٣- أ+ن+ت = ____________ ١٤- أ+ن+ت+م = ____________

١٥- ن+ح+ن = ____________ ١٦- ه+ل+ا+ل = ____________

Vocabulary Repertoire Building: Continue to building up your vocabulary repertoire by learning the words in the following table:

you (fem.)	أَنْتِ	you (mas,)	أَنْتَ	I	أَنا
you (plu.fem.)	أَنْتُنَّ	you (plu.mas)	أَنْتُمْ	we	نَحْنُ
they	هُمْ	she	هِيَ	he	هُوَ
children	أَوْلاد	father	والِد	boy	وَلَد
eye	عَيْن	days	أَيَّام	day	يَوْم
faces	وُجوه	face	وَجْه	two eyes	عَيْنان

Reference Chart on the Arabic Writing System: Showing the Shapes and Forms of Arabic Letters in Initial, Middle and Final Position of Words

Most of the Arabic letters are written in slightly different forms from the way they appear in isolation. These variations depend on whether the letters stand alone, or are joined to a following letter only (initial), or are joined to a following letter and a preceding letter (medial) or are joined to a preceding letter only (final). The following table shows these variations:

Final	Medial	Initial	Isolated
ء / ـأ / ـئ / ـؤ / ـيء	ء / ـأ / ـؤ / ـئـ	أ / إ	ء *
ـا / ا	ـا / ا	ا	ا *
ـب / ب	ـبـ / بـ	بـ	ب
ـت / ت	ـتـ / تـ	تـ	ت
ـث / ث	ـثـ / ثـ	ثـ	ث
ـج / ج	ـجـ / جـ	جـ	ج
ـح / ح	ـحـ / حـ	حـ	ح
ـخ / خ	ـخـ / خـ	خـ	خ

د *	د	ـد / د	ـد / د
ذ *	ذ	ـذ / ذ	ـذ / ذ
ر *	ر	ـر / ر	ـر / ر
ز *	ز	ـز / ز	ـز / ز
س	سـ	ـسـ / سـ	ـس / س
ش	شـ	ـشـ / شـ	ـش / ش
ص	صـ	ـصـ / صـ	ـص / ص
ض	ضـ	ـضـ / ضـ	ـض / ض
ط	طـ	ـطـ / طـ	ـط / ط
ظ	ظـ	ـظـ / ظـ	ـظ / ظ
ع	عـ	ـعـ / عـ	ـع / ع
غ	غـ	ـغـ / غـ	ـغ / غ
ف	فـ	ـفـ / فـ	ـف / ف
ق	قـ	ـقـ / قـ	ـق / ق
ك	كـ	ـكـ / كـ	ـك / ك
ل	لـ	ـلـ / لـ	ـل / ل
م	مـ	ـمـ / مـ	ـم / م
ن	نـ	ـنـ/ نـ	ـن / ن
هـ	هـ	ـهـ / ـهـ / هـ	ـه / ه
و *	و	ـو / و	ـو / و
ي	يـ	ـيـ / يـ	ـي / ي

NOTES:

- The rules of writing the *Hamzah* (ء) are rather complicated; they will be treated under a separate lesson later.
- Note that the letter known as *Alif* (ا) is not a consonant; it is either a **chair** for the *Hamzah* or a long vowel (*aa / ā*).
- When the letter *Alif* (ا) follows an initial or a medial *Laam* (ل), they are written either as (لا) (*the printed form*), or as (لا) (*the hand written form*).
- Note that the letters known as *Wāw* and *Yaa* (و / ي) are writing symbols for consonants as well as long vowels; respectively: (*uu / ū*) and (*ii/ ī*).
- Note that there are six letters which cannot be connected to a following letter; let's call them "one-way-connecters" and they are:

ا / د / ذ / ر / ز / و

* * *

Lesson Thirteen

التَّاءُ الـمَربوطة و الألف الـمَقْصُورَة

The *Alif Maqsūrah* and The *Taa Marbūtah*

(ى) (ـة / ة)

➢ **The *Alif Maqsūrah* (ى):** Besides the already introduced regular *Alif* (ا), there is another form of *Alif*, which appears only at the end of words. This *Alif* is called "***Alif Maqsūrah***", and its Arabic shape is (ى). As you can see, its shape is like that of the ***Yaa*** (ي), but without the dots.

- The phonetic value of this ***Alif Maqsūrah*** is exactly like that of the regular *Alif* ; it requires the prolonging of the sound to correspond to (*aa / ā*).
- When this ***Alif Maqsūrah*** appears at the end of nouns and adjectives, it is in most cases an indication of a feminine gender. However, when it appears at the end of a verb, it is an indication that this verb is a weak one, and that the third consonantal radical of that verb is of *Yaa* (ي) origin; a necessary clue as where to search in the dictionary to find that entry.
- If a suffix is added to a word ending with an *Alif Maqsūrah*, then it changes in shape to a regular *Alif*. Note the examples below:

كُبْرَى ← كُبْـراهُنَّ / صُـغْرَى ← صُغْراكُنَّ / أُخْـرَى ← أُخْراكُمْ

➢ ***The Taa Marbūtah* (ة / ـة)**: Besides the already introduced regular (ت), there is another form of *Taa*, which appears only at the end of nouns and adjectives, but never at the end of verbs. This *Taa* is called "*Taa Marbūtah* ", and its Arabic shape is (ـة / ة). In form, it looks like the consonant *Haa* (ـه / هـ), but obviously without the dots.

- In phonetic value, it has exactly the same sound as that of the regular *Taa*. However, in a pausal situation in the spoken language, the *Taa* sound is normally not enforced if we do not enforce the vowel over it, and in such case it is pronounced as the consonant *Haa* (ـه / هـ).
- Like the ***Alif Maqsūrah***, in nouns and adjectives, the ***Taa Marbūtah* is generally a sign of feminine gender**.
- Also, like the ***Alif Maqsūrah***, if a pronoun is suffixed to a word ending with a ***Taa Marbūtah***, then it changes in shape to a regular *Taa*. Note the examples below:

مَدْرَسَـة ← مَدْرَسَـتُـنا / وَرَقَـة ← وَرَقَـتُـها

سَـيَّارَة ← سَـيَّارَتُـهُ / جامِعَـة ← جامِعَـتُـكُم

* * *

Exercise 1: Listen and repeat first, then read on your own, paying due attention to the sounds and forms of the *Alif Maqsūrah* or the *Taa Marbūtah* at the end of the words:

لَيْلَـى / فاطِمَةُ / سَلْمَى / جَمِيلَـةُ / سُعْدَى / طاوِلَـة / لُبْـنَـى / طالِبَـة /
بُشْرَى / سَلْوَى / جَدِيدَة / كُـبْـرَى / مَدْرَسَة / صُغْرَى / وَرَقَـة / أُخْرَى /
عَطْشَـى / سَـيِّـدَة / عُسْرَى / مُـدَرِّسَـة

* * *

Exercise 2: Listen to your teacher pronouce each pair of words, one pair ending with a regular *Alif* (ـا) versus an *Alif Maqsūrah* (ى) or a regular (ت) versus a *Taa Marbūṭah*, and repeat first, noticing that in each pair, the sounds of the ending letters are identical:

١- مَـهـا / مُـنَـى ٢- رَشا / لَـيْـلَـى ٣- سَـهـا / سُـهَـى

٤- دَعـا / بُـشْـرى ٥- كَـتَـبْـتُ / فـاطِـمَـةُ ٦- دَرَسْـتُ / جَـمـيـلَـةُ

٧- أَكَـلْـتُ / تُـفَّـاحَـةُ ٨- شَـرِبْـتُ / جـامِـعَـةُ

* * *

Exercise 3: Listen to your teacher pronouce the following short sentences and repeat after him / her; and then take turns reading a sentence each:

١- أنـا طـالِـب. ٢- هَـلْ أَنْـتَ طـالِـب؟ ٣- هَـلْ أَنْـتِ طـالِـبـة؟

٤- نَـعَـمْ أنـا طـالِـب. ٥- نَـعَـمْ أنـا طـالِـبَـة. ٦- هُوَ أُسْـتـاذ.

٧- هِـيَ أُسْـتـاذَة. ٨- أَنْـتَ طـالِـب مُـمْـتـاز. ٩- أَنْـتُـمْ طُـلَّاب

مُـمْـتـازون. ١٠- هُـنَّ طـالِـبـات مُـمْـتـازات. ١١- هُـمْ أَصْـدِقـاء.

١٢- نَـحْـنُ مِنْ أَمْريـكـا. ١٣- هَـذا والِـدي وَهَـذِهِ والِـدَتـي.

١٤- نَـحْـنُ نَـدْرُسُ ٱلْـعَـرَبِـيَّـة فـي ٱلْـجـامِـعَـةِ. ١٥- أَشْـرَبُ ٱلشَّـاي

فـي ٱلْـصَّـبـاح. ١٦- نَـشْـرَبُ قَـهْـوَة فـي ٱلْـمَـسـاء.

* * *

Lesson Fourteen

التَّـنْـوِيـنُ وَ (اَلْ) الـتَّـعْـرِيـف

Indefiniteness *(Tanween)* and the Definite Article (الـ)

- In Arabic, regular nouns and adjectives which appear without the "Definite Article" or do not have a possessive pronoun attached to them are said to be in a state of '**indefiniteness**', and end with a final '*Nūn*' sound and are marked with a special sign called '*Tanween*.'
- Nouns with '***Tanween***' correspond in general to English nouns with the indefinite articles '*a*' or '*an*', in words such as: "***a pen***", "***a book***", "***an apple***", or to nouns with the absence of any article, such as: "***water***" or "***students***".
- There are three variations of '***Tanween***', depending on whether a noun is in a Nominative, Accusative or Genitive mode; this is a function of grammar which will be discussed later. However, examples of these variations for initial acquaintance are given in the table below.

- The Arabic 'Definite Article' is: (ألـ/AL); which is a combination of a "*Hamzated Alif +Laam*". However, it is a general practice in writing to leave the *Hamzah* / ء out, and thus the 'Definite Article' will appear as (الـ) at the beginning of a word, and forming an integral part of that word.
- Since the Arabic 'Definite Article' defines a noun that is indefinite; when it is introduced, the '*Tanween*' disappears as being a mark of indefiniteness.

Exercise: Now, listen and repeat first, then study the following table against the explanation above:

Tanween (Genitive)	*Tanween* (Accusative)	*Tanween* (Nominative)
Qalam (*in*) قَلَمٍ	*Qalam* (*an*) قَلَمًا	*Qalam* (*un*) قَلَمٌ
Kitāb (*in*) كِتَابٍ	*Kitāb* (*an*) كِتَابًا	*Kitāb* (*un*) كِتَابٌ
Tuffahat (*in*) تُفَّاحَةٍ	*Tuffāhat* تُفَّاحَةً (*an*)	*Tuffāhat* تُفَّاحَةٌ (*un*)
Mā' (*in*) مَاءٍ	*Mā'* (*an*) مَاءً	*Mā'* (*un*) مَاءٌ

Definite Article (Genitive)	*Definite Article* (Accusative)	*Definite Article* (Nominative)
Al-Qalam (*i*) الْقَلَمِ	Al-Qalam (*a*) الْقَلَمَ	Al-Qalam (*u*) الْقَلَمُ
الْكِتَابِ Al-Kitāb (*i*)	Al-Kitāb (*a*) الْكِتَابَ	Al-Kitāb الْكِتَابُ (*u*)
التُّفَّاحَةِ At-Tuffāhat (*i*)	التُّفَّاحَةَ At-Tuffāḥat (*a*)	التُّفَّاحَةُ At-Tuffāḥat (*u*)
Al-Mā' (*i*) الْمَاءِ	Al-Mā' (*a*) الْمَاءَ	Al-Mā' (*u*) الْمَاءُ

* * *

Lesson Fifteen

الحُرُوفُ الشَّمْسِيَّةُ وَٱلْقَمَرِيَّةُ
Moon Letters and Sun Letters

- In relation to the pronunciation of the Arabic words to which the 'Definite Article' (الـ) has been added, Arabic letters are divided into two groups:
(1) **Moon Letters**, and (2) **Sun Letters**. It will be noted that, depending on the category a particular letter falls under, the pronunciation of the 'Definite Article' and the word it is attached to will be affected.
- So if a noun starts with a '**Moon Letter**', the *Laam* (لْ) of the 'Definite Article' is **fully pronounced**, and it will bear a '***Sukūn***' sign, and there will be no further modification in relation to the pronunciation of the first letter of the defined noun.

- On the other hand, <u>when we attach the 'Definite Article' (ال)</u> to a noun starting with a 'Sun Letter', we **do not pronounce** the *Laam* (ل) of the 'Definite Article'; this *Laam* is, in fact, assimilated into the first letter of that noun, and thus that <u>letter is doubled</u>, and consequently written with a '*Shaddah*' (ّ) sign.

- **Exercise**: Now, listen and repeat first, then study the following table against the explanation above:

Moon Letters

اَلْبِنْتُ	بِنْتٌ	ب	اَلْأَمِيرُ	أَمِيرٌ	أ
اَلْحِمَارُ	حِمَارٌ	ح	اَلْجَمَلُ	جَمَلٌ	ج
اَلْعَيْنُ	عَيْنٌ	ع	اَلْخَيْرُ	خَيْرٌ	خ
اَلْفِيلُ	فِيلٌ	ف	اَلْغَرْبُ	غَرْبٌ	غ
اَلْكَلْبُ	كَلْبٌ	ك	اَلْقَمَرُ	قَمَرٌ	ق
اَلْهَوَاءُ	هَوَاءٌ	هـ	اَلْمَسَاءُ	مَسَاءٌ	م
اَلْيَمِينُ	يَمِينٌ	ي	اَلْوَلَدُ	وَلَدٌ	و

* * *

Sun Letters

اَلثَّانِي	ثَانِي	ث	اَلتِّينُ	تِينٌ	ت
اَلذَّهَبُ	ذَهَبٌ	ذ	اَلدَّارُ	دَارٌ	د
اَلزَّهْرُ	زَهْرٌ	ز	اَلرَّسُولُ	رَسُولٌ	ر
اَلشَّمْسُ	شَمْسٌ	ش	اَلسَّلَامُ	سَلَامٌ	س
اَلضَّرْبُ	ضَرْبٌ	ض	اَلصَّيْفُ	صَيْفٌ	ص
اَلظُّهْرُ	ظُهْرٌ	ظ	اَلطَّيْرُ	طَيْرٌ	ط
اَلنَّهَارُ	نَهَارٌ	ن	اَللَّيْلُ	لَيْلٌ	ل

Exercise 1: **(Oral Activity):** The following are additional nouns given in their indefinite forms; your task is to pronounce each aloud as they are first, then to add the 'Definite Article' to each and pronounce it with the 'Definite Article', applying the rules learned above:

أَهْلٌ	تُرابٌ	بَيْتٌ	ثَـمِينٌ	جَبَلٌ	دَرْبٌ
حُوتٌ	ذَنْبٌ	خَيْطٌ	رَحِيمٌ	عِيدٌ	زَيْتٌ
غَرِيبٌ	سَماءٌ	فَجْرٌ	شَهْرٌ	قَوْلٌ	صَبْرٌ
قَلْبٌ	ضَعِيفٌ	كَلامٌ	طَوِيلٌ	ماءٌ	ظَرِيفٌ
هَمْسٌ	لَطِيفٌ	وَعْدٌ	نَظِيفٌ	يَوْمٌ	

* * *

Exercise 2: Listen and repeat first, then following the given example, identify the letters of the words by writing them in their isolated forms:

كِتابٌ ⇦ ك + ت + ا + ب

١- قَلَم ⇦ ....

٢- طالِب ....

٣- أَمِيـن ⇦ ....

٤- خالِد ....

٥- أَخِي ⇦ ....

٦- هُوَ ....

٧- أَنْتَ ⇦ ....

٨- بَغْدادُ ....

٩- مَكْتَبُ⇦ ....

١٠- لُبْنانُ ....

١١- مِصْرُ⇦ ....

١٢- صَباح ....

* * *

Exercise 3: Following the given example, combine the isolated letters in writing to make up actual words, then read aloud the resultant words:

ء + ن + ا ⇦ أَنـا

١- كَ+يْ+فَ ⇐ .... ٢- نَ+عَ+مْ ⇐ ....

٣- ءَ+يْ+نَ ⇐ .... ٤- مِ+صْ+رُ ⇐ ....

٥- هَـ+ذِ+هِ ⇐ .... ٦- أَ+نْ+تِ ⇐ ....

٧- مَ+رْ+حَ+بَ+ا ⇐ .... ٨- مُ+دِ+يْ+رُ ⇐ ....

٩- شُ+كْ+رًا+ا ⇐ .... ١٠- مُ+دَ+رْ+رِ+سُ ⇐ ....

١١- جَ+دِ+يْ+دٌ ⇐ .... ١٢- أَ+مْ+رِ+يْ+كَ+ا ⇐ ....

* * *

Lesson Sixteen

قَواعِدُ كِتابَةِ ٱلهَمْزَةِ وَهَمْزَةُ المَدّ (آ)

The Rules of Writing the *Hamzah*, And *Hamzah* of *Madd* (آ)

- It has already been stated that *Alif* (ا) is used as a chair for the *Hamzah* (ء). In addition, however, one of the other two weak letters, *Yaa* (ى), without dots, and *Wāw* (و) may serve as a chair for the *Hamzah*.
- Further, the *Hamzah* sometimes occurs without a chair, and is then written either over the line connecting the letters, on either side of it, or by itself.
- The rules governing the chair, or lack of chair therein, are rather complicated, and students are not expected to learn them all at once after this lesson. Exercise and long term close observation will enable the student to internalize these rules, summarized as follows:
    - At the beginning of a word, the chair is always an *Alif* (ا), such as:

أَحْمَد / أَمِين / إِذا / أَنْتَ / أُسْتاذ

- In the middle of a word:

    (a) If only one of the vowels), (◌َ), (◌ُ), (◌ِ), (or two identical vowels) is contiguous to the *Hamzah* (i.e. precedes or is born by it), the chair will be respectively: (ا) or (و) or (ي). Examples:

سَأَلَ / يَسْأَلُ / سُؤَال /يُؤْمِنُ/ رَئِيس/ يُبْدِئ

(b) If two different vowels are contiguous to the ***Hamzah***, the vowel which determines the chair, in accordance with the correspondence given in 2 (***a***) is governed by the following order of preference: (◌ِ), (◌ُ), (◌َ). Examples:

سَئِمَ / فُؤَادُ / سُئِلَ

(c) If the ***Hamzah*** is preceded by a long vowel and bears an (◌َ), then it has no chair. Examples:

سَاءَلَ / مُرُوءَةٌ

(d) If, however, the ***Hamzah*** is preceded by a long vowel and bears a (◌ِ) or a (◌ُ), then the chair usually corresponds to the vowel the ***Hamzah*** bears. Examples:

يُسَائِلُ / تَسَاؤُل

(3) At the end of a word:

(a) The preceding vowel determines the chair, in accordance with the correspondence given in 2 (a). Examples:

بَدَأَ / دَفُؤَ / فَتِئَ

* * *

(b) If there is no preceding short vowel (i.e. if there is a ***Sukūn*** or a long vowel, then there is no chair. Examples:

شَيْءٌ / بَطِيءٌ

* * *

(c) If the final ***Hamzah*** is preceded by a long vowel, then there is no chair; the *Hamzah* stands alone on the line. Examples:

سَمَاءٌ / وُضُوءٌ

* * *

- **The *Hamzah* of *Madd***: If the combination *Alif / Hamzah / Fathah* is followed by a long vowel *Alif* (i.e. ا + أَ), then the *Hamzah* and its vowel are dropped, one *Alif* only is written, and above this *Alif* is written the sign (~); and then will be called the ***Hamzah* of *Madd***. The pronunciation, however, is not changed.

- Similarly, if the combination ***Alif / Hamzah / Fathah*** is followed by a ***Hamzah*** with a ***Sukūn*** above it (i.e. ءْ + أَ), then (آ) is written, and the pronunciation is as in the previous case. Examples:

آدَمُ / آخَرُ / آنَسَ / آكُـلُ / الآنَ (الآنَ)

* * *

Exercise: Listen and repeat first, then read on your own, paying due attention to the sound, form, and position of each ***Hamzah***:

أَهْلاً / سَأَلَ / سُؤَالٌ / جُزْءُ / آمَنَ / رَئِيسُ / بِئْـرٌ / فَأْراً / هَواءٌ /

قَرَأَ / ضَوْءُ / آلامٌ / لُؤْلُؤَةً / أَسْماءُ / مِرْآةٌ / رَأْسُ / مُؤْمِنٌ / إِنَّ /

جَزاءُ / فُؤَادُ / نَشَأَ / الأَرْضُ / السَّماءَ / هَـؤُلاءِ / أَكَلَ / مَأْمُونُ

General Drills and Review / تَـدْريبات عـامَّـة وَمُـراجَـعَـة

Note for Instructors: The following section is designed to be a general drilling and review to reinforce correct pronunciation and writing rules, but not to learn vocabulary and their meanings, or to dwell on theoretical points of grammar. Parts of this section could be used as a basis for student's evaluation or testing. For best results, it is advised that most of these drills be done in a class setting, under the direct supervision of the instructor. Some exercises or parts of longer drills, related to writing, can be assigned as homework.

* * *

Drill 1: *(Oral in Class)* Go back to Lesson 2, pages 4-5, cover up the transliteration parts of the sentences, and:

(a) Listen and repeat first,

(b) Carry on an interactive conversational chain drill, whereby one student initiates the greeting or courtesy expresson and the next student responds and reacts to it.

* * *

Drill 2: (*Oral in Class*) Pronounce each of the following words first, then identify the individual letters that make up these words by saying the name of each letter, as in the given example:

عَلَيْكُمْ = عَيْن + لام + ياء + كاف + ميم

مَرْحَبا / بِخَيْرٍ / لَيْلَى / بَيْرُوتُ / الحَمْدُ / طالِبَةٌ / أَمْرِيكا / مَدْرَسَةٌ / لُبْنانُ / المَكْتَبُ / الآنِسَةُ / جَمِيلَةٌ / زَيْنَبُ / سَمِيرٌ / الخَرْطُومُ / أَهْلاً / نَعَمْ / سُورْيا / وَرَقَةٌ / السَّلامُ / القَمَرُ / مُعَلِّمٌ / الأُولَى / الشَّمْسُ / القاهِرَةُ / مِرْآةٌ / لُؤْلُؤَةٌ .

* * *

Drill 3: (*Homework*) Practice actual Arabic writing by connecting the following groups of letters, to make up actual words which have been introduced before. Add the vowel signs and other diacritical signs as needed once you recognize the word; follow the given example:

ا + ل + سَّ + ل + ا + م = السَّلامُ

١- هَ + ل = ...

٢- جَ + دِ + ي + دٌ = ...

٣- مِ + صْ + رُ = ...

٤- صَ + ب + ا + حَ = ...

٥- ب + ا + بٌ = ...

٦- لَ + يْ + لَ + ى = ...

٧- هَـ + ذِ + هِ = ...

٨- كِ + ت + ا + بٌ = ...

٩- هُـ + وَ = ...

١٠- جَ + م + ا + لُ = ...

١١- أَ + نْ + تِ = ...

١٢- ا + ل + شَّ + مْ + سُ = ...

١٣- ءَ + نْ + ا = ...

١٤- ط + ا + لِ + بٌ = ...

١٥- هُـ + نْ + ا = ...

١٦- بَ + غْ + د + ا + دُ = ...

١٧- مُ + د + ي + رُ = ...

١٨- مَ + دْ + رَ + سَ + ةٍ = ...

١٩- كُ + رْ + سِ + يْ + يٌ = ...

٢٠- مُ + دَ + رْ + رِ + سٍ = ...

* * *

Drill 4: *(Oral in Class)* Listen and repeat to practice contrasting the articulation of Short Vowels versus Long Vowels:

Long Vowel (ا)	Short Vowel (◌َ)	Long Vowel (ا)	Short Vowel (◌َ)
جامَعَ	جَمَعَ	كاتَبَ	كَتَبَ
ظاهَرَ	ظَهَرَ	بارَكَ	بَرَكَ
قاطَعَ	قَطَعَ	دارَسَ	دَرَسَ
غادَرَ	غَدَرَ	واصَلَ	وَصَلَ
خادَعُ	خَدَعَ	فاصَلَ	فَصَلَ

* * *

Long Vowel (ـو)	Short Vowel (◌ُ)	Long Vowel (ـو)	Short Vowel (◌ُ)
قوبِلَ	قُبِلَ	عومِلَ	عُمِلَ
صَدوقُ	صَدُقَ	وَدودُ	وَدُدَ
جومِعَ	جُمِعَ	وَقورُ	وَقُرَ
حوصِرَ	حُصِرَ	طولِبَ	طُلِبَ
كوتِبَ	كُتِبَ	بورِكَ	بُرِكَ

* * *

Long Vowel (ـي)	Short Vowel (◌ِ)	Long Vowel (ـي)	Short Vowel (◌ِ)
سِيري	سِرْ	سَعيدٌ	سَعِدَ
شَهيدٌ	شَهِدَ	عَليمٌ	عَلِمَ
وَريثٌ	وَرِثَ	رَضيعٌ	رَضِعَ
جَريحٌ	جُرِحَ	وَضيعٌ	وَضِعَ
وَليدٌ	وُلِدَ	سَميعٌ	سَمِعَ

* * *

Drill 5: (*Oral in Class*) Listen and repeat to practice contrasting the consonants (*Thaa* / ث and (*Dhaal* / ذ):

(*Dhaal* / ذ)	(*Thaa* / ث)	(*Dhaal* / ذ)	(*Thaa* / ث)
لَذَّةٌ	لَثَّةٌ	ذابَ	ثابَ
بُذورٌ	بُثورٌ	بَذَّ	بَثَّ
ذُمَّ	ثُمَّ	نَذَرَ	نَثَرَ
ذَوّابٌ	ثَوّابٌ	ذِرْوَةٌ	ثَرْوَةٌ

* * *

Drill 6: (*Oral in Class*) Listen and repeat to practice contrasting the consonants (*Thaa* / ث) and (*Seen* /س):

(*Seen* / س)	(*Thaa* / ث)	(*Seen* / س)	(*Thaa* / ث)
سَمِينَةٌ	ثَمِينَةٌ	سابَ	ثابَ
سَمِينٌ	ثَمِينٌ	سَوْرَةٌ	ثَوْرَةٌ
أَسْمَرَ	أَثْمَرَ	سَمَرٌ	ثَمَرٌ
سَقِيفٌ	ثَقِيفٌ	بَسَّ	بَثَّ
سامِرٌ	ثامِرٌ	سَوَى	ثَوَى

* * *

Drill 7: (*Oral in Class*) Listen and repeat to practice contrasting the consonants (*Ĥaa* / ح) and (*'Ayn* / ع):

(*'Ayn*/ ع)	(*Ĥaa* / ح)	(*'Ayn*/ ع)	(*Ĥaa* / ح)
عَمَلُ	حَمَلُ	عَزَمَ	حَزَمَ
العَلِيمُ	الحَلِيمُ	عامِلٌ	حامِلٌ
يَبْعَثُ	يَبْحَثُ	شُعُوبٌ	شُحُوبٌ
ساعَةٌ	ساحَةٌ	عَمِدَ	حَمِدَ
عامِدٌ	حامِدٌ	عَمِيدٌ	حَمِيدٌ

Drill 8: (*Oral in Class*) Listen and repeat to practice contrasting the consonants (***Khaa*** / خ) and (***Kaaf*** / ك):

(*Kaaf* / ك)	(*Khaa* / خ)	(*Kaaf* / ك)	(*Khaa* / خ)
كَليلٌ	خَليلٌ	كَيْلٌ	خَيْلٌ
كَلَّفَ	خَلَّفَ	كَرَّ	خَرَّ
كَرَزَةٌ	خَرَزَةٌ	سَلَكَ	سَلَخَ
ساكِنٌ	ساخِنٌ	كَفيفٌ	خَفيفٌ
كاسِرٌ	خاسِرٌ	كانَ	خانَ

* * *

Drill 9: (*Oral in Class*) Listen and repeat to practice contrasting the consonants (***Ĥaa*** / ح) and (***Khaa*** / خ):

(*Khaa* / خ)	(*Ĥaa* / ح)	(*Khaa* / خ)	(*Ĥaa* / ح)
مَخْروقٌ	مَحْروقٌ	خَرَقَ	حَرَقَ
خَلَقَ	حَلَقَ	خِمارٌ	حِمارٌ
خافَ	حافَ	خامِدٌ	حامِدٌ
خَلَفَ	حَلَفَ	رَخيمٌ	رَحيمٌ
بُخورٌ	بُحورٌ	مُخْتارٌ	مُحْتارٌ

* * *

Drill 10: (*Oral in Class*) Listen and repeat to practice contrasting the consonants (***Khaa*** / خ) and (***Ghayn*** / غ):

(*Ghayn* / غ)	(*Khaa* / خ)	(*Ghayn* / غ)	(*Khaa* / خ)
مَغْبونٌ	مَخْبونٌ	غالٍ	خالٍ
غَمْرٌ	خَمْرٌ	غائِبٌ	خائِبٌ
غَمْسٌ	خَمْسٌ	مَغْمورٌ	مَخْمورٌ

* * *

Drill 11: (*Oral in Class*) <u>Listen and repeat</u> to practice contrasting the consonants (*Daal* / د) and (*Ďaad* / ض):

(Ďaad / ض)	(Daal / د)	(Ďaad / ض)	(Daal / د)
رَكَضَ	رَكَدَ	ضَيْنٌ	دَيْنٌ
بِضْعَةٌ	بِدْعَةٌ	نَقَضَ	نَقَدَ
عَضَّاضٌ	عَدَّادٌ	ضَرْبٌ	دَرْبٌ

* * *

Drill 12: (*Oral in Class*) <u>Listen and repeat</u> to practice contrasting the consonants (*Zaa* / ز) and (*Žaa* / ظ):

(Žaa / ظ)	(Zaa / ز)	(Žaa / ظ)	(Zaa / ز)
ظَلَّ	زَلَّ	ظَهْرٌ	زَهْرٌ
حافِظٌ	حافِزٌ	واعِظٌ	واعِزٌ
ظَفَرَ	زَفَرَ	ظاهِرٌ	زاهِرٌ
ظَهِيرٌ	زَهِيرٌ	عَظِيمَةٌ	عَزِيمَةٌ
أَظْهَرُ	أَزْهَرُ	ظُهورٌ	زُهورٌ

* * *

Drill 13: (*Oral in Class*) <u>Listen and repeat</u> to practice contrasting the consonants (*Dhaal* / ذ) and (*Žaa* / ظ):

(Žaa / ظ)	(Dhaal / ذ)	(Žaa / ظ)	(Dhaal / ذ)
فَظٌّ	فَذٌّ	ظَرَفَ	ذَرَفَ
ظَلِيلٌ	ذَلِيلٌ	ناظِرٌ	ناذِرٌ
مَظَلَّةٌ	مَذَلَّةٌ	مُظِلٌّ	مُذِلٌّ

* * *

Drill 14: (*Oral in Class*) <u>Listen and repeat</u> to practice contrasting the consonants (*Dhaal* / ذ) and (*Zaa* / ز):

(Zaa / ز)	(Dhaal / ذ)	(Zaa / ز)	(Dhaal / ذ)
بَزَّ	بَذَّ	زَلَّ	ذَلَّ

عَـزَّرَ	عَـذَّرَ	زَرَعَ	ذَرَعَ
زَمَّ	ذَمَّ	زَبِيبٌ	ذَبِيبٌ
زَكِيٌّ	ذَكِيٌّ	زادَ	ذادَ
زِمامٌ	ذِمامٌ	زَوْدٌ	ذَوْدٌ

* * *

Drill 15: (*Oral in Class*) Listen and repeat to practice contrasting the consonants (*Seen* / س) and (*Šaad* / ص):

(*Šaad* / ص)	(*Seen* / س)	(*Šaad* / ص)	(*Seen* / س)
صاحَ	ساحَ	صُورَةٌ	سُورَةٌ
الصَّيْفُ	السَّيْفُ	صامَ	سامَ
بَصْمَةٌ	بَسْمَةٌ	صَبَّحَ	سَبَّحَ
صُرَّةٌ	سُرَّةٌ	صَرِيرٌ	سَرِيرٌ

* * *

Drill 16: (*Oral in Class*) Listen and repeat to practice contrasting the consonants (*Kaaf* / ك and (*Qaaf* / ق):

(*Qaaf* / ق)	(*Kaaf* / ك)	(*Qaaf* / ق)	(*Kaaf* / ك)
رَقَدَ	رَكَدَ	قَرَّ	كَرَّ
قُوَّةٌ	كُوَّةٌ	دَقَّ	دَكَّ
قَلَّمَ	كَلَّمَ	مَرْقُومٌ	مَرْكُومٌ

* * *

Drill 17: (*Oral in Class*) Both (*Wāw*/و) and (*Yaa*/ي) letters can function as consonants and as long vowels. First, listen to the pronunciation of the listed words and repeat; and, then mark with either a (C) if it is a consonant, or (LV) if it is a long vowel, as in the given examples:

(C) or (LV)	Word	(C) or (LV)	Word	(C) or (LV)	Word
C	بِخَيْر	LV	جَدِيدٌ	C	وَلَدٌ

	وَرَقَةٌ		مُديرَةٌ		بَيْروتُ
	جَميلَةٌ		طاوِلَةٌ		رَشيدٌ
	صَوْمُ		وَجْهُ		بَيْتُ
	مَأمونُ		رَسولٌ		أَمينُ
	رَءوفٌ		أَميرٌ		يَمينٌ
	إِبْراهيمُ		كُرْسِيٌّ		رَئيسٌ
	وَدودٌ		خَبِيرٌ		سَيِّدٌ

* * *

<u>Drill 18</u>: (Orally & Writing) <u>First</u>, verbally <u>lengthen the short vowel</u> on each of the following consonants to form its <u>corresponding long vowel</u>, then write down the resulting syllable, as in the given examples of the first three cells:

بَ ← با	بِ ← بي	بُ ← بو
ثِ ←	ثُ ←	ثَ ←
حُ ←	حَ ←	حِ ←
خُ ←	خِ ←	خَ ←
ذِ ←	ذَ ←	ذُ ←
رِ ←	رُ ←	رَ ←
صُ ←	صَ ←	صِ ←
ضَ ←	ضِ ←	ضُ ←
طِ ←	طُ ←	طَ ←
عَ ←	عِ ←	عُ ←
غُ ←	غَ ←	غِ ←
قُ ←	قَ ←	قِ ←
كِ ←	كُ ←	كَ ←

لَ ←	لِ ←	لُ ←
هُـ ←	هَـ ←	هِـ ←
وِ ←	وُ ←	وَ ←
يَ ←	يِ ←	يُ ←

* * *

Drill 19: (*Homework*) First, practice writing words with (***Shaddah*** /ّ), by combining the following isolated sets of letters, as in the given example. Second, practice reading by pronouncing the resultant words:

كَ+سْ+سَ+رَ = كَسَّرَ / مُ+دَ+رْ+رِ+سُ = مُدَرِّسُ

١- سُ+لْ+ لَ+مُ= ....

٢- جَ+مْ+مَ+عَ = ...

٣- شَ+دْ+دَ+ةَ= ....

٤- سَ+لْ+لَ+مَ = ...

٥- وَ+دْ+دَ+عَ = ...

٦- عَ+دْ+دَ= ....

٧- عِ+زْ+زَ+ةَ= ....

٨- سَ+يْ+يِ+دٌ = ...

٩- ثُ+مْ+مَ= ....

١٠- مُ+عَ+لْ+لِ+مُ= ....

* * *

Drill 20: (*Oral Classwork & Written Homework*) First, pronounce the following words as they are with (***Tanween*** /ٌ), then add the Definite Article (ال) to each and pronounce it with the Definite Article.

Second, rewrite, in the dotted spaces, the words with the Definite Article, as in the given examples, writing a (***Shaddah***) on the first letter after the (ال) if that letter belongs to the "Sun Letters" group:

قَمَرٌ ← الْقَمَرُ / شَمْسٌ ← الشَّمْسُ

أَخٌ ←	تُفَّاحَةٌ ← ....
بَيْتٌ ←	ثَوْرٌ ← ....

جَدِيدٌ ←	دَواءٌ ← ....
حَمْدٌ ←	ذُبابٌ ← ....
خَيْرٌ ←	رَحْمَةٌ ← ....
عَيْنٌ ←	زَمانٌ ← ....
غُرابٌ ←	سَيِّدٌ ← ....
فَجْرٌ ←	شَرابٌ ← ....
قَلَمٌ ←	صَديقٌ ← ....
كِتابٌ ←	ضَيْفٌ ← ....
مَدْرَسَةٌ ←	طاوِلَةٌ ← ....
هَرَمٌ ←	ظَلامٌ ← ....
وَجْهٌ ←	لَوْنٌ ← ....
يَدٌ ←	نَبيلٌ ← ....

* * *

Drill 21: (*Oral Classwork & Written Homework*) First, pronounce the following words with due attention to the (*Alif Maqṣūrah* /ى) and the (*Taa Marbūṭah* ة / ـة) at the end of these words. Then, rewrite these words in the dotted spaces or on your notebook:

لَيْلى ←	القاهِرَةُ ← ....
عَلى ←	مَدْرَسَةٌ ← ....
إلى ←	مُديرَةٌ ← ....
بُشْرى ←	جَمِيلَةٌ ← ....
كُبْرى ←	وَرَقَةٌ ← ....
صُغْرى ←	طاوِلَةٌ ← ....
لُبْنى ←	زَهْرَةٌ ← ....
سَلْمى ←	شَجَرَةٌ ← ....
هُدى ←	جامِعَةٌ ← ....
وَلْهى ←	لَطيفَةٌ ← ....

.... ← وَرْدَةٌ	بَلى ← ....
.... ← مَدينَةٌ	موسى ← .... *
.... ← مَكْتَبَةٌ	عيسى ← .... *

* * *

Drill 23: (Oral Practice! *Pronunciation, Matching, Writing and Reading*)
Words from the right column are organically connected to words from the left column. Your first task is to match words from the right column with those from the left column; then pronounce them together as a phrase or sentence. Finally, write down the whole structure together as one unit!

▪ السَّلامُ	أَهْلاً وَمَرْحَبا!	____________
▪ صَباح	نَعَمْ ، تَفَضَّل!	____________
▪ مَساء	طَيِّبَة!	____________
▪ كَيْفَ	اَلسَّلام!	____________
▪ مَرْحباً	لا بَأسَ عَلَيْك!	____________
▪ شُكْراً	اَلنُّور!	____________
▪ فُرْصَة	أَشْكُرُكَ / شُكْراً!	____________
▪ إلى	وَسَهْلاً!	____________
▪ مِنْ فَضْلِكَ!	بارَكَ اَللّه فيك!	____________
▪ عَفْواً / مَعْذِرَة!	الخَيْر!	____________
▪ وَعَلَيْكُم	اَلسَّلامَة!	____________
▪ أَهْلاً	إِذْنِكَ!	____________
▪ صَباحَ	عَلَيْكُم!	____________
▪ تَفَضَّلي الشّاي!	جَزيلاً!	____________
▪ مَعَ	اَللِّقاء!	____________
▪ إلى اَللِّقاء!	اَلحال؟	____________
▪ عَنْ	مَعَ السَّلامَة!	____________
▪ مَبْروك!	اَلخَيْر!	____________

Drill 24: (*Reading with Comprehension*) Reading with comprehension is the mother of all aspects of linguistic skills. At this early stage we are going to practice reading simple short sentences as units rather than individual words. For comprehension, one must know the individual meanings of the words that make up the sentences, a process that we will systematically take up in the upcoming parts of this textbook. To facilitate the comprehenshion aspect at this stage, the following sentences will be accompanied by full translation into English. In this first practice, focus will be on using the <u>Arabic Subject Pronouns</u> and <u>Demonstrative Pronouns,</u> which are <u>highlighted in red</u>, contextually:

I am a professor (instructor).	١- أَنَا أُسْتَاذ .
Are you (*masculine*) a student?	٢- هَلْ أَنْتَ طَالِب؟
Yes, I am a student.	٣- نَعَم ، أَنَا طَالِب .
Are you (*feminine*) a student?	٤- هَلْ أَنْتِ طَالِبَة؟
Yes, I am a student.	٥- نَعَم ، أَنَا طَالِبَة .
He is an Arab (*male*) student.	٦- هُوَ طَالِب عَرَبِيّ .
She is an Arab (*female*) student.	٧- هِيَ طَالِبَة عَرَبِيّة .
They are Arab (*male*) students.	٨- هُمْ طُلَّاب عَرَب .
They are Arab (*female*) students.	٩- هُنَّ طَالِبات عَرَبِيّات .
You (*plural*) are excellent students.	١٠- أَنْتُم طُلَّاب مُمْتازون .
You are (*exclusively female*) excellent students.	١١- أَنْتُنَّ طَالِبات مُمتازات .
We study (are studying) Arabic.	١٢- نَحْنُ نَدْرُس العَرَبِيّة .
This is a new house. (*masculine*)	١٤- هَذا بَيْت جَدِيد .
This is a new car. (*feminine*)	١٥- هَذِهِ سَيَّارَة جَدِيدَة .

* * *

Drill 25: (*Reading with Comprehension*) Focus on using some <u>basic verbs conjugated with 1st person singular</u>, highlighted in red:

I drink tea in the morning.	١- أَشْرَبُ ٱلشَّاي فِي الصَّباح .
I eat chicken at dinner.	٢- آكُلُ ٱلدَّجاج فِي ٱلعَشاء .
I study at the library in the evening.	٣- أَدْرُسُ فِي ٱلمَكْتَبَة فِي ٱلمَساء .
I work in the university library.	٤- أَعْمَلُ فِي مَكْتَبَة ٱلجامِعَة .

I love my father and my mother a lot.	٥- أُحِبُّ والِدي وَوالِـدَتـي كَـثِـيـراً .
I play football at the club.	٦- أَلْعَبُ كُـرَةَ ٱلْقَدم فـي النَّادي .

* * *

Drill 26: (*Reading with Comprehension*) Focusing on using some family-related nouns highlighted in red:

This is my father.	١- هَـذا أَبـي . (أب+ي)
This is my mother.	٢- هَـذِهِ أُمِّـي . (أُمّ+ي)
I have one brother.	٣- لِـي أَخ واحِد .
I have one sister.	٤- لِـي أُخْت واحِدَة .
I have one paternal uncle and one paternal aunt.	٥- لِـي عَمّ واحِد وعَـمَّـة واحِدَة .
I have one maternal uncle and one maternal aunt.	٦- لِـي خـال واحِد وخـالَـة واحِدَة .
My grandpa and my grandma live in Lebanon.	٧- يَـعـيشُ جَدِّي وجَدَّتـي فـي لُـبْنان.

* * *

Drill 27: (*Reading with Comprehension*) Focus on using some basic preposition particles highlighted in red:

How are you o my students?	١- كَـيْفَ ٱلـحـال يـا طُـلاَّبـي؟
What is your name, o young lady?	٢- مـا ٱسـمُـكِ يـا آنِـسَـةُ؟
Are you a student at the university?	٣- هَـلْ أَنْـتَ طـالِب فـي ٱلـجامِعَة؟
Where do you live o Adam?	٤- أَيْـنَ تَـسْكُـنُ يـا آدَم؟
When do you go to school?	٥- مَـتى تَـذْهَـبُ إِلـى ٱلـمَدْرَسَة؟
What do you study at the university?	٦- مــاذا تَدْرُسُ فـي ٱلـجـامِـعَـة؟
Why are you sad today?	٧- لِـمـاذا أَنْـتَ فَـرْحـانُ ٱلـيَـوْم؟

*** Now challenge yourself to read the Arabic words for the Arabic countries on this map!**

<u>**Drill 24**</u>**:** Check the most correct statement from each group of the following:

1. ☐ There are 27 consonants in the Arabic language.
   ☐ There are 28 consonants in the Arabic language.
   ☐ There are 29 consonants in the Arabic language.

2. ☐ There are as many vowels in Arabic as there are in English.
   ☐ There are three short vowels and three corresponding long vowels in Arabic.
   ☐ There are only three vowels in Arabic.

3. ☐ All the vowels in Arabic are represented by letter symbols.
   ☐ All the vowels in Arabic are represented by diacritical marks on top or below the consonants.
   ☐ The three short vowels are represented by diacritical marks, while the long vowels are represented by letter symbols.

4. ☐ About nine letters of the Arabic alphabet constitute difficult sounds for English-speaking students.
   ☐ Only a few Arabic consonants have exact sound equivalent in the Englishalphabet.
   ☐ All the Arabic consonants have an exact sound equivalent in the English alphabet.

5. ☐ Arabic, like English, is written from left to right.
   ☐ Arabic is written only from right to left.
   ☐ One can write Arabic either way.

6. ☐ All Arabic letters bear dots: one, two or three.
   ☐ Few Arabic letters bear dots.
   ☐ Almost one half of the Arabic letters bear dots.

7. ☐ Only the ***Wāw*** can be a seat for the ***Hamzah***.
   ☐ The ***Alif***, the ***Wāw*** and the ***Yaa*** can be seats for the ***Hamzah***.
   ☐ Only the ***Alif*** and the ***Wāw*** can be a seat for the ***Hamzah***.

8. ☐ The ***Sukūn*** is another vowel sign.
   ☐ The ***Sukūn*** indicates the absence of a vowel from the consonant bearing it.
   ☐ The ***Sukūn*** indicates that the consonant bearing it is doubled.

9. ▯ The ***Shaddah*** is another vowel sign.
▯ The ***Shaddah*** has no phonetic value.
▯ The ***Shaddah*** results when a consonant occurs twice without a vowel in between.

10. ▯ There are three ***diphthongs*** in Arabic.
▯ There are only two ***diphthongs*** in Arabic.
▯ ***Diphthongs*** are open syllables.

11. ▯ All letters in Arabic can be connected in writing to the letters following them.
▯ Only six Arabic letters cannot be connected to the letters following them.
▯ Twenty-two Arabic letters are non-connectors.

12. ▯ The ***Tanween*** and the **Definite Article** in Arabic do not meet together in one noun.
▯ The ***Tanween*** may occur at any position of a word.
▯ The ***Tanween***, like the **Definite Article**, may occur at the beginning of a word.

13. ▯ There is only one form of ***Tanween*** in Arabic.
▯ There are two variations of ***Tanween*** in Arabic.
▯ There are three variations of ***Tanween*** in Arabic, related to the **nominative**, **accusative** and **genitive** modes.

14. ▯ The "***Laam***" of the Arabic Definite Article is always pronounced.
▯ The "***Laam***" of the Arabic Definite Article is pronounced only when the following letter is a **Sun Letter**.
▯ The "***Laam***" of the Arabic Definite Article is pronounced only when the following letter is a **Moon Letter**.

15. ▯ The sign of the ***Shaddah*** on the letter following the Definite Article is a clue that this letter is a **Sun Letter**.
▯ The sign of the ***Sukūn*** on the letter following the Definite Article is a clue that this letter is a **Sun Letter**.
▯ There is no difference between the Sun Letters and Moon Letters in regard to pronunciation or writing.

16. ▯ The ***Alif Maqsūrah*** may appear at any position in a word.
▯ The ***Alif Maqsūrah*** may appear at the end of a word only.
▯ The ***Alif Maqsūrah*** may appear at the beginning of a word only.

17. ▯ The ***Taa Marbūtah*** may appear at the beginning of a word.
▯ The ***Taa Marbūtah*** may appear at any position in a word.
▯ The ***Taa Marbūtah*** may appear at the end of a word only.

18. ▯ When a <u>suffix</u> is added to a word ending originally with ***Alif Maqsurah***, there is no change in the writing of the *Alif*.
▯ When a <u>suffix</u> is added to a word ending originally with ***Alif Maqsurah***, the shape of the ***Alif Maqsūrah*** changes to a regular ***Alif***.
▯ When a <u>suffix</u> is added to a word ending originally with ***Alif Maqsurah***, the ***Alif Maqsūrah*** is deleted.

19. □ When a <u>suffix</u> is added to a word ending originally with ***Taa Marbūtah***, the shape of the ***Taa Marbūtah*** changes to a regular ***Taa***.
   □ When a <u>suffix</u> is added to a word ending originally with ***Taa Marbūtah***, the ***Taa Marbūtah*** is deleted.
   □ When a <u>suffix</u> is added to a word ending originally with ***Taa Marbūtah***, the shape of the ***Taa Marbūtah*** remains as it is.

20. □ Arabic can be learned easily by self-teaching, without an instructor.
   □ Arabic can be taught by any one who knows another language.
   □ Arabic learning requires hard work, discipline and motivation.

* * *

The following image is another sampling of Arabic Calligraphy, considered the highest form of visual art in the Arabic-Islamic culture. Throughout this book, Arabic calligraphic patterns are introduced as fillers, so you can start relating to and appreciating this aspect of Arabic culture, which is closely related to Arabic as a language!

Part Two / القسم الثانـي

نُصوص حِوارِيَّة مُبَسَّطة

Simplified Conversational Texts

- This part of the textbook contains 15 simplified conversational texts related to the basic themes of greetings, getting acquainted, courtesy expressions and other everyday common conversational themes.
- These conversation patterns are recorded on a CD by native speakers, so that the students will listen to them at home before they come to class and are paired to enact the specific coversation assigned by the instructor. Then the roles are reversed, so that every student gets the chance to enact all parts of the conversation.

صَباح ٱلخَيْر!

المُحادثة ٱلأولى

شادِي : صَباحَ ٱلخَيْرْ!

شادِيَة : صَباحَ ٱلنُّور!

شادِي : اِسْمي شادي!

شادِيَة : وَأنا شادِيَة!

شادِي : أَهْلاً يا شادِيَة!

شادِيَة : أَهْلاً وَسَهْلاً!

* * *

المُحادَثة	the conversation	الأولَى	the first
صَباحَ الخَيْر!	Good morning!	صَباحَ النُّور!	Good morning! (May you have a Bright Morning!) (*response*)
شَادي	***Shādi*** (*a male proper name*)	شادِيَة	***Shādiyah*** (*a female proper name*)
اِسْمي (اِسْم+ـي)	my name	وَأنا	and I (am)
أَهْلاً	Hello! (*and*) welcome!	يا	O ! (*vocative or calling particle, used as a term of endearmen!)*
أَهْلاً وَسَهْلاً	Hello and welcome!		

Notes on the Vocabulary:

1. The two items highlighted above in red, though they look as an integral part of the words they are suffixed to or prefixed to the words, are, in fact, separate words with their independent meaning. The (ـي) suffixed to the end of the noun (اِسْم) is in fact a possessive pronoun, which means "my." And the (وَ) prefixed to the beginning of the pronoun (أنا) is in fact a conjunction particle, which means "and."

2. The Arabic word (النُّور) lierally means, "the light," however, in the greeting above it is used metaphorically to mean "bright."

3. The word (يا), used a lot before the name of a person is considered a "vocative" or "calling" paricle, used as term of endearment or respect, equivalent to the old English"O", in a phrase asuch as, "O' Lord!"

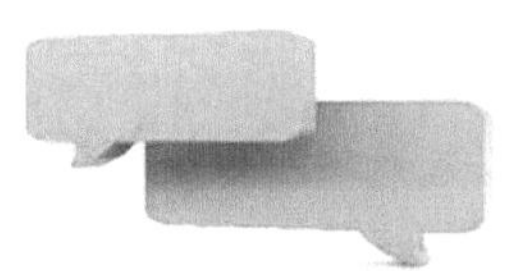

مَساء ٱلخَيْر!

الـمُحادثة ٱلثَّانِيَة

فادي: مَساءَ ٱلخَيْر!

فادِيَة: مَساء ٱلـنُّور!

فادي: كَـيْفَ ٱلحال؟

فادِيَة: لا بَـأْس، الحَمْدُ لِلَّه!

وَأَنْتَ، كَيْفُ حالُكَ؟

فادي: بِخَيْر، الحَمْدُ لِلَّه!

فادِيَة: عَنْ إذْنِكَ، مُسْتَعْجِلَة!

فادي: إذْنُكِ مَعَكِ!

فادِيَة: مَعَ ٱلسَّلامَة!

* * *

Good evening!	مَساء ٱلـخَيْـر!	the second conversation	الـمُحادَثة ٱلثَّانِيَة
Fādi (*a male proper name*)	فادي	May you have a bright evening! *(response)*	مَساءَ ٱلـنُّور!
How are you? *(idiomatically)*	كَيْفَ ٱلـحال؟	*Fādiyah* (*a female proper name*)	فادِيَة
And you, how are you?	وَأَنْتَ، كَيْفَ حالُكَ؟	Not bad, Praise be to God!	لا بَأس، الحَمْدُ لِلَّه!
with your permission	عَنْ إِذْنِكَ!	Fine, in a state of wellbeing!	بِخَيْر
you are excused	إِذْنُكِ مَعَكِ!	(I am) in a rush	مُسْتَعْجِلَة
		Go safely! Goodbye!	مَعَ ٱلسَّلامَة!

Notes on the Vocabulary:

- **Items hilighted in blue are one-letter prepositions that must be written as part of the following words.**
- **Items highlighted in red are again one-letter possessive pronouns that must be written as suffixes to the previous words, and they also designate gender aspect.**

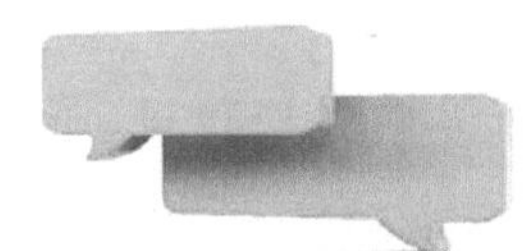

المُحادثة ٱلثَّالِثة

مَرْحباً!

سام: مَـرْحَـبـاً!

حام: أَهْـلاً وَمَـرْحَـبـا!

سام: أَنـا سـام.

حام: وَأَنـا حـام.

سام: مَـنْ هَـذا؟

حام: هُـوَ أَخِـي دانـي.

سام: وَمَـنْ هَـذِهِ؟

حام: هِـيَ أُخْـتـي سَـنـاء.

سام: أَهْـلاً بِـكُـم؟

حام: أَهْـلاً وَمَـرْحَـباً بِـكَ!

* * *

Hello!, Hi!	مَـرْحَـبـاً!	the third conversation	الـمُحادَثة ٱلـثَّـالِـثَة
Ḥām (in Arabic is the father of the Hamitic people)	حـام	*Sām* (*in Arabic is the father of the Semitic people*)	سـام
And I am *Ḥām*	وأنـا حـام	Hello and Welcome!	أَهْـلاً وَمَـرْحَـبـا!
this (masculine)	هَـذا	Who (is)...?	مَـنْ ...؟
Dani (*male proper name*)	دانـي	he is my brother	هُـوَ أخـي (أخ+ـي)
she is my sister	هِـيَ أُخْـتـي (أُخْت+ي)	And who is this? (feminine)	وَمَـنْ هَـذِهِ؟
Welcome to you (all)!	أَهْـلاً بِـكُـم!	*Sanaa'* (*female proper name*)	سَـنـاء
		to you (*masculine singlar*)	بِـكَ (بِـ+ـكَ)

Notes on the Vocabulary:

- Note the prefix (وَ) which means "and", the suffix (ـي) which means "my" and the suffixes (ـكُم) which means "you-plural" and (ـكَ) which means "you-singular."

الـمُحادثة ٱلرَّابِعة

السَّلامُ عَلَيْكُم!

خالِد: السَّـلامُ عَـلَـيْـكُم!

أَمَل: وَعَـلَـيْـكُم السَّلام!

خالِد: كَـيْفُ حالُــكِ؟

أَمَل: طَـيِّــبَــة، وَأَنْـتَ؟

خالد: طَـيِّـب، أَحْمَدُ الله!

أَمَل: مِـنْ أَيْنَ أَنْـتَ؟

خالد: أَنـا مِـنْ قَـطَـر.

أَمَل: وَأَنـا مِنْ ٱلكُوِيت.

خالد: أَهْلاً وَسَهْلاً!

أَمَل: أَهْلاً بِـكَ!

* * *

Peace be upon you!	السَّـلامُ عَـلَـيْـكُم!	the fourth conversation	الـمُحادَثة ٱلرَّابِعَة
Amal *(female proper name)*	أَمَـل	*Khālid* (*male proper name*)	خـالِد
How are you?	كَـيْـفَ حـالُـكِ؟	And Upon you Peace may be!	وَعَـلَـيْـكُمُ ٱلسَّلام!
And what about you?	وَأَنْـتَ؟	Fine, doing well (*feminine form*)	طَـيِّـبَـة
Where are you from?	مِنْ أَيْـنَ أَنْـتَ؟	Well, I am fine, I thank God!	طَـيِّـب، أَحْـمَـدُ ٱلـلّـه!
And I am from Kuwait.	وأَنـا مِنْ ٱلكُوَيت	I am from Qatar.	أَنـا مِـنْ قَـطَـر
Welcome to you!	أَهْـلاً بِـكَ!	Welcome!	أَهْلاً وَسَهْلاً!

Notes on the Vocabulary:

- Note the prefix (وَ) which means "and". However, the (و) prefixed to the word (اللّه) is considered an "oath particle, which means"by."

المُحادثة ٱلخامِسة	مَنْ هَذا؟

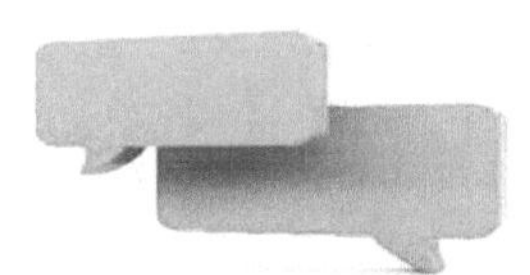

وِسام: مَنْ هَذا يا سامِر!

سامِر: هَذا صاحِبِي نادِر.

وِسام: مَرْحَباً يا نادِر!

سامِر: أَهْلاً يا سامِر!

وِسام: أَنْتَ طالِب؟

سامِر: نَعَم، أَنا طالِب.

وِسام: ماذا تَدْرُس؟

سامِر: أَدْرُس العَرَبِيَّة.

وِسام: أَنا أَدْرُس العَرَبِيّة أَيْضاً.

سامِر: تَشَرَّفْنا!

وِسام: إِلى ٱللِّقاء!

سامِر: مَعَ ٱلسَّلامَة!

* * *

Who is this?	مَنْ هَذا؟	the fifth conversation	المُحادَثة ٱلخامِسَة
O' *Sāmir*	يا سامِر	*Wisām, Nādir, Sāmir* (*three male proper names*)	وِسام، نادِر، سامِر
Welcome, O' *Sāmir*!	أَهْلاً يا سامِر!	Hello O'*Nādir*	مَرْحَباً يا نادِر!
Yes, I am a student.	نَعَم، أَنا طالِب.	Are you a student?	أَنْتَ طالِب؟
I am studying Arabic.	أَدْرُس العَرَبِيَّة.	What are you studying?	ماذا تَدْرُس؟
also, likewisw	أَيْضاً	I am studying Arabic	أَنا أَدْرُس العَرَبِيَّة
Go safely! Goodbye!	مَعَ ٱلسَّلامَة!	Till (we) meet again!	إِلى ٱللِّقاء!

Notes on the Vocabulary:

- **Note the vocative particle (يا) for the old English "O", used extensively in Arabic as a term of endearment before proper names when addressed directly.**

الـمُحادثة ٱلسَّادِسة

الـطَّـقس

كَريم: كَيْفَ ٱلطَّقس ٱليَوْم؟

كَريـمة: ٱلطَّـقْس بارِد.

كَريم: أَنا لا أُحِبّ ٱلبَـرد!

كَريـمة: وأَنا لا أُحِبّ ٱلحَرّ.

كَريم: أَيّ طَقْس تُحِبّ؟

كَريـمة: أُحِبّ طَقْس ٱلـرَّبيع.

كَريم: أَنا أُحِبّ ٱلـخَريف.

كَريـمة: الـصَّـيْـف يَأْتـي حارّاً جِـدّاً أَحْـيـانـاً.

كَريم: الـشِّتاء قَدْ يَأْتـي بارِد جِدّاً.

كَريـمة: إِذَن ٱلـرَّبيع وٱلـخَريف أَحْسَنُ ٱلـفُـصـول.

كَريم: أَنـا مُـوافِـق، هَذا صَحيح!

* * *

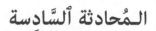

the weather	الطَّقس	the sixth conversation	الـمُحادَثة ٱلسَّادِسَة
How is the weather today?	كَيْفَ ٱلطَّقْس ٱليَوْم؟	*Kareem, Kareema* (*two male proper names*)	كَريـم ، كَريـمة

I do not like	لا أُحِبّ	cold	بارِد
the heat	الـحَرّ	the cold	الـبَرد
I like the Spring weather.	أُحِبّ طَقْس الـرَّبيـع	Which weather do you like?	أيّ طَقْس تُحِبّ؟
the Summer	الـصَّيْف	I like the Fall (Autumn)	أنا أُحِبّ الـخَريف
very hot	حارّاً جِدّاً	comes	يـأتي
might come	قَدْ يَـأتـي	the Winter	الـشِّتاء
then, in this case	إذَن	very cold	بارِد جِدّاً
best of	أحْسَنُ	the Spring and the Fall	الـرَّبيـع والـخَريف
I agree	أنا مُوافِق	the seasons (a season)	الـفُصول (فَصْل)
		this is true	هَذا صَحِيح

Notes on the Vocabulary:

- Note the conjuction (وَ) for the old English "and", prefixed before a pronoun or a noun.

- Note that the seasons of the year in Arabic are considerd "definite nouns" and thus appear mostly with the Definite Article (الـ), highlited in blue color in the table above.

الشَّمْس   غُيُوم وَمَطَر   ثَلْج   رِياح

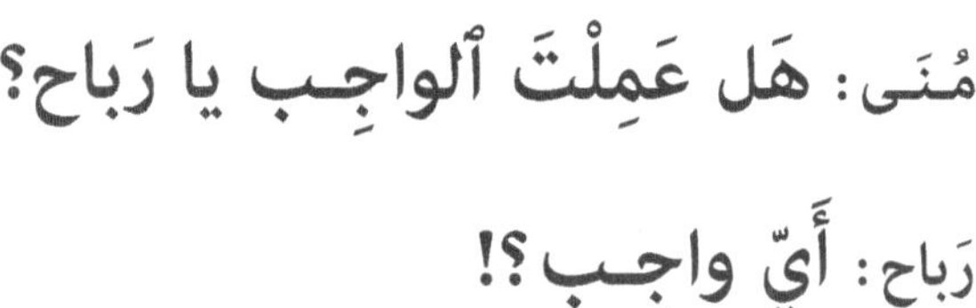

الـمُحادثة ٱلسَّابِـعَـة

الـواجِـب

مُنَى: هَل عَمِلْتَ ٱلواجِـب يا رَباح؟

رَباح: أَيّ واجِـب؟!

مُنَى: واجِـب ٱلـقَـواعِـد ٱلـعَـرَبِـيَّـة.

رَباح: مـا عَـرَفْـتُ كَـيْـفَ أَعْـمَـلُـه!

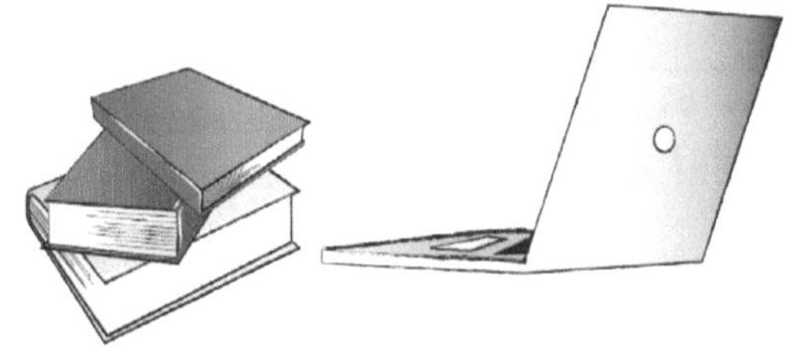

مُنَى: هُـوَ صَـعْـب قَلِيلاً.

رَباح: لازِم أَنْ أُراجِـع ٱلـدَّرْس أَوَّلاً.

مُنَى: فِـكْـرَة جَـيِّـدَة.

رَباح: مُـمْـكِـن أَنْ نَـدْرُسَـهـا مَـعـاً؟

مُـنَـى: نَعَم! لِمَ لا؟

رَباح: هَـيَّا إِلـى ٱلـمَـكْـتَـبَـة!

مُنَى: هَـيَّـا بِـنـا!

* * *

the homework	الواجِـب	the seventh conversation	الـمُحادَثة السَّابِعَة
Did you do the homework?	هَـلْ عَـمِـلْـت ٱلواجِـب؟	*Muna, (female name)* *Rabāḥ* (*male name*)	مُـنَـى / رَبـاح
Which homework?	أَيّ واجِـب؟	O' *Rabāḥ*	يـا رَباح

I did not know	ما عَرَفْت	the Arabic grammar	القَواعِد ٱلعربِيَّة
It is a little difficult	هُو صَعْب قليلاً	how to do it	كَيْفَ أَعْمَلُه
(that) I review	أُراجِع	it is necessary that , it is a must that	يَلْزَمُ أَنْ
first, firstly	أَوَّلاً	the lesson	الدَّرْس
Is it possible that?	مُمْكِن أَنْ	a good idea	فِكْرَة جَيِّدَة
together	مَعاً	we study it	نَدْرُسها
Let's go	هَيَّا إلى	Why not!	لِمَ لا!
Let us go!	هَيَّا بِنا!	to the library	إلى المَكْتَبَة

Notes on the Vocabulary:

- Note the two suffixed pronouns (ـه) and (ـها) attached to verbs and functioning as the direct objects of the verbs they are attached to, these are called "object pronouns."

Other Items related to Academic Life

Srudent (male / female) students	طالِب / طالِبَة / طُلَّاب	instructor (male / female professor	مُدَرِّس / ـة أُسْتاذ / ة
school / schools	مَدْرَسَة / مَدارِس	university / universities	جامِعَة / جامِعات
seat / seats	مَقْعَد / مَقاعِد	classroom	غرْفَةُ الدِّراسَة
Writing board / writing boards	لَوْح / أَلْواح	chair / chairs	كُرْسِيّ / كَراسِي
pen / pens	قَلَم / أَقْلام	book / books	كِتاب / كُتُب
desk / desks	مَكْتَب / مَكاتِب	notebook / notebooks	دَفْتَر / دَفاتِر
computer / computers	حاسُوب / حَواسِيب	library / libraries	مَكْتَبَة / مَكْتَبات

الـمُحادثة ٱلثَّامِنة

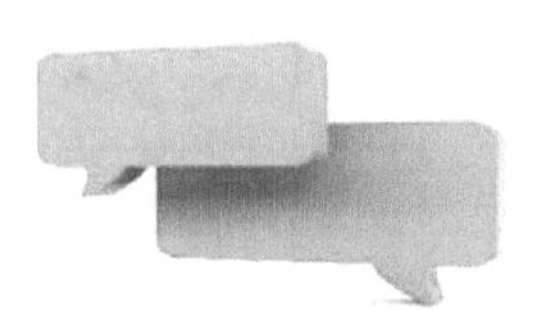

سامـي : أَيْـنَ تَـسْـكُـن أُسْرَتُـكِ يـا سامِـيَـة؟

سامِيَة : تَـسْـكُـنُ أُسْرَتـي هُـنا فـي شِيكاغو.

سامي: أَنْتِ مَحْظوظَة، أَنا وَحـيـد هُـنـا .

سامِيَة: أَفْـهَـمُ مِـن هَـذا أَنَّ أُسْرَتَـكَ فـي أَرْضِ الوَطَـن.

سامي: نَـعَـم ، هُمْ يَعيشونَ فـي الأُرْدُنّ.

سامِيَة : هـذِهِ صورَةُ أُسْرَتـي :أَبـي وأُمِّـي وأَخـي وأَنـا.

سامي: هـذِهِ أُسْرَة صَغيـرَة . أُسْرَتـي أَكْبَـر .

سامِيَة: فـي العـائِلَة عَمّ واحِد وخـالَـة واحِـدَة.

سامي: لـي أَخ وأُخْـت أَكْبَـر مِـنّـي وأَخ وأُخْت أَصْغَـر مِـنّـي.

سامِيَة: ومـاذا عَن الـعـائِـلَـة ؟

سامي: لِـي عَـمّـانِ أَصْغـر مِـن والـدي وعَـمَّـتـان أَكْـبَـرُ مِـنْـه ، وكَذلِكَ لِـي خـال وخـالَـة ، ولَـهُم أَوْلاد كَـثِـيـرون .

سامِيَة: هَـذِهِ عـائِـلَـة كَـبـيـرَة جِـدّاً!

* * *

the nuclear family	الأُسْـرَة	the eighth conversation	الـمُحادَثة ٱلثَّامِنَة
Sāmy, *(male name)* *Sāmiyah* (female name)	سـامـي / سـامِـيَـة	the extended family	الـعـائِـلَـة
lives, resides (verb)	تَـسْـكُـن	Where...?	أَيْـنَ ...؟
O' *Sāmiyah*	يـا سـامِـيَـة	your family	أُسْـرَتُـكِ / ـكَ

here	هُـنـا	my family	أَسْـرَتـي
you're lucky	أَنْـتِ مَـحْـظـوظَـة	in Chicago	فـي شِـيـكـاغُـو
I understand	أَفْـهَـمُ	I am lonely here	أنا وَحـيـد هُـنـا
(are) in the homeland	فـي أَرْض الـوَطَـن	from this that	مِـنْ هَـذا أَنَّ
they are living	هُـم يَـعـيـشـون	yes	نَـعَـم
this is the picture (of)	هَـذِهِ صُـورَة	In Jordan	فـي الأَرْدُنّ
and my brother and I	وأَخـي وأَنـا	my father and my mother	أَبـي وأُمّـي
my family is bigger	أَسْـرَتـــي أَكْــبَـر	this is a small family	هَذِهِ أُسْـرة صَغيـرَة
(there is) one paternal uncle	عَمّ واحِد	in the extended family	فـي العـائِلَة
I have a brother and a sister	لــي أَخ وأُخْـت	and one maternal aunt	وخـالَـة واحِـدَة
and a brother and a sister	وأَخ وأُخْت	older than me	أَكْـبَـر مِـنّـي
And what about the extended family?	ومـاذا عَـن الـعـائِـلَـة؟	younger than me	أَصْغَـر مِـنّـي
younger than my father	أَصْغـر مِـن والـدي	I have two paternal uncles	لِـــي عَـمّـان
and likewise I have	وكَذَلِك لِـي	and two paternal aunts older than him	وعَـمّـتان أَكْـبَـرُ مِـنْـه
and they have many children	ولَـهُـم أَوْلاد كَـثِـيـرون	a maternal uncle and maternal aunt	خـال وخـالَـة
		this is a very big family	هَـذِهِ عـائِـلَـة كَـبِـيـرَة جِـدّاً

Notes on the Vocabulary:

- Note the suffixed pronouns highlited in red, attached to nouns, and corresponding to English possessive pronouns.
- Note also the conjunction (و) prefixed to words and highlited in blue, which means (and) .
- Note the words (عَـمّـان) and (عَـمّـتان) as dual forms, specifically for two in number, which is a third number that does not exist in English.

المُحادثة ٱلتَّاسِعَة

الطَّعام وٱلشَّراب

نَبيل : ما طَعامُكِ ٱلمُفَضَّل يا نَبِيلَة؟

نبيلة : السَّلَطَة وٱلخُضار وشُورَبَة ٱلعَدَس.

نَبيل : أَنْتِ نَباتِيَّة، أَلَيْسَ كَذَلِك؟

نبيلة : نَعَم، وأَنْتَ؟

نَبيل: أَنا آكُل كُلّ شَيء، الحَمْدُ لِلَّه!

نبيلة : ما أَفْضَل أَكْلَة عِنْدَك؟

نبيل : الدَّجاج ٱلمَشْوي مَعَ ٱلرُّز وشُورَبَة ٱلخُضار.

نبيلة : كُنْتُ أُحِبّ ٱلدَّجاج وأَنا صَغيرَة.

نبيل : أَنا أُحِبّ كُلّ أَنْواع ٱللُّحوم: الدَّجاج، وٱلخَروف، والسَّمَك.

نبيلة : ولَكِن لَيْسَ لَحْم ٱلخِنْزير!

نبيل: طَبْعاً لا! وما مَشْروباتُكِ ٱلمُفَضَّلة؟

نبيلة: الماءُ عِنْدي مَلِك ٱلمَشْروبات، وأَحْياناً أَشْرَب ٱلشَّاي وٱلقَهْوَة.

* * *

(the) food and drink	الطَّعام وٱلشَّراب	the ninth conversation	المُحادَثة ٱلتَّاسِعَة
What is your favorite food?	ما طَعامُكِ ٱلمُفَضَّل؟	*Nabeel, (male name) Nabeelah (female name)*	نَبيل / نَبيلَة
salad and vegetables	السَّلَطَة وٱلخُضار	O' *Nabeelah*	يا نَبيلَة
you are vegetarian	أَنْتِ نَباتِيَّة	and lental soup	وشُورَبَة ٱلعَدَس
yes	نَعَمْ	Is'nt that so?	أَلَيْسَ كَذَلِك؟
I do eat	أَنا آكُل	and what about you?	وأَنْت؟

Thanks to God!	الْحَمْدُ لِلَّه !	everything	كُلّ شَيء
for you	عِنْدَك	What's the favorite meal...?	ما أَفْضَل أَكْلَة
With (the) rice	مَعَ الرُّز	broiled (or roasted) chicken	الدَّجاج ٱلْمَشْوي
I used to like chicken	كَنْتُ أُحِبّ ٱلدَّجاج	and vegetable soup	وشُورَبَة ٱلْخُضار
I like	أَنا أَحِبّ	when I was young	وأَنا صَغيرَة
and lamb (meat) and fish	وٱلْخَروف وٱلسَّمَك	all kinds of meats	كُلّ أَنْواع ٱللُّحوم
pork meat	لَحْم ٱلْخِنْزير	however, not	ولَكِن لَيْسَ
And what are your favorite drinks?	وما مَشْروباتُك ٱلْمُفَضَّلة؟	of course not	طَبْعاً لا
(is) the king of all drinks	مَلِك ٱلْمَشْروبات	(the) water for me	الماءُ عِنْدي
(the) tea and (the) coffee	ٱلشَّاي وٱلْقَهْوَة	and sometimes I drink	وأَحْياناً أَشْرَب

Notes on the Vocabulary:

- Note the suffixed pronouns highlited in red, attached to nouns, and <u>corresponding to English possessive pronouns or object pronouns</u>.

- Note also the conjunction (و) prefixed to words and highlited in blue, which means (and) .

- Note also that the Arabic words for specific categories of foods and drinks are considered definite in nature, thus they have the definite article (ٱل) prefixed to them.

- Also note the (أ), prefixed to the word (لَيْسَ) and functioning <u>as an interrogative particle</u>, equivalent to English the English "Is..." or "Are...?"

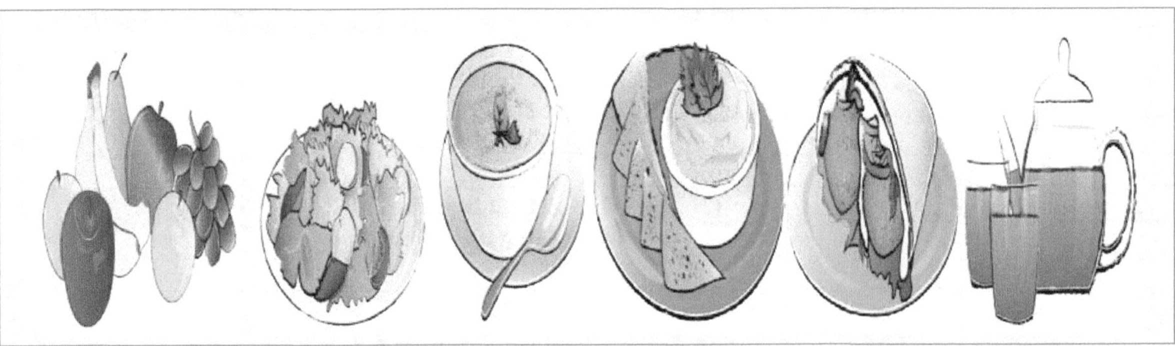

الـمُحادثة ٱلعاشِرَة

الـفُطور في مَطْعَم

الجرسون : صـباحَ ٱلـخَـيـر يا أُسْـتـاذ! ماذا تَـأْمُر؟

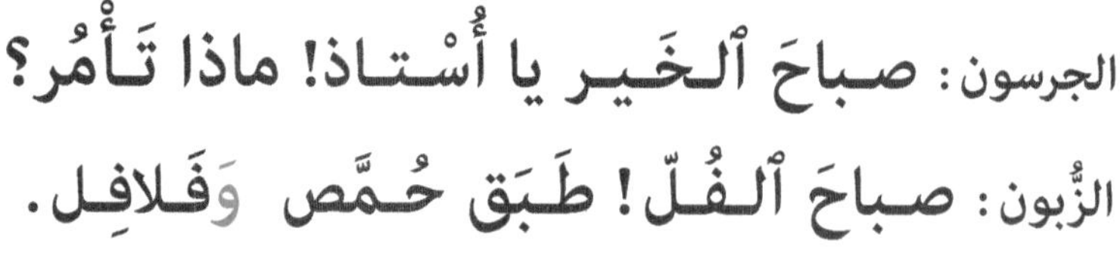

الزُّبون : صـباحَ ٱلـفُـلّ ! طَـبَـق حُـمَّـص وَفَـلافِـل.

الجرسون: حاضِـر، وماذا تَـشْـرَب؟

الزُّبون: فِـنْـجان شـاي بِـٱلـنَّـعْـناع، مِـن فَـضْـلَـك!

الجرسون: أَمْرُك، يا أُسْتاذ!

* * *

الجرسون: تَـفَـضَّـل ٱلفُطُور! بِـٱلـهَـنـاء وٱلـشِّـفاء!

الزُّبون: أَلْف شُكْر! مُـمْـكِـن كـأْس ماء؟

الجرسون: حـاضِـر ، حالاً!

الزُّبون: وَٱلـفـاتُورَة، لَـوَ سَـمَـحْـت!

الجرسون: تَـفَـضَّـل ٱلـمَـاء وَٱلـفاتُـورَة!

الزُّبون: تَـفَـضَّـل ٱلـحِـسـاب، وَٱلـباقِـي "بَخْشِـيـش"!

الجرسون: أَلْـف شُـكْـر يـا أُسْـتـاذ!

* * *

(the) breakfast at a restaurant	الـفُـطور فـي مَـطعم	the tenth conversation	الـمُـحـادَثـة ٱلـعـاشِـرَة
the customer	الـزُّبـون	the waiter, *(adopted from French)*	الـجَـرْسـون
O' Sir!	يا أُسْـتـاذ!	Good morning!	صباحَ الـخَـيْـر!
a "***Hummus***" dip plate	طَـبَـق حُـمُّـص	May it be a fragrant morning as Arabian jasmine!	صباحَ الـفُـلّ!
ready = at your service	حـاضِـر	and ***Falafil***	وَفَـلافِـل

a cup of tea	فِـنْجان شـاي	And what would you like to drink?	ومـاذا تَـشْـرَب؟
kindly, if you please!	مِـن فَـضْـلَـك!	with mint	بِـالـنَّـعْـناع
Please, here's the breakfast	تَـفَـضَّـل الـفُـطُـور!	At your command, O' <u>Sir</u>!	أَمْـرُك، يا أُسْـتـاذ!
Thank you much! *(a thousand thanks)*	أَلْـف شُـكْـر	May it do you much good! *Bon appétit*!	بِـالـهَـناء والـشِّـفاء!
At your command, immediately!	حـاضِـر، حالاً!	If possible, a glass of water!	مُـمْـكِـن كـأس مـاء!
If you permit!	لَـوَ سَـمَـحْـت!	and the bill	وَٱلـفـاتُـورَة
Kindly have the account payment!	تَـفَـضَّـل الـحِـسـاب!	Kindly have the water and the bill!	تَـفَـضَّـل ٱلـمـاء وَٱلـفـاتُـورَة!
a tip *(borrowed from Turkish)*	"بَـخْـشِـيـش"	and (leave) the rest	والـبـاقِـي

<u>**Notes on the Vocabulary**</u>:

- **Note the suffixed pronouns highlited in red, attached to nouns, and <u>corresponding to English possessive pronouns or object pronouns</u>.**
- **Note also the conjunction (و) prefixed to words and highlited in blue, which means (and) . By now you should have observed that Arabic uses the conjunction (و) for (and) more frequently than English!**
- **All the underlined words or phrases are very common Egyptian colloquialism.**
- **The word (بَخْشـيـش) for "tip, gratuity", is borrowed from Turkish and used a lot in colloquial Egyptian.**

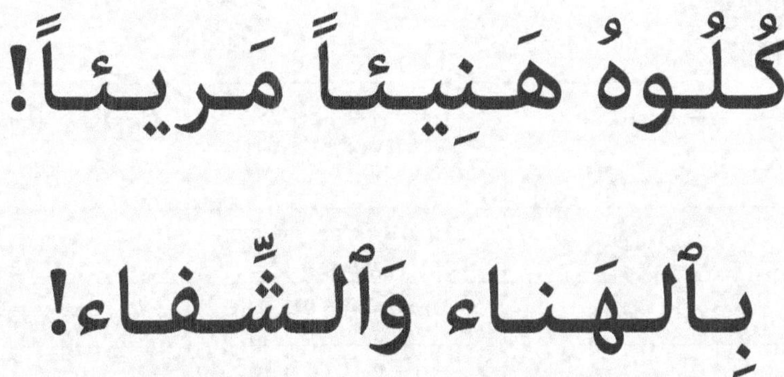

الـمُحادثة ٱلحادِيَة عَشْرة

حَديث عَن ٱلسَّكَن

آدَم: أَيْنَ تَسْكُنيـن يا جولْـيـا؟

جوليا: أَسْكُن فـي سَكَن ٱلطَّالِبات بِـٱلجامِعَة.

آدَم: هَلْ يَسْكُنُ مَعَـكِ أَحَد؟

جوليا: تَسْكُنُ مَعِـي لُورِي، وأَيْنَ تَسْكُنُ أَنْت؟

آدَم: أَسْكُنُ فـي شَقَّة قَريبَة مِنَ ٱلجامِعَة.

جوليا: وهَلْ تَسْكُـنُ وَحْدَك؟

آدَم: يَسْكُن مَعِـي صَديِقِي دانْيال.

جوليا: و كَيْفَ تَحْضُـر إِلَى ٱلجامِعة؟

آدَم: أَحْضُر بِـسَـيَّـارَتِـي.

جوليا: أَنا لا أَحْتاجُ إِلَـى سَيَّارَة، اَلحَمْدُ لِلّه!

آدَم: أَنْتِ مَحْظُوظَة إِذَن، الـبَـنْـزينُ غالـي جِدّاً هَذِهِ الأَيَّام.

جوليا: كانَ ٱللَّهُ فِـي عَوْنِـكَ!

آدَم : شُكْراً جَزيلاً! أَحْتاجُ إِلَـى هَذا العَوْن!

* * *

a talk about housing	حَـديث عَـن ٱلـسَّـكَـن	the eleventh conversation	الـمُـحـادَثـة الـحـاديـة عَـشْـرَة
Julia (*female proper name*)	جـولْـيـا	*Adam* (*male proper name*)	آدَم
O' *Julia*	يا جـولْـيـا	Where do you live?	أَيْـنَ تَـسْـكُـنِـيـن ...؟
female students residence or dorm	سَـكَـن الـطَّـالِـبـات	I live, I reside	أَسْـكُـنُ فـي
Does live...?	هَـلْ يَـسْـكُـن ...؟	at the university	بِـالجامِعَة

one, anyone	أَحَـد	with you	مَـعَـك
my friend *Lauri*	صَـديقَـتـي لُـوري	lives (she) with me	تَـسْـكُن مَـعـي
I live in	أَسْـكُـن فـي	And where do you live?	وأَيْـنَ تَسْكُـن أَنْـت؟
And do you live by yourself	وهَـلْ تَـسْـكُـن وَحْـدَك؟	an apartment near by the university	شَقَّـة قَـرِيبَـة مِـن الـجـامِـعَـة
my friend Daniel	صَـدِيقِي دانْـيـال	with me lives	يَسْكُـن مَعِـي
to the university	إِلَـى الـجـامِـعَـة	And how do you come...?	وَ كَـيْـفَ تَـحْـضُـر؟
I do not need	أَنـا لا أَحْـتـاج	I come by my car	أَحْـضُـرُ بِـسَـيّـارَتـي
You're lucky then	أَنْـتِ مَحْظُوظَة إِذَن	for a car	إِلَـى سَـيّـارَة
these days	هَذِهِ الأَيّـام	the gasoline is very expensive	الـبَـنْـزِين غـالـي جِـدّاً
Many thanks!	شُـكْـراً جَـزِيـلاً!	May God help you!	كـانَ اللّـهُ فـي عَـوْنِـك!
this help	هَـذا الـعَـوْن	I am in need of	أَحْـتـاج إِلَـى

Notes on the Vocabulary:

- Note the usual suffixed pronouns highlited in red, attached to nouns or to particles, and corresponding to English possessive pronouns or object pronouns.
- Note also the usual conjunction (و) prefixed to words and highlited in blue, which means (and) . By now you should have observed that Arabic uses the conjunction (و) for (and) far more frequently than English!
- Note also the preposition (بـ) prefixed twice to nouns. In the first case, it is attached to the noun of place (الجامِعَة), and in this case it means "at." In the second case, it is attached to the noun of transportation vehicle (السَّيّارَة), and in this case it means "by."

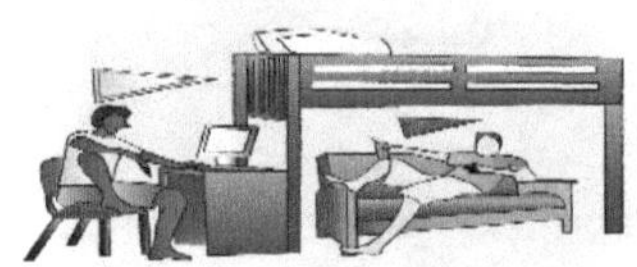

غُـرْفَـة فـي سَـكَـن طُـلاّب

شَـقَّـة فـي عِـمـارَة

بَـيْـت خـاصّ

الـمُحادثة ٱلثَّانية عَشْرة — مُكالَمَة تِليفونِيَّة

هِشام: أَلـو ... مَـرْحَـبـا!

زَيْـنَـب: مَـراحِب! مَنْ يَـتَـكَـلَّم؟ هِـشـام؟

هِشام: نَـعَـمْ أنـا هِـشـام، كَيْفَ أَنْـتِ يـا زَيْـنـب؟

زَيْـنَـب: تَـعْـبـانَـة قَـلـيـلاً!

هِشام: سَـلامَـتُـكِ! خَـيْـراً إِنْ شـاءَ ٱللَّـه!

زَيْـنَـب: يَـبْـدو أَنِّـي أَخَـذْتُ بَـرد.

هِشام: بِٱلسَّـلامَـة! هَـلْ تَـحْـتاجِـيـنَ أَيَّ خِـدْمَـة؟

زَيْـنَـب: أَشْـكُـرُكَ! لازِم أَرْتـاح يَـوْمَـيْـن أَوْ ثَـلاثَـة.

هِشام: طَـبْـعاً، اِنْـتَـبِـهي لِـنَـفْـسِـكِ! وبِٱلـسَّـلامَة مَـرَّة ثـانِـيَـة!

زَيْـنَـب: الـلَّـه يُـسَـلِّـمَـك!

Colloquial Arabic pronunciation of the English "Hello"	أَلـو	the twelfth conversation	الـمُحادَثـة الـثَّـانيـة عَشْرَة
Hishām (*male proper name*)	هِـشـام	Hi, welcome!	مَـرْحَـبا
Plural of مَـرْحَـبا	مَـراحِب	*Zainab* (*female proper name*)	زَيْـنَـب
(Is it) *Hishām*?	هِـشـام؟	Who is speaking?	مَـنْ يَـتَـكَـلَّـم؟

How are you, O' Zainab?	كَـيْـفَ أَنْـتِ يـا زَيْـنَـب؟	Yes, I am *Hishām*	نَـعَمْ، أنـا هِشام
May you be safe!	سَـلامَـتُـكِ!	A little tired!	تَـعْـبانَـة قَـلِـيـلاً
It seems that I	يَـبْـدو أَنِّـي	May it reverts to goodness, God's willing!	خَـيْـراً إِنْ شـاءَ ٱللَّه!
May it be followed by recovery! Get well soon!	بِـٱلسَّـلامَـة	got a cold	أَخَـذْتُ بَـرد
I thank you!	أَشْـكُـرُك	Do you need any service (need)?	هَـلْ تَـحْـتاجِـيـن أيّ خِدْمَـة؟
for two or three days	يَـوْمَـيْـن أَوْ ثَـلاثَـه	I must rest	لازِم أَرْتـاح
Take care of yourself!	اِنْـتَـبِـهِـي لِنَفْسِكِ!	of course	طَـبْـعاً
again, another time	مَرَّة ثانِـيَـة	And wish you recovery! (Idiomatically:Get well soon!	وبِـٱلسَّـلامَـة
		May God keep you safe (too)!	الـلَّـهُ يُـسَـلِّـمَـك!

Notes on the Vocabulary:

- Note the usual suffixed pronouns highlited in red, attached to nouns, particles or verbs, and corresponding to English possessive pronouns or object pronouns.
- Note also the usual conjunction (و) prefixed to words and highlited in blue, which means (and) . By now you should have observed that Arabic uses the conjunction (و) for (and) far more frequently than English!
- Note also the preposition (بـ) prefixed to the noun (السَّلامَـة), and in this case it means "with" or "by."

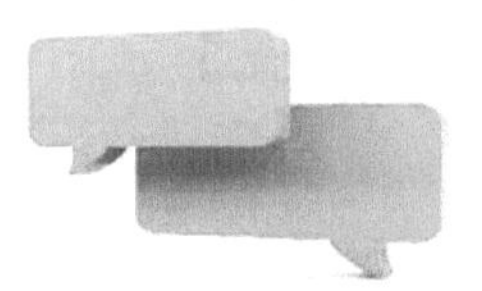

دِ راسَة ٱللُّغات

להתראות
בקרוב

لَطيف: مَرْحَباً يـا آنِسَة!

لَطيفَة: أَهْـلاً يا شـابّ! اِسْـمـي "لَطيفَة".

لَطيف: شَـيء مُـشَوِّق! اِسْمـــي "لَطيف".

لَطيفَة: نَـعَـمْ ، اِسْـمانِ لَـهُـما نَـفْس ٱلـمَـعْنى بِـٱلعَـرَبِيَّـة.

لطيفة

لَطيف

لَطيف: ماذا تَـدْرُسِـين يا "لَطيفَة"؟

لَطيفَة: أَدْرُسُ ٱلـلُّغَـةَ ٱلعِـبْـرِيَّـة.

لَطيف: وأَنا أَدْرُسُ ٱلـلُّغَـةَ ٱلعـرَبِـيَّـة.

لَطيفَة: هـاتـانِ لُـغَـتـان أُخْـتـان سـامِـيَّـتـان!

لَطيف: نَـعَـم، لَكِـنْ لِـماذا تَـدْرُسين ٱلـعِـبْـرِيَّـة؟

لَطيفَة: والِـدي عَـرَبِـيّ، ووالِدَتِـي يَـهُـودِيَّـة لُـغَـتُـهـا ٱلأُمّ ٱلـعِـبْـرِيَّـة!

لَطيف: يـا ٱللَّـه! أَنـا والِـدي يَـهُـودِيّ وأُمّـي عَـرَبِـيَّـة!

لَطيفَة: هـذا وَضْـع عَـجِـيـب ونـادِر!

لَطيف: ولَـكِـنَّـهُ جَـمِـيل ومُـسْـتَـحْـسَـن! أُسْرَتـانـا تُـمَـثِّـلانِ ٱلاِنْـفِـتـاح وٱلـتَّـقَـدُّمِـيَّـة.

لَطيفَة: أَتَّـفِـقُ مَـعَـكَ يـا "ٱبْنَ عَـمِّي"! وهُـما تُـمَـثِّـلان ٱلـمُـسْـتَـقْـبَل وٱلسَّلام!

* * *

the study of languages	دِراسَة ٱلـلُّغات	the eleventh conversation	الـمُحادثة ٱلـثَّـالـثـة عَشْرة

Hello O' Miss!	مَرْحَباً يا آنِسَة!	Masculine/feminine pair of proper nouns from the same root, meaning "gentle, kind."	لَطِيف / لَطِيفَة
My name is *Latīfah*	اِسْمي "لَطيفَة"	Hello, O' young man!	أَهْلاً يا شابّ!
My name is *Latīf*	اِسْمي "لَطيف"	Something interesting!	شَيء مُشَوِّق !
they both have the same meaning	لَهُما نَفْس ٱلمَعْنى	Yes, two names	نَعَمْ ، اِسْمانِ
What are you studying?	ماذا تَدْرُسِين؟	in the Arabic (language)	بِٱلعَرَبِيَّة
And I am studying the Arabic language	وأنا أَدْرُس ٱللُّغَة ٱلعَرَبِيَّة	I am studying the Hebrew language	أَدْرُسُ ٱللُّغَة ٱلعِبْرِيَّة
that are two semitic sister languages	أُخْتان سامِيَّتان	these are two languages	هاتانِ لُغَتان
My father is an Arab	والِدي عَرَبِيّ	Yes, however, why are you studying Hebrew?	نَعَم ، لَكِنْ لِماذا تَدْرُسِين ٱلعِبْرِيَّة؟
her mother tongue is Hebrew	لُغَتُها الأُمّ ٱلعِبْرِيَّة	and my mother is a Jew	ووالِدَتي يَهُودِيَّة
My father is a Jew	أنا والِدي يَهُودِيّ	O my goodness!	يا ٱللّه!
This is a strange and rare situation	هذا وَضْع عَجيب ونادِر	And my mother is an Arab	وأُمّي عَرَبِيَّة
our two families represent	أُسْرَتانا تُمَثِّلانِ	However, it is beautiful and desirable	ولَكِنَّهُ جَميل ومُسْتَحْسَن
I agree with you	أَتَّفِقُ مَعَكَ	openess and progressiveness	ٱلاِنْفِتاح وٱلتَّقَدُّمِيَّة
and they both represent the future and peace	وهُما تُمَثِّلان ٱلمُسْتَقْبَل وٱلسَّلام	O' "my cousin"!	يا "ابْنَ عَمّي"!

Notes on the Vocabulary:

- Note the following sets of words, introduced in the language of the conversation, which represent the "dual number" in Arabic; they include pronouns, nouns, adjectives and verb conjugations and are highlited in violet color:

مَرْحَبَتَيْنِ / اِسْمانِ / لَهُما / هاتانِ لُغَتانِ أُخْتانِ سامِيَّتانِ / أُسْرَتانا تُمَثِّلان / هُما

المُحادثة الرَّابعة عَشْرة

خَدَمات وأَعْمال

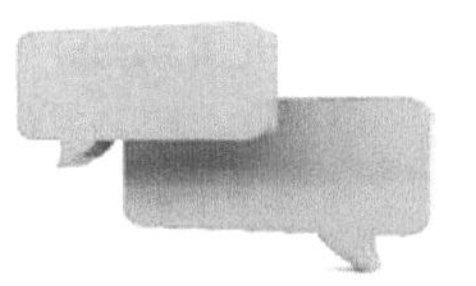

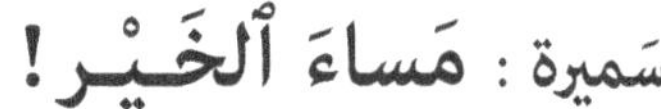

سَميرة : مَساءَ ٱلخَيْر !

سَمير : مَساءَ ٱلنُّور !

سَميرة : كَيْفَ حالُك؟

سَمير : تَمام، أَشْكُرُ ٱللّه !

سَميرة : ما عَمَلُك ؟

سَمير: أَنا تاجِر، وَأَنْتِ ؟

سَميرة: أَنا مُحاسِبة.

سَمير: أَحْتاجُ إِلَى خَدَمات مُحاسَبَة.

سميرة: أَنا في خِدْمَتِكَ !

سَمير: شُكْراً، سَأَزُورُكِ في مَكْتَبِكِ.

سَمير: أَهْلاً بِكَ ! هَذِهِ بِطاقَتي.

سَمير : إِلَى ٱللِّقاء قَريباً !

سميرة: إِلَى ٱللِّقاء، وَمَعَ ٱلسَّلامَة !

* * *

Services and businesses	خَدَمات وأَعْمال	the 14th coversation	المُحادثة ٱلرَّابعة عَشْرة
Good evening!	مَساءَ ٱلخَيْر !	*Sa'eed / Sameer* (*two male proper names*)	سَعيد / سَمير
How are you?	كَيْفَ حالُك؟	Good evening! (*response*)	مَساءَ ٱلنُّور!
I am a merchant, what about you?	أَنا تاجِر ، وَأَنْتِ؟	What's your job?, What's your line of work?	ما عَمَلُك ؟

I need, I am in need for	أَحْتـاجُ إِلَـى	I am an accountant	أَنـا مُـحاسِـبة
accounting	مُـحاسَبَـة	services	خَـدَمـات
Thanks!	شُـكْـراً!	I am at your service	أَنـا فـي خِـدْمَـتِـك
at your office	فـي مَكْـتَبِـكِ (مَكْـتَب+ـكِ)	I will visit you	سَـأَزُورُكِ (سَـ+أَزُورُ +كِ)
Until we meet soon (shortly)!	إلـى ٱلـلِّقـاء قَريـبـا!	This is my card, my business card	هَذِهِ بِـطـاقَـتِـي (بِـطـاقَـة+ـي)
and go safely! Good by!	وَمَـعَ ٱلسَّلامَـة!	until meeting (again)!	إِلَـى ٱلـلِّقاء !

Notes on the Vocabulary:

- Besides the usual conjuncion (وَ) for "and" prefixed before words, and the usual possessive or object pronouns suffixed at the end of nouns, verbs or paricles, and highlited in red, please observe the following:

  (1) The preposition (إِلَـى) following the verb (أَحْتاجُ) and forming with it what is called "verb-preposition idioms." As you encounter more new verbs in the future associated with certain particles, take notice that such verbs have to be learned along with such particles as "verb-preposition idioms."

  (2) In the structure (سَـأَزُورُكَ), the (سَـ) prefixed to the following verb is called in Arabic "the future particle." which is equivalent to the English "will, shall."

الـمُحادثة ٱلخامِسَة عَشْرة	لِقاء في حَرَم ٱلجامِعة

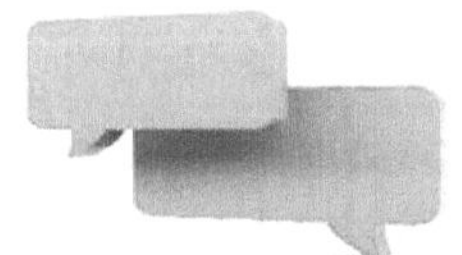

سالِي: أَهْلاً يا سالِم!

سالِم: أَهْـلَـيْـن وَسَهْـلَيْـنِ يا سـالـي! كَـيْفَ أَنْـتِ ٱليَوْم؟

سالِي: بِـخَـيْـر! إِلَـى أَيْنَ أَنْـتَ ذاهِـب؟

سالِم: إِلـى ٱلـمكْـتَـبَـة.

سالِي: سَـأَذْهَـبُ إِلـى ٱلـمكْـتَـبَـة بَـعْـدَ ٱلـغَـداء.

سالِم: أَيْنَ سَـتَـأْكُـلِـين؟

سالِي: فـي كـافِـيـتـريـا ٱلـجامِـعَـة.

سالِم: لَـمْ أَتَـنـاوَلْ ٱلـطَّعام فـي ٱلـجامِـعَة بَـعْـدُ.

سالِي: أَتُـحِـبُّ أَنْ تُـجَـرِّب ٱلـطَّـعـام هُـنـاك؟

سالِم: فِـكْـرَة جَـيِّـدَة، أُجَـرِّب!

سالِي: هَـيَّـا بِـنـا نَـذْهَـب إِلـى ٱلـكـافِـتـيـريـا!

سالِم: وَهُـوَ كَـذَلِك، هَـيَّـا بِـنـا!

* * *

a meeting in the university campus	لِـقـاء فـي حَـرَم ٱلـجـامِـعَـة	the 15th conversation	الـمُحادثة الخامِسَة عَشْرة
Sālim (*male proper name*)	سالِـم	*Sally* (*Arabic transcription*)	سالِـي
<u>Literally</u>: and twice welcome (*dual*)	وَسَهْـلَـيْـن	<u>Literally</u>: twice hello (*dual*)	أَهْلَـيْـن

today	ٱلـيَـوْم	How are you? (*for female*)	كَـيْفَ أَنْـتِ ؟ = كَـيْفَ حالُـكِ؟
Where… to? (*interrogative-preposition combination*)	إِلَـى أَيْـنَ …؟	Fine, in a state of well-being	بِـخَـيْـر
to the library	إِلـى ٱلـمَـكْـتَـبَـة	are you going	أَنْـتَ ذاهِـب
after the lunch	بَـعْـدَ ٱلـغَـداء	I will go	سَـأَذْهَـبُ (سَـ+أَذْهَـبُ)
at the university cafeteria (*borrowed from English*)	في كـافِـتِـيـرْيا ٱلـجـامِـعَـة	Where will you eat? (*feminine*)	أَيْنَ سَـتَـأْكُـلِـيـن (سَـ+تَـأْكُـلِـيـن)
food / (the) food	ٱلطَّعام	I did not have	لَـمْ أَتَـنـاوَلْ
Would you like…?	أَتُـحِـبُّ (أَ+تُحِـبُّ)	yet, till now	بَعْدُ
the food over there	ٱلـطَّـعام هُـنـاك	to try	أَنْ تُـجَـرِّبَ
this is a good idea	هَـذِهِ فِكْـرَة جَـيِّـدَة	there, over there	هُناكَ
let's go = let us go	هَـيَّـا بِـنـا نَـذْهَـب	I try	أُجَرِّبُ
		and let it be so = okay	وَهُوَ كَـذَلِـك

Notes on the Vocabulary:

- Besides the usual conjuncion (وَ) for "and" prefixed before words, and the usual possessive or object pronouns suffixed at the end of nouns, verbs or paricles, and highlited in red, please observe the (سَـ) prefixed twice to two following verbs, and is called in Arabic "the future particle," which is equivalent to the English "will, shall."

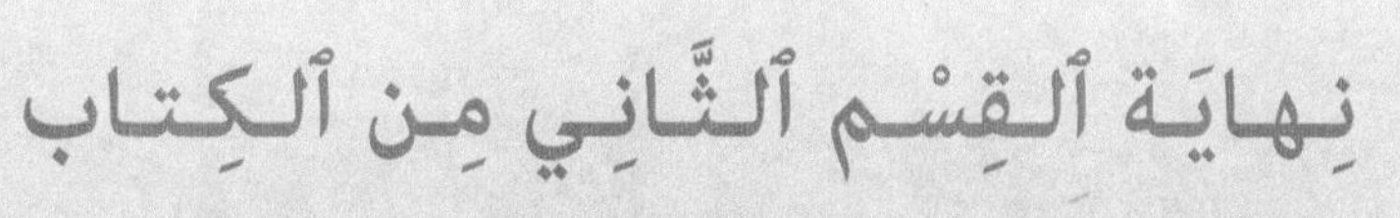

PART THREE .... القِسْمُ الثَّالِثُ

* * *

- نُصُوصٌ حِوارِيّةٌ وأُخرى قَصَصِيَّةٌ لِلقِراءَةِ وٱلفَهْمِ وٱلاِستِيعابِ ....

TEXTS FOR READING AND COMPREHENSION

* * *

- مُفْرَداتٌ وتَراكِيبُ لُغَوِيَّةٌ ....

VOCABULARY AND LINGUISTIC STRUCTURES.

* * *

- قَواعِدُ ٱللُّغَةِ ٱلعَرَبِيَّةِ ....

ARABIC LANGUAGE GRAMMAR

* * *

- تَدْرِيباتٌ وَنَشاطاتٌ لُغَوِيَّةٌ ....

EXERCISES AND LINGUISTIC ACTIVITIES

* * *

- قضايا ثقافِيَّةٌ ونَـماذِجُ مِنَ ٱلحِكَمِ وٱلأَمْثالِ العَرَبِيَّةِ ....

PATTERNS OF ARABIC WISE SAYINGS AND PROVERBS.

* * *

The First Unit / الوحدة الأولى

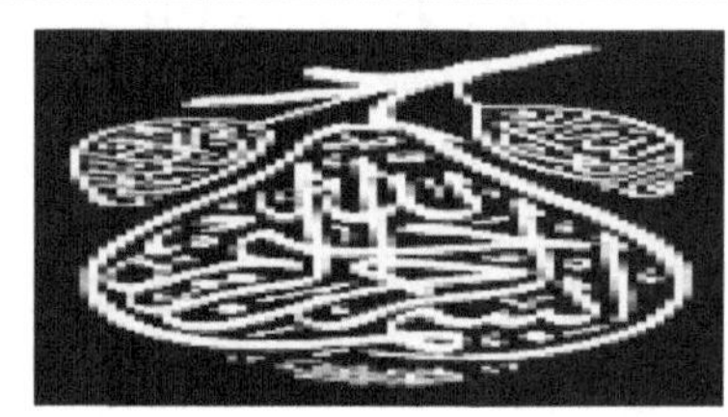

الوِحْدَةُ الأُولَى / 1st Unit

الدَّرسُ الأوَّلُ / 1st Lesson

السَّفَرُ إلى أمْريكا

Traveling to America

اِلْتَقى لُبْنانِيّ وسُورِيَّة في طابور أمامَ السِّفارَة الأمريكِيَّة في بَيْروت، ودارَ بَيْنَهما الحِوار التّالي:

سوزان: مَرْحَبا، اِسْمي سُوزان.

جُورج: أَهْلاً، اِسْمي جُورج.

سوزان: مِنْ أَيْنَ أَنْت؟

جُورج: مِنْ بَيْروت.

سوزان: وأنا مِن دِمَشق.

جُورج: لِماذا أَنْتِ في ٱلطّابور؟

سوزان: أُريد أَنْ أَحْصُل على تَأْشيرَة هِجْرَة؟

جُورج: وأنا أُريد الحُصول على تَأشيرة دِراسَة.

سوزان: في أَيّ جامِعَة سَتَدْرُس؟

جُورج: في جامِعَة "جورج تاوْن" بِواشِنْطُن.

سوزان: أنا سَأُسافِر إلى "فرجِينْيا".

جُورج: لِماذا "فرجِينْيا"؟

سوزان: زَوْجي يَعيش هُناك، وسَأَلْتَحِقُ بِه.

جُورج: أَتَمَنّى لَكِ التَّوْفيق!

سوزان: أَتَمَنّى لَكَ النَّجاح في دِراسَتِك!

مُفْرَدات وتَراكيب الدَّرس الأوَّل

Vocabulary & Linguistic Structures of the First Lesson

I want (to)	أُريد (أَنْ)	entry visa	تَأشِـيرَة	**Nouns**	أَسْـماء
I obtain	أَحْـصُـل (على)	Imigration (gerund)	هِـجْرَة	traveling	السَّفَر
will (you) study	سَـتَـدْرُس	obtaining (gerund)	الحُصُول (على)	America	أَمْريكا
he lives	يَـعيـش	educational, study-related	دِراسِيَّة	a line of people	طابور
I will join	سَـأَلْـتَـحِقُ	which	أَيّ	the embassy	السِّفارَة
I wish	أَتَـمَنَّى	university	جَامِعَة	the American	الأمْريكيَّة
Particles	أَدَوات	*Georgetown*	جُورج تاون	Lebanese (male)	لُبْنانـيّ
to	إلـى	*Washington*	واشِنْطُن	Syrian (female)	سُورِيَّة
in, at	فـي	I	أنـا	Beirut	بَـيْـروت
between	بَـيْـنَ	*Virginia*	فرجِينيا	both of the (dual pronoun)	هُـمـا
from	مِنْ	my husband	زَوْجـي	the dialogue	الـحِوار
Why...?	لِماذا...؟	him	ـهِ	the following	التَّالـي
to	أَنْ	happy outcome	التَّوْفِيق	*Suzan*	سُوزان
which	أَيّ	success	النَّجاح	*George*	جُورج
with, in	بِـ (بِـهِ)	your study	دِراسَتِـكَ	Hello, Hi	مَرْحَبا
for	لَـ (لَـكِ)	**Verbs**	أَفْعال	my name	اِسْمـي
		met	اِلْتَقَى	Welcome! Hello!	أَهْلاً
		took place	دارَ	you (mas./fem.)	أَنْتَ/أَنْتِ

الدَّرْس ٱلثَّانـي : القَواعِد وقَضايا لُغَوِيَّة Grammatical and Linguistic Issues

* * *

١- أقْسامُ الكَلِمَة: Parts of Speech

1.1 Words (Speech) are / is divided into three parts: 1. The **Noun**, 2. The **Verb**, 3. The **Particle**.	١- تَنْقِسِمُ الكَلِمَةُ إلَى ثَلاثَةِ أَقْسامٍ: (١) الاِسْمُ ، (٢) الفِعْلُ ، (٣) الحَرْفُ / الأَداة.
1.2 The **Noun**: Any of a class of words denoting a thing, a person, a place or quality, such as: **Beirut, Damascus, embassy, America, Suzane, George, Virginia, word, noun, verb, particle, lesson, new**	**١-٢** الإِسْمُ : ما يَدُلُّ عَلَى مُسَمًّى قائِمٍ بِذاتِه ، غَيْرِ مُقْتَرِنٍ بِزَمانٍ ، مِثْلُ : بَـيْروت ، دِمَشْق ، السَّفارَة ، أَمْريكا ، سُوزان ، جُورج ، فِرجينيا ، كَلِمَة ، اِسْم ، فِعْل ، أَداة ، دَرْس ، جَديد .
1.3 The **Verb**: Any of a class of words denoting an action related to a specific time in the past, present or future or requesting an action (command); such as: **met, took place / obtain, lives / will study, will join / read, write!**	**١-٣** الفِعْلُ : كَلِمَةٌ تَدُلُّ عَلَى حَدَثٍ مُرْتَبِطٍ بِزَمَنٍ مُعَيَّنٍ ، مِثْلُ : اِلتَقى ، دارَ /أَحْصُل، يَعيش / سَأَدْرُس ، سَأَلْتَحِق / اِقْرَأْ ، اُكْتُبْ!

١-٤ الحَرْفُ (الأَدَاةُ) : كَلِمَةٌ لا تَدُلُّ عَلَى مَعْنَى قائِم بِذاتِهِ ، وَإِنَّـما هِي رَوابِطُ تَكْتَسِبُ مَعْناها مِنْ غَيْرِهَا، مِثْلُ: مِن ، فِـي ، إِلَـى ، عَلى / وَ ، أَوْ / أَيْنَ ...؟ كَيْفَ ... ؟ هَلْ ...؟ ما...؟ لِـماذا ...؟	**1.4** The **Particle**: A short, usually uninflected part of speech used to show syntactical relationships, such as the definite article, prepositions, conjunctions or question particles; examples: **from, in, to, on (*prepositions*) / and, or (*conjunctions*)** **Where...?, How...?, Is / Are...?, What...?, Why...? (*question particles*)**

* * *

٢- الجُملةُ الاِسْمِيَّةُ : الـمُبْتَدأ والْـخَبَـر:

Equational (Nominal) Sentences: Subject and Predicate:

- Arabic contains a type of sentence not found in English. It is called an '**Equational Sentence**.' The following are the most important features related to this type of sentence:
- It does not contain a verb as the opening word in the sentence.
- It consists of two basic parts: the first part is called a '**Subject**' and the second a '**Predicate**.'
- The '**Subject'** may be a **pronoun**, a **proper name**, or a **defined noun**.
- The '**Predicate'** may be a **proper name**, an **indefinite noun**, an **adjective**, an **adverb**, a **prepositional phrase** and a **verbal phrase**.
- The 'Predicate' may either identify the 'Subject' or descibe it.
- Since 'Equational Sentences' have no exact equivalent in English, they are normally best translated to correspond to an English sentence with a verb '**to be**'; i.e. '**am**', '**is**', or '**are**'.
- The following are examples of 'Equational Sentences':

Predicate	Subject	Predicate	Subject
طالِب .	هُـوَ	سُوزان .	اِسْمي
جَديد .	الكِتاب	مِن بَيْروت .	أنـا
أُسْتاذ .	خَليل	فـي فِرجـينا .	زَوْجِي

* * *

٣- الجِنْس: التَّذكـيـر والتَّأنيث فـي الضَّـمائِر والأَسْـماء:

Gender in Pronouns and Nouns:

- While English shows pronoun distinction for the **3rd person** only in the forms of '**he**' and '**she**', Arabic has, furthermore, two pronouns in the **2nd person** to correspond exactly to '**you /male**' and '**you / female**'. These are:

مَنْ أَنْتَ ؟	"**you** / *masculine*"	أَنْتَ
هَلْ أَنْتِ سُورِيَّة ؟	"**you** / *feminine*"	أَنْتِ

- Likewise, while English does not show gender distinction with **Demonstrative Pronouns**, such as '**this, that**', Arabic has masculine / feminine distinction here too, as in the sentences below:

هَـذا طـالِب.	"**this** / *feminine*"	هَـذا
هَذِهِ طالِبَة.	"**this** / *feminine*"	هَذِهِ

- Arabic, likewise, shows gender distinction with **adjectival nouns**, like those referring to **nationalities**, such as '**Arab, American**'.
Let's examine the following pairs of sentences:

هَلْ أَنْتَ لُبْنانِيّ؟ / هَلْ أَنْتِ لُبْنانِيَّة؟

هَلْ أَنْتَ سُورِيّ ؟ / هَلْ أَنْتِ سُورِيَّة ؟

- **Important Note on Gender:** Arabic is a more male-female gender-conscious language than English. However, Arabic has **two genders** only. The English **neuter** '**it**', for inanimate, does not exist in Arabic; therefore Arabic inanimates must be either masculine or feminine in Arabic.

* * *

Interrogative or Question Particles ٤- أَدَوات الاِسْتِفْهام

- Like English, Arabic has a group of words or particles, used to formulate questions. Like English too, if an Arabic structure contains an interrogative particle, then it is placed first in the sentence.

- The interrogative particle (هَلْ) requires an answer starting with '**yes** / نَعَمْ' or '**no** / لا'.
It corresponds to an English question starting with a '**verb to be**'; such as '**Is …?**', '**Am…?**', or '**Are…?**'

- Like English, there are particular **intonation patterns** associated with questions; the student is advised to imitate the model of a native speaker. Now, study the following Arabic question structures for the interrogatives introduced thus far:

هَلْ أَنْتَ عَرَبِيّ؟ / هَلْ أَنْتِ عَرَبِيَّة؟
مَنْ أَنْتَ؟ / مَنْ أَنْتِ؟

- Some "interrogative particles" might combine with a "preposition" to form a question structue. In this case, the preposition comes before the "interrogative particle," such as:

مِنْ أَيْـنَ أَنْتَ؟ which means, "**Where are you from?**"

- Now, let's study the following table which contains all the interrogative particles, used in sentences: (***After reading the sentences, challenge yourself to translate them!)***

Used in a Sentence	English Equivalent	Arabic Particle
أَهَـذا كِـتابُـكَ؟ / أَهُـم طُـلّاب؟	Is ...? Are ...?	أَ
هَلْ هِـيَ لُـبْـنـانِـيَّـة؟ / هَلْ أَنْـتَ سُورِيّ؟	Is ...? Are ...?	هَـلْ
أَيْـنَ تَسْكُـن؟ / أَيْنَ الكِـتاب؟	Where ...?	أَيْـنَ
ما هـذا؟ / مـا اسـمُـكَ؟	What ...?	مـا
مـاذا تُـريـد؟ / ماذا تَـدْرُس؟	What do...?	مـاذا
لِـماذا سَـتُـسافِـرُ إلـى أَمْـريكـا؟	Why...?	لِـمـاذا
مَـنْ أَنْـتَ؟ / مَـنْ يَـعـيش هُـنـا؟	Who...?	مَـنْ
كَـيْـفَ حـالُـكِ؟ كَـيْـفَ تَـفْـعَـل هَـذا؟	How...?	كَـيْـفَ
كَـم طـالـبـاً فـي ٱلـصَّـف؟	How many...?	كَـم
فـي أَيِّ جـامِـعَـة سَـتَـدْرُس؟	Which ...?	أَيّ
مَـتى سَـتُـسـافِـرُ إلـى دِمَـشْـق؟	When...?	مَـتـى

* * *

The Vocative or Calling Particle ٥- حَرف النِّداء (يـا)

- When someone is directly addressed by his / her personal name or title in Arabic, the particle (يـا), known as the '**particle of calling**' is used just before that name or title. This usage implies respect, affection and endearment.

- The proper name or title used after the particle is normally in the nominative mood and bears the ***Ďammah*** at the end, if it is possible to show the ***Ďammah***.
- This particle, very commonly used in classical as well as modern spoken Arabic, has no equivalent in modern English. However, it corresponds to the old English '**O**', as in '**O Lord**!' or '**O King**!'. Now, let's study the following sentences:

يا سوزان ، مَنْ هَذا ؟ or مَنْ هَذا يا سوزان ؟

يا جورج ، هَلْ أَنْتَ عَرَبِـيّ ؟ or هَلْ أَنْتَ عَرَبِـيَ يا جورج ؟

* * *

الدَّرسُ الثَّالِث : تَدْريبات ونَشاطات / Exercises & Activities

Exercise 1: Creating a "Parts of Speech" Table: تَـمْـريـن ١:

On a separate sheet of paper create a table on the model given below and list under each column the words that fall under the appropriate part of speech, using as many words as you can from this unit and previous lessons:

Particle / أداة / حَرف	Verb / فِعل	Noun / إِسْم
وَ	أَدْرُس	بَـيْـروت
هَـل	يُسافِـر	هـذا

* * *

Exercise 2: Recognition of Gender: Masculine / Feminine تَـمْـريـن ٢:

(The teacher supplies the cue, in the form of a pronoun, and the student supplies a male or a female proper name to form with that pronoun an 'Equational Sentence'.)

١- أنا .... ٢- أَنْتَ .... ٣- هَذِهِ ....

٤- هَذا .... ٥- أَنْتِ .... ٦- هُـوَ ....

* * *

Exercise 3: (***Oral Chain Exercise***) **تَمْـرِيـن ٣ :**

Introduction / Asking for Introduction:

(The teacher introduces himself or herself, and asks the 1st student in Arabic: 'Who are you?' Then, in the same manner the 1st student introduces himself by saying: 'I am .... .' Then continuing by asking a 2nd student: 'Who are you?', and so on, in a chain manner to give every student a chance to participate.)

أنا (خَلِيل) ، مَنْ أَنْـتَ (أَنْـتِ) ؟

* * *

Exercise 4: (***Verbal Exercise***) **Question / Answer with (هَلْ):** **تَمْـرِيـن ٤ :**

(The teacher asks each student: هَلْ أَنْتَ (أَنْتِ) ...؟, using a combination of the students' real names, and other than their real names. Depending on the question, the student being questioned will be answering, either affirmatively or negatively, using (نَعَم) or (لا), as in the following example:

هَلْ أَنْتَ آدَمُ ؟ / نَعَمْ، أنا آدَمُ . (or) لاَ، أنا سامِي .

* * *

تَمْـرِيـن ٥ :

Exercise 5: (***Oral Exercise***) **Question Formation with (مَنْ / هَلْ ...؟):**

Form questions with the interrogative particles (هَلْ / مَنْ) to which the following statements can serve as the answers; follow the given example:

نَعَمْ ، هذِهِ مَرْيَم . / هَلْ هَذِهِ مَرْيَم؟

هَذا فَضْل . / مَنْ هَذا؟

١- هَذا آدَم .

٢- لا ، أنا فَضْل .

٣- نَعَمْ ، أَنا نانْسِـي .

٤- هَذِهِ ماري .

٥- لا ، أنا عَرَبِـيّ .

٦- نَعَمْ ، أَنا أَمْرِيكِيَّة .

* * *

Exercise 6: (*Oral Chain Exercise*) **Using the Vocative Particle (يا): : تَـمْرين ٥**

The teacher asks the 1st student about a 2nd student; the 1st student asks the 2nd student: 'Who are you?' Then, after the 2nd student answers, the 1st student answers the original question of the teacher. Follow the following pattern:

> مَنْ هَذِهِ يا آدَمُ ؟ / آدَمُ : مَنْ أَنْتِ ؟
>
> نانْسِي: أَنا نانْسِـي. / آدَمُ: هَذِهِ نانْسِـي.

* * *

الدَّرسُ الرَّابِع: القِراءة الجَهْرِيَّة / Reading Aloud

(يُوسُف إبْراهِيم)

- هاجَرَ "يُوسُف إبراهِيم" مِنْ مِصْر إلَـى أَمريكا قَبْلَ عَشْرِ سَنَوات. وبَعْدَ سَنَة مِنْ إقامَـتِـه حَصَلَ على عَمَل فـي شَرِكَـة تِـجارِيَّة.
- تَعَرَّفَ "يُوسُف" عَلى زَمِيـلَـة فِـي العَمَل اِسْمُـهـا "نانسي". أَحَبَّ "يُوسُف" "نانسـي"، وطَـلَـبَ مِنْـها الزَّواج فَـوافَقَتْ. وبَعْدَ سَنَتَيْـن مِنَ الـزَّواج، أَنْـجَـبَـتْ "نانسي" بِـنـتـاً سَـمَّـتْـها "لِـيـنـا".
- عِنْدما حَصَلَ يوسُف على ٱلـجِنْسِيَّة ٱلأمريكِـيَّـة، غَيَّـرَ اسْمَـهُ إلَـى "جُوزيف أَبْراهام".
- أَرادَ يوسُف أَنْ يَزورَ مِصْر بَعْدَ عَشر سَنَوات مِن هِـجْرَتِـهِ، فَـٱتَّـصَلَ هاتِـفِـيّـاً بِأُخْتِـهِ "سُعاد"، وأَخْبَـرَها بِـمَوْعِدِ حُضُورِهِ إلَـى القاهِرَة.

مُفْرَدات وتَراكيب الدَّرس الرَّابع

Vocabulary & Linguistic Structures of the 4th Lesson

Su'aad	سُعاد	Nouns	أَسْماء
appointed time	مَوْعِد	Joseph Abraham (*Arabic for the two Biblical proper nams*)	يُوسُف إبراهِيم
his coming	حُضورِهِ	Egypt	مِصْر
Cairo	القاهِرَة	America	أمْريكا
Verbs	أفْعال	ten	عَشر
he immigrated	هاجَرَ	years (a year)	سَنوات (سَنَة)
he obtained	حَصَلَ (على)	his residency	إقامَتِه
he got to know	تَعَرَّفَ (على)	job, work	عَمَل
he loved	أَحَبَّ	commercial company	شَرِكَة تِجارِيَّة
he requested	طَلَبَ (مِن)	colleauge	زَمِيلَة
she agreed	وافَقَتْ	the work, the job	العَمَل
she begot, she gave birth	أنْجَبَتْ	her name	اِسْمُها
he changed)	غَيَّرَ	*Nancy*	نانْسي
he wanted (to)	أرادَ (أنْ)	her	ـها
he visits	يَزور	the marriage	الزَّواج
he contacted	اِتَّصَلَ	two years (dual)	سَنَتَيْن (سَنَة)
he informed	أخْبَرَ	a daughter, girl	بِنْتاً = بِنْت
Particles	أدَوات	*Leena*	لِينا
from/ to / before	مِنْ / إلَى / قَبْلَ	the American nationality	الجِنْسِيَّة الأمريكِيَّة
and/ after / in,at	وَ / بَعْدَ / في	his name	اِسْمَهُ
so / of /	فَـ / مِنْ / عِنْدَما	*Joseph Abraham*	جوزيف أبْراهام
of, with	بِـ	his immigration	هِجْرَتِه
to (a verbal particle comes before verbs)	أنْ	his sister	أُخْتِهِ

* * *

أَسْئِلة الفهم والاستيعاب (شَفويّا):

سُؤال
جَواب

١- إلـى أَيْـنَ هـاجَـرَ يُوسُف؟

٢- أَيْـنَ عَـمِلَ يُوسُف؟ ٣- على مَنْ تَـعَـرَّفَ يوسُف ؟

٤- هَل وافَـقَـتْ نانسي على الزَّواج؟

٥- مَتى أَنْـجَـبَـتْ نانْسي البِنْت ؟ ٦- ماذا سَمَّت نانسي بِـنْـتَـها؟

٧- مَتَى غَـيَّـرَ يوسُف اسْمَـهُ؟ ٨- ما ٱسْم يوسُف ٱلجَديد؟

٩- ماذا أَخْـبَـرَ يوسُف أُخْـتَـهُ سُعاد؟

* * *

الدَّرسُ الخامس: الثَّـقـافـة وَٱلـقِـيَـم وَٱلأَمْـثـال
Culture, Values & Proverbs

➢ **Like English, proper names in Arabic include names of people, countries, cities rivers, seas, mountain ranges, names of months, days and seasons. However, Arabic doesn't have the system of capitlization the first letters of such proper names. Proper names might contain the definit article or not.**
Examples of such proper names are:

دِمَشْق	الـمَدينَة	مَكَّة	الأُردن	النِّيل	خالِد	مُحَمَّد
Damascuss	**Medina**	**Mecca**	**Jordan**	**The Nile**	**Khalid**	**Muhammad**

➢ **Proper nouns from foreign languages are normally transcribed into Arabic using Arabic letters, but some times with some modification to accommodate the sound System of Arabic. Examples of such proper names include:**

السَّبْت	مارِس	نوفِمْبَـر	سِبْتِمْبَـر	فَرَنْسا	روسْيا	أَمْريكا
Saturday	**March**	**November**	**September**	**France**	**Russia**	**America**

➢ **Arabic has a unique way of forming compound proper names, specifically for males. This type of names are based on the religious concept of the ninety-nine Beautiful Attributes of God. And the way these names are compounded is to use the word (عَبْدُ), which means "servant" as the first part of the name, to be followed by one of the 99 Atributes of God. Examples of such proper names are:**

عَبْدُ ٱلكَريم	عَبْدُ ٱلسَّلام	عَبْدُ ٱلخالِق	عَبْدُ ٱلرَّحمن	عَبْدُ ٱلـلّـه
The Servant of the Most Generous	**The Servant of Peace**	**The Servant of the Creator**	**The Servant of the Most Merciful**	**The Servant of God**

➤ **Arab Muslims tend to use the Arabic proper names of the Biblical personalities, to name their children. Examples of such proper names are:**

عيسَى	موسَى	يُوسُف	إبراهيم	آدم
Jesus	**Moses**	**Joseph**	**Abraham**	**Adam**

➤ **Another feature particular to Arab culture in giving proper names, as <u>nicknames</u>, using the the words (أَبُو), which means "father of" for a male parent and (أُمّ), which means "mother of," for the female parent, and followed by the given first name of the first botn male or female. Likewise, the word (اِبْن), which means "son of" can be used before the name of the father. This is considered culturally as a celebration of marriage and fertility or preserving the good memory of an ancester . Examples of such nicknames are:**

أمّ حَبيبَة	اِبْنُ خَلدون	أَبو بَكْر	أمّ يوسُف	أَبو إبْراهيم
Mother of Habeebah	**Son of Khaldūn**	**Father of Bakr**	**Mother of Yūsuf**	**Father of Ibrāhīm**

➤ **Another common feature of giving proper names to children, is to use adjective words that have nice linguistic meanings. Examples of such names are:**

آمِنَة	لَطيفَة	جَميلَة	كَريم	سَعيد
The Secure One	**The Gentle, Kind One**	**The Beautiful One**	**The Generous One**	**The Happy One**

➤ **Another type of <u>honorific titles</u>, given or adopted particularly by certain historical figures. Examples of such titles are:**

أمير ٱلمُؤمِنين	المُعتَصِم بِٱللّه	سَيْف الدَّوْلَة	عِماد ٱلدِّين	صَلاح ٱلدِّين
The Prince of the Believers	**He Who is Adhering to God**	**The Sword of the State**	**The Pillar of Religion**	**The Reformer of Religion**

مُختارات مِنَ ٱلحِكَم وٱلأمثال ٱلعربيَّة:
Selections of Arabic Proverbs & Wise Sayings:

الصَّدِيقُ وَقْتُ ٱلضِّيق.
The friend indeed is the friend in need.

العَقْلُ ٱلسَّليمُ فِي ٱلجِسْمِ ٱلسَّليمِ.
The healthy mind is in the healthy body.

السَّلامُ قَبْلَ ٱلكَلام.
Greeting must come before talking.

* * *

General Drills & Review: تَمارين عامَّة ومُراجَعَة

تَمرين ١: **Let's read the following sets of words, recall their meanings and then guess why they were grouped together under one category:**

١- يُوسُف / إبْراهيم / جُورج / سُوزان / سُعاد / نانسي / لِينا .

٢- أنا / أَنْتَ / أَنْتِ / هُوَ / هِيَ / هُمْ / هُنَّ .

٣- إلَى / عَلى / مِنْ / في / بِ .

٤- أَمْريكا / مِصْر / بَيْروت / دِمَشْق .

٥- أمريكِيّ - أَمْريكِيَّة / مِصْرِيّ - مِصْرِيَّة / لُبْنانِيّ - لُبْنانِيَّة .

٦- أَيْنَ / مِن أَيْنَ / أَيّ / في أَيّ / ما / ماذا / كَيْفَ / كَم

٧- تَعرَّفَ (عَلَى) / هاجَرَ (مِن) إلى / حَصَلَ (على) / تَزَوَّجَ / أَنْجَبَتْ / غَيَّرَ / أَحَبَّ / اِتَّصَلَ / طَلَبَ / وافَقَتْ / سَمَّتْ .

٨- إقامَة / عَمَل / شَرِكَة / تِجارِيَّة / زَميلة / الزَّواج / سَنَة / سَنَوات / سَنَتَيْن / الجِنْسِيَّة / هِجْرَة / مَوْعِد / حُضُور .

تـمرين ٢:

From the list of words given in the box below, select the one most suitable to fill in the blanks in the following sentences:

بِأخْتِه / اسْمَهُ / بِـمَوْعِد / مِن / / شَرِكَـة / جوزيف / إلَـى / وافَقَت / نانْسِي/ تَعَرَّفَ / سَمَّتْها / على / يُوسُف / الزَّواج

١- هاجَرَ يوسُف إبراهيم ______ مِصر ______ أمريكا .

٢- عَمِلَ يوسُف فـي ______ تِجاريَّة .

٣- ______ يُوسُف ______ زَمْيلَة لَـه اِسْمُها نانسـي .

٤- أَحَبَّ ______ نانسي ، وطَلَبَ مِنْها ______ .

٥- ______ نانْسي على الزَّواج مِن ______ .

٦- أَنْجَبَتْ نانسي بِنْتاً ______ لِينا .

٧- غَيَّـرَ يُوسُف ______ إلـى ______ أبراهام .

٨- اِتَّصَل يُوسُف ______ سُعاد ، وأَخْبَرَها ______ حُضُوره.

* * *

تـمرين ٣:

Respond verbally in Arabic to the following greetings, courtisies or questions: (*Chain Drill*)

١- مرحباً!

٢- السَّلام عليكم!

٣- صباح الخيـر!

٤- كيف الحال ؟

٥- ما اسمك (اسْمُكِ)؟

٦- مَن أنتَ (أنتِ)؟

٧- مِن أينَ أنتَ (أنتِ)؟

٨- هل أنتَ أمريكـيّ (أنتِ أمريكِيَّة)؟

٩- شُكراً جزيلا!

١٠- إلى اللِّقاء!

نـهايَـةُ الوحْدَة الأولَـى

The Second Unit / الوحدة الثَّانِية

الوِحْدَةُ الثَّانِيةُ / 1st Unit

الدَّرسُ الأَوَّلُ /1st Lesson

فـي ٱلـمَطار
At The Airport

تَقابَلَتْ "سارَة" و"لِينا" فـي مَطارِ "دُبَـيّ"، وجَرى بَيْـنَـهُـما الحِوار التَّالـي:

سارة : إلـى أَيْنَ أَنْتِ مُسافِرَة؟ لِينا : أنا مُسافِرَة إلـى "نيُويورك."

سارة : أَنْتِ أَمْريكِـيَّة؟ لِينا : نَعَم ، أنـا أَمْـريكِـيَّة .

سارة : أنا مِصْرِيَّة. كَـمْ يَوْماً قَـضَـيْـتِ فـي "دُبَـيّ"؟

لِينا : قَـضَـيْـتُ أُسْبوعـاً واحِداً .

سارة : هَـذِهِ زِيـارَة قَـصيـرَة.

لِينا : حَضَرْتُ لِـزِيـارَة والِـدَتـي فـي عُـطْـلَـة ٱلرَّبـيـع .

سارة : هَـلْ أَنْتِ طـالِـبَـة؟

لِينا : نَـعَـمْ، أنـا طـالِـبَـة فـي جـامِـعَـة "نيُويورك."

سارة : أَنـا مُـقيمَة وأَعْـمَـل هُـنـا. لِينا : مـاذا تَـعْـمَـلـيـن؟

سارة : أنا أُسْـتـاذة ٱلـلُّـغـة ٱلـعربـيَّـة فـي "ٱلجـامِـعَـة الأمْـريـكِـيَّة."

لِينا : والِـدَتـي تَـعْـمَـل فـي نَـفْـس ٱلجامِـعَـة، وهِـيَ تُـدَرِّس الـلُّـغـة الإنْـجـلـيـزِيَّـة.

سارة : أُحِـبُّ أَنْ أَتَـعَـرَّفَ عَلَـيْـها .

لِينا : هَـذِهِ بِـطـاقَـتُـها ، وفـيـها ٱسْـمُـها ورَقَـمُ تِـلـيـفـونِـها .

سارة : شُـكْـراً لَـكِ ! وٱلآن ، حـانَ مَـوْعِـدُ سَـفَـري.

لِينا : أَتَـمَنَّـى لَـكِ رِحْـلَـة سَـعـيدَة!

سارة : مَـعَ ٱلـسَّـلامَـة!

مُفْرَدات وتَراكيب الدَّرس الأوَّل

Vocabulary & Linguistic Structures of the 1st Lesson

with	مَعَ	her phone	تِلِيفونِها	Nouns	أَسْماء
		Verbs	**أَفْعال**	airport	مَطار
		met together	تَقابَلَتْ	traveler, passenger	مُسافِرَة
		took place	جَرى	a day	يَوْماً
		you spent (*related to time*)	قَضَيْتِ	one week	أُسْبوعاً واحِداً
		I came	حَضَرْتُ	this (mas./fem.)	هَذا / هَذِهِ
		had arrived (*of time*)	حانَ	short visit	زِيارَة قَصيرَة
		I work	أَعْمَل	visiting my mother	زِيارَة والِدَتي
		she works	تَعْمَل	Spring break	عُطْلَة ٱلرَّبيع
		you work (*feminine singular*)	تَعْمَلين	resident, residing	مُقيمَة
		I like, I love	أُحِبّ	female professor	أُسْتاذَة
		I get to know	أَتَعَرَّف	The Arabic language	اللُّغة ٱلعَرَبِيَّة
		Particles	**أَدوات**	the university	الجامِعَة
		between, among	بَيْنَ	same	نَفْس
		yes	نَعَم	the English language	اللُّغة الإنجليزيَّة
		How many …?	كَمْ ...؟	her card	بِطاقَتُها
		here	هُنا	her name	اِسْمُها
		now	الآن	number (of)	رَقَم

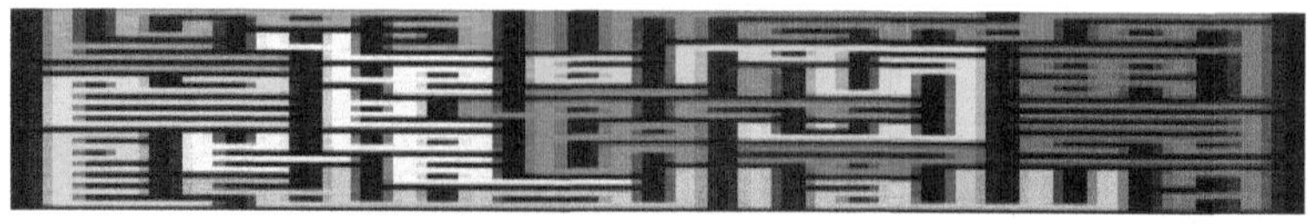

Grammatical and Linguistic Issues الدَّرْس الثَّاني: القَواعِد وقَضايا لُغَوِيَّة

* * *

Interrogative as a Prepositional Phrase ١- أداةُ الاِستِفْهامِ مَعَ حَرْفِ الجَرِّ

- As a general rule, in Arabic, as in English, an interrogative particle comes first in the sentence.
- However, sometimes the nature of the question might involve a preposition, and in such case, that preposition must come before the interrogative particle and forms with it one undivided unit at the beginning of the sentence.
- In English, a phrase like '**From where...?**' may be separated with '**From**' coming at the end; such as: 'Where are you from?' This separation cannot be done in Arabic.
- Now, let's study the following examples that illustrate the facts covered above:

Where is Ibrāhīm from?	مِنْ أَيْنَ إِبْراهيمُ؟ ⇔	Where is Ibrāhīm?	أَيْنَ إِبْراهيم؟
Where is Laylā from?	مِنْ أَيْنَ لَيْلَى؟ ⇔	Where is Laylā?	أَيْنَ لَيْلَى؟

* * *

Tanween (Nunation) Ending with Nouns ٢- التَّنْوِينُ فِي الأَسْماءِ:

- A '*Tanween* / التَّنْوِين ' is the Arabic terminology used for a final '*Noon*' sound, heard at the end of most words that have no Definite Article.
- In this sense, it is a sign of '**indefiniteness**', corresponding in general to the English '**indefinite articles**': '**a**' or '**an**' in expressions such as: '**a student**' or '**an apple**'.

- There are few sub-categories of nouns that do not accept '*Tanween*' any way, even when they do not have the Arabic Definite Article (ال) attached to them. These categories will be treated in future lessons.
- There are three variations of '***Tanween***' depending on the grammatical function of the word in the context of a sentence, as will be explained later. The Arabic written symbols for these three variations are listed in the following box:

"*Tanween Fathah*" (***an*** – اً or ً) / "*Tanween Dammah*" (***un*** – ٌ)
"*Tanween Kasrah*" (***in*** – ٍ)

- Now, let's study some '***nunated***' Arabic words in context, then observe how they would loose the '*Tanween*' when they receive the Arabic Definite Article:

هَذا الطَّالِبُ مِنْ لُبْنان .	⇔	هَذا طالِبٌ . (*un* – ٌ)
This student is from Lebanon.		**This is a student.**
قَرَأْتُ الكِتابَ .	⇔	قَرَأْتُ كِتاباً . (*an* – اً)
I read the book.		**I read a book.**
أَكَلْتُ فِـي الـمَطْعَمِ .	⇔	أَكَلْتُ فِـي مَطْعَمٍ . (*in* – ٍ)
I ate at the restaurant.		**I ate at a restaurant.**

- It is to be noted that some proper names, without the Definite Article, may receive a *Tanween*. However, **names of cities**, **countries** and **female proper names** never take the '*Tanween*' ending; examples:

أَيْنَ بَيْـرُوتُ؟ / بَيْـرُوتُ فِـي لُبْنانَ.
مِنْ أَيْنَ مَرْيَـمُ؟ / مَرْيَمُ مِنْ دِمَشْقَ .

* * *

٣- حالاتُ الإِعْرابِ وعَلاماتُـهُ:

Case-Ending in Nouns: General Introduction:

- Arabic nouns have different ending forms, reflected in what is termed '*case-endings*', known in Arabic grammatical terminology as (*'Alāmāt al-'I 'rāb* / عَلاماتُ الإعراب). These '*case-endings*' reflect the grammatical functions of nouns in sentences.
- There are three forms of '*case-endings*', called (**Nominative** / مَرْفوع), (**Accusative** / مَنْصوب), and (**Genitive** / مَجْرور). The underlined nouns in the table below represent nouns in these different 'case-endings' and show us the different three ending signs for both defined and non-defined nouns.
- Each '*case-ending*' is used for a different grammatical function, and since this topic is considered a topic of "high grammar" it will be introduced systematically, one by one, in subsequent lessons of a second year Arabic.
- Variation in '*case-endings*', however, does not change the basic meanings of the nouns as far as translation is concerned.
- Personal proper names and place names transcribed into Arabic from foreign languages do not receive these '*case-endings*', such as: سُوزان / لينا / نيويورك / فرجينيا .
- Now, let's study the sentences in the following table to further conceptualize the points explained above:

Genitive / مَجْرُور	Accusative / مَنْصُوب	Nominative / مَرْفُوع
سَلَّمْتُ عَلَى مُحَمَّدٍ.	قَـابَلْتُ مُحَمَّداً.	مُحَمَّدٌ طالِبٌ.
تَحَدَّثْتُ إِلَـى الطَّالِبِ العَرَبِـيِّ .	شَكَرْتُ الطَّالِبَ العَرَبِـيَّ.	الطَّالِبُ عَرَبِـيٌّ.
تَعَرَّفْتُ عَلَى سارَةَ.	زُرْتُ سارَةَ فِـي ٱلـمَكْتَبِ.	سارَةُ أُسْتاذَةٌ.

* * *

٤- بَعْضُ حالاتِ رَفْعِ الأَسْماءِ:

Some Functions of Nominative Case-Endings:

- Nouns occurring in titles, headings, lists, grammar notes, and as quotations, which do not constitute full meaningful sentences, are normally listed in the '**Nominative Case**'; such as the underlined nouns in the box below:

الدَّرْسُ ٱلْأَوَّلُ / نَصُّ ٱلدَّرْسِ / طَالِبٌ وَطَالِبَةٌ / التَّحِيَّاتُ وٱلتَّعَارُفْ /
هَلْ هَذا بَابٌ؟ / لُبْنانُ / إِبْراهِيمُ / ٱلتَّنْوِينُ فِي ٱلْأَسْماءِ .

- Nouns functioning as either the '**Subject**' or the '**Predicate**' of '**Equational Sentences**'
- are normally in the '**Nominative Case**'; such as the underlined nouns in the box below:

إِبْراهِيمُ طالِبٌ ./ الطَّالِبُ عَرَبِيٌّ ./ مَرْيَمُ طالِبَةٌ .

- Proper names or title nouns after the '**Vocative** or **Calling Particle**' are normally in the '**Nominative Case**'; however, these nouns in this case never receive the '*Tanween*' form of the '**Nominative**', but only one '*Ďammah*'; such as the underlined nouns of the sentences in the box below:

يا آدَمُ!/ يا إِبْراهِيمُ!/ يا مَرْيَمُ!/ يا طالِبُ!

* * *

٥- التَّذكيرُ وٱلتَّأْنيثُ فِي الأَسْماءِ:

More Notes on Gender in Nouns:

- Arabic nouns and adjectival nouns are either '**Masculine**/مُذَكَّر' or '**Feminine**/مُؤَنَّث', as was stated before.
- There is no '**Neuter**' gender in Arabic, referring to inanimate beings such as in English, as was also stated before.
- Nouns referring to animate beings would have a gender agreeing with the natural gender of the referent. Thus the word for '**mother**' in Arabic would be feminine, and the word for '**father**' would be masculine.
- All names of cities are feminine in gender.
- Names of countries are also mostly feminine in gender; the exceptions to this rule are normally marked in the dictionary and vocabulary lists. The ones listed in the box below are the most common exceptions:

الأُرْدُنَّ	السُّودانُ	العِراقُ	المَغْرِبُ	لُبْنانُ	اليَمَنُ
Jordan	Sudan	Iraq	Morocco	Lebanon	Yemen

- The gender of almost all other nouns depends on the natural gender of the referent or on
- the form of the word itself. Thus the noun (أَخ) for '**brother**' is masculine, and the noun (أُخْت) for '**sister**' is feminine.
- The *Taa Marbūṭah* (ة / ـة) suffixed to the end of nouns, mostly indicates feminine gender; such as : (طالِبَة / فاطِمَة / عَرَبِيَّة). However, there are few exceptions, which will be pointed out as they occur in future lessons.
- It is also a general rule that, whatever comes in male-female pairs in real life, are expressed in Arabic by pairs of words with or without the '*Taa Marbūtah*'; such as:

طالِب - طالِبَة / عَرَبِيّ - عَرَبِيَّة ./ أُسْتاذ - أُسْتاذَة .

- Thus, when a masculine noun with animate referent is listed, it is to be assumed that the feminine counterpart may be automatically formed by adding the '***Taa Marbūṭah***.'
- Gender in Arabic, not only identifies the sex of the referent for animate beings, but also serves an important grammatical function; masculine nouns are replaced by masculine pronouns, and are modified by masculine adjectives; feminine nouns require feminine pronouns and adjectives; for examples:

آدَمُ طالِبٌ عَرَبِيٌّ.	←	هُوَ طالِبٌ عَرَبِيٌّ.
مَرْيَمُ طالِبَةٌ عَرَبِيَّةٌ.	←	هِيَ طالِبَةٌ عَرَبِيَّةٌ.

- Besides the '*Taa Marbūṭah*' as the most prominent suffix for feminine gender, there are two other suffixes applied to a limited categories of nouns and adjectives. These are the *Alif Maqṣūrah* (ى) and the the *Alif-Hamzah* (ـاء), such as: (بُشْرَى) and (حَمْراء). These two categories will be treated with more details in future lessons.

* * *

Exercises & Activities / الدَّرسُ الثَّالِث : تَدْرِيبات وَنَشاطات

Exercise 1: (*Oral Chain Exercise*) Statement / Question with (مِنْ أَيْنَ...؟):
(The teacher makes a personal statement about where is he / she from, followed by

a direct question to a 1st student about where is he or she from, and the 1st student answers the question, then asks the same question to a 2nd student; and so on in a chain drill.)

١- أَنا مِنْ لُبْنان، مِنْ أَيْنَ أَنْتِ؟ ٢- أَنا مِنْ أَمْريكا، مِنْ أَيْنَ أَنْتَ؟

٣- أَنا مِنْ ....، مِنْ أَيْنَ ....؟

* * *

Exercise 2: (*Oral Exercise*) Forming Question with (مِنْ أَيْنَ ...؟):

Read each statement first; then form a question based on it, as in the given example:

سامِي مِنْ لُبْنان. ⇦ مِنْ أَيْنَ سامِي؟

١- هِيَ مِنْ سُورْيا. ٢- مَرْيَمُ مِن بَيْـرُوتَ.

٣- هُوَ مِنْ دِمَشْق. ٤- الطّالِبُ مِن لُبْنان.

٥- أَنـا مِنْ أَمْريكا. ٦- الأُسْتاذُ مِن مِصْرَ.

* * *

Exercise 3: (*Oral or Written*) Recognition of Case and Case-Ending Markers:

Read each sentence first; then indicate whether the underlined noun or nouns are: (**Nominative** / مَرْفوع), (**Accusative** / مَنْصوب), or (**Genitive** /مَجْرور) in **case**, and recognize which **sound- ending** mark the particular case, by choosing from the following list of signs:

(◌ٍ) / (◌ِ) / (اً) / (◌ً) / (◌َ) / (◌ٌ) / (◌ُ)

Follow the given example:

سَلَّمْتُ عَلَى الأُسْتاذِ . (مَجْرُور) (◌ِ)

١- قَرَأْتُ ٱلدَّرْسَ ٱلأَوَّلَ. ٢- سَلَّمْتُ عَلَى ٱلأُسْتاذَةِ ٱلعَرَبِيَّةِ.

٣- قابَلْتُ مَـرْيَمَ . ٤- إِبْراهِيمُ طالِبٌ عَرَبِـيٌّ .

٥- تَحَدَّثْتُ إلَى طالِبَةٍ أَمْرِيكِيَّةٍ. ٦- قَرَأْتُ كِتاباً.

٧- قابَلْتُ أُسْتاذَةً مِنْ لُبْنانَ. ٨- هُوَ أَمْرِيكِيٌّ مِنْ أُوهايُو.

* * *

Exercise 4: (*Oral / Written*) **Meaning and Gender Recognition:**

All the words in the following table are nouns or pronouns, which were introduced in lessons one and two. First, read each word, then indicate its **English meaning**; second, indicate the **gender** of each word, using the Arabic terminology for 'masculine' or 'feminine', as in the first item, done as an example to follow:

Masculine / Feminine مُذَكَّر / مُؤَنَّث	English Meaning / الـمَعنى بِالإنجليزيَّة	The Noun / الاِسْم
مُـذَكَّـر	Lebanon	لُبْنانُ
		نَصٌّ
		الدَّرْسِ
		تَحِيَّة
		سامِي
		صَديق
		مَرْيَم
		صَدِيقَة
		عَرَبِـيّ
		آدَم
		هَذا
		هِيَ
		هَذِهِ

		أمّ
		أب
		طالِبَة
		بَيْـرُوت
		طالِب
		السَّلامَة
		هُوَ

* * *

Exercise 4: (*Oral in Class/Written at Home*) Forming Feminine from Masculine:

Change the followiing nouns from Masculine to Feminine, by adding the (ة / ـة):

١- طالِب ← ....

٢- أُسْتاذ ← ....

٣- عَرَبِـيّ ← ....

٤- صَديق ← ....

٥- أَمْريكِـيّ ← ....

٦- سامِي ← ....

* * *

Exercise 5: (*Oral or Written*) Conjunction with (وَ):

Combine each pair of sentences, using the conjunction (**and** / وَ), as in the given example:

> أَنـا مِنْ لُبْنان . / فَريد مِنْ لُبْنان . ← أَنـا وَفَريد مِنْ لُبْنان .

١- هُوَ مِنْ أَمْريكا . / نانْسِي مِنْ أَمْريكا . ← ....

٢- أَنْتِ مِنْ لُبْنان . / هِيَ مِنْ لُبْنان . ← ....

٣- الأُسْتاذُ مِنْ سُورْيا . / الأُسْتاذَةُ مِنْ سُورْيا. ← ....

٤- الطَّالِبُ مِنْ بَغْداد. / الطَّالِبَةُ مِنْ بَغْداد. ← ....

٥- صَديقِي مِنْ مِصْرَ. / صَديقَتي مِنْ مِصْر. ← ....

* * *

Exercise 6: (*Oral or Written*) Variable Substitution:
Substitute the words in the numbered sentences below for the underlined word in the head sentence inside the box:

أَنـا طالِبٌ مِنْ لُبْنان.

١ - أَنْتِ ....　　٢- هِيَ ....

٢- هُوَ ....　　٤- هَذا ....

٦- هَذِهِ ....　　٦- مَرْيَمُ ....

* * *

الدَّرسُ الرَّابِع: القِراءة الجَهْرِيَّة / Reading Aloud

فِـي مَـطـارِ ٱلـقـاهِـرَة

- سافَـرَ يُوسُف مِن مَطارِ نُيويورك إلَى القاهِرَة. وَعِنْدَما وَصَلَت الطَّائِرَةُ بِسَلام، تَوَجَّهَ يوسُف إلَى قِسْمِ ٱلجَوازات لِلحُصولِ عَلى تَأْشِيـرَةِ الدُّخول.
- نَظَرَ ضابِطُ الأَمْنِ فِي جَوازِ سَفَرِهِ الأَمريكِيِّ وقالَ: ما ٱسْمُكَ ؟ قالَ يُوسُف: اِسْمِي يُوسُف إبراهيم. قالَ الضَّابِطُ: ولَكِنْ ٱسْمُكَ فِـي الجَوازِ "جوزيف أَبراهام! "

- قالَ يُوسُف : هَذا صَحِيح ، لَقَدْ غَيَّـرْتُ ٱسْمِي بَعْدَ أَحْداثِ الحادِي عَشَرَ مِن سِپتِمْبَر لِتُصْبِحَ حياتِـي سَهْلَة فِـي أمريكا .
- قالَ ضابِطُ الأَمْنِ : ولَكِنْ حياتُـكَ سَتَكونُ صَعْبَة عِنْدَما تَحْضُرُ إِلَى هُنا بِـٱسْمٍ أَجْنَبِـيّ !

* * *

مُفْرَدات وتَراكيب الدَّرس الرَّابع
Vocabulary & Linguistic Structures of the 4th Lesson

he headed (to, toward)	تَـوَجَّـهَ (إلـى)	Nouns	أَسْـمـاء
he looked	نَـظَـرَ	Cairo (*capital of Egypt*)	القاهِرَة
he said	قـالَ	the airplane	الطّائِرَة
I changed	غَـيَّـرْتُ	peace, safety (safely)	سَلام (بِسَلام)
it becomes (in order to become)	تُـصْبِـح (لِـتُـصْبِح)	department	قِسْم
it will be	تَـكُـون (سَـتَـكـون)	(of) passports	الـجَوازات (جَـواز)
you come (to)	تَـحْـضُـر (إلـى)	obtaining (*gerund*)	الـحُـصـول (على)
Particles	**أَدوات**	entry (entry visa)	الـدُّخـول (تَـأشِـيـرَة الـدُّخول)
from	مِـنْ	officer	ضـابِـط
to	إلـى	the security (the security officer)	الأَمْـن (ضـابِـط الأمْن)
and	وَ	his passport	جَـواز سَـفَـرِه
when	عِـنْـدَما	true, correct	صَـحـيـح
with	بِـ	events (an event)	أَحْـداث (حَـدَث)

to, in order to	لِـ	the eleventh (of)	الحادي عَشَر
in, at	في	September	سِپتِمْـبَـر
What ...?	ما ...؟	my life	حَـيـاتـي
however, but	وَلَـكِـنْ	easy (*feminine/masculine pair*)	سَـهْـلَـة / سَـهْـل
indeed (*emphasis particle beforepast tense verbs*)	لَـقَـدْ	your life	حَـيـاتُـكَ
after	بَـعْـدَ	difficult (*feminine/masculine pair*)	صَـعْـبَـة / صَـعْـب
here	هُـنـا	foreign (*feminine/masculine pair*)	أَجْـنَـبِـيّ / أَجْـنَـبِـيَّـة
		with a foreign name	بِـٱسْم أَجْـنَـبِـيّ
		Verbs	**أَفْعال**
		it arrived	وَصَـلَـتْ

سُـؤال
جَـواب

* * *

أَسْئِلة الفهم والاستيعاب (شَفويّا):

١- مِنْ أَيْنَ سافَرَ يُوسُف؟

٢- إِلَى أَينَ سافَر يُوسُف؟

٢- إِلَى أَيْنَ تَوَجَّهُ فِـي ٱلـمَطار ، وَلِماذا ؟

٤- لِماذا غَيَّـرَ يوسُف اسْمَهُ؟

٥- ما جَـوابُ ضـابِـطِ الأَمْن؟

الدَّرسُ الخامس: الثقافة وٱلقِيَم وٱلأمْثال:

Culture, Values & Proverbs

- The events of the 9th of September, 2001, had great negative impact on American Arabs and Muslims, who were targetted for attacks, harrassement, as a consequence of guilt by association. Many tried to hide their identities by changing their names to more American-sounding ones, though this is not a commom practice in Arab-Muslim culture.
- Observers compared the Arab-Muslim situation after 9/11 to the what happened to the Japanese after Pearl Harbor events in WWII. Actually, there were extreme voices calling for the the internment of the Arab-Muslims as was done to the Japanese after Pearl Harbor.
- However, after 9/11 there was a noticeable increase in Arab-Muslim culture, and many institutions introduced Arabic teaching into their courses.

* * *

مُختارات من الحِكَم والأمثال العربيَّة :

Selections of Arabic Proverbs & Wise Sayings:

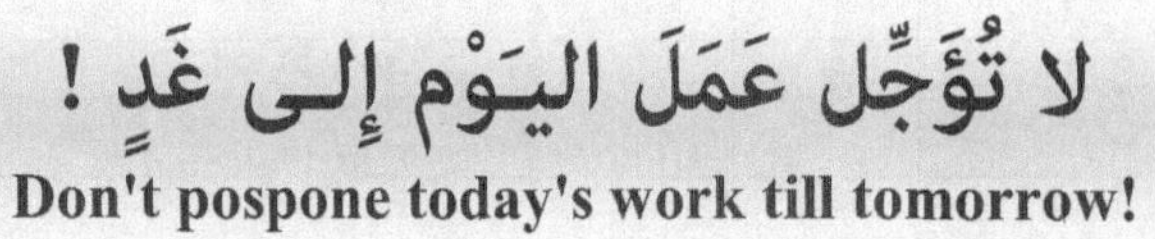

لا تُؤَجِّل عَمَلَ اليَوْم إِلى غَدٍ !

Don't pospone today's work till tomorrow!

أُطْلُبْ ٱلعِلْمَ مِنَ ٱلـمَهْدِ إِلَـى ٱللَّحْدِ !

Seek knowledge from cradle to grave!

الـمرءُ بِأَصْغَرَيْهِ : قَلْبِهِ ولِسانِهِ!

General Drills & Review / تَـمارين عامَّة ومُراجَعَة

تَـمرين ١: **Let's read the following sets of words or phrases, recall their meanings and then guess why they were grouped together under one category:**

١- مَطار / يَوْم / أُسْبُوع / نَفْس/ الرَّبيع.

٢- مُسافِرَة / أَمْريكِيَّة / مَصْرِيَّة / زِيارَة / والِدَة / عُطْلَة / جامِعَة / مُقيمَة / أُسْتاذَة / اللُّغَة العَرَبِيَّة / الإِنْجِليزِيَّة / رِحْلَة / سَعِيدَة / السَّلامَة .

٣- تَقابَلَتْ / جَرَى / قَضَيْـتُ / حَضَرْت .

٤- أَعْمَل / تَعْمَلِيـن / تَعْمَل / تُدَرِّس / أُحِبّ / أَتَعَرَّف / أَتَـمَـنَّـى .

٥- ضابِط (ضُبّاط) / حَدَث (أَحْداث) / طالِب (طُلاَّب) / قِسْم (أَقْسام)

٦- الْوِحْدَةُ الثّانِيَةُ / الطّالِبُ العَرَبِيُّ / الطّالِبَةُ الأَمريكِيَّةُ / الأُسْتاذَةُ العَرَبِيَّةُ .

٧- نَصُّ الدَّرْسِ / مَطارُ القاهِرَةِ / قِسْمُ الْجَوازاتِ / ضابِطُ الأَمْنِ .

٨- قَصِيـرَة / مِصْرِيَّة / أَمْريكِيَّة / سَعِيدَة .

٩- سافَرَ / وَصَلَتْ / تَوَجَّهَ / نَظَرَ / قالَ / غَيَّـرْتُ / تُصْبِحَ / تَحْضُرُ .

١٠- إِلـى أَيْنَ / هَل / ماذا .

تَـمرين ٢: Select any combination of words from the previous exercise to construct full meaningful sentences: (*It's advisable that you write down your sentence (s) on a sheet of paper before delivering it verbally!*)

____

____

تَـمرين ٣: From the list of <u>nouns / pronouns</u> in the shaded box, select the one most suitable tofill in the blanks in the following sentences:

أَجْنَبِـيّ / الطَّائِرَة / مَطارِ / صَحيح / قِسْمِ / القاهِرَة / ضابِط / سَفَره / حَياتـي / صَعْبَة / الحادي عَشَر / الأَمْن

١- سافرَ يوسُف إبراهيم مِن ________ نيويورك إلـى ________ .

٢- وعِندما وَصَلَت ______ بِسلام ، تَوجَّهَ يوسُف إلى ________ الجَوازات .

٣- نَظرَ ______ الأمْن فـي جَوازِ ______ سَفَره الأمريكـيّ .

٤- قالَ يوسُف : هَذا ______ ، لَقد غَـيَّـرْتُ اسْمي بَعْدَ أَحْداثِ________ ________ مِن سِبتِمْبَـر .

٥- قالَ ضابِطُ ______: ولَكِنْ حَياتُكَ سَتَكـونُ ________ عِنْدما تَحْضُـر إلـى هُنا بِاسْم ______ .

٦- غيَّـرتُ اسمي لِـتُـصـبِح ______ سَهْلَة فـي أمريكا .

* * *

تَـمرين ٤: From the list of <u>particles</u> given in the shaded box below, select the one most suitable to fill in the blanks in the following sentences; you may use some particle twice:

ما / إلـى / مَعَ / مِنْ / على / بِـــ

١- هاجَرَ يوسُف _____ مِصر _____ أمريكا. ٢- تَعَرَّفَ يوسُف _____ نانْسِـي.

٣- حَصَلَ يُوسُف _____ الجِنْسِيَّة الأمريكِـيَّة. ٤- تَوَجَّهَ يُوسُف ____ قِسْم الجَوازات.

٥- قالَ ضابِطُ الأَمْن: ____ اسْمُـكَ؟ ٦- اتَّصَلَ يوسُف ___أُخْتِـهِ.

٧- _____ اللِّقاءِ وَ _____ السَّلامَة!

* * *

تَـمرين ٥: **From among the words inside the box below, select the most suitable to fill in the blanks in the following sentences: (*Note that these verbs are from both Units 1 & 2*)**

تَحْضُـر / وَصَلَتْ / سَمَّتْـهـا /حَصَلَ / تَوَجَّهَ / تَعَرَّفَ / أَنْجَبَتْ / سافَرَ / سَتَكون / هاجَرَ / تُصْبِح / غَـيَّـرْتُ / تَزَوَّجَـهـا / قالَ / نَظَر

١- _______ يوسُف مِنْ مِصر إلـى أمريكا.

٢- _______ يوسُف على نانْسِـي و _________ .

٣- _______ نانْسِـي بِنْتاً _________ "لِينا".

٤- _______ يُوسُف على الجِنْسِيَّة الأمريكِـيَّة.

٥- _______ يُوسُف إلى القاهِرَة لِزِيارَة أُخْتِـه.

٦- _______ الطَّائِرَة إلـى مَطارِ القاهِرَة بِسَلام.

٧- فـي مَطارِ القاهِرَة ، _______ يُوسُف إلـى قِسْم الجَوازات.

٨- _______ ضابِطُ الأَمْنِ فـي جَوازِ سَفَر يُوسُف.

٩- _______ضابِطُ الأَمْن لِيُوسُف: ما اسْمُـكَ؟

١٠- قالَ يوسُف: _______ اِسْمـي حَتَّى _______حَياتـي سَهْلَة.

١١- قالَ الضَّابِطُ: ولَكِنْ حَياتُكَ _______ صَعْبَة عِنْدَما _______إلـى هُنا بِاسْم أَجْنَبِـيّ!

تَـمرين ٦: This is an interactive chain activity intended to review the vocabulay of the unit two days before the vocabulary quiz at the end of each unit.
The teacher (or one of the students) starts the activity by adressing one the learners:

- عِنْدي سُؤال لَـكَ / لَـكِ! = I have a question for you!

The addressee student responds by saying: - نَـعَمْ، تَـفَـضَّل / تَـفَـضَّلي !
(Yes, kindly go ahead!)

Then the asking person asks: - ما مَـعْـنى كَـلِمَـة (____) بِـالإنْـجـلـيـزِيَّـة ؟
What is the meaning of the word (____) in English?
(*by using the Arabic word for its English meaning*)

Alternatively, the asking person might say:

- مـا مَـعْـنى كَـلِـمَـة (____) بِـالعَـرَبِـيَّـة ؟
What is the meaning of the word (____) in Arabic?
(*by using the English word for its Arabic meaning*)

If the person being asked gets the right answer, then the questioner might comment, using one of the following Arabic complements:

- أَحْـسَـنْـتَ / أَحْـسَـنْـتِ ! = Well done!
- مُـمْـتـاز / مُـمْـتـازَة ! = Exellent!
- جَـيِّـد / جَـيِّـدَة ! = Good!
- جَـيِّـد جِـدّاً / جَـيِّـدَة جِـدّاً ! = Very good!
- رائِـع / رائِـعَـة ! = Wonderful!

Then the questioner becomes the questioned by another learner, and so on in an interactive chain drill intended to activate the vocabulary.

Let's call this "The Vocabulary Game!" (لُعْبَة الـمُفْرَدات) in Arabic, and practice it as often as possible, inside and outside the classroom!

The Third Unit / الوحدة الثَّالِثَة

الوِحْدَةُ الثَّالِثَة / 3rd Unit
الدَّرسُ الأَوَّلُ/ 1st Lesson

الضِّيافَة
Hospitality

دَعا "سالِم" صَديقَهُ "راشِد" لِلعَشاءِ مَعَهُ في بَيْتِه ، وجَرى بَيْنَهُما الحِوار التَّالي:

سالِم: أَهْلاً وَسَهْلاً ، شَرَّفْتَنا يا صَديقي ٱلعَزيز! راشِد : شَرَّفَ ٱللَّهُ مِقْدارَك!

سالِم: تَفَضَّلْ ، اِجْلِسْ هُنا! راشِد : أَشْكُرُكَ!

سالِم: كَيْفَ حالُ الوالِد والوالِدَة؟

راشِد : هُما بِخَيْر ونِعْمَة .

سالِم : ماذا تُحِبُّ أَنْ تَشْرَبَ قَبْلَ العَشاء؟

راشِد : أُحِبُّ شُرْبَ الشَّاي بَعْدَ العَشاء .

سالِم : جاري "خالِد" يُريد التَّعَرُّف عَلَيْك؟

راشِد : بِكُلِّ سُرور! أَيْنَ هُوَ؟

سالِم : سَيَحْضُرُ بَعْدَ قَليل، ثُمَّ نَأْكُلُ العَشاءَ مَعاً.

راشِد : هَلْ هُوَ مُتَزَوِّج؟

سالِم : لا ، هُوَ أَعزَب مِثْلي ومِثْلَك ، ولَكِنَّهُ قَدْ يَتَزَوَّجُ السَّنَةَ القادِمَة .

راشِد : مَعْنى ذَلِكَ أَنَّهُ خاطِب! سالِم : لا أَدْري بِالضَّبْط .

راشِد : وهَلْ تُفَكِّر في الزَّواج يا "سالِم"؟

سالِم : طَبْعاً، ولَكِن أَحْتاجُ إِلى بَعْضِ الوَقْت .

راشِد : أَنا مُتَرَدِّد في الزَّواج ! سالِم : لِماذا يا صاحِبي؟

راشِد : أَسْمَعُ عَنْ حالاتِ طَلاق كَثيرَة هَذِهِ الأَيَّام!

سالِم : الله يُسْتُر!

مُفْرَدات وتَراكيب الدَّرس الأَوَّل

Vocabulary & Linguistic Structures of the 1st Lesson

get married (he)	يَتَزَوَّج	engaged (he)	خاطِب	Nouns	أَسْماء
know (I)	أَدْري	for sure	بِالضَّبْط	hospitality	الضِّيافَة
think (about) (you)	تُفَكِّر (في)	marriage	الزَّواج	his friend	صَديقُه
need (I)	أَحْتاج	naturally, of course	طَبْعاً	his home	بَيْتِه
hear (I)	أَسْمَعُ	some time	بَعْض الوَقْت	the following dialogue	الحِوارُ التَّالي
(may He) protect!	يُسْتُر	I am hesitant	أنا مُتَرَدِّد	Welcome!	أَهْلاً وَسَهْلاً!
Particles	أَدوات	cases	حالات (حالَة)	my dear friend	صَديقي العَزيز
for	لِـ	divorce	طَلاق	God	اللهُ
with (him)	مَعَهُ	many, lots	كَثيرَة	your status, your value	مِقْدارَك
and	وَ	these days, nowadays	هَذِهِ الأَيَّام	condition, state of well-being	حال
between (both of them)	بَيْنَهُما			the father/ the mother	الوالِد / الوالِدَة
How...?	كَيْفَ ...؟	Verbs	أَفْعال	they (dual)	هُما
in, with	بِـ	to invite	دَعا - يَدْعُو	well / blessing	خَيْر / نِعْمَة
What ...?	ماذا ...؟	took place	دارَ - يَدورُ	drinking (*gerund*)	شُرْب
before / after	قَبْلَ / بَعْدَ	(you) honored (us)	شَرَّفْتَنا	the tea	الشَّاي
to, with	عَلَيْكَ (على)	May honor ...	شَرَّفَ	my neighbor	جاري
Where ...?	أَيْنَ ...؟	kindly, please	تَفَضَّلْ	getting to know (*gerund*)	التَّعَرُّف
then	ثُمَّ	sit down	اِجْلِس	(with) all pleasure	بِكُلِّ سُرور
together	مَعاً	(I) thank you	أَشْكُرُكَ	he	هُوَ
Is ...?	هَلْ ...؟	like (you)	تُحِبّ	a short while	قَليل

no	لا	drink (you)	تَشْرَب	married	مُتزَوِّج
however / but	وَلَكِنَّ / لَكِنْ	like (I)	أُحِبُّ	single	أعْزَب
may, might	قَدْ	wants (he)	يُريد	like you / like me	مِثْلِـي / مِثْلَك
O (vocative particle)	يا	will come (he)	سَيَحْضُر	the next year	السَّنَة القادِمَة
about	عَنْ	eat (we)	نَأكُل	meaning of that	مَعْنَى ذَلِك

* * *

Grammatical and Linguistic الدَّرْس الثَّاني: القَواعِد وقَضايا لُغَوِيَّة

1. The Definite Article (ألْ) .... ١- ألْ التَّعْرِيف
2. The Genitive Case: Object of Prepositions .... ٢- ألْجارُّ والـمَجْرور
3. Subject & Suffixed or Attached Pronouns .... ٣- ألْضَّمائِرُ الـمُنْفَصِلَةُ والـمُتَّصِلَة
4. The Interrogative ماذا and ما .... ٤- "ما" وَ "ماذا" الاِسْتِفْهامِيَّتان
5. The Past Tense Verb and Some of Its Full Conjugation .... ٥- ألْفِعْلُ الـماضي وتَصْرِيفاتُهُ

* * *

Notes Related to the Arabic Definite Article ١- (ال) التَّعْرِيف

- The Definite Article in Arabic is (ال), and it basically means the same as the English (**the**).
- In writing, it might appear as (أَل), with a "***Hamzah***" and a "***Fathah***" over the "***Alif***", or mostly as (اَل), without the "***Hamzah***" but with a "***Fathah***"; or as (ال), with neither the "***Hamzah***" nor the "***Fathah***".
- In pronunciation, it has variations, depending on whether it falls at the beginning of a sound sequence, or in between sound sequence, and also on whether it is followed by a '**Sun Letter**' or a '**Moon Letter**'. *(As was explained in Lesson 8, pages 21-22 of Part 1)*
- Now, let's read the following sets of sentences to further illustrate some notes related to the pronunciation of (اَل):

- اَلأُسْتاذُ مِنَ لُبنان . / اَلخَرْطومُ مَدينَةٌ عَرَبِيَّةٌ . / اَلكِتابُ جَدِيدٌ .
- مِنْ أَيْنَ ٱلأُسْتاذ؟ / أَيْنَ ٱلخُرْطوم؟ / أَيْنَ ٱلكِتابُ ٱلجَدِيدُ؟

- In the box above, the three underlined words in the first set of sentences, all start with an (آل) at the beginning of the sentences, and therefore the ***Hamzated Alif*** is fully and clearly pronounced, regardless of the way it is written. The ***Alif*** of the Definite Article in this case is called "***Hamzat-ul-Qat'*** / هَمْزَةُ الْقَطْع", which means the "**clear and fully articulated *Hamzated Alif***".
- In the box above, the three underlined words, in the second set of sentences, all start with an (آل), but not at the beginning of a sound sequence. Therefore, the '***Hamzah***' is **automatically elided** (i.e. not pronounced) and might be written with a sign of a '***Waslah***' (ٱل), or simply (ال), without any sign over the '***Alif***'. The '***Alif***' of the Definite Article in this case is called "***Hamzat-ul-Wasl*** / هَمْزَةُ الوَصْل", which means the '**elided or to be connected *Hamzated Alif***'.
- The pronunciation of the (ل) part of the Definite Article (ال), is further affected by the consonant which follows it. The words (اَلْقَمَر) for '**the moon**' and (اَلشَّمْس) for '**the sun**' are conventionally used to label the two groups of consonants; thus, (ق) is a '**Moon Letter**' and (ش) is a '**Sun Letter**'.
- In the case of '**Moon Letters**', the (ل) of the Definite Article (ال) is fully and clearly pronounced.
- In the case of '**Sun Letters**', the (ل) of the Definite Article (ال) is not pronounced; it is rather **assimilated in the following consonant**, a process resulting in adding the '***Shaddah***' (ّ) over that letter.
- The 'Sun Letters' are all **dental** or **palatal** and they are:

ت / ث / د / ذ / ر / ز / س / ش / ص / ض / ط / ظ / ل / ن

- The remaining letters are 'Moon Letters'; among these the (ج) and the (ي) are exceptions to the rule, since they are 'Moon Letters' even though they are palatal.
- In Arabic, the Definite Article occurs as an integral part of certain place proper names, and as such they cannot be dropped at will. Examples:

اَلسُّودان / اَلخَرْطوم / اَلسَّعُودِيَّة / اَلرِّياض / اَلقاهِرَة / اَلعِراق / اَلأُرْدُن اَلجَزائِر / اَلـمَغْرِب / اَلرِّباط / اَلكُوَيْت

- It is to be noted that Arabic and English do not necessarilly use the Definite Article on the same names; so each place name must be learned carefully with or without it, as the case may be.

- In English, the Definite Article '**the**' is not usually used with titles followed by names, such as: (Mr. Adam, Pofessor Smith.) In Arabic, however, the Definite Article is used with such titles in referring to the person concerned, but not in addressing him or her directly. For example, we say:

أَيْنَ السَّيِّدُ آدَم ؟ / مِنْ أَيْنَ الأُسْتاذُ وِلْيَم ؟

But we must say:

صَباحَ الخَيْرِ يا سَيِّدُ آدَمُ ! / كَيْفَ الحالُ يا أُسْتاذُ وِلْيَم ؟

* * *

The Genitive Case: Object of Prepositions — ٢- اَلجارُّ والمَجْرور

- Let's first read the following sentences, with due attention to the underlined phrases:

١- اَلخَرْطومُ فـي السُّودانِ .	٢- اَلأُسْتاذُ فـي الصَّفِّ .
٣- اَلقَلَمُ عَلَى المَقْعَدِ .	٤- اَلأُسْتاذَةُ مِنَ الرِّياضِ .
٥- هذا سُؤالٌ مِنْ فَريدٍ .	٦- تَحَدَّثْتُ إِلَى طالِبَةٍ .
٧- اَلكِتابُ لِمَرْيَمَ.	٨- نَحْنُ مِنَ الجَزائِرِ.

- The underlined parts of the sentences above are '**prepositional phrases**'; each consisting of a '**preposition**' and a following '**noun**', functioning as the '<u>object' of that preposition</u>.
- The 'object of a preposition' in Arabic is in the '**genitive case-ending**', called in Arabic (مَجْرُور).
- For the great majority of nouns, the '**genitive case-ending**' is a '***Kasrah***' (◌ِ), as in the first four examples above.
- If the noun after the preposition is indefinite, then the '**genitive case-ending**' is a '***Tanween*** of ***Kasrah***' (◌ٍ◌ٍ), as in the 5th , 6th & 7th examples above.
- For those nouns that do not take '***Tanween***', which are called '<u>**Diptotes**', the '**genitive case-ending**' is a '***Fathah***'</u> (◌َ), as in example number 7 above.

Subject & Possessive or Attached Pronouns ٣- اَلضَّمائِرُ ٱلْـمُنْفَصِلَةُ وٱلْـمُتَّصِلَةُ

- Previously, you have encountered several Arabic pronouns that stand alone, such as:

أنا / هُـوَ / هِيَ / أَنْـتَ / أَنْـتِ / نَـحْـنُ

- These are called "**subject pronouns**" corresponding to the English "**I**, **he**, **she**, **you** (*masculine*) and **you** (*feminine*)." And like English, they stand alone and function as 'subjects' in sentences.
- However, we have another set of corresponding pronouns, called in Arabic '**attached**' or '**suffixed**' pronouns, because they are attached to the end of other nouns to express possessive meaning. Thus, they correspond to the English "**my**, **his**, **her**, **your**, **our**" etc. We have also encountered examples of such pronouns in words such as:

  اسْمِي ، اسْمُكَ ، اسْمُهُ, respectively for "**my name**, **your name** & **his name**."
- In this section, we are going to formally introduce the full set of Arabic "**subject pronouns**" and the full set of the corresponding "**suffixed pronouns**" (i.e. possessive pronouns as they are called in English.)
- Let's first read the following sentences from previous lessons, with due attention to the the underlined parts of the sentences and particularly the part marked in red:

١- إسْمِي يوسُف إبراهيم . (اِسْم+ي) = (**my name**)

٢- مَساءَ ٱلخَيْرِ يا طُلّابِي ! (طُلّاب+ي) = (**my students**)

٣- ما ٱسْمُكَ ؟ (اِسْم+كَ) = (**your name**)

٤- كَيْفَ حالُكُمْ ٱليَوْمَ ؟ (حال+كُمْ) = (**your (*plural*) state of well being**)

- Each underlined part in the sentences above consists actually of two words, though they might look as one word. The first part is a **noun** (اسْم / طُلّاب / اسْم / حال), and the second part is an attached pronoun (ـِي / ـِي / ـكَ / ـكُمْ).
- Pronouns suffixed or attached to the end of nouns in Arabic are used to express possession; thus they are equivalent to English '**Possessive Pronouns**'; such as '**my**, **his**, **her**, **your**, **their**, **our**.'
- The following table contains all **subject pronouns** and their corresponding **attached possessive pronouns**, for the sake of reference and completeness of the subject, though some of these we have not encountered yet in actual sentences:

Used in Context مُسْتَعْمَلاً فِي جُمْلَة	English Equivalent مُقابِلُها بِالإنجليزِيَّة	Suffixed Pronouns اَلضَّمائِرُ الْمُتَّصِلَة	Subject Pronouns ضَمائِرُ الرَّفْعِ الْمُنْفَصِلَة
هَذا كِتابُـهُ .	his	ـهُ / ـهِ	(he) هُوَ
هَذا كِتابُـها .	her	ـها	(she) هِيَ
هَذا كِتابُـكَ .	your (*masculine singular*)	ـكَ	(you- أَنْتَ masculine)
هَذا كِتابُـكِ .	your (*feminine singular*)	ـكِ	(you- أَنْتِ feminine)
هَذا كِتابـي .	my	ـِي	(I-mas.+fem.) أَنا
هَذا كِتابُـهُمْ .	their (*masculine plural*)	ـهُمْ / ـهِمْ	(they-mas.) هُمْ
هَذا كِتابُـهُنَّ .	their (*feminine plural*)	ـهُنَّ / ـهِنَّ	(they-fem.) هُنَّ
هَذا كِتابُـكُمْ .	your (*masculine plural*)	ـكُمْ	(you-mas.) أَنْتُمْ
هَذا كِتابُـكُـنَّ .	your (*feminine plural*)	ـكُنَّ	(you-fem.) أَنْتُـنَّ
هَذا كِتابُـنا .	our (*feminine & masculine plural*)	ـنا	(we-mas.+fem.) نَحْنُ
هَذا كِتابُـهُما .	their (dual) (*feminine & masculine dual*)	ـهُما / ـهِما	(*they-mas.+fem. dual)* هُما
هَذا كِتابُـكُما .	your (dual) (*feminine & masculine dual*)	ـكُما	(you-*mas.+fem. dual)* أَنْتُما

- When a 'suffixed Arabic pronoun' is added to a noun, that noun automatically becomes **defined**, and consequently, it cannot receive '*Tanween*' or the Definite Article.
- In a '**noun-adjective**' phrase, the noun with a suffixed pronoun must therefore have an adjective with the Definite Article (الـ), as in the following examples:

> هَذا صَديقِـي الْـعَرَبِـيُّ . (This is my Arab friend.)
>
> هَذا أُسْتاذُنـا الْأَمريكِـيُّ . (This is our American professor.)

- Whatever 'case-ending' a noun with an attached pronoun should bear, it must appear on the letter before the suffixed pronoun.
- The 1st person singular suffixed pronoun (ـِي), for 'my', does not lend itself to variations in 'case-ending', since the vowel before it must always bear the '***Kasrah***', as an internal part of the process.

- The 3rd person masculine singular, the 3rd person plural, both masculine and feminine, and the 3rd person dual suffixed pronouns, change their vowels to a '***Kasrah***' if the preceding letter bears a '***Kasrah***' or a long vowel (ī / ـيـ).
- Now, let's study the examples below, and observe the points highlighted above:

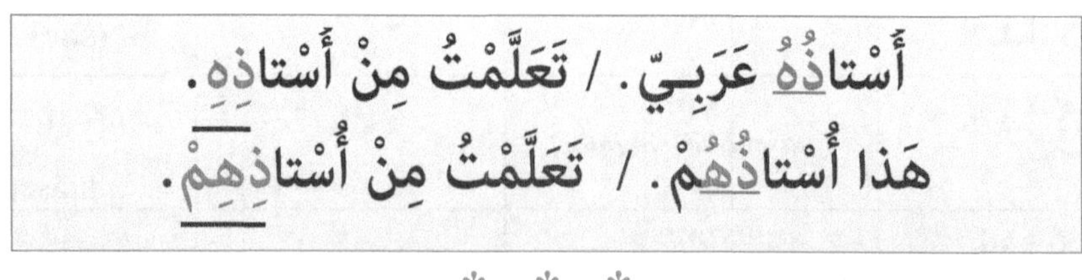

أُسْتاذُهُ عَرَبِيّ. / تَعَلَّمْتُ مِنْ أُسْتاذِهِ.

هَذا أُسْتاذُهُمْ. / تَعَلَّمْتُ مِنْ أُسْتاذِهِمْ.

* * *

٤-"ما" وَ "ماذا" الاِسْتِفْهامِيَّتان / The Interrogative Particles ما and ماذا

- In the text of the lesson, two new interrogative particles were introduced; these are (**ما**) and (**ماذا**). Both these particles will be equivalent to the English '**What…?**'. However, in Arabic they will be used for two different types of sentences.
- Let's now read the following interrogative sentences and observe the pariculars related to each of these particles:

- If we look at the two sets of questions above, we find that in the first set we are asking about the nature of two non-human objects; the first being a '**book**' and the second being a '**picture**'; in this case we will be using the particle (**ما**).
- In the second set of questions, we have pictures of a '**boy**' and a '**cat**' doing something, so the question is about the action being done; therefore the particle (**ماذا**) is followed by a verb.

* * *

٥- اَلفِعْلُ الماضي وتَصْريفاتُهُ

The Past Tense Verb and Some of Its Full Conjugation Paradigm

- The Arabic verb has basically two tenses: '**perfect**' or '**past tense**' and '**imperfect**' or '**present tense**'. The future time is derived from the 'imperfect tense' by means of certain particles which come before it.

- In this sense, the '**tense**' aspect of the Arabic verb is simpler than the English one. However, the 'conjugation' aspect is certainly more complex and elaborate than that of English. Therefore, the Arabic verb system will be introduced in installments over several lessons.
- In this lesson, we will focus on learning the five singular conjugations of the past tense verb. Now let's examine the following table before we explain more specific aspects of our focal point:

Expressed Subject, Gender & Number	**Correspond-ing Pronoun**	**Subject Marker**	**Verb Stem**	**The Verb in a Sentence**
he = آدَمُ **3rd person, masculine, singular**	هُوَ	ـَ **(*a*) over the last consonant**	كَتَبْ	كَتَبَ آدَمُ عَلَى ٱللَّوْحِ .
she = مَرْيَمُ **3rd person, feminine, singular**	هِيَ	ـَتْ (*at*)	كَتَبْ	كَتَبَتْ مَرْيَمُ عَلَى ٱللَّوْحِ .
you = أَنْتَ **2nd person, masculine, singular**	أَنْتَ	ـْتَ (*ta*)	كَتَبْ	ماذا كَتَبْتَ يا آدَمُ ؟
you = أَنْتِ **2nd person, feminine, singular**	أَنْتِ	ـْتِ (*ti*)	كَتَبْ	ماذا كَتَبْتِ يا لَيْلَى؟
I = أَنا **1st person, masculine+feminine singular**	أَنا	ـْتُ (*tu*)	كَتَبْ	كَتَبْتُ عَلَى ٱللَّوحِ .

- Arabic verbs in the '**past tense**' consist of a basic '**stem**' and a '**subject marker**' added at the end of the stem as a suffix. The 'stem' indicates the root of the verb, its basic meaning, and the tense of the verb. The 'subject marker' indicates the person, gender and number of the subject.
- Each verb in Arabic must have a '**subject**'. This 'subject' can either be an expressed noun, as in the first two sentences above, or it can be an implied pronoun, understod from the form the subject marker and context, as in the last three sentences above.
- '**Perfect**' or '**past tense**' verbs in Arabic correspond to an action that has been completed or has taken place just before the time of speaking. It doesn't matter whether the completed action took place minutes ago or a thousand years ago.
- In matters of translations, it is the context and certain contextual clues that will determine whether to use the corresponding English '**simple past**' or the '**present** or **past perfect**, such as, "**have studied**" or "**had studied**".

الدَّرسُ الثَّالِث: تَدْريباتٌ وَنَشاطاتٌ / Exercises & Activities

Exercise 1: (*Oral and Written*) Selecting the Right Preposition — تَمرين ١:

From the prepositions listed in the column to the left, select the appropriate one to fill in the blanks in the following sentences:

from = مِنْ	behind = خَلْفَ
in, at = فِـي	above, on top= فَوْقَ
on = عَلَى	with = مَعَ
to, for = لِـ	
in, with = بِـ	
till, until, to = إلَـى	

١- كُلُّنا ...... خَيْرٍ، اَلحَمْدُ ......لَّهِ!

٢- أَنا ...... لُبْنانَ ، ...... أَيْنَ أَنْتِ؟

٣- اَلكُرْسِيُّ ...... اَلـمَقْعَدِ.

٤- هَذا قَلَمٌ ...... وَرَقَةٍ.

٥- ...... اللِّقاءِ يا طُلّابِي!

٦- ...... السَّلامَةِ يا أُسْتاذُ!

* * *

Exercise 2: (*Oral and Written*) Providing the Correct "Case-Ending" — تَمرين ٢:

In the following sentences, the final vowels of the underlined words were left out. These vowel signs reflect the correct grammatical 'case-ending'. Your task is, first, to read the whole sentence, providing the appropriate missing 'case-ending'; then, second, write in the diacritical mark for the missing 'case-ending'. Follow the given example:
(Attention: To do this drill, you need to use rules learned in Units 2 and 3!)

اَلأُسْتاذ مِنْ اَلقاهِرَة. ⇦ اَلأُسْتاذُ مِنَ اَلقاهِرَةِ.

١- اَلأُسْتاذَة عَرَبِيَّة.

٢- اَلخَرطوم فِـي اَلسُّودان.

٣- اَلكِتاب عَلَى اَلـمَقْعَد.

٤- اَلطَّالِب مِن اَلأُرْدُنّ.

٥- هَلْ أَنْتَ طالِب أَمْريكِـيّ؟

٦- هَذِهِ طالِبَة مِن اَلسَّعُودِيَّة.

٧- اَلبِنْت تَكْتُبُ عَلَى اَلـلَّوْح.

٨- اَلحَمْد لِـلَّـه!

تَـمرين ٣: **Exercise 3**: (*Oral and Written*) **Transformation:** Indefinite ⇨ Definite

Follow the given example to form 'Equational Sentences' from two isolated nouns, by adding the 'Definite Article' to the first word and making it the 'Subject', then provide the correct vowel sign to both 'Subject' and 'Predicate':

أُسْتاذ - عَرَبِـيّ ← اَلأُسْتاذُ عَرَبِـيٌّ.

١- طالِبَة - أَمْريكِيَّة ← ....

٢- أُسْتاذَة - عَرَبِيَّة ← ....

٣- طالِب - أَمْريكِـيّ ← ....

٤- طالِب - عَرَبِـيّ ← ....

٥- أُسْتاذَة - أَمْريكِيَّة ← ....

* * *

تَـمرين ٤:

Exercise 4: (*Oral and Written*) **Forming Questions with** (مَنْ) **or** (ما) **or** (ماذا):

Change the statements below into questions, using (مَنْ), (ما), or (ماذا) as appropriate; follow the given examples:

هَذا أَسْعَدُ. ← مَنْ هَذا؟ / هَذِهِ وَرَقَةٌ. ← ما هَذِهِ؟
اَلـوَلَدُ يَسْأَلُ اَلأُسْتاذَ. ← ماذا يَفْعَلُ اَلـوَلَدُ؟

١- هَذا دَرْسٌ. ← ....؟

٢- هِيَ نانْسي. ← ....؟

٣- هَذِهِ لَيْلَى. ← ....؟

٤- اَلْوَلَدُ يَكْتُبُ. ← ....؟

٥- هَذا كُرْسِيٌّ. ← ....؟

٦- هُوَ أَنْوَرُ. ← ....؟

٧- هذِهِ مَرْيَمُ. ← ....؟

٨- اَلبِنْتُ تَسْأَلُ. ← ....؟

Exercise 5: (*Oral and Written*) Combining Nouns with Possessive Pronouns: تَـمرين ٥

In the following sentences you are given in parenthesis a noun and a pronoun suffix. First, combine them to form a phrase and write them down. Next, translate as in the example:

This is my book.	هَذا (كِتابٌ + ي). ← هَذا كِتابِـي.
How are you (*plural*)?	كَـيْفَ (حالٌ + كُمْ)؟ ← كَـيْفَ حالُـكُـمْ؟

He is my friend | ١- هُوَ (صَديقٌ + ي) . ← هُوَ صديقي.

She is my friend | ٢- هِيَ (صَديقَةٌ + ـهُ). ← هِيَ صديقته

You are our student | ٣- أَنْتُمْ (طُلاَّبٌ + نا). ← أَنْتُمْ طلابنا.

How are you ? | ٤- كَيْفَ (حالٌ + كَ)؟ ← كَيْفَ حالك ؟

Is this her picture | ٥- هَلْ هَذِهِ (صُورَةٌ + ها)؟ ← هَلْ هَذِهِ صورتها؟

Is this your book | ٦- هَلْ هَذا (كِتابٌ + كِ)؟ ← هَلْ هَذا كتابك ؟

* * *

Exercise 6: (*Written / Oral*) Conjugation of Verbs: تَـمرين ٦:

Fill in the blank cells of the following table by writing the appropriate form of the past tense conjugations, then read the five forms of each verb conjugations:

أنا	أَنْتِ	أَنْتَ	هِيَ	هُوَ
استقبلت	استقبلتِ	استقبلتَ	استقبلت	اِسْتَقْبَلَ
جلست	جلستِ	جلستَ	جَلَسَتْ	جلس
ركبت	ركبتِ	رَكِبْتَ	ركبت	ركب
ضحكت	ضَحِكْتِ	ضحكت	ضحكت	ضحك
تَـوَجَّـهْتُ	توجهتِ	توجهتَ	توجهت	توجه
حصلت	حَـصَلْتِ (على)	حصلت	حصلت	حصل
هاجرت	هاجرتِ	هـاجَرْتَ	هاجرت	هاجر

			فَشِلَتْ	
				قالَ

* * *

تَمرين ٧: **Exercise 7: (*Review / Oral*) Question Formation / Noun-Pronoun Substitution:**

The student reads the expressed subject as it is, then he / she asks a question with (مَنْ ...؟), substituting in the process the appropriate corresponding subject pronoun to replace the expressed subject, as in the given example:

الأُسْتاذُ أَسْعَدُ. ← مَنْ هُوَ؟

١- الطَّالِبُ ٱلعَرَبِيُّ ← .... ؟ ٢- ٱلأُسْتاذَةُ ← .... ؟

٣- السَّيِّدُ خَليلٌ ← .... ؟ ٤- ٱلوَلَدُ ← .... ؟

٥- الطَّالِبَةُ ٱلأَمْريكِيَّةُ ← .... ؟ ٦- ٱلصَّديقَةُ ← .... ؟

* * *

تَمرين ٨: سُؤال وَجَواب:

Exercise 8: (*Review / Oral*) Question Formation / Answers Using (مِنْ أَيْنَ؟)

The teacher introduces the pair of words, consisting of a personal proper name and a place proper name; the 1st student forms a question, using the interrogative (مِنْ أَيْنَ ؟) followed by the person's name; then a second student answers the question, using the preposition (مِنْ), followed by the name of the place, as in the given example:

آدَمُ - ٱلسَّعُودِيَّةُ. ← مِنْ أَيْنَ آدَمُ؟ ← مِنَ السَّعُودِيَّةِ.

١- يوسُفُ - مِصْرُ	٢- لَيْلَى - ٱلكُوَيْتُ	٣- مَرْيَمُ - لُبْنانُ
٤- مَرْيَمُ - ٱلرِّياضُ	٥- سامِي - السُّودانُ	٦- أَحْمَدُ - بَغْدادُ
٧- أَسْعَدُ - ٱلخَرْطومُ	٨- فادِيَةُ - ٱلْعِراقُ	٩- إِبْراهِيمُ - ٱلجَزائِرُ
١٠- آدَمُ - ٱلمَغْرِبُ	١١- فَضْلٌ - ٱلرِّباطُ	١٢- مُحَمَّدٌ - ٱلأُرْدُنُّ

Exercise 9: **Reviewing a Reference List:** **تـمرين ٩:**

Go to '**Part 4**' of the book to review the 1st reference list entitled '**The Pronouns: Independent (Subject) and Attached (Possessive)**, **page 336.**

* * *

الدَّرسُ الرَّابع: القِراءة الجَهْرِيَّة / Reading Aloud

فـي بَيْتِ سُعاد وكَمال

- اِسْتَقْبَلَتْ "سُعادُ" وزَوْجُها "كَمال" يوسُف فِـي ٱلْمَطار. ثُمَّ رَكِـبوا سَيَّارَةَ أُجْرَةٍ، وتَـوَجَّهوا إِلَـى ٱلبَيْتِ. أَعَدَّتْ سُعادُ طَعامَ ٱلعَشاءِ، وجَلَسُوا جَمِيعاً إِلَـى مائِدَةِ ٱلطَّعام.
- بَدَأَت سُعادُ ٱلحَديثَ أَثْناءَ ٱلعَشاءِ، وقالَتْ: لَقَدْ نَوَّرْتَ مِصْرَ يا أَخِي ٱلعَزيزُ! رَدَّ يُوسُف: شُكْرا يا أُخْتِي ٱلعَزيزَةُ ويا عَزيزِي كَمال، لَقَدْ اِشتَقْتُ لَكُم كَثيـراً ولِكُلِّ مِصْر.
- قالَ كَمال: كَمْ نَتَمَنَّى لَوْ أَنَّ زَوْجَتَكَ نانْسِي وٱبْنَتَكَ لِينا كانَتا مَعَنا هُنا اليَوْم! سَكَتَ يوسُفُ قَلِيلاً ثُمَّ قالَ: مَعَ الأَسَف، نانْسِي لَمْ تَعُدْ زَوجَتِي!
- تَنَهَّدَتْ سُعادُ وقالَتْ: طَلَّقْتَها؟! رَدَّ يُوسُف: اتَّفَقْنا علَى ٱلطَّلاقِ بَعْدَ أَنْ فَشِلْنا فِـي حَلِّ خِلافاتِنا.
- سَأَلَ كَمال: وَماذا عَن ٱبْنَتِكَ لِينا؟ أَجابَ يوسُف: هِيَ فِي حَضانَةِ أُمِّها، ولِـي حَقُّ ٱلزِّيارَةِ كُلَّ أُسْبُوع.
- سَأَلَتْ سُعادُ: وماذا عَن ٱلبَيْتِ؟ أَجابَ يُوسُف: حَصَلَتْ نانْسِي عَلَيْهِ بِـقَرارٍ مِن ٱلـمَحْكَمَةِ أَيْضاً.
- قالَتْ سُعاد: يَبْدو أَنَّ ٱلقانونَ يَقِفُ إِلَى جانِبِ ٱلـمَرْأَةِ فِي أَمريكا! ما رَأْيُكَ فـي أَنْ نُهاجِرَ إِلَـى أَمريكا يا زَوْجِي ٱلعَزيز؟! ضَحِكَ كَمالُ وقالَ: تُهاجِرينَ وَحْدَكِ يا عَزيزَتـي إِذا أَرَدْتِ!

* * *

الـمُفرَدات (مُرتَّبة حَسَب ورودها فـي النَّصّ):

الكلِمَة العَرَبِيّة	الـمَعْنَى الإنْجليزي	الكلِمَة العَرَبِيّة	الـمَعْنَى الإنْجليزي
بَيْت (بُيوت)	house (houses)	سُعاد / كَمال	*Su'aad* (*female proper name*) *Kamaal* (*male proper name*)
اِسْتَقْبَلَت	welcomed, received (she)	وزَوْجُها (وَ+زَوْج+ها)	and her husband
فـي الـمَطار	at the airport	ثُـمَّ	then (*conjunction particle*)
رَكِـبُـوا	they rode	سَيّارَة (سَيّارات)	a car (cars)
أُجْرَة	rent, hire	سَيّارَة أُجْرَة	a taxi, a cab
وَتَـوَجَّهُـوا إلـى (و+تَـوَجَّهَ+وا)	and they headed for (to)	أَعَدَّتْ	prepared (she)
طَعام العَشاء	supper, dinner food	جَلَسُوا (جَلَس+وا)	they sat
جَميعـاً	all	مائِدَة الطَّعام	the table spread, the dinning table
بَـدَأَتْ	she began	الحَديث	(the) talking
أَثْناءَ العَشاء	during supper	وقالَتْ	and she said
لَـقَدْ نَـوَّرتَ	indeed you have brightened	يا أَخِي (أَخ+ي)	O (*vocative particle*) my brother
العَزيز / العَزيزَة	the dear one (*masculine / feminine*)	رَدَّ يُوسُف قـائِـلاً	Yousuf <u>responded</u> saying
شُـكْـراً	thanks	أُخْتِي ٱلعَزيزَة	my dear sister
عَزيزِي (عَزيز+ي)	my dear	اِشْـتَـقْـتُ إِلَـيْـكُـمْ (إلـى+كُم)	I longed for you all! (<u>Idiomatically</u>: I missed you!)
وَلِـكُـلِّ (و + لِ+كُلّ)	and for all	كَـثِـيـراً	a lot, much
قـالَ	he said	كَمْ نَتَمَّى ...!	How much we wish! (*Idiom for hopeful expectation*)
لَـوْ أَنَّ	if (that)	زَوْجَتَكَ (زَوْجَة+كَ)	your wife
نانْسِي	Nancy (*Arabic transcription for a foreign name*)	وابْنَتَكَ (و+ابْنَة+كَ)	and your daughter
مَعَـنـا (مَعَ+نـا)	with us	سَـكَـتَ	fell silent, paused (he)
قَـلِـيـلاً	a little	ثُـمَّ قالَ	then he said

is no longer (*to be learned as an idiom*)	لَمْ تَعُدْ	regretfully (<u>Literally</u>: with regret!)	مَعَ الأَسَف
sighed (she)	تَنَهَّدَتْ	my wife	زَوْجَتِي
we agreed on	اِتَّفَقْنا عَلَى	you divorced her?	طَلَّقْتَها)
after (that)	بَعْدَ أَنْ	the divorce	الطَّلاق
solving	حَلّ	we failed	فَشِلْنا فِي
(he) asked	سَأَلَ	our disagreements	خِلافاتِنا (خِلاف+ات+نا)
(he) responded	أَجابَ	And what about...?	وَماذا عَنْ ...؟
in the custody of her mother	فِي حَضانَةِ أُمِّها	she (is)	هِيَ
right (rights) (of)	حَقّ (حُقوق)	and I have (*<u>literally</u>: and for me*)	وَلِي (وَ+لِ+ي)
every week	كُلَّ أُسْبُوع (أَسابِيع)	the visitation (*gerund*)	الزِّيارَة
And what about the house?	وماذا عَنِ ٱلبَيْت؟	she asked	سَأَلَتْ
through (by) a decision	بِقَرار (بِ+قَرار)	she got it, she obtained it (*the house*)	حَصَلَتْ عَلَيْهِ (عَلى+هِ)
also, likewise	أَيْضاً	from the court (courts)	مِنَ المَحْكَمَة (مَحاكِم)
the law (laws)	القانونَ (قَوانِين)	it seems that (*to be learned as an idiom*)	يَبْدُو أَنَّ
side (of) (sides)	جانِب (جَوانِب)	stands by, supports	يَقِفُ إِلَى
What's your opinion about? What do you think about?	ما رَأْيُكَ فِي ...؟ (رَأْي+كَ)	the woman (women)	المَرأَةِ (النِّساء) *
over there	هُناكَ	that we immigrate to	أَنْ نُهاجِر إِلَى
laughed (he)	ضَحِكَ	my husband	زَوْجِي (زَوْج+ي)
alone, by yourself	وَحْدَكِ	you immigrate (*2nd person feminine conjugation of the verb*)	تُهاجِرِينَ
if you wish	إِذا أَرَدْتِ	O' my dear one	يا عَزِيزَتِي

أَسْئِلة ٱلفهم وٱلاستيعاب (شَفويّا):

سُـؤال
جَـواب

١- مَن اسْتَقْبَلَ يوسُف فـي ٱلـمَطار؟ ٢- إِلَى أَينَ سافَرَ يُوسُف؟

٣- إِلَـى أَيْنَ تَـوَجَّـهُـوا؟ ٤- ماذا أَعَدَّت سُعادُ؟

٥- أَيْـنَ جَـلَسُوا جَـمِـيعاً؟ ٦- هَلْ سَافَرَتْ نانْسِي ولِينا مَع يوسُف؟

٧- لِماذا اتَّفَقَ يوسُف ونانسي على ٱلطَّلاق؟ ٨- مَنْ حَصَلَ عَلى حَـضانَـةِ لِينا؟

٩- علَى ماذا حَصَلَتْ نانْسِي بِقَرارِ ٱلـمَحْكَمَة؟

١٠- ماذا قالَتْ سُعادُ عَن ٱلقانونِ فـي أَمْريكا؟

* * *

الدَّرسُ الخامس : الثَّقافَة وٱلقِيَم وٱلأَمْثال :Culture, Values & Proverbs

- مُقارَنة بين تقاليد الزَّواج فِي العالَم العربِيّ- الإسلامِيّ والغَرْب عُمومًا؛
- Comparing and contrasting marriage traditions in the Arab-Muslim world with those in the West;
- الطَّلاقُ مَكروه فِي الثَّقافة العربيّة - الإسلامِيَّة (أَبْغَضُ الحلالِ إلى الله الطَّلاق)؛
- Divorce is frowned upon in Arabic-Islamic culture, and is practiced as last resort after mediation failure;
- الفَرْق بَين حضانَة الأَطفال فِي العالَم العَرَبِيّ-الإسلامِيّ والغَرب.
- Comparing and contrasting the issue of children custidy after divorce btween Arab and Western cultures.

* * *

مُختارات مِن الحِكم والأمثال العربيّة:

Selections of Arabic Proverbs & Wise Sayings:

اَلحُبُّ أَعْمَى !

Love is blind!

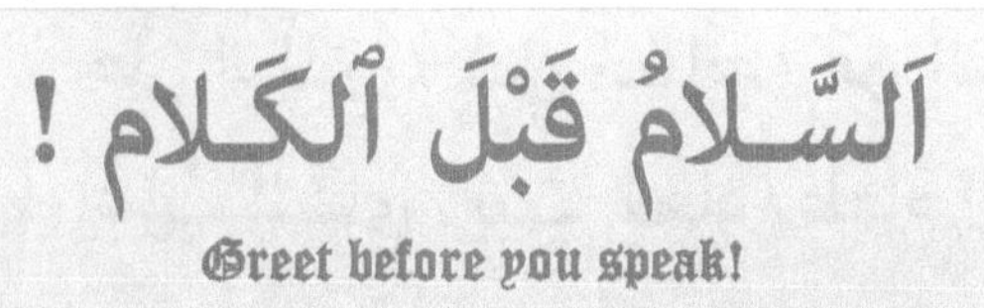
اَلسَّلامُ قَبْلَ ٱلكَلام !
Greet before you speak!

General Drills & Review / تَـمارين عامَّة ومُراجَعَة

تَـمرين ١:

Let's read the following sets of words or phrases, <u>recall their meanings</u> and <u>then guess why they were grouped together under one category</u>:

١- أَهْلاً وسَهْلاً ! / شَرَّفْتَنا ! / شَرَّفَ اللّهُ مِقْدارَك! / تَفَضَّل ! / اللّهُ يُسْتُر ! / بِكُلِّ سُرور!

٢- كَـيْـفَ / مـاذا / لِـمـاذا / هَـلْ / أَيْـنَ / ما .

٣- يـا / هُـنـا / مَعَـهُ / فـي / أَنْ / بَعْدَ / مَعـاً / قَـبْـلَ / لا / ثُمَّ / قَـدْ / إِلـى / عَنْ / عَلَيْكَ / لَكِـنَّـهُ / إِلَـيْـكُمْ / لَـم / لـي / مِنْ / هُـنـاكَ .

٤- هُوَ / هُما / أَنـا / هِيَ .

٥- سالِم / راشِد / سُعاد / كَمال / يُوسُف / نانسـي / لِـينـا .

٦- زَوْج / زَوْجَـة / اِبْـنَـة / أُخْـت / أَخ / والِـد / والِـدَة .

٧- بَيْت / سَيَّارَة / حَضانَة / قَرار / حَلّ / أُسْبُوع / رَأْي / أُجْرَة / طَعام / شَراب / صَديق / جار / أَعْزَب / خاطِب .

٨- البَيْت / العَشاء / الـمائِدَة / العَزيز / الطَّلاق / الـمَحْكَمَة / الزِّيارَة / الشَّاي / القانون / الـمَرْأَة / التَّعَرُّف / الزَّواج / الوَقْت / الضِّيافَة .

٩- شَرَّفَ / قالَ / رَدَّ / أَجابَ / تَـوَجَّـهُـوا / رَكِـبُـوا / جَلَسُوا .

١٠- اِسْتَقْبَلَتْ / بَدَأَتْ / قالَتْ / حَصَلَتْ / أَعَدَّتْ .

١١- أُحِبُّ / أَشْكُـرُ / أَسْمَعُ / تَشْرَبْ / تُفَكِّر / يَتَزَوَّج / أَدري / أَحْتاج / يَسْتُـر / نَـأْكُـل / يَـقِـف / نُـهاجِـر / تُـهاجِـرين / يَـبْـدو .

١٢- طَبْعاً / مَعاً / جَميعاً / كَثيراً / أَيْضاً / قَليلاً .

١٣- فِـي ٱلـمَطارِ / إِلـى ٱلـبَـيْـتِ / عَلى مـائِـدَةِ ٱلطَّعامِ / مَعَ ٱلأَسَفِ / عَلَى الطَّلاقِ / فـي حَضانَةِ / عَنِ ٱلبَيْتِ / بِقَرارٍ / مِن الـمَحْكَمَةِ / إِلـى جانِبِ .

١٤- شُرْبُ ٱلشَّاي / بَيْتِ سُعاد / طَعامَ العَشاءِ / مائِدَةِ الطَّعامِ / حَلِّ خِلافاتِنا .

تـمرين ٢: (واجِب فـي ٱلبَيْت!)

(Homework) Select any combination of words from the previous exercise to construct a full meaningful sentence: (*It's advisable that you write down your sentence (s) on a sheet of paper before delivering it verbally!*)

___

___

* * *

تـمرين ٣:

From the list of nouns in the shaded box, select the one most suitable to fill in the blanks in the following sentences:

مِصْر / لِينا / البَيْتِ / العَزيز / زَوْجُها / الـمَطار / أُجْرَة / جَميعاً / طَعامَ / زَوْجَتَك

١- اِستَقبلتْ سُعاد و ________ كَمال يوسُف فـي ________ .

٢- ركِبوا سَيَّارَة ________ وتَوَجَّهوا إلـى ________ .

٣- أعدَّتْ سُعاد ________ العَشَاءِ ، ثُمَّ جَلسُوا ________إلـى الـمائِدَة.

٤- لَقَدْ نَوَّرْتَ ________ يا أخـي ________!

٥- كَمْ نَتَمَـنَّى لَوْ أَنَّ ________ نانسي وٱبْنَتَك ________ كانتا مَعَنا .

* * *

تـمرين ٤:

From the list of particles given in the shaded box below, select the one most suitable to fill in the blanks in the following sentences

يا / عَنْ / فـي / أَنْ / لـي / على / بِـ / مِنْ / إلـى / إلَـيْكُمْ / لَمْ / مَعَ

١- شَرَّفْتَنا ______ صَديقـي العَزيز!   ٢- ماذا تُحِبُّ______ تَشْرَب ؟

٣- هَلْ تُفَكِّرُ ______ الزَّواج ______ سالِم ؟

٥- أَسْمَعُ ـــــ حالاتِ طَلاقٍ كَثيـرَة .

٦- اِتَّفَقَ يُوسُف ونانْسي ـــــ الطَّلاق .

٧- هِيَ فـي حَضانَةِ أُمِّها ، وَ ـــــ حَقُّ الزِّيارَة .

٨- لَقَدْ اشْتَقْتُ ـــــ كَثيـراً !

٩- يَبْدو ـــــ القانونَ يَقِفُ ـــــ جانِبِ الْمَرأَةِ ـــــ أمْريكا .

١٠- حَصَلَتْ نانسي ـــــ البَيْتِ ـــــ قَرارٍ مِن الـمَحْكَمَة .

١١- قالَ يُوسُف : ـــــ الأَسَفِ ، نانْسي ـــــ تَعُدْ زَوْجَتـي !

* * *

تَـمرين ٥: (صَواب / خَطَأ)

To do the following exercise, let's first learn two additional Arabic words for "true" and "false"! Then based on your general comprehension of the narrative of the *Yusuf*'s story line in the three texts you studied thus far, read the statements below, and then answer whether each is <u>true</u> or <u>false</u>, using one of the following Arabic terms:

false, wrong = خَطأ / true, correct = صَواب

صَواب

خطأ

١- "يوسُف" <u>أَصْلاً</u> مِن "مِصر". ( ) <u>originally</u>

٢- هاجَرَ "يوسُف" إلى "أمريكا" قبلَ خَمس سَنوات. ( )

٣- تعَرَّف "يوسُف" على "نانسِي" في "مِصْر". ( )

٤- غَيَّر "يوسُف" اسمهُ عِندَ حُصولِه على الجِنْسِيَّة الأمريكيَّة. ( )

٥- اِتَّصَلَ يُوسُف بِأُخْتِـهِ سُعاد ، وأَخْبَرَها عَنْ مَوْعِدِ حُضُورِه . ( )

٦- سافر "يوسف" إلى "القاهِرَة" مِن مَطار "شيكاغو". ( )

٧- توجَّهَ "يوسُف" فـي القاهِرة إلى قسم الجَوازات للحُصول على تأشيرة الدّخول. ( )

٨- اسْمُ "يوسُف" في جَواز سَفره الأمريكيّ هو "يوسف إبراهيم." ( )

٩- غَـيَّـر "يوسُف" اسمه بعد أحداث الحادي عشر من "سِبتِمبَر." ( )

١٠- اِستَقبل زَوْجُ "سُعاد" <u>وَحْدَهُ</u> "يوسُف" فـي المطار. ( ) <u>alone</u>

١١- كانت زَوجَة "يوسُف" وابنتُه "لينا" معه في هذه الزِّيارَة. (   )

١٢- اِتَّفَق "يوسُف" و"نانسي" على الطلاق بَعد الفَشَل في حلّ الخِلافات. (   )

١٣- "لينا" في حَضانة "يوسُف" وأمَّها لها حَقُّ الزيارة مرَّة في الأسبوع. (   )

١٤- حَصَلَت "نانسي" على البيت بِقرار مِن المَحكمة. (   )

١٥- "كمال" يُريد أن يُهاجِرَ إلى أمريكا. (   ) wants to

* * *

تَمرين ٦:

Practice the five singular conjugations of the past tense verbs by selecting five
of the verbs you learned thus far to fill in the blanks in the following table:

هُوَ	هِيَ	أَنْتَ	أَنْتِ	أَنا
سافَرَ	سافَرَتْ	سافَرْتَ	سافَرْتِ	سافَرْتُ

* * *

تَـمرين ٧: This is an interactive chain activity intended to review the vocabulay of
the unit, two days before the vocabulary quiz at the end of each unit. The teacher (or one
of the students) starts the activity by adressing one of the learners:

- عِنْدي سُؤال لَكَ / لَكِ! = I have a question for you!

- نَعَمْ ، تَفَضَّل / تَفَضَّلي! The addressee student responds by saying:
(Yes, kindly go ahead!)

Then the asking person asks: - ما مَعْـنى كَـلِـمَـة (____) بِٱلإنْـجـلـيـزِيَّـة ؟

What is the meaning of the word (____) in English?
(*by using the Arabic word for its English meaning*)

Alternatively, the asking person might say:

- ما مَعْـنى كَـلِـمَـة (____) بِٱلـعَرَبِـيَّـة ؟

What is the meaning of the word (____) in Arabic?
(*by using the English word for its Arabic meaning*)

If the person being asked gets the right answer, then the questioner might comment, using one of the following Arabic complements:

- أَحْـسَـنْـتَ / أَحْـسَـنْـتِ ! = Well done!
- مُـمْـتـاز / مُـمْـتـازَة ! = Exellent!
- جَـيِّـد / جَـيِّـدَة ! = Good!
- جَـيِّـد جِـدّاً / جَـيِّـدَة جِـدّاً ! = Very good!
- رائِـع / رائِـعَـة ! = Wonderful!

Then the questioner becomes the questioned by another learner, and so on in An interactive chain drill intended to activate the vocabulary.

Let's call this "The Vocabulary Game!" (لُعْبَة ٱلـمُفْرَدات) in Arabic, and practice it as often as possible, inside and outside the classroom!

نهاية الوحدة الثَّالثة

The Fourth Unit / الوحدةُ الرَّابِعَةُ

اَلوِحْدَةُ ٱلرَّابِعَةُ:
الدَّرْسُ الأَوَّلُ

فِـي ٱلسُّوق

ذَهَبَ آدَمُ وزَمِيلَتُهُ "سالي" إِلى مَتْجَرٍ كَبيرٍ لِلمَلابِسِ يَتَرَدَّدانِ عَلَيْهِ كَثيراً، حَيْثُ أَصْبَحا مَعْرُوفَيْنِ لَدى ٱلبائِعِينَ هُناكَ

- البائِع : أَهْلاً وسَهْلاً يا آنِسَةُ سالي، ويا سَيِّد آدَم!
- سالي :أَهْلاً بِكَ يا سَيِّدُ خالِد!
- آدم : ماذا سَتَشْتَرينَ اليَوْمَ يا سالي؟
- سالي: أَحْتاجُ إِلى مِعْطَفِ جِلْد ، وكَنْزَة صُوف ، ولَفْحَة.
- آدم: أَنا بِحاجَةٍ إِلى قُمْصانٍ شَتَوِيَّة و"پلوڤر" وبَنْطَلون "جِينْز".
- سالي: أَنا أَيْضاً سَأَشْتَري تَنُّورَة طَويلَة وبَعْضَ ٱلجَوارِب .
- آدم: أُنْظُري يا سالي إِلى هَذِهِ ٱلبِدَل، عَلَيْها تَخْفِيض كَبِير!
- سالي: أَنا لا أَراكَ تَلْبَسُ ٱلبِدَل، أَلَيْسَ كَذلِكَ؟
- آدم: أَلْبَسُها في ٱلمُناسَباتِ ٱلرَّسْمِيَّة؛ فَعَلى سَبيلِ ٱلمِثال، عِنْدي مُقابَلَةُ عَمَل في ٱلشَّهْرِ ٱلقادِمِ.
- سالي: وماذا عَنْ عَمَلِكَ ٱلحالِي؟
- آدم: سَأَتْرُكُهُ لِأَنَّ وَقْتَهُ لا يَتَناسَبُ مَعَ جَدْوَلِ فَصْلِ ٱلرَّبِيع.
- سالي: لا أَعْرِفُ كَيْفَ تُوَفِّقُ بَيْنَ ٱلدِّراسَةِ وٱلعَمَل!

– آدم: لَيْسَ عِنْدي خِيار ... يَجِبُ أَنْ أَعْمَل!

– سالي: جَرَّبْتُ العَمَلَ فـي السَّنَةِ الأُولَـى مِنَ الجامِعَة ، ولَـكِنِّـي لَمْ أَسْتَمِرَّ طَويلاً.

– آدم: الوَضْعُ الـمِثالِـيُّ هُوَ التَّـرْكِـيـزُ على الدِّراسَة إِذا كُنْتِ غَـيْـر مُحْتاجَة لِلْعَمَل.

– سالي: الوَقْتُ مَرَّ بِسُرْعَة، هَيَّا بِنا إِلـى الـمُحاسِبِ لِـنَدْفَـعَ ثَـمَنَ الـمَلابِس!

– آدم: وهُوَ كَـذَلِك!

* * *

Vocabulary / اَلـمُفْرَدات

in the market	فـي السُّوق	fourth / the fourth	رابِعَة / الرَّابِعَة
and his colleague Sally	وزَميلَتُـهُ سالـي	Adam went	ذَهَبَ آدَمُ
for clothing	لِـلْمَلابِس	to a big store	إِلى مَتْجَرٍ كَبيرٍ
where they have become known	حَيْثُ أَصْبَحا مَعْرُوفَيْنِ	they (both) frequent it a lot	يَتَرَدَّدانِ عَلَيْـهِ كَثيراً
the selling clerk	البائِع (البائِعين)	by the selling clerks there	لَدى البائِعينَ هُناكَ
O Miss Sally	يـا آنِسَةُ سالـي	Welcome!	أَهْلاً وَسَهْلاً
Hello to you!	أَهْلاً بِـكَ	and O Mr. Adam	ويا سَيِّد آدَم
What will you buy today?	ماذا سَتَشْتَرينَ اليَوْمَ؟	O Mr. Khalid	يا سَيِّدُ خالِد
a leather coat	مِعْطَف جِلْد	I am in need of	أَحْتاجُ إِلـى
and a scarf	ولَفْحَة	and a wool sweater	وكَـنْزَة صُوف
winter shirts	قُمْصان شَتَوِيَّة	I am in need of	أَنا بِـحاجَةٍ إِلـى
and a jeans pants	وبَنْطَلون "جِينْز"	and a pullover	و"پلوڤر"
a long skirt	تَـنُّورَة طَـويلَة	I will also buy	أَنا أَيْضاً سَـأَشْتَـري
Look at...!	أُنْظُري إِلَـى ...!	and some socks	وبَعْضَ الجَـوارِب

on them (there is)	عَلَيْها (عَلَـى+ـها)	these suits (a suit)	هَذِهِ البِدَل (بَدْلَة)
I don't see you	أنا لا أَراكَ	big discount	تَخْـفِيض كَـبِـيـر
Is'nt that so?	أَلَـيْسَ كَـذَلِـكَ؟	wearing suits	تَـلْبَسُ البِدَل
on official occasions (an occasion)	فـي الـمُناسَباتِ الرَّسْمِيَّة (مُناسَبَة)	I wear them	أَلْبَسُها (أَلْبَسُ+ـها)
I have a job interview	عِنْدي مُقابَلَةُ عَمَل	so, for example	فَـعَلى سَبيلِ الـمِثال
And what about your current job?	وماذا عَنْ عَمَلِـكَ الـحالِـي؟	in the coming month (months)	فـي الشَّهْرِ القادِمِ (شُهُور)
because its time	لِأَنَّ وَقْـتَـهُ	I will leave it	سَـأَتْـرُكُـهُ
with the schedule (schedules)	مَعَ جَدْوَلِ (جَداوِل)	does not suit	لا يَـتَـناسَبُ
I do not know	لا أَعْرِفُ	of the Spring Semester (seasons)	فَصْلِ الرَّبِيع (فُصُول)
between studying and working	بَيْـنَ الدِّراسَةِ والعَمَل	how do you balance	كَـيْفَ تُـوَفِّـقُ
I must work	يَـجِبُ أَنْ أَعْمَلَ	there is no choice for me	لَيْسَ عِنْدي خِيار
in the first year	فـي السَّنَةِ الأُولَـى	I tried work	جَـرَّبْتُ الـعَمَلَ
however	ولَـكِـنِّـي	of the university	مِنَ الـجامِعَة
the ideal situation	الوَضْعُ الـمِثالِـيُّ	I did not last long	لَمْ أَسْتَمِرَّ طَويلاً
if you were	إِذا كُـنْـتِ	it is to focus on studying	هُوَ التَّـرْكِيزُ علـى الدِّراسَة
time has passed quickly	الوَقْتُ مَـرَّ بِسُرْعَـة	in no need for work	غَيْـر مُحْتاجَة لِـلْعَمَل
the accountant, the cashier (accountants)	الـمُحاسِبِ (مُحاسِبُون)	Let's go to	هَيَّا بِنا إِلـى
Let it be so! (*idiom to express agreement*)	وهُوَ كَـذَلِـك!	to pay the price of the clothes	لِـنَدْفَعَ ثَـمَنَ الـمَلابِس

Grammatical and Linguistic Notes / اَلدَّرْسُ الثَّانـي : اَلقَواعِدُ وَاَللُّغَوِيّاتُ

1. Notes on Using Some Title Words for Courtesy ١- بَعْض أَلقابِ اَلـمُجامَلَة

- The words (أُسْتاذ / أُسْتاذَة) are the Arabic male-female equivalent of the English title '**professor**' for a higher education instructor. However, the use of the term differs somewhat from English.
- In Arabic common usage, not only a professor at a college is called (أُسْتاذ / أُسْتاذَة), but in general, any person in a learned field, such as lawyers, literary persons, journalists and teachers in schools are called by such titles.
- In addition, the masculine form (أُسْتاذ) is used to address any man who seems to be educted, whether an acquaintance or a stranger on the street, to whom it is appropriate to show courtesy or respect.
- For a lady in these circumstances, one uses the title (آنِسَة) for a '**Miss**', especially non-married young lady, and the word (سَيِّدَة) for a '**Madam**'.
- Moreover, in Arabic, the first name rather than the family name is commonly used with these titles.
- If the speaker is using any of the above title terms to refer to a 3rd person, and not in addressing a person directly, then the Definite Article (ال) is added to them.
- Now, let's read the following sentences and observe the points explained above in context:

أَهْلاً وسَهْلاً يـا آنِسَةُ سالـي! / صَباحَ النُّورِ يـا سَيِّدُ خالِد!

كَيْفَ حالُكِ يـا سَيِّدَةُ مَرْيَم؟ / كَيْفَ حالُكَ يـا أُسْتاذُ آدَم؟

هَلْ أَنْتِ ٱلآنِسَةُ سالـي؟ / مِنْ أَيْنَ ٱلأُسْتاذُ آدم؟

هَلِ ٱلسَّيِّدُ خالِد مَوْجود هُنا؟ / هَلِ ٱلسَّيِّدَةُ مَرْيَمُ فـي مَكْـتَبِـها؟

* * *

2. Demonstrative Phrases .... ٢- تَراكِيبُ أَسْماءِ الإِشارَة

- Let's first read the following sentences, paying attention to the underlined parts of the sentences:

١- هَلْ أَنْتَ بائِعٌ فـي هَـذا ٱلـمَتْجَرِ؟	٢- هَـذِهِ ٱلآنِسَةُ مِنْ أَمْريكا.
٣- هَـذا ٱلقَميصُ شَتَوِيٌّ.	٤- هَـذِهِ ٱلتَّنُّورَةُ طَويلَة.
٥- هَلْ هَـذا ٱلـمِعْطَفُ مِنَ ٱلصُّوف؟	٦- هَلْ هَـذِهِ ٱلبَدْلَـةُ غالِيَة؟

- The underlined parts of the sentences above are examples of Arabic linguistic structures called '**Demonstrative Phrases.**'
- A 'Demonstrative Phrase' consists of a 'Demonstrative Pronoun', such as هَـذا or هَـذِهِ and a noun with the Definite Article.
- The 'Demonstrative Pronoun' must be of the same gender and number as the noun that forms a phrase with it.
- The 'Definite Article' in the noun plays a very important role in the 'Demonstrative Phrase'; since it binds the 'Demonstrative Pronoun' and the noun into a single unit. However, the 'Definite Article' in the 'Demonstrative Phrase' is not translated into English; it serves only to bind the two words into a single unit. If the 'Definite Article' is omitted, the result is two separate units.
- Now, compare the two pairs of sentences below and translate them into English:

هَـذا ٱلـمَتْجَرُ لِـلمَلابِسِ. ⟺ هَـذا مَتْجَرٌ كَبيـرٌ.

هَـذِهِ ٱلبَدْلَـةُ مِنْ ٱلصّوفِ. ⟺ هَـذِهِ بَدْلَـةٌ صُوفِـيَّـةٌ.

* * *

٣- اَلخَبَرُ ٱلصِّفَةُ ومُوَافَقَتُهُ لِلْمُبْتَدَإ

3. Predicate Adjectives and Agreement with the Subjects:

- When we introduced the '**Equational Sentences**' or '**Nominal sentences**' in Unit 1, we said that the 'Predicate' of an 'Equational Sentence' can be a noun that is also an adjective; in the sense that it has adjectival meaning.
- Let's now read and study the following sentences, then further explain the particulars related to this type of linguistic structure:

١- اَلأُسْتاذُ عَرَبِيّ .	⟺	اَلأُسْتاذَةُ عَرَبِيَّة .
٢- هَلْ أَنْتَ أَمرِيكِي؟	⟺	هَلْ أَنْتِ أَمْرِيكِيَّةٌ ؟

- Each underlined word in the sentences above is functioning as a '**predicate**' in an 'equational sentence'.
- Moreover, each of these words is also an **adjective**; in the sense that it further modifies the noun preceding it by providing additional information. An 'adjective' can also be called a '**modifier**' of the 'subject'.
- In Arabic, 'adjectives' in general have varying forms indicating **case**, **definiteness**, **indefiniteness**, **gender** and **number**. However, unlike regular nouns, they do not receive the suffixed pronouns.
- A '**predicate adjective**' is always in the '**nominative case**' and '**indefinite**'.
- However, it varies in both **gender** and **number**. So, if the 'subject' is 'masculine singular', for example, then the 'predicate' must be the same, as in the first two sentences above. But, if the 'subject' is 'feminine singular', for example, then the 'predicate' must be the same, as in the second two sentences of the two sets above.

* * *

4. *Iḍāfah* Linguistic Structures .... ٤- تَراكِيبُ الإِضافَة

- The underlined parts of the sentences below are examples of a very common Arabic linguistic structure called '*Iḍāfah* / الإِضافة'; a word which means '**addition**' or '**annextion**'.
- Let's now read and translate the following sentences, with particular attention to the underlined parts, which are the focus of what we are going to learn about '*Iḍāfah*:

Are you the cashier of the store ? / هَلْ أَنْتِ مُحاسِبَةُ ٱلْمَتْجَرِ؟

This is the schedule of the Spring Semester . / هذا جَدْوَلُ فَصْلِ ٱلرَّبِيعِ .

Let's pay the price of the clothes? / هَيَّا نَدْفَعْ ثَمَنَ ٱلْمَلابِسِ؟

Sally is Adam's colleague in studying. / سالي زَمِيلَةُ آدَم فِي ٱلدِّراسَةِ .

- As we can see from the examples above, the '*Idāfah* in its simplest form is a phrase consisting of two nouns, the second immediately following the first with nothing separating them. These nouns are called in this book the **first term** and the **second term** of the '*Idāfah*.
- The '*Idāfah* is the Arabic way to express a **possessive** relationship between two nouns; the **first term** being the **possessed** and the **second term** being the **possessor**. The second term gives further information about the first term.
- The '*Idāfah* usually corresponds to an English linguistic structure with an '**of-relationship**', as the first three examples above, or to a structure involving the **possessive ('s)** or (s'), as in the fourth example above, or to a structure where the two English nouns are directly juxtaposed, the first modifying the second ; as in the fifth example above.
- The first term of an '*Iḍāfah*' may be in any grammatical case-ending, depending on its function within a sentence. However, the second term must always be '**genitive**', as in the following examples:

هَذا مَـتْـجَـرُ ٱلْـمَـلابِـسِ . / (*first term nominative*)
دَفَـعْتُ ثَـمَـنَ ٱلْـمَـلابِـسِ. / (*first term accusative*)
ذَهَبَ آدَمُ وسالـي إلـى سُوقِ ٱلْـمَدِينَـةِ . / (*first term genitive*)

- The first term of an '*Idāfah*' never receives the Definite Article (ال) or the '*Tanween*'.
- However, the second term may have either. Now, study the following pairs of sentences in comparative perspective:

• هُوَ مُحاسِبُ مَتْجَرٍ .	← هُوَ مُحاسِبُ ٱلْـمَتْجَرِ.
• آدَمُ طالِبُ جامِعَةٍ .	← آدَمُ طالِبُ جامِعَةِ ٱلقاهِرَةِ.
• سالـي طالِبَةُ لُغَةٍ .	← سالـي طالِبَةُ ٱللُّغَةِ ٱلعَرَبِيَّةِ.

- Previously, we have learned that a noun after the 'Vocative Particle (يـا) is in the 'nominative case-ending'; however, if that noun is the first term of an '*Idāfah*', then it is changed to the 'accusative case-ending'. Compare the following pairs of sentences:

يا أُسْـتـاذُ!	← يا أُسْـتـاذَ ٱلـلُّـغَـةِ ٱلـعَـرَبِـيَّـةِ!

* * *

5. The Interrogative Particle (أَ) .... ٥- أَداةُ الاِسْتِفْهام (أَ)

- In addition to (هَلْ) , introduced earlier, there is another 'interrogative particle' with the same general function of introducing a question, which may be answered with "Yes /نَعَمْ or No /لا".
- This particle is the (أَ), and since it consists of only one character, it is written as part of the following word.
- In most cases these two interrogative particles may be used interchangeably, as in the following examples:

هَلْ هُوَ بائِعُ مَلابِس؟	←	أَهُوَ بائِعُ مَلابِس؟
هَلْ هِيَ مِنْ أَمْريكا؟	←	أَهِيَ مِنْ أَمْريكا؟
هَلْ سالي طالِبَةٌ جامِعِيَّةٌ؟	←	أَسالي طالِبَةٌ جامِعِيَّةٌ؟

- However, there are situations where only (هَلْ) is appropriate; and that is with words beginning with the Definite Article (ألْ), such as:

هَلِ ٱلسُّوقُ قَريبٌ؟ / هَلِ ٱلأُسْتاذَةُ جَديدَة ؟

هَلِ ٱلطَّالِبُ فِي مَكْتَبِ ٱلأُسْتاذِ ؟ / هَلِ ٱلآنِسَةُ عَرَبِيَّة؟

- If we want to form a question from a statement that has a negative meaning because of a negative word, such as (لا) or (لَيْسَ), then only the (أَ), is appropriate; such as:

أَلَيْسَ كَذَلِكَ؟ / أَلا تَكْتُبُ دَرْسَكَ؟ / أَلَيْسَ الأُسْتاذُ فِي مَكْتَبِهِ؟

* * *

٦- تَصْريفاتُ ٱلفِعْلُ ٱلماضي في حالاتِ ٱلجَمْع

6. The Past Tense Verb and Its Five Plural Conjugation Paradigm:

- In this lesson, we will focus on learning the five plural conjugations of the past tense verb, corresponding to the five singular ones covered in the previous unit. Now let's examine the following table before we explain more specific aspects of our focal point:

Implied Subject, Gender & Number	Corresponding Pronoun	Subject Marker	Verb Stem	The Verb in a Sentence
they = هُمْ 3rd person, masculine, plural	هُمْ	ـُوا (uu)	ذَهَبْ	ذَهَبُوا إِلى ٱلسُّوقِ .
they = هُنَّ 3rd person, feminine, plural	هُنَّ	ـْنَ (na)	ذَهَبْ	ذَهَبْنَ إِلى ٱلسُّوقِ.
you = أَنْتُمْ 2nd person, masculine, plural	أَنْتُمْ	ـْتُمْ (tum)	ذَهَبْ	لِماذا ذَهَبْتُمْ إِلى ٱلسُّوقِ؟
you = أَنْتُنَّ 2nd person, feminine, plural	أَنْتُنَّ	ـْتُنَّ (tunna)	اِشْتَرَيْ	ماذا اشْتَرَيْتُنَّ مِن ٱلسُّوقِ؟
I = نَحْنُ 1st person, mas. + fem., plural	نَحْنُ	ـْنا (naa)	اِشْتَرَيْ	اِشْتَرَيْنا مَلابِسَ مِنَ ٱلسُّوقِ.

- As you have learned in the previous unit, Arabic verbs in the '**past tense**' consist of a basic '**stem**' and a '**subject marker**' added at the end of the stem as a suffix. The 'stem' indicates the root of the verb, its basic meaning, and the tense of the verb. The 'subject marker' indicates the person, gender and number of the subject.

- Each verb in Arabic must have a '**subject**'. This 'subject' can either be an expressed noun, such as: (الأَوْلادُ كَتَبُوا على ٱللَّوْحِ .) or it can be an implied pronoun, understood from the form the subject marker and context, as in all the sentences in the box above.
- '**Perfect**' or '**past tense**' verbs in Arabic correspond to an action that has been completed or has taken place just before the time of speaking. It doesn't matter whether the completed action took place minutes ago or a thousand years ago.
- In matters of translations, it is the context and certain contextual clues that will determine whether to use the corresponding English 'simple past' or the 'present or past perfect, such as, "have studied" or "had studied".

- In the sentences above, the verb (كَتَبُوا) can be used to refer to an action undertaken by an exclusively male group, of more than two, or to a mixture of males and females. On the other hand, the verb (كَتَبْنَ) is used to refer to an action undertaken by an exclusively female group. (Important Note: the *Alif* in this suffix must be there in writing, though it doesn't have phonetical value (i.e. it's not pronounced)

- In the same manner, the verb (كَتَبْتُمْ) can be used to refer to an action undertaken by an exclusively male group, of more than two, or to a mixture of males and females. Whereas, the verb (كَتَبْتُنَّ) is used to refer to an action undertaken by an exclusively female group.

- As to the 1st person plural conjugation (كَتَبْنا), it has only one form whether the group is exclusively males, exclusively females or a mixture of both genders.

- Now, let's study the following conjugation table of ten past tense verbs introduced thus far in first four units:

نَحْنُ	أَنْتُنَّ	أَنْتُمْ	هُنَّ	هُمْ
دَرَسْنا	دَرَسْتُنَّ	دَرَسْتُمْ	دَرَسْنَ	دَرَسُوا
سَافَرْنا	سَافَرْتُنَّ	سَافَرْتُمْ	سَافَرْنَ	سَافَرُوا
هَاجَرْنا	هَاجَرْتُنَّ	هَاجَرْتُمْ	هَاجَرْنَ	هَاجَرُوا
تَعَرَّفْنا	تَعَرَّفْتُنَّ	تَعَرَّفْتُمْ	تَعَرَّفْنَ	تَعَرَّفُوا
ذَهَبْنا	ذَهَبْتُنَّ	ذَهَبْتُمْ	ذَهَبْنَ	ذَهَبُوا
عَمِلْنا	عَمِلْتُنَّ	عَمِلْتُمْ	عَمِلْنَ	عَمِلُوا
تَقَابَلْنا	تَقَابَلْتُنَّ	تَقَابَلْتُمْ	تَقَابَلْنَ	تَقَابَلُوا
نَظَرْنا	نَظَرْتُنَّ	نَظَرْتُمْ	نَظَرْنَ	نَظَرُوا (إِلَى)
قُلْنا *	قُلْتُنَّ *	قُلْتُمْ *	قُلْنَ *	قَالُوا

* * *

الدَّرْسُ الثّالِثُ: تَدْرِيباتٌ وَنَشاطات / Exercises & Activities

Exercise 1: (*Oral and Written*) **Using the Appropriate Form of CourtesyTitles:**
From among the courtesy titles on the left, select the one form most appropriate to fill in the blanks in the sentences on the right: (*Do not use any one more than once!*)

أَسْتاذُ
الأُسْتاذَةُ
آنِسَةُ
اَلآنِسَةُ
سَيِّدُ
السَّيِّدُ
سَيِّدَةُ
السَّيِّدَةُ

١- صَباحَ ٱلخَيْرِ يا .... أَسْعَد!

٢- كَيْفَ حالُكِ يا .... سالي؟

٣- هَلْ .... مَرْيَمُ فِي ٱلسُّوقِ؟

٤- هَلْ .... آدَمُ فِي غُرْفَتِهِ؟

٥- مَنْ أَنْتِ يا ....؟

٦- أَنا .... ٱلجَدِيدَةُ فادِيَة.

٧- مِنْ أَيْنَ أَنْتَ يا ....؟

٨- إِلى ٱللِّقاءِ يا .... خالِد!

* * *

Exercise 2: (*Oral Chain Exercise*) **Question Formation Using a 'Demonstrative Phrase':**
The teacher introduces 'Equational Sentences' containing 'Demonstrative Pronouns' as their 'Subjects.' The student forms a question with (مَنْ ...؟) and adding the Definite Article (ال) to the noun to form a 'Demonstrative Phrase'; as in the given example:

هَذا طالِب . ⇦ مَنْ هَذا ٱلطّالِب؟

١- هَذا مُدَرِّس.

٢- هَذِهِ طالِبَةٌ جَديدَة.

٣- هَذِهِ رَئِيسَة.

٤ - هَذا أُسْتاذٌ عَرَبِيّ.

٥- هَذا طالِب.

٦- هَذِهِ سِكْرِتيرَةٌ جَديدَة.

٧- هَذِهِ مُدَرِّسَة.

٨- هَذا رَئِيسٌ جَديد.

* * *

Exercise 3: (*Oral and Written*) **Substitution: Predicate Adjective Agreement:**

Substitute the following given subjects for the underlined words in the model sentence, making the appropriate necessary changes to the 'Predicate Adjectives':

اَلْأُسْتاذُ عَرَبِيّ.	اَلْأُسْتاذَةُ عَرَبِيَّة.

١- هُوَ ....   ٢- هِيَ ....

٣- هَلْ أَنْتَ .... ؟   ٤- هَلْ أَنْتِ .... ؟

٥- هَذا ....   ٦- هَذِهِ ....

٧- أَنا ....   ٨- نانسي ....

٩- السَّيِّدُ خليل ....   ١٠- اَلآنِسَةُ سَلْمَى ....

* * *

Exercise 4: (*Oral and Written*) **Recognizing and Marking the *Idāfah* Structure:**

Identify the ***Idāfah*** phrase in each of the following sentences by saying the phrase aloud, then underline it, as in the given example:

سَلْمَى مُحاسِبَةُ ٱلْمَتْجَرِ.

١- خَلِيل مُدَرِّسُ ٱللُّغَةِ ٱلعَرَبِيَّةِ.   ٢- هَذَا قَلَمُ ٱلأُسْتاذِ.

٣- يَكْتُبُ نَصَّ ٱلدَّرْسِ.   ٤- اَلأُسْتاذُ جُورْج رَئِيسُ ٱلقِسْمِ.

٥- كِتابُ ٱلطَّالِبِ جَدِيد.   ٦- قَلَمُ ٱلأُسْتاذِ عَلَى مَقْعَدِ ٱلطَّالِبَةِ.

٧- هَذا مَكْتَبُ ٱلْمُحاسِبَةِ.   ٨- هَلْ هُوَ أُسْتاذُ لُغَةٍ؟

* * *

Exercise 5: (*Oral, Written and Translation*) **Forming *Idāfah* Structures:**

Form ***Idāfah*** relationship between the words in parenthesis, adding or eliminating what is necessary to apply the rules, then translate into English. Follow the given example:

(كِتابٌ - الطَّالِبُ) عَلَى المَقْعَدِ. ⟸ كِتابُ ٱلطَّالِبِ عَلَى ٱلمَقْعَدِ.
The student's book is on the desk.

١- صَديقي فِي (الْمَكْتَبُ - الرَّئِيسُ). ⟸ ....

٢- (سِكْرتِرَةٌ - الْقِسْمُ) جَدِيدَةٌ. ⟸ ....

٣- تَكْتُبُ مَرْيَمُ (نَصٌّ - الدَّرْسُ). ⟸ ....

٤- هَذا (أُسْتَاذٌ - اللُّغَةُ الْعَرَبِيَّةُ). ⟸ ....

٥- (رَئِيسٌ - القِسْمُ) فِي (مَكْتَبُ- السِّكْرتيرَةُ). ⟸ ....

* * *

Exercise 6: Forming Questions with (هَلْ) or (أَ) or Both:

In most cases, (هَلْ) and (أَ) can be used interchangeably. However, in certain situations one or the other must be used. Fill in the blanks with the appropriate interrogative particle. If both can be used then indicate them as in the examples:

هَلْ هَذا دَرْسٌ جَديدٌ؟ / أَهَذا دَرْسٌ جَدِيدٌ؟ /
هَلْ ٱلرَّئِيسُ فِي مَكْتَبِهِ؟ / أَلَيْسَ ٱلأُسْتاذُ فِي مَكْتَبِهِ؟ / أَلَا تَسْأَلُ ٱلْمُدَرِّسَ؟

١- .... هِيَ أَمْريكِيَّةٌ؟
٢- .... لَيْسَ كَذَلِكَ؟
٣- .... لا تَكْتُبُ دَرْسَكَ الآنَ؟
٤- .... السِّكْرتِيرَةُ فِي مَكْتَبِها؟
٥- .... هذا كِتابُكَ؟
٦- .... هُوَ طالِبٌ أَمْريكِيٌّ؟
٧- .... الطَّالِبَةُ ٱلجَدِيدَةُ فِي ٱلصَّفِّ؟
٨- .... لَيْسَ ٱلمُدَرِّسُ فِي الصَّفِّ؟

* * *

Exercise 7: (*Review: Oral*) Combining Nouns with Possessive Pronouns:

In the following sentences you are given a pair of noun-suffix pronouns in parenthesis. Combine them together so you can first read the two as one unit. Then, write them down as one unit and attempt a translation of the sentence, as in the given examples:

كَيْفَ (حالُ + كُمْ) ؟ ← كَيْفَ حالُكُمْ ؟	How are you (*plural*)?

١- هُوَ (صَديقٌ + ي) .
٢- هِيَ (أُسْتَاذَةٌ + ـه) .
٣- هَلْ أَنْتِ (صَدِيقَةٌ + ـهُ) ؟
٤- أَنْتُمْ (طُلاَّبٌ + نـا) .
٥- كَيْفَ (حَالٌ + كَ) ؟
٦- هَلْ هَذِهِ (صُورَةٌ + ها) ؟
٧- هذا (بَيْتٌ + نا) الْجَديدُ.
٨- هَذِهِ (مَلابِسُ + هُمْ) .
٩- هَلْ هذِهِ (سَيَّارَةٌ + أَنْتُم) ؟
١٠- هَلْ هَذِهِ (أَقْلامٌ + أَنْتُنَّ) ؟

* * *

Exercise 8: (*Oral / Written*) Conjugation of Verbs:
Fill in the blank cells in the following table by writing the appropriate form of the conjugation, then reading the five forms of each verb conjugations:

هُمْ	هُنَّ	أَنْتُمْ	أَنْتُنَّ	نَحْنُ
تَرَكُوا				
	ذَهَبْنَ			
		أَحْضَرْتُمْ		
			شَاهَدْتُنَّ	
				بَدَأْنا

Exercise 9: Reviewing Two Reference Lists:

Go to '**Part 4**' of the book to review the reference lists entitled **"Names of Arab Counries, Their Capital Cities, and Related Nationality Words" page 337.**

* * *

الدَّرْسُ الرَّابِعُ: نَـصُّ القِراءَة / Reading Text

فِـي سُوقِ خان ٱلخَلِيلي

- تَرَكَ يوسُف ٱلعَمَلَ فِي الشَّرِكَةِ التِّجارِيَّة، وبَدَأَ يَعْمَلُ فِي ٱلتِّجارَةِ ٱلحُرَّة، كَرَجُلِ أَعْمالٍ مُتَخَصِّص فِي ٱلاِستِيراد وٱلتَّصْدير، حَيْثُ يَسْتَوْرِدُ ٱلتُّحَفِ ٱلفِرعَونِيَّةِ وٱلـمُنْتَجاتِ القُطْنِيَّةِ مِن مِصْر لِيَبيعَها فِي أَمريكا . كَذَلِكَ، فَهُو يُصَدِّرُ بَعْضَ البَضائِع الأَمريكِيَّة إِلَى مِصر .
- ذَهَبَ يوسُف إِلَى سوقِ "خان ٱلْخَلِيلِي" لِيُقابِلَ ٱلحاجّ عَلِيّ الطَّنْطاوِي، وهُوَ تاجِرٌ مَعْرُوفٌ فِي مِصْر .
- قالَ يُوسُف : صَباحَ ٱلخَيْـرِ يا حاجُّ عَلِيّ! رَدَّ ٱلحاجُّ عَلِيّ: صَباحَ ٱلنُّورِ يا أُستاذُ يوسُف! أَهلاً وسَهلاً بِكَ فِي مِصْر!
- قالَ يوسُف: لَقَدْ وَصَلَنِي "فاكْس" بِـٱلبَضائِعِ ٱلَّتِي تُرِيدُها، فَأَحْضَرْتُ لَكَ بَعَضَ ٱلعَيِّنات . قالَ ٱلحاجُّ عَلِيّ : على بَرَكَـةِ ٱلـلَّـه ، دَعْنِي أُشاهِدُها!
- أُعْجِبَ ٱلحاجُّ عَلِيّ بِعَيِّناتِ ٱلأَلعابِ ٱلتَّعلِيمِيَّةِ ومَلابِسِ ٱلرِّياضَة. ثُمَّ اتَّفَقا عَلَى ٱلأَسعارِ، ووَضَعَ طَلَبَ شِراء لِكَـمِّـيَّـةٍ مِنها .

الـمُفردات (مُرتَّبة حَسَب ورودها في النَّصّ):

المَعْنَى الإِنْجليزي	الكلِمَة العَرَبِيّة	المَعْنَى الإِنْجليزي	الكلِمَة العَرَبِيّة
Khan Al-Khalili (*a proper name for a popular traditional market in Cairo*)	خان الْخَليلي	market (markets)	سُوق (أَسْواق)
as a business man	كَـرَجُلِ أعْمال (كَـ+رَجُل)	free trade	التِّجارَةِ الْحُرَّة
importing	الاِسْتِـيراد	specializing (in)	مُتَخَصِّص (فِـي)
whereby	حَيْثُ	and exporting	والتَّصْدير
gift articles (an article of art)	التُّحَفِ (تُحْفَة)	he imports	يَسْتَوْرِدُ
and products	والْمُنْتَجات (مُنْتَج)	Pharaonic	الفِرعَوْنِيَّة
to sell them	لِـيَبيعَها (لِـ+يَبيعَ+ها)	cotton-made	القُطْنِيَّة
merchandise, goods	البَضائِع (بِضاعَة)	he exports	يُصَدِّرُ
the pilgrim (*honorific title*) *	الحاجّ	to meet	لِـيُقابِلَ (لِـ+يُقابِلَ)
a merchant	تاجِر (تُجّار)	*Ali At-Tantawi* (*male proper name*)	عَلِيّ الطَّنْطاوي
responded (he)	رَدَّ	well-known, famous (*masculine/feminine*)	مَعْرُوف / مَعْرُوفَة
fax (*transcription*)	فاكْس	I received (Lit: reached me)	وَصَلَنِي (وَصَلَ+نِـي)
that, which (*relative pronoun*)	الَّتِي	with the goods	بِـالبَضائِع (بِـ+البَضائع)
so I brought	فَـأَحْضَرْتُ (فَـ+أَحْضَرْتُ)	you want (them)	تُرِيدُها (تُرِيدُ+ها)
May it be God's benediction! (*linguistic idiom to express approval and hope*)	على بَرَكَةِ الله	the samples	العَيِّنات (عَيِّنَة)
look at (them)	أُشاهِدُها (أُشاهِدُ+ها)	let me	دَعْنِي

the games	الأَلْعابِ (لُعْبَة)	was pleased with	أَعْجبَ (بِـ)
and clothing, clothes	ومَلابِس (و+مَلابِس)	(the) educational	التَّعليمِيَّة
they (two) agreed on	اِتَّفقا (عَلَى)	sports	الرِّياضَة
and he placed	ووَضَعَ (و+وَضَعَ)	the prices (price)	الأَسعار (سِعْر)
for a quantity	لِـكَمِّيَّة (لِـ+كَمِّيَّة)	a purchase order	طَلَبَ شِراء
		of them	مِنْها (مِنْ+ها)

سُؤال
جَواب

* * *

أَسْئِلة الفهم والاستِيعاب (شَفويّا):

١- ما ٱلعَمَلُ ٱلَّذي تَرَكَهُ يوسُف ؟ which, what ٢- ماذا بَدَأَ يَعْمَلُ يوسُف؟

٣- فِي أَيِّ تِجارَةٍ حُرَّةٍ هُوَ مُتَخَصِّص؟ which ٤- ماذا يَسْتَوْرِدُ يوسُف مِن مِصر؟

٥- ماذا يُصَدِّرُ يوسُف مِن أَمريكا؟ ٦- إِلَى أَيْنَ ذَهَبَ يوسُف؟ولِماذا؟

٧- مَن هُوَ ٱلحاجُّ عَلِيّ الطَّنطاوي؟

٨- ماذا أَحْضَرَ يوسُف لِلحاج عليّ ٱلطَنْطاوي؟

٩- بِـماذا أُعْجِبَ ٱلحاجّ عليّ ٱلطَنْطاوي؟ ١٠- علَى ماذا (عَلامَ) اتَّفَقا؟

* * *

الدَّرْسُ الخامِسُ: الثقافةُ والقِيَمُ والأمثالُ

(أ) يَشرح ٱلْمدرّس / ٱلْـمُدرِّسَة بعض ٱلقَضايا ٱلْـمُتصلة بِـما يلي:

The instructor explains in English some matters related to the following:

- فريضَة ٱلحَجّ فِي الإسلام، وفِكْرَة "الحاجّ" كَلَقَب تَكْريمِيّ؛
- The "Pilgrimage" as a Pillar of Islam, and the idea of the "Pilgrim" as an honorific title.
- الكُنْيَة بِـ(أَبو) و (أُمّ) و (اِبْن) فِي الثَّقافة العربِيَّة الإِسلامِيَّة، ونَماذِج لِذلكَ، مِثل: أَبو بكر، أُمّ الْمُؤمِنين، اِبْنُ خَلْدون؛

- **Nick-namiming by using the "Father of…", "Mother of…", "Son of…", "Prince of…" and examples of this tradition.**

- الأسواق التَّقليدِيَّة القديـمة في العالَم العَربِيّ - الإسلامِيّ ، مِثل: خان الخليلي ، سوق الحميدِيّة، سوق الـموسكِي، وغيرها.

- **The ancient traditional popular "*Sūqs*" in the Arab World and examples of such markets and their features.**

- عَدَمُ انْتِشار ظاهرة الجَمْع بَيْـنَ العَمَلِ والدِّراسَة فـي الـمُجتَمعات العربِيَّة، مُقارنَةً بِـما هُو مألوف فـي أَمريكا.

- **The absence of combining between study and work among the university students in the Arabic societies, as compared with the situation in America.**

* * *

(ب) مُختارات مِن الحِكم والأمثال العربيّة :

لَيْسَ كُـلُّ ما يَلْمَعُ ذَهَباً.
Everything that glitters is not gold.

لاَ تُؤَجِّلْ عَمَلَ ٱليَوْمِ إِلَى غَدٍ!
Do not postpone today's work until tomorrow!

* * *

تَـمارين عامَّة ومُراجَعَة:

تَـمرين ١: **Let's read the following sets of words or phrases, recall their and then guess why they were grouped together under one category:**
(Look for clues in the English phrases in the shaded box at the bottom of the page!

١- صَباحَ الخَيْـر ! - صَباحَ النُّور ! / أَهْلاً وسَهْلاً بِك ! على بَرَكَةِ الله !

٢- كَـ (كَرَجُلٍ) / حَيْثُ / لِـ (لِيَبيعَها) / كَذلِكَ / بِـ (بِكَ) / لَـ (لَكَ) / ثُمَّ .

٣- آنِسَة / تِجارَة / تاجِرَة / حاجَّة / بِضاعَة / عَيِّنَة / كَمِّيَّة / بَرَكَة / لُعْبَة / لُغَة .

٤- أُسْتاذ / أُسْبوع / اِسْم / رَجُل / سُوق / تاجِر / سِعْر .

٥- عَمَل (أَعْمال) / تُحْفَة (تُحَف) / بِضاعَة (بَضائِع) / تاجِر (تُجَّار) / عَيِّنَة (عَيِّنات) / لُعْبَة (أَلْعاب) / سُوق (أَسْواق) / مَكْتَب (مَكاتِب) / سُؤال (أَسْئِلَة) / جَواب (أَجْوِبَة) /رَئِيس (رُؤَساء) / مَقْعَد (مَقاعِد) / أُسْبوع (أَسابِيع).

٦- فِي مَكْتَبٍ / فِي الـمَساءِ / فِي الصَّباحِ / مِنْ أَصْلٍ لُبْنانِـيٍّ / مُسافِرٌ إِلَى الخارِجِ / فِي الشَّرِكَةِ / فِـي التِّجارَةِ / إِلَـى سُوقِ خان الخَلِيلِي / عَلَى بَرَكَةِ اللَّه / عَلى الأَسْعارِ / مَعَ الأَسَفِ / مِن الـمَحْكَمَةِ / إِلَـى جانِبِ.

٧- مِعْطَفُ جِلْدٍ / كَنْزَةُ صُوفٍ / فَصْلُ الرَّبِيعِ/ بَرَكَـةِ اللَّهِ / عَيِّناتُ الأَلْعابِ / مَلابِسُ الرِّياضَةِ.

٨- حَسَناً / أَهْلاً وسَهْلاً / جَمِيعاً / شُكْراً / كَثِيـراً / قَلِيلاً / مَرَّةً / أَيْضاً.

٩- الأُسْبوعَ القادِمَ / الشَّرِكَةِ التِّجارِيَّةِ / التِّجارَةِ الحُرَّةِ / البَضائِعِ الأَمريكِيَّةِ / الأَلْعابِ التَّعْلِيمِيَّةِ.

١٠- تَفَضَّلْ! / اِجْلِسْ! / اُنْظُرِي! / هَيَّا!

١١- سَتَشْتَرِينَ / سَأَشْتَرِي / سَأَحْضُرُ / سَأَتْرُكُـهُ.

١٢- أَحْتاجُ / أَراكَ / أَعْرِفُ / أَدْرِي / أَعْمَلُ / أُحِبُّ / أَسْتَمِرُّ / نَدْفَعُ.

١٣- تَزَوَّجْنا / قُلْنا / رَكِبْنا / تَنَهَّدْنا / حَصَلْنا (عَلى) / وَصَلْنا / ذَهَبْنا / جَلَسْنا.

Past tense verbs conjugated with (We) / Greetings & Courtesy Expressions / Present tense verbs / prefixed particles / Feminine nouns / Future tense verbs / Command (imperative) verbs / Indefinite nouns / Singular-Plural pairs / Noun-adjective phrases / Words used adverbially / *Idaafah* structures / Prepositional phrases .

تَـمْرين ٢: From the list of nouns in in the shaded box, select the one most suitable to fill in the blanks in the following sentences:

الدِّراسَة / قُمْصان / مَتْجَر / صُوف / جِلْد / بَنْطَلُون / القادِمَ / مُقابَلَة / الأولَى / العَمَل

١- ذَهَبَ آدَمُ وسالـي إلـى ________ كَبيـر لِلـمَلابِسِ .

٢- سالـي تَحْتاجُ إلـى مِعْطَفِ ________ وكَنْزَة ________ .

٣- آدَمُ بِحاجَةٍ إلـى ________ شَتَوِيَّة و ________ "جِينْز".

٤- آدَمُ عِنْدَهُ ________ لِـلْعَمَلِ فـي الشَّهْرِ ________ .

٥- لا أَعْرِفُ كَيْفَ تُوَفِّقُ بَـيْـنَ ________ والعَمَلِ.

٦- قالَتْ سالـي: جَرَّبْتُ ________ فـي السَّنَةِ الأُولـى مِنَ الجامِعَةِ.

* * *

تَـمرين ٣: From the list of verbs in in the shaded box, select the one most suitable to fill in the blanks in the following sentences:

يَسْتَوْرِدُ / بَدَأَ / اِتَّفَقا / أُشاهِدُ / وَصَلَنـي / لِيُقابِلَ / تُريدُها / وَضَعَ / يُصَدِّرُ

١- تَرَكَ يُوسُفُ العَمَلَ فـي الشَّرِكَةِ و ________ يَعْمَلُ كَرَجُلِ أَعْمالٍ .

٢- يَعْمَلُ يُوسُفُ فـي الاِسْتِـيرادِ والتَّصْديرِ حَيْثُ ________ التُّحَفَ الفِرْعَوْنِيَّةَ لِيَبِيعَها فـي أَمْريكا .

٣- وكَذَلِكَ ________ يُوسُفُ بَعْضَ البَضائِعِ الأَمْريكِيَّةِ إلـى مِصْر.

٤- ذَهَبَ يُوسُفُ إلـى "خانِ الخَليلي" ________ الحاجَّ علي الطَّنْطاوي.

٥- قالَ يُوسُفُ: لَقَدْ ______ فاكْس بِالبَضائِعِ الَّتي ________.

٦- قالَ الحاجُّ: دَعْنِـي ________ـها.

٧- ثُمَّ ______ علـى السِّعْرِ و ______ الحاجُّ طَلَبَ شِراءِ كَمِّيَّةٍ مِنْها.

* * *

تـمرين ٤: **From the list of <u>particles</u> given in the shaded box below, select the one most suitable to fill in the blanks in the following sentences:**

كَـ / لَـ / مِن / أَ / فِي / على / بِـ / ثُمَّ / إلَـى / لِـ / وَ

١- هُوَ عَرَبِـيّ ، __ لَيْسَ كَذَلِك ؟ ٢- هُوَ مُسافِرٌ ___ الخارِجِ .

٣- بَدَأَ يوسُف يَعْمَلُ ___ التِّجارَةِ الحُرَّةِ __ رَجُلِ أَعمالٍ .

٤- ذَهَبَ يوسُف ___ سُوقِ خان الْخَلِيلي ___ يُقابِلَ الحاجّ الطَّنطاوي .

٥- قالَ الحاجُّ الطَّنْطاوي : أَهلاً __ سَهْلاً __ـكَ فِي مِصر!

٦- قالَ يوسُف : أَحْضَرْتُ __ ـكَ بَعْض عَيِّناتِ البِضاعَةِ.

٧- اتَّفَقا ___الأَسْعارِ ، ___ وَضَعَ الحاجُّ طَلَبَ شِراءٍ __كَمِّيَّةٍ ___ اَلبَضائِع.

* * *

تـمرين ٥: صَواب / خَطأ / **True / False**

Read the following statements and then answer whether each is <u>true</u> or <u>false</u>, using the Arabic terms:

١- لا يَزالُ يوسُف يَعمَلُ فِي الشَّرِكَةِ التِّجارِيَّةِ . (   ) <u>is still</u>

٢- بَدأ يوسُف يعملُ فِي التِّجارَةِ الحُرَّةِ . (   )

٣- يوسُف الآن رَجُلُ أعمالٍ مُتَخصِّص فـي الاِستيراد والتَّصْديرِ . (   )

٤- يَستَورِدُ يوسُف الألعاب التَّعليميَّة وملابِس الرِّياضَة . (   )

٥- يُصَدِّر الحاجّ الطنطاوي التُّحَفَ الفِرعَونِيَّة والـمُنتَجات القطنيَّة . (   )

٦- ذَهَبَ يوسُف إلى سوقٍ "خان الخليلي" لِيُقابِل الحاجَّ الطنطاوي . (   )

٧- الحاجّ الطنطاوي تاجِر مَعروف في أمريكا . (   )

٨- أَحْضَرَ يوسُف بَعضَ عَيِّناتِ البِضاعَةِ للحاجّ الطنطاوي . (   )

٩- <u>ما</u> أَعْجَبَ الحاجُّ الطنطاوي بِعَيِّنات الألعاب التَّعليمِيَّة . (   )   <u>did not</u>

١٠- اِتَّفَقَ الحاجُّ الطنطاوي ويوسُف على الأسعار . (   )

*   *   *

تَمرين ٦: تَصريفات الفِعل (قالَ):

The verb (قالَ) is a <u>weak verb</u> by virtue of having the long vowel (ا) as its middle letter.

You will notice that it has two <u>stems</u>:one where the long vowel (ا) stays, and that's in

three conjugations: two are <u>the 3rd persons masculine and feminine singular</u> and one is <u>the 3rd person masculine plural</u>. In the rest of the conjugations <u>the weak letter is dropped</u>, and the vowel of the <u>first letter is changed to a (*Dammah*)</u>. There are a good number of such verbs in the language, and one should serve as a model for their conjugations.

Corresponding Verb Conjugations	Plural Subject Pronouns	Corresponding Verb Conjugations	Singular Subject Pronouns
قالُوا	هُم	قالَ	هُوَ
قُلْنَ	هُنَّ	قالَتْ	هِيَ
قُلْتُم	أَنْتُم	قُلْتَ	أَنْتَ
قُلْتُنَّ	أَنْتُنَّ	قُلْتِ	أَنْتِ
قُلْنا	نَحْنُ	قُلْتُ	أنا

نِهايَة الوِحَدَةِ الرّابِعَة

The Fifth Unit / الوحدة الخامِسَة

الوِحْدَةُ الخامِسَة / 5th Unit
الدَّرسُ الأَوَّلُ /1st Lesson

ماذا تَفْعَلُ / تَفْعَلِينَ في أَيَّامِ الأُسْبُوعِ؟
What do you do During the Days of the Week?

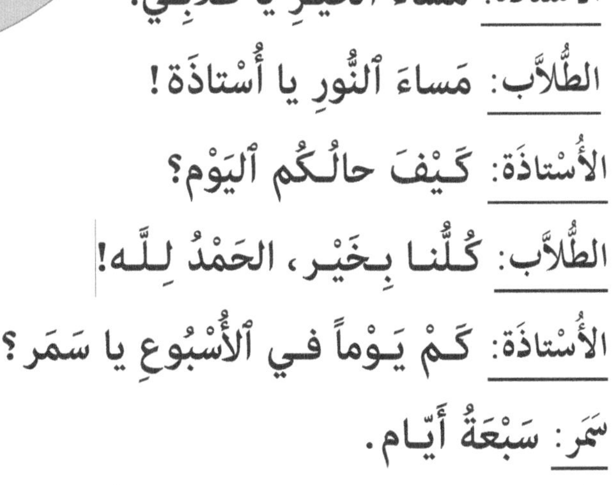

الأُسْتاذَة: مَساءَ ٱلخَيْرِ يا طُلَّابِي!

الطُّلَّاب: مَساءَ ٱلنُّورِ يا أُسْتاذَة!

الأُسْتاذَة: كَيْفَ حالُكُم ٱليَوْم؟

الطُّلَّاب: كُلُّنا بِخَيْر، الحَمْدُ لِلَّه!

الأُسْتاذَة: كَمْ يَوْماً في ٱلأُسْبُوعِ يا سَمَر؟

سَمَر: سَبْعَةُ أَيّام.

الأُسْتاذَة: مَنْ يَعْرِفُ أَسْماءَ أَيّامِ ٱلأُسْبُوع؟

مارغَريت: أَيّامُ ٱلأُسْبُوعِ هِيَ: الأَحَد، الاِثْنَيْن، الثُّلاثاء، الأَرْبِعاء، الخَمِيس، الجُمُعَة، السَّبْت.

الأُسْتاذَة: ماذا تَفْعَلُ يَوْمَ ٱلأَحَدِ يا آدَم؟

آدَم: أَذْهَبُ في ٱلصَّباحِ إِلى ٱلكَنِيسَةِ، وَفي ٱلمَساءِ أَذْهَبُ إِلى ٱلسِّينَما.

الأُسْتاذَة: ماذا تَفْعَلِينَ يَوْمَ ٱلاِثْنَيْنِ يا نانْسِي؟

نانسي: أَحْضُرُ مُحاضَراتِي في ٱلصَّباحِ وَبَعْدَ ٱلظُّهْرِ، ثُمَّ أَذْهَبُ في ٱلمَساءِ إِلَى مَكْتَبَةِ ٱلجامِعَةِ لِلدِّراسَةِ وَٱلبَحْث.

الأُسْتاذَة: ماذا تَفْعَلُ يَوْمَ ٱلثُّلاثاءِ يا سَعِيد؟

سَعِيد: بَعْدَ مُحاضَراتِي في ٱلجامِعَة، أَذْهَبُ إِلى النّادي لِلسِّباحَة.

الأُسْتاذَة: ماذا تَفْعَلِينَ يَوْمَ ٱلجُمُعَةِ يا فاطِمَة؟

فاطِمَة: أُصَلِّي ٱلجُمَعَةَ في ٱلمَسْجِدِ، وفي ٱلمَساءِ أَزُور بَعْضَ صَدِيقاتِي.

الأُسْتاذَة: أَمَّا يَوْمُ ٱلسَّبْتِ، فَأَظُنُّكُمْ تَنامُونَ لِساعاتٍ أَطْوَل، ثُمَّ تَذْهَبُونَ إِلى ٱلسُّوقِ أَوْ تُمارِسُونَ هِواياتٍ شَخَصِيَّة.

* * *

مُفْرَدات وتَراكيب الدَّرس الأوَّل
Vocabulary & Linguistic Structures of the 1st Lesson

the morning	الصَّباح	day	يَوْماً = يَوْم	Nouns	أَسْماء
the church	الكَنِيسَة	Samar *(female proper name)*	سَمَر	the fifth	الخامِسَة
the evening	الـمَساء	seven	سَبْعَةُ / سَبْع	days (a day)	أيّام (يَوْم)
the cinema, the movies	السِّينَما	Who ...?	مَنْ ...؟	the week (weeks)	الأُسْبُوع (أسابِيع)
Nancy *(transcription of female name)*	نانسي	names (name)	أَسْماء (اِسْم)	Good evening!	مَساءَ الخَيْر!
my lectures	مُحاضَراتِي (مُحاضَرَة)	they (are)	هِيَ	my students	طُلَّابِي (طُلَّاب+ي)
library (ies)	مَكْتَبَة (ـات)	Sunday	الأَحَد	Good evening! *(Response)*	مَساءَ النُّور!
the university (ies)	الجامِعَة (ـات)	Monday	الاِثْنَيْن	female professor	أُسْتاذَة
(for) studying	لِلدِّراسَة (لِ+الدِّراسَة)	Tuesday	الثُّلاثاء	your state of wellbeing	حالُكُم (حال+كُم)
(the) research	البَحْث	Wednesday	الأَربِعاء	today	اليَوْم
Sa'eed *(male proper name)*	سَعِيد	Thursday	الخَمِيس	all of us	كُلُّنا
the club	النَّادي	Friday	الجُمُعَة	(in) fine, good	بِخَيْر
		Saturday	السَّبْت	Thanks (to) God!	الحَمْدُ لِلَّه!
				Fāṭimah *(female proper name)*	فاطِمَة

How ...?	كَـيفَ...؟	I go	أَذْهَبُ		
by, in *(always written as part of the following word)*	بِـ	I attend	أَحْضُرُ	the mosque	الـمَسْجِد
for *(always written as part of the following word)*	لِـ	I pray	أُصَلِّي	some (of)	بَعْض
How many...? *(to ask about number)*	كَـمْ ...؟	I visit	أَزُور	my femal friends	صَديقاتِـي (صَديقات+ـي)
How ...?	كَـيفَ...؟	I think (you all)	أَظُنُّ (ـكُم)	(for) hours (an hour)	لِـساعات (سَاعَة)
to	إِلَـى	you *(plural)* sleep	تَنامُونَ	longer	أَطْوَل
and *(always written as part of the following word*	وَ	you *(plural)* go	تَذْهَبُون	the market, the shopping center (markets)	السُّوق (أَسْواق)
after	بَـعْـدَ	Particles	أَدوات	Verbs	أَفْعال
then	ثُـمَّ	What...? *(followed by a verb, to ask about action)*	ماذا ...؟	you do *(masculine)*	تَفْعَل
As for ... (connector)	أَمَّـا ... (فَـ)	in, at, per	فـي	you do *(feminine)*	تَفْعَلِيـنَ
		O *(vocative particle)*	يـا	he knows	يَعْرِفُ

* * *

Grammatical and Linguistic Issues الدَّرْس الثَّانـي: القَواعِد وقَضايا لُغَوِيَّة

1. The Interrogative Particle for "How many....? .... ١- أَداةُ الاِسْتِفْهام (كَمْ ...؟)
2. The Singular Conjugations of the Present Indicative Verb .... ٢- الفِعْلُ الـمُضارِعُ الـمَرْفوعُ(الـمُفْرَد)
3. Helping Vowels at End of Words .... ٣- حَرَكاتُ النُّطْقِ الـمُساعِدَة في أَواخِرِ الكَلِمات
4. The Preposition (لِـ)with defined Nouns .... ٤- حَرْفُ الجَرِّ (لِـ) مَعَ الأَسْماءِ الـمُعَرَّفَةِ بِـ (آل)
5. Numerals for Simple Counting, Ordinal, Adverbial .... ٥- الأَعْدادُ العَدَدِيَّةُ والتَّرْتِيبِيَّةُ والظَّرْفِيَّةُ
6. The Linguistic Structure to Say: (As for ..... Plus (FA) .... ٦- التَّـر كِيبُ اللُّغَوِيُّ: (أَمَّـا .... فَـ)

The Interrogative Particle for "How many.? (كَمْ...؟) ١- أداة الاسْتِفْهامِ

- (كَمْ ...؟) is the Arabic interrogative particle, which is equivalent to the English (**How many?**), used to ask about the <u>number of the subject</u>.
- However, the subject that follows this particle is different from the English in certain aspects. Let's now read the following Arabic sentences to learn the rules pertinent to this particle:

> • كَمْ وَجْبَةً تَأْكُلِينَ فـي اليَوْمِ؟ / كَمْ يَوْماً تَذْهَبُ إلـى الجامِعَةِ؟ /
> • كَمْ طالِباً فـي صَفِّ اللُّغَةِ العَرَبِيَّةِ؟ / كَمْ بَيْضَةً تَأْكُلُ فـي الفُطُورِ؟

- By examining the nouns following the interrogative particle (كَمْ), one should notice two important features: **(1) The noun is in its <u>singular form</u>, rather than the plural form in English; (2)** This noun is in its **<u>indefinite *'nunated'* form</u>**.
- In this sense, the Arabic literal translations of the sentences above should sound like this: "**How many of a meal you eat per day?**", "**How many of a day you go to the university?**", "**How many of a student are there in the Arabic language class?**", "**How many of an egg do you eat for breakfast?**" However, the idiomatic translation in English should be: "**How many meals do you eat per day?**" etc.
- Gramatically, the **<u>singular indefinite *'nunated'* form</u>** of the Arabic structure is called (تَـمييز), **<u>'specification'</u>** which will be dealt with in more details at a more advanced level of grammar.

* * *

٢- تَصريفاتُ الفِعْلِ الـمُضارِعِ الـمَرفوعِ مَعَ ضَمائِرِ الـمُفْرَدِ

The Present Indicative Verb Conjugation with Singular Subjects

- As we learned when we previously introduced the conjugations of the past tense verbs, the Arabic verb system has basically two tenses: (1) **<u>Past</u>** or **<u>Perfect Tense</u>**; (2) **<u>Present</u>** or **<u>Imperfect tense</u>**. The "**future time**" is derived from the "Imperfect Tense" by means of two certain particles which precede the verb, and it will be treated in the next unit. In this lesson, however, we will focus on learning the **five singular conjugations of the "present tense verbs."**
- Now, let's examine the following table before we explain more specific aspects of our focal point:

Expressed Subject, Gender & Number	Correspond-ing Subject Pronoun	Subject Marker	Verb Stem	The Verb in a Sentence
he = سامي 3rd person, masculine singular	هُوَ	يَـ	فْعَل	ماذا يَـفْعَلُ سامي؟

she = رانِية 3rd person, feminine singular	هِيَ	تَـ	أُكُل	رانِيَة تَأْكُلُ ٱلْفُطور.
you = سامي 2nd person, masculine singular	أَنْتَ	تَـ	أُكُل	ماذا تَأْكُلُ يا سامي؟
you = رانِية 2nd person, feminine singular	أَنْتِ	تَـ...ِينَ	أُكُل	ماذا تَأْكُلِينَ يا رانِيَة؟
أَنا 1st person masculine+feminine	أَنا	أَ	تَناوَل	أَتَناوَلُ ٱلعشاءَ في ٱلبَيْتِ.

- Arabic verbs in the **'present tense'** consist of a **'stem'** and a **'subject marker.'** The 'stem' indicates the <u>'root'</u> of the verb, its <u>'basic infinitive meaning'</u> and the <u>'tense'</u> of the verb.
- The 'subject marker' indicates the **'person,'** **'number'** and **'subject'** of the verb.
- **Note the following important points:**
  1. The conjugations of the **3rd person feminine singular** and the **2nd person masculine singular** are <u>identical</u>. Only the context will determine which is which.
  2. The *'Dammah'* short vowel over the last letters of four conjugations of the verbs, and the suffix (ـينَ) in the 2nd person feminine singular <u>indicate the 'mood'</u> of these verbs. In this case, this is called the 'indicative mood'; in Arabic called (*Marfu'* / مَرْفُوع), and this is considered the **default mood**. In future units, we will cover the two other moods along with the specific particles that justify the changing of the default mood to either the **"subjunctive mood"** or the **"jussive mood."**
  3. The first letter of the verb stem is always vowelless (i.e. bears a *Sukoon*); however, the second letter might bear either a *Fathah*, a *Dammah* or a *Kasrah*, which is determined by the lexicon.
  4. Four of the singular conjugations of the present tense verbs have only a **prefix** as the conjugation syllable (i.e. يَـ / تَـ / أَ), and only in the case of the 2nd person feminine is there a combination of the **prefix** (تَـ) and the suffix (ـينَ).
- Like English, each verb in Arabic must have a **'subject'**, and this subject can either be an **expressed noun**, as in the first four examples above, or an implied pronoun, understood from the form of the 'subject marker' and context, as in the last sentence above.
- Unlike modern English, sentences in Arabic has the option of staring with the <u>'subject'</u> or starting with the <u>'verb.'</u>
- <u>'Imperfect'</u> or <u>'Present Tense'</u> verbs in Arabic correspond to two types of verbs in English: One is **'simple present'**, such as: (**he reads, she reads, you read, I read**), and the other is 'present continous' or 'progressive', such as: (**he is writing, she is writing, you are writing, I am writing.**)
- In matters of translations, it is the context and certain contextual clues that will determine whether to use the 'simple present' or the 'progressive.'

- Now, let's study the following conjugation table of five verbs you studied recently, for the purpose of further practice:

أنا	أَنْتِ	أَنْتَ	هِيَ	هُوَ
أَتَناوَلُ	تَـتَناوَلِـيـنَ	تَـتَناوَلُ	تَـتَناوَلُ	يَـتَناوَلُ
أُحِـبُّ	تُحِبِّـيـنَ	تُحِبُّ	تُحِبُّ	يُحِبُّ
أُحاوِلُ	تُـحاوِلِـيـنَ	تُحاوِلُ	تُـحاوِلُ	يُـحاوِلُ
آكُـلُ **	تَـأْكُـلِـيـنَ	تَـأْكُلُ	تَـأْكُلُ	يَـأْكُـلُ
أَجْـلِسُ	تَجْلِسِـيـنَ	تَـجْلِسُ	تَـجْلِسُ	يَـجْلِسُ

* * *

٣- حَرَكاتُ النُّطْقِ الـمُساعِدَة في أَواخِرِ الكَلِمات

Situational Helping Vowels at End of Words

- In Arabic, it is a general rule that no more than two consonants can occur together, no matter whether within a single word, or at the end of a word and the beginning of the next. This is, of course, unlike English where three or more consonants may occur in a row.
- Within a single word, such occurrence never takes place in Arabic; therefore we are left with only one possibility; a situation where a word ends with a "*Sukūn*" and another begins with a '*Waslah*' or "*elided Hamzated Alif*" (ٱ). In such case, in order to eliminate the occurrence of more than two consonants in a row, a "situational heling vowel" is added above or under the letter bearing the "*Sukūn*." This "situational helping vowel" can be a "*Fathah*," a "*Kasrah*," or a "*Dammah*."
- Now, let's examine the working of this process through the following examples:

١- زَميلَـتي + مِنْ + ٱلعِراق .	⟸	زَميلَتي مِـنَ ٱلعِراقِ .
٢- مَنْ + ٱلـمُحاسِبُ + هُنا؟	⟸	مَـنِ ٱلـمُحاسِبُ هُنا؟
٣- هَـلْ + ٱلفُطُورُ + جاهِزٌ؟	⟸	هَـلِ ٱلفُطُورُ جاهِزٌ؟
٤- كَيْفَ + حالُكُمْ + ٱلـيَوْمَ؟	⟸	كَيْفَ حالُكُـمُ ٱلـيَوْمَ؟

- The examples given in the box above represent most of the common situations where 'situational helping vowels' are needed:

1. (مِنْ) its helping vowel will always be a '*Fathah*' to become (مِـنَ).
2. (مَنْ) and (هَلْ) and their helping vowel will always be a '*Kasrah*' to become (مَنِ) and (هَلِ).

3. (هُـمْ) and (كُـمْ) and their helping vowel will always be a 'Dammah' to become (هُـمُ) and (كُـمُ).

* * *

٤- حَرْفُ الجَرِّ (لِـ) مَعَ الأَسْماءِ الـمُعَرَّفَةِ بِـ (ألْ)

The Preposition (لِـ) with Nouns Defined by (ألْ)

- (لِـ) is a one-letter preposition, always written connected to and as part of the following noun. This is also true for all on-letter prepositions that will be learned in the future.
- Attached to a verbal noun or gerund, it means 'for' or '**for the purpose of**.' When attached to a regular noun, it can have the meaning of '**belongs to**.'
- It is a common observance to see this preposition attached to nouns in general, and in particular to verbal nouns which have the Definite Article (ألْ). And when this preposition is attached to such nouns, the ***'Alif'*** of the Definite Article is dropped in writing.
- Now, let's examine the examples in the sentences of the box below to see how this process works:

١- هَذا ٱلْكِتابُ لِطالِبٍ .	⟸ هَذا ٱلْكِتابُ لِلطَّالِبِ.
٢- أَذْهَبُ إِلى ٱلـمَكْتَبَةِ لِقِراءَةِ ٱلْـكُتُبِ.	⟸ أَذْهَبُ إِلى ٱلْـمَكْتَبَةِ لِلقِراءَةِ.
٣- أَذْهَبُ إِلـى الجامِعَةِ لِـدِراسَةِ اللُّغَةِ.	⟸ أَذْهَبُ إِلـى الجامِعَةِ لِـلدِّراسَةِ.
٤- هَذا ٱلْـمَتْجَرُ لِـصَديقـي.	⟸ هَذا ٱلْـمَتْجَرُ لِلأَصْدِقاءِ .

* * *

٥- الأَعْدادُ العَدَدِيَّةُ والتَّرْتيبِيَّةُ والظَّرْفِيَّةُ

Numerals for Simple Counting, Ordinal, Adverbial

- Like English, Arabic numerals have different forms, depending on whether they are used for **simple counting**, as **ordinal with adjectival meaning**, or **adverbially**
- The **counting forms** and the ordinal forms have masculine and feminine variations, needed when they are used contextually due to certain grammatical rules, which will be covered in future grammatical lessons.
- The following table shows the different forms. So, let's practice to learn the numerals from 1 to 10, in these three variations by listening and repeating here in class. Then read on your own and listen to the recorded section, with the aim of learning these by heart!

Adverbial Forms	Ordinal Numerals Masculine & Feminine	Counting Numerals	Arethmetic Symbols
أَوَّلاً	اَلأَوَّل / الأُولَـى	واحِد / واحِدَة	١
ثانِياً	اَلثَّانـي / الثَّانِيَة	اِثْنان / اِثْنَيْـن	٢
ثالِثاً	اَلثَّالِث / الثَّالِثَة	ثَلاث / ثَلاثَة	٣
رابِعاً	اَلرَّابِع / الرَّابِعَة	أَرْبَع / أَرْبَعَة	٤
خامِساً	اَلخامِس / الخامِسَة	خَمْس / خَمْسَة	٥
سادِساً	اَلسَّادِس / السَّادِسَة	سِتّ / سِتَّة	٦
سابِعاً	اَلسَّابِع / السَّابِعَة	سَبْع / سَبْعَة	٧
ثامِناً	اَلثَّامِن / الثَّامِنَة	ثَـمانٍ / ثَـمانِيَة	٨
تاسِعاً	اَلتَّاسِع / التَّاسِعَة	تِسْع / تِسْعَة	٩
عاشِراً	اَلعاشِر / العاشِرَة	عَشْر / عَشْرَة	١٠

- The **counting forms** in the second column are equivalent to the English: **one**, **two**, **three**, **four**, **five**, **six**, **seven**, **eight**, **nine** and **ten**.
- The **ordinal forms** in the third column are equivalent to the English: the **first**, the **second**, the **third**, the **fourth**, the **fifth**, the **sixth**, the **seventh**, the **eighth**, the **ninth** and the **tenth**.
- The adverbial forms in the fourth column are equivalent to the English: **firstly**, **secondly**, **thirdly**, **fourthly**, **fifthly**, **sixthly**, **seventhly**, **eighthly**, **ninthly** and **tenthly**.
- The forms of numerals used for **simple counting** and those used **adverbially** are **fixed**, and should show no variations in literary Arabic. However, they might show slightly slang variations in colloquial Arabic.
- The **ordinal numerals** are also actually **adjectives**, which should show distinction in **gender** (**masculine/feminine**), **definiteness** or **indefiniteness**, and **agreement in case-ending**, (Arabic (**إِعْراب**), with the nouns preceding them, which they modify.
- To put this final note in contextual perspective, let's now read and analyze the following sentences:

اَلدَّرْسُ ٱلأَوَّلُ سَهْل. / أَقْرَأُ ٱلدَّرْسَ الأَوَّلَ. / الكَلِمَةُ فـي ٱلدَّرْسِ الأَوَّلِ.

The word is in the first lesson. / I am reading the first lesson. / The first lesson is easy.

تَحْضُرُ طالِبَةٌ ثالِثَةٌ. / قابَلْتُ طالِبَةً ثالِثَةً. / تَكَلَّمْتُ مَعَ طالِبَةٍ ثالِثَةٍ.

I spoke with a third (female) student. / I met a third (female) student. / A third (female) student is coming.

٦- التَّـر كِيبُ اللُّغَوِيُّ: (أَمَّـا .... فَـ)

The Linguistic Structure to Say: (<u>As for</u> .. Plus (فَـ) as a Linking Particle

- أَمَّـا is a special particle, used to introduce and highlight a specific piece of information, usually related to a more general topic introduced previously.
- You will always find it at the beginning of a sentence, and even more precisely at the beginning of a paragraph to relate the specific to the more general.
- It **<u>must be followed by a noun</u>**, which would be the **<u>subject</u>** of an **'equational sentence**.'
- In translation, the best English equivalent is "**As for**" or "**As to**."
- In a linguistic structure starting with (أَمَّـا), there is a need to connect the information about the subject by means of a connector or linking particle which is (فَـ).
- From a structural point of view, this linking (فَـ) must be there, but it does not have a semantic meaning, and therefore is left untranslated into English. Possibly, a <u>must punctuation</u> '**<u>comma</u>**' before it is a substitution for a specific meaning.
- The clause following the linking (فَـ) can start with a verb, a noun, or a pronoun, as illustrated by the examples below:

> - أَمَّا أَكْلَتِي الـمُفَضَّلَةُ ، فَـهِيَ "الـمُسَخَّن" مِن صُنْعِ أُمِّي .
> - أَمَّا أَنا ، فَـأَكْلَتِي الـمُفَضَّلَةُ هِيَ السَّمَكُ الـمَشْوِيُّ .
> - أَمَّا رانِيَةُ ، فَـتُحِبُّ السَّمَكَ والرُّزَّ مَعَ السَّلطَةِ .

* * *

الدَّرسُ الثّالِث : تَدْريباتٌ وَنَشاطاتٌ / Exercises & Activities

تَـمرين ١ : (*Oral / Written*) Statement ➡ Question with (كَمْ)

Read the following statements first; then form the appropiates to which these statements are the answers. Follow the given example inside the box:

> فـي الأُسْبُوعِ سَبْعَةُ أَيّام . ⬅ كَمْ <u>يَوْماً</u> فـي ٱلأُسْبُوعِ؟

١- يَأْكُلُ سامـي ثَلاثَ وَجباتٍ فـي ٱليَوْمِ . ⬅ ....؟

٢- فـي ٱلصَّفِّ عَشْرَةُ طُلَّابٍ. ⇦ ....؟

٣- فـي ٱلسَّنَةِ أَرْبَعَةُ فُصُولٍ. ⇦ ....؟

٤- لِـي ثَلاثُ أَخَواتٍ. ⇦ ....؟

٥- سامي عِنْدَهُ سَبْعُ قُمْصانٍ. ⇦ ....؟

* * *

(*Oral / Written*) **Converting the Arithmetic Symbols of the : تَـمرين ٢**

Numerals into Letter-Sound Numerals:

In the short answers to the questions below, Arabic numerals were given between parenthesis in their arithmetic symbols. Read each question, then sound out the number for the arithmetic symbol given as an answer and finally write down the numerls in their letter forms. Follow the given example:

كَمْ يَوْماً فِـي الأُسْبُوعِ؟ ⇦ (٧) = سَبْعَة

١- كَمْ أُسْتاذاً فِـي ٱلقِسْمِ؟ ⇦ (٤) = ...

٢- كَمْ طالِبَةً فِـي ٱلصَّفِّ؟ ⇦ (٩) = ...

٣- كَمْ كِتاباً عَلَى ٱلـمَقْعَدِ؟ ⇦ (١٠) = ...

٤- كَمْ دَرْساً تَقْرَأُ فِي ٱلأُسْبُوعِ؟ ⇦ (٥) = ...

٥- كَمْ بَدْلَةً عِنْدَكَ؟ ⇦ (١) = ...

٦- كَمْ مَكْتَبَةً فِي ٱلجامِعَةِ؟ ⇦ (٢) = ...

٧- كَمْ وَرَقَةً عَلَى ٱلـمَقْعَدِ؟ ⇦ (٨) = ...

٨- كَمْ مُقابَلَةً عِنْدَكِ هَذا ٱلشَّهْرِ؟ ⇦ (٦) = ...

٩- كَمْ مِعْطَفاً سَتَشْتَـري سالـي؟ ⇦ (٣) = ...

* * *

(*Oral / Written*) Recognition of the Verbs and Their Subject Pronouns: تَـمرين ٣:

Each sentence below contains one of the 'Five Verbs' conjugations introduced in the grammar notes. Your task is to read the sentence and identify the verb by underlining it; then, give in sound and in writing the corresponding 'subject pronoun' for each conjugation from the list in the column on the left. Follow the given example:

يَـذْهَبُونَ إلـى ٱلسُّوقِ يَـوْمَ السَّبْتِ. (هُـم)

١- هَلْ تَعْرِفُونَ كَيْفَ تَذْهَبُونَ إِلَـى ٱلـمَكْتَبَةِ؟

٢- هَـلْ تَـذْهَبِيـنَ إِلَـى ٱلسُّوقِ يَوْمَ الـجُمُعَـةِ؟

٣- هَلْ تَكْتُبِيـنَ دَرْسَكِ ٱلْجَديدَ؟

٤- لا يَعْرِفُونَ كَيْفَ يَعْمَلُـونَ ٱلتَّمْرين.

٥- لا يَـعْـرَفْـنَ جوابَ هذا السُّؤالِ.

٦- هُـمْ يَضْحَكُونَ وهُـنَّ لا يَضْحَكْـنَ.

أَنْـتِ
أَنْـتُـمْ
أَنْـتُـنَّ
هُـمْ
هُـنَّ

*　*　*

(*Oral / Written*) Practice the Conjugation of the Verbs: تَـمرين ٤:

Fill in the blank cells in the following table with the appropriate conjugations of the verbs according to the 'Subject Pronouns' given on top of the table in the shaded cells. Please take note that this practice contains review of the other conjugations introduced before in Unit 3:

أنـا	أنْـتِ	أنْـتَ	هِـيَ	هُـوَ
				يَـذْهَبُ
			تَـعْرِفُ	
		تَـذْهَـبُ		
أ	تَـفْـعَلِـيـنَ			
أَزُورُ				

تَمرين ٥: (*Oral / Written*) **Reading while Providing and Marking the Appropriate HelpingVowels:**

The sentences were given to you without the situational helping vowels. Your task is to read them appropriately with the helping vowels. Then, mark these vowels in writing. Follow the given example:

كَيْفَ حالُكُمْ ٱليَوْمَ ؟⇐ كَيْفَ حالُكُمُ ٱليَوْمَ؟

١- هَلْ ٱلرَّئِيسُ فِـي مَكْتَبِهِ؟ ⇐ ....?

٢- مَنْ ٱلأُسْتاذُ ٱلجَدِيدُ فِـي ٱلقِسْمِ؟ ⇐ ....?

٣- اَلطَّالِبَةُ ٱلجَدِيدَةُ مِنْ ٱلعِراقِ. ⇐ ....

٤- هَلْ هَذا مَكْتَبُـهُمْ ٱلجَدِيدُ؟ ⇐ ....?

٥- هَذِهِ كُـتُـبُـكُمْ ٱلعَرَبِيَّةُ.⇐ ....

* * *

تَـمرين ٦: (*Writing / Reading*) **Rewriting Words Preceded by the Preposition لِـ Then Reading Them:**

In the following sentences the section in parenthesis shows the actual components of the structure. However, this is not the way they should appear in writing. Your task is, first, rewrite this part as it should appear in actual writing; then, second, read the whole sentence as one unit. Follow the given example:

أَذْهَبُ إِلَى ٱلـمَكْتَبَةِ (لِـ+ال+بَحْثِ). ←أَذْهَبُ إِلَـى الـمَكْتَبَةِ لِلْبَحْثِ.

١- يَذْهَبُ إِلَى ٱلنَّادِي (لِـ+ال+سِباحَةِ). ← ....

٢- تَذْهَبُ إِلَى ٱلـمَسْجِدِ (لِـ+ال+صَلاةِ). ← ....

٣- أَذْهَبُ إِلَى ٱلـمَكْتَبَةِ (لِـ+ال+دِراسَةِ). ← ....

٤- تَذْهَبُ إِلَى ٱلـمَطْعَمِ (لِـ+ال+أَكْلِ). ← ....

٥- هَلْ تَذْهَبِينَ إِلَى ٱلسُّوقِ (لِـ+ال+تَسَوُّقِ)؟← ....

تـمرين ٧: (*Oral / Written*) Using the Ordinal Numerals in Context:

Fill in the dotted spaces of the following sentences with the appropriate form from among those given in parenthesis at the end of the sentences. Follow the given example:

> اَلدَّرْسُ .... سَهْلٌ. (الأُولَى / الأَوَّلُ / الأَوَّل)
>
> ⇦ اَلدَّرْسُ الأَوَّلُ سَهْلٌ.

١- اَلكِتابُ .... جَديدٌ. ⇦ (الثّانِيَةُ / الثّاني / ثانِيَةً)

٢- اَلطّالِبَةُ .... عَرَبِيَّةٌ. ⇦ (الثّالِثُ / الثّالِثَةُ / الثّالِثَة)

٣- أُصَلّي السّاعَةَ .... ⇦ (الْخامِسَ / الْخامِسَةُ / الْخامِسَةَ)

٤- يَقْرَأُ الدَّرْسَ .... مِنَ الْكِتابِ. ⇦ (الرّابِعَ / الرّابِعَةَ / الرّابِعُ)

* * *

تـمرين ٨: (*Oral / Written*) Link the Clauses to Form One Sentence

Using: (أَمَّا ..... فَـ):

Each of the following pairs of clauses can be linked together to form one meaningful sentence using the combination (أَمَّا ..... فَـ). Your task is to go through the process orally, then write down the resultant sentence. Follow the given example:

> يَوْمُ ٱلجُمُعَةِ، / أَتَناوَلُ ٱلعَشاءَ في مَطْعَم. ⇦
>
> ⇩ أَمَّا يَوْمُ الجُمُعَةِ، فَأَتَناوَلُ ٱلعَشاءَ في مَطْعَم.

١- يَوْمُ ٱلسَّبْتِ، / أَتَناوَلُ فُطوري في ٱلبَيْتِ. ....

٢- يَوْمُ ٱلأَحَدِ، / أَذْهَبُ إِلى ٱلسُّوق. ....

٣- يَوْمُ ٱلاِثْنَيْنِ، / أَتَناوَلُ ٱلغَداءَ في الجامِعَة. ....

٤- يَوْمُ ٱلثُّلاثاءِ، / عِنْدي مُحاضَرات في ٱلْمَساءِ. ....

٥- يَوْمُ الأَرْبِعاءِ، / مُحاضَراتي في الصَّباح. ....

٦- يَوْمُ الْخَميسِ، / أَذْهَبُ إِلى السِّينَما. ....

Reviewing Two Reference Lists: **تمرين ٩:**

Go to '**Part 4**' of the book to review the **reference lists** entitled "**Interrogative Particles and Their Usage in Context,**" **page 338**; also "**Prepositions and Adverbs of Place and Time**", **page 339**.

* * *

الدَّرسُ ٱلرَّابعُ: القِراءَةُ ٱلجَهْرِيَّة / Reading Text (Aloud)

بَرْنامَجُ يَوْمِ ٱلجُمُعَةِ

- بَعْدَ أَنْ أَنْهَى يوسُف مَهَمَّتَهُ ٱلتِّجارِيَّة فِي سوقِ خان ٱلْخَليلي ، أَرادَ أَن يَقْضِيَ وَقتاً مُمْتِعاً مَعَ أُخْتِهِ وزَوْجِها. اتَّصَلَ بِهِما مِن فُنْدُقِ "هِيلتون النِّيل" مَساءَ يَومِ ٱلخَميسِ، وأَخْبَرَهُم أَنَّهُ يُريدُ أَنْ يَقْضِيَ يَوْمَ ٱلجُمُعَة كُلَّهُ مَعَهُم.
- فِي ٱلصَّباحِ تَناوَلُوا طَعامَ ٱلفُطورِ فِي مَطْعَم ٱلفُنْدُق. وكانَ ٱلفُطورِ يَتَكَوَّنُ مِن الفولِ المُدَمِّسِ والطَّعْمِيَّةِ (أَوْ الفَلافِل) والبَيْضِ والْجُبْنَةِ والْمُرَبَّى، وَشَرِبوا الشَّايَ والْقَهْوَةَ وعَصِيرَ ٱلبُرتُقال. ثُمَّ تَوَجَّهُوا بَعْدَ ذَلِكَ إِلَى ٱلجامِعِ الأَزْهَرِ لِصَلاةِ ٱلجُمُعَة.
- بَعْدَ ٱلصَّلاةِ، ذَهَبُوا إِلَى حَيِّ "ٱلسَّيِّدَةِ زَيْنَب" ٱلشَّعبِيِّ، وتَجَوَّلُوا بَيْنَ ٱلدَّكاكِينِ ٱلصَّغِيرَةِ هُناكَ. وفِي وَقْتِ ٱلعَصْر، دَخَلُوا مَطْعَماً شَعْبِيّاً وتَناوَلُوا غَداءً مُتَأَخِّراً. فِي ذَلِكَ ٱلمَطْعَمِ أَكَلُوا ٱلأَكْلَةَ ٱلشَّعْبِيَّةَ ٱلمَعْرُوفَةِ بِـ "المُلُوخِيَّةِ بِالأَرانِب" مَع ٱلرُّزِّ وبَعْضِ ٱلسَّلَطاتِ، وشَرِبوا عَصِيرَ ٱلمانْجَةِ ٱلطَّازَج.
- بَعْدَ ٱلْغَداءِ اِسْتَراحُوا قَلِيلاً فِي مَقْهَى شَعْبِيٍّ، ودَخَّنوا ٱلأَرْجِيلَة (النَّارجِيلَة) وشَرِبُوا قَهْوَةً عَرَبِيَّةً.
- قَبْلَ غُرُوبِ ٱلشَّمْسِ بِقَليلٍ، ذَهَبُوا فِي نُزْهَةٍ عَلَى شاطِئِ ٱلنِّيل، حَيْثُ أَكَلُوا ٱلذُّرَةَ ٱلمَشْوِيَّةَ وٱلتُّرْمُسَ وٱلفولَ ٱلسُّودانِي. وبَعْدَ غُرُوبِ ٱلشَّمسِ، اِسْتَأْجَروا مَرْكَباً لِيَتَنَزَّهُوا فِي نَهْرِ ٱلنِّيل.

الـمُفردات (مُرتَّبة حَسَب ورودها في النَّص)

الـمَعْنَى الإِنْجليزي	الكَلِمَة العَرَبِيّة	الـمَعْنَى الإِنْجليزي	الكَلِمَة العَرَبِيّة
day (days)	يَوْم (أيَّام)	program (programs)	بَرْنامَج (بَرامِج)
after that	بَعْدَ أَن	Friday	الجُمُعَة
his mission, his quest	مَهَمَّتَهُ (مَهَمَّة+ـهُ)	he completed	أَنْهَى
enjoyable	مُمْتِعاً / مُمْتِع / مُمْتِعَة	spend (he)	يَقْضِي
(the two of) them	بِـهِما (بِـ+هِما)	he contacted	اِتَّصَلَ بِـ
The Nile Hilton	هِيلتون النِّيل	hotel (hotels)	فُنْدَق (فَنادِق)
Thursday	يَوْم ٱلخَميس	evening	مَساء
that he	أنَّـهُ (أنَّ+ـهُ)	he informed them	أَخْبَرَهُم (أَخْبَرَ+هُمْ)
all long, all of it	كُـلَّـهُ (كُلَّ+ـهُ)	wants to	يُريدُ أَنْ
the breakfast	الإِفْطار = الفُطور	with them	مَعَهُم (مَعَ+هُم)
consisting of	يَـتَـكَـوَّنُ مِن	and it was	وكانَ (وَ+كانَ)
falafil	الطَّعْمِيَّة = الفَلافِل	fava beans dip dish	الفول ٱلـمُدَمَّس
orange juice	عَصِير ٱلبُـرْتُـقـال	they drank	شَرِبُوا
the Luminous Mosque (*proper name*)	الجامِع ٱلأَزْهَر	afterwards	بَـعْدَ ذَلِـكَ
for Friday prayer	لِـصَلاةِ ٱلجُـمُعَـة	for prayer	لِـصَلاة (لِـ+صَلاةِ)
neighborhood, locality	حَيّ (أَحْياء)	they went (to)	ذَهَبُوا (إِلَـى)
popular, folksy	الشَّعْبِيّ / الشَّعْبِيَّة	*Lady Zainab* (*proper name*)	السَّيِّدَة زَيْنَب
among	بَـيْـنَ	they walked around	تَجَوَّلوا
(the) small, the little	الصَّغيـرَة	the shops (a shop)	الدَّكاكِيـن (دُكَّان)
they entered	دَخَـلُوا	late afternoon time	الـعَصْر
late lunch	غَداءً مُـتَـأَخِّراً	popular folksy restaurant,	مَطْعَماً شَعْـبِيّـاً
they ate	أَكَـلُوا	that restaurant	ذَلِـكَ ٱلـمَطْعَم
(the) known as	الـمَعْروفَـة بِـ	popular meal	الأَكْـلَـة الشَّعْـبِـيَّـة

salad (salads)	السَّلَطات (سَلَطَة)	*mulukhiyyah* with rabbet meat	الْمُلوخِيَّة بِٱلأرانِب
the fresh	الطَّازَج	mango	المانْجَة = المانْجا
a little, for a while	قَلِيلاً	they rested	اِسْتَراحُوا
they smoked	دَخَّنُوا	café, a coofee house	مَقْهًى = قَهْوَة (مَقاهي)
Arabic coffee	قَهْوَة عَرَبِيَّة	waterpipe, narghile, hukka	الأَرْجيلَة / النَّارجيلَة / الحُقَّة
sunset	غُروب الشَّمْس	before	قَبْلَ
liesurly walk, liesurly stroll, picnic	فِي نُزْهَة (نُزهات)	by a little	بِقَليل (بِـ+قَليل)
the bank of the Nile	شاطِئ النِّيل	bank, shore (banks, shores)	شاطِئ (شَواطِئ)
lupine beans	التُّرْمُس	grilled corn	الذُّرَة المَشْوِيَّة
they rented	اِسْتَأْجَروا	peanuts	الفول ٱلسُّودانِيّ
to stroll about, to promenade	لِيَتَنَزَّهُوا (لِـ+يَتَنَزَّهوا)	a sailboat (sailboats)	مَرْكَباً / مَرْكَب (مَراكِب)
the Nile River	نَهْر ٱلنِّيل	river (rivers)	نَهْر (أَنْهار)

* * *

سُؤال جَواب

أَسْئِلَة الفهم والاستِيعاب (شَفويّا)/ Comprehension Questions

١- ماذا فَعَلَ يوسُف بَعْدَ أَنْ أَنْهَى مَهَمَّتَهُ ٱلتِّجارِيَّةَ؟

٢- مِن أَيْنَ اتَّصَلَ بِأُخْتِهِ وزَوْجِها؟ ٣- أَيْنَ تَناوَلوا طَعامَ ٱلْفُطُور؟

٤- مِنْ ماذا (مِمَّ) كانَ يَتَكَوَّنُ ٱلْفُطورُ؟

٥- ماذا شَرِبُوا مَعَ الفُطورِ؟ ٦- إِلَى أَيْنَ تَوَجَّهوا بَعْدَ ذَلِكَ؟ ولِماذا؟

٧- إِلَى أَينَ ذَهَبُوا بَعْدَ الصَّلاةِ؟ وماذا فَعَلُوا هُناكَ؟

٨- ماذا فَعَلُوا فِي وَقْتِ ٱلعَصْرِ؟ ٩- ماذا فَعَلُوا بَعْدَ ٱلْغَداءِ؟

١٠- ماذا فَعَلُوا قَبْلَ غُروبِ ٱلشَّمْسِ؟ ١١- ماذا فَعَلُوا بَعْدَ غُروبِ ٱلشَّمْسِ؟

الدَّرْسُ الخامِسُ: الثقافةُ وٱلقِيَمُ وٱلأمثالُ

(أ) يَشرح ٱلـمُدرّس / ٱلـمُدرِّسَة بعض ٱلقَضايا ٱلـمتصلة بِـما يلي:

- أهمِّيَّةُ يَومِ ٱلـجُمعةِ بِٱلنِّسبةِ للمسلميـن؛
  The Importance of Friday for Arab-Muslims
- نُبذة عن ٱلْجامِعِ ٱلأزهر؛
  A conscise piece of information about "*Al-Azhar* "

- الطَّعامُ ٱلشَّعبيُّ ٱلتَّقليديُّ فِي مِصر ودُول عربِيَّة أُخرى؛
  Popular Traditional Foods in Egypt and Other Arab Countries

- الـمعالِمُ ٱلسِّياحِيَّةُ فِـي مِصْر وغَيْـرِها مِن ٱلدُّولِ ٱلعربِيَّة.
  Touristic Landmarks in Egypt and Other Arab Countries

* * *

(ب) مُختاراتٌ مِن ٱلحِكمِ وٱلأمثالِ ٱلعربِيّة:

مَنْ جَدَّ وَجَدَ وَمَنْ زَرَعَ حَصَدَ.

He who strives will achieve, and he who sows shall reap.

عامِلِ ٱلنَّاسَ كَما تُحِبُّ أَنْ يُعامِلُوكَ!

Treat people as you like them to treat you!

عَدُوٌّ عاقِلٌ خَيْرٌ مِنْ صَديقٍ جاهِلٍ.

A sound-minded enemy is better than an ignorant friend.

مَنْ	= he who, the one who
جَدَّ	= strives, works diligently
وَجَدَ	= (will) find (the fruits), will reach
وَمَنْ (وَ+مَنْ)	= and he who
زَرَعَ	= would sow
حَصَدَ	= shall reap
عامِلِ	= treat
النَّاسَ	= (the) people
كَما	= as
تُحِبُّ أَنْ	= you would like that
يُعامِلُوكَ	= they treat you
عَدُوٌّ	= an enemy
عاقِلٌ	= sound-minded
خَيْرٌ مِنْ	= better than
صَديقٍ جاهِلٍ	= ignorant friend

تَـمارين عامَّة ومُراجَعَة:

تَـمرين ١: **Let's read the following sets of words or phrases, recall their meanings and then guess why they were grouped together under one category:**

١- الأَحَد / الاِثْنَيْن / الثُّلاثاء / الأَربِعاء / الْخَمِيس / الْجُمُعَة / السَّبْت.

٢- ماذا / كَيْفَ / كَمْ / مَنْ؟

٣- واحِد / اِثنان / ثلاثَة / أَربَعة / خَمْسَة / سِتَّة / سَبْعَة / ثَـمانِية / تِسْعَة / عَشَرَة.

٤- الأَوَّل / الثَّاني / الثَّالِث / الرَّابِع / الْخامِس / السَّادِس / السَّابِع / الثَّامِن / التَّاسِع / العاشِر.

٥- الأُولَى / الثَّانِيَة / الثَّالِثة / الرَّابِعَة / الْخامِسَة / السَّادِسَة / السَّابِعَة / الثَّامِنَة / التَّاسِعَة / العاشِرَة.

٦- أَوَّلاً / ثانِيًا / ثالِثًا / رابِعًا / خامِسًا / سادِسًا / سابِعًا / ثامِنًا / تاسِعًا / عاشِرًا.

٧- يَوْم (أَيَّام) / اِسْم (أَسْماء) / جامِع (جَوامِع) / مَكْتَبَة (مَكْتَبات) / جامِعَة (جامِعات) / مَسْجِد (مَساجِد) / ساعَة (ساعات) / سُوق (أَسْواق) / بَرْنامَج (بَرامِج) / مَطْعَم (مَطاعِم) / حَيّ (أَحْياء) / دُكَّان (دَكاكِين) / سَلَطَة (سَلَطات) / مَقْهَى (مَقاهِي) / نُزْهَة (نُزْهات) / شاطِئ (شَواطِئ) / مَرْكَب (مَراكِب) / نَهْر (أَنْهار).

٨- قَبْلَ / بَعْدَ / أَنْ / مَعَ / مِن / بَيْنَ / حَيْثُ.

٩- الفول الْمُدَمَّس / الطَّعْمِيَّة / الفَلافِل / البَيْض / الْجُبْنَة / الْمُرَبَّى / الْمُلوخِيَّة بِالأَرانِب / الرُّز / السَّلَطَة / الذُّرَة الْمَشْوِيَّة / الفول السُّودانِـي.

١٠- الشَّاي ، القَهْوَة ، عَصِير البُرْتُقال ، عَصِير الْمانجا.

١١- وَقْتاً مُمْتِعاً / مَطْعَماً شَعْبِيّاً / غداءً مُتَأَخِّراً / قَهْوَةً عَرَبِيَّةً.

تَـمرين ٢: **Select any combination of words from the previous exercise to construct full meaningful sentences: (*It's advisable that you write down your sentence (s) on a sheet of paper before delivering it verbally*)**

____

____

* * *

تَـمرين ٣: **From the list of <u>nouns</u> in in the shaded box, select the one most suitable to fill in the blanks in the following sentences:**

مَطْعَمِ / الفَلافِل / مَقْهى / الفولِ الْمُدَمَّس / الْجُبْنَة / وَقتًا مُمتِعًا / القَهْوَة / البَيْض / غُروبِ الشَّمْسِ / شاطِئ / الأرجِيلَة / الفُطورِ / نُزْهَةٍ / الشّاي / عَصير

١- أراد يوسُف أن يَقضِي ______ ______ مَعَ أختِهِ وزوجِها .

٢- فـي الصَّباحِ تناولوا طعام ______ فـي ______ الفُندُق .

٣- كان الإفطار يتكَوَّنُ مِن ______ ______ و ______
و ______ و ______ .

٤- شَرِبوا ______ و ______ و ______ البُرتُقال .

٥- بعدَ الغداءِ اسْتَراحُوا فـي ______ شَعْبِيّ ودَخَّنوا ______ .

٦- قَبْلَ ______ ______ بِقَلِيل ، ذَهَبوا فـي ______ على ______ النِّيل .

* * *

تَـمرين ٤: **From the list of <u>verbs</u> in in the shaded box, select the one most suitable to fill in the blanks in the following sentences:**

يُريدُ / ذَهَبوا / أَخْبَـرَ / شَرِبُوا / اِسْتَراحُوا / تَنَزَّهُوا / أَشْرَبُ / اِسْتَأْجَروا / تَجَوَّلُوا / أَكَلوا / تَشْرَبُ / يَتَكَوَّنُ

١- ______ يوسُف أخْتَهُ أنَّهُ ______ أن يقضي يوم الجمعة معهم .

٢- كانَ الإفطارُ ______ مِن الفول الـمُدَمَّس والطعمِيَّة والبَيْض .

٣- ______ إلى حَيّ "السَّيِّدَة زَيْنَب" و ______ بَيْـنَ الدَّكاكِيـن .

٤- في ذلِكَ الـمَطعم ______ الـمُـلوخِيَّة بِالأرانِب و ______ العَصير .

٥- بَعدَ الغَداءِ ______ قليلاً في مَقهى شَعبِيّ .

٦- بَعْدَ غُروبِ الشَّمْسِ ______ مَرْكَبًا و ______ فِي نَهْرِ النِّيل .

٧- ______ فِـي نُزْهَةٍ على شاطِئ النِّيل حَيْثُ ______ الذرة الـمَشوِيَّة .

٨- أنا ______ عَصيرَ البُرْتُقال ، وأختي ______ عَصير المانجا .

* * *

تَـمرين ٥: **From the list of particles given in the shaded box below, select the one most suitable to fill in the blanks in the following sentences:**

يا / مَعَ / بَيْـنَ / ماذا / مِن / أَنْ / فِـي / بَعْدَ / بِـ / كَمْ / إلَـى / عَلى / وَ

١- ___ أَنْ أَنْهَى يوسُف مَهَمَّتَهُ التِّجارِيَّة، أرادَ ___ يَقْضي وَقْتاً مُمْتِعاً ___ أُخْتِهِ.

٢- كانَ الفُطورُ يَتَكَوَّنُ ___ ٱلفول وٱلطَّعمِيَّة ___ ٱلبيض وٱلـجُبنَة.

٣- بَعْدَ ٱلصَّلاةِ ذَهَبُوا ___ حَيِّ ٱلسَّيِّدَة زَيْنَبْ وتَجَوَّلُوا ___ ٱلدَّكاكِيـنِ ٱلصَّغيـرَة.

٤- ___ غُرُوبِ ٱلشَّمْسِ __ قَليلٍ ، ذَهبوا ___ نُزْهَةٍ ___ شاطِئِ ٱلنِّيل.

٥- ___ يَوْما فِـي ٱلأُسبوعِ ___ سَمَر؟

٦- ___ تَفْعَلِيـنَ يَوْمَ ٱلجُمُعَةِ يا فاطِمَة؟

* * *

تَـمرين ٦: **Rearrange the Following Sentences to Match the Sequence of the Events in in the Reading Text Text** برنامج يوم الجُمُعَة

Read the following statements and then answer whether each is true or false, using Arabic terms; your answers should be based on your comprehension of the conversational as well as the reading texts of the unit:

١- فـي الصَّباح تَناولوا طَعام الفُطور فـي الفُندق.

٢- بَعْدَ الصَّلاة ذَهبوا إلـى حَيّ السَّيِّدة زَيْنَب .

٣- بَعْدَ الإفطار توَجَّهوا إلـى الجامِع الأزهَر لِصَلاة الجُمُعة .
٤- فـي وَقْت العَصر دَخلوا مَطعماً شَعبيًّا، وتَناولوا غَداءً مُتأخِّراً.
٥- بَعْدَ الغَداء ، اِسْتَراحوا فـي مَقْهى شَعبيّ ودَخَّنوا الأَرجيلة.
٦- بَعْدَ غُروب الشَّمس اِسْتأْجَروا مَركباً لِـيَتَنَزَّهوا عـلى النِّيل .
٧- قَبْلَ غُروب الشَّمس ذَهَبوا فـي نُزْهة عـلى شاطئ النِّيل.

* * *

تَـمرين ٧:

<u>Practice the five singular conjugations of the the present tense verbs</u> by filling in the blanks in the following table:

أنا	أنْتِ	أنْتَ	هِيَ	هُوَ
				يَـأكُـلُ
			تَـشْرَبُ	
		تَـذْهَبُ		
	تَـعْرِفِـيـنَ			
أفْـعَـلُ				

* * *

تَـمرين ٨ : تَصريفات الفِعل (زارَ):

The verb (زارَ) is a weak (hollow), like the verb (قالَ) you studied its conjugation paradigm in the previous unit. Let's see how you fair by conjugating it in its <u>past tense, singular and plural</u> conjugations, to fill in the blanks in the following table!

Corresponding Verb Conjugations	Plural Subject Pronouns	Corresponding Verb Conjugations	Singular Subject Pronouns
	هُم		هُوَ
	هُنَّ		هِيَ
	أنْتُم		أنْتَ
	أنْتُـنَّ		أنْتِ
	نَحْنُ		أنـا

تـمرين ٩: نَشاط لُغَوي: تسلِيَة مع لعبة البَحْثِ عَنِ الكَلِماتِ :

Linguistic Activity : Diversion with the Game of Word Search!
Search the cross-words for the Arabic Days of the Week! (vertically, horizontally, or diagonally):
The words for "Days" and "Week" are done for you as examples:

(السّبت ، الأحد ، الاثنيـن ، الثّلاثاء ، الأربعاء ، الخميس ، الجمعة)

أ	يّ	ا	م	ب	ا	ت	ث	ج	ح	خ	د	ذ	ر	ز
ل	ك	ل	ق	ف	غ	ل	ع	ظ	ط	ض	ص	ا	ش	س
م	ن	أ	هـ	و	ي	ء	أ	ب	ت	ث	ج	ل	ح	خ
غ	ع	س	ظ	ط	ض	ص	ش	ح	س	ز	ر	ج	ذ	د
ف	ذ	ب	ج	ث	ت	ب	ا	ي	د	و	هـ	م	ن	ل
ق	ب	و	ح	ت	ي	هـ	ن	ا	م	ل	ق	ع	س	ك
ا	ث	ع	خ	د	ذ	ر	ز	س	ل	ش	ص	ـة	ض	ق
ل	ف	غ	ا	ل	إ	ث	ن	ي	ن	خ	ع	ظ	ط	ف
س	ق	ك	ل	م	ن	هـ	و	ي	ء	ا	م	ب	ث	غ
ب	ص	ش	ث	س	ز	ر	ذ	د	ح	خ	ج	ي	ت	ع
ت	ض	ز	ل	ض	ظ	غ	ف	ع	ط	ص	ذ	ر	س	ظ
و	ط	د	ا	ل	أ	ر	ب	ع	ا	ء	ح	ج	ث	ط
ي	ظ	ح	ث	س	ص	ط	ظ	ض	ش	ز	د	خ	ت	ض
ا	ب	ت	ا	ث	ج	ح	خ	د	ذ	ر	ز	س	ش	ص
ت	ع	غ	ء	ف	ق	ك	ل	م	ن	هـ	و	ي	ا	ب

نِهاية الوحدة الخامِسَة

The Sixth Unit / الوحدة السَّادِسَة

6th Unit / الوِحْدَةُ ٱلسَّادِسَة
1st Lesson / الدَّرسُ ٱلأَوَّل

فـي قِسْمِ ٱللُّغَةِ ٱلعَرَبِيَّةِ
At the Arabic Language Department

- الطَّالِب : مَرْحَباً يا أُسْتاذَة!
- السِّكْرِتيرَة : أَهْلاً سَيِّدي ! وَلَكِنِّي لَسْتُ أُسْتَاذَةً، أَنا سِكْرِتيـرَةُ ٱلقِسْم.
- الطَّالِب : عَفْواً يا سَيِّدَتـي! مِنْ فَضْلِكِ، أُرِيدُ أَنْ أُقابِلَ أَحَدَ ٱلـمَسْؤُولِيـنَ هُنا.
- السِّكْرِتيرَة : هَلْ أَنْتَ طالِبٌ جَديدٌ فـي هَذِهِ ٱلجامِعَة؟
- الطَّالِب : لا ، لَسْتُ طالِباً جَديداً. وَلَكِنِّي أُرِيدُ أَنْ أَلْتَحِقَ بِٱلقِسْمِ لِدِراسَةِ ٱللُّغَةِ ٱلعَرَبِيَّةِ كَتَخَـصُّصٍ ثـانٍ.
- السِّكْرِتيرَة : حَسَناً! نَحْنُ نُرَحِّبُ بِكَ، وَلَكِنْ يَلْزَمُكَ أَنْ تُـقابِلَ رَئِيسَةَ ٱلقِسْم.
- الطَّالِب : نَعَمْ ، أُقابِلُها الآنَ إِذا كانَتْ مَوْجُودَةً فِـي مَكْـتَـبِها.

- السِّكْرِتيرَة: لِلأَسَفِ! هِيَ لَيْسَتْ مَوْجُودَةً فِـي مَكْـتَبِها الآن.
عِنْدَها مُحاضَرَةٌ حَتَّى السَّاعَةِ الثَّانِيَة.
- الطَّالِب : حَسَناً! سَأَعُودُ ثانِيَةً بَعْدَ ٱلظُّهْر. هَلْ يُـمْكِنُكِ أَنْ تَأْخُذِي لِـي مَوْعِداً مَـعَها؟
- السِّكْرِتيرَة: بِكُـلِّ سُرُورٍ! وَلَكِنْ ما ٱسْمُكَ؟
- الطَّالِب : اِسْمِي صَلاحُ الدِّينِ أَحْمَد، وأَنا طالِبٌ فـي قِسْمِ ٱلعُلُومِ ٱلسِّياسِيَّةِ.
- السِّكْرِتيرَة: شُكْراً يا سَيِّدُ صَلاح! يَبْدُو أَنَّكَ عَرَبِـيٌّ، أَلَيْسَ كَذَلِـكَ؟
- الطَّالِب : لَسْتُ عَرَبِيّاً، أَنا باكِسْتانِـيٌّ، وَلَكِنِّي أُحِبُّ ٱللُّغَةَ ٱلعَرَبِيَّة، إِلَى اللِّقاءِ!
- السِّكْرِتيرَة: أَنا سَعيدَةٌ جِدّاً بِـلِـقـائِـكَ! بِـٱلسَّلامَة!

مُفـرَدات وتَراكيب الدَّرس الأوَّل
Vocabulary & Linguistic Structures of the 1st Lesson

the language (languages)	اللُّغَة (لُغات)	department (departments)	قِسْم (أَقْسام)
however, I am	وَلَكِنِّي (وَ+لَكِنَّ+ي)	the Arabic Language	اللُّغَة العَرَبِيَّة
excuse me! pardon me!	عَفْواً	I am not	لَسْتُ
I want to	أُرِيدُ أَنْ	If you (*feminine*) please!	مِنْ فَضْلِكِ!
one (of)	أَحَدَ	meet (I)	أُقابِلَ
here	هُنا	officials (official)	الـمَسْؤُولِينَ (مَسْؤُول)
in the department	بِـالقِسْمِ (بِـ+ال+قِسْم)	to enroll (in)	أَلْتَحِقَ (بِـ)
as a major, as a specialty	كَـتَخَصُّصٍ (كَـ+تَخَصُّص)	for studying = to study	لِـدِراسَة (لِـ+دِراسَة)
well, fine!	حَسَناً	second (the second)	ثانٍ (الثّانِي)
but, however	وَلَكِنْ	we welcome you	نُرَحِّبُ بِـكَ (بِـ+كَ)
meet (you)	تُقابِلَ	you need to	يَلْزَمُكَ أَنْ (يَلْزَمُ+كَ)
now	الآنَ	I meet her	أُقابِلُـها (أُقابِلُ+ها)
she was	كـانَـتْ	if	إِذا
regretfully	لِـلأَسَف	available, present	مَوْجُودَة
a lecture (lectures)	مُحاضَرَة (مُحاضَرات)	she has	عِنْدَها (عِنْدَ+ها)
the hour, o'clock	السَّاعَة	until	حَتَّى
I will return	سَـأَعُودُ (سَـ+أَعُودُ)	2 o'clock = the 2nd hour	السَّاعَة الثَّانِيَة
(in) the afternoon	بَعْدَ الظُّهْر	again	ثانِيَةً
take, make (*you feminine*)	تَأْخُذِي	it possible for you…? Can you…?	يُـمْكِنُـكِ أَنْ

an appointment	مَوْعِداً	for me	لِي (لـ+ي)
with all	بِكُلِّ (بـ+كُلِّ)	with her	مَعَـها (مَعَ+ها)
What is your name?	ما ٱسْمُكَ ؟	pleasure, happiness / with all pleasure	سُرُور / بِكُلِّ سُرُور
(the) political sciences / a science	العُلُوم السِّياسِيَّة	Salāh ud-Dīn Ahmad (male proper name)	صَلاحُ الدِّين أَحْمَدُ
Isn't that so? (Is not)	أَلَيْسَ كَذَلِكَ ؟ (أَ+لَيْسَ)	it seems that	يَبْدُو أَنَّ
I like, I love	أُحِبُّ	a Pakistani / Pakistan	باكِسْتانِيّ / باكِسْتان
very	جِدّاً	happy, pleased (female-male pair)	سَعِيدَة / سَعِيد
Good bye!	بِالسَّلامَة = مَعَ السَّلامَة	with meeting you	بِلِقائِكَ (بـ+لِقاء+كَ)

Additional Vocabulary:

you are not (*masculine*)	لَسْتَ	he is not / it is not	لَيْسَ
a word (words)	كَلِمَة (كَلِمات)	you are not (*feminine*)	لَسْتِ
will, shall	سَوْفَ = سَـ	a sentence (sentences)	جُمْلَة (جُمَل)

* * *

Grammatical and Linguistic Issues   الدَّرس الثَّاني: القَواعِد وقَضايا لُغَوِيَّة

١- نَفْيُ الجُمَلِ الاسْمِيَّة بـ (لَيْسَ) .... 1. Negating Equational Sentences with لَيْسَ

٢- ٱلأَفْعالُ الـمُرْتَبِطَةُ بِالأَدَوات .... 2. Verbs-Particles Idioms

٣- ٱلفِعْلُ الـمُسْتَقْبَلُ مَعَ الأَدَوات (سَـ/سَوْفَ) 3. The Future Tense with the Particles ....

٤-الصِّفَةُ وَالـمَوْصُوف .... 4. Noun-Adjective Phrases

٥- (جِدًّا) تَرْتِيبُها وَعَلاقَتُها بِالصِّفَة 5. Word Order of the Arabic Equivalent of (Very) ....

٦- تَصْرِيفاتُ الـمُضارِع الْمَرْفُوع في حالاتِ الجَمْع 6. Present Tense Plural Conjugations ....

٧- ٱلـمِيزانُ الصَّرْفِيُّ وَجُذُورُ الكَلِمات: اِسْتِعْمالُ القامُوس الْعَرَبِيِّ ....
7. Morphological Patterning and Root System: Learning to use the Arabic Dictionary

١- نَفْيُ الجُمَلِ الاِسْمِيَّةِ بِـ (لَيْسَ)

1. Negating Equational Sentences with (لَيْسَ) or Its Other Conjugations:

- It has been stated previously that 'Equational Sentences' in Arabic have no verbs. However, they are made negative by the use of a special verb (لَيْسَ) or its derivative conjugational forms.
- (لَيْسَ) or its derivative conjugation forms can be translated into English as '**is not**', '**are not**' or '**am not**', depending on the 'subject' of the sentence.
- The 'subject' of (لَيْسَ) or any of its other related conjugations does not undergo any change in 'case-ending'; it remains in the 'nominative case'.
- If the subject of an 'Equational Sentence' is a personal pronoun, such as '**I**', '**he**' '**she**' or '**you**', then that pronoun is normally omitted when we negate the sentence, since the particular conjugation form of (لَيْسَ) will have the subject pronoun implied in its form.
- Now, let's read the following pairs of sentences, the first having an affirmative meaning and the second being negated by the appropriate form of (لَيْسَ):

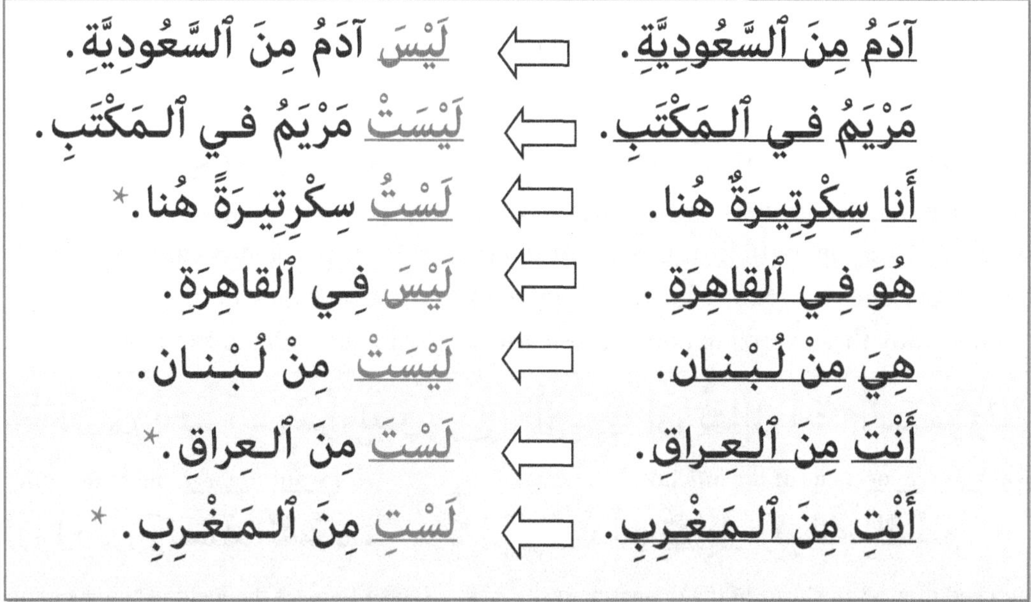

آدَمُ مِنَ ٱلسَّعُودِيَّةِ.	⇦	لَيْسَ آدَمُ مِنَ ٱلسَّعُودِيَّةِ.
مَرْيَمُ فِي ٱلْمَكْتَبِ.	⇦	لَيْسَتْ مَرْيَمُ فِي ٱلْمَكْتَبِ.
أَنَا سِكْرِتِيرَةٌ هُنَا.	⇦	لَسْتُ سِكْرِتِيرَةً هُنَا.*
هُوَ فِي ٱلْقَاهِرَةِ.	⇦	لَيْسَ فِي ٱلْقَاهِرَةِ.
هِيَ مِنْ لُبْنَانَ.	⇦	لَيْسَتْ مِنْ لُبْنَانَ.
أَنْتَ مِنَ ٱلْعِرَاقِ.	⇦	لَسْتَ مِنَ ٱلْعِرَاقِ.*
أَنْتِ مِنَ ٱلْمَغْرِبِ.	⇦	لَسْتِ مِنَ ٱلْمَغْرِبِ.*

- If the '**predicate**' of an 'Equational Sentence' is a single word (as opposed to a prepositional phrase), then when negated by (لَيْسَ) or its other conjugation forms, that 'predicate' becomes 'accusative', as the 'object of (لَيْسَ)', and accordingly should show the '*Fathah*' or the '*Tanween of Fathah*' as its 'case-ending' sign. It must be made clear that this rule explained above applies only when the 'predicate' is a single noun or adjectival noun, or a combination of a 'noun-adjective' phrase, but not if it is a 'prepositional phrase' or an 'adverb'. Here are some examples:

لَيْسَ عُمَرُ ٱلرَّئِيسَ هُنا.	⇦	عُمَرُ ٱلرَّئِيسُ هُنا.
لَيْسَتْ مَرْيَمُ أُسْتاذَةً فـي ٱلقِسْمِ.	⇦	مَرْيَمُ أُسْتاذَةٌ فِي ٱلقِسْمِ.
لَسْتُ سِكْرِتِيرَةً هُنا.	⇦	أَنا سِكْرِتِيرَةٌ هُنا.
أَلَسْتَ طالِباً جَدِيداً؟	⇦	هَلْ أَنْتَ طالِبٌ جَدِيدٌ؟
أَلَسْتِ أُسْتاذَةً عَرَبِيَّةً؟	⇦	هَلْ أَنْتِ أُسْتاذَةٌ عَرَبِيَّةٌ؟

- We have said previously that if the 'subject' of (لَيْسَ), or any other of its conjugations, happened to be a 'personal pronoun', such as **I**, **he**, **she**, or **you**, then that pronoun is normally omitted. However, the 'personal subject pronoun' may be shown if special emphasis is called for, as in the following examples:

لَسْتَ أَنْتَ ٱلرَّئِيسَ هُنا، أَنا ٱلرَّئِيسُ!

لَسْتُ أَنا ٱلطَّالِبَ، أَنْتَ الطَّالِبُ!

* * *

2. Verb-Particle Idioms: (أُرِيدُ أَنْ) , (يَلْزَمُ أَنْ) , (يُـمْكِنُ أَنْ) , (يَبْدُو أَنَّ) -٢

- The verbs above occurred as part of the text of the lesson. As we can see each of them is followed by a certain particle; thus we can say that they are particle-bound and they form with these particles something like an idiom to express specific meanings.
- Let's now study these verbs in context to learn the particulars related to them:

أُرِيدُكَ أَنْ تُقابِلَ أَحَدَ ٱلـمَسْؤُولِيـنَ.	←	أُرِيدُ أَنْ أُقابِلَ أَحَدَ ٱلـمَسْؤُولِيـنَ.
I want you to meet one of the officials.	→	**I want to meet one of the officials.**
يَلْزَمُكَ أَنْ تُقابِلَ رَئِيسَةَ ٱلقِسْمِ.	←	يَلْزَمُ أَنْ أُقابِلَ رَئِيسَةَ ٱلقِسْمِ.
You need to meet the head of the department.	→	**I need to meet the head of the department.**
يُـمْكِنُكَ أَنْ تَدْرُسَ ٱللُّغَةَ ٱلعَرَبِيَّةَ.	←	يُـمْكِنُ أَنْ أَدْرُسَ ٱللُّغَةَ ٱلعَرَبِيَّةَ.
It is possible for you to study the Arabic language.	→	**It is possible that I study the Arabic language.**

- If we examine the usage of the three verbs above, in the three sentences on the right, we will find that each was followed by the particle (أَنْ); this particle belongs to a group of particles in Arabic that are called '**Subjunctive Particles**'. A 'subjunctive particle' requires that a verb in the 'subjunctive mood' should follow.

- The English translation of the particle (أَنْ) is either '**to**', as in the first two examples, or '**that**', as in the third example.
- If we further examine the three parallel sentences on the left we find, in addition to the facts mentioned above, that these same verbs received the 'suffixed pronoun' (ـكَ), and consequently, the conjugation of the following verb was adjusted to correspond to the 'subject' related to this pronoun, which is in this case (أَنْتَ). Obviously, the attachment of the 'suffixed pronoun' (ـكَ), has resulted in a slight change in the meanings of these sentences, as compared to the three previous one.
- Now, let's examine the verb (يَبْدُو) in the following context:

يَبْدُو أَنَّكَ عَرَبِيٌّ. / يَبْدُو أَنَّ الطَّالِبَ عَرَبِيٌّ.
It seems that the student is an Arab. / It seems that you are an Arab.

- Like the previous three verbs, the verb (يَبْدُو) must to be followed by a particular particle, forming with it what we might call a 'Verb-Particle Idiom'.
- However, the particle following this verb is somehow different both in nature and pronunciation. This (أَنَّ), though also translated as '**that**' in English, belongs to a different group of particles, which must be followed by a 'suffixed pronoun' or a regular noun in the 'accusative mood'; unlike the three previous ones which were followed by other verbs.

* * *

3. Future Tense Verbs with the Particles (سَـ) and (سَوْفَ):

- The 'future tense' of Arabic verbs is based on the 'imperfect tense' or 'present tense' stems, preceded by either (سَـ) or (سَوْفَ).
- Since (سَـ), as a one-letter particle, will always be connected to the following verb and forming with it one integrated unit.
- In real everyday language these two particles are used interchangeably. However, in literary Arabic the (سَـ) is used for near future, whereas the (سَوْفَ) is used for distant future.
- Now, let's read the following examples with both future particles:

سَـأَعُودُ ثانِيَةً بَعْدَ ٱلظُّهْرِ. / سَوْفَ أَعُودُ ثانِيَةً، إِنْ شاءَ ٱللَّهُ!
سَـأُقابِلُ أَحَدَ ٱلْـمَسؤُولِينَ بَعْدَ قَلِيلٍ. / سَوْفَ أُقابِلُ أَحَدَ ٱلْمَسؤُولِينَ بَعْدَ أَيّامٍ.
سَـأَذْهَبُ إِلـى ٱلسُّوقِ. / سَوْفَ أَذهَبُ إِلـى ٱلسُّوقِ ٱلأُسْبُوعَ ٱلـقادِمَ.

- Now, let's read the following table containing five conjugations of five verbs to further develop familiarity with verb conjugations that have future meanings:

أنـا	أَنْتِ	أَنْتَ	هِيَ	هُوَ
سَأَعُودُ	سَتَعُودِينَ	سَتَعُودُ	سَتَعُودُ	سَيَعُودُ
سَأُقابِلُ	سَتُقَابِلِيـنَ	سَتُقَابِلُ	سَتُقَابِلُ	سَيُقَابِلُ
سَأُرَحِّبُ	سَتُـرَحِّبِيـنَ	سَتُـرَحِّبُ	سَتُـرَحِّبُ	سَيُـرَحِّبُ
سَأَذْهَبُ	سَتَذْهَبِيـنَ	سَتَذْهَبُ	سَتَذْهَبُ	سَيَذْهَبُ
سَأَفْعَلُ	سَتَفْعَلِيـنَ	سَتَفْعَلُ	سَتَفْعَلُ	سَيَفْعَلُ

* * *

4. Noun-Adjective Phrases .... ٤-الصِّفَةُ وَالـمَوْصُوف

- One of the most common and basic linguistic structures in Arabic is what is known as 'noun-adjective phrase'.
- This structure, in its simplest form, consists of two words. The first is a '**noun**' and the second is an '**adjective**' modifying the noun preceding it or describing it.
- Unlike English, in Arabic, the 'adjective' follows the 'noun' it modifies, rather than preceding it.
- The 'noun-adjective' phrase functions as one single unit in a sentence; the whole phrase serving as 'subject', 'predicate', 'object of a verb' or 'object of a preposition'.
- As such, the 'adjective' agrees with the 'noun' it modifies in several ways:
  1. In **Gender**: If the noun is 'masculine', then the 'adjective' must have its 'masculine' form. If the noun is 'feminine' then the 'adjective' must have its 'feminine' form.
  2. **Definiteness** or **Indefiniteness**: If the 'noun' is 'definite', then the 'adjective' must have the 'Definite Article'; if the 'noun' is 'indefinite', then the 'adjective' must have the appropriate form of '*Tanween*' to reflect that.
  3. **Case-Ending**: If, for example, the 'noun' is ending with a '*Dammah*', because it is 'nominative', then the 'adjective' must bear a '*Dammah*' too.

- Let's now read the following sentences with concentration on the underlined 'noun-adjective phrases' and analyze the points of agreements between the 'nouns' and their 'adjectives':

هَذا بابٌ جَديدٌ. / هَذِهِ طاوِلَةٌ جَديدَةٌ.

مِنْ أَيْنَ ٱلطَّالِبُ ٱلجَديدُ؟ / مِنْ أَيْنَ ٱلطَّالِبَةُ ٱلجَديدَةُ؟

لَيْسَ صَلاحٌ أُسْتاذاً جَديداً. / لَيْسَتْ مَرْيَمُ أُسْتاذَةً جَديدَةً

كَمْ طالِباً سَعيداً فِـي ٱلصَّفِّ؟ / كَمْ طالِبَةً سَعيدَةً فِـي ٱلصَّفِّ؟

هُوَ أُسْتاذٌ فِـي جامِعَةٍ عَرَبِيَّةٍ. / هُوَ أُسْتاذٌ فِـي ٱلجامِعَةِ ٱلعَرَبِيَّةِ.

- Furthermore, there may be more than one 'adjective' modifying the same 'noun' in a 'noun-adjective phrase'; as in the following examples:

هُوَ أُسْتاذٌ عَرَبِـيٌّ مَشْهُورٌ. / هِيَ أُسْتاذَةٌ عَرَبِيَّةٌ مَشْهُورَةٌ.

famous, well-known

- The 'adjective' in a 'noun-adjective phrase' may itself be modified, usually by a simple 'adverb' or by a 'prepositional phrase', as in the following sentences:

هَذا كِتابٌ جَديدٌ جِدّاً. / هَذِهِ آنِسَةٌ سَعيدَةٌ جِدّاً.

- Now, note carefully the distinction between the two following pairs of structures:

اَلأُسْتاذُ مَشْهُورٌ. / اَلأُسْتاذُ ٱلمَشْهُورُ .....

اَلمَكْتَبَةُ جَديدَةٌ. / اَلمَكْتَبَةُ ٱلجَديدَةُ .....

- In the box above, the two statements on the right are both complete sentences, each consisting of a 'subject' and a 'predicate'. As a 'predicate', the 'adjective' agrees with the 'noun subject' in 'gender' but not in 'definiteness'.
- However, the two parallel statements on the left are not full complete sentences, they are 'noun-adjective' phrases; as such, the 'adjectives' agree with their 'nouns' in 'gender', 'definiteness' and 'case-ending'.

5. Word Order for the Arabic Equivalent of "Very / جِدّاً":

- (جِدّاً) is the Arabic equivalent of the English '**very**'.
- In linguistic terminology classification it is considered an '**adverb**', which is invariable, in the sense that it does not have 'case-ending' variations.
- It always follows an 'adjective' and modifies it, rather than preceding it as in English.

هَذا كِتابٌ جَديدٌ جِدّاً. / هَذِهِ أَسْتاذَةٌ مَشْهُورَةٌ جِدّاً.

* * *

6. The Imperfect (Present Tense) Verbs: The Five Verbs ٦-الأَفْعال الخَمْسَة

- We have previously introduced the '**Imperfect**' or '**Present Tense**' verbs, and have limited the conjugation process to only five singular conjugations. (see, 5th point of Lesson 3, under the grammar notes)
- Arabic grammarians have elaborated a group of other conjugations that they call (الأَفْعالُ الْخَمْسَةُ; (i.e. **The Five Verbs**).
- These 'Five Verbs' are derived from the singular forms by suffixing towards the end one of the following: (1) The ***Alif* of the Dual** (two), both for 3rd and 2nd Persons; (2) The ***Wāw* of the Plural**, both for 3rd and 2nd Persons; or (3) The ***Yaa* of the Female 2nd Person**. By following the formula just explaind above, we can derive five extra conjugations, and hence the name '**The Five Verbs**.'
- In the following two tables, we will see first the four singular conjugations of five 'present tense' verbs; then to be followed by the second table, showing '**The Five Verbs**' counterparts of the first group:

أنـا	أَنْتَ	هِيَ	هُوَ
أَفْعَلُ	تَفْعَلُ	تَفْعَلُ	يَفْعَلُ
أَسْأَلُ	تَسْأَلُ	تَسْأَلُ	يَسْأَلُ
أَكْتُبُ	تَكْتُبُ	تَكْتُبُ	يَكْتُبُ
أَذْهَبُ	تَذْهَبُ	تَذْهَبُ	يَذْهَبُ
أَعْرِفُ	تَعْرِفُ	تَعْرِفُ	يَعْرِفُ
Subject Marker Prefix أَ	**Subject Marker Prefix** تَـ	**Subject Marker Prefix** تَـ	**Subject Marker Prefix** يَـ

أنتِ	أنْتُمْ	هُمْ	أنْتُما	هُما
تَـفْعَلِـيـنَ	تَـفْعَلُونَ	يَـفْعَلُونَ	تَـفْعَلانِ	يَـفْعَلانِ
تَـسْأَلِـيـنَ	تَـسْأَلُونَ	يَـسْأَلُونَ	تَـسْأَلانِ	يَـسْأَلانِ
تَـكْـتُـبِـيـنَ	تَـكْـتُـبُـونَ	يَـكْـتُـبُـونَ	تَـكْـتُـبـانِ	يَـكْـتُـبـانِ
تَـذْهَـبِـيـنَ	تَـذْهَـبُـونَ	يَـذْهَـبُـونَ	تَـذْهَـبـانِ	يَـذْهَـبـانِ
تَـعْـرِفِـيـنَ	تَـعْـرِفُـونَ	يَـعْـرِفُـونَ	تَـعْـرِفـانِ	يَـعْـرِفـانِ
Subject Marker Suffix ... Prefix	**Subject Marker Suffix ... Prefix**	**Subject Marker Suffix ... Prefix**	**Subject Marker Suffix ... Prefix**	**Subject Marker Suffix ... Prefix**
تَـ...ـيـنَ	تَـ...ـُونَ	يَـ...ـُونَ	تَـ...ـانِ	يَـ...ـانِ

- If we compare the two tables above, we will notice that, while the four singular conjugations in the first table above had only '**Prefixed Subject Markers**' in the letters (يَـ), (تَـ), and (أَ) before the '**stem**' of the verbs, we find that '**The Five Verbs**' conjugations of the 2nd table above have a combination of both '**Prefixed Subject Markers**' in the letters (يَـ) and (تَـ) before the '**stem**' of the verbs, and '**Suffixed Subject Markers**' in the form of the syllables (ـانِ), (ـُونَ), and (ـِيـنَ); and it is precisely because of this distinguished feature that Arab grammarians labeled them under a special name category.
- Moreover, while the four singular conjugations of the 1st table above, mark "*I'rāb*" or '**Mood Marker Case-Ending**' with short vowel diacritical marks (*Dammah* or *Fathah*), the 'Five Verbs' conjugations mark "*I'rāb*" or '**Mood Marker Case-Ending**' with the presence or the absence of the actual letters (نِ) or (نَ) as will be treated later.

* * *

7. Morphological Patterning and Root System: Prelude to Learning to Use An Arabic Dictionary:

- Let's first read and observe the two following sets of related words:

he wrote = كَـتَـبَ	a lesson = دَرْس
writing = كِـتـابَـة	study, studying = دِراسَـة
a desk, an office = مَـكْـتَـب	a school = مَدْرَسَـة
a library = مَـكْـتَـبَـة	he studied = دَرَسَ

a book = كِتاب	he taught = دَرَّسَ
a letter, something written = مَكْتوب	a (male) teacher = مُدَرِّس
a writer = كاتِب	schools = مَدارِسُ
(ROOT) = (كتب) ك / ت / ب	(ROOT) = (درس) د / ر / س

- If we examine the first set of words in the table above, we will notice that all these words have **three consonants** in common; namely the (د / ر / س). The related words also have various vowels in various arrangements, and some of them have other consonants and long vowel letters.
- Such a set of consonets, in a certain order, common to a number of different words, is called a '**root**', (Arabic جَذْر), and the individual consonants of a 'root' are called '**radicals**'.
- The great majority of 'roots' in Arabic consist of '**three radicals**'; a few contain one, two, four or five. And these 'three radicals' constitute the **entries** in an Arabic dictionary.
- Generally, a given 'root' has associated with it a 'basic meaning' which is relatable to all words derived from it. For example, the 'root د / ر / س' means '**study**'; (دَرْس) '**a lesson**' is a 'thing studied'; (دِراسَة) '**studying**' is the 'activity of studying'; ; (مَدْرَسَة) '**a school**' is a 'place where studying takes place'; (دَرَّسَ) '**he taught**' has the underlying meaning of 'he made someone study'; (مُدَرِّس) '**teacher, instructor**' has the underlying meaning of 'one who teaches'; and so on.
- Furthermore, Arab linguists devised another linguistic device for word association and relations, called '**morphological pattern**'; the Arabic (اَلـمِيزَانُ الصَّرْفِـيُّ).
- Through this '**pattern system**', 'roots' may be conveniently symbolized with the letters (فعل); whereas the (ف) stands for the first radical; the (ع) stands for the second radical; and the (ل) stands for the third radical.
- Now, let's read and examine the following two sets of words, and note that words in each group share one specific 'pattern', based on this linguistic device explained above:

he ate = أَكَلَ	new = جَدِيد
he came = حَضَرَ	modern = حَدِيث

he studied = دَرَسَ	big, large = كَبِير
he went = ذَهَبَ	old = قَدِيم
he returned = رَجَعَ	close by, near = قَرِيب
he wrote = كَتَبَ	happy = سَعِيد
he promised = وَعَدَ	beautiful = جَمِيل
(PATTERN) = (فَعَلَ)	(PATTERN) = (فَعِيل)

- The group in the right hand column above are all examples of a 'pattern' common to 'adjectives' and they all have the 'pattern' (فَعِيل). The 'first radical' in each of them bears the vowel '*Fathah*'; the 'second radical bears the vowel '*Kasrah*'; then there is the '*Yaa* as a long vowel' added after the 'second radical'; then, there is finally the 'third radical'
- The group in the left hand column are all 'verbs' in the 'past tense'. They all have in common a similarity in 'pattern', which is (فَعَلَ), with each of the three 'consonantal radicals' bearing a '***Fathah***'. These verbs and all others that have these common characteristics are accordingly said to be of the 'pattern' (فَعَلَ).
- The great majority of words in Arabic can be analyzed into a '**root**' and a '**pattern**'. This is extremely useful in mastering new vocabulary. As the learners become familiar with more and more 'roots' and 'patterns', they will be able to analyze new words on their own and to associate their meanings with other words they already knew.
- For example, you have learned the words (مَكْتَبَة) and (مَدْرَسَة) for '**a library, a bookstore**' and '**a school**'; they both have the '**pattern**' (مَفْعَلَة), and further have the underlying meanings of '**nouns of places**', since (مَكْتَبَة) is a place where books are to be found, and (مَدْرَسَة) is a place where studying is done. When, in the future, you encounter the word (مَحْكَمَة), for example, you can then analyze it as composed of the 'root' (حكم) '**to judge**' and deduce that its underlying meaning is related to a place where judging takes place; hence its meaning '**court house**'.

- Moreover, an <u>understanding of 'roots' and 'patterns'</u> is essential to the use of Arabic dictionaries where words threin are arranged alphabetically by 'root', and not by their actual physical appearance as is the case with English.

- Now, **to get training in using the Arabic dictionary, follow the following steps**:

  1. Strip the word you want to look up from its non-radical letters it might contain to reduce it to the '**three radical consonants**' which constitute the '**root**'.

  2. Open your dictionary alphabetically, according to the order of the consonants in the 'root' to find the '**entry**' to the word you are trying to look up. The 'root' letters are normally given on the top of the page above a margin line.

  3. Look up alphabetically under the 'entry' till you find the word you are looking for.

- The following are general useful tips to consider when stripping words down to their 'roots':

  1. The '*Taa Marbūtah*' (ـة / ة), the '*Alif Maqsūrah*' (ى) and *Alif*, *Wāw* or *Yaa* (ا / و / ي) <u>as long vowels</u>, are never part of a 'root' and therefore must be the first to be stripped down from a word.

  2. The other consonantal letters that can be 'non-root' letters are confined to the following seven ones:

$$\text{س / أ / ل / ت / م / ن / هـ}$$

- However, these same letters might be 'root radicals' in many words, so do not rush into eliminating them whenever you see them.

- The rest of the Arabic consonantal letters are 'root radicals' and should not be considered at all for elimination.

- The 'non-root' letters, including the three long vowel letters, have been grouped together for easy recalling in the following word:

$$\text{سَأَلْتُمُونِيها}$$

* * *

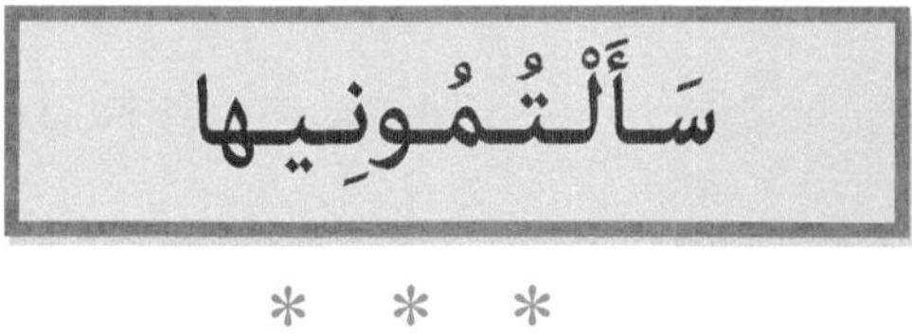

الدَّرسُ الثَّالِثُ: تَدْرِيباتٌ وَنَشاطاتٌ / Exercises & Activities

(*Oral and Written*) Recognizing the Subject Pronoun of (لَيْسَ): تَـمْرِين ١:

Identify the independent pronoun which corresponds to the conjugation form of (لَيْسَ), as in the given example:

لَيْسَ مِنْ لُبْنان. (هُوَ)

١- لَسْتُ طالِباً هُنا. (..............)　　٢- لَيْسَتْ مَرْيَمُ أُسْتاذَةً. (..................)

٣- أَلَسْتِ عَرَبِيَّةً؟ (..............)　　٤- أَلَسْتَ مِنَ ٱلخَرْطومِ؟ (...............)

٥- لَيْسَ مِنَ ٱلكُوَيْتِ. (..............)　　٦- لَسْتُ أُسْتاذَةً هُنا. (...............)

* * *

تَـمْرين ٢: (*Oral and Written*) Negation with (لَيْسَ):

Negate the following affirmative sentences, using the appropriate conjugation form of (لَيْسَ):

هِيَ أُسْتاذَةٌ جَديدَةٌ. ⇐ لَيْسَتْ أُسْتاذَةً جَديدَةً.

١- أَنا مِنَ ٱلسَّعُودِيَّةِ. ⇐ ....

٢- هُوَ طالِبٌ جَديدٌ. ⇐ ....

٣- هِيَ أُسْتاذَةٌ عَرَبِيَّةٌ. ⇐ ....

٤- هَلْ أَنْتِ طالِبَةٌ جَديدَةٌ؟ ⇐ ....

٥- أَنْتَ ٱلرَّئِيسُ هُنا. ⇐ ....

٦- هَذا الأُسْتاذُ عَرَبِيٌّ. ⇐ ....

٧- هَذِهِ الآنِسَةُ أَمْرِيكِيَّةٌ. ⇐ ....

٨- هَذِهِ الْجامِعَةُ مَشْهُورَةٌ. ⇐ ....

٩- الرَّئِيسُ مَوْجُودٌ فِي مَكْتَبِهِ. ⇐ ....

* * *

تَـمْرين٣: (*Oral and Written*) Using the Appropriate Particle with Certain Verbs and Translation:

Use the appropriate particle of (أَنْ) or (أَنَّ) to fill in the blanks in the following sentences, then translate the resultant sentence into English, as in the given examples:

Homework

أُرِيدُ .... أُقابِلَ أَحَدَ ٱلمَسْؤُولِينَ. ←

أُرِيدُ أَنْ أُقابِلَ أَحَدَ ٱلمَسْؤُولِينَ. ↓

I want to meet one of the officials.

١- أُرِيدُ .... أَتَكَلَّمَ مَعَ أَحَدِ ٱلأَساتِذَةِ. ....

٢- يَبْدُو .... ٱلطَّالِبَ ٱلجَدِيدَ عَرَبِيٌّ. ....

٣- يَلْزَمُكَ .... تُقابِلَ رَئِيسَةَ ٱلقِسْمِ. ....

٤- تَبْدُو .... (هِيَ) طالِبَةٌ أَمْرِيكِيَّةٌ. ....

٥- هَلْ يُمْكِنُكِ .... تَأْخُذِي لِي مَوْعِداً؟ ....

٦- نَعَمْ ، يُمْكِنُها .... تُقابِلَ ٱلأُسْتاذَ. ....

٧- يُرِيدُ صَلاحٌ .... يَلْتَحِقَ بِقِسْمِ ٱللُّغَةِ ٱلعَرَبِيَّةِ.

....

* * *

تَمْرِين ٤: (*Oral and Written*) Forming Future Time with (سَـ) and (سَوْفَ):

The following sentences contain verbs that express the 'present' time. Practice making 'future' time by using once the future particle (سَـ) and the future particle (سَوْفَ) another time; follow the given example:

يَذْهَبُ إِلَى السُّوقِ. ← سَيَذْهَبُ إِلَى السُّوقِ. ← سَوْفَ يَذْهَبُ إِلَى السُّوقِ.

١- تُقابِلُ رَئِيسَ ٱلقِسْمِ. ← .... ← ....

٢- أَعُودُ إِلَى مَكْتَبِي. ← .... ← ....

٣- تَكْتُبُ كَلِمَةً جَدِيدَةً. ← .... ← ....

٤- هَلْ تَسْأَلُ ٱلْأُسْتاذَ؟ ← .... ← ....

٥- يَدْرُسُ ٱلدَّرْسَ ٱلسَّادِسَ. ← .... ← ....

٦- أَزُورُ أَصْدِقائِي يَوْمَ ٱلْجُمُعَةِ. ← .... ← ....

* * *

تَمْرين ٥: **(*Oral and Written*) Question Formation with (أَ) + (لَيْسَ):**

Read the following sentences first; then form 'negated questions' using the combination of the interrogative (أ) and the verb of negation (لَيْسَ), as in the given example:

صَلاحٌ طالِبٌ جَديدٌ. ← أَلَيْسَ صَلاحٌ طالِباً جَديداً؟

١- اَلأُسْتاذَةُ مَوْجُودَةٌ في مَكْتَبِها. ← ....؟

٢- هَذِهِ ٱلْمَكْتَبَةُ جَديدَةٌ. ← ....؟

٣- أَنْتِ طالِبَةٌ عَرَبِيَّةٌ. ← ....؟

٤- هَذِهِ جُمْلَةٌ مِنْ نَصِّ ٱلدَّرْسِ. ← ....؟

٥- اَلكَلِمَةُ في ٱلدَّرْسِ ٱلأَوَّلِ. ← ....؟

٦- أَنْتَ رَئِيسُ ٱلقِسْمِ. ← ....؟

* * *

تَمْرين ٦: **(<u>Review</u>: *Written / Oral*) Question Formation:**

From among the interrogative particles in the box below, choose the most appropriate to form questions which focus on the underlined parts of the sentences:

أَ / أَيْنَ / أَلَيْسَ / كَمْ / ما / مَنْ / مِنْ أَيْنَ / هَلْ ؟

١- الطَّالِبُ ٱلجَديدُ مِنَ ٱلْمَغْرِبِ. ⇐ .... ؟

٢- هَذا ٱلْأُسْتاذُ سامِي. ⇦ .... ؟

٣- لَيْسَ هَذا ٱلْأُسْتاذُ مِنَ ٱلرِّباطِ. ⇦ .... ؟

٤- أَنا مَرْيَمُ وَهَذِهِ نانْسِي. ⇦ .... ؟

٥- فِي الصَّفِّ عَشْرَةُ طُلَّابٍ. ⇦ .... ؟

٦- الرَّئِيسُ فِي مَكْتَبِهِ. ⇦ .... ؟

٧- لَسْتَ مِنْ مِصْرَ. ⇦ .... ؟

٨- نَعَمْ، السِّكْرِتِيرَةُ فِي مَكْتَبِها. ⇦ .... ؟

٩- هَذِهِ مَكْتَبَةُ ٱلجامِعَةِ. ⇦ .... ؟

١٠- لا، لَسْتُ عَرَبِيّاً. ⇦ .... ؟

* * *

تَمْرِين ٧: (Review: *Written*) Unscramble to Form Meaningful Sentences and Translation:

Unscramble the following sets of words by writing them in the correct order to form full meaningful sentences; then translate them into English, as in the given example:

> مَوْجُودَةً / أَلَيْسَتِ / مَكْتَبِها / ٱلْأُسْتاذَةُ / فِي ⇦
>
> أَلَيْسَتِ ٱلْأُسْتاذَةُ مَوْجُودَةً فِي مَكْتَبِها؟
>
> **Isn't the (*female*) professor available in her office?**

١- عَرَبِيّ/أَنْتَ / هَلْ . ⇦ .... ؟

٢- يا / أَيْنَ / إِبْراهِيمُ / أَنْتَ / مِنْ . ⇦ .... ؟

٣- عَلَى / يَكْتُبُ / اَلْوَلَدُ / اللَّوْحِ . ⇦ ....

٤- أُسْتاذُ / ٱلسَّعُودِيَّةِ / هُوَ / نَعَمْ / مِنَ ⇦ ....

٥- ثانِيَةً / ٱلظُّهْرِ / سَأَعُودُ / بَعْدَ ⇦ ....

(*Oral / Written*) Recognition of the Verbs and Their Subject Pronouns :تَـمْرين ٨

Each sentence below contains one of the '**Five Verbs**' conjugations introduced in the grammar notes. Your task is to read the sentence and identify the verb by underlining it; then, give in sound and in writing the corresponding 'subject pronoun' for each conjugation from the list in the column on the left. Follow the given example:

كُـلُّهُمْ يَعْرِفُونَ أَيَّامَ ٱلأُسْبُوعِ . (هُمْ)

١- هَلْ تَعْرِفُونَ كَيْفَ تَذْهَبُونَ إِلَى ٱلْـمَكْتَبَةِ ؟

٢- يَذْهَبُونَ إِلـى السُّوقِ يَوْمَ ٱلسَّبْتِ.

٣- هَلْ تَكْتُبِيـنَ دَرْسَكِ ٱلْجَديدَ ؟

٤- لا يَعْرِفـانِ كَيْفَ يَذْهَبـانِ إِلـى ٱلْـمَكْـتَبَةِ.

٥- يَسْأَلانِ ٱلْـمُدَرِّسَ وَيَكْـتُبانِ ٱلْجَوابَ فِـي ٱلصَّفِّ.

٦- هَلْ تَحْضُرُونَ مُحاضَراتِكُمْ فِـي ٱلصَّباحِ أَمِ ٱلْمَساءِ ؟

أَنْتِ
أَنْتُما
أَنْتُمْ
هُمْ
هُما

* * *

(*Oral / Written*) Practice the Conjugation of the Verbs: :تَـمْرين ٩

Fill in the blank cells in the following table with the appropriate conjugations of the verbs according to the 'Subject Pronouns' given on top of the table in the shaded cells. Please take note that this practice contains review of the other conjugations introduced before in Unit 3:

هُمْ	هُما	أَنْتُمْ	أَنْتُما	أَنْتِ	أَنـا	أَنْتَ	هِيَ	هُوَ
يَـكْـتُبُونَ								يَـكْـتُبُ
	يَعْرِفانِ						تَـعْـرِفُ	
		تَذْهَبُونَ				تَذْهَبُ		
			تَسْأَلانِ		أَسْأَلُ			
				تَفْعَلِيـنَ				

(*Oral / Written*) Identifying the 'Root' (جَذْر) and 'Pattern' (وَزْن): تَمْرين ١٠:

Identify the '**root**' and '**pattern**' of each of the following words, then use the dictionary to find out its English meaning; the first two are done as examples:

English Meaning	Pattern	Root	Word
studying, study	فِعالَة	د ر س	دِراسَة
company	فَعِلَة	ش ر ك	شَرِكَة
			ذاهِب
			شَراب
			بُشْرَى
			جِنْسِيَّة
			مُجْتَهِد
			جِهاد
			مَمْنُوع
			مَوْضُوع
			مَحْكَمَة
			طَبِيب
			طَهارَة
			تِجارَة
			اِسْتَعْمَلَ

* * *

(*Oral / Written*) Forming Words Based on Roots and Patterns: تَمْرين ١١:

Form the word which has the 'root' and the 'pattern' given, then look the word up in the dictionary to find its English meaning; one is done for you as an example:

المعنى الإنجليزي English Meaning	الكَلِمَة Actual Word	Pattern / الوَزن	Root / الجَذر
Laboratory	مَعْمَل	مَفْعَل	ع م ل
		فِعَالَة	ت ج ر
		فَعِيل	س ف ر
		فُعُول	و ج ه
		فَعَال	س ل م
		مَفْعَل	د خ ل
		فَعَّال	ب و ب
		فُعُول	ق ع د
		فُعَال	ش ج ع
		مَفْعُول	ج ن ن
		مُفَاعِل	ج ه د
		فَعِيل	س ع د

* * *

Reviewing Two Reference Lists: تَـمْرين ١٢:

Go to '**Part 4**' of the book to review the reference list entitled "**Typical Strong Present Tense Verb Paradigm,**" **page 340**; also "**Conjugations of the Negating Defective Verb (لَيْسَ)**", **page 341**.

الدَّرسُ الرَّابعُ: القِراءَةُ الجَهْرِيَّة / Reading Text (Aloud)

نُزْهَةٌ فـي مَرْكَبٍ عَلَى ٱلنِّيلِ

- بَعْدَ يَوْمٍ طَويلٍ مُمْتعٍ ما بَيْـنَ ٱلفُنْدُقِ وٱلـمَسْجِدِ والأَسواقِ وٱلـمَطاعِمِ وشاطِئِ النِّيلِ، اِسْتَسْلَمَ الْجَميعُ لِلرَّاحَةِ فِـي ٱلـمَرْكَبِ ٱلنِّيلِيِّ ٱلَّذي كانَ يَتحَرَّكُ بِهُدوءٍ فـي جَوٍّ ساحِرٍ حالِم ، بَيْنَما أَضْواءُ ٱلـمَدينَةِ تَنْعَكِسُ على صَفْحَةِ ٱلـمِياهِ قالَتْ سُعادُ: هذِهِ لَيْلَةٌ جَميلَةٌ جِدّاً ، تُذَكِّرُنـي بِـيَـوْمِ زَواجِي!
- قالَ كَمالُ: قاتَـلَ ٱللّـهُ ٱلشَّيْطانَ! لَقَدْ نَسيتُ أَنَّ ٱلْيَوْمَ هُوَ ذِكْرى يَوْمِ زَواجِنا . أَرْجُو أَنْ تُسامِحِيني يا حَبِيبَةَ قَلْبِي !
- قالَ يُوسُف : وَهَلْ هُناكَ أَجْمَلُ مِن هَذا ٱلـمكَانِ وهَذا ٱلْجَوِّ لِلاِحْتِفالِ بِهَذِهِ ٱلـمُناسَبَةِ؟!
- قالَتْ سُعاد: لَقَدْ حَـزِنْتُ كَثيـراً لِـخَـبَـرِ طَلاقِـكَ ، لِذَلِكَ ما أَرَدْتُ أَنْ أَتَحَدَّثَ عَن يَوْمِ زَواجِي .
- قالَ كَمال: هذِهِ فُرْصَةٌ مُناسِبَةٌ لِفَتْحِ مَوْضوعِ زَواجِكَ يا يُوسُف.
- قالَ يُوسُف: زَواجٌ آخَـرُ وأنـا فـي ٱلأَربَعِيـنَ مِن عُمْرِي!
- قالَتْ سُعادُ: لا زِلْتَ شابّاً يا أَخِي ، وأَنْتَ بِـحاجَـةٍ لِامْرَأَةٍ فِـي غُرْبَـتِـكَ!
- قالَ يُوسُف: الزَّواجُ قِسْمَةٌ ونَصِيب ، وما يَشاءُ ٱللّـهُ ويُـقَدِّرُ سَوْفَ يَكونُ!

الـمُفردات مُرتَّبة حَسَب ورودها في النَّصّ):

الْمَعْنَى الإِنْجليزي	الكلِمَة العَرَبِيّة	الْمَعْنَى الإِنْجليزي	الكلِمَة العَرَبِيّة
boat, sail boat (boats)	مَرْكَب (مَراكِب)	pleasure ride, excursion (excursions)	نُزْهَة (نُزُهات)
enjoyable, interesting	مُمْتِع	a long day	يَوْم طَويل
the hotel (hotels)	الفُنْدُق (فَنادِق)	in between (*idiom*)	ما بَيْـنَ
the markets (a market)	الأَسْواق (سوق)	the mosque (mosques)	الـمَسْجِد (مَساجِد)
the bank of the Nile	شاطِئ النِّيل	the restaurants (a restaurant)	الـمَطاعِم (مَطْعَم)
all, everyone	الجَميعُ	succumbed, surrendered	اِسْتَسْلَمَ
the Nile sail-boat	الـمَرْكَب الـنِّـيلـيّ	for resting	لِـلرَّاحَة(لِـ+الرَّاحَة)
was moving	كانَ يَـتَـحَـرَّكُ	which, that (*masculine relative pronoun*)	الَّذي
atmosphere	جَـوّ	calmly, quietly	بِـهُدُوءٍ (بِـ+هُدوء)
dreamy	حـالِـم	magical, charming	سـاحِـر
the lights (light)	أَضْواء (ضَوء)	while	بَـيْـنَـما
reflected on	تَـنْـعَكِسُ (عَلى)	the city	الـمَدينَـة
the waters (water)	الـمِياه (ماء)	surface, also page	صَفْحَة (صَفَحات)
beautiful (*masculine / feminine pair*)	جَمِيلَة / جَميل	a night (nights)	لَيْلَـة (لَيال / اللَّيالي)
reminds me (of)	تُذَكِّرُنـي بِـ (تُذَكِّر+نـي)	very	جِدّاً
my wedding, my marriage	زَواجِي (زَواج+ي)	(of) (the) day	بِـيَوْم (بِـ+يَوْم)
Satan, the Devil	الشَّيْطان	May God fight!	قاتَلَ اللَّهُ!
that today	أَنَّ اليَوْم	I forgot	نَسيتُ
(of) our wedding day	يَوم زَواجِنا (زَواج+نا)	memorial, anniversary	ذِكْرَى
you forgive me	تُسامِحِيـنِي (تُسامِحي+نـي)	I wish that, I hope that	أَرْجو أَنْ

my heart	قَـلْبِي (قَلْب+ي)	O beloved (of)	يا حَبِيبَة
more beautiful (than)	أَجْمَلُ (مِن)	and is there…?	وَهَلْ هُناكَ ...؟
and this atmosphere	وهَذا الـجَوّ	this place	هذا الـمَكان
this occasion	هذِهِ الْمُناسَبَة	for the celebration (of)	لِـلاِحْتِفال (بِـ)
much, a lot	كَثيراً	indeed I was saddened	لَقَدْ حَزِنْتُ
your divorce	طَلاقِـكَ (طَلاقِ+كَ)	for the news (of)	لِـخَبَـر (لِـ+خَبَر)
I didn't want	ما أَرَدْتُ	therfore	لِذَلِكَ
opportunity (opportunities)	فُرْصَة (فُرَص)	to talk, to speak (about)	أَنْ أَتَحَدَّثَ (عَنْ)
for opening	لِـفَتْح (لِـ+فَتْح)	suitable, appropriate	مُناسِبَة
your marriage	زَواجِكَ (زَواج+كَ)	(the) subject (subjects) (of)	مَوْضُوع (مَواضِيع)
another marriage!	زَواج آخَر	another (*masculine / feminine pair*)	آخَرُ / أُخْرَى
of my age	مِن عُمْرِي (عُمْر+ي)	in the forties	فـي الأَرْبَعِيـنَ
a young man	شابّـاً	you're still	لا زِلْتَ
in need	بِـحاجَة (بِـ+حاجَة)	oh my brother	يا أَخِي (أَخ+ي)
your life away from home = diaspora	غُرْبَتِـكَ (غُرْبَة+كَ)	for a woman	لِاِمْرَأَة (لِـ+اِمْرَأَة)
luck, chance	نَصِيب	fate, destiny	قِسْمَة (أَقْسام)
God wills	يَشاءُ الـلَّـه	and that which, and that what (*idiom*)	وما (و+ما)
will be = will pass to be	سَوْفَ يَكُونُ	and ordains, and decrees	ويُـقَدِّرُ (وَ+يُقَدِّر)

* * *

سُؤال

أَسْئِلَةُ الفَهْمِ والاِسْتِيعاب (شَفَوِيّاً)

١- كَيْفَ قَضَى يوسُف وسُعاد وكَمال اليَوْمَ الطَّويلَ الْمُمْتِع؟ spent (time)

٢- أَيْنَ اسْتَسْلَمَ الْجَمِيعُ لِلرَّاحَةِ بَعْدَ يَوْمٍ طَويلٍ مُمْتِعٍ؟

٣- كَيْفَ كانَ يَتَحَرَّكُ الْمَرْكَب؟

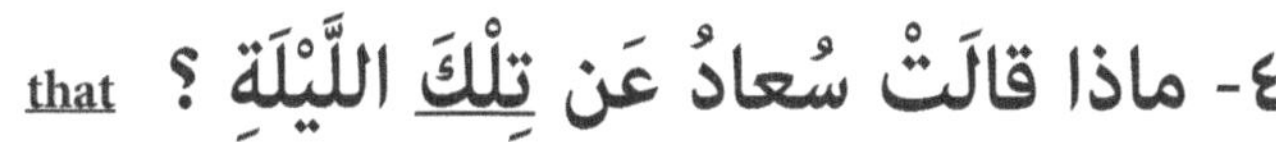

٤- ماذا قالَتْ سُعادُ عَن تِلْكَ اللَّيْلَةِ ؟ that

٥- ماذا قالَ كَمالُ رَدًّا عَلى ما قالَتْ سُعادُ ؟ in response to

جواب

٦- ماذا قالَ يوسُفُ تَعْليقاً عَلى ذَلِكَ ؟ in commenting on

٧- لِماذا حَزِنَتْ سُعادُ كَثيـرًا ؟

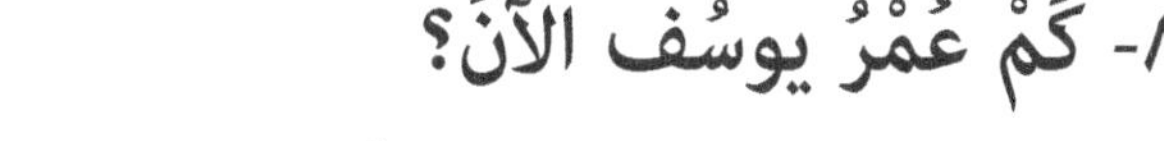

٨- كَمْ عُمْرُ يوسُف الآنَ؟

٩- ماذا قالَ يوسُف عَن الزَّواجِ ؟

* * *

الدَّرسُ الخامِسُ: الثَّقافَةُ والقِيَمُ والأمثال

(أ) يَشرح الْمدرّس / الـمُدرِّسَة بعض القَضايا الـمُتَّصِلة بِـما يلي:

The Instructor Explains Some of the Issues Related to the Following:

- مَفهوم وعادات الزّواج فِي العالَم العرَبِيّ - الإسلامِيّ ؛ والتَّعْليق علـى القولَيـن الدّارِجَـيْـن: الزَّواجُ نِصْفُ الدِّين! ، الزَّواجُ قِسْمَة ونَصِيب!

The concept and traditions related to marriage in the Arabic-Islamic World;

- الزَّواج الْمُرَتَّب فِي الثَّقافة العربِيَّة – الإسلامِيَّة ومُقارَنتِه بِزَواج الغَربِيِّيـن ؛

Arranged or facilitated marriages in the Arabic-Islamic World, in comparison with Western marriages;

- التَّنَزُّه على شاطِئ النِّيل كَوَسيلَةِ استِجْمام فِي مِصْر .

Leisurely strolls and picnics on the banks of the Nile River in Egypt as means of relaxation and socialization.

(ب) مُختارات مِن الحِكم والأمثال العربيّة :

إِنَّ	= indeed, surely, for fact
الطُّيُورَ	= the birds
عَلَى	= on, of
أَشْكالِها	= their own similar
تَقَعُ	= flock together
دِرْهَمُ	= *dirham* weight symbol for a small quantity
وِقايَةٍ	= prevention
خَيْـرٌ مِن	= better than
قِنْطارِ	= *kantar* (large *quantity of some thing*
عِلاجٍ	= remedy, cure,
إِذا	= if
أَرَدْتَ	= you wanted
أَنْ	= to
تُطاعَ	= to be obeyed (you) (
فَـاطْلُبْ	= then ask for
ما	= that which, what
يُسْتَطاعُ	= is being possible

إِنَّ الطُّيُورَ عَلَى أَشْكالِها تَقَعُ .

Birds of a feather flock together.

دِرْهَمُ وِقايَةٍ خَيْـرٌ مِنْ قِنْطارِ عِلاجٍ .

An ounce of prevention is better than pounds of remedy.

إذا أَرَدْتَ أَنْ تُطاعَ ، فَاطْلُبْ ما يُسْتَطاعُ !

If you wish to be obeyed, then ask for what is possible!

تَـمارين عامَّة ومُراجَعَة

تَـمرين ١: **Let's read the following sets of words or phrases, <u>recall their meanings</u> and Then guess why they were grouped together under one category:**

١- مِنْ فَضْلِكِ ! / بِكُلِّ سُرورٍ ! / عَفْوًا يا سَيِّدَتِـي ! / أَهْلاً سَيِّدي ! / لِلأَسَفِ ! سَعِيدَةٌ جِدًّا بِلِقائِكَ ! بِالسَّلامَةِ !

٢- أُسْتاذَة / سِكْرتيـرَة / مُحاضَرَة / مُناسَبَة / صَفْحَة / سَيِّدَة / جامِعَة / لُغَة / رَئِيسَة .

٣- مَرْحَبًا / أَهْلاً / عَفْوًا / حَسَنًا / شُكْرًا / جِدًّا / كَثِيـرًا .

٤- كَـ / إذا / لَكِن / هُنا / هُناكَ / نَعَمْ / لاَ / لِـ / الآنَ / عِنْدَ / حَتَّى / بَعْدَ / ما بَيْنَ / بِـ / لِذَلِكَ / سَوْفَ / سَـ.

٥- لَيْسَ / لَيْسَتْ / لَسْتَ / لَسْتِ / لَسْتُ.

٦- سِكْرتيرَةُ القِسْمِ / رَئِيسَةَ القِسْمِ / قِسْمِ العُلومِ السِّياسِيَّةِ / شاطِئِ النِّيلِ / يَوْمُ الزَّواجِ / صَفْحَةِ الْمِياهِ / أَضْواءُ الْمَدينَةِ.

٧- طالِبٌ جَديدٌ / اللُّغَةِ العَرَبِيَّةِ / السَّاعَةِ الثَّانِيَةِ / يَوْمٍ طَويلٍ مُمْتِعٍ / جَوٍّ ساحِرٍ حالِمٍ لَيْلَةٌ جَميلَةٌ / فُرْصَةٌ مُناسِبَةٌ.

٨- أُريدُ أَنْ / يَلْزَمُكَ أَنْ / يُـمْكِنُكَ أَنْ / أَرْجُو أَنْ / يَبْدُو أَنَّ.

٩- يَتَحَرَّكُ / تَنْعَكِسُ / تُذَكِّرُ / تُسامِحِينَ / أَتَحَدَّثُ / يَشاءُ / يُقَدِّرُ / يَكُونُ / تَأْخُذِينَ / أَعودُ / نُرَحِّبُ / أُقابِلُ / أَلْتَحِقُ (بِـ).

١٠- سَأَعودُ / سَأُقابِلُ / سَأُسافِرُ / سَأَلْتَحِقُ (بِـ) / سَأَدْرُسُ / سَأَتَحَرَّكُ / سَأَكْتُبُ.

١١- اِسْتَسْلَمَ / قالَتْ / نَسِيتُ / أَرَدْتُ / أَكَلوا / شَرِبْنا / ذَهَبْتُم.

١٢- اِمْرَأَة (نِساء) / اِسْم (أَسْماء) / مُناسَبَة (مُناسَبات) / فُرْصَة (فُرَص) / مَوْضوع (مَواضِيع) / صَفْحَة (صَفْحات) / ضَوْء (أَضْواء) / لَيْلَة (لَيالٍ) / نُزْهَة (نُزْهات).

١٣- دَرْسٌ / الدِّراسَةُ / مَدْرَسَةٌ / دَرَسَ / دَرَّسَ / مُدَرِّسٌ / مَدارِسُ.

١٤- كَتَبَ / كِتابَة / مَكْتَب / مَكْتَبَة / كِتاب / مَكْتُوب / كاتِب.

* * *

تَـمرين ٢: **<u>Comprehension</u> Based on the Conversational Text, Page 196**

Read each of the following statements and determine whether it is (True / صَواب) or (False / خَطَأ):

صَواب

١- صَلاحُ الدِّينِ طالِبٌ جَديدٌ فـي الجامِعَةِ. (________)

٢- هُوَ يُريدُ أَنْ يَدْرُسَ اللُّغَةَ العَرَبِيَّةَ. (________)

٣- رَئِيسَةُ القِسْمِ مَوْجُودَةٌ فـي مَكْتَبِها . (______)

٤- رَئِيسَةُ القِسْمِ عِنْدَها مُحاضَرَة . (______)

٥- صَلاحُ الدِّينِ سَيَعُودُ إلـى القِسْمِ غَداً. (______)

٦- صَلاحُ الدِّينِ مُتَخَصِّصٌ فـي العُلُومِ السِّياسِيَّةِ. (______)

٧- صَلاحُ الدِّينِ مِنْ فِلِسْطِيـن. (______)

خَـطـأ

* * *

تَـمرين ٣:

From the list of words in in the shaded box, select the one most suitable to fill in the blanks in the following sentences (*This is based on the Reading Text, page 216*):

اللّه / الأربَعِين / شاباً / تُذَكِّرُنـي / حَزِنْتُ / تُسامِحِيني / لِامْرَأَةٍ / فُرْصَة / نَصِيب / نَسِيتُ

١- هَذِهِ لَيْلَةٌ جَميلَةٌ ______ بِيَوْمِ زَواجي.

٢- لَقَدْ ______ أَنَّ اليَوْمَ ذِكْرى زَواجِنا.

٣- أَرْجُو أَنْ ______ يا حَبِيبَةَ قَلْبي!

٤- لَقَدْ ______ كَثِيراً لِـخَبَـرِ طَلاقِكَ.

٥- هَذِهِ ______ مُناسِبَةٌ لِفَتْحِ مَوْضوعِ زَواجِكَ.

٦- أنا فـي ______ مِنْ عُمْري.

٧- ما زِلْتَ ______ يا أَخـي العَزيز.

٨- أَنْتَ بِحاجَةٍ ______ فـي غُرْبَتِكَ.

٩- الزَّواجُ قِسْمَةٌ و______ !

١٠- ما يَشاءُ ______ سَوْفَ يَكونُ!

تـمرين ٤:

From the list of particles given in the shaded box below, select the one most suitable to fill in the blanks in the following sentences:

إذا / في / بَعْدَ / سَـ / حَتَّى / أَنَّ / ما / إلـى / أَنْ / أ / بِـ / كَـ

١- أُريدُ ___ أُقابِلَ أَحَدَ الْمَسْؤولِيـنَ.

٢- نَحْنُ نُرَحِّبُ ___ـكَ!

٣- أُقابِلُها الآنَ ___ كانَتْ مَوجودَةً ___ مَكْتَبِها.

٤- عِنْدَها مُحاضَرَةٌ ___ السَّاعَةِ الثَّانِيَةِ.

٥- ___أعودُ ثانِيَةً ___ الظُّهْرِ.

٦- يَبْدُو ___ـكَ عَرَبِيٌّ، ___لَيْسَ كَذَلِكَ؟

٧- ___كُلِّ سُرورٍ! وَلَكِنْ ___ ٱسْمُكَ؟

٨- أُريدُ ___ أَدْرُسَ العَرَبِيَّةَ ___ـتَخَصُّصٍ ثانٍ.

٩- أنا طالِبٌ ___ قِسْمِ العُلُومِ السِّياسِيَّةِ.

١٠- ___ اللِّقاءِ!

* * *

تـمرين ٥:

Practice the five plural conjugations of the the present tense verbs by filling in the blanks in the following table to correspond to the given subject pronouns:

نَحْنُ	أَنْتُنَّ	أَنْتُمْ	هُنَّ	هُمْ
				يَـتَحَدَّثُـونَ
			يَـتَحَرَّكْـنَ	

		تُسامِحُونَ		
	تُرَحِّبْنَ			
نُقابِلُ				

* * *

تَمرين ٦: تَصريفات الفِعل (كانَ):

The verb (كانَ) is a <u>weak verb,</u> like the verb (قالَ) which you studied its conjugation paradaim in the previous unit. Let's see how you fair by conjugating it in its <u>past tense,</u> <u>singular and plural</u> conjugations, to fill in the blanks!

Singular Subject Pronouns	Corresponding Verb Conjugations	Plural Subject Pronouns	Corresponding Verb Conjugations
	هُم		هُوَ
	هُنَّ		هِيَ
	أَنْتُم		أَنْتَ
	أَنْتُنَّ		أَنْتِ
	نَحْنُ		أنـا

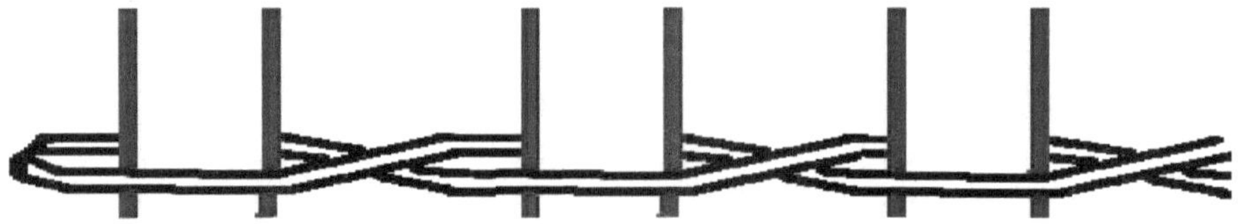

تَـمرين ٧: نَشاط لُغَوي: تسلِيَة مع لعبة البَحْثِ عَنِ الكَلِماتِ :

Linguistic Activity : Diversion with the Game of Word Search:

Search the cross-words for the Arabic given words! (vertically, horizontally, or diagonally) and try to recall their meanings:

(جِدّاً ، سَوْفَ ، لَيْسَ ، لَيْسَتْ ، لَسْتَ ، لَسْتِ ، لَسْتُ)

ز	ر	ذ	د	خ	ح	ج	ث	ت	ا	ب	م	ا	يّ	أ
س	ش	ا	ص	ض	دّ	ظ	ع	ل	غ	ف	ق	ل	ك	ل
خ	اً	دّ	ج	ا	ت	ب	أ	ء	ي	و	هـ	أ	ن	م
د	ذ	ج	ر	ز	س	ح	ش	ص	ض	ط	ظ	س	ع	غ
ل	ن	م	هـ	و	د	ي	ا	ب	ت	ث	ج	و	ذ	ف
ك	ع	س	ي	ل	م	ا	ن	هـ	ي	ت	ح	ف	ب	ق
ق	ض	ـة	ص	ش	ل	س	ز	ر	ذ	د	خ	ع	ث	ا
ف	ط	ظ	ع	خ	ن	ي	ن	ث	إ	ل	ا	تَ	س	ل
غ	ث	ب	م	ا	ء	ي	ثُ	س	ل	م	د	ك	ق	خ
ع	ل	ي	ج	خ	ح	د	ذ	ر	ز	س	ث	ش	ص	ب
ظ	ي	ر	ذ	ص	ط	ع	ف	غ	ظ	ض	ل	ز	ض	ت
ط	س	ج	ح	ء	ا	ع	ب	ر	أ	ل	ا	د	ط	و
ض	ثْ	خ	د	ز	ش	ض	ظ	ط	ص	س	ث	ح	ظ	ي
ص	ش	س	ز	ر	ذ	د	خ	ح	ج	تِ	ا	ت	ب	ا
ب	ا	ي	و	هـ	ن	م	ل	ك	ق	ف	ء	غ	ع	ت

The Seventh Unit / الوحدةُ السَّابِعَةُ

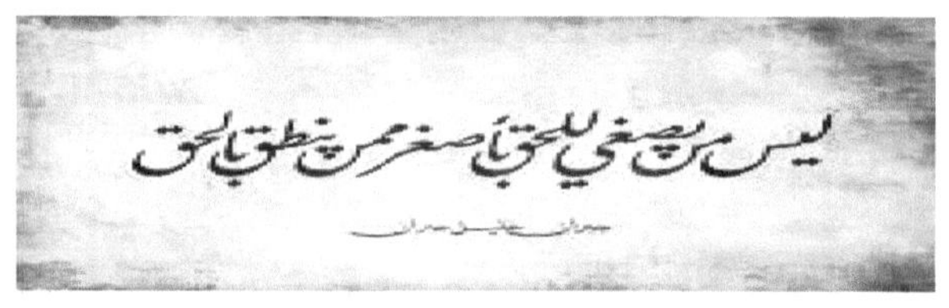

الوِحْدَةُ السَّابِعَةُ 7th Unit
الدَّرْسُ الأَوَّلُ 1st Lesson

أَمامَ ٱلـمُتْحَفِ ٱلوَطَنِيِّ ٱلـمِصْرِيِّ
In Front of the National Egyptian Museum

- الزَّائِر: صَباحَ ٱلخَيْـرِ يـا آنِسَةُ!
- الـمُوَظَّفَة: صَباحَ ٱلنُّورِ يـا أُسْتاذُ!
- الزَّائِر: أَهَذا هُوَ ٱلـمُتْحَفُ ٱلـمِصْرِيُّ ٱلوَطَنِيُّ ٱلقَديـمُ أَمِ ٱلحَديث؟
- الـمُوَظَّفَة: هَذا هُوَ ٱلـمُتْحَفُ ٱلقَديم. اَلـمُتْحَفُ ٱلحَديثُ بِناءٌ بَعيدٌ مِن هُنا.
- الزَّائِر: هَلْ أَنْتِ مُوَظَّـفَـةٌ هُنا؟
- الـمُوَظَّفَة: نَعَمْ، أَنـا سِكْرِتِيـرَةُ ٱلـمُتْحَف.
- الزَّائِر: أَنـا صِحافِـيٌّ فَرَنْسِيٌّ ٱسْمي "شارْل شِيراك". أُرِيدُ أَنْ أُقابِلَ مُديرَ ٱلـمُتْحَف.
- الـمُوَظَّفَة: مُديرُ ٱلـمُتْحَفِ أُسْتاذٌ جامِعِيٌّ مَشْهُورٌ ٱسْمُهُ جَمال بَدَوِي.
- الزَّائِر: هَلْ هُوَ فِـي مَكْـتَـبِـهِ الآن؟

- الـمُوَظَّفَة: نَعَمْ، هُوَ فِـي مَكْـتَـبِه، وَمَكْـتَـبُهُ هُوَ ٱلـمَكْـتَبُ ٱلكَبيـرُ ٱلقَريبُ مِنَ ٱلباب.
- الزَّائِر: هَلْ يَـتَـكَلَّمُ الـلُّـغَـةَ الـفَرَنْسِيَّـة؟
- الْمُوَظَّفَة: نَعَمْ، يَتَكَـلَّمُ الفَرَنْسِيَّـةَ والإِنْجِلِـيـزِيَّـةَ وَبَـعْـضَ الـلُّغاتِ الأُخْرَى.
- الزَّائِر: حَـسَـناً! هَلْ يُـمْـكِـنُـكِ أَنْ تَـأْخُـذِيـنِـي إِلـى مَكْـتَـبِـه؟
- الْمُوَظَّفَة: طَـبْـعاً، بِـكُـلِّ سُرُور. تَـفَـضَّـلْ مَـعِـي يـا أُسْـتـاذُ!
- الزَّائِرُ: شُـكْـرًا جَـزِيلاً يـا آنِـسَـة!

اَلـمُفْرَداتُ والتَّـراكِيبُ اللُّغَوِيَّة
Vocabulary & Linguistic Structures

in front of	أَمامَ	seventh / the seventh	سابِعَة / السَّابِعَة
the national (*mas. / fem. pair*)	الوَطَنِيّ / الوَطَنِيَّة	the museum (*broken plural*)	الـمُتْحَف (مَتاحِف)
the employee, the official (*mas. / fem. pair*)	اَلـمُوَظَّفَة / الـمُوَظَّف	the visitor (*mas. / fem. pair*)	اَلزَّائِر / الزَّائِرَة
Is this...?	أَهَذا ...؟ (أَ + هَذا)	the Egyptian (*mas. / fem. pair*)	الـمِصْرِيّ / الـمِصْرِيَّة
or (*with a helping vowel*)	أَمْ = (أَمِ)	the ancient, the old (*broken plural*)	القَدِيم (قُدَماء)
a building (*broken plural*)	بِناء (أَبْنِيَة)	the modern (*mas. / fem. pair*)	الحَدِيث / الحَدِيثَة
journalist (*mas. / fem. pair*)	صِحافِـيّ / صِحافِيَّة	far (from) (*mas. / fem. pair*)	بَعِيد / بَعِيدَة (عَنْ)
Charles Cherac (*French male proper name*)	شارْل شِيـراك	French (*mas. / fem. pair*)	فَرَنْسِيّ / فَرَنْسِيَّة
meet	أُقابِلَ	I want to	أُرِيدُ أَنْ
university-related (*mas. / fem. pair*)	جامِعِيّ / جامِعِيَّة	director (*mas. / fem. pair*) (*broken plural*)	مُدِير / مُدِيرَة (مُدَراء)
Jamāl Badawi (*male proper name*)	جَمال بَدَوِي	famous, well-known (*mas. / fem. pair*) (*broken plural*)	مَشْهور / مَشْهورَة (مَشاهِيـر)
near by, near to (*mas. / fem. pair*)	القَرِيب / القَرِيبَة (مِنْ)	the big, the large, the important (*mas. / fem. pair*)	الكَبِير / الْكَبِيرَة
he speaks	يَتَكَلَّمُ	the door (*broken plural*)	الباب (أَبْواب)
and some	وبَعْض (و+بَعْض)	and the English (language)	وَالإِنْجِلِيزِيَّة
the other (*mas. / fem. pair*)	الأُخْرَى / الآخَر	the languages (*singular*)	اللُّغات (لُغَة)
of course	طَبْعاً	to take (*you feminine*) me	تَأْخُذِينِي (تَأْخُذِينَ+ي)
with me	مَعِي (مَعَ+ي)	please, come!	تَفَضَّلْ !
		many, a lot / thanks a lot	جَزِيلاً / شُكْرًا جَزِيلاً

* * *

Grammatical and Linguistic Notes / الدَّرْسُ الثَّانِي: اَلقَواعِدُ وَاللُّغَوِيَّاتُ

* * *

1. The Pronoun of Separation .... ١- ضَمِيرُ الفَصْل

- Let's read the following sets of linguistic structures in preparation to explain what the 'pronoun of separation' is:

هَذا مُتْحَفٌ. ←	هَذا اَلْمُتْحَفُ ..... ←	هَذا هُوَ اَلْمُتْحَفُ.
This is a museum.	This museum	This is the museum.
هَذِهِ جامِعَةٌ. ←	هَذِهِ اَلجامِعَةُ ..... ←	هَذِهِ هِيَ اَلجامِعَةُ.
This is a university.	This university	This is the university.
هَذا بِناءٌ. ←	هَذا اَلْبِناءُ ..... ←	هَذا هُوَ اَلْبِناءُ.
This is a building.	This building	This is the building.
هَذِهِ زائِرَةٌ. ←	هَذِهِ اَلزَّائِرَةُ ..... ←	هَذِهِ هِيَ اَلزَّائِرَةُ.
This is a (female) visitor.	This (female) visitor	This is the (female) visitor.

- Note that the first linguistic structure, in each set of structures above, is a full 'Equational Sentence' consisting of a 'subject', which is the 'demonstrative pronoun (هَذا) or (هَذِهِ) and a 'predicate, which is the noun that follows it.
- The second linguistic structure, in each set of structures above, is not a full 'Equational Sentence', but rather a '**demonstrative phrase**', consisting of (هَذا) or (هَذِهِ) and another noun, which forms with it one undivided unit, functioning as the 'subject', but there is no 'predicate' here.

- <u>How then does one say in Arabic</u>, for example, "**This is the museum.**"? The answer to this question is found in the third sentence of each set.
- In such sentence, the pronouns (هُوَ) and (هِيَ) are called "**pronouns of separation**"; serving to separate the 'demonstrative pronoun' from the 'noun with the Definite Article' attached to it, so they are no longer one undivided unit.
- It is to be noted that the 'pronoun of separation' must agree with the 'subject' in '**<u>gender</u>**' and '**<u>number</u>**'.

* * *

2. *Nisbah*: The Relative Adjectives .... ٢- صِفاتُ النِّسْبَة

- A '***Nisbah* Adjective**' is an adjective based on a noun and derived from it. The word '***Nisbah***' means '**<u>related to</u>**'; that is to say an 'adjective related to a noun'.
- Whereas in English there are various devices to derive such adjectives from nouns, in Arabic there is only one.
- Such 'relative adjectives' are particularly important to learn <u>nationalities</u> based on the names of the countries and localities, as will be illustrated by the following examples:

- هُوَ مِنْ لُبْنان. ← هُوَ <u>لُبْنانِيٌّ</u>. | هِيَ مِنْ لُبْنان. ← هِيَ <u>لُبْنانِيَّةٌ</u>.
- هُوَ مِنْ مِصْر. ← هُوَ <u>مِصْرِيٌّ</u>. | هِيَ مِنْ مِصْر. ← هِيَ <u>مِصْرِيَّةٌ</u>.
- هُوَ مِنَ الْعِراق. ← هُوَ <u>عِراقِيٌّ</u>. | هِيَ مِنَ الْعِراق. ← هِيَ <u>عِراقِيَّةٌ</u>.
- هُوَ مِنْ أَمْريكا. ← هُوَ <u>أَمْريكِيٌّ</u>. | هِيَ مِنْ أَمْريكا. ← هِيَ <u>أَمْريكِيَّةٌ</u>.
- هُوَ مِنَ الْكُوَيْت. ← هُوَ <u>كُوَيْتِيٌّ</u>. | هِيَ مِنَ الْكُوَيْت. ← هِيَ <u>كُوَيْتِيَّةٌ</u>.

- By analyzing the underined words above, we will see that making '*nisbah* adjectives' from the names of the countries preceding them is based on one simple device; namely adding the 'suffix' (*iyy* / ـيّ) for the masculine form, and the 'suffix' (*iyyat* / ـيَّة) for the feminine form; these two 'suffixes' are added to the noun in place of any 'case-ending' it might have. Appropriate 'case-endings' are then added after these 'suffixes'.
- The '***Nisbah* adjectives**' follow the same rules of agreement as any other adjective, as has been explained in Lesson 6.

- In forming **'*Nisbah* adjectives'** from a noun, the **'*Nisbah* suffix'** is added to the **'<u>noun stem</u>'**; that is the original noun stripped of any of the following that it might have:
    1. The *Definite Article* (**ال**); thus from (**اَلْعِراقُ**), we get (عِراقِيٌّ / عِراقِيَّةٌ).
    2. The *Tā' Marbūtah* (**ة**); thus from (**اَلْقاهِرَةُ**), we get (قاهِرِيٌّ / قاهِرِيَّةٌ).
    3. The *final long vowel* (**ا**); thus from (**أَمْرِيكا**), we get (أَمْرِيكِيٌّ / أَمْرِيكِيَّةٌ).
- Often, in conversational and spoken Arabic, the 'suffix' (*iyy* / ـِيّ) is pronounced as (*ī* / ـِي) in its **<u>paused form</u>**.
- In the texts of previous lessons, as well as the text of the current lesson, several other '*Nisbah* adjectives' were used. In the following box, you will review these along with the nouns they are derived from:

عَرَب ⇔ عَرَبِيٌّ / عَرَبِيَّةٌ	**أَمْرِيكا** ⇔ أَمْرِيكِيٌّ / أَمْرِيكِيَّةٌ
يَهُود ⇔ يَهُودِيٌّ / يَهُودِيَّةٌ	**سِياسَة** ⇔ سِياسِيٌّ / سِياسِيَّةٌ
باكِسْتان ⇔ باكِسْتانِيٌّ / باكِسْتانِيَّةٌ	**وَطَن** ⇔ وَطَنِيٌّ / وَطَنِيَّةٌ
صِحافَة ⇔ صِحافِيٌّ / صِحافِيَّةٌ	**فَرَنْسا** ⇔ فَرَنْسِيٌّ / فَرَنْسِيَّةٌ
جامِعَة ⇔ جامِعِيٌّ / جامِعِيَّةٌ	**إِنْجِلِيز** ⇔ إِنْجِلِيزِيٌّ / إِنْجِلِيزِيَّةٌ

*　　*　　*

3. More Notes on Masculine and Feminine ..... (تَوَسُّع) ٣- اَلْمُذَكَّرُ والْمُؤَنَّثُ

- Previously, in Lessons 1 and 2, we have made general observations about '**<u>gender</u>**' in the Arabic language. As you can see from what you have studied thus far, <u>Arabic is more 'gender-conscious' than English</u>.
- Based on this fact, pronouns, nouns and adjectives have either been designated as 'masculine' or 'feminine' in vocabulary lists or in grammatical notes.
- Furthermore, 'adjectives' have been listed as 'masculine-feminine' pairs in the vocabulary lists to constantly draw your attention to this feature of gender distinction in Arabic that do not exist in English.
- You have also been taught that the '***Tā' Marbūtah***' and the '***Alif Maqsūrah***' at the end of words are mostly <u>signs of feminine gender</u>; of course there are always few exceptions to these rules.

- We also learned that all names of cities are feminine in gender.
- Likewise, names of countries are mostly feminine; the exceptions here being:

الأُرْدُنُّ / السُّودانُ / العِراقُ / الـمَغْرِبُ / اليَمَنُ / لُبْنانُ

- Beyond the general categories mentioned above, the gender of all other nouns depends on the natural gender of the referent; as illustrated by the following pairs:

أَب ⇔ أُمّ \	أخ ⇔ أُخْت \	حِصان ⇔ فَرَس \	وَلَد ⇔ بِنْت
father / mother	brother / sister	horse / mare	a boy / a girl

- It is highly recommended that the student of Arabic develops the habit of creating his or her own '**reference chart**' on the model of the table below related to 'masculine-feminine' pairs:

Masculine-Feminine Pairs (Adjectives)	Masculine-Feminine Pairs (Nouns)	Masculine-Feminine Pairs (Pronouns)
جَديد - جَدِيدَة	أَب - أُمّ	أَنْتَ - أَنْتِ
عَرَبِـيّ - عَرَبِيَّة	أَخ - أُخْت	هُوَ - هِيَ
أَمْريكِيّ - أَمْريكِيَّة	حِصَان - فَرَس	أَنْتُمْ – أَنْتُـنَّ
سَعيد - سَعيدَة	وَلَد - بِنْت	هُمْ - هُنَّ
قَديـم – قَديـمَة	رَجُل - اِمْرَأَة	هَذا - هَذِهِ
حَديث - حَديثَة	أَسَد - لَبُؤَة	ـهُ - ـها
بَعِيد - بَعِيدَة	آخَر - أُخْرَى	ـكَ - ـكِ
قَرِيب - قَرِيبَة	طالِب - طالِبَة	ـكُمْ - ـكُنَّ

* * *

٤- الاِسْمُ (بَعْض) وَعَلاقَـتُـهُ بِـالاِسْمِ بَعْـدَه:

4. The Noun (بَعْض) and Its Relation to the Noun which Follows It:

- The noun (بَعْض) by its very nature is a quantitative noun, the meaning of which will not be made clear except in conjunction with what follows it.

- It can be followed either by a 'noun' or by a 'suffix pronoun'; as in the following examples:

يَتَكَلَّمُ بَعْضَ ٱللُّغاتِ ٱلأُخْرَى.	يَدْرُسُ بَعْضَها في الجامِعَةِ.
أَقْرَأُ بَعْضَ الكُتُبِ الحَديثَة.	هَلْ يَقْرَأُ بَعْضُكُمْ كُتُباً بِالعَرَبِيَّة؟
بَعْضُ ٱلكَلِماتِ لَيْسَتْ فِي ٱلكِتاب.	بَعْضُها لَيْسَتْ فِي الكِتابِ.
أُحِبُّ بَعْضَ الكِتاب.	أُحِبُّ بَعْضَهُ.
بَعْضُ البِناءِ حَديث.	وَبَعْضُهُ قَديم.

- If we analyze the sentences on the right, we find that in each sentence the word (بَعْضُ) was followed by a noun bearing a '***Kasrah***' indicating that it is in the 'genitive mood'. This is so, because the relationship of the noun (بَعْضُ) to the noun that follows is that of an '***Idāfah***', whereby (بَعْضُ) itself is functioning as the '1st term' of the '*Idāfah*', and the noun following it is functioning as the '2nd term'.
- We will further notice that the noun following (بَعْضُ) can be either in a plural form, as in the first three examples, or a singular form, as in the last two examples.
- If the plural form follows, then the best English rendering is respectively: '**some other languages**', '**some modern books**', and '**some words**'.
- However, if the singular form follows, then the best English rendering is respectively: '**some of the book**' and '**some of the building**'.
- The last vowel of the word (بَعْضُ) itself varies, depending on its grammatical function in the sentence, so it can bear a '*Dammah*', a '*Fathah*' or a '*Kasrah*'.
- In the sentences on the left, the noun (بَعْضُ) was followed by one of the 'suffix pronouns', which were naturally attached to it.
- In these cases, the English translation should be respectively: '**some of them**', '**some of you**', and '**some of them**', '**some of it**' and '**some of it**'.

* * *

5. The Plural and Its Three Types .... ٥- اَلجَمْعُ وأَنْواعُه:

- You might have noticed that in the vocabulary lists, sometimes a singular noun is followed by a note in parenthesis saying that it is a '**broken plural**'.

- Arabic has, in fact, **three types of plurals**; the "broken plural" is one of them, and it is the most common one and the most difficult to master since it would be, in some sense, the equivalent of the English 'irregular plurals', which result by way of internal sounds modifications, and not by adding the common '**s**' or '**es**' to the end of the singular.
- Because of its nature and the difficulty to predict based on the singular form, the 'broken plural' is listed following the singular in Arabic dictionaries and Arabic language instruction books. So the best way to learn the 'broken plurals', in the initial stages of learning Arabic, is to learn them as individual vocabulary in conjunction with the singular forms.
- However, after a student advances in the learning of Arabic, he or she will reach a point of being able to predict the 'broken plural' form from its singular, based on certain common prevalent patterns, which relate the singular pattern to a plural pattern. This is a long term skill that will be learned later, at stages.
- The other two types of plurals are called: (1) **Masculine Sound Plural**, and (2) **Feminine Sound Plural**. As the names indicate, the first one relates to nouns that are masculine in gender, and the second one relates to nouns that are feminine in gender. Both are '**sound**' plurals, as opposed to 'broken', and result regularly by adding certain 'suffixes' to the singular forms.
- Since we have only had very few of these two types of plurals, we will introduce in the following table a few examples of each, for the purpose of initial acquaintance and familiarity; let's read first some examples representing '**masculine sound plurals**':

آَلصِّحافِيُّ الـمِصْرِيُّ يَزُورُ أَمْريكا.	←	آَلصِّحافِيُّونَ الـمِصْرِيُّونَ يَزُورُونَ أَمْريكا.
آَلـمُدَرِّسُ فِي مَكْتَبِه.	←	آَلـمُدَرِّسُونَ فِي مَكاتِبِهِمْ.
هُوَ مُسافِرٌ إِلَـى الخارِج.	←	هُمْ مُسافِرُونَ إِلَـى الْخارِج.
هُوَ مَوْجودٌ فِي مَكْـتَـبِـه.	←	هُمْ مَوْجُودُونَ فِي مَكاتِبِهِمْ.
هُوَ أُسْتاذٌ جامِعِيٌّ مَشْهُور.	←	هُمْ أَساتِذَةٌ جامِعِيُّونَ مَشْهُورُونَ.

- In the parallel sentences of the box above, the underlined nouns in the sentences on the right are singular forms of words that have been introduced previously.
- The underlined nouns, in the parallel sentences on the left, represent 'masculine sound plural' forms of the parallel singular forms.
- Through close examination, you will find that the 'masculine sound plurals' of the singular forms have resulted by adding the '**suffix**' (ـُونَ) to them; all these plurals are in the

‘nominative case-ending’. When they are in the ‘accusative’ or ‘genitive’ case, then the ‘masculine sound plural’ ending will be (ـِينَ). This will be treated with more details and elaboration in future lessons.

- Now, let’s read the sentences in the box below to gain initial insight on the formation of ‘**feminine sound plurals**’:

الصِّحافِيَّةُ ٱلـمِصْرِيَّةُ تَزُورُ أَمْريكا. ⟵ الصِّحافِيَّاتُ ٱلـمِصْرِيَّاتُ يَزُرْنَ أَمْريكا.

الـمُدَرِّسَةُ فِـي مَكْتَبِها. ⟵ الـمُدَرِّساتُ فِي مَكاتِبِهِنَّ.

هِيَ مُسافِرَةٌ إِلَـى ٱلخارِج. ⟵ هُنَّ مُسافِراتٌ إِلَـى ٱلخارِج.

هِيَ مَوْجُودَةٌ فِي مَكْتَبِها. ⟵ هُنَّ مَوْجُوداتٌ فِـي مَكاتِبِهِنَّ.

هِيَ أُسْتاذَةٌ جامِعِيَّةٌ مَشْهُورَة. ⟵ هُنَّ أُسْتاذاتٌ جامِعِيَّاتٌ مَشْهُورات.

- In the parallel sentences inside the box above, the underlined nouns in the sentences on the right are singular forms of feminine words that have been introduced previously.
- The underlined nouns in the parallel sentences on the left, represent the ‘feminine sound plural’ forms of the parallel singular forms.
- Through close examination, you will find that the ‘feminine sound plural’ forms of the singular forms have resulted by adding the ‘**suffix**’ (ات) to them, after dropping the *Taa’ Marbūtah* of the singulars. all these plurals are in the ‘nominative case-ending’. When they are in the ‘accusative’ or ‘genitive’ case, then the vowels over the ‘***Taa***’ will change to one ‘*Kasrah*’ or a ‘*Tanween Kasrah*’ to look like (اتِ) or (اتٍ); and this aspect will be treated with more details and elaboration in future lessons.
- Thus, from now on, it would be easy for you to identify both ‘masculine sound plural’ nouns and ‘feminine sound plural nouns’ by observing the particular ‘suffixes’ introduced above.
- Now, the following table contains a cataloguing of all the ‘**broken plurals**’ of singulars related to nouns introduced thus far. It would be a good learning habit to keep expanding on this list as new nouns are introduced in future lessons:

دَرْس (دُرُوس)	نَصّ (نُصُوص)	عَرَبِـيّ (عَرَب)	صَديق (أَصْدِقاء)
سُؤال (أَسْئِلَة)	أُسْتاذ (أَساتِذَة)	صَفّ (صُفُوف)	طالِب (طُلَّاب)
كُرْسِيّ (كَراسِي)	مَقْعَد (مَقاعِد)	كِتاب (كُتُب)	جَواب (أَجْوِبَة)
وَرَقَة (أَوْراق)	قَلَم (أَقْلام)	صُورَة (صُوَر)	حائِط (حِيطان)

لَوْح (أَلْواح)	مَكْتَب (مَكاتِب)	جَديد (جُدُد)	رَئِيس (رُؤَساء)
قِسْم (أَقْسام)	أَصْل (أُصُول)	أُسْبُوع (أَسابِيع)	يَوْم (أَيّام)
حال (أَحْوال)	اِسْم (أَسْماء)	بَحْث (أَبْحاث)	كَنِيسَة (كَنائِس)
مَسْجِد (مَساجِد)	سُوق (أَسْواق)	مَوْعِد (مَواعِيد)	عِلْم (عُلُوم)
سَعِيد (سُعَداء)	سَيِّد (سادَة)	جُمْلَة (جُمَل)	مُتْحَف (مَتاحِف)
قَديم (قُدَماء)	حَديث (حُدَثاء)	بِناء (أَبْنِيَة)	مُدِير (مُدَراء)
مَشْهور (مَشاهِير) → also مَشْهُورُونَ	كَبِير (كُبَراء) (كِبار)	باب (أَبْواب)	

* * *

الدَّرسُ الثَّالِثُ: تَدْرِيباتٌ وَنَشاطاتٌ / Exercises & Activities

Exercise 1: (*Oral and Written*) Using the Pronouns of Separation (هُوَ) or (هِيَ):

Transform the following 'demonstrative phrases' into full meaningful sentences, by insering the appropriate pronoun of separation between the 'demonstrative pronoun' and the noun following it; follow the given example:

هَذا ٱلبِناءُ ٱلكَبِيرُ ..... ⇐ هَذا هُوَ ٱلبِناءُ ٱلكَبِيرُ.

١- هَذِهِ الكَلِمَةُ الجَدِيدَةُ ..... ⇐ ....

٢- هَذا الـمُتْحَفُ القَدِيمُ ..... ⇐ ....

٣- هَذا الأُسْتاذُ الـمَشْهورُ ..... ⇐ ....

٤- هَذِهِ الـمَكْتَبَةُ الحَدِيثَةُ ..... ⇐ ....

٥- هَذِهِ الـمُوَظَّفَةُ الجامِعِيَّةُ ..... ⇐ ....

* * *

Exercise 2: (*Oral and Written*) **Transformation: Prepositional Phrase *Nisbah* Adjective:**

Follow the given example to transform the underlined prepositional phrase into a '***Nisbah* Adjective**':

الأُسْتاذُ مِنْ لُبْنان. ⇦ الأُسْتاذُ لُبْنانِيٌّ.

١- الأُسْتاذَةُ مِنْ مِصْر . ⇦ ....

٢- الجامِعَةُ فِي أَمْريكا. ⇦ ....

٣- الـمُتْحَفُ فِي فَرَنْسا. ⇦ ....

٤- الـمُوَظَّفَةُ مِنْ بَيْروت. ⇦ ....

٥- الـمُديرُ مِنَ ٱلأُرْدُنّ. ⇦ ....

٦- الـمَكْتَبَةُ فِي ٱلجامِعَة. ⇦ ....

* * *

Exercise 3: (*Oral and Written*) **Substitution: *Nisbah* Adjectives with (أَمْ):**

In the following sentences, substitute the two nouns of places with two '***Nisbah* adjectives**' related to them, while inserting the particle (أَمْ) between the two; follow the given example:

هَلِ الـمُديرُ مِنْ لُبْنان أَمْ مِصْر؟ ⇦ هَلِ الْمُديرُ لُبْنانِيّ أَمْ مِصْرِيّ؟

١- هَلِ ٱلأُسْتاذُ مِنْ أَمْريكا أَمْ فَرَنْسا ؟ ⇦ ....؟

٢- هَلِ ٱلـمُوَظَّفَةُ مِنْ بَغْداد أَمْ بَيْروت ؟ ⇦ ....؟

٣- هَلِ ٱلجامِعَةُ فِي سُوريا أَمْ لِيبْيا؟ ⇦ ....؟

٤- هَلِ ٱلـمُتْحَفُ فِي ٱلرِّياض أَمِ ٱلرِّباط ؟ ⇦ ....؟

Exercise 4: **(*Oral and Written*) Transformation: Masculine to Feminine or Feminine to Masculine:**

Reproduce the following sentences, changing all masculine nouns and adjectives to feminine and all feminine nouns and adjectives to masculine, as in the given examples:

- الـمُديرُ ٱلجَديدُ لُبْنانـيّ. ⇦ الـمُديرَةُ ٱلجَديدَةُ لُبْنانِيَّة.
- الأُسْتاذَةُ ٱلعَرَبِيَّةُ عِراقِيَّة. ⇦ الأُسْتاذُ ٱلعَرَبِـيُّ عِراقِيّ.

١- الزّائِرَةُ ٱلأَجْنَبِيَّةُ صِحافِيَّة. ⇦ ....

٢- الـمُوَظَّفُ ٱلجَديدُ أَمْريكِـيّ. ⇦ ....

٣- الأُسْتاذُ ٱلجامِعِيُّ مَشْهور. ⇦ ....

٤- الـمُدَرِّسَةُ ٱلـمِصْرِيَّةُ جَديدَة. ⇦ ....

٥- الزّائِرُ ٱلأَجْنَبِيُّ صِحافِـيّ. ⇦ ....

٦- السِّكْرِتيـرَةُ ٱلجَديدَةُ عَرَبِيَّة. ⇦ ....

٧- الطّالِبُ ٱلجَديدُ فَرَنْسِيّ. ⇦ ....

* * *

Exercise 5: **(*Oral, Written and English Meaning*) Suffix Pronouns with (بَعْض):**

Attach to the word (بَعْض) the 'suffix pronouns' which correspond to the 'subject pronouns' provided in parenthesis, then give the English meanings of the new combinations; follow the given examples:

بَعْض (هُوَ) = بَعْضُهُ = some of it ⇦ بَعْض (هُمْ) = بَعْضُهُمْ = some of them

بَعْض (هُنَّ) ⇦ = ... = ... بَعْض (أَنْتُمْ) ⇦ = ... = ...

بَعْض (نَحْنُ) ⇦ = ... = ... بَعْض (هُمْ) ⇦ = ... = ...

بَعْض (أَنْتُـنَّ) ⇦ = ... = ... بَعْض (هِيَ) ⇦ = ... = ...

Exercise 6: Marking the Plural Nouns and Identifying the Plural Type:

Read the following sentences first, then mark each plural noun or adjective by underlining it, then finally mention whether it is "**broken plural**", "**masculine sound plural**" or "**feminine sound plural**", as in the given examples:

الطُّلاَّبُ ٱلأَمْرِيكِيُّونَ يَدْرُسونَ ٱلعَرَبِيَّةَ . (broken plural / masculine sound plural)
الطَّالِباتُ ٱلجَديداتُ عَرَبِيَّاتٌ . (all three are feminine sound plurals)

١- هُنَّ مُوَظَّفاتٌ جَديدات . (..........)

٢- هُمْ أَساتِذَةٌ زائِرُونَ . (..........)

٣- هَلْ أَنْتُنَّ صِحافِيَّاتٌ فَرَنْسِيَّات ؟ (..........)

٤- هَلْ أَنْتُمْ طُلاَّبٌ جُدُد ؟ (..........)

٥- نَحْنُ آنِساتٌ عَرَبِيَّات . (..........)

٦- الأَصْدِقاءُ ٱلزَّائِرونَ مِنْ أَمْرِيكا . (..........)

٧- الـمُدَراءُ ٱلجُدُدُ جامِعِيُّونَ . (..........)

٨- الطَّالِباتُ ٱلعَرَبِيَّاتُ يَدْرُسْنَ لُغاتٍ أُخْرَى . (..........)

٩- هُمْ مُوَظَّفُونَ كِبارٌ فِي ٱلجامِعَةِ . (..........)

١٠- ما أَسْماءُ ٱلصِّحافِيِّينَ ٱلعَرَب ؟ (..........)

* * *

Exercise 7: (***Review: Oral and Written***) **Identifying Noun-Adjective Phrases and Recognizing the Aspects of Agreement Between the Noun and Its Adjective:**

Mark the 'noun-adjective' phrases in the following sentences by underlyning them, then mention the features of agreement between them, in regard to: **definiteness** or **indefiniteness**, **gender**, **number** and **case-ending**, as in the given example:

الطَّالِبُ ٱلجَديدُ أَمْريكِـيّ. ←	(both are definite, both are masculine, both are singular and both are nominative)

١- هَذِهِ مُوَظَّفَةٌ جَديدَة. (...)

٢- الـمُديرُ أَمامَ ٱلـمُتْحَفِ ٱلوَطَنِيّ. (...)

٣- هَذِهِ هِيَ ٱلجامِعَةُ ٱلوَطَنِيَّة. (...)

٤- هَذا هُوَ ٱلكِتابُ ٱلجَديد. (...)

٥- أُدَرِّسُ ٱللُّغَةَ ٱلعَرَبِيَّة. (...)

٦- أَذْهَبُ إِلَى ٱلـمَكْتَبَةِ ٱلحَديثَة. (...)

٧- هَذا بِناءٌ حَديثٌ جِدًّا. (...)

٨- قابَلْتُ الزَّائِرَةَ الفَرَنْسِيَّة. (...)

* * *

Exercise 8: (Review: *Oral*) Responses to Greetings , Courtesies or Requests:

Give verbal responses to the following greetings, courtesies or requests:

مَرْحَباً!	السَّلامُ عَلَيْكُمْ!	شُكْراً جَزيلاً يا سَيِّدُ!
مَساءَ الخَيْـر!	تَفَضَّلْ اِجْلِسْ!	كَيْفَ الحالُ ؟ / كَيْفَ حَالُكَ؟
تَشَرَّفْتُ بِـمعْرِفَتِك!	صَباحَ الْخَيْر!	هَلْ يُـمْكِنُ أَنْ أُقابِلَ الأُسْتاذ ؟
مِنْ فَضْلِكُمْ اِجْلِسُوا!	أَنا سَعيدٌ بِلِقَائِكَ!	إِلَـى اللِّقاء!

* * *

Exercise 9: (Review: *Oral and Written*) Conjugation of Verbs:

Fill in the blank cells in the following table bywriting the appropriate form of the conjugation, then reading the whole paradigm of each verb conjugations:

أنـا	أنْتِ	أنْتَ	هِيَ	هُوَ
				يَـتَكَـلَّمُ
			تُـرِيدُ	
		تَـأْخُذُ		
	تُـحِبِّـيـنَ			
أَدْرُسُ				
	تُـرَحِّـبِـيـنَ			
		تُـقَـابِلُ		
			تَـعُودُ	
				يَـكْـتُـبُ
			تَـلْـتَحِقُ	
		تَـذْهَـبُ		
أَتَشَرَّفُ				

* * *

Exercise 10: Reviewing a Reference List:

Go to '**Part 4**' of the book to review the reference list entitled "**Conjugation Paradigm of the Defective Verb (كـانَ)**," **page 342**.

* * *

الدَّرْسُ الرَّابِعُ: نَصُّ مُحادَثَةٍ / Conversational Text

البَحْثُ عَن عَروسٍ لِيوسُف

- سُعاد: يُقْلِقُنِي مَوْضوعُ عُزوبِيَّةِ يُوسُف، وأُريدُ أَنْ أُساعِدَهُ فِي ٱلبَحْثِ عَنْ عَروس.

- كَمال: ولَكِنْ رُبَّما لا يُريدُ يُوسف أَنْ يَتَزَوَّجَ ثانِيَةً! اِسْأَلِي أَخاكِ أَوَّلاً إِذا كانَ يَرْغَبُ فِي الزَّواجِ.

- سُعاد: لَقَدْ لَمَّحَ لِي بِأَنَّهُ إِذا فَكَّرَ فِي ٱلزَّواجِ فَإِنَّهُ يَرْغَبُ فِي ٱلزَّواجِ مِنْ مِصْرَيَّة.

- كَمال: حَسَناً! على بَرَكَةِ ٱللَّه! عَلَيْكِ إِذَنْ أَنْ تَنْشَطِي فِي هذا ٱلمَوضوع!

- سُعاد: لِي زَمِيلَةٌ فِي ٱلعَمَلِ اِسْمُها لَيْلى، وهِيَ جَميلَةٌ وسُمْعَتُها جَيِّدَة.

- كَمال: إِذَنْ عَلَيْكِ أَنْ تُرَتِّبِي لِمُناسَبَةٍ حَتَّى يَتَقابَلا.

- سُعاد: أُفَكِّرُ أَنْ أَدْعو لَيْلَى ويوسُف إِلَى عِيدِ مِيلادي حَتَّى يُمْكِنُهُما أَنْ يَتَقابَلا.

- كَمال: جَمِيلٌ جِدّاً! وأَنا أَقومُ بِإِعْدادِ كُلِّ ما يَلْزَمُ لِلحَفْلَةِ.

- سُعاد: حَسَناً اِتَّفَقْنا! ولا تَنْسَ أَنَّ عِيدَ مِيلادِي هُوَ يَوْمُ ٱلجُمُعَةِ ٱلقادِمِ.

- كَمال: وَلَوْ! وهَلْ يَنْسَى زَوْجٌ مَحْظوظٌ مِثْلِي أَجْمَلَ عِيدِ مِيلادٍ فِي الدُّنْيا؟!

مُفْرَداتُ الدَّرْسِ الرَّابِعِ

bride / bridegroom	عَروس / عَريس	searching (for)	البَحْثُ (عَنْ)
it bothers me, it worries me	يُقْلِقُنِي (يُقْلِقُ+نِـي)	for Yusuf	لِيوسُف (لِـ+يوسف)
being bacholer	عُزُوبِيَّة	(the) subject (of)	مَوْضُوع (مَواضيع)
help him	أُساعِدَهُ (أُساعِد+ـهُ)	and I want (to)	وَأُريدُ (أَنْ)
perhaps, maybe	رُبَّـما	however	وَلَكِنْ
get married	يَتزَوَّج	he does not want (to)	لا يُريدُ (أَنْ)
ask	اِسْأَلِـي	again	ثانِيَةً
firstly	أَوَّلاً	your brother	أخاكِ (أَخا+كِ)
he would desire (in)	كَانَ يَرْغَبُ (فِـي)	if	إِذا
indeed	لَقَدْ	getting married	الزَّواج
to me	لِـي (لِـ+ي)	he insinuted (to) (that	لَمَّحَ (لِـ) (بِـ)
if he would think (about)	إِذا فَكَّـرَ (فِـي)	that he	بِـأَنَّـهُ (بِـ+أَنَّ+ـهُ)
would desire (to)	يَرْغَبُ (فِـي)	then he	فَـإِنَّـهُ (فَـ+إِنَّ+ـهُ)
well, fine	حَسَناً	to an Egyptian	مِنْ مِصْرِيَّة
it is incombent on you (to)	عَلَيْـكِ أَنْ (عَلَى+كِ)	*Idiom*: let it be left for God's Blessing!	عَلَى بَرَكَةِ ٱللَّـهِ
become active (in regard to)	تَنْشَطِي (فِـي)	then, in such case	إِذَنْ
I have	لِـي	this subject	هذا الـمَوْضوع
at work	فِـي العَمَلِ	a colleague	زَمِيلَة
and she is beautiful	وهِيَ جَمِيلَة	her name (is)	اِسْمُها (اِسْمُ+ها)
good	جَيِّدَة	and her reputation (is)	وسُـمْـعَـتُـها (و+سُمْعَةُ+ها)
for an occasion	لِـمُناسَبَةٍ (لِـ+مُناسَبَةٍ)	you arrange (for)	تُرَتِّبِي (لِـ)

they (two) would meet	يَتَقابَلا	so that, in order that	حَتَّى
invite (to)	أَدْعُو (إلَـى)	I am thinking (to)	أُفَكِّرُ (أَنْ)
it be possible for (the two of) them	يُـمكِـنُـهُما	my birthday	عِيدِ مِيلادي
very beautiful	جَمِيلٌ جِدًّا	to meet (each other)	أَنْ يَتَقابَلا
(to) prepare	بِـإعْدادِ (بِـ+إعْدادِ)	and I undertake	وأنا أَقومُ (وَ+أنا) بِـ
is necessary (for)	يَـلْـزَمُ (لِـ)	all that	كُـلِّ ما
Literally: we agreed; *Idiomatically*: we are on agreement	اِتَّـفَـقْـنـا	(for) the party, the celebration	لِـلْحَفْلَةِ (لِـ+الْحَفْلَةِ)
the coming Friday (is)	يَوْمُ الجُمُعَةِ القادِمِ	and don't forget that	ولا تَنْسَ أَنَّ
and is it possible to forget	وَهَلْ يَنْسَى	*a colloquial idiom meaning* "How possible!"	وَلَوْ
like me, like myself	مِثْلِـي (مِثْل+ي)	a lucky husband	زَوْجٌ مَحْظوظٌ
birthday	عِيدِ مِيلادٍ	(the) most beautiful	أَجْمَلَ
		in the world	فِـي الدُّنْيا

* * *

أَسْئِلَةُ الفَهْمِ والاِسْتيعابِ لِنَصِّ الدَّرْسِ الرَّابِعِ (شَفَوِيًّا)

سُؤال

جَواب

١- ماذا يُـقْـلِـقُ سُعاد؟

٢- فِيمَ (فِـي+ماذا) تُريدُ سُعادُ أَنْ تُساعِدَ أَخاها يوسُف؟

٣- ماذا طَلَبَ كَمال مِن سُعاد أَنْ تَسْأَلَ أَخاها؟

٤- هلْ لَمَّحَ يُوسُف إِلَى أَنَّهُ يُريدُ الزَّواج؟ وكَيْفَ فَعَلَ ذَلِكَ؟

٥- ماذا قالَت سُعادُ عَنْ زَميلَتِها فِي العَمَلِ؟

٦- لِماذا تُفَكِّرُ سُعادُ أَنْ تَدْعُو يوسف ولَيْلى إلى عِيدِ مِيلادِها؟

٧- مَنْ سَيَقومُ بِإعدادِ كُلِّ ما يَلْزَمُ لِلحَفْلَةِ؟

٨- مَتَى سَيَكونُ عِيدُ مِيلادِ سُعاد؟ ٩- ماذا قالَ كَمال عَن عِيدِ مِيلادِ سُعاد؟

الدَّرْسُ الخامِسُ: الثَّقافَةُ والقِيَمُ والأمثال

Culture, Values & Proverbs

(أ) يَشرح الْمدرّس / الـمُدرِّسَة بعض القَضايا الـمُتَّصِلة بِـما يلي :

The Instructor Explains Some of the Issues Related to the Following:

- الطَّلاقُ فِي الثَّقافَةِ العَربِيَّة - الإسلامِيَّة ؛
- **Divorce in the Arabic-Islamic Culture; Divorce is frawned upon, and is considered the last resort.**
- حَضانَةُ الأَطْفالِ وحُقوقُ الأبِ والأُمِّ.
- **The custody of Children the Arabic-Islamic Culture, and the rights of Father and Mother.**

Explain the meaning of the Prophetic saying:؛ (أبْغَضُ الْحَلالِ إلَى اللهِ الطَّلاقُ)

* * *

(ب) مُختارات مِن الحِكم والأمثال العربيّة :

اَلـقَـناعَـةُ كَـنْـزٌ لاَ يَـفْـنَى.

Contentment is a lasting treasure.

الأَقْـرَبُونَ أَوْلَـى بِـٱلـمَـعْـرُوف.

Charity begins at home.

إذا كانَ ٱلـكَـلامُ مِنْ فِـضَّـة،
فَـٱلسُّـكُـوتُ مِـنْ ذَهَـب.

Speech is silver, silence is gold.

الْقَناعَة =	(the) contentment
كَنْز =	(is) a treasure
لا يَفْنَى =	that does not perish = lasts
الأَقْرَبُونَ =	the relatives, those who are near
أَوْلَى (بِـ) =	more desrving (of)
بِالْمَعْرُوف =	kindness = charity
إذا =	if
كانَ =	was to be
الْكَلام =	the speech, talking
مِنْ =	(made) from
فِضَّة =	silver
فَالسُّكُوت =	then silence
ذَهَب =	gold

تَـمارين عامّة ومُراجَعَة
General Drills & Review

تَـمرين ١: **Let's read the following sets of words or phrases, <u>recall their meanings</u> and then guess why they were grouped together under one category:**

١- صَباحَ الخَيْـر ! / صَباحَ النُّور ! / بِكُـلِّ سُرور ! / تَفَضَّلْ مَعي يا أُسْتاذ ! / شُكْـراً جَزيلاً!

٢- الـمُتْحَفُ الـمِصْرِيُّ / الـمُتْحَفُ الوَطَنِيُّ / الـمُتْحَفُ القَديمُ / الـمُتْحَفُ الحَديثُ / الـمَكْتَبُ الكَبيـرُ.

٣- صِحافِـيٌّ فَرَنْسِيٌّ / أُسْتاذٌ جامِعِيٌّ / لِيَوْمٍ واحِدٍ.

٥- فـي مَكْتَبِهِ / إِلَى مَكْتَبِهِ / مِن البابِ / عَلى مائِدَةٍ / بِالقاهِرَةِ / عَنْ حَياتِهِ / بِصورَةٍ / فِـي الأُسبوعِ.

٦- سِكْرِتيـرَةُ الـمُتْحَفِ / مُديرُ الـمُتْحَفِ / مائِدَةُ العَشاءِ / بَيْتُ الأُسْرَةِ.

* * *

تَـمرين ٢: **Read each of the following statement, then determine whether it is <u>True</u> (صواب) or <u>False</u> (خَطـأ): (Comprehension Questions based on the text on page 228)**

١- الـمُوَظَّفَةُ سِكْـرِيرَةُ الـمُتْحَفِ. (__________)

٢- الصِّحافِـيُّ أَمْريـكِـيّ. (__________)

٣- مُديرُ الـمُتْحَفِ مَوْجودٌ فـي مَكْتَبِهِ. (__________)

٤- مُديرُ الـمُتْحَفِ لا يَتَكَلَّمُ الفَرَنْسِيَّةَ. (__________)

٥- الـمُتْحَفُ الحَديثُ بِناءٌ بَعيد. (__________)

٦- الصِّحافِـيُّ يُريدُ أَنْ يُقابِلَ مُديرَ الـمُتْحَفِ. (__________)

* * *

تَـمرين ٣: **Fill in the blank in the following sentences with the most appropiate word From among those in the shaded box below:**

مَـعي / سِكْرِتـيـرَةُ / أُسْتاذ / فَرَنْسِيّ / أُقابِلَ / الكَبِيـر / يَتَكَلَّمُ / البابِ

١- أَنا ______ الـمُتْحَفِ.   ٢- تَفَضَّل ______ بِكُلِّ سُرُورٍ!

٣- أُريدُ أَنْ ______ مُديرَ الـمُتْحَفِ.

٤- مُديرُ الـمُتْحَفِ ______ جامِعِيٌّ.

٥- مَكْتَبُهُ هُوَ الـمَكْتَبُ ______ القَريبُ مِنَ ______.

٦- مُديرُ الـمُتْحَفِ ______ الفَرَنْسِيَّةَ والإِنْجليزِيَّةَ.

* * *

تَـمرين ٤: (تَرْجَمَة إلى الإنجليزيَّة) **Translate the following sentences into English:**

١- أُريدُ أَنْ أُساعِدَ أَخِـي فـي البَحْثِ عَنْ عَروس.

______

٢- يُوسُفُ يَرْغَبُ فـي الزَّواجِ مِنْ ٱمرَأَةٍ مِصْرِيَّةٍ.

______

٣- لِـي زَمِيلَةٌ فـي العَمَلِ ٱسْمُها لَيْلـى ، وهِيَ جَميلَة وسُمْعَتُها جَيِّدَة.

______

٤- أُفَكِّرُ أَنْ أَدْعُو لَيْلـى إِلـى عِيدِ مِيلادي.

______

٥- أَنا أَقُومُ بِـإِعْدادِ كُـلِّ ما يَلْزَمُ لِحَفْلِ عِيدِ الـميلاد .

______

٦- لا تَنْسَ أَنَّ عِيدَ مِيلادي يَوْمُ الجُمُعَةِ القادِمِ .

٧- كَيْفَ أَنْسَى أَجْمَلَ عِيدِ مِيلادٍ فـي الدُّنْيا!

---

* * *

تـمرين ٥: **Practice forming the five singular and plural conjugations of the the past tense verbs by filling in the blanks in the following two tables to correspond to the given subject pronouns:**

أنـا	أنتِ	أنتَ	هِيَ	هُو
				ضَحِـكَ
			طَـلَـبَـتْ	
		اِجْـتَـمَـعْـتَ		
	ذَكَـرْتِ			

نَحْنُ	أَنْتُـنَّ	أَنْتُمْ	هُنَّ	هُمْ
				تَـكَـلَّمُوا
			أَخَـذْنَ	
		ضَحِـكْـتُـم		
	بَـدَأْتُـنَّ			
قُـلْـنا				

تـمرين ٦: نَشاط لُغَوي: تسلِيَة مع لعبة ٱلبَحْثِ عَنِ ٱلكَلِماتِ :

Linguistic Activity : Diversion with the Game of Word Search:

Search the cross-words for the following Arabic words inside the box (vertically, horizontally, or diagonally), the first three words are done for you!

بعض / بعضهم / أصدقاء / طلاب / متاحف / عربيّ / لبنانيّة / مُشكلة / مائدة / عشرة

و	يّ	ا	م	ب	ا	ت	ث	ج	ح	خ	أ	ذ	ر	ز
ل	ا	ل	ق	ف	ع	ل	ل	ظ	ط	ض	ص	ا	ش	س
ب	ن	ح	هـ	ب	ع	ض	ث	م	إ	ث	د	ا	ن	خ
ن	ع	س	د	ط	ض	ص	هُـ	ح	س	ز	ق	ج	ذ	د
ا	ذ	ب	ج	ث	ت	ب	ـة	م	د	و	ا	م	ن	ل
ن	ب	و	ح	ت	ي	هـ	ن	ا	م	ل	ء	ع	د	ك
يّ	ب	ن	ا	ن	ي	ي	ة	س	ب	ع	ـة	ن	ض	ق
ـة	ر	ب	ع	ـة	ب	ث	ن	ي	ن	خ	ع	ظ	ط	ف
ث	ق	ك	ت	م	ن	هـ	و	ي	ء	ا	م	ب	ل	غ
م	ا	ئـ	د	ة	ت	ر	ذ	ع	ر	ب	يّ	ي	ل	ع
ا	ض	ز	ل	ض	ع	ا	ف	م	ط	م	ذ	ر	ب	ظ
ئـ	ط	د	ا	ل	ر	ـة	ح	ع	ش	س	ح	ج	ث	ط
د	ظ	ح	ث	س	ب	ط	ظ	ف	ش	ك	د	خ	ت	ض
ة	ب	ت	ا	ث	ي	ح	خ	د	ذ	س	ل	ش	ر	ة
ت	ع	غ	ء	ع	ش	ر	ة	م	ن	هـ	و	ة	ا	ب

نهاية الوحدة السابعة

The Eighth Unit / الوحدةُ الثَّامِنَةُ

أُطْلُبِ ٱلعِلْمَ مِنَ ٱلـمَهْدِ إلى ٱللَّحْد!

الوِحْدَةُ الثَّامِنَةُ 8th Unit
الدَّرْسُ الأَوَّلُ 1st Lesson

الدِّراسَةُ فـي ٱلخارِجِ
Studying Abroad

يُسافِرُ عَدَدٌ كَبيرٌ مِنَ ٱلطُّلَّابِ ٱلعَرَبِ إِلـى أَمْرِيكا وأَوْروبّا لِلدِّراسَةِ فـي جامِعاتِها. وَمِنْ بَيْنِ هَؤُلاءِ ٱلَّذينَ سافَرُوا إِلَى ٱلخارِجِ لِلدِّراسَةِ سَمِير وَسَميرَة، اللَّذانِ قُبِلا في جامِعَةِ "آن آرْبَر" في وِلايَةِ "مِيتْشِعان". اِلتَقى سَمِير وَسَميرَة في مَكْتَبِ ٱلتَّسْجِيلِ بِٱلجامِعَةِ، قَبْلَ بَدْءِ ٱلدِّراسَةِ بِأُسْبوعَيْنِ، ودارَ بَيْنَهُما ٱلحِوارُ ٱلتّالـي:

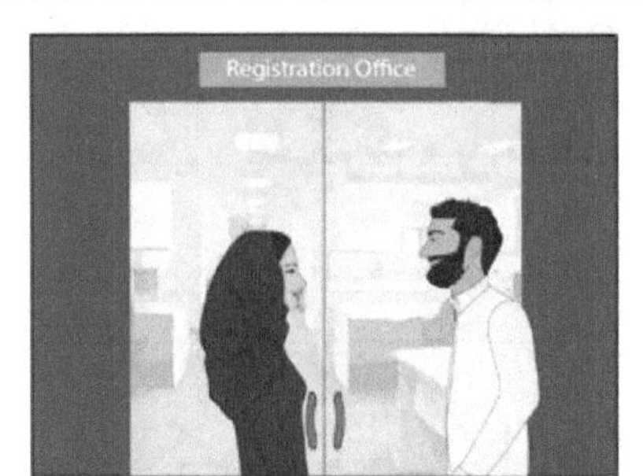

- سَمِير: مَرْحَباً يا آنِسَة! يَبْدُو مِنْ سِماتِكِ أَنَّكِ عَرَبِيَّة.
- سَمِيرَة: نَعَمْ، هَذا صَحيح! أَنا عَرَبِيَّة مِنْ لُبْنان.
- سَمِير: وأَنا مِنْ مِصْر.
- سَمِيرَة: تَشَرَّفْتُ! أَنْتَ طالِب جَديد؟

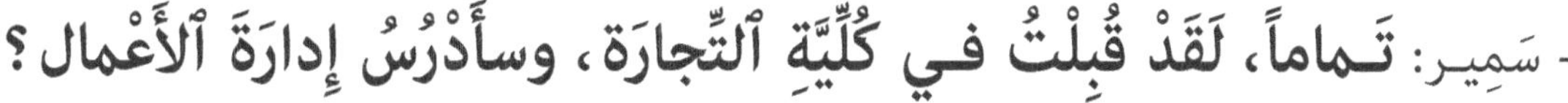
- سَمِير: تَماماً، لَقَدْ قُبِلْتُ فـي كُلِّيَّةِ ٱلتِّجارَة، وسأَدْرُس إِدارَةَ ٱلأَعْمال؟
- سَمِيرَة: وأَنا طالِبَةٌ جَديدَةٌ أَيْضاً، وسَأَدْرُسُ ٱلأَدَبَ ٱلإِنْجِليـزِيّ.
- سَمِير: هَلْ سَتُقيمِـينَ فـي سَكَنِ ٱلطَّالِباتِ؟
- سَمِيرَة: فـي ٱلحَقيقَة، كُنْتُ أُفَضِّلُ ذَلِك، ولَكِن والِدَتـي أَوْصَتْـني بِٱلسَّكَنِ مَعَ خالَتِي، الَّتي تُقِيمُ قَريباً مِنَ ٱلجامِعَة.
- سَمِير: أَنْتِ مَحْظُوظَة بِوُجودِ خالَتِكِ هُنا؟
- سَمِيرَة: هَذا صَحيح، ولَكِنّي لا أُريدُ أَنْ أَتَحَدَّثَ بِٱلعَرَبِيَّةِ كَثِيـراً، وهَذا ما يُزْعِجُنِي.
- سَمِير: أَظُنُّ أَنَّ خالَتَكِ تَفْهَمُ ذَلِكَ جَيِّداً!
- سَمِيرَة: أَرْجُو ذَلِك!

- سَمِير: هَلْ تُفَكِّرِينَ بِٱلرُّجُوعِ إِلـى ٱلوَطَنِ بَعْدَ ٱلتَّخَرُّج؟

- سَمِيرَة: والِدايَ لَنْ يَسْمَحا لِـي بِٱلبَقاءِ هُنا.

- سَمِير: أَنا أُفَكِّرُ بِدِراسَةِ "ٱلـماجِسْتِير" بَعْدَ ٱلحُصولِ على "ٱلبَكالُورْيُوس."

- سَمِيرَة: ولَكِنْ هَلْ سَتَعُودُ إِلـى مِصْر فـي ٱلنِّهايَة؟

- سَمِير: أَنا أَمِيلُ إِلـى ٱلبقاءِ هنا، إِذا سَمَحَتِ ٱلظُّرُوف.

- سَمِيرَة: وماذا عَنْ والِدَيْكَ؟

- سَمِير: هُما لا يُـمانِعانِ ما دُمْتُ قادِراً عَلى تَوْفِيرِ مَصارِيفِي.

- سَمِيرَة: أَتَـمَنَّى لَكَ التَّوْفِيق!

- سَمِير: أَشْكُرُكِ، وأَتَـمَنَّى لَكِ سَنَةً دِراسِيَّةً جَيِّدَة!

* * *

اَلـمُفْرَداتُ والتَّراكِيبُ اللُّغَوِيَّةُ (مُرَتَّبَةٌ حَسَبَ تَسَلْسُلِ وُرودِها فِي النَّص)

study / (the) studying, (*verbal noun*)	دِراسَة / الدِّراسَة - (ـات)	eighth / the eighth	ثامِنَة / الثَّامِنَة
travel, travels (to)- traveling	يُسافِرُ (إِلـى) (سَفَر)	abroad, the outside (of a country)	الخارِج
large, big (*masculine / feminine pair*)	كَبِير / كَبِيـرَة	a number (of) (*broken plural*)	عَدَد (مِن) (أَعْداد)
to America	إِلـى أَمْرِيكا	of Arab students	مِنَ الطُّلَّابِ العَرَب
for studying (*verbal noun*)	لِـلدِّراسَة (لِ+ال+دِراسَةِ)	and Europe	وَأُوْرُوبَّا
and from among	وَمِنْ بَيْـنِ (وَ+مِنْ)	their universities (*singular*)	جَامِعاتِـها (جامِعَة)
those who (*plural form of relative pronoun*)	الَّذِينَ	these, those (*the singular demonstrative pronouns*)	هَؤُلاءِ (هَذا / هَذِهِ)

Sameer (*male proper name*)	سَـمِـيـر	traveled (they) (traveling)	سافَرُوا (سَفَر)
the two of whom (*dual form of relative pronoun*)	اللَّذانِ	*Sameera* (*female proper name*)	سَـمِـيـرَة
Ann Arbour University	جامِعَةِ "آن آرْبَر"	both were admitted to	قُبِلا فـي
met	اِلْتَقى	in the State of Michigan	فـي وِلايَةِ "مِيتِشِغان"
at the University	بِـٱلجامِعَة	in the registration office	فـي مَكْتَبِ ٱلتَّسْجِيل
the beginning of schol	بَدْءِ ٱلدِّراسَة	before	قَبْلَ
and took place	وَدارَ	by two weeks (a week)	بِـأَسْبُوعَيْـنِ (أَسْبوع)
the following dialogue	الحِوارُ ٱلتَّالـي	between (the two of them)	بَـيْـنَـهُما
it looks	يَبْدُو	Hello, O Miss!	مَرْحَباً يا آنِسَة !
that you are an Arab	أَنَّـكِ عَرَبِيَّة	from your features	مِنْ سِماتِـكِ
I am an Arab	أَنـا عَرَبِيَّة	yes, this is true	نَعَمْ ، هَذا صَحِيح
and I am from Egypt	وَأَنـا مِنْ مِصْر	from Lebanon	مِنْ لُبْنان
Are you a new student?	أَنْتَ طالِب جَدِيد؟	I am honored	تَشَرَّفْـتُ
I have been admitted	لَقَدْ قُبِلْتُ	exactly, correct	تَـماماً
and I will be studying	وَسَـأَدْرُس	Into the Business College	فـي كُـلِّـيَّةِ ٱلتِّجارَة
and I am a new student	وَأَنـا طالِبَة جَدِيدَة	business administration	إِدارَة ٱلأَعْمال
English literature	الأَدَبَ ٱلإِنْجِلِيـزِيّ	also, likewise	أَيْـضاً
in the students' housing	فـي سَكَنِ ٱلطَّالِباتِ	Will you be residing...?	هَلْ سَـتُقِيمِيـنَ ...؟
I would have preferred that	كُنْتُ أُفَضِّلُ ذَلِك	in fact	فـي ٱلحَقِيقَة
bed me, counselled me	أَوْصَتْـنـي	however, my mother	ولَكِنَّ والِدَتـي
with my (maternal) aunt	مَعَ خـالَـتِـي	to reside, to live	بِـٱلسَّكَنِ
near by the university	قَـرِيبـاً مِنَ ٱلجامِعَة	who is residing	الَّتي تُـقِـيـمُ
by the presence of your aunt here	بِـوُجُودِ خـالَـتُـكِ هُنا	you are lucky	أَنْتِ مَحْظوظَة
I do not want to	لا أُرِيدُ أَنْ	however, I	ولَكِنِّي

a lot, often	كَـثِـيـراً	to speak in Arabic	أَتَـحَدَّث بِـٱلـعَـرَبِـيَّـة
I guess that	أَظُـنُّ أَنَّ	and this is what disturbs me	وهَـذا ما يُـزْعِـجُـنِـي
understants that well	تَـفْـهَـمُ ذَلِكَ جَـيِّـداً	your aunt	خـالَـتَـكِ
Are you thinking (of)...?	هَـلْ تُـفَـكِّـرِينَ	I hope so	أَرْجُو ذَلِـكَ
to the homeland	إِلـى ٱلوَطَنِ	of returning	بِـٱلـرُّجُـوع
my (two) parents	والِـدايَ	after graduation	بَـعْـدَ ٱلـتَّـخَـرُّج
(by) staying here	بِـٱلـبَـقـاءِ هُـنـا	will not permit me	لَنْ يَـسْمَحا لِـي
about studying for the Masters (degree)	بِـدِراسَـةِ ٱلـماجِـسْـتِـيـر	I am thinking about	أَنـا أُفَـكِّـرُ بِـ
the B.A. (degree)	الـبَـكـالُـورِيُوس	after obtaining (earning)	بَـعْـدَ ٱلحُصُولِ على
Will you be returning...?	هَـلْ سَـتَـعُـودُ ...؟	howeber, but	ولَـكِـنْ
at the end	فـي ٱلـنِّـهـايَـة	to Egypt	إِلَـى مِصْر
staying here	الـبَـقـاءِ هُـنـا	I am inclined to	أَنـا أَمِـيـلُ إِلـى
And what about your (two) parents?	وماذا عَنْ والِدَيْـكَ؟	if circumstances permit	إِذا سَـمَـحَـتْ ٱلـظُّـرُوف
do not object	لا يُـمـانِـعـانِ	they both	هُما
able to	قـادِراً عـلـى	as long I am	ما دُمْـتُ
I wish you happy outcome! (*idiom*)	أَتَـمَنَّى لَـكَ ٱلتَّوْفِيق!	to cover my expenses	تَـوْفِـيـر مَـصـارِيـفِـي

* * *

Collective Translation in Class / تَرْجَمَةٌ جَماعِيَّةٌ فـي ٱلصَّفِّ

The authors of this work strongly believe that the skill of translation is very important when one is learning a second language. Therefore, in an attempt to train students in this skill, some time and effort should be invested in this! To achieve this objective, students are paired and asked to translate the conversational text above into English. Instead of using the traditional dictionary, which they are not fully trained to do at this stage, the students already have the list of vocabulary and linguistic structures listed after the text. After each pair of students translate their individual part, two students are assigned to collect the different parts of translation, while one of them reads one line of the Arabic text, the second student is asked to read the translation of what has been read. This process will reinforce improved reading and comprehension of written texts. Go for it!

الدَّرْسُ ٱلثَّاني: القَواعِدُ وَٱللُّغَوِيَّاتُ / Grammatical and Linguistic Notes

* * *

١- الـمَصْدَرُ و (ال) التَّعْريف / The Verbal Nouns and the Definite Article (أَل):

- '**Verbal Nouns**' are nouns derived from and related to verbs, to indicate the concept of the action indicated by the verb. For example, the verb '**studied**' has the 'verbal noun' '**studying**' to indicate the concept implied by the verb.
- Arabic 'verbal nouns' correspond to English gerunds ending in '**ing**'.
- Let's now introduce the verb-verbal nouns pairs related to this lesson:

> دَرَس - دِراسَة / سافَرَ - سَفَر / حَصَلَ - حُصُول / حَضَرَ - حُضُور
> اِلْتَحَقَ - اِلْتِحاق / تَقابَلَ - تَقابُل / تَعارَفَ - تَعارُف / أَحَبَّ - حُبّ
> تَزَوَّجَ - تَزَوُّج (زَواج) / اِنْتَهَى - اِنْتِهاء / رَجَعَ - رُجُوع /
> عَمِلَ - عَمَل.

- The first words in these sets of pairs are '**past tense verbs**', while the second ones are '**verbal nouns**'.
- 'Verbal nouns' in Arabic are nouns *per se*, and as such they have all the characteristics and features of any other regular noun, including the feature of receiving the 'Definite Article (ال)' and receiving a 'case-ending' depending on their function in sentences.
- Now, let's read the following sentences and examine the underlined 'verbal nouns' in context and compare them with their English translations:

- الدِّراسَةُ فِـي ٱلخارِجِ.
- اِلْتَقى هَيْثَم وَهِنْد فـي مَكْتَبِ ٱلتَّسْجِيل.
- والِدَتـي أَوْصَتْني بِـٱلسَّكَنِ مَعَ خالَتِي.
- هَلْ تُفَكِّرينَ بِـٱلرُّجوعِ إِلـى ٱلوَطَنِ بَعْدَ ٱلتَّخَرُّجِ؟
- أَنا أَميلُ إِلـى ٱلبَقاءِ هُنا.
- أُفَكِّرُ بِـدِراسَةِ ٱلـماجِسْتِير بَعْدَ ٱلحُصُولِ عَلى ٱلبَكالوريوس.

By examing the underlined 'verbal nouns' above, we notice that they mostly receive the 'Definite Article (ال)'; something that is not usually done in English and this is one important point to remember for the purpose of idiomatic translations.

* * *

The Verbal Sentences .... ٢- الجُمْلَةُ الفِعْلِيَّة

- Arab linguists have defined a **'verbal sentence' as one which starts with a 'verb'**. A sentence which starts with a noun, and yet has a verb in it, will not be considered a 'verbal sentence'; it is called a 'nominal sentence'.
- In light of this, a 'verbal sentence' in its simplest form consists of only one word- the verb itself; the 'subject' being implied by the form of the verb:

* رَجَعَ . (He returned.)   * رَجَعَتْ . (She returned.)

- A 'verbal sentence' may also contain an 'expressed subject', which could be only one single noun or a 'noun-adjective' phrase. The 'subject' of a 'verb' is always in the 'nominative case'.
- The 'verb' agrees with its 'subject' in gender; so if the 'subject' is 'masculine', then the 'verb conjugation' should reflect the 'masculine' form. If the 'subject' is 'feminine', then the 'verb conjugation' should reflect that also; as in the following examples:

رَجَعَ سَمِـيـرٌ إِلـى الشَّرْقِ الأَوْسَطِ. / رَجَعَتْ سَمِـيـرَةُ إِلَـى الشَّرْقِ الأَوْسَطِ.

> يَدْرُسُ سَمِيرٌ إِدَارَةَ ٱلْأَعْمَالِ. / تَدْرُسُ سَمِيرَةُ ٱلْأَدَبَ ٱلْإِنْجْلِيزِيَّ.

- As you can see from the sentences above, a 'verbal sentence' can be expanded to include a 'prepositional phrase' or an 'object of the verb' if it happened to be a 'transitive verb'.

- If a 'feminine subject' follows the 'verb', but is separated from it by another word or phrase, then the 'verb' may be either 'masculine' or 'feminine', as illustrated by the examples below:

> حَضَرَتْ إِلَى ٱلْجَامِعَةِ زَائِرَةٌ أَجْنَبِيَّةٌ. (or) حَضَرَ إِلَى ٱلْجَامِعَةِ زَائِرَةٌ أَجْنَبِيَّةٌ.

- The 'subject' of a 'verb' may be a '**compound subject**', joined together by the connecter (**and** = وَ); in such a case, the 'verb' agrees in 'gender' with the first member of such 'subject', as in the following examples:

> رَجَعَ هَيْثَمُ وَهِنْدُ إِلَى ٱلشَّرْقِ ٱلْأَوْسَطِ.
> رَجَعَتْ هِنْدُ وَهَيْثَمُ إِلَى ٱلشَّرْقِ ٱلْأَوْسَطِ.

- A 'verbal sentence' may contain an 'object' of the 'verb', if that 'verb' is 'transitive' in nature. In this case, the usual order is ('verb' ⟶ 'subject' ⟶ 'object). The 'object' of a 'verb' must reflect the 'accusative case'; as in the following examples:

> دَرَسَ آدَمُ ٱللُّغَةَ ٱلْعَرَبِيَّةَ.
> دَرَسَتْ سُعَادُ لُغَةً أَجْنَبِيَّةً.

- Furthermore, a 'verbal sentence' may contain one or more 'adverbs' or 'adverbial phrases', modifying the 'subject'. These 'adverbial modifiers' are typically words or phrases that answer questions such as: 'Where…?', 'Where to …?', 'Where from …' or 'When…?' 'Adverbial modifiers' may occur in various positions within the 'verbal sentence'; as the ones underlined in the following examples:

> بَعْدَ سَنَةٍ، رَجَعَتْ إِلَى بَلَدِهَا.
> حَضَرَ سَمِيرٌ إِلَى أَمْرِيكَا مِنْ لُبْنَانَ.

- It must be further noticed that in Arabic, sentences of any type may be introduced or joined by a '**conjunction**'; such as (وَ / أَوْ / أَمْ). It is also much more common for an Arabic sentence to begin with the 'conjunction (وَ)' than it is for an English sentence to begin with '**and**'. Let's examine the following sentences:

أَنا أُسْتاذٌ، وَأَنْتَ طَالِبٌ.
حَضَرَ هَيْثَمُ مِنْ لُبْنان، وَدَرَسَ فِي جامِعَةِ آنْ آرْبَرْ.
وَبَعْدَ سَنَةٍ مِنَ الدِّراسَةِ، رَجَعَتْ لَيْلَى إِلـى بَلَدِها.

* * *

Adjectives with Non-Human Plural Nouns: ٣-الصِّفاتُ مَعَ جَمْعِ غَيْـرِ ٱلعاقِلِ

- When we previously introduced 'noun-adjective' phrases, we said that generally the 'adjective' would agree with the 'noun' it modifies in some aspects, including 'number'.
- However, we need to modify this general rule to include a sub-rule, which should say that **if the 'noun' being modified is a 'non-human plural', then the 'adjective' modifying it should be in its 'feminine singular' form**. This rule applies whether the 'plural noun' being modified is in the form of a '**feminine sound plural**' or in the form of a '**broken plural**', as long as it refers to 'non-human'.
- To illustrate this point in context, let's now examine the following sentences in comparative perspective:

الطَّالِباتُ ٱلعَرَبِيّاتُ جَديداتٌ .	⇐	الجامِعاتُ ٱلعَرَبِيَّةُ تُدَرِّسُ ٱلإِنْجِليزِيَّةَ.
الـمُوَظَّفاتُ ٱلجَديداتُ مِنْ أَمْريكا.	⇐	يَتَعَلَّمُ ٱلطُّلاَّبُ لُغاتٍ أَجْنَبِيَّةً.
الأُسْتاذاتُ ٱلزَّائِراتُ مِنْ مِصْرَ .	⇐	الكُتُبُ ٱلجَديدَةُ عَرَبِيَّةٌ.
الطَّاوِلَةُ الكَبيـرَةُ لَيْسَتْ هُنا.	⇐	الطَّاوِلاتُ الكَبيـرَةُ لَيْسَتْ هُنا.

- The above rule actually extends to 'pronouns'; so if we have a 'non-human plural noun' that we need to refer to it in terms of 'pronouns', then we use the 'feminine singular' forms of such 'pronouns'; as in the following examples:

هَذا لَوْحٌ.⇦هَذِهِ أَلْواحٌ.	هَذِهِ طاوِلَةٌ.⇦ هَذِهِ طَاوِلاتٌ.

* * *

Demonstrative Pronouns: Plural Form for Humans (هَؤُلاءِ): ٤- اِسْمُ الإِشارة

- We are by now too much familiar with the two 'demonstrative pronouns': (هَذا) for 'masculine singular' and (هَذِهِ) for 'feminine singular'.
- In the text of this lesson, the 'plural demonstrative pronoun' (هَؤُلاءِ) was introduced; this 'plural' form has no 'gender' distinction, and thus can equally be used for 'masculine plural' as well as 'feminine plural'.
- Like the singular forms of 'demonstrative pronouns', this 'plural' form is invariable, in the sense that it does not change its internal vowels, nor the vowel at the end.
- However, its usage is limited only to 'plurals' which refer to human beings only. With 'plurals' referring to non-human, the 'feminine singular' form (هَذِهِ) is used.
- Let's now study the examples in the following box to see these rules in context:

هَذا صِحافِيٌّ فَرَنْسِيٌّ.	⇦	هَؤُلاءِ صِحافِيُّونَ فَرَنْسِيُّونَ.
هَذِهِ أُسْتاذَةٌ جَديدَةٌ.	⇦	هَؤُلاءِ أُسْتاذاتٌ جَديداتٌ.
	but	
هَذِهِ جامِعَةٌ مَشْهُورَةٌ.	⇦	هَذِهِ جامِعاتٌ مَشْهُورَةٌ.

* * *

Ordinal Numerals .... ٥- الأَعْدادُ ٱلتَّرتيبِيَّة

- Besides the cardinal numerals used for simple counting, Arabic, like English, has two other sets of numerals, one of them is called "**ordinal**." Ordinal numerals, as the term indicates, are used to convey the idea of ordering the numbers in descending order.
- In the table below we will introduce the Arabic numerals categorized in three groups: The first group represents the cardinal numerals; the second group represents the ordinal numerals used as adjectives; and the third group is a variation of ordinal numeral, used adverbially:

Adverbial Use	Ordinal Numerals Feminine / Masculine	Counting Numerals	Arithmetic Symbols
أَوَّلاً	الأَوَّل / الأُولى	واحِد / واحِدَة	١
ثانياً	الثَّانـي / الثَّانِيَة	اِثْنان – اِثْنَيْـنِ / اِثْنَتان – اِثْنَتَيْـنِ	٢
ثالثاً	الثَّالِث / الثَّالِثَة	ثَلاث / ثَلاثَة	٣
رابعاً	الرَّابِع / الرَّابِعَة	أَرْبَع / أَرْبَعَة	٤
خامساً	الْخامِسُ / الْخامِسَةُ	خَمْس / خَمْسَة	٥
سادساً	السَّادِس / السَّادِسَة	سِتّ / سِتَّة	٦
سابعاً	السَّابِع / السَّابِعَة	سَبْع / سَبْعَة	٧
ثامناً	الثَّامِن / الثَّامِنَة	ثَمانـي / ثَمانِيَة	٨
تاسعاً	التَّاسِع / التَّاسِعَة	تِسْع / تِسْعَة	٩
عاشراً	العاشِر / العاشِرَة	عَشْر / عَشْرَة	١٠
حادِيَ عَشَرَ	الحادِيَ عَشَرَ / الحادِيَةَ عَشْرَةَ	أَحَدَ عَشَرَ / إحْدى عَشْرَةَ	١١
ثانِيَ عَشَرَ	الثَّانِيَ عَشَرَ / الثَّانِيَةَ عَشْرَةَ	اِثْنا عَشَرَ / اِثْنَتا عَشْرَةَ	١٢
ثالِثَ عَشَرَ	الثَّالِثَ عَشَرَ / الثَّالِثَةَ عَشْرَةَ	ثَلاثَةَ عَشَرَ / ثَلاثَ عَشْرَةَ	١٣
رابِعَ عَشَرَ	الرَّابِعَ عَشَرَ / الرَّابِعَةَ عَشْرَةَ	أَرْبَعَةَ عَشَرَ / أَرْبَعَ عَشْرَةَ	١٤
خامِسَ عَشَرَ	الخامِسَ عَشَرَ / الخامِسَةَ عَشْرَةَ	خَمْسَةَ عَشَرَ / خَمْسَ عَشْرَةَ	١٥
سادِسَ عَشَرَ	السَّادِسَ عَشَرَ / السادِسَةَ عَشْرَةَ	سِتَّةَ عَشَرَ / سِتَّ عَشْرَةَ	١٦

سابِعَ عَشَرَ	السَّابِعَ عَشَرَ / السَّابِعَةَ عَشْرَةَ	سَبْعَ عَشْرَةَ / سَبْعَةَ عَشَر	١٧
ثامِنَ عَشَرَ	الثَّامِنَ عَشَرَ / الثَّامِنَةَ عَشْرَةَ	ثَـمانِـي عَشْرَةَ / ثَـمانِيَةَ عَشَرَ	١٨
تاسِعَ عَشَرَ	التَّاسِعَ عَشَرَ / التَّاسِعَةَ عَشْرَةَ	تِسْعَ عَشْرَةَ / تِسْعَةَ عَشَرَ	١٩
عِشْرِينَ	العِشْرُونَ / العِشْرِينَ	عِشْرُونَ / عِشْرِينَ	٢٠
	الحادي والْعِشْرونَ - والعِشْرِينَ / الحادِيَةُ والعِشْرُونَ - والعِشْرِين	واحِدٌ وعِشْرُونَ / واحِدًا وعِشْرِينَ / واحِدٍ وعشرين	٢١
	الثَّانِـي والعِشْرونَ - الثَّانِـي والعِشْرِينَ / الثَّانِيَةُ والعِشْرِينَ	اِثْنانِ وعِشْرُونَ - اِثْنَيْـنِ وعِشْرِينَ / اِثْنَتانِ وعِشْرُونِ - اِثْنَتَيْـنِ وعِشْرِين	٢٢

- Using the cardinal numerals for simple counting constitutes no problem, for one can use either the masculine or the feminine forms.
- However, when these cardinal numerals are used in a context along with their counted nouns, a rule of reversed agreement applies whereby the masculine form of the number is used with a feminine counted noun and a feminine form of the number is used with a masculine noun. This is rather a complex and unusual characteristic of formal Arabic that will be visited at a higher level of learning.
- As for the ordinal numerals, they are mostly used as adjectives in a definite noun-adjective phrases. Hence they have to agree with the gender of the preceding nouns in a way that the masculine form of the number must follow a masculine gender noun and vice versa, as can be seen in the following examples:

الجُمْلَةُ ٱلأُولـى قَصِيـرَةٌ.	الدَّرْسُ ٱلأَوَّلُ سَهْلٌ.
تَرْجَمْتُ ٱلجُمْلَةَ ٱلثَّالِثَةَ.	قَرَأْتُ ٱلدَّرْسَ ٱلثَّالِثَ.
نَسْكُنُ فـي ٱلبِنايَةِ ٱلسَّابِعَةِ.	أَسْكُنُ فـي ٱلشَّارِعِ ٱلسَّابِعِ.

* * *

الدَّرْسُ ٱلثَّالِث : تَدْرِيباتٌ وَنَشاطاتٌ / Exercises & Activities

تَـمْرين ١: (*Oral / Written*) Recognition: The Verbal Noun and Its Verb

Read the following sentences identify the 'verbal nouns' by underlining them and give their corresponding verbs in their 3rd person, masculine, singular conjugations. Follow the given example:

> يُسافِرُ ٱلطُّلاَّبُ ٱلعَرَبُ إِلَـى ٱلخارِجِ لِلدِّراسَةِ. ⇦ (دَرَسَ)

١- يَسْتَعِدُّ لِلسَّفَرِ إِلـى أَمْرِيكا. he is getting ready ⇦ (..........)

٢- رَجَعَ إِلَى بَلَدِهِ بَعْدَ ٱلحُصُولِ عَلَى شَهادَةٍ. ⇦ (..........)

٣- اِلْتَحَقَ بِٱلجامِعَةِ بَعْدَ حُضُورِهِ إِلـى أَمْرِيكا. ⇦ (..........)

٤- سافَرَ إِلـى ٱلشَّرْقِ ٱلأَوْسَطِ لِلْعَمَلِ هُناكَ. ⇦ (..........)

٥- تَزَوَّجَتْ سَمِيرَةُ بَعْدَ رُجُوعِها إِلـى بَلَدِها. ⇦ (..........)

* * *

تَـمْرين ٢: (*Oral / Written*) Recognition: The Verb and Its subject:

The following sentences contain 'past tense verbs' corresponding to one of the 'implied subjects (هُوَ) or (هِيَ) or to an 'expressed subject'; your task is to read the sentence, identify the 'verb' by underlining it and identify the 'implied' or 'expressed' 'subject', as in the given examples:

دَرَسَ ٱللُّغَةَ ٱلعَرَبِيَّةَ . (هُوَ) | رَجَعَتْ سَميرَةُ إِلَى بَلَدِها. (سَميرَةُ)

١- حَضَرَتْ إِلـى ٱلصَّفِّ ٱلسَّاعَةَ ٱلواحِدَةَ. (..........................)

٢- دَرَسَ سَميـرٌ إِدارَةَ ٱلأَعْمالِ. (..........................)

٣- رَجَعَ إِلـى بَلَدِهِ بَعْدَ ٱلدِّراسَةِ فـي أَمْريكا. (..........................)

٤- تَزَوَّجَ سَميـرٌ مِنْ سَميـرَةَ بَعْدَ ٱلتَّخَرُّجِ مِنَ ٱلجامِعَةِ. (..........................)

٥- سافَرَتْ إِلَـى ٱلشَّرْقِ ٱلأَوْسَطِ لِلْعَمَلِ هُناكَ. (..........................)

٦- دَرَسَتْ مَرْيَمُ فِي جامِعَةٍ أَجْنَبِيَّةٍ. (..........................)

٧- حَصَلَ عَلَى شَهادَتِهِ فِي إِدارَةِ ٱلأَعْمالِ بِتَفَوُّقٍ. (..........................)

٨- بَعْدَ ٱلتَّخَرُّجِ مِنَ ٱلجامِعَةِ عَمِلَ إِبْراهيمُ فِـي ٱلسَّعُودِيَّةِ. (..........................)

* * *

تَـمْرين ٣: (*Oral*) Substitution: Verbal Sentences

Substitute the following numbered words or phrases for the underlined 'subject of the verb' in the model sentence inside the box, note that the conjugation of the verb might need to be modified:

سافَرَ سامِـي إِلـى ٱلشَّرْقِ ٱلأَوْسَطِ.

١- هِنْد ٢- الأُسْتاذُ ٣- الرَّئِيسُ ٤- الـمُوَظَّفَةُ ٱلعَرَبِيَّةُ ٥- مَرْيَمُ

٦- سامِي ٧- الأُسْتاذَةُ ٨- الصِّحافِيَّةُ ٱلفَرَنْسِيَّةُ ٩- الصِّحافـيُّ

١٠- الطَّـالِبَةُ ١١- الزّائِرُ ١٢- الشّابُّ اللُّبْنانـيُّ ١٣- مُديرُ ٱلـمُتْحَفِ

١٤- سِكْرِتيـرَةُ ٱلقِسْمِ ١٥- الآنِسَةُ سُعادُ

* * *

تَـمْرِين ٤: (*Oral / Written*) Recognizing the Components of the Verbal Sentence:

Read each of the following sentences and identify its '**verb**', its '**subject**', its '**direct object**', its '**object of preposition**' and its '**adverbial modifier**', whichever exists in the sentence. Then write each under its category in the table which follows. The first sentence is done for you as an example:

١- دَرَسَتْ سَميـرَةُ ٱللُّغَةَ ٱلإِنْجِليزِيَّةَ فِـي أَمْرِيكا.

٢- سافَرَ رَئِيسُ ٱلقِسْمِ إِلَـى ٱلقاهِرَةِ.

٣- رَجَعَتِ ٱلصِّحافِيَّةُ ٱلأَمْرِيكِيَّةُ مِنَ ٱلعِراقِ.

٤- تَزَوَّجَ هَيْثَمُ وَهِنْدُ بَعْدَ تَخَرُّجِهِما مِنَ ٱلجامِعَةِ.

٥- حَضَرَ مُدِيرُ ٱلـمُتْحَفِ إِلَى مَكْتَبِهِ.

٦- حَصَلَتْ مَرْيَمُ عَلَى شَهادَةٍ جامِعِيَّةٍ.

٧- رَجَعَ مِنْ عَمَلِهِ فِـي ٱلـمَساءِ.

Adverbial Modifier	Direct Object	Subject	Verb
فِـي أَمْرِيكا	ٱللُّغَةَ ٱلإِنْجِلِيزِيَّةَ	هِـنـدُ	دَرَسَتْ

تَمْرين ٥: (*Oral / Written*) Using the Appropriate Form of the Adjectives in Relation to Gender and Number:

Select the appropriate form of the '**adjective**' from among those given in parenthesis at the end of the sentences; note that you should pay special attention to the '**gender**' and '**number**' of the 'nouns' these 'adjectives' modify and also to whether they refer to '**humans**' or '**non-humans**'; follow the given example:

الطُّلاَّبُ .... مِنَ ٱلشَّرْقِ ٱلأَوْسَطِ. (الجَديدُ / الجُدُدُ / الجَديدَةُ) ⇩

⇦ اَلطُّلاَّبُ ٱلجُدُدُ مِنَ ٱلشَّرْقِ ٱلأَوْسَطِ.

١- هَلْ هَذِهِ هِيَ ٱلطَّالِبَةُ .... ؟ (العَرَبِيُّ / العَرَبِيَّةُ / العَرَبِيَّاتُ)

٢- هَلِ ٱلأُسْتاذُ .... فـي مَكْتَبِهِ؟ (الزَّائِرَةُ / الزَّائِرُونَ / الزَّائِرُ)

٣- الرَّئِيسُ .... يَزُورُ أَمْريكا. (الـمِصْرِيَّةُ / الـمِصْرِيُّ / الـمِصْرِيُّونَ)

٤- دَرَسْتُ فِي جامِعاتٍ .... (أَجْنَبِيَّةٍ / أَجْنَبِيَّاتٍ / أَجْنَبِيٍّ)

٥- عَمِلَتْ مُدَرِّسَةً فِي مَدْرَسَةٍ .... (ثانَوِيٍّ / ثانَوِيَّةٍ / ثانَوِيَّةٌ)

٦- اَلكُتُبُ .... عَلَى مَكْتَبِ ٱلرَّئِيسِ. (الجَديداتُ / الجُدُدُ / الجَديدَةُ)

* * *

تَمْرين ٦: (*Oral / Written*) Using the Correct Demonstrative Pronoun:

From the list of the three 'demonstrative pronouns' in the shaded box on the left, select the appropriate one to fill in the blanks in the following sentences:

هَذا
هَذِهِ
هَؤُلاءِ

١- .... طُلاَّبٌ جُدُدٌ.

٢- .... مَكْتَبَةٌ حَديثَةٌ.

٣- مَنْ .... ٱلزَّائِرُ ٱلجَديدُ؟

٤- تَخَرَّجْتُ مِنَ .... ٱلجامِعَةِ قَبْلَ ثَلاثِ سَنَواتٍ.

٥- .... ٱلسَّيِّداتُ مِنَ ٱلشَّرْقِ ٱلأَوْسَطِ.

(Review: *Oral / Written*) Comprehension Questions: تَـمْرين ٧:

Read again the text of Lesson 1, pages 251-252, then answer the following questions verbally first, then in writing:

١- لِماذا يُسَافِرُ ٱلطُّلاَّبُ ٱلعَرَبُ إِلـى ٱلخارِجِ ؟ **Why** ...?

٢- أَيْنَ ٱلْتَقى سَمِيـر وَسَـمِـيـرَة؟

٣- مِنْ أَيْنَ سَمِيـر ، ومِنْ أَيْنَ سَـمِـيـرَة ؟

٤- ماذا سَيَدْرُسُ سَمِيـر ، وماذا سَتَدْرُسُ سَـمِـيـرَة؟

٥- أَيْنَ سَتَسْكُنُ سَـمِـيـرَة ، ولِماذا؟

٦- ما الَّذي يُزعِجُ سَـمِـيـرَة مِنَ ٱلسَّكَنِ مَعَ خالَتِها؟

٧- هَلْ ستَـرْجِعُ سَـمِـيـرَة إِلـى لُبْنان بَعْدَ ٱلتَّخَرُّج؟

٨- ماذا يُفَضِّلُ سَمِيـر ، العَوْدَة إِلـى مِصر أَمْ ٱلبَقاء فـي أَمْريكا؟

٩- هَلْ سَيَسْمَحُ والِدا سَمِيـر لَـهُ بِٱلبَقاءِ فـي أَمْريكا؟

* * *

(Review: *Oral / Written*) Reviewing the Arabic Numerals: 1-10: تَـمْرين ٨:

Fill in the empty cells in the following table with the appropriate form of the numerals; first orally, then in writing:

Adverbial Use	Ordinal Numerals Feminine / Masculine	Counting Numerals	Arithmetic Symbols
....	.... / الأَوَّل	واحِد	١
ثانِياً	الثَّانِيَة /	....	٢
....	.... /	ثَلاثَة	٣
رابِعاً	.... / الرَّابِعُ	....	٤
....	الخامِسَةُ /	خَمْسَة	٥
سادِساً	.... / السَّادِسُ	....	٦

٧	سَبْعَة	.... / السَّابِعَةُ	....
٨	....	الثَّامِنُ /	ثامِناً
٩	تِسْعَة	.... / التَّاسِعَةُ	....
١٠	....	العاشِرُ /	عاشِراً

* * *

تَمْرين ٨: **Reviewing a Reference List:** Go to the reference lists section to review the "Conjugations Paradigm of a Typical Past Tense Verb, page 343.

* * *

الدَّرْسُ الرَّابِعُ : نَصٌّ حِوارِيٌّ (٢) Conversational Text (2)

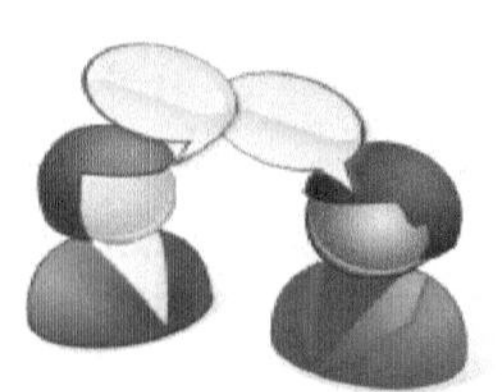

حَدِيثٌ عَنِ ٱلزّواجِ وٱلحُبِّ وٱلأُسْرَة

سُعاد : أُريدُ أَنْ أَفْتَحَ مَعَكَ مَوْضُوعَ الزَّواجِ يا أَخِي، فَأَرْجُو أَنْ تَفْتَحَ لي قَلْبَكَ وَتَسْمَعَني !

يُوسُف : وَكَيْفَ لا أَفْتَحُ قَلْبِي وَصَدْرِي لِأُخْتِي العَزيزَةِ الوَحيدَةِ! تَفَضَّلِي وقُولِي ما تُريدينَ!

سُعاد : لَقَدْ ساءَنا خَبَرُ طَلاقِكَ مِنْ زَوْجَتِكَ السَّابِقَةِ نانْسِي مُنْذُ شَهْرَيْنِ فقَطْ، خُصُوصاً أَنَّكَ تَزَوَّجْتَها بَعْدَ قِصَّةِ حُبٍّ جَميلَة .

يُوسُف : نَعَمْ ، وَلَكِنْ لِلأَسَف، الحُبُّ لا يَدومُ طَوِيلاً فِي هَذِهِ الأَيَّامِ!

كَمال : دَعْكَ مِنَ التَّشاؤُمِ وَالْحُزْنِ يا أَخِي! أَنا وَأُخْتُكَ مُتَزَوِّجانِ مُنْذُ عِشْرِينَ سَنَةً ، وَلا يَزالُ حُبُّنا يَكْبُرُ كُلَّ يَوْمٍ .

سُعاد : اَلمُهِمُّ أَنَّكَ بِحاجَةٍ إِلَى زَوْجَةٍ وَرَفيقَةٍ وَأُمٍّ لِوَلَدٍ يَحمِلُ ٱسْمَ العائِلَةِ وَأَنْتَ الاِبْنُ الوَحيدُ. لي صَديقَةٌ في العَمَلِ مُثَقَّفَةٌ وَجَميلَةٌ وَمِنْ أُسْرَةٍ كَرِيمَة !

يُوسُف: أَشْعُرُ أَنَّ الوَقْتَ غَيْـرَ مُناسِبٍ لِلدُّخولِ فـي تَجْرِبَةِ زَواجٍ أُخْرى!

كَمال: دَعْ عَنْكَ هَذا الوَهْم! فَـلَسْتَ أَوَّلَ مَنْ يَفْشَلُ فـي زَواجِهِ الأَوَّل، وَخَيْـرُ البِـرِّ عاجِلُـهُ.

سُعاد: الـمُهِمُّ الآنَ أَنْ تُوافِقَ عَلَى مَبْدَإِ مُقابَلَةِ صَدِيقَتِي لَيْلَى، والتَّعَرُّفِ عَلَيْها!

يُوسُف: حَسَناً! أَتْرُكُ لَكِ أَمْرَ تَرْتِيبِ اللِّقاءِ، وَأَتَوَكَّلُ عَلَى اللهِ فـي أَمْرِ تَرْتِيبِ الأَقْدارِ.

الـزَّواج قِـسْمَـة وَنَـصِـيـب!

* * *

الـمُفْرَداتُ والتَّراكيبُ اللُّغَوِيَّةُ لِلدَّرْسِ الرَّابِعِ (مُرتَّبة حَسَبَ وُرودِها في النَّصِّ)

the marriage	الزَّواج	a talk about	حَديث عَنْ
and the family	والأُسْرَة (و+الأُسْرَة)	and the love	وَالحُبّ (و+الْحُبّ)
open with you	أَفْتَحَ مَعَـكَ	I want to	أُريدُ أَنْ
so I hope that	فَـأَرْجُو أَنْ (فَـ+أَرجُو)	(the) subject (of)	مَوْضُوع
your heart	قَلْبَـكَ (قَلْبَ+كَ)	you open for me	تَفْتَحَ لـي (لِـ+ي)
and how (is it possible)	وكَيْفَ (و+كَيْفَ)	and hear me, and listen to me	وَتَسْمَعَـنِي
my heart	قَلْبِـي (قَلْب+ي)	not to open	لا أَفْـتَـحُ
to my sister	لِأُخْتِـي (لِـ+أُخْت+ي)	and my chest (breast)	وَصَدْرِي (و+صَدْر+ي)
the only one	الوَحِيدَة	the dear one	العَزيزَة
and say	وقولـي (و+قولـي)	please go ahead	تَفَضَّلـي
you want	تُـريـدِينَ	that which *(relative pronoun)*	ما
It pained us, it displeased us	ساءَنـا (ساءَ+نـا)	indeed	لَقَدْ

your divorce	طَلاقِـكَ (طَلاق+كَ)	the news (of)	خَبَـرُ
your wife	زَوْجَتِـكَ (زَوْجَة+ك)	from	مِن
Nancy (*transliteration*)	نانسِي	former, ex	السَّابِقَة
two months (a month)	شَهْرَيْنِ (شَهْر)	ago	مُـنْـذُ
particularly, especiallyy	خُصوصاً	only	فَـقَـط
have married her	تزَوَّجْتَها (تَزَوَّجْتَ+ها)	that you	أنَّـكَ (أَنَّ+كَ)
story (stories)	قِصَّة (قِصَص)	after	بَـعْـدَ
beautiful	جَـمـيـلَـة	love	حُـبّ
however, but	ولَـكِـنْ	yes	نَـعَـمْ
does not last	لا يَدُومُ	regretfully	لِـلأَسَف
in these days	فـي هَذِهِ الأيَّـام	long, for long	طَـويـلاً
and sadness	والحُـزْنِ	cast aside pessimism	دَعْـكَ مِنَ التَّـشاؤُم
I and your sister	أَنا وأُخْـتُـكَ (و+أُخْت+ك)	O' My brother	يـا أخـي
since twenty years ago	مُنْذُ عِشْرينَ سَنَة	(are) married (*dual*)	مُـتَـزَوِّجانِ (مُتَزَوِّج)
our love	حُبُّـنـا (حُـبّ+نـا)	and is still	ولا يَـزالُ
every day	كُـلَّ يَوْم	is growing	يَـكْـبُـرُ
that you (are)	أَنَّـكَ (أَنَّ+كَ)	the inportant (matter) is	الـمُهِمُّ
a wife	زَوْجَـة	in need of	بِحاجَة إلـى (بِـ+حاجَة)
and a mother	وأُمّ (و+أُمّ)	and a companion	ورَفِـيقَـة (و+رفيقَة)
to carry, to bear	يَـحْـمِـلُ	for a child	لِـوَلَـد (لِـ+وَلَـد)
and you are	وأنْـتَ (و+أَنْـتَ)	the name of the family	اسْمَ الـعـائِـلَـة
the lone, the only	الـوَحِـيـد	the son	ٱلاِبْـنُ
a friend	صَـديـقَـة	I have	لـي (لِـ+ي)
cultured, educated	مُـثَـقَّـفَـة	at work	فـي الـعَـمَـل

and from = comes from	ومِـن (و+مِن)	and beautiful	وَجَـمـيـلَـة (و+جَميلة)
noble, good	كَـريـمَـة	family (families)	أُسْـرَة (أُسَـر)
the time	الـوَقْـتَ	I feel that	أَشْـعُـرُ أَنَّ
for entering into	لِـلدُّخُـولِ فـي	Is not suitable	غَـيْـرَ مُـنـاسِب
another	أُخْـرَى	marriage experience	تَـجْـرِبَـةِ زَواج
this erroneous impression	هَـذا الـوَهْـمَ	cast aside, set aside (*to be learned as an idiom*)	دَعْ عَـنْـكَ
(the) first	أَوَّل	for you are not	فَـلَـسْـتَ
who fails in	يَـفْـشَـلُ فـي	who	مَـنْ
and the sooner the better (*to be learned as an idiom*)	وَخَـيْـرُ ٱلْـبِرِّ عـاجِلُـه	his first marriage	زَواجِـهِ الأَوَّلِ
that you agree on	أَنْ تُـوافِـقَ عَلى	the important (thing) now	الـمُهِمُّ الآنَ
meeting	مُـقـابَـلَـة	(the) principle (of)	مَـبْـدَإ (مَـبادئ)
Layla or Laila (*female proper name*)	لَـيْـلَى	my friend	صَدِيقَتِي (صَديقَة+ي)
well, fine	حَـسَـنـاً	and getting to know her	والـتَّـعَـرُّف عَـلَـيْـها
(the) matter (of)	أَمْـر (أُمور)	I leave it to you	أَتْـرُكُ لَـكِ (لَ+كِ)
the meeting, the get together	الـلِّـقـاء	arranging for	تَـرْتِـيـب
the destined matters (a destined matter, a fated matter)	الأَقْـدار (قَدَر)	and I put my trust in God	وأَتَـوَكَّـلُ على ٱلـلَّـهِ
		arranging for the destined matters	تَـرْتِـيـب الأَقْـدار

* * *

Comprehension Questions (Orally) (شَفَوِيًّا) أَسْئِلَةُ الفَهْمِ والاِسْتيعابِ

سُؤال

١- أَيَّ مَوْضُوعٍ تُريدُ سُعادُ أَنْ تَفتَحَ مَعَ أَخيها يوسُف؟

٢- ماذا تَرْجُو سُعادُ مِن يوسُف أَنْ يَفْعَل؟

٣- ماذا قالَ يُوسُف رَدًّا على رَجاءِ سُعاد؟ in response to / the hope

جَواب

٤- ما الخَبَرُ الَّذي ساءَ سُعاد وزَوْجَها؟

٥- ماذا قالَ يُوسُف عَن الحُبّ هذِه الأيَّام؟

٦- ماذا قالَ كَمال رَدًّا على تَشاؤُم يُوسُف؟

٧- ماذا قالَتْ سُعاد عَنْ حاجَةِ يُوسُف؟

٨- ماذا قالَت سُعاد عَن صَديقَتِها في العَمَل؟

٩- كَيْفَ يَشْعُرُ يُوسُفُ الآنَ بِالنِّسْبَةِ لِتَجْرِبَةِ زَواجٍ أُخْرى؟

١٠- ماذا قالَ كَمال لِيُوسُف عَنْ الوَهْمِ؟

١١- ماذا قالَ يُوسُف عَنْ مَبْدَأ مُقابَلَة لَيْلى؟

* * *

الدَّرْسُ الخامِسُ: الثَّقافَةُ وٱلقِيَمُ وٱلأمْثالُ
Culture, Values & Proverbs

(أ) يَشْرَحُ المُدرِّسُ/المُدَرِّسَة بَعْضَ القَضايا الْمُتَّصِلَةِ بِما يَلي:

The instructor explaims some of the values and cultural issues related to the following:

❖ أَهَمِّيَّةُ الزَّواجِ كَواجِبٍ دينِيٍّ وٱجْتِماعِيٍّ في الثَّقافَةِ العربيَّة الإسلامِيَّة.

The importance of marriage as a religious and social value in the Arabic-Islamic culture.

❖ دَوْرُ الأُمَّهاتِ والأَخَواتِ في اخْتِيارِ العَرائِس لِرِجالِ الأُسْرَة.

The role of mothers and sisters in exploring issues related to choosing brides for the males of the family;

❖ السَّفرُ إلى الْخارِجِ في طَلَبِ العِلْمِ تقليدٌ راسِخٌ في الثَّقافَةِ العربيَّة الإسلامِيَّة.

Travelling abroad in pursuit of knowledge is a well-established tradition in the Arabic-Islamic culture and value system.

﴿طَلَبُ العِلْمِ فَريضَةٌ عَلى كُلِّ مُسْلِمٍ ومُسْلِمَة.﴾

(Seeking knowledge is a sacred duty upon each male and female Muslim.)

﴿أُطْلُبُ ٱلعِلْمَ وَلَوْ في الصِّين!﴾

(Seek knowledge even as far as China!)

(ب) مُخْتاراتٌ مِن الحِكَمِ والأَمْثالِ العَرَبِيَّةِ:

أُطْلُبِ العِلْمَ مِنَ الـمَهْدِ إلى اللَّحْدِ!
Seek knowledge from cradle to grave!

الجارُ قَبْلَ الدَّارِ!
(Seek) the neighbor before the house!

السَّماءُ لا تُـمْطِرُ ذَهَباً!
The heavens do not rain gold.

seek = أُطْلُبْ
knowledge = العِلْمَ
from = مِنْ
the cradle = الـمَهْد
to = إلـى
the frave = اللَّحْد
the neighbor = اَلجارُ
before = قَبْلَ
the house = الدَّارِ
the heaven, the sky = السَّماءُ
does not = لا
rain = تُـمْطِرُ
gold = ذَهَباً

* * *

تَـمارين عامّة ومُراجَعَة
General Drills & Review

تَـمرين ١: **Let's read the following sets of words or phrases, recall their meanings and then guess why they were grouped together under one category:**

١- اِلْتَقَى/دارَ/قُبِلْتُ/أَوْصَتْـني/قُبِلا/تَشَرَّفْتُ/سَمَحَتْ/ما دُمْتُ/سافَرُوا.

٢- يُسافِرُ/يَبْدُو/أُفَضِّلُ/تُقِيمُ/أَتَحَدَّثُ/يُزْعِجُني/أَظُنُّ/تَفْهَمُ/أَرْجُو/تُفَكِّرِينَ/ يَسْمَحانِ/أُفَكِّرُ/أَميلُ/يُـمانِعانِ/أَتَـمَنَّى.

٣- الدِّراسَة/بَدْء/سَكَن/وُجود/الرُّجُوع/البَقاء/الحُصُول/النِّهايَة/تَوْفيـر/التَّوْفيق.

٤- سَـأَدْرُسُ/سَـتَسْكُنِيـنَ/سَـتُقِيمِيـنَ/سَـتَعُودُ.

٥- جامِعَةُ آن آرْبَر / وِلايَةُ مِيتشِيغان / إدارَةَ الأَعمالِ / كُلِّيَّةُ التِّجارَة / سَكَنُ الطَّالِبات / مَكْتَبُ التَّسْجِيل / دِراسَةُ الـماجِسْتِيـر .

٦- سَنَة دِراسِيَّة / طالِبَة جَديدَة / طالِب جَديد / عَدَد كَبِيـر / الطُّلاَّبُ العَرَب / اللُّغَةُ الإِنْجليزِيَّة .

The group of words / phrases above fall under one of the following categories: (1) Noun-adjective phrases, (2) Past tense verbs, (3) ***Idāfah*** structures, (4) Verbal nouns (gerunds), (5) Present tense verbs, (6) Future tense verbs.

* * *

تـمرين ٣: **Fill in the blanks with suitable words from these you learned from the text of Lesson four, entitled:** حديث عن الزَّواج والحُبّ والأسرَة

١- سَمِيـر مِن __________ .

٢- سَمِيـرَة مِنْ __________ .

٣- هُما قُبِلا فـي __________ آن آربَر بِـ __________ مِيتشِغان .

٤- سَمِيـر سَيَدْرُسُ فـي كُلِّيَّةِ ______ ، وسَميـرَة سَتَدْرُسُ ______ الإنْجِلِيزِيّ .

٥- سَمير سَيَدْرُسُ ______ الأَعْمال .

٦- سَمِيـرَة سَتَسْكُنُ مَعَ __________ .

٧- بَيْتُ خالَتِها __________ مِنَ الجامِعَةِ .

٨- والِدا سَميـرَة لَنْ ________ لَها بِـالبَقاءِ فـي أَمْريكا .

٩- سَمِيـر سَيَدْرُسُ ________ بَعْدَ الحُصُولِ عَلى ________ .

١٠- سَمِيـر يُفَضِّلُ ________ فـي أَمْريكا إذا سَمَحَت ________ .

* * *

تـمرين ٤: Translate into English the following sentences from the coversational text of Lesson four, entitled: حديث عن الزَّواج والحُبّ والأسرَة

١- أَرْجُو أَنْ تَفْتَحَ لـي قَلْبَكَ وتَسْمَعَني !

٢- لَقَد ساءَنا خَبَـرُ طَلاقِكَ مِن زَوْجَتِكَ نانْسي .

٣- الحُبُّ لا يَدُومُ طَويلاً هَذِهِ الأَيَّام .

٤- لـي صَديقَة فـي العَمَلِ مُثَقَّفَة وجَميلَة ومِن أُسْرَة كَريـمَة .

٥- لَسْتَ أَوَّل مَنْ يَفْشَلُ فـي زَواجِهِ الأَوَّل .

* * *

تـمرين ٥: صَواب / خَطأ - True / False

Read the following statements and then answer whether each is true or false, using the Arabic terms; your answers should be based on your comprehension of the texts of the current unit:

١- يُسافِرُ عَددٌ كَبيرٌ مِن الطلاّبِ العرب إلى أَمْريكا وأَوْرُوبّا لِلدِّراسة . (   )

٢- لا يَدرُسُ الطلاب العرب في جامِعاتٍ أمريكيّة أو أوروبِيَّة . (   )

٣- حَضَرَ سمير إلى أمريكا لِلدِّراسة في جامِعة آن أربر بـِميشغان . (   )

٤- حَضَرَتْ سميرة مِن بلدها لبنان لِلدِّراسة في أمريكا . (   )

٥- سَتَدْرُسُ سميرة لِلحُصُولِ على شهادة الـماجستير في إدارة الأعمال . (   )

٦- دَرَسَ سمير إدارة الأعمال وحَصَل على الـماجستير السَّنَةَ الـماضِيَة. (   )

٧- بَعْد الاِنتِهاء مِن الدِّراسة يُفَضِّلُ سمير البَقاء فـي أَمريكا. (   )

٨- لا تُريد سُعاد أن تُساعد أخاها يوسف في البَحْثِ عن عروس. (   )

٩- ليلى زميلة سُعاد في العمل ، وهي جميلة وسُمعتها جَيِّدة . (   )

١٠- وافقَ يُوسُفُ على اقْتِراحِ أُخْتِه بِمقابَلة لَيْلى . (   )

* * *

تمرين ٦: **Practice forming the five singular and plural conjugations of the following past and present tense verbs by filling in the blanks in the following two tables to correspond to the given subject pronouns:**

أنا	أنتِ	أنتَ	هِيَ	هُو
				يُسافِرُ
			لَمَّحَتْ	
		تَنْشَطُ		
	رَجَعْتِ			
أَتَزَوَّجُ				

نَحْنُ	أنْتُنَّ	أَنْتُمْ	هُنَّ	هُمْ
				يَرْغَبونَ
			اِلْتَحَقْنَ	
		تُرَتِّبونَ		
	دَرَسْتُنَّ			
نَعْمَلُ				

* * *

تَمرين ٧: **Chain Drill > Prompting:** **The instructor prompts a student to produce another word related to a word in the list below either in root, singular-plural relationship, masculine- feminine relationship, verb-gerund relationship, or past-present tense relationship. The first student prompts another student with the next item on the list; and so on in a chain drill whereby each student takes the two roles of being prompter and prompted:**

	سافَرَ		جامِعَة		الدِّراسَة
	يَتزَوَّج		عَريس		بَحَثَ عَن
	سَنَوات		تَخَرُّج		مَرَّات
	مُناسَبات		هذا		زَميلَة
	هَؤُلاء		طالِب		كَبير
	تُفَكِّرينَ		جَديدَة		العَمَل
	الرُّجوع		أَنْتَ		شابّ
	أَخْبار		هُوَ		أَجْنَبِيَّة
	الحُبّ		حَصَلَ (على)		مُدَرِّسَة
	يَوْم		سَأَسْكُنُ		مَكْتَب
	الأَوَّل		والِد		عَرَبِيّ
	جَميلَة		الدُّخول		أَنا

* * *

تَمرين ٨: Practice finding the root and patern of the following words, as in the first given example:

English Meaning	Pattern (وزن)	Root (جذر)	Word (كَلِمَة)
beautiful	فَعِيلَة	ج م ل	جَميلَة
			والِد
			رُجُوع
			مُناسَبات
			مُدَرِّسَة
			الجُمُعَة
			دِراسَة
			كَبيرَة

تَـمرين ٩: نَشاط لُغَوي: تسلِيَة مع لعبة البَحْثِ عَنِ الكَلِماتِ:

Linguistic Activity : Diversion with the Game of Word Search:

Search (vertically, horizontally, or diagonally) for the hidden 'Arabic Pronouns' given in the box: (one is done for you!)

هذا / هذه / هؤلاء / هو / هي / أنت / أنا / نـحن / هم / هنّ / أنتم

ز	هـ	ذ	د	خ	ح	ج	ث	ت	ا	ب	م	ا	ن	أ
و	ش	ا	ص	ض	ط	ظ	ع	ل	غ	ف	ق	ل	ك	ل
خ	ح	ل	ج	ث	ت	ب	أ	ء	ا	ذ	هـ	أ	ن	م
د	ذ	ج	ر	ز	س	ح	ش	ص	ض	ط	ن	س	ع	غ
ل	ن	م	هـ	و	د	ي	ا	ب	ت	ت	هـ	ب	ذ	ف
ك	ح	ع	ق	ء	ا	ل	ؤ	هـ	ي	ت	ح	و	ب	ق
ق	ن	ـة	ص	ش	ل	س	ز	ر	ذ	د	خ	ع	ث	ك
ف	ط	ظ	ع	خ	ن	ي	ن	ث	إ	ل	ا	غ	ف	ل
غ	ث	ب	م	ا	ء	ي	و	هـ	ن	م	ل	ك	ق	م
م	ت	ن	أ	خ	ح	د	ذ	ي	ز	س	ث	ش	ص	ش
ظ	س	ر	ذ	ص	ط	ع	ف	غ	ظ	ض	ل	ز	ض	هـ
ط	ث	ج	ح	ء	ص	ع	ب	ر	أ	ل	س	د	م	و
ض	ت	خ	د	ز	ش	ض	ظ	ن	ص	س	ث	ح	ظ	ي
ص	ش	س	ز	ر	ذ	د	ت	ح	ج	ث	ا	ن	ب	م
ب	ا	ي	نّ	هـ	ن	م	ل	ك	ق	ف	ء	غ	ع	ت

نهاية الوحدة الثامنة

The Ninth Unit / الوحدةُ التَّاسِعَةُ

الوِحْدَةُ التَّاسِعَةُ 9th Unit
الدَّرْسُ الأَوَّلُ 1st Lesson

مُحادَثَةٌ بَيْـنَ رَجُلٍ عَرَبِـيٍّ وَامْرَأَةٍ أَمْريكِيَّةٍ

تَقابَلَ رَجُلٌ عَرَبِـيٌّ وَامْرَأَةٌ أَمْريكِيَّةٌ فـي مُتْحَفٍ قُرْبَ مَيْدانِ التَّحْريرِ بِالقاهِرَةِ، ودارَ بَيْـنَهُـما الحِوارُ التَّالـي:

- الرَّجُل : أَنْتِ تَتَكَلَّمِيـنَ العَرَبِيَّةَ جَيِّداً ، فَـأَيْنَ تَعَلَّمْتِ لُغَـتَـنا يا سَيِّدَتِـي؟
- الـمَرْأَة : دَرَسْتُها فِي الجامِعَةِ لِمُدَّةِ ثَلاثِ سَنواتٍ ، عِنْدَما كُنْتُ مُتَخَصِّصَةً في العَلاقاتِ الدُّوَلِيَّة.
- الرَّجُل: ولَكِنْ هَذا لا يَكْـفِي لِإتْـقانِـكِ الـلُّغَةَ بِهَذِهِ الصُّورَة.
- الـمَرْأَة : هَذا صَحِيح ، فَـقَدْ حَضَرْتُ بَعْدَ ذَلِكَ إلى مِصْر، وقَـضَيْـتُ حَوالَـيْ

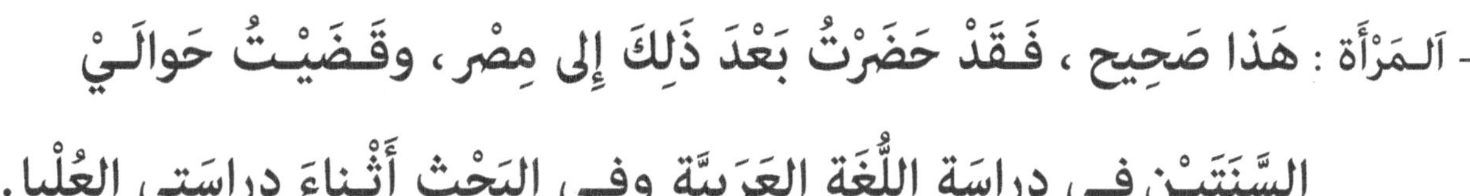

السَّنَتَيْـنِ فـي دِراسَةِ اللُّغَةِ العَرَبِيَّةِ وفـي البَحْثِ أَثْـنَاءَ دِراسَتِي العُلْيا.
- الرَّجُل : وما تَـخَـصُّـصُـكِ؟
- الْمَرْأَة : دَرَسْتُ التَّاريخَ الـمِصرِيَّ القَديم فـي مَرْحَلَةِ الـماجِسْتِيـر والدُّكْتُوراه، وأَصْبَحْتُ أُسْتاذَةً في قِسْمِ التَّاريخِ بِـجامِعَـةِ شِيكاغو.
- الرَّجُل : أَنا تَخَرَّجْتُ مِنْ جامِعَةِ شيكاغو أَيْضاً، حَيْثُ حَصَلْتُ عَلى الـماجِسْتِير والدُّكْتُوراه فـي العُلُومِ السِّياسِيَّة.

- اَلْمَرْأَة : وماذا تَعْمَلُ الآن؟

- الرَّجُل : أَنا أُسْتاذ فـي قِسْمِ العُلُومِ السِّياسِيَّةِ فـي الجامِعَةِ الأمْريكِيَّةِ بِالقاهِرَة.

- اَلْمَرْأَة : وما رَأْيُكَ فـي الاِنْتِخاباتِ الأَخِيـرَة، والَّتي فازَ بِها الحِزْبُ الحاكِم؟

- الرَّجُل : أَنْتِ رُبَّـما تُدْرِكِيـنَ أَكْثَـرَ مِنْ غَيْـرِكِ أَنَّها اَنْتِخاباتٌ غَيْـرُ حُرَّة.

- اَلْمَرْأَة : أَتَـمَنَّى أَنْ تَكونَ أَكْـثَـرَ دِيـموقْراطِيَّـةً فـي الـمَرَّةِ القادِمَة!

- الرَّجُل : لَدَيَّ شُعُورٌ قَـوِيٌّ أَنَّ الوَضْعَ لَنْ يَسْتَمِرَّ على هَذِهِ الحالَة!

* * *

اَلـمُفْرَداتُ وٱلتَّـراكِيبُ ٱللُّغَوِيَّةُ (مُرَتَّبَةٌ حَسَبَ تَسَلْسُلِ وُرودِها في النَّص)

an Arab man	رَجُـلٌ عَرَبِـيٌّ	met	تَـقـابَـلَ
at a museum	فـي مُـتْـحَـفٍ	and an American woman	وَٱمْرَأَةٌ أَمْريكِـيَّـةٌ
At-Tahreer Square	مَـيْدانِ الـتَّـحْـريـرِ	near by	قُـرْبَ
and took place between the two of them	ودارَ بَـيْـنَـهُـما	in Cairo	بِـالقاهِرَةِ
you speak (*feminine singular conjugation*)	أَنْتِ تَـتَـكَلَّمِـيـنَ	the following dialogue	الحِوارُ الـتَّـالـي
well, good	جَـيِّـداً	Arabic = the Arabic language	العَرَبِيَّة = اللُّغَة العَرَبِـيَّـة
did you learn (*feminine singular*)	تَـعَـلَّـمْـتِ	so where ...?	فَـأَيْـنَ ...؟(فَـ+أَيْنَ)
my lady	سَيِّـدَتِـي (سَيِّدَة+ي)	our language	لُـغَـتَـنـا (لُغَة+نا)
at the university	فـي الـجـامِـعَـةِ	I studied it	دَرَسْتُها (دَرَسْتُ+ها)
three years	ثَـلاثَ سَنَوات	for a period (of)	لِـمُدَّةِ (لِـ+مُـدَّة)
majoring in	مُـتَـخَـصِّـصَـة فـي	when I was	عِـنْـدَما كُـنْـتُ

however, but	وَلَكِنْ	(the) International Relations	العَلاقاتِ الدَّوَلِيَّة
for your mastering	لِإتْقانِكِ	this is not sufficient	هَذا لا يَكْفي
in such a way	بِهَذِهِ الصُّورَة	the language (languages)	اللُّغَة (لُغات)
for indeed I came	فَقَدْ حَضَرْتُ	this is correct	هَذا صَحيح
and spent	وقَضَيْتُ	to Egypt	إلى مِصْر
in studying	في دِراسَةِ	approximately two years	حَوالَيْ السَّنَتَيْن
and in doing research	وفي البَحْث	the Arabic language	اللُّغَة العَرَبِيَّةِ
my graduate study	دِراسَتي العُلْيا	during	أَثْناءَ
I studied	دَرَسْتُ	And what is your specialty?	وما تَخَصُّصُكِ؟
in the stage	في مَرْحَلَة	the Egyptian History	التَّاريخ المِصْريّ
and I became a professor	وأَصْبَحْتُ أُسْتاذَةً	of Masters and Doctorate (degrees)	الماجِسْتير والدُّكْتُوراه
at Chicago University	بِجامِعَةِ شِيكاغو	in the History Department	في قِسْمِ التَّاريخ
the University of Chicago	جامِعَةِ شِيكاغو	I graduated from	أنا تَخَرَّجْتُ مِنْ
where I earned	حَيْثُ حَصَلْتُ عَلى	also, likewise	أَيْضاً
And what are you doing now?	وماذا تَعْمَلُ ألآنَ؟	in Political Sciences	في العُلُومِ السِّياسِيَّة
in the department (of)	في قِسْمِ	I am a professor	أنا أُسْتاذ
And what is your opinion about …	وما رَأْيُكَ فِي...؟	at the American University	في الجامِعَةِ الأَمْريكِيَّة
in which there won	الَّتي فازَ بِها	the latest elections	الاِنْتِخابات الأخِيرَة
Perhaps you might realize	أَنْتِ رُبَّما تُدْرِكِين	the ruling party	الحِزْبُ الحاكِم
that they are elections	أَنَّها اَنْتِخابات	more than other than you	أَكْثَرَ مِنْ غَيْرِكِ
I wish it will be	أَتَمَنَّى أَنْ تَكُونَ	which are not free	غَيْرُ حُرَّة
in the next time	في المَرَّةِ القادِمَة	more democratic	أَكْثَرَ دِيموقْراطِيَّةً
that the situation	أَنَّ الوَضْعَ	I have a strong feeling	لَدَيَّ شُعُورٌ قَوِيٌّ
on this way or state	على هَذِهِ الحالَة	will not continue to be	لَنْ يَسْتَمِرَّ

الدَّرْسُ الثَّانــي: القَواعِدُ وَٱللُّغَوِيَّاتُ / Grammatical and Linguistic Notes

١- تَصْرِيفُ الفِعْلِ الـمَاضِي: ٱلـمُخاطَبُ الـمُفْرَدُ الـمُذَكَّرُ وَالـمُؤَنَّثُ ، والـمُفْرَدُ الـمُتَكَلِّمُ ....

1. The Conjugation of Past Tense Verbs: 2nd Person Singular, Masculine & Feminine and 1st Person Singular

٢- ضَمائِرُ المَفْعُولِيَّةِ الْمُتَّصِلَةُ بِالأَفْعالِ .... 2. Object Suffixed Pronouns with Verbs:

٣- اِسْمَ الإِسْتِفْهامِ (أَيٍّ) وَخُصُوصِيَّاتُهُ .... 3. The Interrogative Noun أَيٌّ

٤- الْفِعْلُ (كانَ) وعَمَلُهُ .... 4. The Verb (كَانَ)

٥- أَلْفاظُ ٱلعُقُودِ وٱلـمِئَةُ وٱلأَلْفُ وقِراءَةُ وَكِتابَةُ ٱلسِّنِينَ ....

5. Multiple of Tens Numerals, the Hundred, the thousand and Reading and Writing Years in Letter Forms

* * *

١- تَصْرِيفُ الفِعْلِ الـمَاضِي: ٱلـمُخاطَبُ الـمُفْرَدُ الـمُذَكَّرُ وَالـمُؤَنَّثُ ، والـمُفْرَدُ الـمُتَكَلِّمُ
The Conjugation of Past Tense Verbs: 2nd Person Singular, Masculine & Feminine and 1st Person Singular

- Let's first read the following sentences and focus on the underlined verbs:

أَيْنَ دَرَسْتَ العَرَبِيَّةَ يا مارك؟ | دَرَسْتُ الْعَرَبِيَّةَ فِي كُـلِّيَّةِ "لِيك فُورِسْت."

أَيْنَ دَرَسْتِ العَرَبِيَّةَ يا آنِسَةُ؟ | دَرَسْتُ العَرَبِيَّةَ فِي جامِعَةِ شِيكاغُو.

أَيْنَ تَعَلَّمْتَ العَرَبِيَّةَ يا كرِيس؟ | تَعَلَّمْتُ العَرَبِيَّةَ فِي كُـلِّيَّةِ لِيك فُورِسْت.

أَيْنَ تَعَلَّمْتِ العَرَبِيَّةَ يا مـاري؟ | تَعَلَّمْتُ العَرَبِيَّةَ فِي جامِعَةِ جونْز هُوبْكِنْز.

عَلَى أَيِّ شَهادَةٍ حَصَلْتَ؟ | حَصَلْتُ عَلَى شَهادَةِ البَكالُورِيُوس.

إِلَـى أَيِّ بَلَدٍ سافَرْتِ يا آن؟ | سافَرْتُ إِلَى مِصْرَ لِدِراسَةِ الـعَرَبِيَّةِ.

- In the first sentence on the right, the question is directed to a 'male person'; therefore the 'subject-marker' of the underlined verb is (ـتَ), which indicates that the 'subject' is a '**2nd person masculine singular**'; that is corresponding to the 'subject pronoun' (أَنْتَ).
- In the parallel sentence on the left, the 'male person' being asked answers in the '**1st Person**'; therefore the 'subject-marker' of the underlined verb is (ـتُ), which indicates that the 'subject' is a '**1st person masculine singular**'; that is corresponding to the 'subject pronoun' (أنا).
- In the second sentence on the right, the question is directed to a 'female person'; therefore the 'subject-marker' of the underlined verb is (ـتِ), which indicates that the 'subject' is a '**2nd person feminine singular**'; that is corresponding to the 'subject pronoun' (أَنْتِ).
- The same process is repeated with other verbs in senteces 3 & 4 , and again in sentences 5 & 6.
- It is to be noted that for the '**1st Person Singular**' the conjugation of the verb is identical, whether the speaker is a male or a female.
- ***Important Note:** In dictionaries, Arabic verbs are customarily listed in their 3rd person masculine singular of the past tense, because this is the shortest of all the conjugations. For the verb (دَرَسَ), for example, this is literally, "He studied." But the English equivalent is usually listed as the 'infinitive'-'to study'.*
- The following table contains the five singular conjugations of the 'past tense verbs' introduced thus far in this lesson and the previous one:

1st Person Masc. + Fem. Singular (أنـا)	2nd Person Feminine Singular (أَنْتِ)	2nd Person Masculine Singular (أَنْتَ)	3rd Person Feminine Singular (هِيَ)	3rd Person Masculine Singular (هُوَ)	Stem
دَرَسْتُ	دَرَسْتِ	دَرَسْتَ	دَرَسَتْ	دَرَسَ	دَرَسْ
حَضَرْتُ	حَضَرْتِ	حَضَرْتَ	حَضَرَتْ	حَضَرَ	حَضَرْ
حَصَلْتُ	حَصَلْتِ	حَصَلْتَ	حَصَلَتْ	حَصَلَ	حَصَلْ
رَجَعْتُ	رَجَعْتِ	رَجَعْتَ	رَجَعَتْ	رَجَعَ	رَجَعْ
عَمِلْتُ	عَمِلْتِ	عَمِلْتَ	عَمِلَتْ	عَمِلَ	عَمِلْ
سَافَرْتُ	سَافَرْتِ	سَافَرْتَ	سَافَرَتْ	سَافَرَ	سَافَرْ
اِلْتَحَقْتُ	اِلْتَحَقْتِ	اِلْتَحَقْتَ	اِلْتَحَقَتْ	اِلْتَحَقَ	اِلْتَحَقْ

تَقابَلْتُ	تَقابَلْتِ	تَقابَلْتَ	تَقابَلَتْ	تَقابَلَ	تَقابَلْ
تَعارَفْتُ	تَعارَفْتِ	تَعارَفْتَ	تَعارَفَتْ	تَعارَفَ	تَعارَفْ
تَزَوَّجْتُ	تَزَوَّجْتِ	تَزَوَّجْتَ	تَزَوَّجَتْ	تَزَوَّجَ	تَزَوَّجْ
تَعَلَّمْتُ	تَعَلَّمْتِ	تَعَلَّمْتَ	تَعَلَّمَتْ	تَعَلَّمَ	تَعَلَّمْ
أَكْمَلْتُ	أَكْمَلْتِ	أَكْمَلْتَ	أَكْمَلَتْ	أَكْمَلَ	أَكْمَلْ
تَخَصَّصْتُ	تَخَصَّصْتِ	تَخَصَّصْتَ	تَخَصَّصَتْ	تَخَصَّصَ	تَخَصَّصْ
تَغَيَّرْتُ	تَغَيَّرْتِ	تَغَيَّرْتَ	تَغَيَّرَتْ	تَغَيَّرَ	تَغَيَّرْ
سَعِدْتُ	سَعِدْتِ	سَعِدْتَ	سَعِدَتْ	سَعِدَ	سَعِدْ
ـْتُ	ـْتِ	ـْتَ	ـَتْ	/	**Subject-Markers**

* * *

Object Suffixed Pronouns with Verbs / ٢- ضَمائِرُ الْمَفْعُولِيَّةِ الْمُتَّصِلَةُ بِالأَفْعالِ

- We have previously seen what we called 'suffixed' or 'attached pronouns' in relation to nouns. In this case, these 'suffixed pronouns' are equivalent to what we call in English 'possessive pronouns'.
- Let's now study the following examples as a review of what we learned before:

هَذا قَلَمُهُ . (قَلَمُ+ـهُ)

This is his pen.

هَذا قَلَمُها . (قَلَمُ+ـها)

This is her pen

هَذا قَلَمُكَ . (قَلَمُ+ـكَ)

This is your pen. (*masculine*)

هَذا قَلَمُكِ . (قَلَمُ+ـكِ)

This is your pen. (*feminine*)

هَذا قَلَمِي . (قَلَمُ+ـي)

This is my pen.

هَذا قَلَمُنا . (قَلَمُ+نا)

This is our pen.

هَذا قَلَمُكُمْ . (قَلَمُ+كُمْ)

This is your pen. (*masculine plural*)

هَذا قَلَمُكُنَّ . (قَلَمُ+كُنَّ)

This is your pen. (*feminine plural*))

هَذا قَلَمُهُمْ . (قَلَمُ+هُمْ)

This is their pen. (*masculine plural*)

هَذا قَلَمُهُنَّ . (قَلَمُ+هُنَّ)

This is their pen. (*feminine plural*))

- In the following examples we will see the same set of 'suffixed pronouns' attached to the end of 'verbs'. In this case, these pronouns are called '**object pronouns**' since they function as the objects of the verbs they are attached to.
- Now, let's study the following examples, with special concentration on the underlined parts of the sentences:

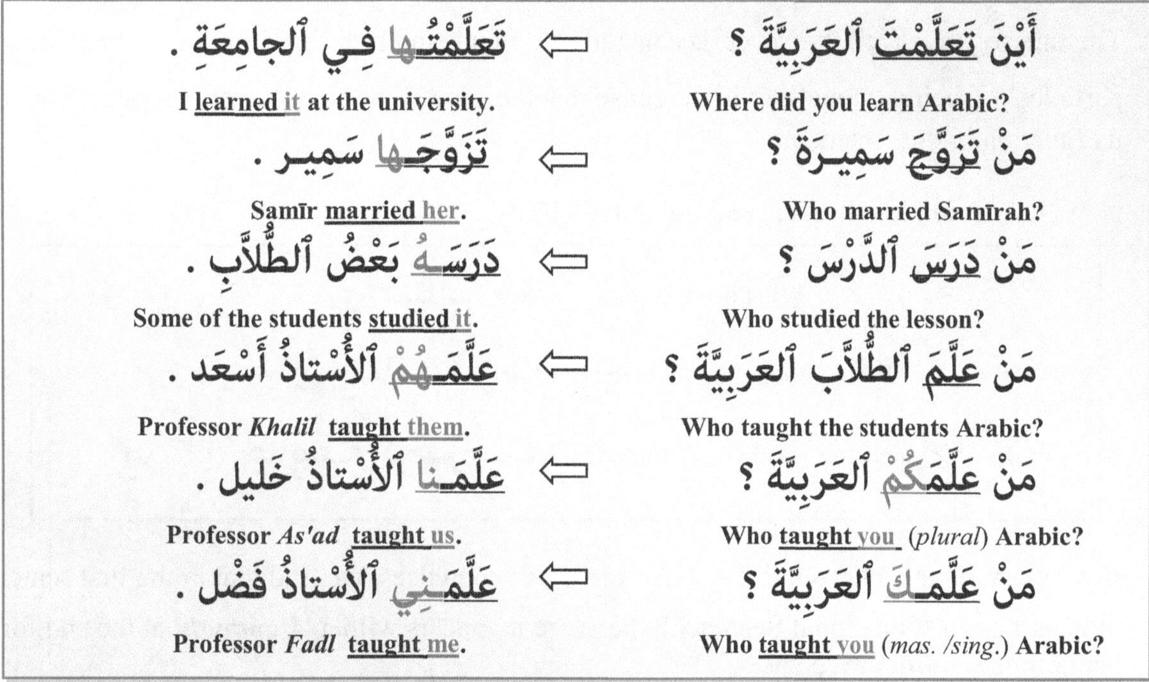

أَيْنَ تَعَلَّمْتَ ٱلْعَرَبِيَّةَ ؟	⇦	تَعَلَّمْتُهَا فِي الجامعةِ .
Where did you learn Arabic?		**I learned it at the university.**
مَنْ تَزَوَّجَ سَمِيرَةَ ؟	⇦	تَزَوَّجَهَا سَمِير .
Who married Samīrah?		**Samīr married her.**
مَنْ دَرَسَ ٱلدَّرْسَ ؟	⇦	دَرَسَهُ بَعْضُ ٱلطُّلَّابِ .
Who studied the lesson?		**Some of the students studied it.**
مَنْ عَلَّمَ ٱلطُّلَّابَ ٱلْعَرَبِيَّةَ ؟	⇦	عَلَّمَهُمْ ٱلأُسْتَاذُ أَسْعَد .
Who taught the students Arabic?		**Professor *Khalil* taught them.**
مَنْ عَلَّمَكُمْ ٱلْعَرَبِيَّةَ ؟	⇦	عَلَّمَنَا ٱلأُسْتَاذُ خليل .
Who taught you (*plural*) Arabic?		**Professor *As'ad* taught us.**
مَنْ عَلَّمَكَ ٱلْعَرَبِيَّةَ ؟	⇦	عَلَّمَنِي ٱلأُسْتَاذُ فَضْل .
Who taught you (*mas. /sing.*) Arabic?		**Professor *Fadl* taught me.**

- As you can see from the examples above, we have seen here the same identical 'suffix pronouns' attached to the end of the verbs to function as the 'objects' of these verbs.
- However, there is only one minor modification with the '**1st person singular suffix pronoun**' (ـي), when attached to a verb versus when it is attached to a noun. Let's study the two following examples in comparative perspective to see the difference:

هَذا كِتَابِي (كِتاب+ـي) . ⇦ عَلَّمَنِي الأُسْتاذُ خَـلِـيل . (عَلَّمَ+نِي)

- When the 'suffix pronoun' (ـي) was attached to the noun of the first example, we have done so directly, without adding any extra letters. However, in the second example, we have added between the end of the verb and the 'suffix' (ـي) an extra (ـنـ), called the '***Noon* of Protection**' to bear the '***Kasrah***' vowel, which can't be born by an original letter of a verb.

* * *

The Interrogative Noun أَيٌّ and Its Particulars ٣- اِسْمَ ٱلاِسْتَفْهامِ (أَيٌّ) وَخُصُوصِيّاتُـهُ

- We have introduced, thus far, several 'interrogative particles' used to ask questions.
- A common feature of these particles is that they were all invariable; which means that they end with a fixed vowel sign that does not change at the end, as is the case with regular nouns.
- The interrogative (أَيٌّ), however, is considered a noun, and it differs from other 'interrogative particles' by being '**variable**'; in the sense that the 'vowel' at its end changes, depending on its function in the sentence.

- Now, let's read the following examples and observe this feature in context:

What book is this?	أَيُّ كِتابٍ هَذا؟
Which book did you read?	أَيَّ كِتابٍ قَرَأْتَ؟
From which university did you graduate?	مِنْ أَيِّ جامِعَةٍ تَخَرَّجْتَ؟

If we examine the interrogative (أَيٌّ) in the above sentences, we find that in the first sentence it is part of an 'Equational Sentence'; therefore it appears with a '***Dammah***' at the end for being in the '**nominative case**'.

- In the second sentence, it appears with a '***Fathah***' at the end for being in the '**accusative case**' as the object of the verb (قَرَأْتَ).
- And in the third sentence, it appears with a '***Kasrah***' at the end for being in the '**genitive case**' as the object of the preposition (فِـي).
- In all three sentences, (أَيٌّ) is followed by an '**indefinite noun**' in the '***nunated* genitive ending**' for being the '**2nd term of an *Idāfah***'; and this is another important feature of this 'interrogative noun', which distinguishes it from other 'interrogative particles'.
- As to its English translation, the 'interrogative' (أَيٌّ) can be translated as '**What…?**' or as '**Which…?**'.

*　*　*

The Verb (كَانَ): Its Nature and Its Grammatical Function ٤- الفِعْلُ (كانَ) وعَمَلُهُ

(Arab linguists describe the verb (كَانَ) as being a '**defective past tense auxiliary verb**', equivalent in meaning to the English '**was**' or '**were**'.

- As a ‘verb’ it is subject to the conjugation variations that apply to any other verb.
- However, as ‘**defective**’ and ‘**auxiliary**’, it differs from other verbs in the sense that it does not require a ‘**subject**’ or an ‘**object**’, but rather serves to render the ‘**present**’ meaning of ‘**Equational sentences**’ into ‘**past time**’.
- Let’s now read the following sentences, with due concentration on the underlined parts of each sentence:

Present		Past
فَضْل أُسْتاذٌ فِي جامِعَةِ تُولِيدُو.	⇦	كَانَ فَضْل أُسْتاذاً فِي جامِعَةِ تُولِيدُو.
Fadl is a professor at the university of Toledo.		Fadl was a professor at the university of Toledo.
مَرْيَمُ مُدَرِّسَةٌ فِي مَدْرَسَةٍ ثانَوِيَّةٍ.	⇦	كانَتْ مَرْيَمُ مُدَرِّسَةً فِي مَدْرَسَةٍ ثانَوِيَّةٍ.
Maryam is a teacher at a secondary school.		Maryam was a teacher at a secondary school.
هَلْ أَنْتَ مُوَظَّفٌ هُنا؟	⇦	هَلْ كُنْتَ مُوَظَّفًا هُنا؟
Are you an employee here?		Were you (male) an employee here?
هَلْ أَنْتِ طالِبَةٌ فِي هَذِهِ ٱلْمَدْرَسَةِ؟	⇦	هَلْ كُنْتِ طالِبَةً فِي هَذِهِ ٱلْمَدْرَسَةِ؟
Are you a student at this school?		Were you (female) a student at this school?
أَنا ٱلْمُدِيرُ فِي هَذا ٱلْمَكْتَبِ.	⇦	كُنْتُ ٱلْمُدِيرَ فِي هَذا ٱلْمَكْتَبِ.
I am the manager in this office.		I was the manager in this office.

* * *

Present		Past
هُمْ أَساتِذَةٌ فِي جامِعَةِ شِيكاغُو.	⇦	كانُوا أَساتِذَةً فِي جامِعَةِ شِيكاغُو.
They are professors at the University of Chicago.		They were professors at the University of Chicago.
هُنَّ مُدَرِّساتٌ فِي مَدْرَسَةٍ ثانَوِيَّةٍ.	⇦	كُنَّ مُدَرِّساتٍ فِي مَدْرَسَةٍ ثانَوِيَّةٍ.
They are teachers at a secondary school.		They were teachers at a secondary school.
هَلْ أَنْتُمْ مُوَظَّفُونَ هُنا؟	⇦	هَلْ كُنْتُمْ مُوَظَّفِينَ هُنا؟
Are you employees here?		Were you (*male*) employees here?
هَلْ أَنْتُنَّ طالِباتٌ فِي ٱلْمَدْرَسَةِ؟	⇦	هَلْ كُنْتُنَّ طالِباتٍ فِي ٱلْمَدْرَسَةِ؟
Are you students at the school?		Were you (*female*) students at the school?
نَحْنُ طُلَّابٌ فِي ٱلْكُلِّيَّةِ.	⇦	كُنَّا طُلَّاباً فِي ٱلْكُلِّيَّةِ.
We are students at the college.		We were students at the college.

- All the sentences on the right, in the box above, are '**equational sentences**', containing as their basic elements '**subjects'** and '**predicates**'. Let's remember that 'equational sentences' in Arabic do not contain verbs at all. However, when we translate them into English, we must use a '**present verb-to-be**'; such as: '**is**', '**are**', or '**am**'. In terms of '**time**,' all 'equational sentences' have a **<u>present time implied</u>** in them, though there is no verb.
- If we want to change the 'present time' aspect of an 'equational sentence' to 'past time', then we must introduce the appropriate conjugation of the verb (كَانَ), as the parallel sentences on the left show.
- Moreover, (كَانَ) and another group of similar verbs, known together as (**<u>كَانَ and Its Sisters</u>**), command a change in the 'predicate' of the 'equational sentences', resulting in changing it from 'nominative case' to '**accusative case**', as the underlined nouns following (كَانَ) above demonstrate.
- In the table below, all the conjugations of (كَانَ), along with their corresponding 'subject pronouns' are shown for the purpose of reference. Since no "dual conjugations" were given in the examples above, these **<u>dual</u>** conjugations will be listed in table below:

Plural Conjugations and Corresponding Subject Pronouns			**Singular Conjugations and Corresponding Subject Pronouns**		
(هُمْ)	(they were/*masculine*)	كَانُوا	(هُوَ)	(he was)	كَانَ
(هُنَّ)	(they were/*feminine*)	كُنَّ	(هِيَ)	(she was)	كَانَتْ
(أَنْتُمْ)	(you were/*mas. plural*)	كُنْتُمْ	(أَنْتَ)	(you were/*mas. sing.*)	كُنْتَ
(أَنْتُنَّ)	(you were/*fem. plural*)	كُنْتُنَّ	(أَنْتِ)	(you were/*fem. sing.*)	كُنْتِ
(نَحْنُ)	(we were/*fem. +mas.*)	كُنَّا	(أَنَا)	(I was /*fem. +mas.*)	كُنْتُ
Dual Conjugations			**Dual Conjugations**		
They (both) were	(*masculine dual*)		(هُمَا)		كَانَا
They (both) were	(*feminine dual*)		(هُمَا)		كَانَتَا
You (both) were	(*masculine+feminine dual*)		(أَنْتُمَا)		كُنْتُمَا

٥- أَلْفاظُ ٱلعُقُودِ وٱلـمِئَةُ وٱلأَلْفُ وقِراءَةُ وَكِتابَةُ ٱلسِّنِيـنَ

Multiple of Tens Numerals, the Hundred, the thousand and Reading and WritingYears in Letter Forms

- Let's first study the following Arabic numerls in preparation to be able to read years in letter forms:

English Equivalent	Multiple of Tens in Accusative and Genitive Forms	Multiple of Tens in Nominative Forms	Arithmetic Numerals
twenty	عِشْرِينَ	عِشْرُونَ	٢٠
thirty	ثَلاثِيـنَ	ثَلاثُونَ	٣٠
forty	أَرْبَعِيـنَ	أَرْبَعُونَ	٤٠
fifty	خَمْسِيـنَ	خَمْسُونَ	٥٠
sixty	سِتِّيـنَ	سِتُّونَ	٦٠
seventy	سَبْعِيـنَ	سَبْعُونَ	٧٠
eighty	ثَـمانِيـنَ	ثَـمانُونَ	٨٠
ninety	تِسْعِيـنَ	تِسْعُونَ	٩٠

(hundreds) مِئات	مِئَتانِ / مِئَتَيْـنِ (two hundreds)	(one hundred) مِئَة / مِائَة	١٠٠/ ٢٠٠
(thousands) آلاف	أَلْفانِ / أَلْفَيْـنِ (two thousands)	(one thousand) أَلْف	١٠٠٠/ ٢٠٠٠

- In classical Arabic, the reading and writing of years would start with the smaller units, moving upward to the larger units (tens first, then hundreds, then finally the thousands), as in the following examples:

سَنَةَ ثَـمانِيـنَ وَتِسْعِمِئَةٍ وَأَلْفٍ .	١٩٨٠
سَنَةَ خَمْسٍ وَثَـمانِيـنَ وَتِسْعِمِئَةٍ وَأَلْفٍ .	١٩٨٥
سَنَةَ أَرْبَعٍ وَأَلْفَيْـنِ .	٢٠٠٤

- However, in modern Arabic, it is more common to start the reading and writing of years with the larger units (thousands), moving downward to the hundreds, then the the single units (1-10), and finaly, the multiple of tens units as in the following examples:

سَنَةَ أَلْفٍ وَتِسْعِمِئَةٍ وثَمانِيـنَ .	١٩٨٠
سَنَةَ أَلْفٍ وَتِسْعِمِئَةٍ وَخَمْسٍ وَثَمانِيـنَ .	١٩٨٥
سَنَةَ أَلْفَيْـنِ وَأَرْبَعٍ .	٢٠٠٤

- Notice that the word (سَنَةَ) in all the examples above ends with a '*Fatḥah*' for being in 'adverbial of time' mood. However, the numeral that follows is ending with a '***Kasrah***' for being a '**2nd term of *Iḍāfah***' in relation to (سَنَةَ), then the other units are related to it through the conjunction (وَ) resulting in all of them being in the '**genitive case ending**'.

* * *

الدَّرسُ الثَّالث : تَدْرِيباتٌ وَنَشاطاتٌ / Exercises & Activities

(*Oral and Written*) Recognizing the Verb and Its Subject: تَـمْرين ١:

Identify the verbs in the following sentences by underlining them, then identify the independent subject pronouns which correspond to the conjugations of the verbs, as in the given examples:

تَعَلَّمَ ٱلعَرَبِيَّةَ فِـي ٱلجامِعَةِ. (هُوَ) | بَعْدَ ٱلدِّراسَةِ رَجَعْتُ إِلَـى بَلَدِي. (أَنا)

١- حَضَرَتْ أُمّي لِزِيارَتِنا. (..............) ٢- كُنْتُ أُسْتاذَةً فِي ٱلجامِعَةِ. (..............)

٣- هَلْ سافَرْتَ إِلَى مِصْرَ؟ (..............) ٤- هَلْ أَكْمَلْتِ دِراسَتَكِ؟ (..............)

٥- تَزَوَّجَ سَميرٌ سَميرَةَ. (..............) ٦- تَخَصَّصَتْ فِي إِدارَةِ ٱلأَعْمالِ. (..............)

٧- عَمِلْتُ أُسْتاذاً فِي ٱلجامِعَةِ. (..............) ٨- تَخَرَّجْتُ مِنْ جامِعَةِ شِيكاغو. (..............)

* * *

تَمْرين ٢: تَصْرِيفُ الأَفْعال (*Oral and Written*) Conjugation of the Verb:

Conjugate the verb in the model sentence inside the box to correspond to the subjects given below:

(أَنا) ⇦ دَرَسْتُ ٱللُّغَةَ ٱلعَرَبِيَّةَ فِي ٱلجامِعَةِ.

١- (أَنْتِ) ⇦.................... ٢- (آدَمُ) ⇦.................... ٣- (هُوَ) ⇦....................

٤- (مَرْيَمُ) ⇦.................... ٥- (هِيَ) ⇦.................... ٦- (أَنْتَ) ⇦....................

٧- (أَنا) ⇦.................... ٨- (آن) ⇦.................... ٩- (جُورْج) ⇦....................

١٠- (الطَّالِبَةُ الجَدِيدَةُ) ⇦.................... ١١- (اَلصِّحَافِيُّ الأَجْنَبِيُّ) ⇦....................

* * *

تَمْرين ٣: تَصْرِيفُ ٱلأَفْعال (*Oral and Written*) Conjugations of Verbs:

Fill in the blanks of the following sentences with the correct conjugation of the '**verb stem**' given in parenthesis at the end of the sentences, to correspond to the underlined expressed '**subject**'; follow the given example:

.... مَرْيَمُ ٱلدَّرْسَ ٱلتَّاسِعَ. (دَرْس) ← دَرَسَتْ مَرْيَمُ ٱلدَّرْسَ ٱلتَّاسِعَ.

١- أَنا .... ٱلدِّراسَةَ فِي جامِعَةِ ٱلقاهِرَةِ. (أَكْمَلْ)

٢- .... ٱلأُسْتاذَةُ ٱلزَّائِرَةُ إِلَى ٱلشَّرْقِ ٱلأَوْسَطِ. (رَجَعْ)

٣- يا باسِمُ، هَلْ .... ٱللُّغَةَ ٱلإِنْجِلِيزِيَّةَ فِي أَمْرِيكا؟ (تَعَلَّمْ)

٤- .... ٱلأُسْتاذُ أَسْعَدُ امْرَأَةً أَمْرِيكِيَّةً. (تَزَوَّجْ)

٥- يا نانْسِي، مِنْ أَيْنَ .... عَلَى شَهادَةِ ٱلدُّكْتُوراه؟ (حَصَلْ)

٦- .... سَمِيرٌ وَسَمِيرَةٌ مِنَ ٱلشَّرْقِ ٱلْأَوْسَطِ لِلدِّرَاسَةِ فِي أَمْرِيكا. (حَضَرْ)

٧- .... سَمِيرَةٌ مُدَرِّسَةً فِي مَدْرَسَةٍ ثانَوِيَّةٍ. (عَمِلْ)

* * *

(*Oral*) Conjugations of Verbs: تَمْرِين ٤: تَصْرِيفُ ٱلْأَفْعال

Give personal answers to the following direct questions, remembering that in all your answers you will be using the '**1ˢᵗ person conjugation**' of the verb; follow the given example:

أَيْنَ دَرَسْتَ ٱللُّغَةَ ٱلْعَرَبِيَّةَ يا هِنْري؟ ← دَرَسْتُ ٱللُّغَةَ ٱلْعَرَبِيَّةَ فِي ٱلْجامِعَةِ.

١- ماذا تَعَلَّمْتِ فِي ٱلْجامِعَةِ يا سُوزان؟ ←

٢- إِلَى أَيِّ بَلَدٍ سافَرْتَ يا آدَمُ؟ ←

٣- يا نِينا، هَلْ رَجَعْتِ إِلَى فَرَنْسا بَعْدَ ٱلدِّراسَةِ فِي أَمْرِيكا؟ ←

٤- يا باسِمُ، عَلَى أَيِّ شَهادَةٍ جامِعِيَّةٍ حَصَلْتَ؟ ←

٥- هَلْ عَمِلْتِ فِي بَلَدٍ أَجْنَبِيٍّ يا ماري؟ ←

٦- يا سَمِيرُ، هَلْ تَخَصَّصْتَ فِي إِدارَةِ ٱلْأَعْمالِ؟ ←

٧- كَمْ كِتاباً قَرَأْتِ هَذِهِ ٱلسَّنَةَ يا سَمِيرَةُ؟ ←

* * *

(*Oral and Written*) Using the Appropriate Case-Ending with (أَيُّ): تَمْرِين ٥

Fill in the dotted spaces of the following sentences with the appropriate form of the 'interrogative noun' (أَيُّ), from among the three possibilities given in parenthesis at the end of the sentences; follow the given example:

عَلَى أَيِّ شَهادَةٍ حَصَلْتَ مِنَ ٱلْجامِعَةِ؟ (أَيُّ / أَيَّ / أَيِّ)

١- .... كِتابٍ قَرَأْتَ هَذا ٱلْأُسْبُوع؟ (أَيُّ / أَيَّ / أَيِّ)

٢- .... رَجُلٍ هَذا؟ (أَيُّ / أَيَّ / أَيِّ)

٣- فـي .... كُلِّيَّةٍ تَعَلَّمْتَ ٱلعَرَبِيَّةَ؟ (أَيُّ / أَيَّ / أَيِّ)

٤- .... امْرَأَةٍ تَزَوَّجْتَ يا سَمِيـر؟ (أَيُّ / أَيَّ / أَيِّ)

٥- مِنْ .... بَلَدٍ عَرَبِـيٍّ أَنْتَ يا عُمَر؟ (أَيُّ / أَيَّ / أَيِّ)

٦- .... مَدْرَسَةٍ هَذِهِ؟ (أَيُّ / أَيَّ / أَيِّ)

* * *

تَـمْرين ٦: **Exercise 6: (*Oral / Written*) Using Object Pronouns with Verbs:**

Change the 'object pronoun' in the model sentence to correspond to the 'subject pronouns' given in the shaded box on the left below:

عَلَّمَـهُ ٱلعَرَبِيَّةَ فِي ٱلجامِعَةِ. (هُوَ)

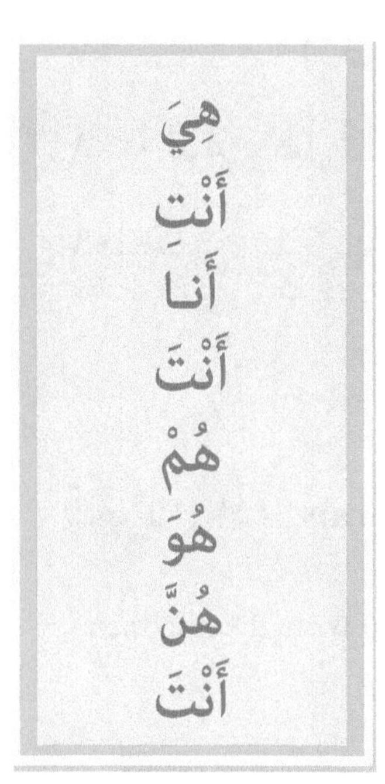

١- ....

٢- ....

٣- ....

٤- ....

٥- ....

٦- ....

٧- ....

٨- ....

* * *

تَـمْرين ٧: **(*Oral / Written*) Using the Appropriate Conjugation of the Verb (كانَ):**

From among the different conjugations of the 'defective' or 'weak' verb (كانَ) in the shaded box on the left, select the appropriate conjugation suitable to fill in the blanks of the following sentences; follow the given examples:

كانَتْ مَرْيَمُ طالِبَةً فِـي ٱلجامِعَةِ. | كانُوا مُوَظَّفِيـنَ فِـي ٱلـمُتْحَفِ.

١- .... (أنـا) أُسْتاذاً في جامِعَةِ تُولِيدُو.

٢- .... مُوَظَّفاتٍ في الْمُتْحَفِ.

٣- .... أَساتِذَةً زائِرينَ في جامعاتٍ عَرَبِيَّةٍ.

٤- يا سَميرَةُ، هَلْ .... مُدَرِّسَةً في الشَّرْقِ الأَوْسَطِ؟

٥- .... ماري صِحافِيَّةً في الْعِراقِ.

٦- هَلْ .... (أَنْتُـنَّ) مَعَهُمْ في الـمَطْعَمِ العَرَبِيِّ؟

٧- .... (نَحْنُ) طُلاَّبًا في جامِعاتٍ أَمْريكِيَّةٍ.

٨- يا آدَمُ، هَلْ .... مَعَهُمْ في الـمَدْرَسَةِ الثّانَوِيَّةِ؟

٩- .... نانْسي سِكْرِتيـرَةً فِـي قِسْمِ اللُّغَةِ الْعَرَبِيَّةِ.

١٠- .... مُدَرِّسيـنَ في السَّعُودِيَّةِ.

كانَ / كانُوا

كانَتْ / كُنَّ

كُنْتَ / كُنْتُمْ

كُنْتِ / كُنْتُـنَّ

كُنْتُ / كُـنّا

* * *

تَـمْرين ٨: **(*Oral / Written*) Pronouncing and Converting Arithmetic Numerals In Written words forms and Reading Years:**

First, say the letter-forms of the arithmetic numerals in the table below, then write them in their letter-forms; follow the given examples:

٣٠ = ثَلاثُونَ / ٩٠ = تِسْعُونَ / ١٠٠ = مِئَة / ٢٠٠٠ = أَلْفانِ / سَنَةَ ١٩٩٩ = سَنَةَ أَلْفٍ وَتِسْعمِئَةٍ وَتِسْعٍ وَتِسْعِيـنَ / سَنَةَ ٢٠١٠ = سَنَةَ أَلْفَيْـنِ وعَشْرَة

Letter Foms of Numerals	Arithmetic Symbols of Numerals	Letter Forms of Numerals	Arithmetic Symbols of Numerals	Letter Forms of Numerals	Arithmetic Symbols of Numerals
	٦٠		٤٠		٢٠
	٥٠		٣٠		٨٠
	١٠٠		٩٠		٧٠
	سَنَة ٢٠٠٠		سَنَة ١٧٠٠		سَنَة ٥٠٠
	سَنَة ٢٠٠٣		سَنَة ٢٠٠٢		سَنَة ٢٠٠١
	سَنَة ٢٠٠٦		سَنَة ٢٠٠٥		سَنَة ٢٠٠٤

* * *

تَـمْرين ٩:

(*Oral / Written*) Unscramble to Form Meaningful Sentences and Translation:

Unscramble the following sets of words by writing them in the correct order to form full meaningful sentences; then translate them into English, as in the given example:

لُغَتَنا / يا / تَعَلَّمْتِ / أَيْنَ / سَيِّدَتـي ⇩

أَيْنَ تَعَلَّمْتِ لُغَتَنا يا سَيِّدَتِـي؟ **Where did you learn our language my lady?**

١- فِـي / كُنْتُ / دَرَسْتُها / مُتَخَصِّصَة / الدُّوَلِيَّةِ / الجامِعَةِ / العَلاقاتِ / فـي / عِنْدَما ⇦

....

....

٢- القَديم / فـي / دَرَسْتُ / الـمِصْرِيّ / مِصْر / التَّاريخ ⇦

....

....

٣- لِلعُلُومِ / فـي / أَنا / شِيكاغو / أُسْتاذ / السِّياسِيَّة / جامِعَة ⇦

....

....

٤- فـي / الاِنْتِخاباتِ / رَأْيُكَ / ما ..؟ / بِـمِصْر / الأَخيرَة ⇦

....

....

٥- أَنْ / تَكُون / أَكْثَـر / القادِمَة / دِيـمُقراطِيَّة / أَتَـمَنَّى / الـمَرَّة ⇦

....

* * *

تَـمْرين ١٠: Transformation Using *Nisbah* Adjectives: (Review: *Oral / Written*)

Transform the underlined part of each of the following sentences to a '***Nisbah*** **adjective**' as in the given example:

دَرَسَ ٱلطَّالِبُ فِي جامِعَةٍ فِـي مِصْر. ← دَرَسَ ٱلطَّالِبُ فِي جامِعَةٍ مِصْرِيَّةٍ.

١- هَلْ أُسْتَاذُكَ مِنْ أَمْرِيكا؟ ← ....؟

٢- تَخَرَّجْتُ مِن جامِعَةٍ فِي ٱلـمَغْرِبِ. ← ....

٣- هَذا ٱلرَّجُلُ مِنَ ٱلعِراقِ. ← ....

٤- الطَّالِبَةُ ٱلجَدِيدَةُ مِنْ فَرَنْسا. ← ....

٥- هَلْ أَنْتَ مِنْ لُبْنانَ أَمْ مِنْ سُورْيا؟ ← ....؟

٦- تَعَلَّمْتُ ٱلعَرَبِيَّةَ مِن صَدِيقَةٍ مِنْ لُبْنان. ← ....

٧- هَلْ أَنْتَ مِنْ بَيْرُوت أَمْ مِنْ دِمَشْق؟ ← ....؟

٨- هُوَ مِن السَّعودِيَّةِ، وهِيَ مِن ٱلكُوَيْتِ. ← ....

٩- هَلْ أَنْتِ مِن ٱلـمَغْرِبِ أَمْ مِن ٱلجَزائِر. ← ....؟

Exercise 11: **Reviewing a Reference List:**

Go to '**Part 4**' of the book to review the reference list entitled **'The Months of the Year According to Three Calendar System, the Days of the Week & the Four Seasons of the Year,'** **page 344.**

* * *

الدَّرْسُ ٱلرَّابِعُ : نَصُّ القِراءَة / Reading Text

حَفْلُ عِيدِ مِيلادِ سُعاد

❖ دَعَتْ سُعادُ لَيْلَى وأُمَّها وأُخْتَها يَوْمَ ٱلجُمُعَةِ التَّالِـي إِلَى حَفْلَةِ عِيدِ مِيلادِها، كَما دَعَتْ أَخاها يُوسف وبَعْضَ ٱلأَصدِقاءِ والصَّديقاتِ الآخَرينَ.

❖ حَضَرَتْ لَيْلَى وأُمُّها وأُخْتُها الصَّغيرَةُ إِلَى بَيْتِ سُعاد ، يَحْمِلْنَ هَدِيَّةً لِسُعاد بِـمُناسَبَةِ عيدِ ميلادِها . وقَدَّمَتْ سُعادُ أَخاها يُوسُف لِلْضُيوفِ .

❖ أَحْضَرَ كَمال ، زَوْجُ سُعاد ، كَعْكَةَ عيدِ الْميلاد ، وزَرَعَ فِيها أَرْبَعَ شَمْعاتٍ كَبيرَةٍ ، تُـمَثِّلُ كُلُّ شَمْعَةٍ عَشْرَ سَنَواتٍ .

❖ أَطْفَأَتْ سُعادُ الشَّمْعاتِ، وغَنَّى الجَميعُ لَها "سَنَة حِلْوَة يا جَميل!" بارَكَ الجَميعُ لِسُعاد بِعِيدِ مِيلادِها، وقَطَعَ يُوسُف الكَعْكَةَ قِطَعاً صَغيرَةً، وأَكَلَ الجَميعُ وشَرِبُوا الـمُرَطِّباتِ، ثُمَّ قَدَّموا لِسُعاد بَعْضَ الْهَدايا. وبَعْدَ وَقْتٍ مُمْتِعٍ وأَحاديثَ مُشَوِّقَةٍ، غادَرَ الْجَميعُ بَيْتَ سُعاد إِلاَّ يُوسُف.

❖ سَأَلَتْ سُعادُ يُوسُف: "ما رَأْيُكَ في لَيْلَى؟" قالَ يُوسُف: "أَعْجَبَتْنِي كَثِيـراً، إِنْسانَةٌ طَيِّبَةٌ ومُثَقَّفَةٌ ... ذَوقُكِ حُلْو يا أُخْتِي العَزيزَة."

❖ اِبْتَسَمَتْ سُعادُ ابْتِسامَةً واسِعَةً وقالَتْ: "الباقِي عَلَيَّ يا أَخِي العَزيز!"

* * *

الـمُفْرَداتُ والتَّراكيبُ اللُّغَوِيَّةُ لِلدَّرْسِ الرّابِعِ (مُرتَّبة حَسَبَ وُرودِها في النَّصّ)

birthday / her birth	عِيدُ مِيلاد / مِيلادِها	party, celebration	حَفْل = حَفْلَة
her mother	أُمَّها (أُمّ+ها)	she invited	دَعَتْ
the following Friday	يَوْمَ الجُمُعَةَ التَّالِـي	her sister	أُخْتَها (أُخْت+ها)
her brother	أخاها (أخا+ها)	additionaly, likewise	كَما
friends (male friend)	الأَصدِقاء (صَديق)	and some (of)	وبَعْض (و+بَعْض)
(the) others	الآخَرين	female friends (a female friend)	الصَّديقات (صَدِيقَة)
Su'ad's house	بَيْتِ سُعاد	she came (to)	حضَرَتْ (إلَـى)
a gift, a present (presents)	هَدِيَّة (هَدايا)	carrying (*feminine plural conjugation*)	يَحْمِلْنَ
and she presented	وقَدَّمَتْ (و+قَدَّمَت)	on the occasion (of)	بِـمُناسَبَة
(he) brought	أَحْضَرَ	to the guests (a guest)	لِـلضُّيُوف (ضَيْف) (لِـ+الضُّيوف)
a cake	كَعْكَة	Su'ad's husband	زَوْجُ سُعاد
in it	فِـيها (فِـي+ها)	and he planted (placed)	وزَرَعَ (وَ+زَرَعَ)
candles (a candle)	شَمْعات (شَمْعَة)	four (*masculine/feminine pair*)	أَرْبَعَ / أَرْبَعَة
(they/it) represent(s)	تُـمَثِّلُ	big (*masculine / feminine pair*)	كَبِيـرَة / كَبيـر
ten (*masculine/feminine pair*)	عَشْرَ / عَشْرَة	each candle	كُلّ شَمْعَة
she distinguished, she put off	أَطْفَأَتْ	years (a year)	سَنَوات (سَنَة)
all	الجَميعُ	and sang	وَغَنَّى (وَ+غَنَّى)
beautiful (sweet) year	سَنَة حِلْوَة	for her	لَـها (لَـ+ها)
congratulated / for	بارَكَ لِـ / بِـ	O' beautiful one	يا جَميل

small pieces	قِطَعاً صَغيـرَة	and (he) cut	وقَطَعَ (و+قَطَعَ)
and they drank	وَشَرِبُوا (و+شَرِبُوا)	and ate (he/ they)	وأَكَلَ (و+أَكَلَ)
then, and then	ثُمَّ	the refreshments	الـمُرَطِّبات
some (the) gifts	بَعْضَ الهَدايا	they offered to, the presented to	قَدَّموا لِـ
time (times)	وَقْت (أَوْقات)	and after	وبَعْدَ (وَ+بَعْدَ)
and conversations, talks	وأَحاديث (و+أحاديث)	enjoyable	مُـمْـتِـع
departed, left	غادَرَ	interesting	مُشَوِّقَـة
(she) asked	سَأَلَتْ	except, but	إلاَّ
he said / she said	قالَ / قالَتْ	What's your opinion about? What do you think about?	ما رَأْيُـكَ فِـي...؟
much, a lot	كَـثِيـرًا	I liked her; (<u>Literally</u>: she pleased me)	أَعْـجَـبَـتْـنِي
good, nice, pleasant	طَيِّبَة	a human being	إنْسَانَة
your taste (is)	ذَوْقُـكِ (ذَوْق+كِ)	and cultured	ومُثَقَّفَة (و+مُثَقَّفَة)
O' my dear sister	يا أُخْتِي العَزيزَة	sweet, nice, beautiful	حُلْو
a broad (big) smile	اِبْتِسامَة واسِعَة	she smiled	اِبْتَسَمَتْ
O' my dear brother	يا أَخِي العَزيز	the rest is on me	الباقِي عَلَـيَّ (عَلى+ي)

* * *

أَسْئِلَةُ الفَهْمِ والاِسْتيعابِ (شَفوِيًّا) Comprehension Questions (Orally)

١- مَنْ دَعَتْ لَيْلَى إِلَى حَفْلَةِ عِيدِ مِيلادِها ؟

٢- مَنْ حَضَرَتْ إِلَى بَيْتِ سُعاد بِـمُناسَبَةِ عِيدِ مِيلادِها؟

٣- مَنْ قَدَّمَتْ سُعادُ لِلضُّيوف؟

٤- ماذا أَحْضَرَ كَمال؟

٥- كَمْ شَمْعَةً زَرَعَ كَمال فِي كَعْكَةِ عيدِ الـميلاد؟ وماذا تُـمَثِّلُ كُلُّ شَمْعَة؟

٦- ماذا غَنَّى الجَميعُ؟ ٧- مَنْ قَطَعَ الكَعْكَةَ قِطَعاً صَغِيـرَةً؟

٨- ماذا قَدَّمَ الجَميعُ لِسُعاد؟ ٩- ماذا سَأَلَتْ سُعادُ أخاها يُوسُف؟

١٠- ماذا قالَ يُوسُف رَدّاً عَلى سُؤالِ أُخْتِهِ سُعاد؟ in response to

* * *

الدَّرْسُ ٱلخامِسُ: الثَّقافَةُ وٱلقِيَمُ وٱلأمْثالُ
Culture, Values & Proverbs

(أ) يَشْرَحُ الْمُدرِّسُ/الْمُدَرِّسَة بَعْضَ القَضايا الْمُتَّصِلَةِ بِـما يَلي:

- الاِحْتِفالُ بِعيدِ الْميلادِ ثَقافَةٌ دَخيلَةٌ عَلَى الثَّقافَةِ العَرَبِيَّةِ.

Celebrating birthdays is not universal in Arabic culture, since it is borrowed from the West.

- الَّذينَ يَحْتَفِلونُ بِأَعيادِ الْميلادِ هُم الْمُتَأَثِّرونَ بِالثَّقافاتِ الغَرْبِيَّة.

Those who celebrate birthdays in Arab culture are mostly influenced by Western culture.

- لُبْنانُ ومِصرُ مِثالانِ لِلدُّوَلِ العَرَبِيَّةِ الْمُتَأَثِّرَةِ بِالثَّقافاتِ الغَرْبِيَّةِ، والسَّعودِيَّةُ مِثالٌ لِلدُّوَلِ العَرَبِيَّةِ الْمُحافِظَةِ نِسْبِيًّا.

Lebanon and Egypt are two of the Arab countries where many people celebrate birthdays, whereas in Saudi Arabia and Sudan people are less likely to celebrate birthdays!

* * *

(ب) مُخْتاراتٌ مِن ٱلحِكَمِ وٱلأَمْثالِ ٱلعَرَبِيَّةِ:

خَيـرُ ٱلكَـلامِ ما قَـلَّ وَدَلَّ.
The best speech is that which is short but to the point.

اَلـيَـدُ ٱلواحِدَةُ لا تُـصَـفِّـق.
(The) one hand does not clap.

فِـي ٱلتَّأَنّـي السَّلامَة، وَفِـي ٱلعَجَلَةِ ٱلنَّدامَة.
There is safety in patience, and regret in haste.

تَـمارين عامّة ومُراجَعَة

General Drills & Review

تَـمرين ١: **Let's read the following sets of words or phrases, recall their English meanings and then guess why they were grouped together under one category:** (***To be done as small groups activity in class***)

١- دَعَتْ / حَضَرَتْ (إلَى) / يَحْمِلْنَ / قَدَّمَتْ / أَحْضَرَ / زَرَعَ / تُـمَثِّلُ / أَطْفَأَتْ / غَنَّى / بارَكَ / قَطَعَ / أَكَلَ / شَرِبُوا / قَدَّمُوا / غادَرَ / سَأَلَتْ / قالَ / أَعْجَبَتْ / اِبْتَسَمَتْ / قالَتْ .

٢- الأَصْدِقاء / الصَّديقات / الآخرينَ / الضُّيوف / شَمْعات / سَنَوات / الْمُرَطَّبات / الهَدايا / أَحادِيث .

٣- أُخْتُها الصَّغيرَةُ / شَمْعاتٍ كَبيرَةٍ / قِطَعًا صَغيرَةً / وَقْتٍ مُمْتِعٍ / أَحاديثَ مُشَوِّقَةً / إِنْسانَةٌ طَيِّبَةٌ / ذَوْقُكِ حُلْو / أُخْتي العَزيزَةُ / أَخِي العَزيزُ / اِبْتِسامَةً واسِعَةً .

٤- إِلَـى حَفْلَةِ / إِلَـى بَيْتِ / بِـمُناسَبَةِ / لِلضُّيوفِ / بَعْدَ وَقْتٍ / بِعِيدِ مِيلادِها .

٥- أُمُّها / أُخْتُها / أَخاها / مِيلادِها .

٦- كَما / يا / ثُمَّ / بَعْدَ / إلاَّ / ما...؟ / إِلَـى / فِـي .

* * *

تَـمرين ٣: **From the list of words in the shaded box select the one most suitable to fill in the blanks in the following sentences:** (***to be done in class in small groups***)

اِبْتِسامَةً / مِيلادِها / الآخَرينَ / شَمْعاتٍ / حَفْلَةِ / عِيدِ / هَدِيَّةً / أَخاها / لِلضُّيوفِ / العَزيزُ / مُشَوِّقَة / جَمِيل / رَأْيُكِ / مُمْتِع / مُثَقَّفَة / الْمُرَطَّبات / إلاَّ / الباقِي / اِبْتَسَمَتْ / أَعْجَبَتْنِي / سَأَلَتْ / زَرَعَ / دَعَتْ / قَطَعَ / قَدَّمَتْ / حَضَرَتْ / غَنَّى / شَرِبُوا / كَـما .

١- ______ سُعاد ليلى وأمَّها يَوْمَ الجُمُعة إلـى ______ عِيد ______.

٢- ______ دَعَت ______ يُوسُف وبَعْض الأصدِقاء ______.

٣- ______ ليلى وأمُّها وأختُها إلى بَيْتِ سُعاد يَحْمِلنَ ______ لِسُعاد .

٤- ______ سُعادُ أخاها يوسُف ______.

٥- ______ كمال أربَعَ ______ كَبيرَة في كَعْكَةِ ______ الـمِيلادِ .

٦- ______ الجميعُ لِسُعاد "سَنَة حِلوَة يا ______"!

٧- ______ يُوسُف الكعكة وأكَلَ الْجميعُ و______ ______ .

٨- وبَعْد وقت ______ وأحاديث ______ غادرَ الجَميعُ ______ يُوسُف.

٩- ______ سُعاد يوسُف : ما ______ في ليلى؟

١٠- قال يُوسف: ______ كثيراً ، إنسانَة طيِّبة و ______ .

١١- ______ سُعاد ______ واسِعَة وقالت:______ عَلَيَّ يا أخي ______ .

* * *

تَمرين ٤: صَواب / خَطأ _ True / False

Read the following statements and then answer whether each is true or false, using the Arabic terms for true or false; your answers should be based on your comprehension of the conversational as well as the reading texts of the unit:

١- الـمَرأة الأمريكيَّة تَتكلَّمُ العربيَّة جَيِّداً. (______)

٢- الـمَرأة الأمريكيَّة دَرَسَتْ اللّغة العربيَّة لِـمُدَّة سَنة واحدة فـي الجامِعة.(______)

٣- تَخَصَّصت الـمَرأة الأمريكيَّة فـي التَّاريخ الـمصريّ القديم .(______)

٤- أَمْضَت الـمَرأة الأمريكيَّة سنتَيْن فـي تعلُّم العربيَّة والبحث فـي سُوريا. (______)

٥- الرَّجل الـمِصريّ دَرسَ الـماجِستير والدكتوراه فـي أمريكا.(______)

٦- الرَّجل المِصريّ أُستاذ للعلوم السِّياسيَّة في جامِعة القاهِرة. (________)

٧- تقابلَ الرّجل والمرأة في "مَيْدان التَّحرير" بِالقاهِرَة. (________)

٨- دَعَت سُعادُ لَيلى فَقَط إلى حَفلة عيد ميلادها. (________) only

٩- دَعَت سُعاد بَعض الأصدقاء والصَّديقات إلى حَفلة عيد ميلادها. (________)

١٠- قدَّمَت سُعاد أخاها يوسُف لِلضُّيوف. (________)

١١- أحْضَرَت ليلى ، صديقة سُعاد ، كعكة عيد الميلاد. (________)

١٢- زرع كمال أربع شمعات كبيرة في كعكة عيد الميلاد. (________)

١٣- أكل الجَميع وشَربوا المُرطبات، ثمَّ قدَّموا لِسُعاد بعض الهدايا. (________)

١٤- غادر الجميع بيت سُعاد إلاّ يوسُف. (________)

١٥- ما أعجبت يوسف ليلى. (________)

١٦- عُمْرُ سُعاد أربعونَ سَنَة. (________)

١٧- غنَّى الجميعُ لِسُعاد : "سَنَة حِلوَة يا جميل!" (________)

صَواب

خطأ

* * *

تَمرين ٥: **Practice** forming the **five singular and plural conjugations of** the following **past and present tense verbs** by filling in the blanks in the following two tables to correspond to the given subject pronouns

أنا	أنتِ	أنتَ	هِيَ	هُو
				حَضَرَ
			تَحْمِلُ	
		قَدَّمْتَ		
	أَحْضَرْتِ			
زَرَعْتُ				

نَحْنُ	أَنْتُـنَّ	أَنْتُمْ	هُنَّ	هُمْ
				بـارَكُـوا
			يَـحْـمِـلْـنَ	
		غـادَرتُـمْ		
	سَألْـتُـنَّ			
نَـبْـتَـسِمُ				

* * *

تَـمرين ٦:

__Chain Drill > Prompting:__ **The first student in the chain is prompted to produce another word related to it either in __root__, __singular-plural relationship__, __masculine- feminine relationship__, __verb-gerund relationship__, __past-present tense relationship__ or __antonym relationship.__**

The first student prompts another student with the next item on the list; and so on in a chain drill whereby each student takes the two roles of being prompter and prompted:

؟	سَأَلَتْ	؟	سَنَة	؟	صَديقات	؟	صَديق
؟	صَغِيـرَة	؟	اِبْتَسَمَت	؟	شَمْعات	؟	ضَيْف
؟	حَديث	؟	سَنَوات	؟	تَحْضُرُ	؟	صَديقة
؟	قَديم	؟	حَضَرَتْ	؟	كَبيـرَة	؟	أَصْدِقاء

تـمرين ٧: نَشاط لُغَوي: تسلِيَة مع لعبة البَحْثِ عَنِ الكَلِماتِ :

Linguistic Activity : Diversion with the Game of Word Search:

Search (vertically, horizontally, or diagonally) **the cross-words for the hidden multiples of tens in Arabic numerals and numerals related to 'hundred' and 'thousand' given in the box below:**

عشرون / ثَلاثيـن / أربعون / خمسين / ستّون / سبعين / ثـمانون / تسعين / مئة / ألف / ألفين / آلاف / مئتان / مئات

أ	ن	ا	م	ب	ا	ت	ث	ل	ا	ث	ي	ن	ع	ز
ل	ر	ل	ق	ئ	غ	ل	ع	ظ	ط	ض	ص	ا	ش	و
ف	ن	ب	هـ	ذ	ة	ء	أ	ب	ت	ث	ج	ل	ر	خ
و	ع	س	ع	ط	ض	ا	ش	ح	س	ز	ر	ج	و	د
س	ذ	ب	ه	و	ت	ب	ن	ي	م	و	هـ	م	ن	ل
ق	ب	و	ح	ت	ن	هـ	ؤ	ل	ا	ئ	ق	ع	ح	ك
ك	ث	ع	آ	د	ذ	ر	ز	س	ل	ش	ة	خ	ن	ق
ل	م	غ	ي	ل	إ	ث	م	ئ	ت	ا	ن	ظ	ط	ف
م	ا	ك	ل	ن	ا	هـ	و	ي	ء	ا	م	ب	ث	غ
ش	ن	ش	ث	س	ز	ف	ذ	د	ح	خ	م	س	ي	ن
ت	و	ز	ل	ت	ظ	غ	ف	ع	ط	ص	ذ	ب	س	ظ
و	ن	د	س	ت	أ	ل	ف	ي	ن	ء	ح	ع	ب	ط
ي	ظ	ع	ث	و	ص	ن	ظ	ض	ش	ز	د	ي	ع	ض
م	ب	ن	ي	ن	ج	م	ئ	ا	ت	س	ع	ن	ي	ص
ت	ع	غ	ء	ن	ق	ك	ل	م	ن	هـ	ح	ي	ن	ب

نِـهايَـة الـوحـدة الـتَّـاسِعَـة

The Tenth Unit / الوحدةُ العاشِرَة

اَلوِحْدَةُ ٱلعاشِرَة 10th Unit
اَلدَّرْسُ ٱلأَوَّلُ 1st Lesson

دَرْسُ مُراجَعَةٍ لِلْقَواعِد

قَرَّرَ ٱلأُسْتاذُ مُراجَعَةَ أَهَمّ ٱلقَواعِدِ ٱلَّتي دُرِسَتْ في هَذا ٱلكِتابِ لِإعْدادِ ٱلطُّلابِ وٱلطَّالِباتِ لِلامْتِحانِ ٱلنِّهائِيِّ.

- الأُسْتاذُ : أَيُّها ٱلطُّلّابُ وأَيَّتُها ٱلطَّالِباتُ، السَّلامَ عَلَيْكُم!
- الطّلابُ والطَّالِباتُ: وعَلَيْكُمُ السَّلامُ يا أُسْتاذ!
- الأُسْتاذُ : سَيَكُونُ دَرسُنا ٱليَوْمَ مُراجَعَةً عامَّةً لِلقَواعِدِ ٱلَّتي دَرَسْتُموها، على طَريقَةِ ٱلسُّؤالِ وٱلجَوابِ ، فَهَلْ أَنْتُمْ مُسْتَعِدُّونَ؟
- الطّلابُ والطَّالِباتُ: نَعَمْ ، نَحْنُ جاهِزُونَ لِأَسْئِلَتِكَ يا أُستاذُ، تَفَضَّلْ وٱسْأَل!
- الأُسْتاذُ : ما أَقْسامُ "ٱلكَلِمَةِ" بِٱللُّغَةِ ٱلعَرَبِيَّةِ يا "رايَنْ"؟
- رايَنْ : الكَلِمَةُ ثَلاثَةُ أَقْسامٍ ، وهِيَ : "ٱلاِسْمُ" و"ٱلفِعْلُ" و"ٱلحَرْفُ" أَوْ "ٱلأَداة".
- الأُسْتاذُ : أَحْسَنْتَ ! مَنْ يَعْرِفُ خاصِّيَّةً أَوْ خاصِّيَّتَيْنِ لِلاِسْمِ؟
- بَرايَنْ : الاِسْمُ يَقْبَل "ٱلتَّعْريف بـ "ال" ويَقْبَلُ "عَلاماتِ ٱلإِعْراب" عَلى آخِرِهِ.
- الأُسْتاذُ : مُمْتاز يا "برايَنْ" ، وماذا عَنِ ٱلفِعْلِ يا "نُور"؟
- نُور : الفِعْلُ لا يَقْبَلُ "ال" ٱلتَّعْريف ، ولَكنَّهُ يُصَرَّفُ ، وهُناكَ ثَلاثَةَ عَشَرَ تَصريفاً لِلفِعْلِ في ٱللُّغَةِ ٱلعَرَبِيَّةِ .
- الأُسْتاذُ : رائِع يا "نُور" ، وماذا عَنِ ٱلأَداةِ يا "كاثي"؟
- كاثي : الأدواتُ تُعْتَبَرُ رَوابِط، ولَها صُورَةٌ واحِدَة؛ أَيْ لا تَقْبَلُ "ال التَّعْريف" ولا "ٱلإِعْراب".
- الأُسْتاذُ : شُكْراً يا "كاثي"؟ والآنَ ، مَنْ يَذْكُرُ لَنا بَعْضَ "أَدَواتِ ٱلاِسْتِفْهامِ"؟
- دِينا : مَنْ ، ما ، ماذا ، لِماذا ، كَيْفَ ، أَيْنَ ، و كَم .
- الأُسْتاذُ : أَحْسَنْتِ يا "دِينا" ، والآن، ما مَعْنَى "ٱلاِسْمُ ٱلمَعْرِفَة"؟

- جَميلَة : **هُوَ ٱلاِسْمُ الـمُعرَّفُ بِـ "ال"، مِثْلُ (الكِتابُ) أَو "اِسْمُ ٱلعَلَمِ"، مِثْلُ: (مِصْر) أَو "اِسْمٌ مُضافٌ إِلـى مَعْرِفَة"، مِثْل (كِتابُ ٱلأُسْتاذِ).**

- الأُسْتاذُ : **جَميل يا "جَميلَة"، والآن، ماذا يُسَمَّى ٱلتَّركيبُ ٱللُّغَوِيُّ (كِتابُ ٱلأُسْتاذ)؟**

- سوزان : **يُسَمَّى هَذا ٱلتَّـركيبُ "الإِضافَة" ، وهُوَ عِبارَةٌ مُكَوَّنَةٌ مِنْ ٱسْمَيْـنِ، الأَوَّلُ "نَكِرَة" وٱلثّانـي "مَعْرِفَة".**

- الأُسْتاذُ : **تَـمام يا "سُوزان"، والآن، هُناكَ نَوْعانِ مِنَ ٱلجُمَلِ فـي ٱللُّغَةِ ٱلعَرَبِيَّةِ، فَما هُما؟**

- ريم : **هُما "الجُمْلَةُ الاِسْمِيَّة"، وَ"الجُمْلَةُ الفِعْلِيَّة". أَمّا "ٱلجُمْلَةُ ٱلاِسْمِيَّة" فَـهِيَ ٱلجُمْلَةُ الَّتي تَبْدَأُ بِٱسْمٍ أَو بِضَميـر ، أَمّا "ٱلجُمْلَةُ ٱلفِعْلِيَّة" فَتَبْدأُ بِفِعْلٍ.**

- الأُسْتاذُ : **مُمْتازَة يا "ريم"، والآن، مِمَّ تَتَكَوَّنُ "ٱلجُمْلَةُ ٱلاِسْمِيَّة" و"الجُمْلَةُ الفِعْلِيَّة"؟**

- روبَرت : **تَتَكَوَّنُ "ٱلجُمْلَةُ ٱلاِسْمِيَّة" مِن "مُبْتَدَأ" و "خَبَـر". وتَتَكَوَّنُ "ٱلجُمْلَةُ ٱلفِعْلِيَّة"مِنْ "فِعْل" و "فاعِل" وقَدْ تَحْتَوي على "مَفْعُول بِـه" إِذا كانَ ٱلفِعْلُ " مُتَعَدِّيـاً".**

- الأُسْتاذُ : **جَميل جِدّاً يا "روبَرت"، ما هِيَ "ضَمائِر ٱلـمُخاطَب"؟**

- ياسْمين : **هِيَ "أَنْتَ" و"أَنْتِ" و"أَنْتُما" و"أَنْتُمْ" و"أَنْتُـنَّ".**

- الأُسْتاذُ : **يا سَلام "ياسْمين"! وٱلآن، ما هِيَ "ضَمائِر ٱلغائِب"؟**

- جوليا : **هِيَ "هُوَ" و"هِيَ" و"هُما" و"هُمْ" و"هُنَّ".**

- الأُسْتاذُ : **أَحْسَنْتِ يا "جولْيا"! والآن، ما هِيَ "ضَمائِر ٱلـمُتَكَلِّم"؟**

- سارة : **هِيَ ٱثْنانِ فَقَط "أَنـا" و"نَحْنُ".**

- الأُسْتاذُ : **أَحْسَنْتُمْ وشُكْراً لَكُم جَميعاً! والآن ، أُريدُ مِن كُلِّ واحِدٍ مِنْكُم أَنْ يُصَرِّفَ ٱلفِعْلَ ٱلـماضي "دَرَس" مَع جَميعِ ٱلضَّمائِر، وكَذَلِكَ ٱلفِعْلَ ٱلـمُضارِعَ "يَدْرُسُ" على وَرَقَة ويُقَدِّمُها خِلال رُبْـعِ سـاعَـة!**

آلمُفْرَداتُ والتّراكِيبُ اللُّغوِيَّةُ (مُرَتَّبَةٌ حَسَبَ تَسَلْسُلِ وُرودِها في النَّص)

on reviewing, to review	مُراجَعَة	the professor decided	قَرَّرَ الأُسْتاذ
which were studied	الَّتي دُرِسَتْ	the most important grammar	أَهَمّ القَواعِد
for (to) preparing male and female students	لِإعْداد الطُّلاب والطَّالِبات	in this book	فِي هَذا الكِتاب
O' You male students	أَيُّها الطُّلاَّب	for the final exam	لِلامْتِحانِ ٱلنِّهائِيِّ
Greetings of Peace!	السَّلامُ عَلَيْكُم!	and O' You female students	وأَيَّتُها الطَّالِباتُ
O' You Professor!	يا أُسْتاذ!	And may Peace be with you too!	وعَلَيْكُمُ السَّلام!
a general review of the grammar	مُراجَعَة عامَّة لِلقَواعِد	Our lesson today will be	سَيَكُونُ دَرْسُنا ٱليَوْم
in the format of	على طَريقَة	that you studied (them)	ٱلَّتي دَرَسْتُموها
So, are you ready?	فَهَلْ أَنْتُمْ مُسْتَعِدُّون؟	the question and the answer	السُّؤَالِ والجَوابِ
for your questions	لِأَسْئِلَتِكَ	Yes, we are ready	نَعَمْ، نَحْنُ جاهِزُونَ
What are the parts of speech?	ما أَقْسام "الكَلِمَة"	Please go ahead and ask!	تَفَضَّلْ واْسْأَلْ!
three pats	ثَلاثَةُ أَقْسام	in the Arabic language	بِاللُّغَة العَرَبِيَّة
the verb	الفِعْل	and they are: the noun	وهِيَ: الاِسْم
Well done you!	أَحْسَنْتَ !	the particle	الحَرْف = الأداة
one characteristic or two	خَاصِّيَّة أَو خاصِّيَّتَيْن	Who does know…?	مَنْ يَعْرِفُ ...؟
(it) accepts	يَقْبَل	for the noun	لِلاِسْمِ
the case-ending markers	"عَلاماتِ الإِعْراب"	defined by the "Al"	"التَّعْريف بـ "ال"
Excellent O'You Brian!	مُمْتاز يا "برايَنْ"!	at its end, over its end	عَلى آخِرِهِ
O' You Noor!	يا "نُور"	And what about the verb ?	وماذا عَنِ ٱلفِعْل؟
the definite article	"ال" التَّعْريف"	it does not accept	لا يَقْبَلُ
and there are thirteen	وهُناكَ ثَلاثَة عَشَرَ	but it is conjugated	ولَكِنَّهُ يُصَرَّفُ

Wonderful!	رائِع!	conjugation for the verb	تَصْريفاً لِلفِعْل
O' You Kathy	يا "كاثي"	And what about the particle?	وماذا عَنِ ٱلأَداةِ ؟
and they have one form, they have one pattern	ولَها صُورَة واحِدَة	particles are considered links	الأدواتُ تُعْتَبَرُ رَوابِط
Thanks, O'Cathy!	شُكْراً يا "كاثي"!	which means they do not accept	أَيْ لا تَقْبَلُ
who would mention to us	مَنْ يَذْكُرُ لَنا	and now	والآن
interrogative particles	"أَدَوات ٱلِاسْتِفْهام"	some (of)	بَعْض
What…?	ما ...؟	Who …?	مَنْ ...؟
Why …?	لِماذا ....؟	What…? (*followed by a verb*)	ماذا ...؟
Where …?	أَينَ ...؟	How …?	كَيْفَ ...؟
Well done, O' Deena	أَحْسَنْتِ يا "دِينا"	How many …?	كَم ...؟
"the Definite Noun"	"الِاسْم ٱلْمَعْرِفَة"	What is the meaning …?	ما مَعْنَى ...؟
which is defined by the "Al"	الْمُعَرَّفُ بِـ "ال"	it is the noun	هُوَ ٱلِاسْم
or "the Proper Noun"	أو "ٱسْم ٱلعَلَم"	such as (the book)	مِثْل (الْكِتابُ)
a noun added to another definite noun to show possessive relationship	" اِسْم مُضاف إلى مَعْرِفَة"	such as (Egypt)	مِثْلُ (مِصْر)
Beautiful, O' *Jameela*!	جَميل يا "جَميلَة"	such as (the book of the professor) or (the professor's book)	مِثْل (كِتاب الأُسْتاذِ)
the linguistic structure	التَّرْكيب اللُّغَوِيّ	What is it called …?	ماذا يُسَمَّى ...؟
the "*Idāfah*" = (literally adding one noun to another to express possessive relationship)	"الإِضافَة"	this structure is called	يُسَمَّى هَذا التَّرْكيب
consisting of two nouns	مُكَوَّنَة مِنْ ٱسْمَيْن	and it is a phrase	وهُوَ عِبارَة
and the second is "definite"	والثَّاني"مَعْرِفَة"	the first is "indefinite"	الأَوَّلُ "نَكِرَة"
there are two types of sentences	هُناكَ نَوْعانِ من ٱلجُمَل	Perfect, O' Suzanne!	تَمام يا "سُوزان"!
they (the two) are: "the nominal" = "equational sentence"	هُما "الجُمْلَة الاِسْمِيَّة"	So, what are they? (*dual*)	فَما هُما؟
As for …,	أَمَّا	and the "verbal sentence"	وَٱلجُمْلَة الفِعْلِيَّة

which begins with a noun	اَلَّتِي تَبْدَأُ بِٱسْم	it is the sentence	فَهِيَ ٱلجُمْلَة
it begins with a verb	فَتَبْدأُ بِفِعْل	or with a pronoun	أو بِضَمِير
Of what does it consist…?	مِمَّ تَتَكَوَّنُ ...؟ (مِنْ+ماذا)	Excellent, O' You Reem!	مُمْتازَة يا "رِيم"
"Verb" and "Subject of the verb"	"فِعْل" و "فاعِل"	"Subject" and "Predicate"	"مُبْتَدَأ" و "خَبَر"
"a direct object of the verb"	"مَفْعُول بِهِ"	and it might contain	وقَدْ تَحْتَوي على
Very beautifully done, O' Robert!	جَمِيل جِدّاً يا "روبَرت"	if the verv was "transitive"	إذا كانَ الفِعْل "مُتَعَدِّياً"
the second person (adresee) pronouns	"ضَمائِر ٱلمُخاطَب"	What are (they)…?	ما هِيَ ...؟
and "You" (*feminine*)	و "أَنْتِ"	They are: "You" (*masculine*)	هِيَ "أَنْتَ "
and "You all" (*masculine*)	و "أَنْتُمْ"	and "The Two of You" (mas.+*fem.*)	و "أَنْتُما"
What a Peace, O' Jasmine! (*Exclamation of being pleased*!)	يا سَلام "ياسْمِين"!	and "You all" (*feminine*)	و "أَنْتُنَّ"
"he"	"هُوَ"	the third person (absentee) pronouns	"ضَمائِر ٱلغائِب"
and "they" (*dual for two, masculine of feminine*)	و "هُما"	and "she"	و "هِيَ"
and "they" (*exclusively feminine group*)	و "هُنَّ"	and "they" (*exclusively masculine group or mix of two genders*)	و "هُمْ"
the first person (speaker) pronouns	"ضَمائِر ٱلمُتَكَلِّم"	Well done, O' *Julia*!	أَحْسَنْتِ يا "جولْيا"!
"I" and "We"	"أنا" و "نَحْنُ"	they are two only	هِيَ ٱثْنانِ فَقَط
and thank you all!	وشُكْراً لَكُم جَميعاً	Well done (all of you)!	أَحْسَنْتُمْ!
each one of you	كُلُّ واحِد مِنْكُم	I want from	أُريدُ مِن
the past tense verb	ٱلفِعْل ٱلماضِي	to conjugate	أَنْ يُصَرِّفَ
with all the pronouns	مَع جَمِيعِ ٱلضَّمائِر	"he studied," "he studies	"دَرَسَ" "يَدْرُسُ"
the present tense	الفِعْل المُضارِع	and likewise	وكَذلِكَ
within a quarter of an hour = 15 minutes	خِلال رُبْعِ ساعَة	and present it	ويُقَدِّمَها

* * *

Collective Translation in Class / تَرْجَمَةٌ جَماعِيَّةٌ في ٱلصَّفِّ

الدَّرْسُ الثَّانِي: القَواعِدُ وَٱللُّغَوِيَّاتُ / Grammatical and Linguistic Notes

* * *

١- نِداءُ ٱلْمُعَرَّفِ بِـ (ال) بِٱلأَدَواتِ (أَيُّها) و (أَيَّتُها):

Calling Particles for Nouns with the Definite Article: (أَيُّها) and (أَيَّتُها):

- We have previously introduced the 'Vocative' or 'Calling Particle' (يا) to be used before a proper name or a title noun. If we go back to review the usage of this particle, then we would notice that none of the nouns following (يا) had the Arabic 'Definite 'Article (أَل) attached to it.
- Now, let's study the sentences in the box below and learn the two new 'Vocative Particles, used to call upon nouns that have the Arabic 'Definite Article':

أَيُّها الطُّلّابُ، كَيْفَ حالُكُمْ ؟	O' (the male) students, how are you?
أَيَّتُها الطّالِباتُ، كَيْفَ حالُكُنَّ ؟	O' (the female) students, how are you?
أَيُّها ٱلسَّيِّداتُ وَٱلسّادَةُ، السَّلامُ عَلَيْكُم!	O' (the) ladies and gentlemen, Peace Be upon you!
أَيُّها الأَبُ، عَلِّمْ أَوْلادَكَ الأَخْلاقَ !	O' (the) father, teach your children the good manners!
أَيَّتُها الأُمُّ، عَلِّمي أَوْلادَكِ الأَخْلاقَ !	O' (the) mother, teach your children the good manners!

- In the sentences above, the nouns following the "vocative particles" are being called upon and they all start with 'Definite Article' (آل).
- Therefore, we used the particle (أَيُّها) if the following noun is '**masculine**' in gender, and we used the particle (أَيَّتُها) if the following noun is '**feminine**' in gender.
- If the the noun following the "vocative particle" is a 'compound' one, one is 'masculine' in gender and the other is 'feminine' in gender, then we use (أَيُّها); as in the 3rd example above.
- The nouns being called upon by these two particles can be in the 'plural' form, as in the first three examples above, or they can be in the 'singular' form, as in the last two examples.
- The usage of these two "vocative particles" has implied in them elements of seriousness and formality.

* * *

The Complex or Expanded *Iḍāfah*: ٢- ٱلإضافَةُ ٱلْمُرَكَّبَةُ:

- It has been stated previously that the '*Iḍāfah*' structure consists mostly of two terms, each being most commonly a single noun. (see Unit 4)
- In this lesson, however, we will learn more about other expanded forms of '*Iḍāfah*', which we will call '*Complex Iḍāfah*'.
- Now, let's read and examine the following sentences:

١- قَرَّرَ ٱلأُسْتاذُ مُراجَعَةَ قَواعِدِ وِحْداتِ ٱلكِتابِ.
The professor decided on reviewing the grammar of the units of the book.

٢- يَسْتَعِدُّ ٱلطُّلَّابُ لِامْتِحانِ ٱللُّغَةِ ٱلعَرَبِيَّةِ النِّهائِيِّ.
The are getting ready for the final exam of the Arabic language.

٣- هَذا مَكْتَبُ رَئِيسِ جامِعَةِ ٱلقاهِرَةِ .
This is the office of the president of Cairo University.

٤- قَرَأْتُ كِتابَ أُسْتاذِ ٱللُّغَةِ ٱلعَرَبِيَّةِ .
I read the book of the professor of the Arabic language.

٥- ذَهَبَ ٱلصَّحافِيُّ إِلَى مَكْتَبِ مُدِيرِ ٱلمُتْحَفِ ٱلجَدِيدِ .
The journalist went to the office of the director of the new museum.

- Each of the sentences above is an example of a '*Complex Iḍāfah*', whereas we see that there are more than two terms involved in the '***Iḍāfah***' relationship.
- The following statements apply to a '**complex *Iḍāfah***':
  The first word in the string may be any 'case-ending', depending on its function in the sentence; all the other terms are '**genitive**'.
- Only the last noun in the string may have the 'Definite Article' or '*Tanween*' if it happened to be indefinite.

- The last noun of any simple '***Iḍāfah***' may be itself the first term in relation to the following noun in another '***Iḍāfah***' relationship, thus expanding the number of nouns involved in the '***Iḍāfah***' structure, and forming in the process a 'complex ***Iḍāfah***'; so that strings of three, four and even more nouns sometimes occur, as in the examples above.
- The last term of an expanded 'complex ***Iḍāfah***' may be a 'noun-adjective' phrase, as in the first, second, fourth and fifth examples above.

* * *

٣-اَلصِّفَةُ ٱلَّتِي تَصِفُ ٱلْمُضافَ إِلَيْهِ

The Adjective Modifying the First Term of an *Iḍāfah*:

- The '***Iḍāfah***' is one undivided unit, where the 2nd term follows the 1st term directly, without anything separating them. This being the case, an important question is raised: "Since an 'adjective' is also supposed to follow the noun it modifies, and given that the two terms of an '***Iḍāfah***' cannot be separated, is it possible to have a structure where we still can modify the 1st term of an '***Iḍāfah***'? The answer to this question is '**yes, it is possible**' and the following examples will illustrate that:

١- مِنْ أَيْنَ أُسْتاذُ ٱللُّغَةِ ٱلْعَرَبِيَّةِ ٱلْجَدِيدُ؟

٢- قَرَّرَ ٱلْأُسْتاذُ مُراجَعَةَ قَواعِدِ ٱلدَّرْسِ ٱلعاشِرِ.

٣-مُدِيرَةُ ٱلْمُتْحَفِ ٱلْجَدِيدَةُ فِي مَكْتَبِها ٱلآنَ.

٤- سَأَقُومُ بِمُراجَعَةِ ٱلْقَواعِدِ ٱلسَّابِقَةِ.

- In the sentences above, the underlined words constitute '***Iḍāfah***' structures; and as we explained previously, they might contain '***adjectival nouns***' that are part of the ***Iḍāfah***.
- In the first sentence above, the word (الْجَدِيدُ) is modifying the word (أُسْتاذُ). However, because it is modifying the first term of the underlined ***Iḍāfah***, it must be placed at the end of the end of that ***Iḍāfah*** and agree with the noun it modifies it in the '**masculine**' gender and the '**nominative case-ending**' and in being '**singular**' in number. Therefore, the word (الْجَدِيدُ) is not really part of the ***Iḍāfah*** structure,
- Because, in the second sentence, the word (العاشِرِ) is modifying the word (الدَّرْسِ), which is part of the ***Iḍāfah*** structure, it must agree with it in the '**genitive case-ending**' and thus constitute part of ***Iḍāfah***.
- Because, in the third sentence, the word (الْجَدِيدَةُ) is modifying the word (مُدِيرَةُ),

which is itself is the first term of the ***Iḍāfah,*** it must placed after the second term of the ***Iḍāfah***, but agree with the first term in the '**feminine**' gender and the '**nominative case-ending**,' and thus the adjective is not part of the simple ***Iḍāfah***, consisting of two nouns only.

- Because, in the fourth sentence, the word (السَّابِقَةِ) is modifying the word (القَواعِدِ), which itself the second term of the ***Iḍāfah***, it must agree with it in the '**feminine**' gender and the '**genitive case-ending**' and thus forming a part of a '*Complex Iḍāfah*.'
- One final important observation is that all these 'adjectives' have received the 'Definite Article' (أَل) while the nouns they modify do not have it; is there then a discrepancy here or there is a rational answer?! ***(Use your critical thinking in light of all that your learned about the Iḍāfah to answer this question!)***

* * *

٤- نَفْيُ ٱلأَفْعالِ بِـ (لا) وَ (ما) وَ (لَمْ) و (لَنْ)

Negating the Verb in Arabic: The Negating Particles: (لا) , (ما) and (لَمْ) (لَنْ)

- Sentences in any language may have affirmative meanings or negated meanings. Arabic uses certain words, which we might call '**negating particles**' to negate sentences.
- We have already studied (لَيْسَ) and its different conjugations as a negating tool to negate 'Equational Sentences'.
- Now, we are going to introduce particles used to negate verbs; so let's read and examine the following sentences:

يَتَعَلَّمُ جُورْج ٱللُّغَةَ ٱلعَرَبِيَّةَ.	⇐	لا يَتَعَلَّمُ جُورْج ٱللُّغَةَ ٱلعَرَبِيَّةَ.
هِيَ تَتَكَلَّمُ ٱلعَرَبِيَّةَ جَيِّداً.	⇐	هِيَ لا تَتَكَلَّمُ ٱلعَرَبِيَّةَ جَيِّداً.
نَذْهَبُ إِلَى ٱلجامِعَةِ كُلَّ يَوْمٍ.	⇐	لا نَذْهَبُ إِلَى ٱلْجامِعَةِ كُلَّ يَوْمٍ.
كُلُّ ٱلطُّلّابِ يَدْرُسُونَ ٱلتّارِيخَ.	⇐	كُلُّ ٱلطُّلّابِ لا يَدْرُسُونَ ٱلتّارِيخَ.
أَسْمَعُ نَشْرَةَ ٱلأَخْبارِ كُلَّ يَوْمٍ.	⇐	لا أَسْمَعُ نَشْرَةَ ٱلأَخْبارِ كُلَّ يَوْمٍ.

- The sentences on the right in the box above all have affirmative meanings. Each contains a verb in the '**present tense conjugation**'; so in the parallel sentences on the left, when we negated the meanings of these sentences, we simply placed the negative particle (لا) before the verbs; there is no further change or modification required.

- Now, let's study another group of parallel sentences to observe the usage of the negating particle (ما):

سافَرَتْ مَرْيَمُ إِلَى ٱلخارِجِ.	⇦	ما سافَرَتْ مَرْيَمُ إِلَى ٱلخارِجِ.
تَخَصَّصْتُ فِي ٱلعُلومِ السِّياسِيَّةِ.	⇦	ما تَخَصَّصْتُ فِي ٱلعُلومِ ٱلسِّياسِيَّةِ.
تَغَيَّرَتِ الأُسْتاذَةُ كَثِيراً.	⇦	ما تَغَيَّرَتِ ٱلأُسْتاذَةُ كَثِيراً.
ذَهَبْنا إِلَى مَطْعَمٍ عَرَبِيٍّ.	⇦	ما ذَهَبْنا إِلَى مَطْعَمٍ عَرَبِيٍّ.

- The sentences on the right in the box above all have affirmative meanings. Each contains a verb in the '**past tense conjugation**'; so in the parallel sentences on the left, when we negated the meanings of these sentences, we simply placed the negative particle (ما) before the verbs; there is no further change or modification required.
- Now, let's study another group of parallel sentences to observe the usage of the negating particle (لَمْ):

سافَرَتْ مَرْيَمُ إِلَى ٱلخارِجِ.	⇦	لَمْ تُسافِرْ مَرْيَمُ إِلَى ٱلخارِجِ.
تَخَصَّصْتُ فِي ٱلعُلومِ ٱلسِّياسِيَّةِ.	⇦	لَمْ أَتَخَصَّصْ فِي ٱلعُلومِ ٱلسِّياسِيَّةِ.
دَرَسْتُ ٱللُّغَةَ ٱلعَرَبِيَّةَ.	⇦	لَمْ أَدْرُسْ ٱللُّغَةَ ٱلعَرَبِيَّةَ.
قَرَأْنا ٱلدَّرْسَ ٱلعاشِرَ.	⇦	لَمْ نَقْرَأْ ٱلدَّرْسَ ٱلعاشِرَ.
سَمِعُوا ا نَشْرَةَ ٱلأَخْبارِ.	⇦	لَمْ يَسْمَعُوا نَشْرَةَ ٱلأَخْبارِ.

- The sentences on the right in the box above all have affirmative meanings. Each contains a verb in the '**past tense conjugation**'; so in the parallel sentences on the left, when we negated the meanings of these sentences, we did three things: first, placed the negative particle (لَمْ) before the verbs; second, **changed the 'past tense conjugations of the verbs'** to '**present tense conjugations**'; and third, **changed the ending vowels of the verbs to reflect what we call the 'jussive mood', which in this case is a '*Sukūn*' over the last original consonant of the verbs.**
- Therefore, the particle (لَمْ) is more than a simple negating particle, and thus it is called also a '**jussive particle**', whereas the verb following it must undergo a transformation from the 'indicative mood' to the 'jussive mood'. The three 'moods' of the 'imperfect conjugations' of verbs will be treated with more detail in future lessons.
- Needless to say, using the particle (لَمْ) for negation is more complex than using the other

two particles. However, its usage is similar to the English negation process of, say for example: '**I studied**.' versus , ' **I did not study**.' Here, the past tense '**studied**' reverted to the imperfect '**study**' when we negated it.

- Now, let's study another group of parallel sentences to observe the usage of the negating particle (لَـنْ):

١- سَـأُسافِرُ إلـى مِصْـر بَعْدَ أُسْبُوع .⇐ لَنْ أُسافِـرَ إلـى مِصْـر بَعْدَ أُسْبُوع .

٢- سَـنَـذْهَـبُ إلـى ٱلنَّادي غَداً . ⇐ لَنْ نَذْهَـبَ إلـى ٱلنَّادي غَداً .

٣- سَوْفَ يَحْضُرُونَ لِـزِيارَتِـنـا . ⇐ لَنْ يَحْضُرُوا لِـزِيارَتِـنـا .

٤- سَوْفَ يَدْرُسُونَ فـي ٱلخارِجِ . ⇐ لَنْ يَدْرُسُوا فـي ٱلخارِجِ .

- The sentences on the right in the box above all have affirmative future meanings, expressed through the (سَـوْفَ / سَـ) particles before the **present indicative verbs** . In the parallel sentences on the left, we used the negating particle (لَـنْ) to negate the meanings of these sentences. Since the particle (لَـنْ) is also a **subjunctive particle**, the present tense verbs following it change their case-endings to reflect the "**subjunctive mood**."

* * *

٥- اِرْتِـبـاطُ ٱلأَفْعالِ وَٱلـمَـصـادِرِ بِـٱلأَدَواتِ

Verbs-Prepositions and Verbal Nouns-Particles Idioms:

- You must have observed, by now, that there are certain verbs and verbal nouns (gerunds) in Arabic which are followed by and are associated with specific particles, necessary to fulfil the meanings of these verbs or verbal nouns. This association between a specific verb or verbal noun and a specific particle is known in linguistic terminology as '**Verb-Particles Idioms**' or '**Verbal Noun- Particles Idioms**', and it is to be found in all languages. Therefore, when you learn such verbs or verbal nouns, you must also learn the particular particles associated with them as '**idioms**'.
- To make you aware, as a learner, about the significance of this topic, let's first review the examples in the following table:

- سافَـرَ إلـى أَمْريكا لِـلدِّراسَةِ . (سافَـرَ إلـى)
- تَخَرَّجْتُ مِن جامِعةِ شيكاغو . (تَخَرَّجْتُ مِن)
- تَخَصَّصْتُ فـي ٱلعُلومِ السِّياسِيَّة . (تَخَصَّصْتُ فـي)
- نَتَمَنَّى أَنْ تَكونَ أَكْثَـرَ ديـمُقراطِيَّة فـي ٱلـمَرَّةِ ٱلقادِمة. (نَتَمَنَّى أَنْ)
- يَدْرُسُ لِـلحُصولِ على شَهادَةِ الدُّكتوراه . (الحُصول على)
- أُحِبُّ ٱلاِسْتِماعَ إلـى ٱلـمُوسيقى العَرَبِيَّة . (الاِستِماع إلـى)

- It should be noted that though, in many cases, there is some level of correspondence between Arabic and English in regard to 'Verb-Particle Idioms' , there are many cases also that there is not. Now study the following sentence and observe that in the first case of the 'verb' (رَجَعَتْ إِلَى) there is correspondence with the English (**she returned to**); however, with the Arabic 'verbal noun' (الْحُصُولِ عَلَى), the English is rendered as '**obtaining**' without any particular particle.

رَجَعَتْ إِلَى بَلَدِها بَعْدَ ٱلْحُصُولِ عَلَى شَهادَتِها.

She **returned to** her country after **obtaining** her degree.

---

*　*　*

٦- اَلْأَسْماءُ ٱلْمَوْصُولَةُ : (اَلَّذِي / اَلَّتِي / اَلَّذِينَ)

The Relative Pronouns: (اَلَّذِي), (اَلَّتِي) and (اَلَّذِينَ):

- Besides the 'personal subject pronouns', the 'possessive pronouns', the 'object pronouns' and the 'demonstrative pronouns', we have another set of pronouns, called in English '**relative pronouns**', though Arabic linguists call them 'relative nouns'.

- The most commonly used of these are: (اَلَّذِي), (اَلَّتِي) and (اَلَّذِينَ), each of which has two possible meanings, depending on whether the reference is to '**human**' or '**non-human**' antecedent, as will be explained after examining the following sentences:

This is the (male) student <u>who</u> studied Arabic.	هَذا هُوَ ٱلطَّالِبُ ٱلَّذِي دَرَسَ ٱلْعَرَبِيَّةَ.
This is the (female) student <u>who</u> studied Arabic.	هَذِهِ هِيَ ٱلطَّالِبَةُ ٱلَّتِي دَرَسَتِ ٱلْعَرَبِيَّةَ.
Those are the (male) students <u>who</u> studied Arabic .	هَؤُلاءِ هُمُ ٱلطُّلَّابُ ٱلَّذِينَ دَرَسُوا ٱلْعَرَبِيَّةَ.
I read the book <u>which (that)</u> the professor wrote.	قَرَأْتُ ٱلْكِتابَ ٱلَّذِي كَتَبَهُ ٱلْأُسْتاذُ.
I read the word <u>which (that)</u> the professor wrote.	قَرَأْتُ ٱلْكَلِمَةَ ٱلَّتِي كَتَبَها ٱلْأُسْتاذُ.
I read the books <u>which (that)</u> the professor wrote.	قَرَأْتُ ٱلْكُتُبَ ٱلَّتِي كَتَبَها ٱلْأُسْتاذُ.

- By examining the sentences above, we find that the 'relative pronouns': (الَّذِي), (الَّتِي) and (الَّذِينَ), were rendered into English as '**who**', but precisely the Arabic implies '**he who**', '**she who**' and '**they who**' respectively, when reference is related to '**humans**' as in the first three sentences above.
- In the last three sentences, the 'relative pronouns' were used in reference to '**non-humans**'; respectively, 'the book', 'the word' and 'the books'. The English rendering of these 'relative pronouns' is '**which**' or '**that**' in this case.
- The words underlined twice before these 'relative pronouns' are called '**antecedents**', and they should always be '**definite**'.
- There should always be agreement in '**gender**' and '**number**' between the 'relative pronoun' we use and its 'antecedent' when the 'antecedent' is related to 'humans'. In this case (الَّذِي) is used for 'masculine singular antecedent'; (الَّتِي) for 'feminine singular antecedent'; and (الَّذِينَ) for 'masculine plural antecedent'.
- However, **if the 'antecedent' refers to 'non-human plural', then we use (الَّتِي) as its related 'relative pronoun**, as in the last example of the sentences above. Now study the following examples to reinforce the last point stated above:

> هَذِهِ هِيَ ٱلْمَسَاجِدُ ٱلَّتِي يُصَلِّي فِيهَا ٱلْمُسْلِمونَ.
>
> هَذِهِ هِيَ ٱلْكَنَائِسُ ٱلَّتِي يُصَلِّي فِيهَا ٱلْمَسِيحِيُّونَ.
>
> هَلْ سَمِعْتُمُ ٱلأَخْبَارَ ٱلَّتِي قَدَّمَتْهَا قَنَاةُ ٱلْجَزِيرَةِ؟

* * *

Synonyms and Antonyms in Arabic: ٧- التَّرَادُفُ وَٱلتَّضَادُ فِي ٱلْمَعْنَى

- A '**Synonym**' is a '**word that has the same or nearly the same meaning as another in the same language**'. And an '**Antonym**' is a '**word that is opposite in meaning to another word in the same language.**' As such, 'synonyms' and 'antonyms' are to be found in every living language.
- For a student of Arabic, being aware of 'synonyms' and 'antonyms' serves a practical way to learn new vocabulary and expand on one's vocabulary repertoire, and it also helps to improve one's verbal and written skills. In light of this, it is highly recommended that learners develop good habits by making their own lists of words that are 'synonymous'

or 'antonymous' as 'easy- to- refer- to- lists'. However, for the purpose of initial acquaintance, let's read in the following parallel sentences that contain '**synonyms**':

* نَعَمْ، نَحْنُ مُسْتَعِدُّونَ. ⇐ نَعَمْ، نَحْنُ جاهِزُونَ.
* أُحِبُّ أَبي وَأُمِّي. ⇐ أُحِبُّ والِدِي وَوالِدَتِي.
* بَعْدَ تَخَرُّجِهِ عَمِلَ بِٱلتِّجارَةِ. ⇐ بَعْدَ تَخَرُّجِهِ ٱشْتَغَلَ بِٱلتِّجارَةِ.
* رَجَعَ الطُّلابُ إلى بَلَدِهِمْ. ⇐ عادَ الطُّلَّابُ إلى بَلَدِهِمْ.
* هِيَ مُدَرِّسَةٌ في هَذِهِ ٱلمَدْرَسَةِ. ⇐ هِيَ مُعَلِّمَةٌ في هَذِهِ ٱلمَدْرَسَةِ.

- Now, let's read in the following box few parallel sentences that contain '**antonyms**':

* ذَهَبْتُ إلى ٱلجامِعَةِ قَبْلَ ٱلظُّهْرِ. ⇐ ذَهَبْتُ إلى ٱلجامِعَةِ بَعْدَ ٱلظُّهْرِ.
* أُحِبُّ ٱلعِلْمَ وٱلعُلَماءَ. ⇐ أَكْرَهُ ٱلسِّياسَةَ وَٱلسِّياسِيِّينَ.
* هَذِهِ ٱلمَكْتَبَةُ حَديثَةٌ. ⇐ تِلْكَ ٱلمَكْتَبَةُ قَديمَةٌ.
* هَذا ٱلكِتابُ جَديدٌ. ⇐ ذَلِكَ ٱلكِتابُ قَديمٌ.
* هَذا ٱلوَلَدُ طَويلٌ. ⇐ هَذِهِ ٱلبِنتُ قَصيرَةٌ.

* * *

اَلدَّرسُ الثَّالث: تَدْرِيباتٌ وَنَشاطاتٌ / Exercises & Activities

تَمْرين ١: (*Oral / Written*) Using the Appropriate 'Calling Particle':

From among the three 'calling particles' in the boxed shaded column on the left, select the most appropriate one to fill in the blanks of the following sentences:

يا ، أَيُّها ، أَيَّتُها

١- .... ٱلطُّلَّابُ وٱلطَّالِباتُ، السَّلامُ عَلَيْكُم!

٢- أَيْنَ تَعَلَّمْتِ ٱلعَرَبِيَّةَ .... سَيِّدَتِـي ؟

٣- .... ٱلأُمَّهاتُ ! عَلِّمْنَ أَوْلادَكُنَّ ٱلأَخْلاقَ ٱلصَّالِحَةَ !

٤- مِنَ أَيْنَ حَصَلْتَ عَلَى شَهَادَتِكَ .... آدَمُ ؟

٥- .... ٱلآباءُ! عَلِّمُوا أَوْلادَكُمْ ٱلأَخْلاقَ ٱلصَّالِحَةَ !

* * *

تَـمْرين ٢: (*Oral / Written*) **Recognition of the Complex *Iḍāfah* and Translation:**

The following sentences contain '**complex *Iḍāfah***'. Your task is to identify the nouns involved in the 'complex *Idāfah*' by underlining them , then translate the sentences into English, as in the given example:

هَذا رَئِيسُ جامِعَةِ ٱلقاهِرَةِ. ⇐ **This is** the president of the university of Cairo.

١- قابَلْتُ مُديرَ مَتْحَفِ ٱلقاهِرَةِ ٱلْوَطَنِيِّ . ⇐ ....

٢- اِسْتَمَعْتُ إِلَـى نَشْرَةِ أَخْبارِ قَناةِ ٱلْجَزيرَةِ. ⇐ ....

٣- وُزَراءُ خارِجِيَّةِ ٱلدُّوَلِ ٱلعَرَبِيَّةِ يَجْتَمِعُونَ ٱليَوْمَ. ⇐ ....

٤- مَجْلِسُ ٱلأَمْنِ يَنْتَقِدُ مِلَفَّ حُقُوقِ ٱلإِنْسانِ فِي سُوريا. ⇐ ....

٥- هَذِهِ مَكْتَبَةُ قِسْمِ ٱللُّغَةِ ٱلعَرَبِيَّةِ . ⇐ ....

* * *

تَـمْرين ٣: (*Oral & Written*) **Using Adjectives to modify the First Term of an *Iḍāfah*:**

From among the 'adjectives' given in parenthesis at the end of the sentences, select the appropriate one to fill in the blanks of the following sentences; follow the given example:

كُتُبُ ٱلطُّلّابِ .... فِـي مَكْـتَبِ ٱلـقِسْـمِ. (الجُدُدُ / الجَديدَةُ / الجَديدَةِ)

كُتُبُ ٱلطُّلّابِ ٱلجَديدَةُ فِـي مَكْـتَبِ ٱلـقِسْـمِ .

١- مُتْحَفُ ٱلقاهِرَةِ .... بَعيدٌ مِنْ هُنا. (القَديـمِ/ القَديـمَةِ / القَديـمُ)

٢- تَعَلَّمْتُ فِي مَعْهَدِ اللُّغَةِ الْعَرَبِيَّةِ .... (الحَديثِ / الحَديثَةِ / حَديثٍ)

٣- هَذِهِ مُدَرِّسَةُ ٱلتَّاريخِ .... (الجَديدِ / الجَديدَةِ / الجَديدَةُ)

٤- قابَلْتَ مُديرَ ٱلـمُتْحَفِ .... (الـمَشْهورِ / الـمَشْهورَ / مَشْهورًا)

٥- وُزَراءُ ٱلخارِجِيَّةِ .... يَجْتَمِعُونَ فِـي القاهِرَةِ. (العَرَبُ / العَرَبِيَّةُ / العَرَبِيَّةِ)

* * *

تَـمْرين ٤: (*Oral / Written*) Using the Right Particle to Negate the Verb:

From among the three 'negating particles' inside the shaded column on the left, select the appropriate one to fill in the blanks of the following sentences:

لا
ما
لَمْ

١- .... دَرَسَتْ سَميـرَةُ ٱلـلُّـغَـةَ ٱلإِنْجـلـيزِيَّـةَ فِـي أَمْـريكا.

٢- .... يُسافِـرُ رَئِـيسُ ٱلـقِسْمِ إِلَـى ٱلقاهِرَةِ.

٣- .... تَـرْجِـعْ مَـرْيَـمُ مِـنَ ٱلـعِـراقِ.

٤- .... تَـزَوَّجَ سَميـرٌ وَسَميـرَةُ بَعْدَ تَـخَرُّجِـهِما مِنَ ٱلجامِعَةِ.

٥- .... يَـحْـضُـرْ مُـديرُ ٱلـمُـتْـحَفِ إِلـى مَكْـتَـبِـهِ ٱلـيَـوْمَ.

٦- وُزَراءُ ٱلـخارِجِيَّـةِ ٱلـعَـرَبُ .... يَـتَـجـاوَزُونَ خِـلافـاتِـهِـمْ.

* * *

تَـمْرين ٥: Exercise 5: (*Oral / Written*) Identifying Verb-Particle or Verbal Noun- Particle Idioms and Translation:

Each of the following sentences contains a 'verb-preposion' or 'verbal noun-preposition idiom'; your task is to read the sentence first, identify the idiom, then attempt a translation of the sentence; follow the given example:

> رَجَـعَ إِلَـى بَـلَـدِهِ بَـعْـدَ ٱلـحُـصُولِ عَلَى شَهادَتِـهِ ٱلـجامِـعِـيَّـةِ.
>
> He returned to his country after obtaining his university degree.

١- أَبْحَثُ عَنْ تاجِرِ جُمْلَةٍ لِـيُـزَوِّدَنـي بِـٱلتُّحَفِ ٱلفِرْعَوْنِيَّةِ. ....

٢- تَشَرَّفْتُ بِمَعْرِفَتِكُمْ أَيُّها ٱلطُّلاَّبُ ٱلجُدُدُ! ....

٣- كُلُّنا بِخَيْر، وٱلحَمْدُ لِلَّهِ! ....

٤- وَصَلَ الزُّوّارُ إِلى مَطارِ ٱلقاهِرَةِ بِالسَّلامَةِ. ....

٥- أُريدُ أَنْ أَلْتَحِقَ بِقِسْمِ ٱللُّغَةِ ٱلعَرَبِيَّةِ. ....

٦- يُسافِرُ عَدَدٌ كَبيرٌ إِلَى ٱلخارِجِ لِلدِّراسَةِ. ....

* * *

تَمْرين ٦: (*Oral / Written*) Using the Correct Relative Pronoun:

From the list of the three 'relative pronouns' in the shaded column on the left, select the appropriate one to fill in the blanks of the following sentences:

١- دَرَسْتُ فِي نَفْسِ ٱلجامِعَةِ .... دَرَسَ فِيها أَبِي.

٢- هَذا هُوَ ٱلكِتابُ .... كَتَبَهُ ٱلأُسْتاذُ خَليل.

٣- هَؤُلاءِ هُمُ ٱلصِّحافِيُّونَ .... يَعْمَلُونَ فِي قَناةِ ٱلجَزيرَة.

٤- أَسْمَعُ ٱلأَخْبارَ .... تَنْقُلُها قَناةُ ٱلجَزيرَة.

٥- لا أُحِبُّ ٱلرُّؤَساءَ .... يُعْلِنُونَ ٱلحُرُوبَ عَلَى بِلادٍ أُخْرَى.

الَّذي
الَّتي
الَّذينَ

* * *

تَمْرين ٧: (*Oral / Written*) : Recognizing <u>Synonyms</u> and <u>Antonyms</u>:

The words in the table below have either a 'synonym' or an 'antonym' in relation to the words listed inside the shaded column on the right. Your task is to select the right '**synonym**' or '**antonym**' and write it down in the empty parallel cells, then give their English meanings; two are done for you as examples:

قَديم / old	جَديد / new
	أَخْبار
	السَّلاَم
	كُلّ
	صَديق
	لَكَ
	بَيْت
والِدٌ / father	أَب / father
	قَبْلَ
	رَجَعَ
	عَاقِل
	الدَّواء
	تَفْصِيل
	قَرِيب
	مُعَلِّم

قَديم
والِد
جَميع
أَنْباء
مُدَرِّس
الدَّاء
اَلْحَرب
جاهِل
بَعْدَ
عادَ
بَعيد
عَلَيْك
مُوجَز
دار
عَدُوّ

* * *

تَـمْرين ٨:

Reviewing a Reference Lists:

Go to '**Part 4**' of this book to review the **reference list** entitled 'Time-Related Terms and Common Words Used Adverbially', **page 345.**

الدَّرْسُ ٱلرَّابِعُ: نَصُّ القِراءَة / Reading Text

يوسُف يَخْطُبُ لَـيْـلـى

- بَعْدَ أَنْ قابَلَ "يوسُف" "ليلى"، لِأَوَّلِ مَرَّة، فـي حَفْلِ عيدِ ميلادِ أُخْتِـهِ "سُعاد"، أَبْدى إِعْجابَهُ بِـها، وَوافَقَ على طَلَبِ يَدِها كَما أَرادَتْ أُخْتُهُ "سُعاد".
- وَلِذَلِكَ ٱتَّصَلَ "يوسُف" بِخالِـهِ "حامِد"، وطَلَبَ مِنْـهُ أَنْ يُـمَثِّلَهُ أَمامَ عائِلَةِ "ليلى". وَضَرَبَتْ "سُعاد" مَوْعِداً مَعَ عائِلَةِ "ليلى"، لِلْقِيامِ بِزِيارَتِهِم بِغَرَضِ التَّقَدُّمِ رَسْمِياً لِخِطْبَةِ "ليلى".
- وَصَلَ خالُ "يوسُف" عَصْـرَ يَوْمِ الجُمُعَةِ إِلـى بَيْتِ "سُعاد". وَبَعْدَ الأَسْتِـراحة، وَتَناوُلِ ٱلشَّاي، رَكِبَ ٱلجَميعُ سَيَّارَةَ أُجْرَة، وذَهَبوا إِلـى بَيْتِ "سُعاد" فـي حَيِّ ٱلعَبَّاسِيَّةِ بِٱلقاهِرة.
- كانَ فـي ٱسْتِقْبالِهِم والِدُ "ليلى"وَوالِدَتُها وَعَمُّها وَعَمَّتُها، وَرَحَّبُوا بِهِم أَيَّـما تَرْحيب.
- جَلَسَ "حامِد" وَ"كَمال"، زَوْجُ "سُعاد"، وَ"يوسُف" وأُخْتُهُ "سُعاد" فـي غُرْفَةِ ٱلاِسْتِقْبال، وَقامَتْ "ليلى" وأُخْتُها ٱلصَّغيـرَةُ بِتَقْديمِ ٱلقَهْوَةِ لِلضُّيُوف.
- قالَ "حامِد"، خالُ "يوسُف"، نَشْـرَبُ ٱلقَهْوَةَ إِذا وافَقْتُم على طَلَبِنا. وقالَ والِدُ "ليلى": أَنْتُم ضُيُوفٌ كِرامٌ فـي بَيْتِنا، وطَلَباتُكُم على ٱلعَيْـنِ وٱلرَّاس.
- قالَ "حامِد": كَما تَعْلَمُون، نَحْنُ هُنا لِطَلَبِ يَدِ كَريـمَتِكُم "ليلى" لِٱبْنِنا "يوسُف"، وَنَحْنُ نَرْجُو كَرَمَكُم فـي تَلْبِيَةِ طَلَبِنا. و"يوسُف" - بِٱلـمُناسبة -

رَجُلُ أَعْمالٍ ناجِح، وَيَعْمَلُ فـي ٱلاِسْتِيـرادِ وٱلتَّصْدِيرِ بَيْـنَ مِصْر وأَمْرِيكا، وَيُقِيمُ حالِيّاً فـي أمريكا، ويُسْعِدُهُ ويُشَـرِّفُـهُ ٱلقُرْبُ مِنْكُم.

- رَدَّ والِدُ "ليلى": الرَّأْيُ أَوَّلاً وَأَخِيـراً لِلْعَرُوسَة. لَـمْ تَنْبِسْ "ليلى" بِبِنْتِ شَفَة، وَطَأْطَأَتْ رَأْسَها خَجَلاً.
- قـالَ "حامِد": السُّكُوتُ عَلامَةُ ٱلرِّضَى!
- و قـالَ ٱلوالِد: على بَرَكَةِ ٱللَّه، هَيَّا بِنا نَقْرَأْ "ٱلفاتِحَة"!
- قَرَأَ ٱلجَميعُ "ٱلفاتِحَة"، وَقالُوا: آمِيـن!
- صافَحَ والِدُ "ليلى" ضُيُوفَـهُ، وقالَ لِيوسُف: مَبْـرُوك يا ٱبْنِي! وبَدَأَتْ والِدَةُ "ليلى" تُزَغْرِد، وَرَدَّتْ عَلَيْها عَمَّةُ "ليلى" وَ "سُعاد".
- قامَ "يوسُف"، وأَلْبَسَ "ليلى" خاتَمَ ٱلخُطُوبَة، وقالَ لَها: مَبْـرُوك! وأَلْبَسَتْ "ليلى" "يوسُف" خاتَمَ ٱلخُطُوبَة، وبارَكَ ٱلجَمِيعُ لِلْعَرُوسِ وٱلعَرِيس.
- أَحْضَـرَتْ أُمُّ "ليلى" وأُخْتُها ٱلشَّـرْبات، وَشَـرِبَ ٱلجَمِيعُ شَـرْباتِ ٱلفَرَح. وَجاءَ ٱلجِيـرانُ لِيُبارِكوا لِلَيْلى بَعْدَ أَنْ سَمِعُوا ٱلزَّغارِيد.

* * *

اَلـمُفْرَداتُ والتَّـراكِيبُ اللُّغَوِيَّةُ الجديدة (مُرَتَّبَةٌ حَسَبَ تَسَلْسُلِ وُرودِها في النَّص)

showed his admiration	أَبْدى إعْجابَـه	to seek engagement	يَخْطُب
asking for her hand	طَلَبَ يَدَها	he agreed to	وافَقَ على
he requested from	طَلَبَ من	maternal uncle	خال
she set up an appointment	ضَرَبَت مَوْعِداً	to represent him	يُـمَثِّلـه
a visit to them, to pay them a visit	بِـزِيارتِـهم	to undertake, to pay	لِـلقِيام

formally making an advancement	التَّقَدُّم رَسْمِيّا	for the purpose of	بِـغَرَض
afternoon	عَصْـر	for asking the hand in engagement	لِـخِطْبَة
rode, took a ride	رَكِبَ	resting	الِاسْتِـراحة
at their reception	ٱستِقْبالِـهِم	the *'Abbasiyyah* neighborhood	حيّ العبَّاسِية
her paternal aunt	عمَّتها	her paternal uncle	عمُّها
a warm welcome (*IDIOM*)	أيَّـما تَرحِيب	they welcomed them	رحَّبوا بِـهِم
she undertook	قامَتْ	guest room, reception salon	غُرفة الِاستِقبال
our request	طَلَبِـنا	if you agreed to	وافَقْتُم على
honorable guests	ضُيوف كِرام	your requests	طلباتـكم
for asking the hand of	لِـطَلَبِ يَد	upon the eye and the head (*idiom for honoring a request*)	على العَيْن والرَّاس
we hope for your generosity	نرجو كَرَمَـكُم	your kind daughter	كَريـمَتِـكُم
by the way (*idiom*)	بِـٱلـمُناسبة	in responding to our request	تلبية طلبـنا
he works in	يَعْمَل فـي	a successful business man	رَجُل أَعْمال ناجِح
it will give him pleasure	يُسعِدُه	import-export	الِاستِيراد والتَّصْدير
to be related to you (*in marriage*)	القُرب مِنكم	it will honor him	يُشرِّفـه
the opinion	الرَّأي	he responded	رَدَّ
goes back to the bride (to be)	لِـلعَروسة	firstly and lastly	أولاً وأخيراً
she lowered her head	طَأطَأت رأسَها	she did not utter a word (*idiom*)	لَـمْ تَنبس بِبِنت شَفة
(the) silence	السُّكوت	in a shyness way	خجلاً
Congratulations!	مبروك !	a sign of consent,satisfaction, agreement	علامة الرِّضَى
The Opening Chapter of the Qur'an	الفاتِحة	Let us recite	هيَّا بِنا نَقْرأ
he shook the hands (of)	صافَحَ	Amin!	آمِين
O' My Son	يا ٱبني	his guests	ضُيوفـه

echoed her (in voice cheering)	ردَّت عليها	she began voice-cheering	بدأت تُزَغْرِد
and dressed (her finger)	ألْبَسَ	he stood up	قامَ
she brought	أَحْضَرت	with the engagement ring	خاتَم الخُطُوبة
sherbets of celebration	شَربات الفَرَح	the sherbets	الشَّربات
the neighbors	الجيران	came	جاءَ
after that	بَعْدَما	to congratulate	لِيُبارِكوا
the voice-cheering	الزَّغاريد	they heard	سَمِعوا

* * *

أَسْئِلَةُ الفَهْمِ والاِسْتيعابِ (شَفَوِيًّا) Comprehension Questions (Orally)

١- ماذا طَلَبَ "يُوسُف" مِن خالِه "حامِد" ؟

٢- متى وَصَلَ خالُه إلى بَيتِ "سُعاد"؟

٣- مَنْ قَدَّمَتْ سُعادُ لِلضُّيوف؟ ٤- أيْنَ تَسْكُن عائِلة "ليلى"؟

٥- مَن كانَ في اسْتِقبالِ "يُوسُف" وأقارِبِه؟ his relatives

٦- كَيْف اَسْتَقبَلَت عائِلة "ليلى" الضُّيوف؟

٧- أيْنَ جَلَسَ "يُوسُف" وأقارِبِه؟

٨- ماذا قَدَّمَت "ليلى" وأخْتُها لِلضُّيوف؟

٩- ماذا قالَ "حامِد" قَبْلَ شُرب القهوة؟

١٠- ماذا كانَ رَدُّ والِد "ليلى" على طَلَبِ"حامِد"؟

١١- ماذا كانَ رَدُّ "ليلى"؟

١٢- ماذا قَرَأَ الجَميعُ قَبْلَ المُبارَكة؟

١٣- ماذا ألْبَسَ "يُوسُف" "ليلى"؟

١٤- ماذا أحْضَرَت أُمُّ "ليلى" وأُخْتُها؟

الدَّرْسُ الخامِسُ: الثَّقافَةُ والقِيَمُ والأمْثالُ

Culture, Values & Proverbs

(أ) يَشْرَحُ الْمُدرِّسُ / الْمُدَرِّسَة بَعْضَ القَضايا الْمُتَّصِلَةِ بِما يَلي:

❖ الحَديثُ عن مَراسِمِ وطُقُوس الخُطوبة في الثَّقافة العربيَّة.

A general view of engagement traditions and procedures in the Arabic culture.

❖ دَوْرُ العائِلة ، وخُصوصاً نِساءِ العائِلة ، في ترتيب أُمور الخُطوبة والزَّواج .

The role of family members, and especially the women, in arranging the affairs of engagement and marriage.

❖ شَرْحُ فِكْرة (إكْمال نِصْف الدِّين.)

Explaining the common belief that getting married is a "kind of completing the missing half of one's religion."

❖ أَهَمِّيَّةُ قِراءة "سورة الفاتِحة" كَرَمْز لِقداسة وأَهَمِّيَّة العامل الدِّينِيِّ في أُمور الزَّواج .

The importance of sealing an engagement and marriage agreement with reading the "OPENING CHAPTER" of the Qur'an, as a symbol of fulfilling the religious aspect of one's life.

(ب) مُخْتاراتٌ مِن الْحِكَمِ والأَمْثالِ العَرَبِيَّةِ:

اَلـمَكْـتُوبُ على اَلْـجَـبِـيـن لازِم تِـشوفُـه اَلْـعَـيْـن!

What has been written on the forehead, must be witnessed by the eye!

(A cultural adage to express the idea fate plays in our lives.)

طَـنْـجَـرَة ولاقَـتْ غَطـاهـا!

It's a pot finding its perfect cover!

(A cultural adage said to express the idea of finding the right match.)

تَـمارين عامّة ومُراجَعَة
General Drills & Review

تَـمرين ١:

Let's read the following sets of words or phrases, recall their English meanings and then guess why they were grouped together under one category: (*To be done as small groups activity in class*)

١- مَنْ / مـا / ماذا / كَيْف / كَمْ / أَيْنَ / لِماذا / مِنْ أَيْنَ / مَعَ مَنْ .

٢- أَنـا / نَحْنُ / أَنْتَ / أَنْتِ / أَنْتُما / أَنْتُم / أَنْتُـنَّ / هُوَ / هِيَ / هُما / هُم / هُنَّ .

٣- أَحْسَنْت / عَظِيم / شُكْراً / مُمْتازَة / جَيِّدَة / رائِع / أَشْكُرُك / يا سَلام / جَميل جِدّاً.

٤- أَدَواتُ ٱلاِسْتِفْهام / النَّكِرَة / الـمَعْرِفَة / الجُمْلَةُ الاِسْمِيَّة / الجُمْلَةُ الفِعْلِيَّة / الضَّمائِر / أَقْسامُ الكَلِمَة / الإِضافة / ال التَّعْريف / الـمُبْتَدَأ / الخَبَر / الفِعْل / الفاعِل / الـمَفْعُول بِـهِ / الصِّفَة / تَصْريفُ الفِعْل .

٥- الطُّلاَّب / الطَّالِبات / الأَسْئِلَة / القَواعِد / جاهِزُون / أَقْسام / أَدَوات / ضَمائِر / دَقائِق .

٦- يـا / أَيُّـها / أَيَّـتُها .

٧- الَّذي / الَّتي / الَّذينَ .

٨- لا / ما / لَم .

The categories fall under one of the following:

1. Verbs negating particles,
2. Pronouns,
3. Plural nouns,
4. Vocative (Calling) particles,
5. Relative pronouns,
6. Well-done expressions,
7. Interrogative particles,
8. Plural nouns.

* * *

تمرين ٢: **Select any combination of words from the previous exercise to construct full meaningful sentences: (*It's advisable that you write down your sentence (s) on a sheet of paper before delivering it verbally!*)**

____

____

* * *

تمرين ٣: صَواب / خَطأ - True / False

Read the following statements and then answer whether each is <u>true</u> or <u>false</u>, using the Arabic terms for <u>true</u> or <u>false</u>; your answers should be based on your comprehension of the <u>conversational</u> as well as the <u>reading texts</u> of the unit:

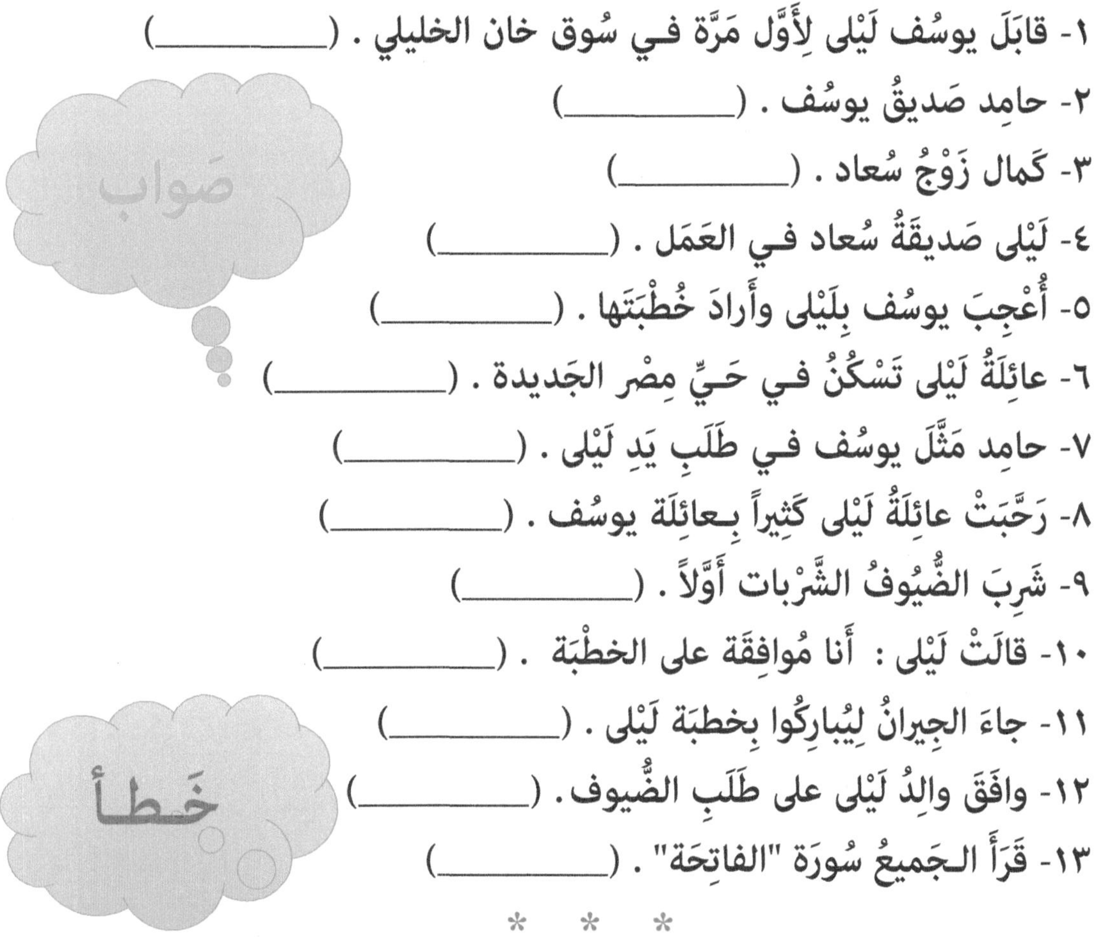

١- قابَلَ يوسُف لَيْلى لِأَوَّل مَرَّة في سُوق خان الخليلي . (__________)

٢- حامِد صَديقُ يوسُف . (__________)

٣- كَمال زَوْجُ سُعاد . (__________)

٤- لَيْلى صَديقَةُ سُعاد في العَمَل . (__________)

٥- أُعْجِبَ يوسُف بِلَيْلى وأَرادَ خُطْبَتَها . (__________)

٦- عائِلَةُ لَيْلى تَسْكُنُ في حَيِّ مِصْر الجَديدة . (__________)

٧- حامِد مَثَّلَ يوسُف في طَلَبِ يَدِ لَيْلى . (__________)

٨- رَحَّبَتْ عائِلَةُ لَيْلى كَثيراً بِعائِلَة يوسُف . (__________)

٩- شَرِبَ الضُّيوفُ الشَّرْبات أَوَّلاً . (__________)

١٠- قالَتْ لَيْلى : أَنا مُوافِقَة على الخطْبَة . (__________)

١١- جاءَ الجِيرانُ لِيُبارِكُوا بِخطبَة لَيْلى . (__________)

١٢- وافَقَ والِدُ لَيْلى على طَلَبِ الضُّيوف. (__________)

١٣- قَرَأَ الجَميعُ سُورَة "الفاتِحَة" . (__________)

* * *

تمرين ٤: **The following sentences are missing an <u>important link</u> in the form of a <u>specisific particle or preposition</u>. Your task is to select the appropriate one from among the particles listed inside the box, at left on the following page, to fill in the appropriate blank in the sentences:**

١- سافَرَ يوسُف _____ أَمْريكا لِلدِّراسَةِ والعَمَل.
٢- تَخَرَّجْتُ _____ جامِعةِ شيكاغو.
٣- يَعْمَلُ يُوسُف _____ تِجارَةِ الاِسْتِيراد والتَّصْدير.
٤- نَتَمَنَّى ____ تَكونَ أَكْثَر ديمُقراطِيَّة ____ الْمَرَّةِ الْقادِمة.
٥- يَدْرُسُ لِلحُصولِ _____ شَهادَةِ الدُّكتوراه.
٦- أُحِبُّ الاِسْتِماعَ _____ الْموسيقى العَرَبِيَّة.
٧- ضَرَبَتْ سُعادُ مَوْعِداً ____ عائِلَةِ لَيْلى.
٨- جاءَ الجِيرانُ ____ يُباركُوا لِلَيْلى.

ل
مِنْ
عَلى
أَنْ
إلى
في
مَعَ

* * *

تَمرين ٥: تَرْجَمَة إلى الإنْجليزِيَّة: Translate the following sentences into English:

ترجمة إلى الإنجليزيَّة

١- أَبْدى يُوسُف إِعْجابَهُ بِلَيْلى، وَأَرادَ طَلَبَ يَدِها.
٢- ضَرَبَتْ سُعادُ مَوْعِداً مَعَ عائِلَةِ لَيْلى لِلزِّيارَة.
٣- جَلَسَ الضُّيُوفُ في غُرْفَةِ الاِسْتِقْبالِ.
٤- قَدَّمَتْ ليلى وأُخْتُها الصَّغِيرَةُ القَهْوَةَ لِلضُّيُوف.
٥- يوسُف رَجُلُ أَعْمالٍ ناجِح، وَيَعْمَلُ في الاِسْتِيرادِ والتَّصْدِيرِ.
٦- الرَّأْيُ أَوَّلاً وَأَخِيراً لِلْعَرُوسَة.
٧- السُّكُوتُ عَلامَةُ الرِّضَى!
٨- صافَحَ والِدُ ليلى ضُيُوفَهُ، وقالَ: مَبْرُوك!
٩- أَلْبَسَ يوسُف ليلى خاتَمَ الخُطُوبَة.
١٠- جاءَ الجِيرانُ لِيُبارِكوا لِلَيْلى بَعْدَ أَنْ سَمِعُوا الزَّغاريد.

مَبْرُوك!

* * *

تـمرين ٦:

<u>Practice</u> forming the <u>five singular and plural conjugations of</u> the following <u>past and present tense verbs</u> by filling in the blanks in the following two tables to correspond to the given subject pronouns: (*All the verbs in the first table are present tense, and all the verbs in the second table are past tense*)

أنا	أنتِ	أنتَ	هِيَ	هُو
				أَلْبَسَ
			جَلَسَتْ	
		قَدَّمْتَ		
	صافَحْتِ			
أَشْرَبُ				

نَحْنُ	أَنْـتُـنَّ	أَنْـتُـمْ	هُنَّ	هُمْ
				سَمِـعُـوا
			يُـبـارِكْـنَ	
		تُـوافِـقُـونَ		
	تُرَحِّـبْـنَ			
نَسْكُـنُ				

* * *

تـمرين ٦:

<u>Chain Drill > Prompting:</u> The first student in the chain is prompted by the instructor to produce another word related to the first in the listed words below, either in <u>root</u>, <u>singular-plural relationship</u>, <u>singular-dual relationship</u>, <u>masculine- feminine relationship</u>, <u>verb-gerund relationship</u>, <u>past-present tense relationship</u>, <u>antonym relationship</u> or <u>synonym relationship.</u> The first student prompts another student with the next item on the list; and so on in a chain drill whereby each student takes the two roles of being prompter and prompted:

؟	أَكْرَهُ	؟	زَوْجَة	؟	الطّالِبات	؟	أَنْتُمْ
؟	طالِبَة	؟	جار	؟	أَنْتُـنَّ	؟	الخُطوبَة
؟	جِيران	؟	أُحِبُّ	؟	يَخْطُبُ	؟	الزَّواج
؟	جَميع	؟	رَفيق	؟	صَديق	؟	كُـلّ

تَـمرين ٧: نَشاط لُغَوي: تسلِيَة مع لعبة ٱلبَحْثِ عَنِ ٱلكَـلِماتِ:

Linguistic Activity : Diversion with the Game of Word Search:

Search (vertically, horizontally, or diagonally) the cross-words for the hidden words given in the box below:

هذا / هذه / هؤلاء / الَّذي / الَّتِي / الَّذينَ / هو / هِي / هُمْ / أَيُّها / أَيَّتُها

ز	هـ	ن	ي	ي	ذ	لّ	ا	ت	ا	ب	م	ا	ن	هـ
و	ش	ا	ص	ض	ط	ظ	ع	ل	غ	ـئـ	ق	ل	ذ	ل
خ	ر	ل	ا	ـهـ	ت	يّ	أ	ء	ـة	ذ	هـ	ه	ن	ف
د	و	ج	ر	ز	س	ح	ش	ا	ض	ط	ع	س	ع	و
ل	ن	م	هـ	و	م	ي	ن	ب	ت	و	ه	ب	ذ	س
ك	ح	ع	ق	ـئـ	ل	ا	ذ	هـ	ن	ت	ح	و	ب	ق
ق	ن	خ	ـة	ش	ل	س	ز	ر	ذ	د	آ	ع	ث	ا
ف	ط	ظ	ن	ا	ت	ـئـ	م	ث	إ	ل	ا	غ	م	لّ
غ	ث	ب	م	أ	ء	ي	و	هـ	ا	م	ل	ك	ا	ت
هـ	ي	س	م	يّ	ح	د	ذ	م	ز	س	ث	ش	ن	ي
ؤ	س	ب	ذ	ـهـ	ط	ع	ف	غ	ظ	ت	ل	ز	و	ت
ل	ب	ع	ح	ا	ن	ي	ف	ل	أ	ت	س	د	ن	و
ا	ع	ي	د	ز	ش	ض	ظ	ن	ص	و	ث	ع	ظ	ي
ء	ي	ن	ز	ر	ت	ا	ـئـ	م	ج	ن	ي	ن	ب	هـ
ب	ن	ي	ح	ن	ي	ذ	لّ	ا	ق	ن	ء	غ	ي	ت

نهاية الوحدة العاشرة

ونهاية دروس الكتاب

PART FOUR .... القسم الرَّابعُ

ARBIC REFERENCE LISTS .... قَوائِمُ مَرْجِعِيَّةٌ •

مَسْرَدٌ عَرَبِيٌّ - إِنْجِلِيزِيٌّ لِمُفْرَداتِ دُروسِ ٱلْقِسْمِ ٱلثَّالِثِ .... •

• Arabic-English Glossary

اَلضَّمَائِرُ ٱلْمُنْفَصِلَةُ وَٱلْمُتَّصِلَةُ

THE PRONOUNS: INDEPENDENT & SUFFIXED (Possessive)

اَلشَّخْصُ وَٱلْجِنْسُ Person & Gender	مُتَّصِلٌ بِفِعْلٍ Suffixed to a Verb	مُتَّصِلٌ بِٱسْمٍ Suffixed to a Noun	مُنْفَصِلٌ Independent
SINGULAR Forms	اَلْمُفْرَدُ	*SINGULAR Forms*	اَلْمُفْرَدُ
3rd person masculine	شَكَرَهُ / هُ (ـهُ)	كِتابُهُ / ـهُ (ـهِ)	هُوَ
3rd person feminine	شَكَرَها / ها (ـها)	كِتابُها / ـهَا	هِيَ
2nd person masculine	شَكَرَكَ / كَ (ـكَ)	كِتابُكَ / ـكَ	أَنْتَ
2nd person feminine	شَكَرَكِ / كِ (ـكِ)	كِتابُكِ / ـكِ	أَنْتِ
1st person Mas. & Fem.	شَكَرَنِي / نِي (ـنِي)	كِتابِي / ـِي	أَنا
PLURAL Forms	اَلْجَمْعُ	*PLURAL Forms*	اَلْجَمْعُ
3rd person masculine	شَكَرَهُم / هُمْ (ـهُمْ)	كِتابُهُمْ / ـهُمْ ـهِمْ	هُمْ
3rd person feminine	شَكَرَهُنَّ / هُنَّ (ـهُنَّ)	كِتابُهُنَّ/ ـهُنَّ / ـهِنَّ	هُنَّ
2nd person masculine	شَكَرَكُمْ / كُمْ (ـكُمْ)	كِتابُكُمْ / ـكُمْ	أَنْتُمْ
2nd person feminine	شَكَرَكُنَّ / كُنَّ (ـكُنَّ)	كِتابُكُنَّ / ـكُنَّ	أَنْتُنَّ
1st person mas. & fem.	شَكَرَنا / نا (ـنا)	كِتابُنا / ـنا	نَحْنُ
Dual Forms	اَلْمُثَنَّى	*Dual Forms*	اَلْمُثَنَّى
3rd person masc. & fem.	شَكَرَهُما / هُما (ـهُما)	كِتابُهُما / ـهُما	هُما
2nd person masc. & fem.	شَكَرَكُما / كُما (ـكُما)	كِتابُكُما / ـكُما	أَنْتُما

Important Notes: (1) When pronouns are **suffixed to nouns**, then they correspond to the following ***English Possessive Pronouns***: **His**, **Her**, **Your** (m+f), **My**, **Their** (m+f), **Your** (Plu. m+f) and **Our**. (2) However, when they are **suffixed to verbs**, then they correspond to ***English Object Pronouns***: **Him**, **Her**, **You** (m+f), **Me**, **Them** (m+f), **You** (m+f) and **Us**, respectively.

اَلدُّوَلُ ٱلعَرَبِيَّةُ وَعَوَاصِمُها وَٱلْجِنْسِيَّاتُ

ARABIC-SPEAKING STATES, NATIONALITIES & CAPITAL CITIES

اَلـمَعْنَى الإِنجِلِيزِي English Equivalent	اَلعاصِمَةُ Capital City	اَلجِنسِيَّةُ Related Nationality	اِسْمُ ٱلدَّوْلَةِ State Name
Jordan / Amman	عَمَّان	أَرْدُنِّي / أَرْدُنِّيَّة	اَلْأُرْدُنّ
United Arab Emirates / Abu Dhabi	أَبُو ظَبْي	إماراتِيّ / إماراتِيَّة	الْإِماراتُ ٱلعَرَبِيَّةُ ٱلْمُتَّحِدَةُ
Bahrain / Al-Manama	اَلـمَنامَة	بَحْرَيْنِي / بَحْرَيْنِيَّة	اَلبَحْرَيْن
Algeria / Algeria	اَلجَزائِر	جَزائِرِيّ / جَزائِرِيَّة	اَلجَزائِر
Saudi Arabia / Riyadh	اَلرِّياض	سَعُودِيّ / سَعُودِيَّة	اَلسَّعُودِيَّة
Sudan / Khartoum	اَلخَرْطُوم	سُودانِيّ/ سُودانِيَّة	اَلسُّودان
Iraq / Baghdad	بَغْداد	عِراقِيّ / عِراقِيَّة	اَلعِراق
Kuwait / Kuwait	اَلكُوَيْت	كُوَيْتِيّ / كُوَيْتِيَّة	الكُوَيْت
Morocco / Rabat	اَلرِّباط	مَغْرِبِيّ/ مَغْرِبِيَّة	اَلـمَغْرِب
Yemen / Sanaa	صَنْعاء	يَمَنِيّ / يَمَنِيَّة	اَليَمَن
Tunisia / Tunis	تُونِس	تُونِسِيّ / تُونِسِيَّة	تُونِس
Syria / Damascus	دِمَشْق	سُورِيّ / سُورِيَّة	سُورْيا / سُورِيَّة
Oman / Masqat	مَسْقَط	عُمانِيّ/ عُمانِيَّة	عُمان
Palestine / Jerusalem	اَلقُدْس	فِلِسْطِينِيّ / فِلِسْطِينِيَّة	فِلِسْطِين
Qatar / Doha	اَلدَّوْحَة	قَطَرِيّ / قَطَرِيَّة	قَطَر
Lebanon/ Beirut	بَيْرُوت	لُبْنانِيّ / لُبْنانِيَّة	لُبْنان
Libya / Tripoli	طَرابُلُس	لِيبِيّ / لِيبِيَّة	لِيبْيا
Egypt / Cairo	اَلقاهِرَة	مِصْرِيّ / مِصْرِيَّة	مِصْر

Interrogative (Question) Particles / أَدَواتُ الاِسْتِفْهامِ

مُسْتَعْمَلاً فِي جُمْلَةٍ Used in a Sentence	اَلـمَعْنَى بِالْإِنْجِلِيزِيَّةِ English Meaning	أَداةُ ٱلاِسْتِفْهام Interrogative Particle
أَهُوَ عَرَبِـيٌّ؟ / أَلَسْتَ عَرَبِيّاً؟ / أَلَسْتُ واحِداً مِنْكُمْ؟	Is...? / Are...? / Am...?	أَ ...؟
أَيْنَ ٱلْكِتابُ؟ / مِنْ أَيْنَ أَنْتِ؟ / إِلَـى أَيْنَ تَذْهَبُ؟	Where ...? / Where from ...? / Where to ...?	أَيْنَ ..؟/ مِنْ أَيْنَ...؟ / إِلـى أَيْنَ ...؟
أَيُّ كِتابٍ هَذا؟ / أَيَّ كِتابٍ قَرَأْتَ؟ فِـي أَيِّ جامِعَةٍ تَعَلَّمْتَ؟	Which ...?	أَيُّ / أَيَّ / أَيِّ ...؟
كَمْ طالِباً يَدْرُسُ الْعَرَبِيَّةَ؟ / كَمْ ثَـمَنُ هَذا ٱلْكِتابِ؟	How many ...? How much ...?	كَمْ ...؟
كَيْفَ حالُكُمْ؟ / كَيْفَ تَفْعَلُ هَذا؟	How ...?	كَيْفَ ...؟
لِماذا سافَرْتَ إِلَـى مِصْرَ؟	Why ...?	لِماذا ...؟
ما هَذا الصَّوْتُ؟ / ما هَذِهِ ٱلبِنايَةُ؟	What ...?	مـا ...؟
ماذا أَكَلْتَ ٱليَوْمَ؟ / ماذا تُرِيدُ أَنْ تَأْكُلَ؟	What ...? (*to ask about the action*)	ماذا ...؟
مَتَى تُسافِرُ إِلَى بَلَدِكَ؟ مَتَى مَوْعِدُ وُصولِ الطَّائِرَةِ؟	When ...?	مَتَى ...؟
مَنْ هَذا الرَّجُلُ؟ / مَنْ قابَلْتَ فِي طَرِيقِكَ؟ / لِمَنْ هَذا ٱلْقَلَمُ؟	Who ...? Whom...? / Whose ...?	مَنْ / لِمَنْ ...؟
هَلْ أَنْتَ طالِبٌ هُنا؟ / هَلْ تَدْرُسُ العَرَبِيَّةَ؟ / هَلْ دَرَسْتَ فِي أَمْرِيكا؟	Are ...? / Do / Does ...? Did ...?	هَلْ ...؟

PREPOSITIONS, ADVERBS OF PLACE & TIME / حُرُوفُ ٱلجَرِّ وَأَسْماءُ ٱلزَّمانِ وَٱلـمَكانِ

مُسْتَعْمَلاً في جُمْلَةٍ Used in a Sentence	الـمَعْنَى بِالإِنْجِلِيزِيَّةِ English Meaning	حَرْفُ الجَرِّ Preposition
حَضَرَ ٱلطَّالِبُ إِلَـى ٱلـمَدْرَسَةِ.	to	إِلَـى
كَتَبَ ٱلجُمْلَةَ بِٱلقَلَمِ.	with, by	بِـ
اَلكِتابُ عَلَى الطَّاوِلَةِ.	on	عَلَى
كَتَبَ كِتاباً عَنْ تـارِيخِ أَمْرِيكا.	about	عَنْ
اَلْأُسْتاذُ فِـي ٱلـمَكْتَبِ.	in, at	فِـي
اَلوَقْتُ كَـالسَّيْفِ إِنْ لَمْ تَقْطَعْهُ قَطَعَكَ.	as, like	كَـ
هَذا ٱلكِتَابُ لِـخالِد.	for, belongs to	لِـ
اَلطَّالِبَةُ ٱلجَدِيدَةُ مِنْ لُبْنان.	from	مِنْ
مُسْتَعْمَلاً في جُمْلَةٍ Used in a Sentence	الْمَعْنَى بِالْإِنْجِلِيزِيَّةِ English Meaning	ظَرْفُ الزَّمانِ أَوِ الـمَكانِ *ADVERBS*
مَرْيَمُ أَمامَ بابِ ٱلبَيْتِ.	in front of	أَمامَ
حَضَرَ بَعْدَ ٱلظُّهْرِ.	after	بَعْدَ
القَلَمُ تَحْتَ ٱلكِتابِ.	under, beneath	تَحْتَ
اَلـمَكْتَبَةُ خَلْفَ ٱلـمُتْحَفِ.	behind	خَلْفَ
مَكْتَبُ ٱلـمُدِيرِ فَوْقَ مَكْتَبِ ٱلسِّكْرِتِيـرَةِ.	above, on top of	فَوْقَ
حَضَرْتُ قَبْلَ ٱلظُّهْرِ.	before	قَبْلَ
ذَهَبْتُ مَعَ ٱلْأُسْتاذِ إِلَـى ٱلـمَطْعَمِ.	with	مَعَ

Important Note: ***Adverbs of Time*** or ***Place*** function like ***Prepositions*** in taking the nouns after them as "**objects**". The "**objects**" of ***Adverbs*** and ***Prepositions*** are in the "***Genitive Case-Ending***".

ARABIC REFERENCE LISTS (5)

اَلْفِعْلُ ٱلْمُضارِعُ ٱلْمَرْفُوعُ

VERB CONJUGATION: PRESENT INDICATIVE *

Corresponding Pronoun	Mood Marker	Subject Marker Suffix	Subject Marker Prefix	Verb Form
		Singular Forms		
هُوَ	ـُ above the last radical		يَـ	يَدْرُسُ
هِيَ	ـُ above the last radical		تَـ	تَدْرُسُ
أَنْتَ	ـُ above the last radical		تَـ	تَدْرُسُ
أَنْتِ	نَ	ـيـ	تَـ	تَدْرُسِينَ
أَنا	ـُ above the last radical		أَ	أَدْرُسُ
		Plural Forms		
هُمْ	نَ	ـو	يَـ	يَدْرُسُونَ
هُنَّ	No mood marker	ـنَ	يَـ	يَدْرُسْنَ
أَنْتُمْ	نَ	ـو	تَـ	تَدْرُسُونَ
أَنْتُنَّ	No mood marker	ـنَ	تَـ	تَدْرُسْنَ
نَحْنُ	ـُ above the last radical		نَـ	نَدْرُسُ
		Dual Forms		
(Mas.) هُما	نِ	ـا	يَـ	يَدْرُسانِ
(Fem.) هُما	نِ	ـا	تَـ	تَدْرُسانِ
أَنْتُما (Mas. + Fem.)	نِ	ـا	تَـ	تَدْرُسانِ

Note: ***Present (Imperfect) Indicative*** verbs correspond to English ***Simple Present*** or to ***Progressive Constructions*** with "***is / are / am***" and a verb in the "*...ing*" form; such as: ***He studies. They study. She is studying. I am studying.***

كل عام وأنتم بخير

اَلفِعْلُ ٱلـمَاضِي ٱلجَامِدُ " لَيْسَ " / VERB CHART: " لَيْسَ"

English Equivalent	Subject Marker Suffix	Verb Form	Corresponding Pronoun
Singular Forms			
He is not	ـَ	لَيْسَ	هُوَ
She is not	ـَتْ	لَيْسَتْ	هِيَ
You are not (*masculine*)	ـْتَ	لَسْتَ	أَنْتَ
You are not (*feminine*)	ـْتِ	لَسْتِ	أَنْتِ
I am not	ـْتُ	لَسْتُ	أنـا
Plural Forms			
They are not (*masculine*)	ـُوا	لَيْسُوا	هُمْ
They are not (*feminine*)	ـْنَ	لَسْنَ	هُنَّ
You are not (*masculine*)	ـْتُم	لَسْتُمْ	أَنْتُمْ
You are not (*feminine*)	ـْتُنَّ	لَسْتُنَّ	أَنْتُنَّ
We are not (*masculine* & *feminine*)	ـْنا	لَـسْـنـا	نَحْنُ
Dual Forms			
They are not (*two males*)	ـا	لَـيْـسا	هُما
They are not (*two females*)	ـَتا	لَـيْـسَـتا	هُما
You are not (*identical for two males or two females*)	ـْـتُـما	لَـسْـتُـما	أَنْتُما

Notes:

- *Linguists consider this verb as "**defective**" or "**weak**" verb. It is weak because it does not have an "imperfect stem" as strong verbs do. It is a verb, because, in its "perfect stem", it is conjugated like all verbs to correspond to different subjects.*
- *It is a **negating verb**, used specifically to negate "**Equational Sentences**" and corresponds to English "**am not, is not, are not**".*
- *This verb has the effect of changing the vowel ending of the "**predicate**" part of the "Equational Sentence" to "**accusative**" from "**nominative**"; note the following two examples:*

سَمِيرٌ طَالِبٌ. ⇐ لَيْسَ سَمِيرٌ طَالِباً. هُمْ طُلَّابٌ. ⇐ لَيْسُوا طُلَّاباً.

THE CONJUGATIONS OF THE VERB تَصْرِيفَاتُ ٱلْفِعْلِ (كَانَ)

Imperative (Command)	Subjunctive (لَنْ)	Jussive (لَمْ)	Present Indicative (Imperfect)	Past Tense (Perfect)	Subject Pronoun
Singular Forms					
X	يَكُونَ	يَكُنْ	يَكُونُ	كَانَ	هُوَ
X	تَكُونَ	تَكُنْ	تَكُونُ	كَانَتْ	هِيَ
كُنْ	تَكُونَ	تَكُنْ	تَكُونُ	كُنْتَ	أَنْتَ
كُونِي	تَكُونِي	تَكُونِي	تَكُونِينَ	كُنْتِ	أَنْتِ
X	أَكُونَ	أَكُنْ	أَكُونُ	كُنْتُ	أَنَا
Plural Forms					
X	يَكُونُوا	يَكُونُوا	يَكُونُونَ	كَانُوا	هُمْ
X	يَكُنَّ	يَكُنَّ	يَكُنَّ	كُنَّ	هُنَّ
كُونُوا	تَكُونُوا	تَكُونُوا	تَكُونُونَ	كُنْتُمْ	أَنْتُمْ
كُنَّ	تَكُنَّ	تَكُنَّ	تَكُنَّ	كُنْتُنَّ	أَنْتُنَّ
X	نَكُونَ	نَكُنْ	نَكُونُ	كُنَّا	نَحْنُ
Dual Forms					
X	يَكُونا	يَكُونا	يَكُونانِ	كَانا	هُما Mas.
X	تَكُونا	تَكُونا	تَكُونانِ	كَانَتا	هُما Fem.
كُونا	تَكُونا	تَكُونا	تَكُونانِ	كُنْتُما	أَنْتُما Both

Notes: (1) *This verb is the English equivalent of the verb "to be". In its past tense form it corresponds to the English "was"; in its present indicative form it corresponds to English "is" or "are"; in its Jussive form, it corresponds to English "was not" or "were not." In its Subjunctive form the exact meaning is determined by the meaning of the subjunctive particle which precedes it.*

(2) *It is the leading verb in a group of verbs called "KANA and its Sisters" because they are all precede "Equational Sentences" to modify the time element of these sentences from present to past.*

(3) *This verb along with all its sisters has the effect of changing the vowel ending or the grammatical mood of the "predicate" part of the "Equational Sentence" to "accusative" from "nominative."*

تَصْرِيفُ ٱلفِعْلِ ٱلـمَاضِي
PAST TENSE (PERFECT) CONJUGATION CHART

English Equivalent	Subject-Marker Suffix	Verb Form	Corresponding Pronoun
Singular Forms	***Singular Forms***	***Singular Forms***	***Singular Forms***
He studied.	above last letter (*a*) ـَ	دَرَسَ	هُوَ
She studied	(*at*) ـَتْ	دَرَسَتْ	هِيَ
You studied. *(masculine)*	(*ta*) ـْتَ	دَرَسْتَ	أَنْتَ
You studied. *(feminine)*	(*ti*) ـْتِ	دَرَسْتِ	أَنْتِ
I studied. *(masculine & feminine)*	(*tu*) ـْتُ	دَرَسْتُ	أنـا
Plural Forms	***Plural Forms***	***Plural Forms***	***Plural Forms***
They studied. *(masculine)*	(*uu*) ـُوا	دَرَسُوا	هُمْ
They studied. *(feminine)*	(*na*) ـْنَ	دَرَسْنَ	هُنَّ
You studied. *(masculine)*	(*tum*) ـْتُمْ	دَرَسْتُمْ	أَنْتُمْ
You studied. *(feminine)*	(*tunna*) ـْتُنَّ	دَرَسْتُنَّ	أَنْتُنَّ
We studied. *(masculine & feminine)*	(*naa*) ـْنا	دَرَسْنا	نَحْنُ
Dual Forms	***Dual Forms***	***Dual Forms***	***Dual Forms***
They studied. *(two males)*	(*aa*) ـا	دَرَسا	هُما
They studied. *(two females)*	(*ataa*) ـَتا	دَرَسَتَا	هُما
You studied. *(two males or females)*	(*tumaa*) ـْتُما	دَرَسْتُمَا	أَنْتُما

Note: Past Tense (Perfect) verbs are used to inform about actions that took place sometime in the past, before the time of speaking. They correspond to English 'simple past tense', to 'present perfect' and 'past perfect;' such as: **He studied. / He has studied. / He had studied.**

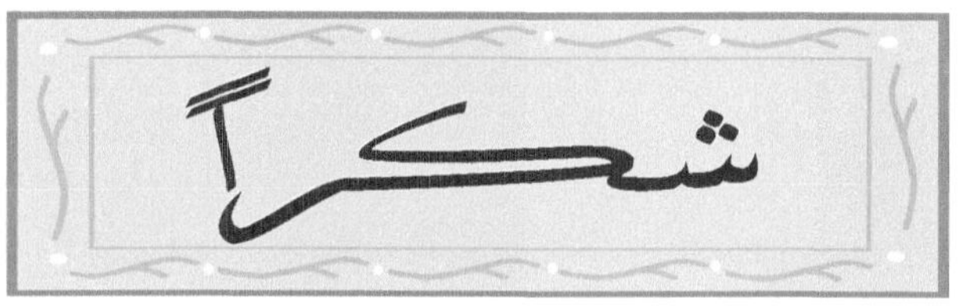

أَشْهُرُ ٱلسَّنَةِ بِناءاً عَلَى ثَلاثَةِ تَقاوِيمَ وَأَيَّامُ ٱلأُسْبُوعِ وَفُصُولُ ٱلسَّنَةِ

THE MONTHS OF THE YEAR ACCORDING TO THREE CALENDAR SYSTEMS, THE DAYS OF THE WEEK & THE FOUR SEASONS OF THE YEAR

Syriac Origin Calendar Months	Arabized Gregorian Calendar Months	Islamic Calendar Months	Numerical Order
كانُونُ ٱلثَّانِي	يَنايِر	مُحَرَّم	١
شُبَاط	فِبْرَايِر	صَفَر	٢
آذار	مارْس	رَبِيعُ ٱلأَوَّلُ	٣
نِيسان	أَبْرِيل	رَبِيعُ ٱلثَّانِي	٤
أَيَّار	مايُو	جُمادَى ٱلأُولَى	٥
حُزَيْران	يُونْيُو	جُمادَى ٱلثَّانِية	٦
تَمُّوز	يُولْيُو	رَجَب	٧
آب	أَغُسْطُس	شَعْبان	٨
أَيْلُول	سِبْتِمْبَر	رَمَضان	٩
تَشْرِينُ الأَوَّل	أَكْتُوبَر	شَوَّال	١٠
تَشْرِينُ الثَّانِي	نُوفِمْبَر	ذُو ٱلقِعْدَة	١١
كانُونُ الأَوَّل	دِيسِمْبَر	ذُو ٱلحِجَّة	١٢

* * *

الثُّلاثاء Tuesday	الإِثْنَيْن Monday	الأَحَد Sunday	السَّبْت Saturday
	الجُمُعَة Friday	الخَمِيس Thursday	الأَرْبِعَاء Wednesday

* * *

Fall, Autumn الخَرِيف	Summer الصَّيْف
Spring الرَّبِيع	Winter الشِّتاء

أَلْفاظٌ ذاتُ صِلَةٍ بِالْوَقْتِ، ومُفْرَداتٌ مَنْصُوبَةٌ عَلَى الظَّرفِيَّة

TIME-RELATED TERMS and COMMON WORDS USED ADVERBIALLY

the present	الحاضِر	now	الآنَ
the future	الـمُسْتَقْبَل	the past	الـمـاضِي
yesterday	أَمْسِ	today	اليَوْم
a second / seconds	ثـانِيَة (ثـوانٍ)	after	بَعْدَ
time, age	زَمَن / زَمان (أَزْمِنَة)	a minute	دَقِيقَة (دَقائِق)
trice	ثـالِثَةً	again,	ثَانِيَةً
a year / years	سَنَة (سِنِيـن- سَنَوات	an hour / an hour time	ساعَة / ساعَة
a month / months	شَهْرٌ (أَشْهُر- شُهُور)	yearly	سَنَوِيّـاً
morning / at morning time	صَباح / صَباحًا	monthly	شَهْرِيّـاً
noon / at noon time	ظُهْر / ظُهْراً	Lengthy, for a long time	طَوِيلاً
at night-fall	عِشَاءً	a year (*masculine*) / a year time	عام (أَعْوام)/ عاماً
a decade / a decade time	عَقْد (عُقُود) / عَقْداً	afternoon / afternoon time	عَصْر / عَصْراً
a period of time	فَتْـرَة (فَتَرات)/ فَتْـرَةً	tomorrow	غَداً
before	قَبْلَ	dawn / at dawn time	فَجْر / فَجْرًا
shortly, soon	قَرِيباً	a century / a century time	قَـرْن (قُـرُون)
once, one time	مَرَّةً	night / at night time	لَيْل (لَيالٍ) / لَيْلاً
sunset / at sunset time	مَغْرِب / مَغْرِباً	evening / at evening time	مَساء (أَمْسِيات)
day time / at day time	نَهار / نَهاراً	since	مُنْذُ
a day / a day time/ daily	يَوْم (أَيّـام) / يَوْمِيّاً	time	وَقْت (أَوْقات)

<u>Note</u>: Some of the words above are purely adverbs, which are invariable. However, most of them are nouns that can be used adverbially by adding a "*Tanween of Fathah*" at the end.

ARABIC-ENGLISH GLOSSARY

About This Glossary

- Words in this glossary are listed alphabetically according to their actual physical appearance, and not according to the '**Root**' system used in most bilingual dictionaries.
- All nouns that appeared with the **Definite Article** (ألْ) in the texts are stripped of it, and then they are listed alphabetically accordingly. The exceptions are some proper names of Arabic countries, cities and proper names of localities, where what appears as a "Definite Article" is actually an integral part of the name that cannot be dropped at will.
- If the listed word is a **singular noun**, then its **plural** follows between **(.....)**; and if it is **plural**, then its **singular** follows in between **(.....)**, such as أَب (آباء) or أَبْواب (باب).
- If a noun is **masculine** in gender, then its **feminine** counterpart, if it exists, is introduced after a **slash** (/) and vise-versa.
- If a listed item is "**gerund**" or "**verbal noun**," then it is followed by a listing of its related verb inside brackets, such as (آمَنَ) after إيمان.
- **A star in red (*)** preceding a listed item alerts you of a **compound of two parts or more** and functioning as a **linguistic idiom**.
- Un-vowelled three- letter listings, such as: {جمع}, indicate the '**Root**' of the word listed.
- If a **verb** or a **verbal noun** is listed followed by a **preposition** in parenthesis, like this, أَبْحَثُ (عَنْ), then it is an indication that they form together a **verb** or **verbal noun-preposition idiom and should be learned as verb or verbal noun-particle idiom**.
- A noun listed like this, أُسْتاذَة - ات indicates that it takes the regular "**Feminine Sound Plural.**"
- A noun listed like this, مُدَرِّس - ـُونَ indicates that it takes the regular "**Masculine Sound Plural.**"
- A phrase after a red star, such as, * مَا أَجْمَلَ!, indicates that the listed item is used in a **special linguistic construction, consisting of more than one part of speech,** or as an **idiom**.
- Words in italics inside parenthesis stand for explanatory notes, such as (*male-female pairs*).
- All one-letter particles will always be written prefixed to the following word, and will be highlighted in blue color.
- What in English is called possessive pronouns or object pronouns, which follow nouns and verbs, are also suffixed to these nouns and verbs, and are highlighted in red color.

Glossary / مَسْرَدُ ٱلْمُفْرَدات

ء / أ / آ / أُ / اِ

The form of writing the *Hamzah* at the beginning of a word	أ	Written symbol for the first Arabic consonant and its name	ء (هَمْزَة)
A subject-marker at the beginning of a present tense verb stem for 1st person singular; such as I love. →	أ أُحِبُّ	Is...? / Are...? (*Interrogative particle used interchangeably with* هَل)	أ
ruins, traces (trace)	آثار (أَثَر) {أثر}	This is called the *Hamzah of Madd* (a combination of a *Hamzated Alif* and an *Alif* as a long vowel.)	آ = (أ + ا)
its end * it cetera	آخِـرِهِ {أخر} * إِلَـى آخِـرِهِ	another *(masculine / feminine pair/ and plural)*	آخَـر / أُخْـرى / آخَرِينَ {أخر}
March *(the third month of the Syriac calendar)*	آذار {أذر}	Adam *(the first man, male proper name)*	آدَم {أدم}
pains (pain))	آلام (أَلَـم) {ألم}	I eat *(two Hamzas in a row become* آ*)*	آكُـلُ (أ+أكَـل) {أكل}
Miss, unmarried young lady (young ladies)	آنِسَـة (آنِسـات) {أنس}	he amused, he entertained, he comforted (comforting, entertaining)	آنَس (إِينـاس) {أنس}
father (*broken plural*) * dear father *(classic form)* * your father * my father	أَب (آباء)، * أَبَـتِ * أَبُـوكَ * أَبِـي	he believed (believing)	آمَـنَ (إِيمـان) {أمن}
she smiled (smiling) * a wide big smile	اِبْتَسَـمَـتْ (اِبْتِسام) * اِبْتِسامَة واسِعَة	I look (for), I am searching (for) (searching for)	أَبْحَـثُ (بَحْـث) (عَنْ)
he showed (showing) * he showed his admiration for her	أَبْـدَى (إِبْـداء) {بدي} * أَبْـدَى إِعْجابَـهُ بِـها	eternal, eternity, endless (eternal time)	أَبَـد (آبـاد) {أبد}
leprous (leprous ones) (*takes broken plural*)	أَبْـرَص (بُـرْص) {برص}	needles (a needle)	إِبَـر (إِبْـرَة) {أبر}

son (sons) * the only son	اِبْـن (أَبْـنـاء) {بنو} * الاِبْـنُ الـوَحِـيـد	pitcher, kettle *(takes broken plural)*	إِبْـريق (أَبـارِيـق) {برق}
doors (a door) *(broken plural)*	أَبْـواب (بـاب) {بوب}	daughter (daughters) * your daughter	اِبْـنـة (بَـنـات) {بنت} * اِبْـنَـتَـكَ
she came (coming)	أَتَـتْ (إِتْـيـان) {أتـي}	white color *(takes broken plural)*	أَبْـيَـض (بِـيـض) {بيض}
I speak (about) (speaking, speech)	أَتَـحَـدَّثُ (عَنْ) (حَدِيث) {حدث}	Would you like (to) …?	أَتُـحِـبُّ (أَنْ) {حبب} (أَ+تُـحِـبُّ)
I feel honored, I am honored (honoring)	أَتَـشَرَّفُ (تَشَرُّف) {شرف}	I leave (leaving) * I leave it for you (feminine)	أَتْـرُكُ (تَـرْك) {ترك} * أَتْـرُكُ لَـكِ
I get to know, I get acquainted (with)	أَتَـعَـرَّفُ (عَلَى) (تَعَرُّف) {عرف}	he established contact (with) (contacting)	اِتَّـصَـلَ (اِتِّـصـال) (بِـ)
* they (dual) agreed upon	* اِتَّـفَـقـا عَـلـى {وفق}	I agree (with) (agreement)	أَتَّـفِـقُ (اِتِّـفـاق) (مَع) {وفق}
mastery, (he mastered) * for your mastery (of)	اِتْـقـان (أَتْـقَـنَ) {تقن} * لِاِتْـقـانِـكِ) (لِـ+اِتْـقـان+ـكَ)	* We agreed upon	* اِتَّـفَـقْـنـا عَـلـى {وفق}
I wish (to, that) (wishing) * I wish you success!	أَتَـمَنَّى (أَنْ) (الـتَّـمَنِّي) {مني} * أَتَـمَنَّـى لَـكَ الـتَّـوْفِـيـق!	I speak, I talk (talking, speech)	أَتَـكَـلَّـمُ (كَـلام) {كلم}
I trust (in), I put my reliance (on) (trusting)	أَتَـوَكَّـلُ (عَلَى) (تَـوَكُّـل) {وكل}	I take up, I deal with, I have (a meal) (taking up, dealing) * I did not have, I did not deal with	أَتَـنـاوَلُ (تَـنـاوُل) {نول} * لَـمْ أَتَـنـاوَلْ
two (nominative-accusative pair)	اِثْـنـانِ / اِثْـنَـيْـنِ {ثني}	trace, effect (traces, effects)	أَثَـر (آثـار) {أثـر}
vacation, break (breaks)	إجازَة (إجازات) {جوز}	he answered, he responded (answering, responding)	أَجابَ (إِجـابَـة) {جوب}
I try, I'll try (trying, experimenting)	أُجَرِّبُ (تَجْرِبَة) {جرب}	you *(masculine singular)* met (meeting)	اِجْـتَـمَـعْـتَ (اِجْـتِـمـاع) {جمع}
sake * for the sake of	أَجْـل {أجل} * مِنْ أَجْـلِ	fair, fee, price * taxi, car for hire	أُجْـرَة {أجـر} * سَيّارَة أُجْرَة

more beautiful * How beautiful!	أَجْمَل {جمل} * ما أَجْمَلَ!	You sit down! *(command verb for masculine singular, feminine singular and plural)*	اِجْلِسْ / اِجْلِسي / اِجْلِسُوا! {جلس}
answers (answer)	أَجْوِبَة (جَواب) {جوب}	foreign, foreigner, alien (takes broken plural) / *(masculine / feminine pair)*	أَجْنَبِيّ (أَجانِب) / أَجْنَبِيَّة {جنب}
Conversations, talks (a conversation, a talk) * interesting conversations	أَحادِيث (حَدِيث) * أَحاديث مُشَوِّقَة {حدث}	I answer, I respond (responding, response)	أُجِيبُ (إِجابَة) {جوب}
I need, I am in need (of) (needing)	أَحْتاجُ (اِحْتِياج) (إِلَى) {حوج}	I love, I like (liking, loving) * he loved	أُحِبُّ (حُبّ) * أَحَبَّ {حبب}
one, uniquely one, anyone * eleven * one of the officials	أَحَد {وحد} * أَحَدَ عَشَرَ * أَحَد المَسْؤُولِين	celebration (of) (he celebrated)	اِحْتِفال (بِـ) {حفل} (اِحْتَفَلَ) (بِـ)
he obtained, he achieved, he won (obtaining, achieving)	أَحْرَزَ (إِحْراز) {حرز}	events (an event) *(broken plural)*	أَحْداث (حَدَث) {حدث}
he felt, he sensed (feeling)	أَحَسَّ (إِحْساس) {حسس}	belts (a belt)	أَحْزِمَة (حِزام) {حزم}
You excelled, you did excellent! *(used to complement a male, a female and a group)*	أَحْسَنْتَ / أَحْسَنْتِ / أَحْسَنْتُمْ! {حسن}	he did well, he excelled, he offered a charity (doing well, offering charity)	أَحْسَنَ (إِحْسان) {حسن}
she brought (bringing)	أَحْضَرَتْ (إِحْضار) {حضر}	I attend (attending, attendance)	أَحْضُرُ (حُضُور) {حضر}
conditions (a condition)	أَحْوال (حال) {حول}	I praise, Ahmad *(as a male proper name)* (praise, praising) * I praise God!	أَحْمَدُ (حَمْد) {حمد} * أَحْمَدُ ٱللَّه!
news (a piece of news) * news bulletin	أَخْبار (خَبَر) {خبر} * نَشْرَةُ الأَخْبار	brother (brothers) * my dear brother * your brother (accusative mood)	أَخ (إِخْوَة) {أخو} * أَخِي العَزِيز * أَخاكَ
* his sister * her sister * my dear sister	* أُخْتُهُ * أُخْتُها * أُخْتِي العَزِيزة {أخو}	sister (sisters) * two sisters	أُخْت (أَخَوات) {أخو} * أُخْتانِ

he took (taking) * he took me * I had a cold, I contracted a cold	أَخَـذَ (أَخْـذ) {أخذ} * أَخَـذَنِـي * أَخَـذَتْ بَـرد	invention / the invention (inventions) *(feminine sound plural)*	اِخْتِـراع / الإِخْتِـراع (اِخْتِـراعات) {خرع}
other, another *(masculine / feminine pair)* * for another	آخَـر / أُخْرَى {أخر} * بِـأُخْرَى	they *(feminine plural)* took (taking)	أَخَـذْنَ (أَخْـذ) {أخذ}
green color (green ones)	أَخْـضَـر (خُـضْـر) {خضر}	You come out! You go ! out! *(command verb for a male, a female and a group)*	أُخْـرُجْ / أُخْـرُجِـي / أُخْـرُجُـوا! {خرج}
my sisters (a sister)	أَخَـواتِـي (أُخْت) {أخو}	manners (a trait, a manner) / the manners, the moral traits	أَخْلاق (خُـلُـق) / الأَخْلاق {خلق}
latest / the latest * the latest elections	أَخِـيـرَة / الأَخِـيـرَة {أخر} * الاِنْتِخابات الأَخِـيـرَة	my brothers (a brother)	إِخْـوَتِـي (أَخ) {أخو}
particle, tool (particles, tools) * interrogative (question) particles	أَداة (أَدَوات) {أدو} * أَدَوات الاِسْتِفْهام	administration (administrations) * business administration	إِدارَة (إِدارات) {دير} * إِدارَة ٱلأَعْـمـال
* You enter! * You enter! *(feminine)* * You enter! *(plural)* * Please come in!	* أُدْخُـلْ! {دخل} * أُدْخُـلِـي * أُدْخُـلُـوا! * تَـفَـضَّـلْ أُدْخُـلْ!	literature (literatures) * the English literature	أَدَب (آداب) {أدب} * الأَدَب الإِنْـجِـلِـيـزِيّ
I study, I am studying (studying, study)	أَدْرُسُ (الـدِّراسَة) {درس}	* You study! *(command verb for a male, a female and a group)*	* أُدْرُسْ! {درس} * أُدْرُسِـي ! * أُدْرُسُـوا!
I study, I am studying (studying, study) * I do not know	أَدْرِي (دِرايَـة) {درس} * لا أَدْرِي	* I teach *(Form II)* (teaching)	* أُدَرِّسُ (تَدْرِيس) {درس}
If * if you *(feminine)* wanted	إِذا * إِذا أَرَدْتِ	since	إِذْ
therefore, then, in that case	إِذَن {أذن}	permission * With your permission! *(to a male / female) /* * You go with your permission! *(response to a male / female)*	إِذْن {أذن} * عَـنْ إِذْنِـكَ! / عَـنْ إِذْنِـكِ! * إِذْنُـكَ / ـكِ مَعَـكَ / ـكِ!
I review, I go back (review, reviewing)	أُراجِـعُ (مُراجَعَة) {رجع}	I go (to) *(subjunctive ending)* (going)	أَذْهَـبَ (ذَهاب) (إِلَـى) {ذهب}
she wanted (wanting, will)	أَرادَتْ (إِرادَة) {ريد}	he wanted (wanting, will) * he wanted to spend	أَرادَ (إِرادَة) {ريد}

		(time)	* أرادَ أنْ يَقْضِـيَ
I see (seeing, sight) * I see you	أَرَى (رُؤْيـا) {رأي} * أَراكَ (أَرَى+كَ)	rabbits (a rabbit) * Jew's mallow with rabbits (a dish)	أرانِب (أَرْنَـب) * مُـلُوخِيَّـة بِـالأَرانِب
forty (*nominative / accusative pair*)	أَرْبَعُونَ / أَرْبَـعِـيـنَ {ربع}	four (*masculine / feminine pair*)	أَرْبَع / أَرْبَـعَـة {ربع}
connection (to), bonding (with) (verbal noun	اِرْتِـبـاط (بِـ) {ربط}	I rest (resting)	أَرْتـاح (إِرْتِياح) {ريح}
water-pipe = Hokka	أَرْجِـيلَـة / الأَرجيلة (أَراجِـيـل) {رجل}	I hope (that) * so I hope that	أَرْجُـو (أَنْ) {رجو} * فَـأَرْجُو (أَنْ)
you wanted (to) * I wanted (to)	أَرَدْتَ (أَنْ) (إِرادَة) * أَرَدْتُ (أَنْ) {ريد}	he dated, he wrote a history, he recorded (writing a history, recording)	أَرَّخَ (تَـأْرِيـخ) {أرخ}
rice (*collective noun*)	أَرُزّ = رُزّ	* if you would want	* إذا أَرَدْتَ
I want (wanting, will) * I want (to)	أُرِيـدُ (إِرادَة) {ريد} * أُرِيدُ (أَنْ)	land, terrain, ground, floor * the Earth * the homeland	أَرْض (أَراضِـي) {أرض} * الأَرْض * أَرْضُ الوَطَن
I visit (visiting) (*verbal noun*) * I visit you	أَزُورُ (زِيـارَة) {زور} * أَزُورُكَ	luminous * the Luminous *Azhar* (*a proper name for one of the oldest universities in Egypt*)	أَزْهَـر {زهر} * الأَزْهَـر الشَّرِيف
I ask (asking, a question)	أَسْـأَلُ (سُـؤال) {سأل}	humming, buzzing, whizz (it buzzed, it hummed)	أَزِيـز (أَزَّ) {أزز}
* You ask! (*command for male and female*)	* اِسْـأَلْ ! * اِسْأَلِـي! {سأل}	questions (question)	أَسْـئِـلَـة (سُـؤال) {سأل}
foundation (foundations)	أَسـاس (أُسُس) {أسس}	professors (a professor) (*masculine broken plural*)	أَسـاتِـذَة (أُسْـتـاذ) {أستذ}
I swim (swimming)	أَسْـبَـحُ (سِـبـاحَـة) {سبح}	basic – (*masculine / feminine pair of Nisbah adjective*) (basics)	أَساسِـيّ / أَساسِـيَّـة (أَسـاسِـيَّـات) {أسس}
* one *week (used adverbially)* * by two weeks	* أُسْـبُـوعـاً واحِـداً {سبع} * بِـأُسْبُـوعَـيْـنِ	week (weeks) * days of the week	أُسْـبُـوع (أَسابِـيـع) {سبع} * أَيَّامُ الأُسْـبُـوع

a professor (professors) (*masculine singular*)	أُسْـتـاذ (أَساتِـذَة) {أستذ}	they rented (renting) * they rented a boat	اِسْـتَـأْجَـرُوا (اِسْتِئجار) {أجر} * اِسْتَأْجَرُوا مَرْكَباً
reception place, resting time (he rested) *at the reception hall	اِسْتِـراحَـة (اِسْتَـراحَ) {روح} * فـي صَـالَـةِ الاِسْـتِـقْـبـال	they rested (resting)	اِسْـتَـراحُـوا {روح} (اِسْتِـراحَة)
I can, I am capable (of)	أَسْـتَـطِـيع (أَنْ) {طوع}	he / they surrendered (surrendering)	اِسْـتَسْـلَـمَ (اِسْتِسْلام) (لِـ) {سلم}
* usage, utilization (he used, he utilized) * using, utilization of the dictionary	اِسْـتِـعْـمال (اِسْـتَـعْـمَلَ) {عمل} * اِسْـتِـعْـمال اَلْقـامُـوس	readiness (he got ready) * being ready to or for	اِسْـتِـعْـداد (اِسْـتَـعَـدَّ) {عدد} * عَلَى اسْـتِـعْـدادٍ أَنْ
reception (he received, he welcomed) *at the reception hall	اِسْـتِـقْـبال (اِسْـتَـقْـبَلَ) {قبل} * فِـي صَالَةِ الاِسْتِقْـبـال	he / they used, utilized (using, utilization)	اِسْـتَـعْـمَلَ (اِسْـتِـعْـمال) {عمل}
* he welcomed me * their reception	* اِسْـتَـقْـبَـلَـنِي * اِسْـتِـقْـبـالِـهِـم	he welcomed, he received she welcomed, she received	اِسْـتَـقْـبَـلَ {قبل} اِسْـتَـقْـبَـلَـتْ
he listened (to) (listening to)	اِسْـتَـمَـعَ (اِسْـتِـماع) (إِلَـى / لِـ) {سمع}	it (she) continued (continuity) * I did not continue	اِسْـتَـمَـرَّتْ (اِسْـتِـمْـرار) {مرر} * لَـمْ أَسْـتَـمِـرَّ
they listened (to)	اِسْـتَـمَـعُـوا (اِسْـتِـماع) (إِلَـى) {سمع}	* You listen (to)! *(command verb for male, female and plural)*	اِسْـتَـمِـعْ! (إِلَـى / لِـ) / اِسْـتَـمِـعِـي! / اِسْـتَـمِـعُـوا! {سمع}
lion (lions)	أَسَـد (أُسُـود) {أسد}	import, importing (he imported)	اِسْـتِـيراد (اِسْـتَـوْرَدَ) {ورد}
secrets (a secret)	أَسْـرار (سِـرّ) {سرر}	Israeli (Israel)	إِسْـرائِـيلِـيَّـة (إِسْـرائِيل)
our two families (a family)	* أُسْـرَتـانـا (أُسْـرَة) {أسر}	family (families) * a noble family	أُسْـرَة (أُسَـر) {أسر} * أُسْـرَة كَـرِيـمَـة

happier	أَسْعَد {سعد}	prices (a price) * with most suitable prices	أَسْعار (سِعْر) {سعر} * بِأَنْسَب الأَسْعار
* You hush! *(command verb for masculine singular, feminine singular and plural)*	* أُسْكُتْ! {سكت} * أُسْكُتِي * أُسْكُتُوا!	regret * Regretfully, being sorry!	أَسَف {أسف} * لِلأَسَف!
Islamic (*masculine / feminine pair*)	إِسْلامِيّ / إِسْلامِيَّة {سلم}	I reside, I live (living, residing, residence)	* أَسْكُنُ (سَكَن) {سكن}
name (names) * your name (*masculine / feminine*) * his name * her name	اِسْم (أَسْماء) {سمي} * اِسْمُكَ / ـكِ * اِسْمُهُ * اِسْمُها	weapons, arms	أَسْلِحَة (سِلاح) {سلح}
two nouns, two names *(dual for nominative / accusative forms)*	اِسْمانِ / اِسْمَيْنِ (اِسْم) {سمي}	name (names) * fore name * demonstrative pronouns	اِسْم (أَسْماء) {سمي} * اِسْم أَجْنَبِيّ * أَسْماء الإِشارَة
I hear (hearing, listening)	أَسْمَعُ (سَماع) {سمع}	* Definite noun * Indefinite noun * Proper names *(grammatical terms)*	* اِسْم مَعْرِفَة * اِسْم نَكِرَة {سمي} * اِسْم العَلَم
markets / the markets (a market)	أَسْواق / الأَسْواق (سُوق) {سوق}	easier * easier (than)	أَسْهَل {سهل} * أَسْهَلُ (مِنْ)
I watch, I see (watching, seeing) * I watch her	أُشاهِدُ (مُشاهَدَة) {شهد} * أُشاهِدُها	prisoner (prisoners)	أَسِير (أَسْرى) {أسر}
I drink (drinking)	أَشْرَبُ (شُرْب) {شرب}	I missed, I longed for * I missed you, I longed for you	اِشْتَقْتُ (اِشْتِياق) {شوق} * اِشْتَقْتُ لَكُم
I thank (thanking) * I thank you! *(masculine / feminine)*	أَشْكُرُ (شُكْر) {شكر} * أَشْكُرُكَ / كِ!	I feel (that) (feeling)	أَشْعُرُ (أَنَّ) (شُعُور) {شعر}
things (a thing)	أَشْياء (شَيْء) {شيأ}	their likes, their looks, their shapes, their similar ones	* أَشْكالها (شَكْل) {شكل} (أَشْكال+ ها)
she / it became * I became	أَصْبَحَتْ {صبح} * أَصْبَحْتُ	he / it became * the two of them became	أَصْبَحَ {صبح} * أَصْبَحا

she / it published (publishing)	أَصْدَرَتْ (إِصْدار) {صدر}	finger (fingers)	إِصْبَع (أَصابِع) {صبع}
more difficult * more difficult (than)	أَصْعَب {صعب} * أَصْعَبُ (مِن)	friends (a friend) (*broken plural*) * my friends	أَصْدِقاء (صَدِيق) {صدق} * أَصْدِقائِي
origin (origins)	أَصْل (أُصُول) {أصل}	younger (than), smaller (than)	أَصْغَر (مِنْ) {صغر}
a grammatical Arabic term of the juxtaposing two nouns to create a possessive relationship, equivalent to saying in English, "the student's book"	إِضافَة (الإِضافَة) {ضيف}	original (*masculine / feminine pair*)	أَصْلِيّ / أَصْلِيَّة {أصل}
Lights (a light) * the lights of the city	أَضْواء (ضَوْء) {ضوء} * أَضْواءُ الـمَدينَـة	I beat, I multiply (beating, multiplication)	أَضْرِبُ (الضَّرب) {ضرب}
babies, young children (a baby, a child)	أَطْفال (طِفْل) {طفل}	she extinguished, she put out (putting out)	أَطْفَأَتْ (إِطْفاء) {طفأ}
You seek, pursue, search for! (*command conjugation*)	أُطْلُبْ! {طلب}	releasing, setting free, firing (of a gun) (he freed, he fired)	إِطْلاق (أَطْلَقَ) {طلق}
better, more delicious (than)	أَطْيَب (مِنْ) {طيب}	longer, taller (than)	أَطْوَل (مِنْ) {طول}
I believe (that)	أَعْتَقِدُ (أَنَّ) {عقد}	I believe (that), I guess (that) * so I guess you all	أَظُنُّ (أَنَّ) {ظنن} * فَأَظُنُّكُم
preparatory = junior / the junior school * the ordinal numerals	أَعْداد (عَدَد) {عدد} * الأَعْدادُ ٱلتَّرْتيبِيَّة	she / it pleased = liked * I liked her a lot, she pleased me a lot * was pleased (with)	أَعْجَبَ {عجب} * أَعْجَبَتْنِي كَثيراً * أُعْجِبَ (بِـ)
preparatory = junior / the junior school	إِعْدادِيَّة / الإِعْدادِيَّة {عدد}	she prepared (preparation)	أَعَدَّتْ (إِعْداد) {عدد}
I know (knowledge, information) * I know you	أَعْرِفُ (مَعْرِفَة) {عرف} * أَعْرِفُكَ	showing the case endings at the end of nouns to indicate whether they are nominative, accusative or genitive (a grammatical issue not found in English)	إِعْراب (الإِعْراب) {عرب}
* I inform you (*plural*)	* أُعْلِمُكُم {علم}	single, bachelor (*masculine / feminine pair*)	أَعْزَب / عَزْباء {عزب}
I work, I do (a work, a job)	أَعْمَلُ (عَمَل) {عمل}	works, businesses (a work, a job)	أَعْمال (عَمَل) {عمل}

I work (in) (working (in)	أَعْمَلُ (فِي) (العَمَلُ فِي) {عمل}	blind (blind ones) *(broken plural)*	أَعْمَى (عُمْيان) {عمي}
I live (living)	أَعِيشُ (عَيْش) {عيش}	I return (returning)	أَعُودُ (عَوْدَة) {عود}
inauguration (he inaugurated)	اِفْتِتاح (اِفْتَتَحَ) {فتح}	* its closure, its shut down	* إِغْلاقِها (أَغْلَقَ) {غلق}
You open! *(command verb for singular male, singular female and plural)*	اِفْتَحْ! اِفْتَحِي! اِفْتَحُوا! {فتح}	I open (opening)	أَفْتَحُ (فَتْح) {فتح}
better (than)	أَفْضَل (مِنْ) {فضل}	he dumfounded, he silenced with arguments (dumfounding)	أَفْحَمَ (إِفْحام) {فحم}
Verbs, actions / the verbs, the actions (a verb, an action) * the five verbs which share two features of conjugation	أَفْعال / الأَفْعال (فِعْل) {فعل} * الأَفْعالُ الخَمْسة	breakfast, breaking the fast (he had breakfast)	إِفْطار (أَفْطَرَ) {فطر}
he made someone understand (make understanding) (Form IV)	أَفْهَمَ (إِفْهام) {فهم}	I am thinking (about) (thinking)	أُفَكِّرُ (بِـ) (تَفْكِير) {فكر}
I meet (meeting) * I meet her	أُقابِلُ (مُقابَلَة) {قبل} * أُقابِلُها	I understand (understanding)	أَفْهَمُ (فَهْم) {فهم}
fated matters (fate)	أَقْدار (قَدَر) {قدر}	I suggest (that) (suggestion)	أَقْتَرِحُ (أَنْ) (اِقْتِراح) {قرح}
You read! *(command verb for singular male, singular female and plural)*	اِقْرَأْ! / اِقْرَئِي! / اِقْرَؤُوا! {قرأ}	I offer, I present (offering)	أُقَدِّمُ (تَقْدِيم) {قدم}
departments, divisions (a department, a division) * its department, its division * parts of speech	أَقْسام (قِسْم) * أَقْسامِها {قسم} * أَقْسام الكَلِمَة	those who are near, those who are related (a relative)	أَقْرَبُونَ / الأَقْرَبُونَ (قَرِيب) {قرب}
I carry (on), I undertake (undertaking)	أَقُومُ (القِيام) (بِـ) {قوم}	less (than)	أَقَلّ (مِنْ) {قلل}
I write (writing)	أَكْتُبُ (كِتابة) {كتب}	bigger, older (than)	أَكْبَر (مِنْ)
more (than) * more democratic	أَكْثَر (مِنْ) * أَكْثَر دِيمُقْراطِيَّة	You write! *(command verb for singular male, singular female and plural)*	اُكْتُبْ! / اُكْتُبِي! / اُكْتُبُوا! {كتب}

I eat (eating)	آكُـلُ (أكْـل) {أكل}	I hate (hate, hating)	أَكْـرَهُ (كُـرْه) {كره}
I ate * My favorite meal	أَكَـلْـتُ {أكـل} * أَكْـلَـتِـي الـمُفَضَّلَة	he ate (eating)	أَكَـلَ (أكْـل) {أكل}
you completed, you finished (*feminine singular*)	أَكْـمَـلْـتِ {كمل}	* You ate (*Masculine Plural*) * They ate	* أَكَـلْـتُـمْ * أَكَـلُـوا
the (*the Arabic definite article*, which is always prefixed before nouns)	اَلْـ / الـ * (ال) الـتَّـعْـريف	I dress up, I wear clothes) (dressing up) * I wear them (clothes)	أَلْـبَـسُ (لِـبْـس) {لبس} * أَلْـبَـسُـهـا
This is a *Yaa*-shaped letter without the dots, but pronounces as the long *Alif*, and it appears only at the end of words!	* أَلِفُ مَـقْـصُـورَة = ى	is the name of this form of *Alif*, which is either a combination of two *Hamzated Alif*, or a *Hamzated Alif* and *Alif* as a long vowel	* أَلِـفُ ٱلْـمَـدِّ = آ
now	الآنَ (الـ+آنَ)	except, but	إِلاَّ
Monday	الاِثْـنَـيْـنِ	to (*preposition*) * to you (*plural*) * Until (we) meet (again)! {*idiom*}	إِلَـى * إِلَـيْـكُـمْ * إِلَـى الـلِّـقـاء! {لقي}
Wednesday	الأَرْبِـعَـاء	Sunday	الأَحَـد
Al-Azhar (*a proper name for the oldest university in Egypt*)	الأَزْهَـر	Jordan (*an Arab country masculine*)	الأُرْدُنّ
the proverbs, the wise-saying (a proverb)	الأَمْـثـال (مَـثَـل) {مثل}	Alexandria (a coastal city *in Egypt*)	الإِسْـكَـنْـدَرِيَّـة
I enrolled, I joined (in) (enrolment, joining)	اِلْـتَـحَـقْـتُ (بِـ) (اِلْـتِـحاق) {لحق}	I enroll, I join (in) (enrolment, joining)	أَلْـتَـحِـقُ (بِـ) (اِلْـتِـحاق) {لحق}
Tuesday	الـثُّـلاثـاء	he met (with) (meeting with)	اِلْـتَـقَـى (بِـ) (اِلْـتِـقـاء) {لقي}
Friday	الـجُـمُـعَـة	Algeria	الـجَـزائِـر
Khartoum (*capital of Sudan*)	الـخَـرْطُـوم	(the) praise * The Praise belongs to God!	الـحَـمْـد * الـحَـمْـدُ لِـلَّـه!
Rabat (*capital of Morocco*)	الـرِّبـاط	Thursday	الـخَـمِـيس
Saturday	الـسَّـبْـت	Riyadh (*capital of Saudi Arabia*)	الـرِّيـاض
Sudan (*masculine*)	الـسُّودان	Saudi Arabia	الـسَّـعُـودِيَّـة
Iraq (*masculine*)	الـعِـراق	the Middle East	الـشَّـرْق ٱلأَوْسَـط

Kuwait	الـكُـوَيْـت	Cairo	الـقـاهِـرَة
(she) who (*relative pronoun*)	الَّـتـي	but, except	إلاَّ
(those) who (*plural relative pronoun*)	الَّذِينَ	(he) who (*relative pronoun*)	الَّـذي
thousand (thousands) / two thousands	أَلْـف (آلاف) / أَلْـفـانِ	I play, I am playing (play, playing)	أَلْـعَـبُ (لَعِب) {لعب}
honorific titles nick names (an honorific title, a nick name)	أَلْـقـاب (لَـقَـب) {لقب}	vocabulary, utterances (a word, an utterance * multiples of tens words	أَلْـفاظ (لَـفْـظ) {لفظ} * أَلْـفاظ الـعُـقُـود
* Is not…? = Is not…? * Isn't that so?	* أَلَـيْـسَ؟ (أ+لَـيْسَ) * أَلَـيْـسَ كَـذَلِـكَ؟	God = The One God * to God * Praise be to God!	الـلَّـهُ * لِـلَّـهِ (لِـ+الله) * اَلْـحَـمْـدُ لِـلَّـه!
or (*used as related to the English either… or*)	أَمْ	Morocco	الـمَـغْـرِب {غرب}
* As for… (it/he/she)	* أَمَّا ... فَـ	mother (mothers)	أُمّ (أُمَّـهـات) {امم}
religious leader (leaders)	إِمامَ (أَئِـمَّـة) {أمم}	in front of (*adverb & preposition*)	أَمـامَ {أمم}
matter, affair (matters, affairs)	أَمْـر (أُمُـور) {أمر}	exam, test (tests, exams) * for the grammar test	إِمْتِحان (إِمْتِحانات) {محن} * لِامْـتِـحـان القَواعِد
America	أَمْـريكـا	a woman / the woman (women) * Note that the plural is not related in root to the singular	اِمْـرَأَة / الْـمَـرْأَة} {مرأ} * (نِساء) {نسو}
yesterday	أَمْـس {مسي}	American (*masculine / feminine pair*)	أَمْـريـكِـيّ / أَمْـريـكِـيَّـة
security-related (*masculine / feminine pair*)	أَمْـنِـيّ / أَمْـنِـيَّـة {أمن}	security / the security * The Security officer	أَمْـن / الأَمْـن {أمن} * ضـابِـطُ الأَمْـن
I am inclined (to), (inclination towards)	أَمِـيلُ (إِلَـى) (الـمَيْلُ إِلَـى) {ميل}	prince (princes)	أَمِـيـر (أُمَـراء) {أمر}
trustworthy (trustworthy ones)	أَمِـيـن (أُمَـنـاء) {أمن}	Amin! (in Arabic, it means, "May God answer the prayer!"	آمِـيـن! {أمن}
if (*conditional particle*) * If God so wills!	إِنْ * إِنْ شـاءَ ٱلـلـهُ!	that, to (*subjunctive particle*)	أَنْ
that * that you * that I	أَنَّ * أَنَّـكَ * أَنَّـنِـي	I	أَنـا
you (*masculine singular*)	أَنْـتَ	verily, surely, indeed (*particle of emphasis*)	إِنَّ
elections (election)	اِنْـتِـخـابـات (اِنْتِخاب) {نخب}	you (*feminine singular*)	أَنْـتِ

moving, transferring (*verbal noun*) (he moved, he transferred)	اِنْـتِـقـال (اِنْـتَـقَـلَ) {نقل}	waiting (he waited) * on the waiting for you, awaiting for you	اِنْـتِـظـار (اِنْـتَـظَـرَ) {نظر} * بِـاْنْـتِـظـارِكَ
you (*masculine plural*)	أَنْـتُـمْ	she moved, she transferred	اِنْـتَـقَـلَـتْ (إِلَـى) {نقل}
finishing, coming to an end * after finishing from	اِنْـتِـهـاء (اِنْـتَـهَـى) {نهي} * بَـعْـدَ اْلاِنْـتِـهـاء مِنْ	you (*feminine plural*)	أَنْـتُـنَّ
English (*masculine-feminine pair; notice the two ways of writing*)	إِنْـجِـلِـيـزِيّ (إِنْكِليزِيّ) إِنْجِلِيزِيَّة (إِنْـكِـلِـيزِيَّة)	she begot, she gave birth to (giving birth to)	أَنْـجَـبَـتْ (إِنْـجـاب) {نجب}
man, mankind, human being (*masculine / feminine pair*) * human rights	إِنْـسـان / إِنْسانَـة {أنس} *حُـقُـوق اْلإِنْـسان	sections, directions, sides	أَنْحاء {نحو}
You look! (to a *female) * You look at ...!	* أُنْـظُـرِي! {نظر} * أُنْـظُـرِي إِلَـى ...!	Miss, young lady	آنِـسَـة / الآنِسَة – ات {أنس}
types, varieties (a type, a variety*)*	أَنْـواع (نَـوْع) {نوع}	he completed, he finished (completion, finishing)	أَنْـهَـى (إِنْـهـاء) {نهي}
Is this ...?	أَهَـذا ...؟ (أَ+هَـذا)	neat, tidy, well-dressed (*masculine / feminine pair*)	أَنِـيـق / أَنِـيقَـة {أنق}
Hello! * Welcome! *(idiom)*	أَهْـلاً! * أَهْـلاً وَسَـهْـلاً !	family, relatives * My family	أَهْـل * أَهْـلِـي {أهل}
* Welcome to you! {*masculine / feminine)* * Welcome to you! *(plural)*	* أَهْـلاً بِـكَ! / بِـكِ * أَهْـلاً بِـكُـمْ!	two hellos (*colloquial for returning a warmer greeting*)	أَهْـلَـيْـن!
or	أَوْ	more important (important)	أَهَـمّ (مُـهِـمّ)
middle / the middle * the Middle East	أَوْسَـط / الأَوْسَـط {وسط} * الشَّـرْق الأَوْسَـط	Europe European (*male/female pair*)	أُورُوبّـا أُورُوبِّـيّ / أُورُوبِّـيَّـة
first / the first * the first (*feminine*) * firstly * first and last	أَوَّل / الأَوَّل {أول} * الأُولَـى * أَوَّلاً * أَوَّلاً وَأَخِـيـراً	he advised, he recommended (advice, recommendation) * she advised me (to)	أَوْصَـى (تَـوْصِـيَـة) {وصي} * أَوْصَـتْـنِـي (بِـ)
boys, children (boy, child)	أَوْلاد (وَلَـد) {ولد}	more deserving, have more right, have priority	أَوْلَـى {ولي}

Which? *(interrogative noun which can end with one of the three short vowels, depending on the context)*	أَيٌّ / أَيَّ / أَيٍّ	which means, that's to say, in other words *(explanatory particle)*	أَيْ
* days of the week * these days	* أَيَّـامُ ٱلأُسْـبُـوع * هَـذِهِ الأَيَّـام	days (a day) * today, the day	أَيَّـام (يَـوْم) {يوم} * الـيَـوْم
export, exporting	إِيْـراد {ورد}	O you! *(calling particle for defined feminine plural)*	أَيَّـتُـها
Where...? *(interrogative particle)* * So where ...? * Where from...?	أَيْـنَ...؟ * فَـأَيْـنَ...؟ / * مِنْ أَيْـنَ...؟	also, likewise	أَيْـضاً {أيض}
		O you! *(calling particle for definite masculine plural)*	أَيُّـها

* in the name (of) * in the name of God	بِـاْسْمِ = بِـسْـمِ * بِـسْـمِ ٱللَّـهِ	in, by, of, with, for *(preposition always written as part of the following noun)*	بِـ
* with their visit, by their visit	* بِـزِيـارَتِـهِـم {زور} (بِـ + زِيـارَةِ + ـهِـم)	* fine, good (Lit., in a state of well being *{idiom}*)	* بِـخَـيْـر (بِـ + خَـيْـر)
* for the purpose	* بِـغَـرَضِ {غرض} (بِـ + غَـرَض)	* safely, with safety, in safety	* بِـٱلسَّـلامَـةِ {سلم} (بِـ + السَّـلامَـة)
* of charity, of good deed	* بِـٱلـمَـعْـرُوف {عرف} (بِـ + الْـمَـعْـرُوف)	* by car	* بِـٱلـسَّـيَّـارَة {سير} (بِـ + الـسَّـيَّـارَة)
* with mint * tea with mint (a common favorite drink)	* بِـٱلـنَّـعْـنـاع {نعنع} * شـاي بِـٱلنَّعْناع	* by the way	* بِـٱلـمُـنـاسَـبَـةِ {نسب} (بِـ + الـمُـنـاسَـبَـة)
* as a result, because	* بِـسَـبَـب {سبب} (بِـ + سَـبَـب)	* May it be agreeable and healthy!	* بِـٱلـهَـنـاء وَٱلـشِّـفـاء {هنئ} {شفي}
* by meeting you	* بِـلِـقـائِـكَ {لقي} (بِـ + لِقاء + ـكَ)	* by a little	* بِـقَـلِـيـل {قلل} (بِـ + قَـلِـيـل)
* of my marriage day	* بِـيَـوْمِ زَواجِـي {يوم} (بِـ + يَـوْم)	* with calmness = calmly	* بِـهُـدُوء {هدأ} (بِـ + هُـدُوء)

harm, worry * Don't you worry! You take it easy!	بَأْس * لا بَأْسَ عَلَيْكَ!	he came back, he returned (coming back, returning)	باءَ (بَوْء) {بوء}
door (doors)	باب (أَبْواب) {بوب}	seller / the seller *(takes masculine sound plural)*	بائِع / البائِع (بائِعين) {بيع}
he spent the night (spending the night)	باتَ (بَيات) {بيب}	dad *(baby language)*	بابا {أب}
a researcher, a seeker (he researched)	باحِث (بَحَثَ) {بحث}	it became known, he divulged (divulged, becoming known)	باحَ (بَوْح) {بوح}
cold *(masculine / feminine adjective)*	بارِد / بارِدَة {برد}	it perished, it became extinct	بادَتْ {بيد}
* May God bless you! (Said as a response to مَبْرُوك!)	* بارَكَ اللّهُ فِيكَ! {برك}	skillful, proficient *(masculine / feminine adjective)*	بارِع / بارِعة {برع}
he sold (selling)	باعَ (بَيْع) {بيع}	falcon (falcons)	باز (أَبْواز) {بوز}
remainder, rest (the remainder, the rest) * the rest is on me	باقِي / الباقِي {بقي} * الباقِي عَلَيّ	it laid eggs *(said of birds)*	باضَتْ {بيض}
mind, state of awareness	بال / البال {بيل}	Pakistan Pakistani *(male / female pair)*	باكِسْتان باكِسْتانِيّ / باكِسْتانِيَّة
he cut off, he severed	بَتَرَ (بَتْر) {بتر}	well (wells) *(of water or oil)*	بِئْر (آبار) {بئر}
he spread, he scattered, he disseminated	بَثَّ (بَثّ) {بثث}	he cut off, he achieved, he decided	بَتَّ (بَتّات) {بتت}
in need (of)	بِحاجَة (إِلَى)	pimples, pustules (a pimple, a pustule)	بُثُور (بَثْر) {بثر}
search, research *(takes broken plural)*	بَحْث (أَبْحاث) {بحث}	he searched (for), * researching for	بَحَثَ (عَنْ) {بحث} * البَحْثُ عَن
vapor, fume (vapor, fumes) *(broken plural)*	بُخار (أَبْخِرَة) {بخر}	sea (seas) *(takes two patterns of broken plural)*	بَحْر (بُحُور، بِحار) {بحر}
way out, escape * it is a must *(to be learned as an idiom)*	بُدّ * لا بُدَّ أَنْ	* in a state of wellbeing, fine, well	* بِخَيْر (خَيْرات) {خير}
I began, I started (beginning)	بَدَأْتُ (بِدايَة) {بدأ}	he began, he started (beginning) * he began the work	بَدَأَ (بِدايَة) {بدأ} * بَدَأَ العَمَلَ

a start, a beginning (beginnings) *(takes feminine sound plural)*	بِـدايـة (بِدايات) {بدأ}	she began (beginning) * you *(feminine plural)* began	بَدَأَتْ (بِدايَـة) {بدأ} * بَـدَأْتُـنَّ
suit (suits) / the suits	بَـدْلَـة (بِـدَل) / الـبِـدَل {بدل}	full moon (full moons)	بَـدْر (بُـدُور) {بدر}
seeds (a seed)	بُـذُور (بِـذْرَة) {بذر}	he surpassed, he beated (surpassing)	بَـذَّ (بَـذّ) {بذذ}
a blessing (blessings) * Go with God's Blessings!	بَـرَكَـة (بَـرَكَـات) {برك} * عَـلى بَرَكَـةِ ٱلـلّـه!	cold (noun)	بَـرْد {برد}
program, schedule *(takes broken plural)*	بَـرْنـامَج (بَـرامِـج) {برمج}	* his blessings (a blessing)	* بَـرَكـاتُـهُ (بَـرَكَـة) (بَرَكاتُ+ـهُ) {برك}
he announced good news (announcing good news)	بَـشَّـرَ (تَبْشِـيـر) {بشر}	he defeated, he outstripped (defeating, outstripping)	بَـزَّ (بَـزّ) {بزز}
nions *(collective noun)* (an onion)	بَـصَـل (بَصَلَة) {بصل}	a good piece of news *(takes feminine sound plural)*	بُـشْـرى (بُشْرَيات) {بشر}
merchandise *(takes broken plural)*	بِـضـاعَـة (بَـضـائِـع) {بضع}	acutely aware, having insight *(masculine / feminine adjective)*	بَـصِـيـر / بَـصِـيـرَة {بصر}
potatoes *(collective noun)*	بَـطـاطـا {بطط}	ducks *(collective noun)* (a duck)	بَـطّ (بَـطَّـة) {بطط}
he became vainly proud (vainly pride)	بَـطَـرَ (بَـطَـر) {بطر}	card (cards) * my card	بِـطـاقَـة (بِـطـاقـات) {بطق} * بِـطـاقَـتِـي
watermelon *(collective noun)* (a watermelon)	بَـطِّـيخ (بَـطِّـيـخَـة) {بطخ}	slow *(masculine / feminine adjective)*	بَـطِـيء / بَطِيئَـة {بطء}
yet, as yet *(adverb)*	بَـعْـدُ	after * after that, afterwards, later *{idiom}* * after he obtained	بَـعْـدَ * بَـعْـدَ ذَلِـكَ * بَـعْـدَ أَنْ حَـصَـلَ
distant, far (from) / *(feminine-masculine pair)*	بَـعِـيـدَة / بَـعِـيـد (مِنْ) / (عَنْ) {بعد}	some * some of them	بَـعْـض * بَـعْـضُـهُـمْ (بَـعْـضُ+ـهُـم)
hateful, odious *(masculine / feminine adjective)*	بَـغِـيـض / بَـغِـيـضَـة	Baghdad *(capital of Iraq)*	بَـغْـداد
to you *(masculine & feminine singular)*, to you *(plural)* * Welcome to you all!	بِـكَ / بِـكِ (بِـ+ـكَ / ـكِ) بِـكُـمْ (بِـ+كُـمْ) * أَهْـلاً بِـكُـمْ!	remaining, staying *(masculine / feminine adjective)*	بَـقـاء / الـبَـقـاء

without	بِلا (بِـ + لا)	Bachelor (Degree) The Bachelor Degree	بَكالُوريُوس / البَكالُوريُوس
country (*broken plural*) * their country	بَلَد (بِلاد) * بَلَدِهِمْ	countries (*broken plural*) (a country) * his country * her country * my country	بِلاد (بَلَد) * بَلَدِه * بَلَدِها * بَلَدِي
* pullover *(adopted colloquially from English)*	* بِلوفَر (بِلُوفَرات)	dates *(collective noun)* (a single date)	بَلَح (بَلَحَة) {بلح}
with us * Let us go! (*idiom*)	بِنا (بِـ + نا) * هَيَّا بِنا!	for knowing you *(masculine / feminine pair)*	بِمَعْرِفَتِكَ / ـكِ {عرف} (بِـ+مَعْرِفَة+ـكَ / ـكِ)
girl, daughter (girls, daughters) * to your *(both of you)* daughter	بِنْت (بَنات) * لِبِنْتِكُما	a building (buildings) / the building	بِناء (أَبْنِيَة) / البِناء {بني}
* pants *(adopted colloquially from Spanish)* * jeans pants	*بَنْطَلُون (بَنْطَلُونات) * بَنْطَلُون جِينْز	gasoline	بَنْزِين {بنزن}
glad, happy, wonderful (*masculine / feminine pair*)	بَهِيج / بَهِيجَة {بهج}	bank (*broken plural*) (*borrowed from English*)	بَنْك (بُنُوك) {بنك}
house (*broken plural*) * their house * to (the) house (of)	بَيْت (بُيُوت) * بَيْتِهِمْ * لِبَيْتِ	door-man, door keeper	بَوّاب (بَوّابِين) {بوب}
Beirut (*capital of Lebanon*)	بَيْرُوت	desert (deserts) (*broken plural*)	بَيْداء (بِيد) {بيد}
white color (*feminine form / masculine form*)	بَيْضاء / أَبْيَض	eggs (*collective noun*) (an egg)	بَيْض (بَيْضَة)
a seller, a shop keeper (sellers, shop keepers)	بَيّاع (بَيّاعُونَ) {بيع}	selling (he sold / he sells	بَيْع (باعَ / يَبِيعُ) {بيع}
between both of them *(dual attached pronoun)*	* بَيْنَهُما (بَيْنَ+ـهُما)	between * between me * and from among	بَيْنَ * بَيْنِي (بَيْنَ+ـي) * وَمِنْ بَيْن
		while, meanwhile	بَيْنَما

suffixed to perfect stem verbs for "you" (*masculine*), "you" (*feminine*) and "I"	ـتَ / ـتِ / ـتُ	prefixed to an imperfect stem verbs for "she" and "you", plus all 2nd persons	تَـ / تُـ
to postpone (you) * Don't postpone!	تُـؤَجِّـلْ {أجل} * لا تُـؤَجِّـلْ!	*Taa' Marbūṭah (a special character that appears only at the end of nouns, and is mostly to indicate feminine gender)*	* تـاء مَرْبُـوطَـة = ة / ـة
you (*feminine*) take me	* تَـأْخُـذِيـنِـي {أخذ} (تَـأْخُـذِي + نِـي)	you take, she takes (taking) * you take (*feminine singular*)	تَـأْخُـذُ (أَخْـذ) {أخذ} * تَـأْخُـذِي
* the entry visa * study visa * emigration visa	* تَأْشِيـرَة الدُّخُول * تَأْشِيـرَة دِراسَة تَـأْشِيـرَة هِجْرَة	visa (visas)	تَـأْشِيـرَة (تَـأْشِيـرات) {أشر}
you command, she commands (commanding, ordering)	تَـأْمُـرُ (أَمْـر) {أمر}	you eat, you are eating (*feminine singular*) (eating)	تَـأْكُـلِـيـنَ (أَكْـل) {أكل}
he repented (repentance)	تـابَ (تَـوْبَـة) {توب}	being patient, being careful	تَـأَنِّـي / الـتَّـأَنِّـي {أنـي}
I pursued, I followed up (pursuing, following up)	تـابَـعْـتُ (مُـتـابَـعَـة) {تبع}	follower (followers) (*takes masculine sound plural*)	تـابِـع (تـابِـعُـونَ) {تبع}
merchant (*broken plural*) * a whole-sale merchant * a well-known merchant	تـاجِـر (تُـجَّـار) {تجر} * تـاجِـر جُـمْـلَـة * تـاجِـر مَـعْـرُوف	crown (crowns) (*broken plural*)	تـاج (تِـيـجـان) {توج}
ninth / the ninth ninthly	تـاسِع / الـتَّـاسِـع / تـاسِـعـاً {تسع}	history / the history * The Ancient Egyptian History	تـاريخ / الـتَّـارِيخ {أرخ} * الـتَّاريخ الـمِصْرِيّ القَديـم
next, following / the next, the following	تـالِـي / الـتَّـالِـي {تلو}	* By God! (*the prefixed Taa' is an oath particle*)	* تَـأَلـلَّـهِ ! (تَـ+الـلَّـه)
there remains (remaining) * so there remains	تَـبْـقَـى (بَقاء) {بقي} * فَـتَـبْـقَـى	it ((*non-human*) begins	تَـبْـدَأُ (بَـدْء) {بقي}
it (*non-human*) consist (of)	تَـتَـكَـوَّنُ (مِنْ) (تَـكَـوُّن) {كون}	you (*feminine singular*) speak	تَـتَـكَـلَّـمِـيـنَ (تَـكَـلُّم) {كلم}

trade, trading, business (he traded, he did business) * the private business, the free trade	تِجارَة (تاجَر) {تجر} * التِّجارَة ٱلحُرَّة	you take up (food), you deal with (subject) (taking up, dealing with)	تَتَناوَلُ (تَناوُل) {نول}
* we moved around (moving around) * they moved around among	* تَجَوَّلْنا (تَجَوُّل) (تَجَوَّلَ+نا) {جول} * تَجَوَّلُوا بَيْنَ	you try, you are trying (try, experimentation)	تُجَرِّبُ (تَجْرِبَة) {جرب}
under, beneath	تَحْتَ {تحت}	you like , you love (*masculine / feminine pair*) * you would like to drink	تُحِبُّ / تُحِبِّينَ {حبب} * تُحِبُّ أَنْ تَشْرَب
it *(non-human)* contains	تَحْتَوي (على) (احْتِواء) {حوي}	you need (needing) (*second person feminine singular*)	تَحْتاجِينَ (احْتِياج) {حوج}
antique gifts (an antique gift) * with antique gifts * Pharaonic antique gifts	تُحَف (تُحْفَة) {تحف} * بِالتُّحَف * التُّحَف الفِرعَوْنِيَّة	you attend , you come (to) (*masculine / feminine pair*)	تَحْضُرُ / تَحْضُرِينَ (إِلَى) {حضر}
I graduated (from) (graduation (from))	تَخَرَّجْتُ (تَخَرُّج) (مِن) {خرج}	greetings (a greeting) * A pleasant greeting!	تَحِيَّات (تَحِيَّة) {حيي} * تَحِيَّةً طَيِّبَةً!
* graduation (from) * his graduation	* التَّخَرُّج (مِنْ) {خرج} * تَخَرُّجِهِ	* their graduation *(referring to two)*	* تَخَرُّجِهِما {خرج} (تَخَرُّج + هِما)
price-reduction sale *(takes feminine sound plural)* * big price-reduction sale	تَخْفِيض {خفض} (تَخْفِيضات) * تَخْفِيض كَبِير	I specialized, I majored (in) (majoring in) * your specialization	تَخَصَّصْتُ {خصص} (تَخَصُّص) (في) * تَخَصُّصِكِ
you study (*second person feminine singular*)	تَدْرُسِينَ (دِراسَة) {درس}	you study, she studies (studying)	تَدْرُس (دِراسَة) {درس}
you realize (*second person feminine singular conjugation)*	تُدْرِكِينَ (إِدْراك) {درك}	teaching, instruction (he taught)	تَدْرِيس (دَرَّسَ) {درس}
she goes, you *(masculine singular)* go (going)	تَذْهَبُ (ذَهاب) {ذهب}	it reminds me (of) (reminder)	تُذَكِّرُني (بِـ) (تَذْكِير) {ذكر}

synonymy (it became synonymous)	تَرادُف (تَرادَفَ) {ردف}	soil, , dust, earth (soils)	تُراب (أَتْرِبَة) {ترب}
arrangement, arranging (he arranged)	تَرْتيب (رَتَّبَ) {رتب}	Structures (a structure) * linguistic structures	تَراكِيب (تَرْكِيب) {ركب} * تَراكِيب لُغَوِيَّة
translation (he translated)	تَرْجَمَة (تَرْجَمَ) {ترجم}	* arranging for the meeting * arranging for the fated things	* تَرْتِيب ٱللِّقاء * تَرْتِيب ٱلأَقْدار
you (feminine singular) welcome (welcoming)	تُرَحِّبِينَ (تَرْحِيب) {رحب}	you (feminine plural) welcome (welcoming)	تُرَحِّبْنَ (تَرْحِيب) {رحب}
Turkey Turkish (masculine/feminine pair)	تُرْكِيا تُرْكِيّ / تُرْكِيَّة	he left, he departed (leaving, departing)	تَرَكَ (تَرْك) {ترك}
lupine / the lupine	تُرْمُس / التُّرْمُس	focusing, concentration / the focusing * focusing (on), concentration (on)	تَرْكِيز / التَّرْكِيز * التَّرْكِيزُ (عَلَى) {ركز}
you (feminine singular) want (wanting) * that which you want	تُرِيدِينَ (إرادة) {ريد} * ما تُرِيدِينَ	you (masculine. Singular) want (to) (wanting)	تُرِيدُ (أَنْ) {ريد} (إرادَة)
it / she ceases * does not cease = continue to be, still	تَزالُ {زول} * لا تَزالُ	* you (masculine plural) want (to)	* تُرِيدُونَ (أَنْ)
she utters shrills of joy (done be Arab women only)	تُزَغْرِدُ (زَغْرَدَة) {زغرد}	she / it increases (increasing)	تَزْدادُ (ازْدِياد) {زيد}
you visit (masculine singular), she visits (visiting, a visit)	تَزُورُ (زِيارَة) {زور}	he married / she married / they (both) married	تَزَوَّجَ / تَزَوَّجَتْ / تَزَوَّجا {زوج}
you ask (masculine singular), she asks (inquiry)	تَسْأَلُ (تَساؤُل) {سأل}	supplying you, providing you * supplying you with what you want	* تَزْوِيدَكَ (زَوَّدَ) (تَزْوِيد+كَ) {زود} * تَزْوِيدُكَ بِما تُرِيدُ
you forgive me (feminine singular) (tolerance, forgiveness)	تُسامِحِينِي (تَسامُح) {سمح}	you forgive (masculine plural) (tolerance, forgiveness)	تُسامِحُونَ (تَسامُح) {سمح}
nine (masculine / feminine pair)	تِسْع / تِسْعَة {تسع}	you can, you are able (to) (masculine singular), she can, she is able (to)	تَسْتَطِيعُ (أَنْ) {طوع}
you live (masculine singular), she lives	تَسْكُنُ (سَكَن) {سكن}	ninety (nominative / accusative pair)	تِسْعُونَ / تِسْعِينَ {تسع}

you hear *(masculine singular)* me	* تَسْمَعَنِي {سمع} (تَسْمَعَ + نِي)	you live, you reside *(second person feminine singular)*	تَسْكُنِينَ (سَكَن) {سكن}
you *(masculine singular)* drink, she drinks (drinking)	تَشْرَبُ (شُرْب) {شرب}	pessimism / the state of pessimism	تَشاؤُم / التَّشاؤُم {شئم}
* I am (have already been) honored! * We are honored!	* تَشَرَّفْتُ! {شرف} * تَشَرَّفْنا!	you *(plural)* drink *(jussive & subjunctive mood)*	تَشْرَبُوا (شُرْب) {شرب}
exporting / the export (he exported)	تَصْدِير / التَّصْدِير (صَدَّرَ) {صدر}	she / it see it * must the eye see it *(colloquial idiom)*	* تِشُوفُه * لازِم تِشُوفُه العَيْن
she describes (description)	تَصِفُ (وَصْف) {وصف}	conjugation (of verbs) he conjugated * Verbs conjugation	تَصْرِيف / تَصْرِيفاً (صَرَّفَ) {صرف} * تَصْرِيفُ الأَفْعال
antonymous	تَضاد {ضدد}	it / she claps, it / she applauds (clapping, applauding)	تُصَفِّقُ (تَصْفِيق) {صفق}
you light up, you kindle (kindling, lighting up)	تُضِيء (إضاءَة) {ضوء}	solidarity, support * in solidarity with	تَضامُن (تَضامَنَ) مَعَ {ضمن} * بِالتَّضامُنِ مَعَ
she / it overlooks (on)	تُطِلُّ (إطْلال) (عَلى) {طلل}	you to be obeyed *(passive voice)*	تُطاع (إطاعَة) {طوع}
they (both) got acquainted (getting acquainted) * getting to know her	تَعارَفا (تَعارُف) {عرف} * التَّعَرُّفُ عَلَيْها	getting acquainted, getting to know each other (they got acquainted)	تَعارُف (تَعارَفَ) {عرف}
dealing (they dealt with each other)	تَعامُل (تَعامَلَ) (مَعَ) {عمل}	You come here! *(command verb for masculine singular, feminine singular and plural)*	تَعالَ / تَعالَيْ / تَعالَوا {علو}
tired, exhausted *(masculine / feminine adjectives)*	تَعْبان / تَعْبانَة {تعب}	cooperation (with), he cooperated (with)	تَعاوُن (تَعاوَنَ) (مَعَ) {عون}
is considered (consideration) *(passive voice verb)*	تُعْتَبَرُ (اِعْتِبار) {عبر}	expression, composition (he expressed	تَعْبِير (عَبَّرَ) {عبر}

exposure (to) (he exposed (to)	تَعَرُّض (تَعَرَّضَ) (لِـ) {عرض}	I wondered (wondering)	تَعَجَّبْتُ (تَعَجُّب) {عجب}
he got acquainted (with) (getting acquainted) * getting to know you	تَعَرَّفَ (عَلَى) {عرف} (تَعارُف) * التَّعَرُّفُ عَلَيْكَ	she / you *(masculine singular)* know (knowledge)	تَعْرِفُ (مَعْرِفَة) {عرف}
* I got acquainted with him * getting to know her	* تَعَرَّفْتُ عَلَيْهِ * التَّعَرُّف عَلَيْها	I got acquainted (with)	تَعَرَّفْتُ (تَعَرُّف) (عَلَى) {عرف}
he learned you learned *(masculine / feminine singular)*	تَعَلَّمَ (تَعَلُّم) {علم} تَعَلَّمْتَ / تَعَلَّمْتِ	defining (verbal noun) * making a noun definite by adding the definite article	تَعرِيف {عرف} * التَّعْرِيف بِأل
you learned *(masculine plural)*	تَعْلَمُونَ (عِلْم) {علم}	I learned (learning)	تَعَلَّمْتُ (تَعَلُّم) {علم}
she works, you work *(masculine singular)* * you work *(feminine singular)*	تَعْمَلُ (عَمَل) {عمل} * تَعْمَلِينَ	educational (*masculine/feminine pair*) * educational games	تَعْليميّ / تَعْليميّة {علم} * الألعاب ٱلتَّعْلِيمِيَّة
you *(feminine singular)* have changed (changing)	تَغَيَّرْتِ (تَغَيُّر) {غير}	she returns, you return (*Masculine./Singular*) (returning)	تَعُودُ (عَوْدَة) {عود}
you open (*Mas./ Sing.*), she opens * that you open your heart for me	تَفْتَحُ (فَتْح) {فتح} * أَنْ تَفْتَحَ لِي قَلْبَكَ	an apple (apples)	تُفّاحَة (تُفّاح) {تفح}
* Kindly, you come with me!	* تَفَضَّلْ مَعِي! {فضل}	Kindly have! Kindly come in! Kindly take! *(Polite request (command) verb for masculine singular, feminine singular and plural)*	تَفَضَّلْ! / تَفَضَّلِي! / تَفَضَّلُوا! {فضل}
you do *(feminine singular)* (doing, action)	تَفْعَلِينَ (فِعْل) {فعل}	you do *(masculine singular)* (doing, action)	تَفْعَلُ (فِعْل) {فعل}
she thinks about, you think about *(masculine singular)* (thinking)	تُفَكِّر (في) (تَفْكِير) {فكر}	you do (*masculine plural*) (doing, action)	تَفْعَلُونَ (فِعْل) {فعل}
she, you understand (understanding)	تَفْهَمُ (فَهْم) {فهم}	you think (about) *(feminine singular)* (thinking)	تُفَكِّرِينَ (بِـ) (تَفْكِير) {فكر}
he / they met (meeting)	تَقابَلَ (تَقابُل)	distinction (he was superior, he achieved	تَفَوُّق (تَفَوَّقَ)

(meeting each other)	{قبل}	distinction) * with distinction, with honors	{فوق} * بِـتَـفَـوُّق
she / you accept (acceptance) *(meeting each other)*	تَـقْـبَـلُ (قُـبُـول) {قبل}	they (females) met (meeting) *(meeting each other)*	تَـقـابَـلَـتْ (تَـقـابُـل) {قبل}
progressiveness (he progressed)	تَـقَـدُّمِـيَّـة (تَـقَـدَّمَ) {قدم}	he approached (for) (approaching (for)	تَـقَـدَّمَ (لِـ) (الـتَّـقَـدُّم) {قدم}
nearly, approximately	تَـقْـرِيـبـاً {قرب}	offering, introducing *(verbal noun)* (he offered, he introduced)	تَـقْـدِيـم (قَـدَّمَ) {قدم}
they (birds) flock, gather around, it is located	تَـقَـعُ (عَلَى) (وُقُـوع) {وقع}	his report	تَـقْـرِيـرِه (تَـقْـرِيـر+ه) {قرر}
you write *(Masculine Plural)*	تَـكْـتُـبُـونَ (كِـتـابَـة) {كتب}	she writes, you *(Masculine Singular* write	تَـكْـتُـبُ (كِـتـابَة) {كتب}
to be *(jussive form)* * she / you was not, were not	تَـكُـنْ {كون} * لَـمْ تَـكُـنْ	he spoke (speaking) * they spoke	تَـكَـلَّـمَ (كَـلام) {كلم} * تَـكَـلَّـمُـوا
you wear, you dress in *(masculine singular)* she wears, she dresses in	تَـلْـبَـسُ (لِـبْـس) {لبس}	to be (*You Masculine* Singular) to be (*She*) *(indicative mood)*	تَـكُـونُ {كون}
you enroll (in) *(masculine singular)*, she enrolls (in)	تَـلْـتَـحِقُ (الْـتِـحاق) (بِـ) {لحق}	responding positively, compliance (he responded positively) * responding positively to our request	تَـلْـبِـيَـة (لَـبَّـى) * تَـلْـبِـيَـة طَـلَـبِـنـا
that *(feminine. demonstrative pronoun)*	تِـلْـكَ	you curse *(masculine singular)* (cursing)	تَـلْـعَنَ (لَـعْـنَـة) {لعن}
took place, was concluded (conclusion)	تَـمَّ (تَـمـام) {تـمم}	telephone (telephones) *(adopted from English)*	تِـلِـيـفُـون (تِلِيفونات) {تلفن}
exercises, drills (an exercise, a drill) * general drills	تَـمـارِيـن (تَـمْـرِيـن) {مرن} * تَـمـارِيـن عـامَّـة	you practice, you exercise *(masculine plural)*	تُـمـارِسُـونَ (مُـمـارَسَـة) {مرس}
it / she represents (representation) * they *(dual feminine)* represent	تُـمَـثِّـلُ (تَـمْـثِـيـل) * تُـمَـثِّـلانِ (مثل)	All right! Perfect! * exactly, perfectly	تَـمـام! {تـمم} * تَـمـامـاً

we had, we took *(food or drink)*, we dealt with *(subject)*	تَـنـاوَلْـنـا (تَـنـاوَلْ+نا) {نول}	it rains (rain)	تُـمْـطِـرُ (مطر)
you *(masculine singular)* forget * Don't you forget!	تَـنْـسَـى (نِسْيان) {نسي} * لا تَـنْـسَ!	she utters * she did not utter a word	تَـنْـبِـسُ (نَـبْـس) {نبس} * لَمْ تَـنْـبِسْ بِـبِـنْـتِ شَـفَـة
skirt (skirts) *(takes broken plural)* * a long skirt	تَـنُّـورَة (تَـنـانِـيـر) {تـنـر} * تَـنُّـورَة طَـوِيلَة	it reflects (upon)	تَـنْـعَـكِـسُ (عَلَى) {عكس} (اِنْعِكاس)
you emigrate *(feminine singular)* (emigration)	تُـهـاجِـرِيـنَ (هِجْرَة) {هجر}	a final "noon" sound which appears at the end of nouns and is represented by certain diacritical marks	تَـنْـوِيـن / التَّـنْـوِيـن {نون}
mulberry (collective noun) (one mulberry)	تُـوت (تُـوتَـة) {تـوت}	you / it / she agree (s) (on)	تُـوافِـق (عَلَى) {وفـق} (مُـوافَـقَـة) (عَلَى)
you accommodate, you reconcile, you harmonize (between)	تُـوَفِّـقُ (بَيْـنَ) {وفـق} (تَـوْفِـيـق)	he headed (towards) (heading towards) * they headed (towards)	تَـوَجَّـهَ (إِلَـى) {وجه} (تَـوَجُّـه) * تَـوَجَّـهُـوا (إِلَـى)
happy outcome, success (he had success)	تَـوْفِـيق (وَفَّـقَ) {وفق}	making available (he saved, he made available	تَـوْفِـيـر (وَفَّـرَ) {وفر}
Tunis, Tunisia *(an Arab country in north Africa)*	تُـونِـس	stopping, stoppage (it / he stopped	تَـوَقُّـف (تَـوَقَّـفَ) {وقف}

ث

steady, fixed *(masculine / feminine pair)*	ثـابِـت / ثـابِـتَـة {ثبت}	he returned / he repented (repentance)	ثـابَ (ثَـواب) {ثـوب}
eighth / the eighth / eighthly	ثـامِـن / الـثَّـامِـن / ثـامِـنـاً {ثـمن}	third / the third / thirdly	ثـالِث / الـثَّـالِث / ثـالِـثـاً {ثلث}
a second of time (seconds of time) second in order *(feminine form)*	ثـانِـيَـة (ثَـوانِـي) ثـانِـيَـة {ثـني}	second / the second / secondly	ثـانِـي / الـثَّـانِـي / ثـانِـيـاً {ثني}

culture / the culture	ثَـقـافَـة / الـثَّـقـافَـة {ثـقـف}	secondary (*masculine / feminine. pair*)	ثـانَـوِيّ / ثـانَـوِيَّـة {ثني}
Tuesday	ثُـلاثـاء / الـثُّـلاثـاء {ثلث}	three (*masculine / feminine pair*) * thirteen	ثَلاث / ثَـلاثَـة {ثلث} * ثَـلاثَـةَ عَـشَـرَ
one-third = 1/3 (the one-third)	ثُـلُـث (الـثُّـلُـث) {ثلث}	thirty (*nominative / accusative pair*)	ثَـلاثُـونَ / ثَـلاثِـيـنَ {ثلث}
eight (*masculine / feminine pair*)	ثَـمانِـي / ثَـمانِيَة {ثـمن}	eighty (*nominative / accusative pair*)	ثَـمـانُـونَ / ثَـمـانِـيـنَ {ثـمن}
then, and then	ثُـمَّ	fruits (a fruit)	ثَـمَر (ثَـمَـرَة) {ثـمر}
* the price of the cloths	* ثَـمَـن الـمَـلابِـس {لبس} {ثـمن}	price (prices)	ثَـمَـن (أَثْـمـان) {ثـمن}
reward	ثَـواب {ثـوب}	precious, expensive (*masculine / feminine pair*)	ثَـمِـيـن / ثَـمِـيـنَـة {ثـمن}
garlic (generic noun) (one clove of garlic)	ثُـوم (فَـصّ ثُـوم) {ثـوم}	dress, garment (dresses, garments) * my dress	ثَـوْب (أَثْـواب) {ثـوب} * ثَـوْبِـي

ج

he came (coming)	جـاءَ (مَـجِـيء) {جيء}	I came (coming)	جِـئْـتُ (مَـجِـيء) {جيء}
neighbor / the neighbor (neighbors) (takes *broken plural*)	جـار / الـجـار (جِـيـران) {جور}	he traversed, he roamed	جـابَ (جَـوْب) {جوب}
current, happening now / the current, the on-going	جـاري / الـجـاري {جري}	preposition / object of a preposition * a linguistic term for a prepositional phrase	جـارّ، مَـجْـرُور {جور} * الـجـارُّ وَالـمَـجْـرُور
a sitting man / a sitting woman (*active participle, masculine / feminine pair*)	جـالِـس / جـالِـسَـة {جلس}	spy (spies) (*takes broken plural*)	جـاسُوس (جَـواسِيس) {جسس}

university-related (*masculine/feminine pair*)	جامِعِيّ / جامِعِيَّة {جمع}	university (universities) your (*plural.*) university	جامِعَة (جامِعات) {جمع} *جامِعَتُكُمْ
we are ready (I am ready) (*masculine sound plural*)	جاهِزُونَ (جاهِز) {جهز}	side (sides) * the side of the woman in support	جانِب (جَوانِب) {جنب} *جانِبِ المَرْأة
mighty in power *(as a God's attribute)*, tyrant *(as related to man's attribute)*	جَبّار (جَبابِرَة) {جبر}	ignorant (ignorant ones) (*takes broken plural*)	جاهِل (جُهَلاء) {جهل}
ass (asses) (*takes broken plural*)	جَحْش (جُحُوش) {جحش}	mountain (mountains) (*takes broken plural*)	جَبَل (جِبال) {جبل}
he strived hard, he worked diligently (striving hard, working seriously)	جَدَّ (الجِدّ) {جدد}	wall (walls) (*broken plural*)	جِدار (جُدْران) {جدر}
program, schedule (schedules) (*broken plural*)	جَدْوَل (جَداوِل) {جدل}	very	جِدّاً {جدد}
roots (root) (*broken plural*) * the roots of words	جُذُور (جَذْر) {جذر} * جُذُور الكَلِمات	new (new ones) (*feminine form / singular / plural*)	جَدِيد (جُدُد) {جدد} جَدِيدَة (جَدِيدات)
It took place, it flowed (taking place, flowing)	جَرَى (جَرَيان) {جري}	I tried (trying) * I tried working	جَرَّبْتُ (تَجْرِيب) {جرب} * جَرَّبْتُ العَمَلَ
requital, recompense	جَزاء {جزي}	waiter (*broken plural*) (*adopted from French*)	جَرْسُون = نادِل
lot, plenty, many * Thanks a lot!	جَزِيلاً {جزل} * شُكْراً جَزِيلاً!	peninsula / the peninsula * *Al-Jazeera* Channel	جَزِيرَة / الجَزِيرَة * قَناة الْجَزِيرَة
body (bodies) (*takes broken plural*)	جِسْم (أجْسام) {جسم}	body (bodies) (*broken plural*)	جَسَد (أجْساد) {جسد}
he sat (sitting)	جَلَسَ (جُلُوس) {جلس}	he was great, lofty, exalted (loftiness, sublimity *(mostly related to God)*	جَلَّ (جَلال) {جلل}
beauty, *Jamaal* (*common proper name*)	جَمال {جمل}	sitting companion (*takes broken plural*)	جَلِيس (جُلَساء) {جلس}

he amassed, he gathered (amassing, gathering)	جَمَّعَ (تَجْمِيع) {جمع}	plural / the plural (as a grammatical term) * all, altogether	جَمْع / الجَمْع * الجَمِيع {جمع}
camel (camels) (*takes broken plural*)	جَمَل (جِمال) {جمل}	a Friday, Friday	جُمُعَة / الجُمُعَة {جمع}
whole-sale * whole-sale merchant	جُمْلَة {جمل} * تاجِر جُمْلَة	sentence (sentences) * the nominal sentence * the verbal sentence	جُمْلَة (جُمَل) {جمل} * الجُمْلَة الاِسْمِيَّة * الجُمْلَة الفِعْلِيَّة
all * everyone, all	جَمِيع {جمع} * الجَمِيع	republican (*masculine / feminine pair*) republic	جُمْهُورِيّ / جُمْهُورِيَّة جُمْهُورِيَّة {جمهر}
* all that relates (to)	* جَمِيع ما يَتَعَلَّق (بِـ) {جمع} {علق}	all together (*adverbial usage*)	جَمِيعاً {جمع}
garden, paradise / the Paradise (gardens) (*broken plural + feminine sound plural*)	جَنَّة / الجَنَّة {جنن} (جِنان / جَنَّات)	beautiful (*masculine*) beautiful (*feminine*) * very beautiful	جَمِيل - ونَ {جمل} جَمِيلَة - ات * جَمِيل جِدًّا
soldiers (a soldier)	جُنُود (جُنْدِيّ) {جند}	nationality / the nationality	جِنْسِيَّة / الجِنْسِيَّة {جنس}
effort (efforts)	جُهْد (جُهُود) {جهد}	struggle, strive, effort (he struggled, he strived)	جِهاد (جاهَدَ) {جهد}
Hell-Fire	جَهَنَّم {جهنم}	ignorance (he was ignorant)	جَهْل (جَهِلَ) {جهل}
answer (answers) (*takes broken plural*)	جَواب (أَجْوِبَة) {جوب}	atmosphere, weather / the atmosphere, the weather * magical atmosphere	جَوّ / الجَوّ {جوو} * جَوّ ساحِر
permission, pass (passes) (*takes feminine sound plural*) * his passport	جَواز (جَوازات) {جوز} * جَوازُ سَفَرِهِ	socks / the socks (one sock) (*broken plural*)	جَوارِب / الجَوارِب (جَوْرَب) {جورب}
weather-related, atmospheric-related (*Nisbah adjective, feminine / masculine*)	جَوِّيَّة / جَوِّيّ {جوو}	excursion, tour, outing (excursions) (*Feminine Sound Plural*)	جَوْلَة (جَوْلات) {جول}
army (armies) (*takes broken plural*)	جَيْش (جُيُوش) {جيش}	good (*masculine / feminine pair*) * in a good way	جَيِّد / جَيِّدَة {جود} * جَيِّداً

ح

pilgrim / the pilgrim (*honorific title*)	حاجّ / الحاجّ {حجج}	wall (walls) (*broken plural*)	حائِط (حِيطان) {حوط}
the one before ten to make the number eleven * the eleventh	حادي / الحادي {أحد} * الحادي عَشَر	need, necessity / the need (needs, necessities) (*takes feminine sound plural*)	حاجَة / الحاجَة (حاجات) {حوج}
* Ready to serve you! (*said as an affirmative kind response to a request*)	* حاضِر / حاضِرَة! {حضر}	hot (*masculine / feminine adjective*) * very hot	حارّ / حارَّة {حرر} * حارّ جِدّاً
case, instance (cases, instances) * in this case, in this instance	حالَة (حالات) {حول} * فِي هَذِه الحالَة	condition (conditions) (*takes broken plural*) * How are you? * How are you? (*specific-male or female*)	حال (أَحْوال) {حول} * كَيْفَ الْحال؟ * كَيْفَ حالُكَ / كِ؟
current, present / the current	حالي / الحالي {حول}	dreamy (*masculine / feminine adjectival pair*)	حالِم / حالِمَة {حلم}
has come, has arrived (*said of time*)	حانَ (حَيْن) {حين}	at the present time (*adverb*)	حالِيّاً {حول}
seeds (a seed) (*broken plural*)	حُبُوب (حَبَّة) {حبب}	love / the love * our love * a talk about love	حُبّ / الحُبّ {حبب} * حُبُّنا (حُبُّ+نا) * حَدِيث عَن الحُبّ
till, until * so that the two of them would meet	حَتَّى * حَتَّى يَتَقابَلا	beloved, sweetheart (*masculine / feminine pair*) * the beloved of my heart	حَبِيب / حَبِيبَة {حبب} * حَبِيبَة قَلْبي
veil / the veil	حِجاب / الحِجاب {حجب}	he performed pilgrimage (pilgrimage)	حَجَّ (حَجٌّ / الحَجّ) (حجج)
a stone (stones) (*takes broken plural*)	حَجَر (حِجارَة) (حجر)	he covered, he screened, he veiled (veiling, screening)	حَجَبَ (حِجاب) (حجب)
he related, he spoke, he narrated (speech, narration)	حَدَّثَ (حَدِيث) {حدث}	it happened (to) (happening (to))	حَدَثَ (حُدُوث) (لِـ) {حدث}

a talk (about) (talks about)	حَـدِيـث (أَحـادِيـث) (عَنْ) {حدث}	* Relate to us, Talk to us! *(Imperative verb)*	* حَـدِّثْـنـا {حدث} (حَـدِّثْ+نـا)
iron / the iron (*collective noun*)	حَـدِيـد / الـحَـدِيد {حدد}	modern / the modern *(feminine form)*	حَـدِيـث / الـحَـدِيـث (حَـدِيـثَـة) {حدث}
caution	حَـذَر {حذر}	shoe (shoes) *(takes broken plural)*	حِـذاء (أَحْـذِية) {حذو}
letter, particle (letters, particles) *(takes broken plural)* * the preposition	حَـرْف (حُـرُوف) {حرف} * حَـرْفُ الـجَـرّ	war (wars) *(takes broken plural)*	حَـرْب (حُـرُوب) {حرب}
he declared it sacred or prohibited (declaration of prohibition)	حَـرَّمَ (تَـحْـرِيـم) {حرم}	campus, sanctuary (sanctuaries, campuses) * the university campus	حَـرَم (أَحْـرام) {حرم} * الـحَـرَم الـجامِـعِـيّ
letters (a letter)	حُرُوف (حَرْف) {حرف}	wars (a war)	حُرُوب (حَرْب) {حرب}
* sun letters * moon letters	* حُـرُوف شَمْسِيَّة * حُـرُوف قَـمَـرِيَّة {حرف}	* preposition particles * the spelling letters = the alphabet	* حُـرُوفُ ٱلـجَـرّ * حُـرُوف ٱلـهِـجاء {حرف}
party (parties) (as related to ideology) *(takes broken plural)* * the ruling party	حِـزْب (أَحْزاب) {حزب} * الـحِـزْبُ الـحاكِـم	silk *(collective noun)*	حَـرِيـر {حرر}
sadness (sad occasions) (*takes broken plural*)	حُـزْن (أَحْزان) {حزن}	he tied up, he bundled, he took matters firmly (determination)	حَـزَمَ (حَـزْم) {حزم}
arithmetic, calculus, account	حِـسـاب {حسب}	I felt sad (sadness)	حَـزِنْـتُ (حُـزْن) {حزن}
nice, good (a common proper noun)	حَـسَـن {حسن}	he envied (envy)	حَـسَـدَ (حَسَد) {حسد}
hashish, grass (generic)	حَـشِيـش {حشش}	well, fine *(adverb)*	حَـسَـنـاً {حسن}
he reaped, he harvested (reaping, harvesting)	حَـصَـدَ (حَـصـاد) {حصد}	horse (horses) (*broken plural*)	حِـصـان (أَحْـصِـنَـة) {حصن}
I obtained, I earned	حَـصَلْـتُ (عَلَى) {حصل}	class periods, shares (a class period, a share) (*broken plural*)	حِـصَـص (حِـصَّـة) {حصص}
obtaining *(verbal noun)* * after obtaining	حُـصُـول (عَلَى) {حصل} * بَعْدَ ٱلـحُـصُول (عَلَى)	I obtained, I earned * she obtained it, she got it	حَـصَـلَـتْ (عَـلى) {حصل} * حَـصَـلَـتْ عَـلَـيْـهِ

he came (to) (from), he attended she came (to) (from), she attended	حَضَرَ (إِلَى) (مِنْ) حَضَرَتْ (إِلَى) (مِنْ)	custody (custodies) * her mother's custody	حَضانَة (حَضانات) {حضن} * حَضانَة أُمِّها
firewood (*takes broken plural*)	حَطَب (أَحْطاب) {حطب}	coming, attendance (*verbal noun*)	حُضُور (إِلَى) (مِنْ) {حضر}
prohibition, ban, embargo (*takes broken plural*)	حَظْر (حُظُور) {حظر}	luck, fortune, portion (*takes broken plural*)	حَظّ (حُظُوظ) {حظظ}
grandchild (grandchildren) (*takes broken plural*)	حَفِيد (أَحْفاد) {حفد}	party / party (parties) (*takes feminine sound plural*)	حَفْل / حَفْلَة {حفل} (حَفْلات)
* their rights *(for feminine plural)*	* حُقُوقُهُنَّ (حُقُوق + هُنَّ)	right, duty (rights, duties) (*broken plural*) * human rights	حَقّ (حُقُوق) {حقق} * حُقُوق الإِنْسان
solution, resolution *(takes broken plural)* * the resolution of our disagreements	حَلّ (حُلُول) {حلل} * حَلّ خِلافاتِنا	proverbs, wise-sayings / a proverb, a wise-saying (*broken plural*)	حِكَم / الحِكَم (حِكْمَة) {حكم}
sweet one, beautiful one (feminine form)	حُلْوَة (حُلْوات) {حلو}	barber (barbers) (*takes masculine sound plural*)	حَلّاق (حَلّاقُونَ) {حلق}
praise / the praise * Praise be to God! (*idiom*)	حَمْد / الحَمْد * الْحَمْدُ لِلّه!	donkey (donkeys) (*takes broken plural*)	حِمار (حَمِير) {حمر}
diet, abstention (diets, abstentions)	حِمْيَة (حِمْيات) {حمي}	chick-peas, the dip made from chick-peas, *hummus*	حُمُّص {حمص}
whale (whales) (*takes broken plural*)	حُوت (حِيتان) {حوت}	dialogue, conversation *(takes feminine sound plural)* * the following dialogue	حِوار (حِوارات) {حور} * الحِوارُ ٱلتّالِي
about, around, concerning, related to	حَوْلَ {حول}	water basin, container (basins, containers) (*takes broken plural*)	حَوْض (أَحْواض) {حوض}
life / the life * your life * my life	حَياة / الحَياة {حيي} * حَياتُكَ (حَياة+كَ) * حَياتِي	nearly, approximately	حَوالَيْ {حول}

a neighborhood, a living entity (neighborhoods, living things) (*takes broken plural*)	حَيّ (أَحْياء) {حيو}	where, wherever since, whereas (*adverb of time & place*)	حَيْثُ
		* the neighborhood of lady *Zaynab* * the *'Abbasiyyah* neighborhood *(in Cairo)*	* حَيُّ ٱلسَّيِّدَة زَيْنَب * حَيّ ٱلعَبَّاسِيَّة

she failed, she was disappointed (failure, disappointment	خابَتْ (خَيْبَة) {خيب}	he failed, he was disappointed (failure, disappointment	خابَ (خَيْبَة) {خيب}
abroad / the outside (of a place)	خارِج / الخارِج {خرج}	ring (rings) * the engagement ring	خاتَم (خَواتِم) {ختم} * خاتَم ٱلخُطُوبَة
private, special (*masculine / feminine*)	خاصّ / خاصَّة {خصص}	foreign, outside / the exterior, the outside * minister of foreign affairs, secretary of state (*American*)	خارِجِيَّة / الخارِجِيَّة {خرج} * وَزِير ٱلخارِجِيَّة
engaged, one who is engaged *(takes broken plural)*	خاطِبَ (خُطّاب) {خطب}	Characteristic * two characteristic	خاصِّيَّة {خصص} * خاصِّيَّتَيْن
eternal, immortal, everlasting / a common proper name) (takes *masculine sound plural*)	خالِد (خالِدُونَ) {خلد}	maternal uncle / maternal aunt (maternal uncles / maternal aunts) * his maternal uncle	خال / خالَة (أَخْوال) (خالات) {خول} * خالِهِ
Khan Al-Kaleeli *(a famous popular market in Cairo)*	* خان الخَلِيلِي	fifth / the fifth / fifthly	خامِس / الخامِس / خامِساً {خمس}
predicate / the predicate *(a grammatical term for the second part of the nominal sentence)*	خَبَر / الخَبَر {خبر}	a piece of news *(takes broken plural)* * for the piece of news	خَبَر (أَخْبار) {خبر} * لِخَبَرِ
bread (he baked)	خُبْز (خَبَزَ) {خبز}	he informed, he announced the news (informing)	خَبَّرَ (إِخْبار) {خبر}
in a state of being shy, out of bashfulness / shyness, bashfulness	خَجَلاً / الخَجَل {خجل}	wicked, malicious, noxious *(masculine / feminine pair and their plurals)*	خَبِيث / خَبِيثَة (خُبَثاء / خَبِيثات) {خبث}

You take! *(command or imperative verb for masculine singular, feminine singular and plural)*	خُـذْ / خُـذي / خُـذُوا! (أَخْـذ) {أخذ}	services (a service) * At your service!	خَـدَمات (خِـدْمَـة) {خدم} * فِـي خِـدْمَـتِـكَ!
map (maps) *(takes broken plural)*	خَـرِيطَـة (خَـرائِـط) {خرط}	it murmured, it bubbled (purling of running water)	خَـرَّ (خَـرِيـر) {خرر}
especially *(adverb)*	خُـصُوصاً {خصص}	autumn, the fall season	خَـرِيف / الـخَـرِيف {خرف}
it became vacant, it became empty, it became devoid (seclusion) * he secluded himself	خَـلا (خِـلْـوَة) {خلو} * خَـلا بِـنَـفْـسِـهِ	vegetables / the vegetables	خُـضـار / الـخُـضـار {خضر}
during	خِـلالَ {خلل}	* their disagreements (a disagreement)	* خِـلافاتِـهِـم (خِلاف) {خلف}
a friend, a companion, a male proper name	خَـلِـيـل (أَخِـلاَّء) {خلل}	behind (adverb of place)	خَـلْـفَ {خلف}
fifty *(nominative / accusative pair)*	خَـمْسُونَ / خَـمْسِـيـنَ {خمس}	five *(masculine-feminine pair)*	خَـمْـس / خَـمْـسَـة {خمس}
pig, swine (pigs) *(takes broken plural)*	خِـنْزِيـر (خَـنازِيـر) {خنزر}	Thursday	خَـمِـيس / الـخَـمِـيس {خمس}
* its choices (a choice) * I do not have a choice	* خَـياراتِـهِ (خَـيـار) (خَـيـارات+ـه) {خير} * لَيْسَ عِـنْـدي خَـيـار	peaches, plums (a peach, a plumb)	خَـوْخ (خَـوْخَـة) {خوخ}
better (than)	خَـيْـر (مِنْ)	good, better / the good * Doing good, doing fine! * Good morning!	خَـيْـر / الـخَـيْـر * بِـخَـيْـر * صَـباحَ ٱلـخَـيْـر!
May it be good! *(idiom)*	* خَـيْـراً! {خيـر}	* the sooner the better *(to be learned as an idiom)*	* خَـيْـرُ الـبِـرِّ عـاجِـلُـه
		thread, cord (threads, cords)	خَـيْـط (خُـيُـوط) {خيـط}

د

internal, interior, local (*masculine/feminine pair*) * domestic policy	داخِلِيّ / داخِلِيَّة {دخل} * السِّياسَة الدّاخِلِيَّة	illness, sickness (takes *broken plural*)	داء (أَدواء) {دوي}
made the rounds, took place (taking place)	دارَ (دَوَران) {دور}	home, house / the home, the house *(takes broken plural)*	دار / الدّار (دُور) {دور}
bear (bears) *(takes broken plural)*	دُبّ / الدُّب (دِبَبَة) {دبب}	lasted, may last (lasting) * May your favor continue to last!	دامَ (دَوام) {دوم} * دامَ فَضْلُكُمْ!
hens, chickens (a hen, a chicken)	دَجاج (دَجاجَة) {دجج}	Dubai (one of the United Arab Emirates city)	دُبَيّ {دبي}
they smoked (smoking)	دَخَّنوا (تَدْخِين) {دخن}	they entered (entering)	دَخَلوا (دُخُول) {دخل}
path, trail, mountain pass *(takes broken plural)*	دَرْب (دُرُوب) {درب}	it flowed, it streamed (flowing copiously)	دَرَّ (دَرّ) {درر}
chat, leisurely talk	دَرْدَشَة {دردش}	study, studying / (the) study * His study * My study	دِراسَة / الدِّراسَة {درس} * دِراسَتِه * دِراسَتِي
lesson / the lesson (lessons) *(takes broken plural)* * our lesson	دَرْس / الدَّرْس {درس} (دُرُوس) * دَرْسُنا	he studied (studying) * were studied *(passive voice)*	دَرَسَ (دِراسَة) {درس} * دُرِسَتْ
she studied (studying)	دَرَسَتْ (دِراسَة) {درس}	he taught (teaching)	دَرَّسَ (تَدْرِيس) {درس}
you studied (*masculine singular*) * you (all) studied them	دَرَسْتَ {درس} * دَرَسْتُمُوها	she taught (teaching)	دَرَّسَتْ (تَدْرِيس) {درس}
dirham, drachma (a *weight equal to 3.12 grams*)	دِرْهَم (دَراهِم) {درهم}	I studied / I studied it * My graduate studies	دَرَسْتُ / دَرَسْتُها {درس} * دِراسَتِي العُلْيا
she invited (inviting, invitation)	دَعَتْ (دَعْوَة) {دعو}	he called (to / for) (calling on)	دَعا (إلى / لِـ) (دَعْوَة) {دعو}
Let me!	دَعْنِي! {ودع}	You stop, abandon, leave aside! *(said to a male)*	دَعْكَ! {ودع}

a note book, a writing pad (*takes broken plural*)	دَفْتَر (دَفاتِر) {دفتر}	it became warm, he felt warm (feeling warm, being warm)	دَفُؤَ (دِفْء) {دفأ}
fine, thin, delicate, fragile, exact (*masculine / feminine adjective*)	دَقِيق / دَقِيقَة {دقق}	it became thin, fine, fragile (getting fragile, thin or fine)	دَقَّ (دِقَّة) {دقق}
he made flat, he leveled, he pressed down, he demolished	دَكَّ (دَكّ) {دكك}	minute (minutes) as units of time	دَقِيقَة (دَقائِق) {دقق}
Doctorate degree / the Doctorate degree	دُكْتُوراه / الدُّكْتُوراه	Doctor, Ph.D. (*borrowed from English*)	دُكْتُور / الدُّكْتُور
bucket, pail (*takes broken plural*)	دَلْو (دِلاء) {دلو}	pointed to, was to the point	دَلَّ {دلل}
Damascus (*capital of Syria*)	دِمَشْق	destruction	دَمار {دمر}
a patrol (*takes feminine sound plural*)	دَوْرِيَّة (دَوْرِيَّات) {دور}	cure, medicine (*takes broken plural*)	دَواء (أَدْوِيَة) {دوي}
international (*masculine / feminine pair*)	دُوَلِيّ / دُوَلِيَّة {دول}	a state, a country (*broken plural*) * the Arab Countries	دَوْلَة (دُوَل) {دول} * الدُّوَلُ العَرَبِيَّة
democracy, democratic (*adopted from English*)	دِيمُقْراطِيَّة	cock, rooster (*takes two broken plural forms*)	دِيك (دِيَكَة / دُيُوك) {ديك}

going = one who goes (*active participle, takes masculine sound plural*)	ذاهِب (ذاهِبُونَ) (إِلَى) {ذهب}	it melted (melting) (*said of ice or snow*)	ذابَ (ذَوَبان) {ذوب}
corn / the corn * the grilled corn	ذُرَة / الذُّرَة * الذُّرَة المَشْوِيَّة	flies (a fly) (*takes broken plural*)	ذُباب (ذُبابَة) {ذبب}
anniversary, memory (*takes feminine sound plural*) * the anniversary of our marriage day	ذِكْرَى (ذِكْرَيات) {ذكر} * ذِكْرَى يَوْمِ زَواجِنا	you (*feminine singular*) mentioned	ذَكَرْتِ (ذِكْر) {ذكر}
sin (sins) (*takes broken plural*)	ذَنْب (ذُنُوب) {ذنب}	that (*demonstrative pronoun*)	ذَلِكَ
he went (going) (to)	ذَهَبَ (إِلَى) (ذَهاب) {ذهب}	going (to) = the act of going (*verbal noun*)	ذَهاب (إِلَى) {ذهب}

I went (to)	ذَهَـبْـتُ (إلَـى) {ذهب}	gold *(nominative / accusative ending)*	ذهَبٌ (ذَهَـباً) {ذهب}
they went (to) *(feminine Plural)*	ذَهَـبْـنَ (إلَـى) {ذهب}	you *(plural)* went (to) *(masculine plural)*	ذَهَـبْـتُـمْ (إلَـى) {ذهب}
taste (tastes) * your taste is beautiful, you have a beautiful taste	ذَوْق (أَذْواق) {ذوق} * ذَوْقُـكِ حُلْـو	we went (to)	ذَهَبْـنـا (إلَـى) {ذهب}

Wonderful! *(masculine / feminine adjectival pair)*	رَائِـع / رائِـعَـة! {روع}	**head (heads)** *(takes broken plural)*	رَأس (رُؤُوس) {رءس}
* the department's chair *(masculine / feminine pair)*	* رَئِـيس / رَئِـيـسَـة ٱلْقِسْـمِ {رءس}	**president** *(masculine, takes broken plural)* **president** *(feminine, takes feminine sound plural)*	رَئِـيس (رُؤَساء) {رءس} رَئِـيسَـة (رَئِـيـسات)
* your opinion (about) * So, what is your opinion?	* رَأْيُـكُـمْ (بِـ) * فَـمـا رَأْيُـكُـمْ ...؟	**opinion (opinions)** * your opinion	رَأْي (آراء) {رأي} * رَأْيُـكَ
wonderful *(masculine / feminine pair)*	رائِـع / رائِـعَـة {روع}	**principal, major** *(masculine / feminine pair)*	رَئِـيسِـيّ / رَئِـيسِـيَّـة {رءس}
desiring (of) (desire) *(active participle)*	راغِـب (فِـي) (رَغْـبَـة) {رغب}	**fourth / the fourth / fourthly**	رابِـع / الـرَّابِـع / رابِـعـاً {ربع}
he gained, he profited (gain, profit)	رَبِـحَ (رِبْـح) {ربح}	**ribbon, band, bandage** *(takes broken plural)*	رِبـاط (أَرْبِطَـة) {ربط}
a Spring / the Spring season, *(also a male proper name)*	رَبِـيـع / الـرَّبِـيـع {ربع}	**perhaps, may be**	رُبَّـمـا {ربب}
she returned (to) / (from)	رَجَـعَـتْ (إلَـى) (مِنْ) {رجع}	**he returned (to) (from) (returning)**	رَجَـعَ (إلَـى) (مِنْ) (رُجُوع) {رجع}
man (men) * business man	رَجُـل (رِجـال) {رجل} * رَجُـل أَعْـمـال	**I returned (returning)**	رَجَـعْـتُ (إلَـى) (مِنْ) (رُجُوع) {رجع}
they welcomed (welcoming) * they welcomed them	رَحَّـبُـوا (تَـرْحِـيب) * رَحَّـبُـوا بِـهِـم {رحب}	**returning, return** *(verbal noun)*	رُجُـوع (إلَـى) (مِنْ) {رجع}
Merciful / the Most Merciful One *(one of the beautiful names of God)*	رَحْـمـان / الـرَّحْـمٰـن {رحم}	**a journey, a trip (trips, journeys)**	رِحْـلَـة (رَحَلات) {رحل}

Merciful / the Most Merciful One (*one of the beautiful names of God*)	رَحِيـم / الـرَّحِيـم {رحم}	mercy (*takes feminine sound plural*) * and the Mercy of God	رَحْمَة (رَحْمات) {رحم} * وَرَحْمَةُ ٱللّٰه
You repeat aloud! *(command verb for masculine / feminine singular and plural)*	رَدِّدْ / رَدِّدِي / رَدِّدُوا ! (تَـرْدِيد) {ردد}	he responded, he reciprocated *(response)* * she responded to her	رَدَّ (رَدّ) {ردد} * رَدَّتْ عَلَـيْـهـا
drizzle	رَذاذ {رذذ}	responses, answers (a response)	رُدُود (رَدّ) {ردد}
a letter (letters) * my letter	رِسالَـة (رَسائِـل) * رِسالَـتِـي {رسل}	rice	رُزّ = أَرُزّ
formally, officially, in a formal way	رَسْـمِـيّاً {رسم}	messenger / The Messenger *(title for the Prophet)* (Messengers)	رَسُول / الـرَّسُـول (رُسُـل) {رسل}
bruises, contusions / a bruise	رُضُـوض / رَضَّـة {رضض}	approval, satisfaction * the sign of approval, satisfaction	رِضـى / الـرِّضَـى {رضي} * عَـلامَـةُ الـرِّضَـى
companion *(masculine / feminine pair)*	رَفِـيـق / رَفِـيقَـة {رفق}	he lifted, he raised (lifting, raising)	رَفَـعَ (رَفْـع) {رفع}
delicate, tender, gentle, friendly *(masculine / feminine pair)*	رَقِـيـق / رَقِـيقَـة {رقق}	number (numbers) *(takes broken plural)* * her phone number	رَقَـم (أَرْقـام) {رقم} * رَقَـم تِـلِـيفُـونِـهـا
he ran, he raced (running, racing)	رَكَـضَ (رَكْـض) {ركض}	he rode, he mounted (riding, mounting) * they rode, they mounted	رَكِـبَ (رُكُـوب) {ركب} * رَكِـبُـوا
Ramadan *(9th month of Islamic calendar, month of fasting)*	رَمَـضـان {رمض}	weak, feeble, meager *(masculine / feminine pair)*	رَكِيـك / رَكِـيكَـة {ركك}
bonds, connection (a bond, a connection)	رَوابِـط (رابِـط) {ربط}	garden, meadow (gardens) * Riyadh *(capital of Saudi Arabia)*	رَوْض (رِيـاض) * الـرِّيـاض {رسل}
		sport * sports clothing	رِيـاضَـة {ريض} * مَـلابِـس الـرِّيـاضَـة

ز

visitor / the visitor (visitors) (*feminine sound plural*) * a foreign female visitor	زائِـرَة / الـزّائِـرَة (زائِـرات) {زور} * زائِـرَة أَجْـنَـبِـيَّـة	visitor / the visitor (visitors) (*This word takes both Mas. Sound Plu. & broken plural*)	زائِـر / الـزّائِـر (زائِـرُونَ / زُوّار) {زور}

he visited (visiting) * for visiting, for the purpose of visiting	زارَ (زِيـارَة) {زور} * لِـزِيـارَة	he / it increased (increasing)	زادَ (زِيـادَة) {زيد}
raisins *(collective noun)*	زَبِـيـب {زبب}	customer (customers) (*takes broken plural*)	زُبُـون / الـزُّبُـون (زَبـائِـن) {زبن}
thyme (*an herb*), a dipping product powder from thyme	زَعْـتَـر / سَعْـتَـر {زعتر}	he sowed, he planted (sowing, planting)	زَرَعَ (زِراعَـة) {زرع}
colleague, classmate, companion *(masculine / feminine pair)* * his female colleague	زَمِـيـل / زَمِـيـلَـة {زمل} * زَمِـيـلَـتُـهُ	the trilling cries of joy by Arab women	زَغـارِيـد {زغرد}
marriage / the marriage as an institution	زَواج / الـزَّواج {زوج}	flowers (*collective noun*) (a flower)	زَهـر (زَهْـرَة) {زهر}
wife (wives) *(takes feminine sound plural)* * your ex-wife	زَوْجَة (زَوْجات) {زوج} * زَوْجَـتُـكَ الـسَّابِـقَـة	husband (husbands) *(takes broken plural)* * her husband * my husband	زَوْج (أَزْواج) {زوج} * زَوْجُـهـا * زَوْجِـي
oil *(collective noun)* (oils)	زَيْـت (زُيُـوت) {زيت}	jar made of porous clay *(takes broken plural)* * a short visit	زِيـارَة (زارَ / يَـزورُ) {زور} * زِيـارَة قَـصِـيـرَة
jar made of porous clay *(takes broken plural)*	زِيـر (أَزْيـار) {زير}	olive trees, olives *(as produce) (collective noun)* (one olive item)	زَيْـتُـون (زَيْـتُـونَـة) {زيت}
		Zaynab (female proper name) * Lady *Zaynab*	زَيْـنَـب * الـسَّـيِّـدَة زَيْـنَـب

س

* I will leave it	* سَـأَتْـرُكُـهُ (سَـ + أَتْـرُكُ+ ـهُ) {ترك}	will, shall (*particle prefixed before the present tense verb to indicate future time*)	سَـ
I will go	سَـأَذْهَـبُ {ذهب} (سَـ + أَذْهَـبُ)	I will study	سَـأَدْرُسُ (سَـ + أَدْرُسُ) {درس}
I will return	سَـأَعُـودُ {عود} (سَـ + أَعُـودُ)	I will visit * I will visit you	سَـأَزُورُ (سَـ + أَزُورُ) * سَـأَزُورُكَ {زور}
h asked, he questioned (question)	سَـأَلَ (سُـؤال) {سأل}	I will undertake	سَـأَقُـومُ (بِـ) {قوم} (سَـ + أَقُـومُ)

question (questions) *(takes broken plural)*	سُؤال (أَسْئِلَة) {سأل}	he interrogated (interrogation)	سَاءَلَ (مُساءَلَة) {سأل}
he became weary, he became bored (weariness, boredom)	سَئِمَ (سَأم) {سئم}	he was interrogated, he was asked (interrogation) *(passive voice)*	سُئِلَ (مُساءَلَة) {سأل}
it displeased us = we were unhappy	ساءَنا (ساءَ+نا) {سوء}	prevailing (prevailing ones) *(masculine sound plural)*	سائِد (سائِدُونَ) {سود}
magical, fascinating *(masculine / feminine adjectives)*	ساحِر / ساحِرَة {سحر}	seventh / the seventh / seventhly	سابِع / السَّابِع / سابِعاً {سبع}
he marched (to) (marching to)	سارَ (السَّيْر) (إِلَى) {سير}	sixth / the sixth / sixthly	سادِس / السَّادِس / سادِساً {سدس}
hour, watch / the hour, the watch *(takes feminine sound plural)* * the second hour, 2 o'clock	ساعَة / السَّاعَة {سعي} * السَّاعَة الثَّانِيَة	hour, watch *(takes feminine sound plural)* * for longer hours	ساعَة (ساعات) {سعي} * لِساعات أَطْوَل
he traveled (to) (traveling to) * they travelled	سافَرَ (السَّفَر) (إِلَى) {سفر} * سافَرُوا	You help! *(command verb for masculine singular)*	ساعِدْ! (مُساعَدَة) {سعد}
she traveled (to) (traveling to)	سافَرَتْ (السَّفَر) (إِلَى) {سفر}	I traveled (to) (traveling to)	سافَرْتُ (السَّفَر) (إِلَى) {سفر}
two Semitic *(dual form)*	سامِيَّتانِ {سمو}	one who is silent / the one who is silent	ساكِت / السَّاكِت {سكت}
reason, cause * because (of)	سَبَب {سبب} * بِسَبَب	swimming / the swimming * for swimming	سِباحَة / السِّباحَة {سبح} * لِلسِّباحَة
seven *(masculine / feminine pair)*	سَبْع / سَبْعَة {سبع}	he examined, he probed (examining, probing)	سَبَرَ (سَبْر) {سبر}
he castes (a metal), he molded (casting, molding, formulating)	سَبَكَ (سَبْك) {سبك}	he preceded, he outstripped (preceding, coming before others)	سَبَقَ (سَبْق / سِباق) {سبق}
you will buy *(feminine singular)*	سَتَشْتَرِينَ {شري} (سَـ + تَشْتَرِينَ)	you will eat *(feminine singular)*	سَتَأْكُلِينَ {أكل} (سَـ + تَأْكُلِينَ)

you will return *(masculine singular)*	سَـتَـعُـودُ {عود} (سَـ + تَـعُـودُ)	six *(masculine / feminine pair)*	سِـتّ / سِـتَّـة {ستت}
It / she / you (masculine) will be	سَـتَـكُونُ {كون} (سَـ + تَـكُونُ)	you will stay *(feminine singular)*	سَـتُـقِـيـمِـيـن {قوم} (سَـ + تُـقِـيـمِـيـن)
mirage, phantom	سَراب {سَرَب}	dawn, early morning *(takes broken plural)*	سَـحَـر (أَسْـحـار) {سَحر}
pleasure, happiness * With all pleasure!	سُـرُور {سرر} * بِـكُـلِّ سُـرُور!	release, liberty * their *(dual)* liberty	سَـراح {سَرَحَ} * سَـراحَـهُـما
he was happy (happiness) I was delighted (with), I was happy (with)	سَـعِـدَ (سَعادَة) {سعد} سَـعِـدْتُ (بِـ)	bed, couch, elevated seat (beds, couches) *(takes two forms of broken plural)*	سَـرِيـر (أَسِـرَّة / سُـرُر) {سرر}
happy *(masculine / feminine pair)*	سَعِـيـد / سَـعِـيـدَة {سعد}	price (prices / the prices) *(takes broken plural)*	سِعْـر (أَسْـعار / الأَسْعار) {سعر}
ambassador (ambassadors) *(takes broken plural)*	سَـفِـيـر (سُـفَـراء) {سفر}	embassy (embassies) *(takes feminine sound plural)* * the American embassy	سِـفـارَة (سِـفـارات) {سفر} * السِّـفـارَة الأَمريـكِـيَّـة
secretary *(masculine / feminine pair, adopted from English)*	سِكْـرِتـيـر / سِـكْـرِتـيـرَة	he fell silent, he paused (silence / the silence)	سَـكَـتَ (سُـكُـوت / السُّـكُـوت) {سكت}
silence / the silence	سُـكُـوت / الـسُّـكُـوت {سكت}	residence / the residence	سَـكَـن / السَّـكَـن
peace / the peace * Peace be upon you! *{idiom}* * What a peace! *(exclamatory admiration)* * Peacefully	سَـلام / الـسَّـلام {سلم} * الـسَّـلامُ عَـلَـيْـكُـمْ! * يـا سَـلامُ! * بِـسَـلام	calm, tranquility, peace * the "*Sukoon*" sign (ْ) indicating vowel-less consonant	سُكُون / السُّكُون {سكن} * عَلامَة السُّكُون
a salad (*takes feminine sound plural*)	سَلَطَـة (سَلَطات) {سلط}	safety / the safety * Wishing for your safety! * You go accompanied with safety! *(idioms)*	سَـلامَـة / السَّـلامَـة {سلم} * سَلامَـتُـكَ / ـكِ! * بِـٱلسَّـلامَـة!
he followed a path (comport, path of behavior)	سَـلَـكَ (سُـلُـوك) {سلك}	he boiled (boiling in water)	سَـلَـقَ (سَـلْـق) {سلق}
ladder, stairs (ladders) *(takes broken plural)*	سُـلَّـم (سَـلالِم) {سلم}	he saluted, he saved (salutation) * Convey salutation!	سَـلَّـمَ (تَـسْلِيم) {سلم} * سَـلِّـمْ!

sky, heaven / the sky *(takes feminine plural)*	سَماء / السَّماء (سَماوات) {سمو}	sound, healthy / the sound, the healthy	سَلِيم / السَّلِيم {سلم}
she named her	سَمَّتْها {سمي} (سَمَّتْ+ها)	features, characteristics (a feature, a characteristic * your features	سِمات (سِمَة) {وسم} * سِماتِكِ
she / it permitted * if circumstances would permit	سَمَحَتْ (سَماح) {سمح} * إذا سَمَحَتْ الظُّرُوف	you forgave, you permitted *(masculine / feminine singular)* (forgiving, permitting) * If you would permit! / With your permission!	سَمَحْتَ / سَمَحْتِ (سَماح) {سمح} * لَوْ سَمَحْتَ / ـتِ!
I heard (hearing)	سَمِعْتُ (سَماع) {سمع}	he heard (hearing)	سَمِعَ (سَماع) {سمع}
her reputation	سُمْعَتُها {سمع} (سُمْعَة+ها)	you heard *(masculine plural)* (hearing)	سَمِعْتُم (سَماع) {سمع}
a fish (fishes) (*collective noun*) * grilled fish	سَمَكَة (سَمَك) {سمك} * السَّمَك المَشْوِيّ	they heard (hearing) *(masculine plural)*	سَمِعُوا (سَماع) {سمع}
* after a year * May it be a sweet year!	* بَعْدَ سَنَة {سنو} * سَنَة حِلْوَة!	year (years) *(takes feminine and masculine sound plurals)* * the next year, the coming year	سَنَة (سَنَوات / سِنُون / سِنِين) {سنو} * السَّنَة القادِمَة
sandwich *(singular / plural; transcribed from English)*	سانْدَوتْش (سانْدَوتْشات)	yearly, annually *(Nisbah adjective, masculine / feminine pair)*	سَنَوِيّ / سَنَوِيَّة {سنو}
night assembly, evening gathering *(takes feminine sound plural)*	سَهْرَة (سَهْرات) {سهر}	he stayed late at night (night assembly, evening social gathering	سَهِرَ (سَهَر) {سهر}
Treading leveled grounds, easy coming! * two easy paths (*idiom*) * Welcome to you (all), You are welcome!	سَهْلاً! {سهل} * سَهْلَيْن (سَهْل) * أَهْلاً وَسَهْلاً بِكُمْ!	easy *(masculine / feminine adjective pair)*	سَهْل / سَهْلَة {سهل}
wall, fence *(takes broken plural)*	سُور (أَسْوار) {سور}	bad, being bad, evil, ill, inequity, offence *(takes broken plural)*	سُوء (أَسْواء) {سوء}
will, shall * it / he will be	سَوْفَ = سَـ * سَوْفَ يَكُونُ	Syria Syrian *(masculine / feminine pair)*	سُوْريا، سُورِيَّة {سور} سُورِيّ / سُورِيَّة

policy, politics	سِياسَة (سِيَاسات) {سيس}	market (markets) *(takes broken plural)*	سُوق (أَسْواق) {سوق}
a car (cars) * by car	سَيَّارَة (سَيَّارات) * بِٱلسَّيَّارَة {سير}	* domestic policy	* السِّياسَة الدَّاخِلِيَّة {سيس}
political *(masculine / feminine pair)* * the politicians	سِياسِيّ / سِياسِيَّة {سيس} * السِّياسِيِّينَ	* a taxi, a car for hire	* سَيَّارة أُجْرَة {سير} {أجر}
Mr., Sir, master (Misters) * my dear sir	سَيِّد / السَّيِّد (سادَة) {سود} * سَيِّدِي	he will attend, he will come (coming, attendance)	سَيَحْضُرُ (حُضُور) {حضر}
sword (swords) *(takes broken plural)*	سَيْف (سُيُوف) {سيف}	Mrs., lady * My lady * My ladies and gentlemen!	سَيِّدَة (سَيِّدات) {سود} * سَيِّدَتي * سَيِّداتِي سادَتِي!
		cinema, movies *(feminine, adopted from English)*	سِينَما / السِّينَما

he willed / he wills * God's willing!	شَاءَ / يَشاءُ {شيأ} * إِنْ شَاءَ ٱللَّه!	matters, affairs * governmental affairs	شُؤُون (شَأْن) {شأن} * الشُّؤُون ٱلحُكُومِيَّة
shore, bank (of a river) *the bank of the Nile	شَاطِئ (شَواطِئ) {شطأ} * شَاطِئ النِّيل	young man *(nominative, accusative cases)* / young woman (youth)	شابّ ، شابّاً / شابَّة (شَباب) {شبب}
they saw, they watched *(feminine plural conjugation)*	شاهَدْنَ (شاهَدْ+نَ) {شهد}	comprehensive, massive *(masculine / feminine adjectival pair)*	شامِل / شامِلَة {شمل}
window *(takes broken plural)*	شُبَّاك (شَبابِيك) {شبك}	tea / the tea	شاي / الشَّاي
courageous, brave *(takes broken plural)*	شُجاع (شُجْعان) {شجع}	winter / the winter	شِتاء / الشِّتاء {شتي}

paleness, pallor (he became pale, he became sickly looking	شُحُوب (شَحُبَ) {شحب}	a tree *(takes broken plural)*	شَجَرَة (أَشْجار) {شجر}
personality (personalities) *(takes feminine sound plural)*	شَخْصِيَّة / (شَخْصِيَّات) {شخص}	personal *(masculine / feminine pair)*	شَخْصَيّ / شَخْصِيَّة {شخص}
severe, strong *(takes broken plural)*	شَدِيد / شَدِيدَة (أَشِدَّاءُ) {شدد}	he tightened, he stressed * the "*Shaddah*" sign (ّ) to indicate a double consonant	شَدَّ (شَدّ) {شدد} * الشَّدَّة
he drank (drinking) * We drank	شَرِبَ (شُرْب) {شرب} * شَرِبْنا (شَرِبْ+نا)	drink (drinks, sweetened drinks)	شَراب (أَشْرِبَة، شَرْبات) {شرب}
honor * I am honored too! *(idiom)*	شَرَف {شرف} * الشَّرَف لِي!	I drank (drink, sherbet) * the sweet drinks of joy	شَرِبْتُ (شَراب) {شرب} * شَرْبات الفَرَح
east * The Middle East	شَرْق {شرق} * الشَّرْق الأَوْسَط	* You have honored us! * May God honor your dignity! *(a courtesy and rsponce to it)*	* شَرَّفْتَنا ! {شرف} * الشَّرَف لِي! * شَرَّفَ ٱللّهُ مِقدارَك!
conditions (a condition) * dealing conditions	شُرُوط (شَرْط) {شرط} * شُرُوط التَّعامُل	a company (companies) *(takes feminine sound plural)* * the commercial company	شَرِكَة (شَرِكات) {شرك} * الشَّرِكَة التِّجارِيَّة
to be splintered, to be shattered	شَظَى {شظي}	honorable, illustrious * The Illustrious *Azhar*	شَرِيف {شرف} * الأَزْهَر الشَّرِيف
he felt (feeling) * strong feeling	شَعَرَ (شُعُور) {شعر} * شُعُور قَوِيّ	popular, the popular	شَعْبِيَّة / الشَّعْبِيَّة {شعب}
* thanks, thank (you) * thanksgiving * Many thanks, thanks a lot!	* شُكْراً! {شكر} * الشُّكْر * شُكْراً جَزِيلاً!	cure, healing (he cured, he healed)	شِفاء (شَفَى) {شفي}
sun / the Sun * the Sun-related (الـ)	شَمْس / الشَّمْس {شمس} * الـ الشَّمْسِيَّة	shape, look *(broken plural)*	شَكْل (أَشْكال) {شكل}
a certificate, a diploma, a degree (diplomas,	شَهادَة (شَهادات)	candle (candles) *(takes feminine sound*	شَمْعَة (شَمْعات /

degrees) * his diploma, his degree * her diploma or degree	{شهد} * شَـهادَتِـهِ * شَـهادَتِـها	*plural and broken plural*)	شُمُوع) {شمع}
turning into gray color (*said of hair turning gray)*	شُـهُـوب {شهب}	month (months) *(takes two patterns of broken plural)* * the coming month, the next month	شَـهْـر (شُهُور / أَشْهُـر) {شهر} * الشَّـهْـر ٱلـقـادِم
thing, something (things) (*nominative / accusative*)	شَـيء، شَـيْـئـاً (أَشْـيـاءُ) {شيأ}	soup (soups) (*takes feminine sound plural*)	شُـورَبَـة (شُـورَبـات) {شرب}
		Devil, Satin (takes *broken plural*)	شَيْطـان (شَياطِـيـن) {شيطن}

companion, friend *(takes broken plural)* * My friend, my companion	صاحِـب (أَصْـحـاب) {صحب} * صاحِبِـي	patient, enduring, perseverant (patient ones) *(takes masculine sound plural)*	صابِـر (صابِـرُونَ) {صبـر}
he / it became (becoming)	صارَ (صَـيْـرورَة) {صيـر}	he hunted (hunting)	صادَ (صَـيْـد) {صيد}
morning * Good morning! * Good morning! (*response*)	صَـبـاح {صبح} * صَـبـاحَ ٱلـخَـيْـر! * صَـبـاحَ ٱلـنُّـور!	he shook hand (shaking hand)	صافَـحَ (مُـصـافَـحَـة) {صفح}
he was patient, he endured (Patience, endurance / the patience)	صَـبَـرَ (صَـبْـر) {صبـر} صَـبْـر / الـصَّـبْـر	* this morning * at morning time (adverb	* صَـبـاحَ ٱلـيَـوْم * صَـبـاحـاً
journalist *(masculine / feminine pair)* * the journalists	صِحافِـيّ / صِحافِـيَّـة {صحف} * الصِّحافِيُّونَ	he dyed, , he painted (dying, painting)	صَـبَـغَ (صَـبْـغ) {صبـغ}
true, right, correct	صَحِـيـح {صحح}	* your health	* صِـحَّـتُـكَ {صحح} (صِـحَّـة+كَ)
he believed you	* صَـدَّقَـكَ (صَدَّقَ+كَ) {صدق}	* my chest, my breast	* صَـدْرِي (صَـدْر+ي) {صدر}

a female friend (female friends)	صَدِيقَة {صدق} (صَديقات)	friend / the friend (friends) *(broken plural)* * My friend	صَدِيق / الصَّدِيق (أَصْدِقاء) {صدق} * صَدِيقِي
small, little, young (feminine singular & plural) * the youngest among them (females)	صُغْرَى (صُغْرَيات) {صغر} * صُغْراهُنَّ	difficult *(masculin / feminine pair)*	صَعْب/ صَعْبَة {صعب}
class, classroom *(takes broken plural)*	صَفّ (صُفُوف) {صفف}	small, little, young *(broken plural)* *(feminine singular & plural)*	صَغِير (صِغار) {صغر} صَغِيرَة - ات
page (pages) *(takes feminine sound plural)*	صَفْحَة (صَفَحات) {صفح}	adjective (the adjective) (adjectives) *(takes feminine sound plural)*	صِفَة (الصِّفَة) (صِفات) {وصف}
* *Nisbaah* adjectives *(adjectives based on nouns, to describe a relation to the noun)*	* صِفات ٱلنِّسْبَة {وصف} {نسب}	* the surface of the bodies of waters *(idiomatic)*	* صَفْحَةُ ٱلمِياه {صفح}
he clapped, he applauded (clapping, applauding)	صَفَّقَ (تَصْفِيق) {صفق}	* the adjective and the noun being modified by it *(a grammatical term for a noun-adjective phrase)*	* الصِّفَة وَالمَوْصُوف {وصف}
correct, true	صَواب {صوب}	prayer, praying * for praying	صَلاة (صَلَوَات) {صلو} * لِلصَّلاة
fasting (he fasted)	صَوْم (صامَ) {صوم}	a picture, way, manner *(takes broken plural)* * in this manner, in this way	صُورَة (صُوَر) {صور} * عَلَى هَذِه الصُّورَة
		Summer (the Summer)	صَيْف (الصَّيْف) {صيف}

ض

harmful *(masculine / feminine pair)*	ضارّ / ضارَّة {ضرر}	officer *(takes broken plural)* * Security officer	ضابِط (ضُبّاط) {ضبط} * ضابِط الأَمْن
* you *(plural)* laughed	* ضَحِكْتُمْ {ضحك}	he laughed (laughing)	ضَحِكَ (ضَحِك) {ضحك}
he has beaten, he stroked (beating, striking, multiplication in math)	ضَرَبَ (ضَرْب) {ضرب}	he harmed (harming, harm)	ضَرَّ (ضَرَر) {ضرر}

weak, disadvantaged *(masculine / feminine pair)*	ضَعِيف / ضَعِيفَة {ضعف}	* she set up an appointment *(to be learned as an idiom)*	* ضَرَبَتْ مَوْعِداً {ضرب} {وعد}
a pronoun (pronouns) *(takes broken plural)* * Pronoun of separation	ضَمِير (ضَمائِر) {ضمر} * ضَمِير الفَصْل	* Ďammah is the name for one of the short vowels which appear over consonant letters	* ضَمَّة (ُ◌) {ضمم}
* speaker pronouns = 1st person pronouns	* ضَمائِر ٱلمُتَكَلِّم {ضمر} {كلم}	* absentee pronouns = 3rd person pronouns	* ضَمائِر ٱلغائِب {ضمر} {غيب}
* attached or suffixed pronouns	* الضَمائِر ٱلمُتَّصِلَة {ضمر} {وصل}	* addressee pronouns = 2nd person pronouns	* ضَمائِر ٱلمُخاطَب {ضمر} {خطب}
light (lights) *(takes broken plural)*	ضَوْء (أَضْواء) {ضوء}	* separat or subject pronouns	* الضَمائِر ٱلمُنْفَصِلَة {ضمر} {فصل}
hospitality / the hospitality	ضِيافَة / الضِّيافَة) {ضيف}	suburbs (a suburb) *(takes broken plural)*	ضَواحِي (ضاحِيَة) {ضحي}
* his guest * honorable guests	* ضَيْفُهُ (ضَيْف+ـهُ) {ضيف} * ضُيُوف كِرام	a guest (guests) *(takes broken plural)* * to (for) the guests	ضَيْف (ضُيُوف) {ضيف} * لِلضُّيُوف
		difficulty, hardship	ضِيق / الضِّيق {ضيق}

ط

* she bowed her head *(as a sign of being bashful)*	* طَأْطَأَتْ رَأْسَها {طأطأ}	she bent, she bowed (her head) (bending, bowing of head)	طَأْطَأَتْ (طَأْطَأَة) {طأطأ}
it became good, pleasant, agreeable (goodness, geniality)	طابَ (طِيبَة) {طيب}	an airplane / the airplane * by airplane	طائِرَة / الطّائِرَة {طير} * بِٱلطّائِرَة
fresh / the fresh	طازَج / الطّازَج {طزج}	impress, stamp, mark, character (stamps, characters)	طابِع (طَوابِع) {طبع}
a line. a single file of people (lines, single files of people) *(takes broken plural)*	طابُور (طَوابِير) {طبر}	a student (students) *(female)* student (students) * the Arab students	طالِب (طُلّاب) {طلب} طالِبَة (طالِبات) * الطُّلّاب العَرَب

medicine / the medicinal science)	طِبّ / الطِّبّ {طبب}	a table (tables) *(takes feminine sound plural)*	طاوِلَة (طاوِلات) {طول}
of course, naturally *(adverb)*	طَبْعاً {طبع}	he printed (printing)	طَبَعَ (طِباعَة) {طبع}
drum (drums) *(takes broken plural)*	طَبْل (طُبُول) {طبل}	dish, plate *(takes broken plural)* * Today's dish * Hummus plate	طَبَق (أَطْباق) * طَبَقُ ٱليَوْمِ * طَبَق حُمُّص
he knocked, he banged (knocking, banging)	طَرَقَ (طَرْق) {طرق}	medical doctor (medical doctors) *(masculine / feminine forms and their corresponding plurals)*	طَبِيب (أَطِبَّاء) / طَبِيبَة (طَبِيبات) {طبب}
food (foods) *(takes broken plural)* * my fovarite food * the supper food, the supper meal	طَعام (أَطْعِمَة) {طعم} * طَعَامِي المُفَضَّل * طَعام العَشاء	a way, a method * in a way	طَرِيقَة {طرق} * بِطَرِيقَةٍ
baby, young child *(takes broken plural)*	طِفْل (أَطْفال) {طفل}	the Egyptian term for *Falafil*	طَعمِيَّة / الطَّعْمِيَّة {طعم}
divorce / the divorce * your divorce * you divorced her * divorce cases	طَلاق / الطَّلاق {طلق} * طَلاقِكَ * طَلَّقْتَها * حالات طَلاق	weather / the weather	طَقْس / الطَّقْس {طقس}
* He asked for her hand * our request, our demand, our order * he requested from him	* طَلَبَ يَدَها {طلب} * طَلَبَ مِنْهُ	request, demand, order * she requested * our request, our demand, our order	طَلَب {طلب} * طَلَبَتْ * طَلَبُنا (طَلَب+نا)
* a purchase order	* طَلَب شِراء {طلب} {شري}	* your requests *(for plural)*	* طَلَباتِكُمْ {طلب}
it was purified (purification)	طَهُرَ (طَهارَة) {طهر}	cooking pot (cooking pots) *(takes broken plural)*	طَنْجَرَة (طَناجِر) {طنجر}
for long time, for long *(adverbial usage)*	طَوِيلاً {طول}	long, tall *(masculine / broken plural)* long, tall *(feminine plural)*	طَوِيل (طِوال) {طول} طَوِيلَة (طَوِيلات)

birds / the birds (a bird)	طُيُور / الطُّيُور (طَيْر) {طير}	good, pleasant * Good greeting!	طَيِّباً / طَيِّبَةً {طيب} * تَحِيَّةً طَيِّبَةً!
		pilot / the pilot	طَيَّار / الطَّيَّار {طير}

ظ

envelope (envelopes), circumstance (circumstances) *(takes broken plural)*	ظَرْف (ظُرُوف) {ظرف}	gazelle (gazelles) *(takes broken plural)*	ظَبْي (ظِباء) {ظبي}
shades *(broken plural)* (shade)	ظِلال (ظِلّ) {ظلل}	elegant, graceful, charming *(masculine / feminine pair)*	ظَرِيف / ظَرِيفَة {ظرف}
he appeared (appearance)	ظَهَرَ (ظُهُور) {ظهر}	darkness / the darkness	ظَلام / الظَّلام {ظلم}
noon / the noon time * in the after noon	ظُهْر / الظُّهْر {ظهر} * بَعْدَ الظُّهْر	back, rear part of the body	ظَهْر (ظُهُور) {ظهر}

ع

family-related *(masculine / feminine pair)*	عائِلِيّ / عائِلِيَّة {عيل}	family (families) *(takes feminine sound plural)* * his family	عائِلَة (عائِلات) {عيل} * عائِلَتِه
tenth / the tenth / tenthly	عاشِر / العاشِر / عاشِراً {عشر}	he returned (returning)	عادَ / يَعُودُ (عَوْدَة) {عود}
sound-minded *(masculine / feminine pair)*	عاقِل / عاقِلَة {عقل}	a storm *(takes broken plural)*	عاصِفَة (عَواصِف) {عصف}
scientist, scholar (scientists, scholars) *(takes broken plural)*	عالِم (عُلَماء) {علم}	world *(takes broken plural)*	عالَم (عَوالِم) {علم}
public / the public * general drills	عامَّة / العامَّة {عمم} * تَمارين عامَّة	You treat! *(command verb for masculine singular)*	عامِلْ! {عمل}
admonition, lessens to be learned (an admonition, a lesson learned)	عِبَر (عِبْرَة) {عبر}	he worshiped (worshiping)	عَبَدَ (عِبادَة) {عبد}

he expressed (expression)	عَبَّرَ (تَعْبِير) {عبر}	expression, phrase (expressions, phrases) *(takes feminine sound plural)*	عِبارَة (عِبارات) {عبر}
he stumbled, he tripped, he found, he discovered (stumbling, finding)	عَثَرَ (عُثُور) {عثر}	Hebrew * the Hebrew Language	عِبْرِيَّة * اللُّغَة العِبْرِيَّة {عبر}
strange, wonder-causing *(masculine / feminine pair)*	عَجِيب / عَجِيبَة {عجب}	haste, rush	عَجَلَة / العَجَلَة {عجل}
you returned	عُدْتَ {عود}	he counted, he considered (counting, consideration)	عَدَّ (العَدّ) {عدد}
several	عِدَّة {عدد}	a number (of) * a large number	عَدَد (مِنْ) {عدد} * عَدَد كَبِير
enemy (enemies) *(takes broken plural)*	عَدُوّ (أَعْداء) {عدو}	lentil / the lentil * lentil soup	عَدَس / العَدَس {عدس} * شُورَبَة ٱلعَدَس
* Arabic (as a language) * The Arabic Language	*العَرَبِيَّة {عرب} *اللُّغَة ٱلعَرَبِيَّة	Arab, Arabic *(masculine / feminine pair)*	عَرَبِيّ (عَرَب) {عرب} عَرَبِيَّة (عَرَبِيّات)
bride *(takes feminine sound plural and broken plural)*	عَرُوس = عَرُوسَة (عَرُوسات / عَرائِس) {عرس}	I knew, I learned that (knowing, learning that)	عَرَفْتُ (مَعْرِفَة) {عرف}
the state of being bachelor or single (noun)	عُزُوبِيَّة {عزب}	groom *(takes broken plural)*	عَرِيس (عِرْسان) {عرس}
difficulty, hardship *(feminine gender noun)*	عُسْرَى {عسر}	dear (dear ones) *(masculine / feminine pair and their corresponding plurals)*	عَزِيز (أَعِزَّاء) {عزز} عَزِيزَة (عَزِيزات)
supper, dinner / the supper * for supper	عَشاء / العَشاء {عشي} * لِلعَشاء	military *(masculine / feminine pair)*	عَسْكَرِيّ / عَسْكَرِيَّة {عسكر}
twenty *(nominative / accusative pair)*	عِشْرُونَ / عِشْرِينَ {عشر}	ten *(masculine / feminine pair)* * ten minutes	عَشر / عَشْرَة {عشر} * عَشْرُ دَقائِق
juice * mango juice	عَصِير {عصر} {منج} *عَصِيرُ ٱلمانْجَة	afternoon time / at afternoon time	عَصْرَ / عَصْراً {عصر}
perfume, scent (perfumes) *(takes broken plural)*	عِطْر (عُطُور) {عطر}	he / it has bitten (biting)	عَضَّ (العَضّ) {عضض}

break, vacation (breaks, vacations) *(takes broken plural)* * Spring break	عُطْلَة (عُطَل) {عطل} *عُطْلَة الرَّبِيع	thirsty *(feminine / masculine adjective pair)*	عَطْشَى / عَطْشَان {عطش}
chaste, modest, virtuous, decent *(masculine / feminine adjective pair)*	عَفِيف / عَفِيفَة {عفف}	* Welcome! (*as a response to* شُكْراً) * Excuse me! * Pardoning (of)	* عَفْواً! {عفو} * عَفْواً! * العَفْوُ (عَنْ)
a necklace (necklaces) *(takes broken plural)*	عِقْد (عُقُود) {عقد}	a decade, a contract (decades, contracts) *(takes broken plural)*	عَقْد (عُقُود) {عقد}
mind / the mind	عَقْل / العَقْل {عقل}	a scorpion (scorpions) *(takes broken plural)*	عَقْرَب (عَقَارِب) {عقرب}
* <u>Literally</u>: on my eye and head, <u>Idiomatically</u>: it is of the greatest consideration in approval	* عَلَى ٱلعَيْنِ {عين} وَٱلراس! {رأس}	on, above * ready for, prepared to	عَلَى {علو} * عَلَى ٱسْتِعْدَاد (لِـ) {عدد}
* May it be with God's Blessings! *(An idiom said as a statement of approval)*	* عَلَى بَرَكَةِ ٱللّه! {علو} {برك}	* at the family level	* عَلَى ٱلمُسْتَوَى ٱلعائِلِيّ
* by way of	* عَلَى طَرِيقَة {طرق}	* By way of example, for example! *(treat it as an idiom)*	* عَلَى سَبِيل ٱلمِثال {علو} {سبل} {مثل}
relation (relations) * International Relations	عَلاقَة (عَلاقات) {علق} * العَلاقات الدُّوَلِيَّة	remedy, cure (remedies, cures)	عِلاج (عِلاجات) {علج}
* the sign of satisfaction and acceptance	* عَلامَةُ الرِّضَى {علم} {رضي}	a sign, a symbol (signs, symbols) *(singular / plural pair)* * signs of case-ending inflections	عَلامَة (عَلامات) * عَلامات الإعْراب {علم} {عرب}
* on you, against you * you must	* عَلَيْكَ (عَلَى+كَ) * عَلَيْكَ (أَنْ)	she / it flew high (ascending high)	عَلَتْ (عُلُوّ) {علو}
* on both of them, both of them must	* عَلَيْهِما (عَلَى+هِما)	you *(feminine)* have to, it falls upon you *(to be learned as an idiom)*	* عَلَيْكِ أَنْ {علو} (على+كِ)
he taught, he instructed (teaching, education)	عَلَّمَ (تَعْلِيم) {علم}	knowledge, science * political sciences	عِلْم (عُلُوم) {علم} * العُلُوم السِّياسِيَّة

scholars, scientists (a scholar, a scientist) *(plural / singular pair)*	عُلَماء (عالِم) {علم}	You teach! *(command verb for a male-female pair and for plural)*	عَلِّمْ!/ عَلِّمِي!/ عَلِّمُوا! {علم}
age, (ages) *(takes broken plural)*	عُمْر (أَعْمار) {عمر}	paternal uncle (uncles) paternal aunt (aunts)	عَمّ (أَعْمام) {عمم} عَمَّة (عَمَّات)
* her paternal uncle	عَمُّها (عَمّ+ها) {عمم}	* my age	عُمْري (عُمْر+ي) {عمم}
work, job *(broken plural)* * to work (for), working towards	عَمَل (أَعْمال) {عمل} * لِلْعَمَلِ (عَلَى)	* her paternal aunt	عَمَّتُها {عمم} (عَمَّة+ها)
I worked * your current job	عَمِلْتُ {عمل} * عَمَلُكَ ٱلحالِيّ	he worked - he works she worked- she works	عَمِلَ - يَعْمَلُ عَمِلَتْ - تَعْمَلُ
about, with * With your permission! *(to masculine / feminine)*	عَنْ * عَنْ إِذْنِكَ / كِ! {أذن}	* two paternal uncles / two paternal aunts *(dual forms for nominative and accusative moods)*	عَمّانِ/ عَمَّيْنِ {عمم} * عَمَّتانِ / عَمَّتَيْنِ
when, at *(adverb of time and place)* * when, at the time when	عِنْدَ * عِنْدَما	grapes (grapes) *(collective noun and its plural)*	عِنَب (أَعْناب) {عنب}
title, address (addresses, titles) * by (under) the title	عُنْوان (عَناوِين) {عنون} * بِعُنْوان	with, in possession of : * he has * she has * I have *(though this is a particle, when attached to pronouns, it assumes the meaning of the verb "to have")*	عِنْدَ * عِنْدَهُ * عِنْدَها * عِنْدِي
help, aid (the help, the aid)	عَوْن (العَوْن) {عود}	* my return, my going back	عَوْدَتِي {عود} (عَوْدَة+ـي)
eye / the eye (two eyes) (eyes) *(takes broken plural)*	عَيْن / العَيْن {عين} (عَيْنانِ) (عُيُون)	holiday, festival (holidays, festivals) *(takes broken plural)* * birthday	عِيد (أَعْياد) {عيد} * عِيدُ مِيلاد
* some samples	* بَعْضُ العَيِّنات {عين}	a sample (samples) *(takes feminine sound plural)*	عَيِّنَة (عَيِّنات) {عين}

an absentee *(masculine / feminine pair)*	غـائـب / غـائِـبَـة {غيب}	he was absent / she was absent (absenteeism)	غـابَ / غـابَـتْ (غِـيـاب) {غيب}
expensive, precious (*masculine / feminine adjective pair)*	غـالِـي / غـالِـيَـة {غلو}	he/ they/it departed, left (*departure, leaving)*	غـادَرَ (مُغادَرَة) {غدر}
he / it soiled, covered with dust	غَـبَّـرَ {غـبـر}	dust	غُـبـار {غـبـر}
lunch / the lunch * late lunch	غَـداء / الـغَـداء {غدي} * غَـداءً مُـتَـأَخِّـراً	tomorrow / at morrow time *(adverbial)*	غَـد / غَـداً
raven (ravens) (takes *broken plural*)	غُـراب (غِرْبان) {غرب}	he misled, he deceived (deception, delusion)	غَـرَّ (غُـرُور) {غرر}
◦ in your life of diaspora	* غُـرْبَـتِـكِ {غرب}	feeling of estrangement outside one's homeland = diaspora	غُـرْبَـة / الـغُـرْبَـة {غرب}
rooms (a room) (*takes broken plural*)	غُـرَف (غُـرْفَـة) {غرف}	west / * the West *(as opposed to the East)*	غَـرْب / * اَلـغَـرْب {غرب}
sunset	* غُـرُوبُ الـشَّـمْـس {غرب} {شمس}	◦ the reception room, the guest room	* غُـرْفَـة {غرف} اَلاِسْـتِـقْـبـال {قبل}
deceived, misled *(masculine / feminine adjective forms)*	غَـرِيـر / غَـرِيـرَة {غرر}	stranger, strange, odd *(masculine / feminine adjective forms)*	غَـرِيـب / غَـرِيـبَـة {غرب}
he / it / they sang (singing)	غَـنَّـى (غِـنـاء) {غني}	it became expensive, (high price, high cost)	غَـلَـت (غَـلاء) {غلو}
other than, different from, unlike, no, not *(specific meaning will be determined by context)*	غَـيْـر {غيـر}	absence	غِـيـاب {غيب}
* non-free, not free	* غَـيْـرُ حُـرَّة	he changed (changing)	غَـيَّـرَ (تَـغْـيِـيـر) {غيـر}
* <u>Literally</u>: the non-reasoning subject = <u>Idiomatically</u>: non-human subject *(as a grammatical term)*	* غَـيْـرِ ٱلـعـاقِـل	* other than you	* غَـيْـرِكَ {غيـر}

ف

mouse *(nominative / accusative forms)* (mice) *(takes broken plural)*	فَـأر / فَـأراً (فِـئْـران) {فأر}	so, then, hence, therefore *(as a one letter connector, it will be always written prefixed to the following word)*	فَـ

….. , then you ask! *(command verb)*	فَـاْطْـلُـبْ! {طلب} (فَـ+اطْـلُـبْ)	* …, so I hope	* فَـأَرْجُـو (فَـ + أَرْجُـو) {رجو}
opener / * the Opening Chapter of the Qur'an	فـاتِـحَـة / * الـفـاتِـحَـة {فتح}	heart (hearts) *(takes broken plural)*	فُـؤاد (أَفْـئِـدَة) {فأد}
he / it won (in) * won in it	فـازَ (بِـ) (فَـوْز) {فوز} * فـازَ بِـهـا	deluxe, of high quality *(masculine / feminine adjective pair)*	فـاخِر / فـاخِـرَة {فخر}
doer, actor / the subject of the verb *(as a grammatical term)*	فـاعِـل / الـفـاعِـل {فعل}	abstainer, *Fatimah* *(a female proper name)*	فـاطِـمَـةُ {فطم}
… it begins (with) (beginning)	فَـتَـبْـدَأُ (بِـ) (بِـدايَـة) {بدأ}	he / it desisted, refrained, ceased * he / it continued to be *(idiom)*	فَـتِـئَ {فـتـأ} * مـا فَـتِـئَ
"*Fatḥah*" is one of the three short vowels written above a consonant * an opening, gap (openings)	فَـتْـحَـة (َ◌) {فـتح} * فَـتْـحَـة (فَـتَـحـات)	he opened, conquered (opening, conquering) * opening for	فَـتَـحَ (فَـتْـح) {فـتح} * فَـتْـح لِـ
he / it abated, became languid (abating, cooling off)	فَـتَـرَ (فُـتُـور) {فـتـر}	they opened *(masculine plural conjugation)*	فَـتَـحُـوا (فَـتْـح) {فتح}
girls, young ladies (a girl, a young lady)	فَـتَـيـات (فَـتـاة) {فتو}	period of time * for a period of time	فَـتْـرَة {فـتـر} * لِـفَـتْـرَة (لِـ+فَـتْـرَة)
relief, ease from difficulty	فَـرَج / الـفَـرَج {فرج}	dawn, daybreak / the day-breaking time	فَـجْـر / الفَـجْـر {فجر}
mare, hare (mares) *(takes broken plural)* * horsemanship, chivalry	فَـرَس (أَفْـراس) {فرس} * الـفُـرُوسِـيَّـة	member, individual (members, individuals)	فَـرد (أَفْـراد) {فرد}
duty, decree, ordinance (duties, decrees, ordinances) *(takes broken plural)*	فَـرْض (فُـرُوض) {فرض}	opportunity, chance *(takes broken plural)* * It is a good opportunity meeting you*! (idiom)*	فُـرْصَـة (فُـرَص) {فرص} * فُـرْصَـة طَـيِّـبَـة! * فُـرْصَـة مُـنـاسِـبَـة
France French *(masculine / feminine pair)*	فَـرَنْـسا فَـرَنْـسِـيّ / فَـرَنْـسِـيَّـة	Pharaoh Pharaonic *(masculine / feminine pair)* * Pharaonic antiquities	فِـرْعَـوْن {فرعن} فِـرْعَـوْنـيّ / فِـرْعَـوْنِـيَّـة * الـتُّـحَـف الْـفِـرْعَـوْنِـيَّـة
seasons, classes (a season, a class) *(broken plural)* * the spring season	فُـصُـول (فَـصْـل) {فصل} * فَـصْـلُ الـرَّبِـيـع	He failed (failing) * we failed (in)	فَـشِـلَ (فَـشَـل) {فشل} * فَـشِـلْـنـا (فـي)

favor, bounty, grace, surplus (favors, bounties, surpluses) *(takes broken plural)*	فَـضْـل (أَفْـضـال) {فضل}	silver *(generic)*	فِـضَّـة {فضض}
your (*plural*) favor, your kindness * May your favor last!	فَـضْـلُـكُـمْ {فضل} (فَـضْـل+كُمْ) * دامَ فَـضْـلُـكُـمْ !	your favor, your bounty, your grace * If you gracefully please! (*idiom*)	فَـضْـلِـكَ (فَـضْـل+كَ) { فضل} * مِـنْ فَـضْـلِـكَ / ـكِ!
he did (doing) * the verb she did	فَـعَـلَ (فِـعْـل) / * الـفِـعْل فَـعَـلَـتْ (فَـعَـلَ+تْ)	he split, he cleaved, he created (splitting, creating) *(verbal noun)* * breaking of the fast, having breakfast	فَـطَـرَ (فُـطُـور) {فطر} * فُـطُـور
* the past tense verb * the present tense verb	* الـفِـعْـلُ الـمـاضِـي * الـفِـعْـلُ الـمُـضـارِع	you did (*masculine*) you did (*feminine*) you did (*masculine plural*)	فَـعَـلْـتَ (فَعَلَ+تَ) فَـعَـلْـتِ (فَعَلَ+تِ) فَـعَـلْـتُـمْ (فَعَلْ+تُمْ)
idea (ideas) * Good idea!	فِـكْـرَة (أَفْـكـار) {فكر} * فِـكْـرَة جَـيِّـدَة!	only	فَـقَـطْ
mouth (mouths) *(takes broken plural)*	فَـمّ (أَفْـواه) {فوه}	Palestine	فِـلِـسْـطِـيـن
cup, coffee / tea cup (cups) * cup of tea	فِـنْـجـان (فَـنـاجِـيـن) {فنجن} * فِـنْـجـان شـاي	So, what…?	فَـمـا …؟
So, is (are)…?	فَـهَـل…؟	hotel, inn / the hotel, the inn (hotels, inns) *(takes broken plural)*	فُـنْـدُق / الـفُـنْـدُق (فَـنـادِق) {فندق}
broad bean * peanuts * the fava beans dip	فُـول {فول} {سود} * الـفُول السُّودانِـيّ * الـفُول الـمُـدَمَّس	then, she / it is	فَـهِـيَ
elephant (elephants) *(takes broken plural)*	فِـيـل (فِـيَـلَـة) {فيل}	in, at *(preposition)* * in it, there is in it * in fact	فِـي * فِـيـهـا * فِـي الـحَـقِـيـقَـة
		a film, a movie *(adopted from English)* *(broken plural)*	فِـيـلْـم (أَفْـلام)

he met (meeting) * I met	قابَلَ (مُقابَلَة) قابَلْتُ (قابَلْ+تُ) {قبل}	list (broken plural) * price list * food menu	قائِمَة (قَوائِم) {قوم} * قائِمَةُ ٱلأَسْعَار * قائِمَةُ ٱلطَّعام
he led, he drove steer (a car) (leading, driving)	قادَ (قِيادَة) {قود}	to fight (fighting) * May God fight the Devil! (an idiomatic supplication said when some failure takes place)	قاتَلَ (مُقاتَلَة) * قاتَلَ ٱللَّهُ ٱلشَّيْطانَ! {قتل}
coming, upcoming (the coming)	قادِمَة / القادِمَة {قدم}	capable (of), able (to) (adverbial use, singular / plural)	قادِراً (عَلَى) قادِرِينَ (عَلَى) / (قادِر) {قدر}
he stood up (standing up) * he undertook (a task) (undertaking) * she undertook	قامَ (قِيام) {قوم} * قامَ (القِيام بِ) * قامَتْ (بِ)	he said (leading, saying) * they said * we said	قالَ (قَوْل) {قول} * قالُوا * قُلْنا
before	قَبْلَ	law / the law (laws) (takes broken plural)	قانُون / القانُون (قَوانِين) {قنن}
surely, indeed (a particle of emphasis before a past tense verb) * and might (if it precedes a present tense verb)	قَدْ = لَقَدْ * وَقَدْ	I was accepted, I was admitted (passive voice verb for first person singular) * they were (dual) accepted	قُبِلْتُ (قُبُول) * قُبِلا
old, ancient (broken plural- masculine) (feminine and its feminine sound plural)	قَدِيم (قُدَماء) {قدم} قَدِيمَة (قَدِيمات)	holiness, sacredness, sanctity * Jerusalem * the Most Holy (attribute of God)	قُدْس {قدس} * القُدْس * القُدُّوس
* she introduced her	* قَدَّمَتْها {قدم} (قَدَّمَتْ+ها)	he introduced, he offered (introduction, offering)	قَدَّمَ (تَقْدِيم) {قدم}
he settled down, he established (settling down)	قَرَّ (قَرار) {قرر}	* they introduced, they offered	* قَدَّمُوا {قدم} (قَدَّم+ـوا)
a decision (genitive / accusative forms) * by court decision	قَرار / قَراراً {قرر} * بِقَرار ٱلمَحْكَمَة	he read (reading) I read (past tense)	قَرَأَ (قِراءَة) {قرأ} قَرَأْتُ (قَرَأْ+تُ)
near, nearby (adverb)	قُرْبَ {قرب}	he came closer (to) * getting closer to you (through marriage in your family)	قَرُبَ (مِنْ) {قرب} * القُرْب مِنْكُم
near (to), close (by) (masculine / feminine adjective pairs)	قَرِيب (مِنْ) / قَرِيبَة (مِنْ) {قرب}	he decided (decision, report)	قَرَّرَ (تَقْرِير) {قرر}

department (departments) * I enrolled in the department (of) * the passports department	قِسْم (أَقْسام) {قسم} * اِلْتَحَقْتُ بِقِسْم * قِسْمِ الجَوازات	shortly, soon *(adverb)*	قَريباً {قرب}
story (stories) *(takes broken plural)*	قِصَّة (قِصَص) {قصص}	a determined share or luck	قِسْمَة (أَقْسام) {قسم}
he spent (time), he passed – he passes, he spends (time) * I spent, I passed * you (female) spent time	قَضَى - يَقْضِي * قَضَيْتُ {قضي} * قَضَيْتِ	short (short ones) *(feminine form and its plural)*	قَصير (قِصار) قَصيرَة - ات {قصر}
Qatar *(name of a gulf Arab country)* * in Qatar	قَطَر * بِقَطَر	issue, matter, cause *(takes broken plural)*	قَضِيَّة (قَضايا) {قضي}
cotton * high quality cotton	قُطْن {قطن} * القُطْن الفاخِر	he cut (cutting); he covered (a distance)	قَطَعَ (قَطْع) {قطع}
heart * your hear * my heart	قَلْب {قلب} * قَلْبَكَ (قَلْبَ+كَ) * قَلْبِي (قَلْب+ـي)	he sat down, he became idle (setting down)	قَعَدَ (قُعُود) {قعد}
became less, became short *(in quantity)* / to be less, to become less	قَلَّ / يَقِلُّ {قلل}	* You say! (saying) *(command verb, masculine singular and feminine singular)*	* قُلْ! (قَوْل) {قول} * قُولِي!
little (little ones) *(feminine form and its plural)*	قَليل (أَقِلاَّء) {قلل} قَليلَة (قَليلات)	pen (pens) *(takes broken plural)*	قَلَم (أَقْلام) {قلم}
moon (moons) *(takes broken plural)*	قَمَر (أَقْمار) {قمر}	of small quantity or occurrence *(adverb)*	قَليلاً {قلل}
winter shirts *(takes broken plural)*	* قُمْصان شَتَوِيَّة {قمص}	shirt (shirts) *(takes broken plural)*	قَميص (قُمْصان) {قمص}
contentment	قَناعَة / القَناعَة {قنع}	channel (channels) * Aljazeera TV channel	قَناة (قَنَوات) {قنو} * قَناةُ الجَزيرَة
coffee, coffee-house / the coffee	قَهْوَة / القَهْوَة {قهو}	*quintal, kantar (a large weight equal to about 45 kilograms) (takes broken plural)*	قِنْطار {قنطر} (قَناطير)
values / the values system (a value)	قِيَم / القِيَم (قِيمَة) {قيم}	grammatical rules, bases (a grammatical rule, a base) * Arabic Grammar	قَواعِد (قاعِدَة) {قعد} * القَواعِد ٱلعَرَبِيَّة

ك

your (*suffixed possessive pronouns for "your"; masculine / feminine*)	ـكَ / ـكِ	* as, like (as a one-letter particle, it is always written prefixed to the following word)	* كَـ
he deceived, he duped (deceiving, duping) (*verbal noun*)	كـادَ (كَـيْـد) {كيد}	a writer, an author (writers, authors) (*takes broken plural*)	كـاتِـب (كُـتّـاب) {كتب}
he measured, he weighed (measuring, weighing)	كـالَ (كَـيْـل) {كيل}	cafeteria (*adopted from English*)	كـافِـتِـيرْيـا
Kabob (pronounced as "*Kabaab*")	كَـبـاب / الـكَـبـاب {كبب}	he was (being, universe) * May God be helping you!	كـانَ (كَـوْن) {كون} * كـانَ ٱللَّـهُ فـي عَـوْنِـكَ!
big, large (*Masculine / Feminine pair and their plural*)	كَـبِـيـر (كِـبـار) {كبـر} كَـبِـيـرَة (كَـبِـيـرات)	oldest, biggest (*feminine form*) * the oldest among them (*feminine plural for humans only*)	كُـبْـرى {كبـر} * كُـبْـراهُـنَّ (كُـبْـرَى + هُـنَّ)
he wrote (writing) * I wrote	كَـتَـبَ (كِـتـابَـة) {كتب} * كَـتَـبْـتُ	a book (books) (*takes broken plural*)	كِـتـاب (كُـتُـب) {كتب}
many, plenty (*masculine sound plural*)	كَـثِـيـرُونَ (كَـثِـيـر) {كثـر}	* as a second major, as a second field of specialty	* كَـتَـخَـصُّـص ثـانٍ {خصص} (كَـ + تَـخَـصُّـص)
likewise, also * Is not that so?	كَـذَلِـكَ * أَلَـيْـسَ كَـذَلِـكَ؟	a lot, much (*adverb*)	كَـثِـيـراً {كثـر}
he attacked, he charged maneuvering (attacking) (*verbal noun*)	كَـرَّ (الـكَـرّ) {كرر}	* as a business man	* كَـرَجُـلِ أَعْـمـال
generous, kind, noble (*masculine / feminine pairs*) (*both are proper names*)	كَـرِيـم / كَـرِيـمَـة {كرم}	chair (chairs / the chairs)	كُـرْسِـيّ {كرس} (كَـراسٍ / الـكَـراسِـي)
"*Kasrah*" *is one of the three diacritical marks of short vowel, appearing under the consonant letters)*	كَـسْـرَة (ـِـ)	* honorable ones (*plural*) * your generosity	* كِـرام * كَـرَمُـكُـمْ

kafta (also pronounced as "*kufta*")	كُفْتَة / الكُفْتَة	cake (cakes) * the birthday cake	كَعْكَة {كعك} كَعْكات * كَعْكَةُ عِيد المِيلاد
* all of it * every year	* كُلُّهُ * كُلَّ سَنَة	all, all (of) * all of us * every week	كُلّ {كلل} * كُلُّنا * كُلّ أُسْبُوع
* each one of the two * each one * with all pleasure	* كُلّ مِنْهُما * كُلُّ واحِد * بِكُلِّ سُرُور	he became tired, exhausted (tiredness, exhaustion)	كَلَّ (كَلال) {كلل}
a dog (dogs) *(takes broken plural)*	كَلْب (كِلاب) {كلب}	speech, talking / the speech	كَلام / الكَلام {كلم}
he talked, he spoke (talking, speaking)	كَلَّمَ (تَكْلِيم) {كلم}	a word (words) *(takes feminine sound plural)*	كَلِمَة (كَلِمات) {كلم}
/ How many...? * For how much...? * how much we wish	كَمْ ...؟ * بِكَمْ ...؟ * كَمْ نَتَمَنَّى	college (colleges) *(takes feminine sound plural)* * business school or college	كُلِّيَّة (كُلِّيّات) {كلل} * كُلِّيَّة التِّجارَة
* as a teacher *(female)* (female teachers)	* كَمُدَرِّسَة {درس} (مُدَرِّسات)	your *(masculine plural suffix pronoun)*	ـكُمْ
quantity (quantities) *(tales feminine sound plural)*	كَمِّيَّة (كَمِّيّات) {كمم}	as, in the same way as, likewise, additionally	كَما
woolen sweater *(takes feminine sound plural)*	كَنْزَة صُوف (كَنْزات) {كنز} {صوف}	a treasure (treasures) *(takes broken plural)*	كَنْز (كُنُوز) {كنز}
church (churches) *(takes broken plural)*	كَنِيسَة (كَنائِس) {كنس}	your *(feminine plural suffix pronoun)*	ـكُنَّ
congress / the Congress *(transcription of the English word)*	كُونْغْرِس / الكُونْغْرِس	courses of study (a course of study *(adopted from English)*	كُورْسات (كُورْس)
How...? * How are you? *(generic idiom)*	كَيْفَ ...؟ * كَيْفَ الحال؟	in order to, so that, for *(a subjunctive particle which precedes verbs and make them in subjunctive mood)*	كَيْ
		* How are you? *(specific for one male / female)*	* كَيْفَ حالُكَ / ـكِ؟

ل

no * does not *(if followed by a verb)* * neither / nor * you are still a young man	لا * لا / * وَلا * لا زِلْتَ شابّاً	to, belonging to, for *(preposition)*	لِـ
* for your questions	* لِـأَسْـئِـلَـتِـكَ {سأل} (لِـ+أَسْـئِـلَة+كَ)	* for our son	* لِـابْـنِـنـا {إبن} (لِـ+اِبْنِ+نـا)
* for the preparation	* لِـإِعْـدادِ {عدد} (لِـ+إِعْـداد)	* for your mastery	* لِـإِتْـقـانِـكَ {تقن} (لِـ+إِتْـقَـان+كَ)
* for the first time	* لِـأَوَّلِ مَـرَّة {أول} (لِـ+أَوَّلِ)	* because	* لِأَنَّ (لِـ+أَنَّ)
pearls (a pearl) *(takes broken plural)*	لُـؤْلُـؤَة (لآلِـئ) {لألأ}	* for a period (of time)	* لِـمُـدَّةِ {مدد} (لِـ+مُـدَّةِ)
he took refuge (a place of refuge)	لاذَ (مَـلاذ) {لوذ}	he / it appeared, showed, loomed, emerged (appearing)	لاح (لَـوْح) {لوح}
a player (players) *(takes masculine sound plural)*	لاعِـب (لاعِـبُـونَ) {لعب}	must, necessary (to) * I must rest	لازِم (أَنْ) {لزم} * لازِم أَرْتـاح
dress, garment (dresses) *(takes broken plural)*	لِـبـاس (أَلْبِـسَـة) {لبس}	she / it met, she / it found (meeting, finding)	لاقَـت (لِـقـاء) {لقي}
* in order to become	* لِـتُـصْـبِـحَ (لِـ+تُـصْـبِـحَ) {صبح}	Lebanon Lebanese *(masculine / feminine pair)*	لُـبْـنـان لُـبْـنـانِـيّ / لُـبْـنـانِـيَّـة
committee (committees) *(takes broken plural)*	لَـجْـنَـة (لِـجان) {لجن}	* for having, for taking up (he had, he took up)	* لِـتَـنـاوُل (تَـنـاوَلَ) {نول}
grave / the grave (graves) *(takes broken plural)*	لَـحْـد / الـلَّـحْـد (لُحُود) {لحد}	cover, blanket, quilt (quilts) *(takes broken plural)*	لِـحـاف (لُـحُـف) {لحف}
* for the engagement (of)	* لِـخِـطْـبَـةِ {خطب}	meat (meats) *(takes broken plural)*	لَـحْـم (لُـحُـوم) {لحم}

therefore *(invariable connecter)*	لِـذَلِـكَ	with, at, have *(adverb)* * with me, I have	لَـدَى {لدي} * لَـدَيَّ
you are not *(masculine singular)*	لَـسْـتَ {ليس}	I am not	لَـسْـتُ {ليس}
you are not *(masculine plural)*	لَـسْـتُـمْ {ليس}	you are not *(feminine singular)*	لَـسْـتِ {ليس}
you are not *(feminine plural)*	لَـسْـتُـنَّ {ليس}	you are not *(masculine & feminine dual)*	لَـسْـتُـمـا {ليس}
for asking, for requesting	لِـطَـلَـبِ {طلب}	they are not *(feminine plural)*	لَـسْـنَ {ليس}
game (games) * the game of vocabulary activation	لُـعْـبَـة (لُعَب) {لعب} * لُـعْـبَـة تَـفْـعِـيـل الـمُـفْـرَدات	kind, gentle *(feminine / masculine adjective pair, also common proper names)*	لَـطِـيـفَـة / لَـطِـيـف {لطف}
a language * our language * her mother tongue	لُـغَـة (لُـغـات) {لغو} * لُـغَـتَـنـا (لُـغَـة+نـا) * لُـغَـتُـهـا الأَمّ	a language (languages) * two languages * the Hebrew Language	لُـغَـة (لُـغـات) {لغو} * لُـغَـتـانِ * اللُّغَـة الـعِـبْـرِيَّـة
for opening	لِـفَـتْـحِ {فتح} (لِـ+فَـتْـح)	linguistic (*Nisbah adjective of* لُـغَـة)	لُـغَـوِيّ / لُـغَـوِيَّـة {لغو}
		scarf (scarfs) *(takes feminine sound plural)*	لَـفْـحَـة (لَـفْـحات) {لفح}
indeed, verily, surely * indeed you have enlightened	لَـقَـدْ * لَـقَـدْ نَـوَّرْتَ	meeting, encounter (he met) * Until we meet again! *(idiom said upon leaving)* * I am happy for meeting you!	لِـقـاء (لَـقِـيَ) {لقي} * إِلَـى الـلِّـقـاء! * سَـعِـدْتُ بِـلِـقـائِـكَ / ـكِ!
for each, for every	لِـكُـلِّ (لِـ + كُـلّ)	for you *(masculine)* for you *(feminine)*	لَـكَ (لَـ + كَ) لَـكِ (لَـ + كِ)
* regretfully = Literally: for the regret	* لِـلأَسَـف {اسف}	but, however * but he * but I am	لَـكِـنْ / لَـكِـنَّ * لَـكِـنَّـهُ * لَـكِـنِّـي
* for the exam	* لِـلـإِمْـتِـحـانِ {محن}	* for the celebration (of)	* لِـلإِحْـتِـفـال (بِـ) {حفل}

* for the studying	* لِـلـدِّراسَـة {درس} (لِـ+الـدِّراسَـة)	* for obtaining	* لِـلـحُـصُـولِ (عَلى) {حصل} (لِـ+الحُصُول)
* for the bride	* لِـلـعَـرُوسَـة {عرس} (لِـ + ال + عَـرُوسَـة)	* for the guests	* لِـلـضُّـيُـوف {ضيف} (لِـ+ال+ضُـيُـوف)
* for the verb	* لِـلـفِـعْـلِ {فعل} (لِـ + ال + فِـعْـل)	for the languages	لِـلُّـغَـات {لغو} (لِـ + الـ + لُـغات)
* for the clothing	* لِـلـمَـلابِـس {لبس} (لِـ+الـ+مَـلابِـس)	* for the undertaking	* لِـلـقِـيـام {قوم} (لِـ+ال+قِـيـام)
did not *(jussive particle, takes the following verb in jussive mood)*	لَـمْ	* to God * The Praise be to God!	* لِـلَّـهِ {أله} (لِـ+اللَّه) * الـحَـمْـدُ لِـلَّـه! {حمد}
Why...?	لِـمـاذا ...؟	* Why not!	* لِـمَ لا !
will not *(a subjunctive particle negates the future time of verbs)* * will not continue * the two of them will not permit	لَـن * لَـنْ يَـسْـتَـمِـرَّ {مرر} * لَـنْ يَـسْـمَـحـا {سمح}	he insinuated (insinuation) * he insinuated to me, he hinted to me	لَـمَّـحَ (تَـلْـمِـيـح) {لـمح} * لَـمَّـحَ لِـي
* in order for us to pay *(before the verb this is a subjunctive particle and the verb after it is in a subjunctive mood)*	* لِـنَـدْفَـعَ {دفع} (لِـ + نَـدْفَـعَ)	* for us	* لَـنـا (لَـ + نـا)
* for her	* لَـهـا (لَـ + ـهـا)	* for yourself	* لِـنَـفْـسِـكَ {نفس} (لِـ + نَـفْـسِ + كَ)
if * If you would permit!	لَـو * لَـوْ سَـمَـحْـتَ!	* for the two of them * for all of them	* لَـهُـما (لَـ + ـهُـما) * لَـهُـمْ (لَـ + ـهُـم)
board, blackboard, writing board *(takes broken plural)*	لَـوْح (أَلْـواح) {لوح}	* if not for	* لَـوْلا
for me, I have, belongs to me	لِـي (لِـ + ـي)	color (colors) *(takes broken plural)*	لَـون (أَلْـوان) {لون}
in order for them to congratulate	لِـيُـبـارِكُـوا {برك} (لِـ + يُـبـارِك + ـوا)	Libya Libyan *(masculine / feminine pair)*	لِـيـبْـيـا لِـيـبِـيّ / لِـيـبِـيَّـة

lion (lions) *(takes broken plural)*	لَـيْـث (لُـيُـوث) {ليث}	to Yusuf	لِـيُـوسُـف {يسف} (لِـ + يُـوسُـف)
a night / the night, tonight (nights) *(takes broken plural)*	لَـيْـلَـة / الـلَّـيْـلَـة (لَـيالِـي)	he is not * she is not * they are not *(masculine)* * Isn't that so?	لَـيْـسَ {ليس} * لَـيْـسَـتْ * لَـيْـسُـوا * أَلَـيْـسَ كَـذَلِـكَ؟
		lemons (collective noun) (one lemon)	لَـيْـمُـون (لَـيْـمُـونَـة)

What...? *(interrogative particle used to ask about non-human nouns)*	مـا ...؟	abbreviation for A.D., C.E. *(Christian era calendar)*	م = مِـيـلَادِيَّـة {ولد}
that, which, that which (*relative pronoun)* * in between, that which is in between	مـا * مـا بَـيْـنَ	did not *(a negating particle that negates the past tense verb)* * I did not want (to)	مـا * مـا أَرَدْتُ (أَنْ)
hundred / hundreds / two hundred	مِـئَـة / مِـئـات / مِـئَـتـانِ {مأو}	How…! *(exclamation particle to express admiration and wonder)* * How beautiful spring is!	مـا ...! * مـا أَجْـمَـلَ ٱلـرَّبِـيع!
believer (believers) *(takes masculine sound plural)*	مُـؤْمِـن (مُـؤْمِـنُـونَ) {أمن}	convention (conventions) *(takes feminine sound plural)*	مُـؤْتَـمَـر (مُـؤْتَـمَـرات) {أمر}
feminine / the feminine (grammatical term)	مُـؤَنَّـث / الـمُـؤَنَّـث {أنث}	trustworthy, reliable (trust worthy ones) *(passive participle form)* *(takes masculine sound plural)*	مَـأْمُـون (مَـأْمُـونُـونَ) {أمن}
a table spread (table spreads) *(takes broken plural)* * the food table spread	مـائِـدَة (مَـوائِـد) {مود} * مـائِـدَة الطَّعام	water / the water	مـاء / الـمـاء {موه}
What do (did)…? (*question particle to ask about the action, thus followed by a verb*) * What do you do? * What about …?	مـاذا ...؟ * مـاذا تَـفْـعَـلُـونَ؟ * مـاذا عَـنْ ...؟	* Master's Degree *(adopted from English and Arabized)* * The Master Degree	* مـاجِـسْـتِـيـر / * الـمـاجِـسْـتِـيـر
principle / the principle * as a matter of principle	مَـبْـدَأ / الـمَـبْـدَأ {بدأ} * مِـنْ حَـيْـثُ الـمَـبْـدَإِ	mango * mango juice	مـانْـجَـة / مـانْـجُـو / * عَـصِـيـر ٱلـمـانْـجَـة

subject / the subject of a nominal sentence (linguistic term)	مُبْتَدَأ / الـمُبْتَدأ {بدأ}	Blessed, May it be blessed! / Congratulation!	مُبارَك / مَبْرُوك! {برك}
When ...? *(interrogative particle for time)*	مَتَى ...؟	late *(masculine / feminine pair)*	مُتَأَخِّراً / مُتَأَخِّرَةً {أخر}
museum (museums) *(takes broken plural)*	مُتْحَف (مَتاحِف) {تحف}	store (stores) *(takes broken plural)* * a clothing store	مَتْجَر (مَتاجِر) {تجر} * مَتْجَر مَلابِس
hesitant *(masculine / feminine pair)* * two married pair	مُتَرَدِّد / مُتَرَدِّدَة {ردد}	specialist (in) *(feminine)*	مُتَخَصِّصَة (فِي) {خصص}
transitive * the transitive verb	مُتَعَدٍّ {عدو} * الفِعْلُ المُتَعَدِّي	a married person *(masculine / feminine pair)* * two married pair	مُتَزَوِّج / مُتَزَوِّج * مُتَزَوِّجانِ {زوج}
educated, cultured *(masculine / feminine pair)*	مُثَقَّف / مُثَقَّفَة {ثقف}	speaker / the speaker = first person *(as a grammatical term)*	مُتَكَلِّم / المُتَكَلِّم {كلم}
courtesy (courtesies) *(takes feminine sound plural*	مُجامَلَة (مُجامَلات) {جمل}	such as, similar * like you, similar to you * like me, similar to me	مِثْل {مثل} * مِثْلُكَ (مِثْلُ+كَ) * مِثْلِي (مِثل+ي)
industrious, hardworking *(masculine / feminine pairs and their corresponding plurals)*	مُجْتَهِد (مُجْتَهِدُونَ) مُجْتَهِدَة (مُجْتَهِدات) {جهد}	One who struggles for a cause, warrior, freedom fighter *(takes masculine sound plural*	مُجاهِد (مُجاهِدُونَ) {جهد}
council (councils) *(broken plural)* * security council	مَجْلِس (مَجالِس) {جلس} *مَجْلِسُ الأَمْن	object of a preposition *(grammatical term)*	مَجْرُور {جرر}
crazy, insane, possessed *(takes broken plural)*	مَجْنُون (مَجانِين) {جنن}	group, variety * for a group of, for a variety of	مَجْمُوعَة (مِنْ) {جمع} * لِمَجْمُوعَة مِنْ
accountant (accountants) *(feminine / masculine pair and their corresponding sound plurals)*	مُحاسِبَة / مُحاسِب (مُحاسِبات) / مُحاسِبُون {حسب}	conversation, talk (the *plural form has the meaning of* "negotiations")	مُحادَثَة (مُحادَثات) {حدث}

a lecture (lectures) *(takes feminine sound plural)*	مُحاضَرَة (مُحاضَرات) {حضر}	accounting, accountability (to do accounting)	مُحاسَبَة (حاسَبَ) {حسب}
lucky one, lucky (for) *(masculine / feminine adjective pair)*	مَحْظُوظ / مَحْظوظَة (بِـ) {حظظ}	she. it is in need (of) *(takes feminine sound plural)* * not needy, not in need (of)	مُحْتاجَة (إلى) (مُحْتاجات) {حوج} * غَيْرُ مُحْتاجَة
praise-worthy one *(two very common proper male names)*	مُحَمَّد / مَحْمُود {حمد}	a court house *(takes broken plural)*	مَحْكَمَة (مَحاكِم) {حكم}
sincere / the sincere, sincerely	مُخْلِص / المُخْلِص {خلص}	selections (a selection)	مُخْتارات (مُخْتارَة) {خلص}
teacher (teachers) *(takes masculine sound plural))* teacher (teachers) *(takes feminine sound plural)*	مُدَرِّس (مُدَرِّسُونَ) {درس} مُدَرِّسَة (مُدَرِّسات)	entrance (entrances) *(takes broken plural))*	مَدْخَل (مَداخِل) {دخل}
he extended, he laid out (extending)	مَدَّ (المَدّ) {مدد}	a school (schools) *(takes broken plural)* * Our school	مَدْرَسَة (مَدارِس) * مَدْرَسَتُنا {درس}
director (directors) *(male / broken plural)* director *(female / feminine sound plural)*	مُدِير (مُدَراء) مُدِيرَة - ات {دير}	he extended, he laid out (extending) * for a period of	مُدَّة {مدد} * لِمُدَّة
masculine / the masculine *(grammatical term to refer to male gender nouns)*	مُذَكَّر / المُذَكَّر {ذكر}	city (cities) *(takes broken plural)*	مَدِينَة (مُدُن) {مدن}
woman / the woman (women- *note that plural is based on a different root)*	مَرأة / المَرْأة (نِساء) {مرأ} {نسو}	passed by (passing by) * time has passed by quickly	مَرَّ (مُرُور) {مرر} * مَرَّ الوَقْتُ بِسُرْعَة
times (one time) *(takes feminine sound plural)* * a second time, again * the next time	مَرَّات (مَرَّة) {مرر} * مَرَّة ثانِيَة * المَرَّة القادِمَة	a mirror (mirrors) *(takes broken plural)*	مِرآة (مَرايا) {رأي}
jam, preserved fruit (the jam, the preserved fruit)	مُرَبَّى (المُرَبَّى) {ربو}	review (reviews) *(takes feminine sound plural)*	مُراجَعَة (مُراجَعات) {رجع}
refreshments (a refreshment)	مُرَطِّبات (مُرَطِّب) {رطب}	Hello, welcome!	مَرْحَباً! / مَرْحَبا! {رحب}

a boat (boats) *(takes broken plural)*	مَـرْكَـب / مَـرْكَـبـاً (مَـراكِـب) {ركب}	nominative case-ending *(grammatical term*	مَـرْفُـوع {ركب}
Maryam = Mary, Maria *(Arabic proper name corresponding to Mary in English and Maria in Latin)*	مَـرْيَـم {مري}	ideal of manhood (valor, chivalry, generosity, sense of honor) *(takes feminine sound plural)*	مُـرُوءَة (مُـرُوءات) {مرأ}
official, in charge *(masculine / feminine forms with their corresponding plurals)*	مَـسْـؤُول (مَسْؤُولِـيـنَ) مَـسْـؤُولَـة (مَسْؤُولات) {سأل}	more (of)	مَـزِيداً (مِنْ) {زيد}
help, aid / the help, the aid	مُساعَـدَة / الـمُـساعَـدَة {سعد}	evening / the evening * Good evening! * Good evening! *(response)*	مَساء / الـمَـسَاء {مسي} * مَساءَ ٱلـخَـيْـر! / * مَساءَ الـنُّـور!
desirable *(takes masculine sound plural)*	مُـسْـتَـحْـسَـن {حسن} (مُـسْـتَـحْـسَـنُـونَ)	a traveler, traveling *(masculine / feminine forms with their corresponding plurals)*	مُسافِـر (مُسافِـرونَ) مُسافِـرَة (مُسافِـرات) {سفر}
you are ready (*masculine sound plural)* I am. he, you ready *(the singular can be used by all masculine singular subjects)*	مُـسْـتَـعِـدُّونَ (مُـسْـتَـعِـدّ) {عدد}	I am in a hurry (female) *(takes feminine sound plural)*	مُـسْـتَـعْـجِـلَـة {عجل} (مُـسْـتَـعْـجِـلات)
level (levels) (*Takes feminine sound plural after converting the Alif Maqsurah into a Yaa.*)	مُـسْـتَـوَى (مُـسْـتَـوَيـات) {سوي}	future / the future	مُـسْـتَـقْـبَـل / {قبل} الـمُـسْـتَـقْـبَـل
a theater (theatres) *(takes broken plural)*	مَـسْـرَح (مَـسارِح) {سرح}	a mosque (mosques) *(takes broken plural)*	مَـسْـجِـد (مَـساجِـد) {سجد}
longing (for), eager (to)	مُـشْـتـاقـاً (إلَـى) {شوق}	Muslims *(masculine sound plural)* (a Muslim)	مُـسْـلِـمُـونَ (مُسْلِم) {سلم}
varied, variety, mixed *(masculine / feminine pair)*	مُشَكَّـل / مُـشَـكَّـلَـة {شكل}	a problem (problems) *(takes broken plural and feminine sound plural)*	مُـشْـكِـلَـة (مَشاكِـل / مُشْكِلات) {شكل}
exciting *(masculine / feminine pair)*	مُـشَـوِّق / مُـشَـوِّقَـة {شوق}	famous (*masculine*) famous (*feminine*) *(famous ones / masculine / feminine plurals)*	مَـشْـهُـور (مَـشْـهُـورُونَ) مَـشْـهُـورَة (مَـشْـهُـورات) {شهر}

* the broiled chicken	* الدَّجاج المشْوِي {شوي}	broiled, roasted (the roasted)	مَشْوِيّ / المَشْوِي {شوي}
gerund, verbal noun, source *(takes broken plural)*	مَصْدَر (مَصادِر) {صدر}	expenses (expense) * my expenses	مَصارِيف (مَصْرُوف) * مَصارِيفِي
a factory (factories) *(takes broken plural)*	مَصْنَع (مَصانِع) {صنع}	Egypt Egyptian *(masculine / feminine pair)*	مِصْر {مصر} مِصْرِيّ / مِصْرِيَّة
a grammatical term for the first term of an *Iḍāfah* structure	مُضاف / المُضاف {ضيف}	made (from)	مَصْنُوعَة (مِنْ) {صنع}
an airport / the airport (airports) *(takes feminine sound plural)*	مَطار / المَطار (مَطارات) {طير}	* a grammatical term for the second term of an *Iḍāfah* structure *(literally: juxtaposed to it)*	مُضاف إِلَيْهِ / {ضيف} * المُضاف إِلَيْهِ
divorced *(dual number)* (a divorcee)	مُطَلَّقانِ (مُطَلَّق) {طلق}	a restaurant (restaurants) *(takes broken plural)* * an Arabic restaurant * a popular restaurant	مَطْعَم (مَطاعِم) * مَطْعَم عَرَبِيّ {طعم} * مَطْعَماً شَعْبِيّاً
with * with me * with us * Good by! *(idiom)* literally: (go with safety!) * Regretfully!	مَعَ * مَعِي * مَعَنا * مَعَ السَّلامَة! * مَعَ ٱلأَسَف!	demonstrations (a demonstration)	مُظاهَرات (مُظاهَرَة) {ظهر}
Excuse me! Pardon me! Sorry!	مَعْذِرَة! {عذر}	hostile (to), against	مُعادِيَة (لِـ) {عدو}
definite, defined / the definite noun *(a grammatical term)*	مَعْرِفَة / المَعْرِفَة {عرف}	noun being defined, / the noun being defined *(a grammatical term)*	مُعَرَّف / المُعَرَّف {عرف}
known as / the one known as	مَعْرُوفَة (بِـ) / {عرف} المَعْرُوفَة (بِـ)	charity, good deed, known, recognized * more deserving of charity	مَعْرُوف / المَعْرُوف * أَوْلَى بِٱلمَعْرُوف
a coat, an overcoat *(nominative / accusative forms)* * a leather overcoat	مِعْطَف / مِعْطَفاً {عطف} * مِعْطَفُ جِلد	* two people known as *(dual form)*	* مَعْرُوفَيْنِ (بِـ) {عرف}
teacher *(masculine / feminine pair)*	مُعَلِّم / مُعَلِّمَة {علم}	* with you *(masculine / feminine pair)*	* مَعَكَ / مَعَكِ

lab (labs) *(takes broken plural)* * the language lab	مَعْمَل (مَعامِل) {عمل} * مَعْمَلُ ٱللُّغَة	information (a piece of information)	مَعْلُومات (مَعْلُومَة) {علم}
* with her, with it *(if non-human)* * with them * with me	* مَعَها (مَعَ + ها) * مَعَهُم (مَعَ+هُم) * مَعِي (مَعَ + ي)	meaning / the meanings (meanings)	مَعْنَى / مَعْنًى / المَعْنَى (مَعانٍ) {عني}
departure, leaving (he departed)	مُغادَرَة (غادَرَ) {غدر}	institute (institutes) *(takes broken plural)*	مَعْهَد (مَعاهِد) {عهد}
vocabulary word (vocabularies) *(feminine sound plural)*	مُفْرَدَة (مُفْرَدات) {فرد}	key (keys) *(takes broken plural)*	مِفْتاح (مَفاتِيح) {فتح}
* direct object of a verb *(linguistic term)*	* مَفْعُول بِهِ {فعل}	favorite / the favorite	مُفَضَّل / المُفَضَّل {فضل}
meeting, interview (interviews) (he met, he interviewed)	مُقابَلَة (مُقابَلات) (قابَلَ) {قبل}	across from, opposite to, in exchange for	مُقابِل {قبل}
seat / the seat (seats) *(takes broken plural)*	مَقْعَد / المَقْعَد (مَقاعِد) {قعد}	resident (in) *(masculine / feminine form)*	مُقِيم / مُقِيمَة (في) {قيم}
office (offices) *(takes broken plural)* * the registrar's office	مَكْتَب (مَكاتِب) {كتب} * مَكْتَب ٱلتَّسْجِيل	coffee house *(takes two forms of broken plural)* * a popular coffee house	مَقْهَى (مَقاهٍ / المَقاهِي) {قهو} * مَقْهَى شَعْبِيّ
your office *(for masculine singular & feminine singular)*	مَكْتَبُكَ / ـكِ {كتب} (مَكْتَبُ+ـكَ / ـكِ)	their offices *(for masculine plural)*	مَكاتِبِهِم {كتب} (مَكاتِب+هِم)
her office	مَكْتَبُها {كتب} (مَكْتَبُ+ـها)	his office	مَكْتَبِه {كتب} (مَكْتَبُ+ـهُ)
written / the written (on) *(literally)* * what has been fated (for) *(idiomatically)*	مَكْتُوب / {كتب} * المَكْتُوب (عَلى)	my office	مَكْتَبِي (مَكْتَبِ+ـي) {كتب}
clothes (a garment) * sports clothing	مَلابِس (مَلْبَس) {لبس} * مَلابِس ٱلرِّياضَة	consisting (of)	مُكَوَّنَة (مِنْ) {كون}
file (files) *(takes feminine sound plural)*	مِلَفّ (مِلَفّات) {لفف}	notes, observations (a note, an observation)	مُلاحَظات (مُلاحَظَة) {لحظ}

exercising, practicing, pursuing *(takes feminine sound plural)*	مُمارَسَة (مُمارَسات) {مرس}	Jew's mallow * Jew's mallow with rabbit (meat)	مُلُوخِيَّة {ملخ} * مُلُوخِيَّة بِالأَرانِب
enjoyable, interesting *(feminine / masculine pair)*	مُمْتِعَة / مُمْتِع {متع}	distinguished, excellent *(for male, female and their corresponding plurals)*	مُمْتاز / مُمْتازَة (مُمْتازُونَ) / مُمْتازات {ميز}
Who...? (*interrogative particle for humans*)	مَنْ ...؟	it is possible (to)	مُمْكِن (أَنْ) {مكن}
* Kindly, please! *(idiom)* * It is clear that … *(idiom)*	* مِنْ فَضْلِكَ/ كِ! * مِنَ ٱلْوَاضِحِ أَنَّ ...	from, of, than (*preposition*) * from me * from among you all from both of them, from among both of them	مِنْ ...؟ * مِنِّي (مِنْ +ي) * مِنْكُم مِنْهُما (مِنْ+هُما)
occasion / the occasion (occasions) *(takes feminine sound plural)* * on the occasion	مُناسَبَة / المُناسَبَة {نسب} (مُناسَبات) * بِمُناسَبَةِ	suitable *(masculine / feminine pair)*	مُناسِب / مُناسِبَة {نسب}
wish, hope *(a common female proper name)*	مُنَى {منو}	the formal occasions	* المُناسَباتُ ٱلرَّسْمِيَّة
cotton-made products	المُنْتَجات القُطْنِيَّة	towels (a towel) *(broken plural)*	مَناشِف (مِنْشَفَة) {نشف}
accusative mood of case-ending *(grammatical term)*	مَنْصُوب {نصب}	since, ago	مُنْذُ
forbidding (he forbade)	مَنْع (مَنَعَ) {منع}	sight, scene (sights, scenes) *(takes broken plural)*	مَنْظَر (مَناظِر) {نظر}
cradle / the cradle (cradles) (takes *broken plural*)	مَهْد / المَهْد (مُهُود) {مهد}	wild cow *(known for its wide beautiful eyes) (hence* it is a common female proper name	مَها = مَهاة {مهو}
mission, concern *(takes feminine sound plural)* * his commercial mission	مَهَمَّة (مَهَمَّات) {همم} * مَهَمَّتَهُ التِّجارِيَّة	important * what matters is that you	مُهِمّ {همم} * المُهِمُّ أَنَّكَ
corresponding to, to be agreeable with * its suitability for, its agreement with	مُوافِق / المُوافِق {وفق} * مُوافَقَتِهِ لِـ	forbidden / the forbidden	مَمْنُوع / المَمْنُوع {منع}

present, available *(masculine plural)* present, available *(feminine plural)*	مَـوْجُـود (مَـوْجُـودُونَ) مَـوْجُودَة (مَوْجُودات) {وجد}	summary / the summary (of news)	مُـوجَـز / الـمُـوجَـز {وجز}
employee *(masculine plural)* employee *(feminine plural)*	مُـوَظَّـف (مُوَظَّـفُـونَ) مُـوَظَّـفَة (مُوَظَّفات) {وظف}	subject, topic *(takes broken plural)*	مَـوْضُـوع (مَـواضِـيع) {وضع}
location (locations) *(takes broken plural)*	مَـوْقِـع (مَواقِـع) {وقع}	appointed time, appointment *(takes broken plural)*	مَـوْعِـد / مَـوْعِـداً (مَـواعِـيـد) {وعد}
public square (public squares) *(takes broken plural)* * *At-Taḥrīr* (= Liberation) Square	مَيْدان (مَيادِين) {مدن} * مَـيْـدانُ ٱلتَّـحْـريـر	birth * birthday	مَـوْلِـد / مِـيـلاد {ولد} * عِـيـد مِـيـلاد
AD., CE. (*Christian era calendar*)	مِـيـلادِيَّـة {ولد}	Scale, balance *(takes broken plural)* * the morphological pattern *(a linguistic term)*	مِـيزان (مَوازِين) {وزن} * الـمِيـزان ٱلـصَّرفِـيّ

Suffixed at the end of verbs, both perfect and imperfect, to indicate feminine plural	ـنَ	Subject-marker for the 1st person plural in the conjugation of present tense verbs = we	نَـ
we eat, we are eating (eating / *as a gerund*)	نَـأكُـلُ (الأَكْـل) {أكل}	(our, us, we) Subject-marker for the 1st person plural in the conjugation of past tense verb; also possessive suffix pronoun with nouns	ـنـا
people / the people *(collective noun)* (a human being)	نـاس / الـنَّـاس (إِنْـسان) {أنس}	successful (successful ones) *(takes masculine plural)*	نـاجِـح (نـاجِـحُـونَ) {نجح}
unique (masculine / feminine adjective pair); also common proper names	نـادِر / نـادِرَة {ندر}	he slept (sleeping)	نـامَ (نَـوْم) {نوم}
plants-related, vegetarian *(masculine / feminine adjective pair)*	نَـباتِـيَّـة / نَـبـاتِـيّ {نبت}	club / the club (clubs) *(takes broken plural)*	نـادِي / الـنَّـادِي (نَوادِي) {ندو}
we speak (over)	نَـتَـحَـدَّثُ (عَلـى) {حدث}	noble *(masculine / feminine adjective pair)*; also common proper names for both genders	نَـبِـيـل / نَـبِـيـلَـة {نبل}

we talk (about)	نَـتَـكَـلَّـمُ (عَنْ) {كلم}	we have lunch	نَـتَـغَـدَّى {غدو}
we wish (that)	نَـتَـمَـنَّـى (أَنْ) {مني}	we take a walk, we stroll (at)	نَـتَـمَـشَّـى (عَلَى) {مشي}
as a result of	نَـتِـيـجَـةً (لِـ) {نتج}	we have, we take (food); we deal with (topic) * in order to have, so we can have	نَـتَـنـاوَلُ {نول} * لِـنَـتَـنـاوَلَ
we	نَـحْـنُ	we need, we are in need (of)	نَـحْـتـاجُ (إِلَـى) {حوج}
regret, being regretful / the regret	نَـدامَـة / الـنَّـدامَـة {ندم}	calling (he called) * a vocative particle	نِـداء (نـادى) {ندي} * حَـرْفُ نِـداء
he vowed, he consecrated (vowing, consecrating	نَـذَرَ (نَـذْر) {نذر}	we pay (to) (paying, payment)	نَـدْفَـعُ (لِـ) (دَفْـع) {دفع}
consecrated to God, solemnly pledged, warner, harbinger	نَـذِيـر {نذر}	we go, we are going (to) (the act of going)	نَـذْهَـبُ (إِلَـى) (ذَهاب) {ذهب}
we hope, we wish	نَـرْجُـو (رَجاء) {رجو}	we see, we are seeing	نَـرَى (رُؤْيَـة) {رأي}
we want (to)	نُـرِيدُ (أَنْ) {ريد}	we welcome * we welcome you	نُـرَحِّـبُ (بِـ) {رحب} * نُـرَحِّـبُ بِـكَ
women (a woman) * female, womanly *(nisbah adjective)*	نِـساء (امْـرَأَة) {نسو} * نِـسَـائِـيّ	picnic (picnics) *(takes feminine sound plural)*	نُـزْهَـة (نُـزُهـات) {نزه}
he grew up, he / it came into being, evolved (growing up, coming into being)	نَـشَـأَ (نَـشْـأَة) {نشأ}	I forgot (forgetting)	نَـسِـيـتُ (نِـسْـيـان) {نسي}
bulletin * news bulletin	نَـشْـرَة {نشر} * نَـشْـرَة الأَخْـبـار	we drink (drinking)	نَـشْـرَبُ (شُـرْب) {شرب}
we arrive (at), we reach (at) * to reach (at)	نَـصِـلَ (إِلَـى) {وصل} * لِـنَـصِـلَ (إِلَـى)	text (texts) *(takes broken plural)*	نَـصّ (نُـصُـوص) {نصص}
he looked at, he glanced at (looking, glancing)	نَـظَـرَ (إِلَـى) (نَـظَـر) {نظر}	luck, portion *(takes broken plural)*	نَـصِـيـب (أَنْـصِـبَـة) {نصب}
clean *(masculine / feminine pair of adjectives)*	نَـظِـيـف / نَـظِـيـفَـة {نظف}	equal, matching, similar, opposite (equals, opposites)	نَـظِـيـر (نُـظَـراء) {نظر}

yes	نَعَمْ {نعم}	we know (knowledge)	نَعْرِفُ (مَعْرِفَة) {عرف}
soul, self * yourself * even against your own self	نَفْس * نَفْسكَ * وَلَوْ عَلَى نَفْسِكَ	a blessing (blessings) *(takes broken plural)*	نِعْمَة (نِعَم) {نعم}
we do, we are doing (deed, action)	نَفْعَلُ (فِعْل) {فعل}	crude oil / the crude oil	نَفْط / النَّفْط {نفط}
we meet (meeting, interview)	نُقابِلُ (مُقابَلَة) {قبل}	negation / the negation *(as a linguistic term)* * negating particles	نَفْي / النَّفْي {نفي} * أَدَواتُ النَّفْي
we read (reading)	نَقْرَأُ (قِراءَة) {قرأ}	we offer (to), we transmit (to)	نُقَدِّمُ (إِلَى / لِـ) {قدم}
indefinite / the indefinite noun *(takes feminine sound plural)*	نَكِرَة / النَّكِرَة (نَكِرات) {نكر}	we write (writing)	نَكْتُبُ (كِتابَة) {كتب}
we emigrate (emigration)	نُهاجِرُ (هِجْرَة) {هجر}	we play (playing)	نَلْعَبُ (لَعِب) {لعب}
final *(masculine / feminine pair of Nisbah adjectives)* * in a conclusive way, as a final step *(adverb)*	نِهائِيّ / نِهائِيَّة * نِهائِيّاً {نهي}	daytime / the daytime *(as opposed to night time)*	نَهار / (النَّهار) {نهر}
river (rivers) *(takes broken plural)* * the Nile River	نَهْر (أَنْهار) {نهر} * نَهْرُ النِّيل	end, termination, conclusion (ends, conclusions)	نِهايَة (نِهايات) {نهي}
representatives (a representative) * the House (Council) of Representatives	نُوّاب (نائِب) {نوب} * مَجْلِسُ النُّوّابِ	light / the light * Good morning! *(as a response)* * Good evening! *(as a response)*	نُور / النُّور {نور} * صَباحَ النُّور! * مَساءَ النُّور!
type, kind, variety (types, varieties) *(takes broken plural)* * two types, two varieties *(nominative / accusative forms)*	نَوْع (أَنْواع) {نوع} * نَوْعانِ / نَوْعَيْنِ	you brought lite, you brightened	نَوَّرْتَ (تَنْوير) {نور}
		Nile / the Nile (river)	نِيل / النِّيل {نيل}

his, it, him (*suffix pronoun attached to nouns, prepositions or verbs*)	ه / ـهُ / ـهِ	abbreviation for the *Hijri* Islamic calendar	هـ = هِجْرِيَّة
these, those (*demonstrative pronoun for human plurals only*)	هَـؤُلاءِ {هاء}	her, hers, it (*suffix pronoun attached to nouns, prepositions or verbs*)	ها / ـها
these two, those two (*dual forms of demonstrative pronouns in nominative / accusative forms*)	هاتانِ / هاتَيْنِ	You bring! You give! You Provide! (*a special command verb which has no past or present forms in three form for masculine singular, feminine singular and plural*)	هاتِ! / هاتِي! / هاتُوا!
a guide / the guide	هادِي / الهادي {هدي}	he emigrated (emigration)	هاجَرَ (هِجْرَة) {هدي}
emigration (he emigrated)	هِجْرَة (هاجَرَ) {هجر}	blowing of the wind (it blew, it started to blow)	هُبُوب (هَبَّ) {هبب}
gift, present (gifts, presents) (*takes broken plural*)	هَدِيَّة (هَدايا) {هدي}	calmness (he / it calmed down) * with calmness = calmly	هُدُوء (هَدَأَ) {هدأ} * بِهُدُوء
this (*feminine singular; also used for non-human plurals*)	هَذِهِ	this (*masculine, singular demonstrative pronoun*)	هَذا
flight, escape, fleeing, running away (he escaped, he ran away)	هُرُوب (هَرَبَ) {هرب}	pyramid (pyramids) (*takes broken plural plus feminine sound plural*)	هَرَم (أَهْرام / أَهْرامات) {هرم}
Is.../ Are...? (*interrogative particle*)	هَلْ ...؟	he defeated (defeat)	هَزَمَ (هَزِيمَة) {هزم}
they (*masculine plural subject pronoun*)	هُمْ	it / he appeared, showed, it set in (crescent, new moon)	هَلَّ (هِلال) {هلل}
they (*subject pronoun for dual number, both masculine or feminine*)	هُما	their, them (*suffix pronoun attached to nouns, prepositions or verbs*)	هُمْ / ـهُمْ / ـهِمْ
the glottal stop consonant considered the first letter of the Arabic Alphabet	هَمْزَة (ء) {همز}	their, them (*suffix pronoun for dual number, attached to nouns, prepositions or verbs*)	هُما / ـهُما / ـهِما
here	هُنا	whispering (he whispered)	هَمْس (هَمَسَ) {همس}
they (*feminine*)	هُنَّ	there, over there, there is	هُناكَ
he	هُوَ	their, them (*suffix pronoun for feminine plural, attached to nouns, prepositions or verbs*)	هُنَّ / ـهِنَّ

she	هِيَ	hobby (hobbies) *(takes feminine sound plural)* * personal hobbies	هِواية (هِوايات) {هوي} * هِـوايات شَـخْـصِـيَّة
		Let go! * Let us go! * Let's go to!	هَـيَّا * هَـيَّا بِـنـا! * هَـيَّا إِلـى!

و

By God! *(called the "Waw" of making an oath prefixed to the word "God")*	وَ * وَٱلـلَّـهِ! (وَ+ٱلـلَّـهِ)	and *(conjunction always written as part of the following word)*	وَ
one *(masculine / feminine pair)* * once, one time * by yourself *(masculine / feminine)*	واحِـد / واحِـدَة {وحد} * مَـرَّةً واحِـدَةً * وَحْـدَكَ / وَحْـدَكِ	this is the long vowel (*oo*) which occurs only in medial position of words and sounds "*oo*" in a word like "room"	ـُو (أَبُـوهُ)
clear / the clear * it is clear that {*idiom*}	واضِـح / الـواضِـح {وضح} * مِـنَ الـواضِـحِ أَنَّ	duty, something incumbent * Don't mention it; for nothing!	واجِـب {وجب} * لا شُـكْـرَ عَـلى وَاجِب!
she agreed (upon) (agreement upon)	وافَـقَـت (عَـلَى) {وفق} (مُوافَـقَـة) (عَـلَى)	he agreed (upon) (agreement upon)	وافَـقَ (عَـلَى) {وفق} (مُوافَـقَـة) (عَـلَى)
parent *(male / female)* = father/ mother	والِـد / والِـدَة {ولد} = أَب / أُمّ	* you *(plural)* agreed (upon) (agreement upon)	* وافَـقْـتُـم (عَـلَى) {وفق}
* my father * his father	* والِـدِي (والِـد+ـي) * والِـدُهُ (والِـد+هُ) {ولد}	* my mother, * her mother	* والِـدَتِـي * والِـدَتُـها (والِـدَة+ـي / ها) {ولد}
a meal (meals) *(takes feminine sound plural)* * the lunch meal	وَجْـبَـة (وَجْـبـات) {وجب} * وَجْـبَـة الـغَـداء	flimsy, trivial *(masculine / feminine pair)* * Put aside the flimsy excuses!	واهِي / واهِـيَـة {وهي} * دَعْـكَ مِـنَ ٱلأعْـذار ٱلـواهِـيَـة!
a face (faces) *(takes broken plural)*	وَجْـه (وُجُـوه) {وجه}	he found, he would find (finding, existence)	وَجَـدَ (وُجُـود)

unit, oneness (units) *(masculine / feminine one)*	وِحْـدَة (وِحْـدات) {وحد}	notable, eminent *(takes broken plural)*	وَجِيـه (وُجَـهاء) {وجه}
lonely *(masculine / feminine one)* the only one	وَحِيد / وَحِـيدَة {وحد} الـوَحِـيـد / الـوَحِـيـدَة	* you alone, you by yourself * alone, all by myself	* وَحْـدَكِ * وَحْـدِي {وحد}
he bid farewell (bidding farewell)	وَدَّعَ (وِداع) {ودع}	he loved, he liked (love, liking)	وَدَّ (وُدّ) {ودد}
devoted, fond, friendly *(masculine / feminine adjective pair)*	وَدُود / وَدُودَة {ودد}	love, friendship *(a common female proper name)*	وِداد {ودد}
minister *(a political office)* *(takes broken plural)*	وَزِيـر (وُزَراء) {وزر}	a sheet of paper, a leaf *(takes broken plural and feminine sound plural)* * your sheet of paper	وَرَقَـة (أَوْراق / وَرَقـات) {ورق} * وَرَقَـتُـكَ
he arrived (at) * she / it arrived (at) * it reached me = I received	وَصَـلَ (إِلَـى) {وصل} * وَصَـلَـتْ * وَصَـلَـنِـي	amid (of), in the middle (of)	وَسَـطَ {وجه}
situation (situations) *(takes broken plural)* * the ideal situation	وَضْـع (أَوْضـاع) {وضع} * الـوَضْـع الـمِـثـالِـيّ	* my arrival * your arrival	* وُصُـولِـي {وصل} * وُصُـولـكَ / ـكِ
homeland, patria * the homeland, the patria	وَطَـن (أَوْطـان) * أَرْضُ الـوَطَـن {وطن}	ritual ablution before prayer (he made ablution)	وَضُـوء (تَـوَضَّـأَ) {وضء}
he employed (employment)	وَظَّـفَ (تَـوْظِـيـف) {وظف}	national, nationalistic (*nisbah* from وَطَن)	وَطَـنِـيّ / وَطَـنِـيَّـة {وطن}
he promised (promising)	وَعَـدَ (وَعْـد) {وعد}	position, job / the position (positions, jobs)	وَظِيفَـة / الـوَظِـيفَـة (وَظـائِـف) {وظف}
time (times) / the time *(takes feminine sound plural)* * an enjoyable time	وَقْـت (أَوْقـات) / الـوَقْـت {وقت} * وَقْت مُـمْـتِـع	prevention, protection *(takes feminine sound plural)*	وِقـايَـة (وِقـايـات) {وقي}
stopping, stop (he stopped) * to stopping	وَقْـف (وَقَـفَ) {وقف} * بِـوَقْـفِ	* an enjoyable time *(adverbial use)* * the afternoon time * his time	* وَقْـتـاً مُـمْـتِـعـاً * وَقْـتَ الـعَـصْـر * وَقْـتُـهُ
child, boy (boys, children *(takes broken plural)* * to a child, to a son	وَلَـد (أَوْلاد) {ولد} * لِـوَلَـد	my authorized agent	وَكِـيلِـي (وَكِـيـل+ـي) {وكل}

* and therefore	* وَلِـذَلِـكَ (وَ+لِـذَلِـكَ)	province, state (provinces, states) * the United States of America	وِلايَـة (وِلايـات) {ولي} * الوِلايات الـمُتَّحِدَة الأمريكِيَّة
delusive imagination, erroneous impression *(takes broken plural)*	وَهْـم (أَوْهـام) {وهم}	* even though, even if * How possible! *(idiom)* * and even if against	* وَلَـوْ * وَلَـوْ عَـلى
woe, affliction, distress (unto, for) (woes, afflictions) *(takes feminine sound plural)*	وَيْـل (لِـ) (وَيْـلات)	* Okay *(idiomatically)* * let it be like that *(literally)*	* وَهُـوَ كَـذَلِـكَ!

ي

my, me *(suffix for first person singular possessive and object pronouns)*	ـِي / ي	(He / They) subject-marker prefix for 3rd person imperfect verb conjugations only	يَـ / يُـ
Vocative or calling particle, equivalent to old English "O!", such as: "O Lord!" * What a peace! *(exclamation to express wonder and admiration)*	يا * يا سَلام! {سلم}	*ee* (this is the sound of the "*Yaa*" in middle and final positions of words as the long vowel "*ee*", such as in the word "seed"	◌ِيـ / ـِيـ / ـِي يُـرِيـد / سَـعِـيـد
despair, hopelessness / the despair	يَـأْس / الـيَـأْس {يئس}	he comes, he approaches (coming, approaching)	يَـأْتِـي (إِتْـيـان) {أتـي}
he congratulates (congratulation)	يُبارِكُ (مُبارَكَة) {برك}	he believes (believing, belief)	يُـؤْمِـنُ (إِيـمان) {أمن}
he brings out anew, he initiates (bringing out, initiating)	يُـبْـدِئُ (إِبْـداء) {بدأ}	so they would congratulate (congratulation)	* لِـيُـبـارِكُـوا (مُـبـارَكَـة)
(they) forgo, surpass, disregard	يَـتَـجـاوَزُونَ {جوز}	it seems (that) * it seems that I am * it seems that you are *(masculine / feminine)*	يَـبْـدُو (أَنَّ) {بدو} * يَـبْـدُو أَنَّـنِـي * يَـبْـدُو أَنَّـكَ / ـكِ
they move, they are moving (movement) *(feminine plural conjugation)*	يَـتَـحَـرَّكْـنَ (حَـرَكَـة) {حرك}	they speak, they are speaking (speech)	يَـتَـحَـدَّثُـونَ (حَـدِيـث) {حدث}
it relates (to) (relating (to)	يَـتَـعَـلَّـقُ (بِـ) (تَعَـلُّـق) (بِـ) {علق}	they *(masculine dual)* frequent (frequenting)	يَـتَـرَدَّدانِ (تَـرَدُّد) {ردد}

they both meet each other (meeting) *(dual subjunctive mood)*	يَـتَـقـابَـلا (تَـقـابُـل) {قبل}	he learns (learning)	يَـتَـعَـلَّـمُ (تَـعـلُّـم) {علم}
it consists (of)	يَـتَـكَـوَّنُ (مِنْ) {كون}	he speaks, he is speaking (speaking, speech)	يَـتَـكَـلَّمُ (كَـلام) {كلم}
he / it harmonizes (with), be compatable with, be suitable to (suitability with)	يَـتَـنـاسَـبُ (مَعَ) (تَـنـاسُـب) {نسب}	they wish (to) (wishing) (to) *(feminine plural conjugation)*	يَـتَـمَـنَّـيْـنَ (أَنْ) (تَـمَـنِّـي) {مني}
he carries (carrying) * they are carrying *(feminine plural)*	يَـحْـمِلُ (حَمْل) {حمل} * يَـحْـمِـلْـنَ	it must (to) (must) * it is a must that I work = I must work	يَـجِـبُ (أَنْ) (وُجُـوب) {وجب} * يَـجِـبُ أَنْ أَعْـمَـلَ
hand / the hand *(takes broken plural)* * the hand of your daughter	يَـد / الـيَـد (أَيْـدِي ، أَيـادِي) {أيد} * يَـد كَـريـمَـتِـكُـم	he seeks to be engaged (engagement)	يَـخْـطُـبُ (خُـطُـوبَـة) {خطب}
it lasts, it continues to exist (lasting, continuation)	يَـدُومُ (دَوام) {دوم}	he studies, he is studying (study, studying)	يَـدْرُسُ (دِراسَـة) {درس}
he desires (to) (desiring)	يَـرْغَـبُ (فِـي) (رَغْـبَـة)	he goes (going)	يَـذْهَـبُ (ذَهاب) {ذهب}
it / he ceases, stop * it still, continues to be	يَـزالُ {زول} * لا يَـزالُ	he wants (to) (wanting, willing)	يُـرِيـدُ (إِرادَة) (أَنْ) {ريد}
it bothers me	يُـزْعِـجُـنِـي {زعج} (يُـزْعِـجُ + نِـي)	they visit (visiting, visit) *(feminine plural conjugation)*	يَـزُرْنَ (زِيـارَة) {زور}
he supplies me (with) * in order to supply me (with)	يُـزَوِّدُنِـي (بِـ) (يُـزَوِّدُ+نِـي) {زود} * لِـيُـزَوِّدَنِـي (بِـ)	he visits, he is visiting (visit, visiting) they visit, they are visiting	يَـزُورُ (زِيـارَة) {زور} يَـزُورُونَ (زِيـارَة)
(he / they) interrogate question (interrogation, questioning)	يُـسـائِـلُ (سُـؤال) {سأل}	(he / they) ask (asking)	يَـسـأَلُ (سُـؤال) {سأل}
he protects (protection) * May God protect!	يَـسْـتُـرُ (سَـتـر) {ستر} * الـلّـه يَـسْـتُـر!	(he / they) travel (to) (travel, traveling)	يُـسـافِـرُ (سَـفَـر) (إِلَـى) {سفر}

(he / they) get ready (for) (getting ready, readiness)	يَسْتَعِدُّ {عدد} (اِسْتِعْداد) (لِـ)	that which is possible, what is feasible *(passive conjugation)* (possibility)	يُسْتَطاع (اِسْتِطاعَة) (طوع)
(he / they) lives/ live (living, residing)	يَسكُنُ (سَكَن) {سكن}	it pleases me (to) / it pleases him (to) (pleasing, making happy)	يُسْعِدُنِي / يُسْعِدُهُ (أَنْ) (إِسْعاد) {سعد}
(he / they) wills / will (willingness) * God wills, God is willing	يَشاءُ (مَشيئَة) {شيأ} * يَشاءُ اللّهُ	(he / it) is called, is named (naming) *(passive voice verb)*	يُسَمَّى (تَسْمِيَة) {سمي}
it honors him (that) (honoring)	يُشَرِّفُهُ (تَشْرِيف) (أَنْ) {شرف}	(he / they) drinks / drink (drinking)	يَشْرَبُ (شُرْب) {شرب}
it is conjugated (conjugation) he conjugates	يُصَرَّفُ (تَصْرِيف) يُصَرِّف {صرف}	they issue, they declare (issuing, declaring)	يُصْدِرُونَ (إِصْدار) {صدر}
he prays (pray, praying)	يُصَلِّي (صَلاة) {صلو}	he / they votes, vote (on) (voting)	يُصَوِّتُ (عَلَى) (تَصْوِيت) {صوت}
they treat you (treating, treatment)	يُعامِلُوكَ (مُعامَلَة) {عمل} (يُعامِلُ+و+كَ)	he / it demands * demanding it to	يُطالِبُ {طلب} * يُطالِبُها بِأَنْ
he knows (knowing, knowledge)	يَعْرِفُ (مَعْرِفَة) {عرف}	he admits, he confesses, he recognizes (confession, recognition)	يَعْتَرِفُ (اِعْتِراف) (أَمامَ) {عرف}
they declare (declaration)	يُعْلِنُونَ (إِعْلان) {علن}	Jacob *(Arabic form of this proper noun)*	يَعْقُوب {عقب}
he goes back, he returns to * they are not any more capable *(idiom)*	يَعُود (عَوْدَة) {عود} * لَمْ يَعُودُوا قادِرِينَ	he works (in) (working, work)	يَعْمَلُ (فِي) (عَمَل) {عمل}
they live, they reside (living, residing)	يَعِيشُونَ (عَيْش) {عيش}	he lives (in), he resides (in) (living, residing)	يَعِيشُ (فِي) (عَيْش) {عيش}
(he / it) perishes, gets exhausted, comes to an end (perishing, ending)	يَفْنَى (فَناء) {فني}	he fails (failing)	يَفْشَلُ (فَشَل) {فشل}
he makes it a fated matter, he evaluates (making fateful, evaluation)	يُقَدِّرُ (تَقْدِير) {قدر}	he accepts (accepting	يَقْبَلُ (قُبُول) {قبل}

it stands by (stopping, standing)	يَـقِـفُ (إِلَـى) (وُقُـوف) {وقف}	he introduces her / it (introduction)	يُـقَـدِّمُـهـا (تَـقْـدِيـم) {قدم}
(it / he) grows up (growing up, getting bigger)	يَـكْـبُـرُ (كِـبَـر) {كبـر}	it annoys me, it worries me (annoyment, worrying)	يُـقْـلِـقُـنِـي (إِقْلاق) {قلق}
they visit (visiting, visit) *(feminine plural conjugation)*	يَـكْـتُـبْـنَ (كِـتـابَـة) {كتب}	he writes, he is writing (writing)	يَـكْـتُـبُ (كِـتـابَـة) {كتب}
he is, he be * he will be	يَـكُـونُ (كَـوْن) {كون} * سَـيَـكُـونُ	it suffices, it is enough (sufficing)	يَـكْـفِـي (كِـفـايَـة) {كفي}
it is necessary (that) * you need (to)	يَـلْـزَمُ (أَنْ) {لزم} (لُـزُوم) * يَـلْـزَمُـكَ (أَنْ)	he enrolls (in), he joins (in) (enrollment, joining)	يَـلْـتَـحِـقُ (بِـ) (الْـتِـحـاق) {لحق}
the two of them *(dual conjugation)* object (objection)	يُـمـانِـعـانِ (مُـمـانَـعَـة) {منع}	it glitters (glittering, shining)	يَـلْـمَـعُ (لَـمَـعـان) {لـمع}
it is possible (to) (possibility)	يُـمْـكِـنُ (أَنْ) (إِمْـكـان) {مكن}	he represents him (representation)	يُـمَـثِّـلُـهُ (تَـمْـثِـيـل) {مثل}
January *(Arabized form of the English)*	يَـنـايِر	* you can, it is possible for you * she can, it is possible for her (to)	* يُـمْـكِـنُـكَ (أَنْ) * يُـمْـكِـنُـهـا (أَنْ)
he forgets (forgetting)	يَـنْـسَـى (نِـسْـيـان) {نسي}	he criticizes (criticizing, criticism)	يَـنْـتَـقِـدُ (انْـتِـقـاد) {نقد}
Jewish *(feminine / masculine nisbah adjective forms)* * Judaism	يَـهُـودِيَّـة / يَـهُـودِيّ * الـيَـهُـودِيَّـة {هود}	he threatens (to) (threatening, threat)	يُـهَـدِّدُ (بِـ) (تَـهْـدِيـد) {هدد}
July *(Arabized form of the English)*	يُـولْـيُـو	Joseph	يُـوسُـف
* today * two days	* الـيَـوْم * يَـوْمَـيْـنِ	day (days) *(takes broken plural)* * the following Friday	يَـوْم (أَيّـام) {يوم} * يَـوْمُ الـجُـمُـعَـةِ الـتَّـالِـي